TWILIGHT OF THE PAST

Probing Indian History and Archaeology

TWILIGHT OF THE PAST

Probing Indian History and Archaeology

Editor

N. Chandramouli

ARYAN BOOKS INTERNATIONAL

New Delhi

in association with

PONDICHERRY UNIVERSITY

Pondicherry

TWILIGHT OF THE PAST

ISBN: 978-81-7305-419-8

First Published in **2012** by
ARYAN BOOKS INTERNATIONAL
Pooja Apartments, 4B, Ansari Road, Darya Ganj, New Delhi-110 002 (India)
Tel.: 23287589, 23255799; Fax: 91-11-23270385
E-mail: aryanbooks@gmail.com
www.aryanbooks.co.in

in association with

PONDICHERRY UNIVERSITY
Pondicherry

Computer Typeset and Printed in India at
ABI Prints & Publishing Co., New Delhi

पाण्डिच्चेरी विश्वविद्यालय
PONDICHERRY UNIVERSITY
(केन्द्रीय विश्वविद्यालय)
(A Central University)

आचार्य जे.ए.के. तरीन
Prof. J.A.K. TAREEN
कुलपति
Vice-Chancellor

आर. वेन्कटरामन नगर
R. Venkataraman Nagar
कालापेट Kalapet
पुदूच्चेरी ६०५ ०१४
Puducherry - 605 014
भारत. India.

March 23, 2011

Foreword

Archaeology and Earth Sciences share a very close relationship with each other. In the 19th century, some of the earliest scholars who investigated the antiquity of man were geologists and palaeontologists. Thus, scholars such as Charles Lyell, Hugh Falconer, Joseph Prestwich and others laid the foundations for modern prehistory through their analyses of the Pleistocene gravel deposits at Boucher de perthes in France and other regions of the Old World.

In 19th century India, the same may be said of Robert Bruce Foote, who worked in the Geological Survey, but who is best remembered for his contributions in the field of archaeology, specifically the prehistoric past of the Peninsular India. Foote not only discovered the first prehistoric stone tool in the subcontinent, but went on to discover and study hundreds of prehistoric and protohistoric sites in most parts of Southern and Western India. Foote's knowledge of geology not only aided in establishing the stratigraphic sequence of sites, but also helped understand geomorphological processes, past environments and even investigate natural processes affecting the distribution and preservation of archaeological sites. Foote, along with his colleague, W. King, discovered many palaeolithic occurrences in stratified contexts in Andhra, Karnataka and other regions of South India.

Bruce Foote's work on prehistoric sites occurring within the laterites and *Teris* in Tamil Nadu and Neolithic ash mounds in Karnataka were of particular importance. In fact, Foote's notable contribution was assigning an age to some of the geological formations based on the archaeological material found within.

The contributions of the geologists and geomorphologists were also significant in other related fields of archaeology, particularly rock-art. Rock paintings in India were recorded by Archibald Carllyle in the forested region of the Mirzapur district of Uttar Pradesh about a decade earlier to the famous discovery of Altamira Cave paintings of the Upper Palaeolithic age in Spain. It is, indeed, heartening to note that even in those times when the very study of the rock-art was at a nascent stage, Carllyle could identify and recognize the prehistoricity of the rock paintings discovered by him.

In later years, this close connection between geology and archaeology continued. This is noticeable in the works of scholars like V.D. Krishnaswami who had basic training as a geologist, and who participated in the famous Yale-Cambridge Expedition of the 1930s investigating the relationship between Ice Ages and prehistoric cultures in North-Western part of the subcontinent. He later worked extensively in Tamil Nadu, correlating palaeolithic cultures and river terraces.

Multidisciplinary studies involving teams of scientists are also a feature of modern research projects in archaeology. Satellite remote sensing and GIS are also being adopted increasingly, not only for research purposes but also for impact assessment studies, particularly on the heritage sites of our country, as the papers by Shanti Pappu *et al.*, P. Vijaya Prakash, S. Nagaraju and D. Dayalan and others in the present volume indicate. The paper by G.L. Badam described the recent developments in the scientific approaches to archaeological research in India.

Similarly, archaeology and history are two inseparable components in the study and analysis of the human cultural progress. The two (partly social/humanistic and partly scientific) disciplines of archaeology and history have been going hand in hand in unravelling India's past. Significant developments can be delineated in the theoretical and methodological aspects of the archaeological researches in post-Independent India. M.L.K. Murty's paper in this volume highlighted the conceptual and methodological shifts in the prehistoric studies, particularly in South India. Sundara's paper on the proto-historical cultures of the Karnataka region brought out the salient features of the cultural developments during that period.

Issues which troubled contemporary Indian society have also been taken care of by these two disciplines. The Aryan problem, the issues of Iron Age, the megalithic societies and their spatio-temporal dynamics, the rise of chiefdoms and subsequent rise of empires were addressed, and significant theories and concepts have been proposed to understand the various facets of Early Historical societies.

Growth of religious dogmas and ideas, social, political and cultural dimensions of the religious institutions, processes of urbanization and state formation, the role played by the subaltern sections of the society in shaping the historical events during the Early Historic and Medieval periods were put to intensive analyses, and new perspectives were added to the existing historical knowledge on these issues.

In the domain of folkloristics; numismatics; iconography; art & architecture; secular/ religious forms of the terracotta art of the Prehistoric, Protohistoric and Historical periods and their continuation in the ethnographic present, advanced researches were carried out and many new perspectives were added. Y.A. Sudhakara Reddy's paper brought out the latest trends and developments in the field of folkloristics on a global scale.

The rise of Colonialism and its exploitative strategies, the struggle for freedom in colonial India, the subaltern histories, the post-Modernist trends in historical writings constitute the other critical areas of focus in historical discourses today. K.A. Manikumar's paper is focused on the theoretical issues of the subaltern histories in the post-Modernist era.

I am happy to see the well-researched papers in this volume, contributed by distinguished scholars across the country, on all the issues enumerated above. I am particularly happy to see the papers on various aspects of the history of pre- and post-Colonial Pondicherry and other issues of regional history of South India, some of which are contributed by the research scholars and faculty of this University and the faculty of the Kanchi Mamunivar Centre for Post-Graduate Studies (autonomous), Puducherry. I congratulate the editor for the academic exercise of not just organizing a National Seminar, but making its academic deliberations available for wider readership, in the form of this proceedings volume. I am sure this volume will be receiving accolades from the researchers, students and lay readers alike.

Prof. J.A.K. Tareen
Vice-Chancellor

Preface

Globalization in/of India opened up the nation's economy to the market forces, which in turn brought about tremendous changes in the fields of technological advancement, spread of monetary economy, materialistic prosperity of a few, rise of neo-rich middle class, specifically of the software youth, easy availability of such items of once luxury goods now turned to be the essential commodities and more. These changes brought forth by the government and private agencies heralded equally significant changes in the general outlook of the people towards the acquisition of knowledge, personal relations both at the family and professional levels, outlook towards the society and nation at large, personal habits, and so on.

The consequences of globalization encompassed the entire gamut of the Indian society and changed its face beyond recognition within a span of less than a decade or more. Gone are the days of *panch varsh pranalika* (five-year plans executed on yearly basis), even the government budgetary allocations are being made in 'Q' installments as the private corporate firms and the targets are accordingly modified. This phenomenon is to be seen in most of the state governments in India. It is *consumerism* now, which is the watch word for the Indians and its government as well.

The so-called political unification of the country under the British which got consolidated during the Freedom movement is becoming a thing of the past. The *Swadeshi* is a forgotten word as India became a heaven for multinational companies, luxury cars and suites, designer jewellery of *de beers* and so on. One should talk of measuring wealth in crores/millions and billions of rupees and dollars. The *lakhpatis* are now endangered species, if not extinct ones. Against this glorious backdrop, India appears to be a divided nation on regional, linguistic, caste and political lines. When India is touted as an emerging 'Super Power', within the country we are a divided lot and are not able to live harmoniously side by side. In the name of language, region, religion and caste, notions of superiority are being preached; movement of people is being restricted; natural resources are being owned as their personal property of respective States/regions; heritage is a commodity for marketing; historical past is remembered symbolically to arouse parochial feelings; historical/religious personalities and reformers are owned by selfish caste groups; history is studied and interpreted to suit the convenience of disparate human groups divided on a variety of lines and alliances. The intellectual discourses in the country are focused on global economies, global villages and global histories, whereas in our own backyard agricultural suicides are on the rise. No economist is bothered to look at the reasons for poverty in the agricultural sector and the excessive riches in the services sector. For the American President, the main reason for the global increase in prices is due to the Indians who are spending much on food and luxury goods.

The changes in the social structure are even more pronounced. Attempts to highlight caste identities have been one of the most unique features of globalization. History is being attempted to be rewritten on caste lines. During the ancient and medieval times, people tried to elevate their social status via economic and religious media to move up in the vertical social order. In India, today there is a reversal of that practice; many of the caste groups clamour for the *status* of scheduled caste/tribe to enjoy the benefits of government employment while the State itself is retreating from the social responsibilities of education, health and sanitation and employment generation. The historical dynasties/mythical personalities are 'owned' by the caste groups to elevate their social status, without bothering to practice the preachings of those mythical and religious personalities. Even distinguished social reformers and political thinkers of modern era were brought under the blanket of *caste* as its perpetrators while during their lifetime they have actually denounced it and fought against it.

Religion as a social institution played a leading role in the efflorescence of arts and letters, music and dance, economic and agricultural development, trade and urban centres, monumental temple-complexes and many more necessary things for the society at large during the early historical and medieval times. Most of the festivals, fairs and ritual paraphernalia of all the religious systems of the country today were the inheritance of the medieval times, which in those times helped the knitting of people of different social, economic, cultural and ritual strata together. The meaning, structure and purpose of religion today are witnessing tumultuous changes. Religion goes high-tech and the believers/pilgrims are now enjoying air-conditioned waiting rooms to have the *Darshan* of the Almighty. The God together with His blessings is available online. Religious organizations are brimming with funds and this has resulted in the plaguing problems of low moral values in all the religious systems. Sexual abuse, money laundering, excessive spending on religious propagation, luxurious life of the religious teachers, involvement in political squabbles and discourses are some of the grave concerns troubling all the religious systems in India today. Religion has become another commodity in the *culture of disposables*. Religion is no more a social institution meant for keeping the people together; on the contrary, it has become a divisive force. Religious institutions are no more places of spiritual significance; religious teachers are no more a respected lot. Religion has become another by-product of consumerism, which is all about profits and losses.

The greatest impact of globalization is to be seen in the agricultural sector. We can rarely see nowadays the bent backs of the rural folk involved in agricultural activities. The melodious songs of the agricultural folk can only be seen in published books and on DVDs of private sponsored publicity blitzkrieg. Festivals are now symbols of *Cultural Property* and for corporate *Heritage Management* or *Culture Resource Management*. The changes in the economic and social structures have led to the exodus of rural agricultural labour in search of state-sponsored 'Employment Generation Programmes' making it difficult to find the needed work-force for agricultural activities. The labour-intensive Indian agriculture sector is being taken over by the machines of *John Deers*. Fertile lands are either converted into 'real estates' or handed over to

Special Economic Zones at throwaway prices. The petty farmers are driven out of their lands with the lure of lucrative jobs which will never come anyway. Agriculture is no more a welcome occupation in India; on the other hand, it is one which is driving the farmers towards suicides. Inflation nears '0' levels and the food products cost a treasure for the middle class community. The paradoxes are innumerable. A cup of tea costs Rs. 6/- and the State supplies rice at Rs. 1/- a kilo. The prices fluctuate on hourly basis equally in the case of essential commodities as well as precious metals. No economist will attempt to explain the reason, except making a statement that the market forces are deciding the pricing regime.

People in most of the towns and cities now are not bold enough to drink water that is not *e*-boiled, *ozone* treated and without oxygen additives. In the countryside, the women walk for miles to have a pot of potable/muddy water. The income of the government through the excise department is continuously on the rise despite the movements of the women against the intoxicants. Even small hamlets have well-maintained liquor shops besides local arrack markets, even if they do not have provision for the supply of safe drinking water. We, however, declare and observe symbolic holiday for liquor sales on October 2nd every year. Population control is no more a watch-word for the government. We no longer worry about the population increase. The paradox in this context is the intensive as well as extensive mechanization in all aspects of social life. Human relations even in a 'we two – ours one' scenario are on the decline. We listen to the news of child trade every day. Even the *Slum Dog Millionaire* children are no exceptions. Health insurance, as a consequence, has been the fancy slogan for the government as well as corporate, multinational giants. You should get a disease and become bed-ridden to see and enjoy the corporate treatment in 5 Star hospitals, where even the dead bodies are treated with *intensive care.*

The growth of the neo-rich middle class during the last decade or more is one of the most important changes in the contemporary Indian society. The most potent cause for this is the software boom. Young, college/university fresh graduates become executives overnight earning salaries over and above 'fifty K'. This sudden rush of money developed a community of tech-savvy, laptop using (to produce false CVs) youngsters riding designer bikes which are oil guzzlers, shuttling between offices in cabs, taking burgers and pizzas, attending week-end pubs and discotheques, savouring hot drinks in the company of girl friends and performing heroic deeds of riding their bikes and cars in that intoxicated condition at breakneck speeds. This generation has led to the phenomenal growth of shopping malls, luxury cars, designer bikes, real estate prices, house rents and so on. In majority, they do not care for the social values and stigmas. The direct aftermath of the growth of technical, software and engineering jobs is the decline of the social sciences, humanities and other pure sciences.

The disciplines of Archaeology and History are the most suffered in this regard. In the changed political, social and economic conditions, the didactic role of History is forgotten by the practitioners, teachers and students of History alike as also the general public, and that could be one of the reasons why the contemporary society is plagued with serious problems. In the mad rush for monetary gains, people are not bothered to think about anything, let alone their past, wherein the roots of the present are to be identified.

If the decline of employment opportunities has driven the students away from the disciplines of History and Archaeology, the policies of the government has played their role in the disappearance of many historical and archaeological sites. The rampant destruction of archaeological sites through mining activities is the biggest blow in this regard. As part of the restructuring of the curriculum, History is linked to *tourism studies* and the result is that History has become a subsidiary to tourism studies at the graduate and post-graduate levels in many colleges and universities. Heritage tours and walks, adventure tourism and the like are more for a media hype directed towards publicity marketing and revenue generation than towards addressing the issues of the historical significance of the monuments, historical places and archaeological sites.

The maladies being experienced by the contemporary Indian society are countless starting from the SEZs to the decline of social structure as a whole. All of them can be addressed by a historical study of the social institutions at least to identify the reasons for the present state of affairs, let alone to find solutions if any. Most of the papers in this volume are in that direction.

Without a proper comprehension of the prehistoric past, the understanding of the early social formations cannot be possible. M.L.K. Murty's paper brings out the salient features of research trends in prehistoric archeology of South India. Starting from the Paleolithic age, he made a thorough analysis of the archeological data in the light of theoretical and methodological developments. Bringing out the knowledge of prehistoric archeology of South India up to date, he put forth some interesting avenues for future research, particularly the ethnographic approach to understand the evolutionary changes from hunting-gathering to agro-pastoral economies, which can be applied in a pan-Indian archaeological study as well.

The papers on different topics of prehistoric archaeology by P. Vijaya Prakash, V. Selvakumar and P.C. Venkata Subbaiah present the results of their significant field investigations in respective study areas. P. Vijaya Prakash presented the mesolithic cultural data of north-eastern Andhra Pradesh from a geo-ecological perspective. His analysis of the Mesolithic cultural adaptations has brought out yet another interesting facet of hunter-gatherer adoptive strategies in diversified ecological settings. V. Selvakumar's paper presented the results of his recent field investigations in the lower Kaveri valley of Tamil Nadu. P.C. Venkata Subbaiah, in his paper, has discussed the man-land relationship in the Upper and Central Pennar basin of Andhra during the Neolithic phase. Extensive field investigations done by him in the study area resulted in discovery of a large number of Neolithic habitation sites distributed in varying density in the upper and central Pennar zones. He looked at the ecological determinants for the distributional pattern of the agro-pastoral settlements in the Pennar basin.

Multi-disciplinary studies have become a common feature of archaeological researches in India in recent times. G.L. Badam, in his paper, has brought out the advances in the application of scientific analyses in the interpretation and dating of archeological cultures in India, such as dental history, bio-molecular studies, taphonomic analysis of fossils, etc. He has also shown how the paleo-ecological model is useful to study the Indian rock art as also the significance of ostrich egg shells to the rock art analysis. Bansi Lal Malla, in his paper, has proposed some alternative approaches for the understanding of the meaning of rock art in the light of the launching of *Adi Drishya* Project by Indira Gandhi National Centre for the Arts (IGNCA), New Delhi.

Discussing a variety of issues related to the proto-historical period, A. Sundara has brought out many new avenues for investigation in the upper Krishna region of Karnataka, along with the valleys of its tributaries, such as Malaprabha and Bheema. His hypothesis of the southern origin of the Salvada ware in relation to the ash-mound occurrences is quite interesting seen in the light of existence of large number of Savalda culture sites in the upper Krishna region. He also analysed the rock art depictions of megalithic burials and the *puranic* descriptions of death rituals. He makes a clarion call for the urgent need of systematic documentation of all surviving archaeological sites using latest scientific tools, before all the surface evidences of archaeological sites disappear on account of ignorant vandalism and deliberate destruction in the wake of rapid developmental programmes. Following the observations of A. Sundara, the paper by Shanti Pappu and Kumar Akhilesh presents an overview of the nature of impact of developmental activities and expansion of human settlements on the survival of prehistoric sites based on their pioneering study in Tamil Nadu and also suggest some necessary steps to preserve the prehistoric sites as part of their broader research and heritage management project.

S. Nagaraju's paper advocates the linking of the practice of archaeology with the modern necessities of sustainable development. By the application of his alternative action archaeology, he tried to provide alternative strategies for the preservation of productive agricultural land for future needs, which is now being distributed indiscriminately to the SEZs. His ideas on the utilization of the medieval monumental structures for a variety of modern necessities offer interesting avenues for planners in designing their developmental schemes.

Terracotta art is the most primitive, rustic and mundane of all the early art forms in India and elsewhere. Its widespread occurrence in terms of space, volume and variety makes the terracotta art one of the most important evidences to study and understand the genesis of codified religion. S. Murali Mohan in his paper has discussed the archeological context of the terracotta figurines of early historic Andhra Pradesh found in various sites and in the variety of contexts. Going beyond the typo technological descriptive pattern, his study concentrates on the evolutionary pattern of different symbols on the terracotta figurines into codified religious/ ritual symbolism of later times. He also stressed the need to take note of the contextual occurrence of terracotta finds in the archeological excavations. Another paper on terracotta art is that of S. Vasanthi. She analysed the 'mother and the child' terracotta figurines found in different excavated sites in Tamil Nadu, most of which are datable to the Medieval Period.

Kirankranth Choudary's paper brings out interesting evidence of medicine and medical practices in the Buddhist tradition and literature. The literary texts of Little and Great vehicles contain voluminous information about diseases and their symptoms, medicines for their cure, methods of preparation of medicines, their ingredients, individual hygiene and cleanliness, preparation of ointments from the leaves and barks of trees, etc. It was in Buddhism that the early Indian medicinal knowledge gets codified, consolidated and elaborated to cater to the needs of a wider clientele.

The medieval phase in the history of peninsular India was one of the most vibrant epochs in the Indian history as a whole. It was during this period that the traditional four-fold society emerges in a diversified form facilitating the vertical mobility of the lower sections of the society in the social order. The 'Boya ascendancy' was one of such dimensions of the vertical social mobility of the marginalized sections during the medieval times in Andhra. C. Somasundara Rao in his paper presents the historiographical analysis of the Boya community in medieval Andhra. Basing his analysis on a wealth of inscriptional data, datable between 7th-16th centuries, he has discussed the integration of the Boya community into the Andhra society.

The same vertical social mobility of the marginalized sections of the society forms the theme of P.S. Kanaka Durga's paper. She took up the theoretical premise of kingship and state formation in the medieval Andhra between 7th-13th centuries for her critical analysis. Starting her discussion with the historiographical analysis of the state and kingship in early Indian literature, she links up different stages in the development of kingship and the creation of myths and legends for the assertion of the sovereigneity starting from the Chalukyas. She also analysed the socio-economic and political factors of the medieval era in the changing contexts of the evolution of kingship. The cultural and ritual institutions, such as *Sapta santhanas*, temples, *Agraharas*, etc. and their role in the legitimization of sovereignity was also effectively analyzed.

R. Nagaswamy, in his paper, argued for the disapproval of certain oral traditions about the religious conditions of Chola rule in Tamil Nadu, which are being portrayed as religious bigotry even in the popular cinema medium recently. The analysis of the inscription of Kulottunga Chola II is an eye-opener against such historical misinterpretations.

A. Gurumurthy and E. Sobhan Babu studied the patterns of urbanization in the south-western part of Andhra Pradesh under the Vijayanagara rule. They classified the urban centres on the basis of their size, structure and nature. Besides the trade, Vijayanagara urbanism was mainly sustained by religion as a result of which temple urbanism prospered during this period. Many of the fairs, rituals and festivals that are still popular today in South India are a legacy inherited from this period. This paper describes in detail a host of urban centres and towns that were established during the Vijayanagara times across the peninsula.

The paper by S.M. Nagabhushana discusses the role of ancient Belgaum in north-western Karnataka as an important commercial and trade centre in the history of peninsular India. His analysis of the ancient and medieval inscriptions brings out the items of merchandise and the trade guilds of Belgaum.

D. Dayalan, in his paper, has described the history of conservation and management activities of the Taj Mahal. Being a man involved in its conservation and preservation projects for a long time, Dayalan gives a personal touch to the description of the various issues involved.

Historical writings in India were initiated by the Oriental and Utilitarian schools of thought. After 1905, Indian historical writings were strongly influenced by the Nationalist School followed by the Leftist schools of historical thought, during and after Indian freedom struggle. Tremendous changes in historical writings were subsequently brought forth by the Subaltern school of thought emphasizing on the creation and promotion of 'grassroots history' by Karl Marx, Antonio Gramsci and others. Under the influence of the philosophy of the Subaltern thought, a band of historians under the stewardship of Ranajit Guha in the 80s of the last century started the Subaltern school of historical writings in India. They argued for the creation of *History from Below* (grassroots history) as opposed to the *History from Above* (remember the *Feudalism from Above* and *Feudalism from Below* of D.D. Kosambi) which hitherto gave importance only to the history of *elite minority*. This *History from Below* is aimed at the creation of the history of the *popular majority* through the examination and analysis of the subaltern sections of the society. The historical events led to the growth of researches into the role and participation of tribal, peasant, folk and other marginalized groups during and after the Indian Independence movement. K.A. Manikumar, Y.A. Sudhakara Reddy, G. Chandhrika, S. Manikandan, P. Sumabala, M. Amrithalingam and Lalitha Ramadurai in their papers present their individual contributions in related fields.

K.A. Manikumar's paper is on the theoretical underpinnings of subaltern history and post-modernism. Discussing the theoretical prepositions of noted western historians and philosophers, he traces out how the post-modernist theoretical developments led to the birth of Subaltern school of historical writings in India. Drawing parallels in philosophy and methods between post-modernists and subalterns, Manikumar also reviews the response from the intellectual world of historians towards these two highly influential schools of historical thought and writings.

Y.A. Sudhakara Reddy has discussed the current research trends in the field of folk culture studies. He brings out the theoretical developments in the fields of literature and anthropology as the stimulating factors for the emergence of folklore studies as a separate and independent discipline. Through a review of the pioneering works of the western scholars like Alan Dundes, Bakhtin, E.B. Tylor and Ben-Amos, etc., he delineates the major theoretical and methodological shifts in folkloristics. The theoretical developments of post-modern and post-structural phases led to the creation of new conceptual frameworks to look at the ethnographic context of 'folk and related areas' and the data through which the 'folk' is approached.

G. Chandhrika's paper looks at the *folk* perspective of the early Christian writings whose identification of a Dravidian folk and language groups in southern India as opposed to the Northern and Aryan language and race. The Christian writings have made a profound impact on the minds of the people of Tamil Nadu which permeates into the 21st century when it comes to the identification of purity and hoary antiquity of the Tamil language and the greatness of Dravidian race is concerned.

S. Manikandan's paper interprets the folk songs and ballads of the famous palegar Virapandya Kattabomman of Tirunelveli district of Tamil Nadu. The ballads and folk songs narrated in the region were collected and published as *'veerapandya kattabommu kathai padal'*. This paper discusses the significance of this work as a primary source for the reconstruction of the contemporary historical events.

P. Sumabala, in her paper, discusses the issue of environmental conservation from a historical perspective. She traces out different forms of worship prevalent in India which helped in the environmental conservation with a religious sanction. The role of religion in the environmental preservation and protection right from the ancient times into the present shows how India maintained a time-tested method of environmental conservation successfully even before the much publicised western oriented conservation movements.

M. Amrutalingam's paper has discussed the ancient Tamil literary background of nature conservation. The sacred groves as the natural habitats preserved by the people for their intrinsic value were also found mentioned in the ancient Tamil literature. These natural sanctuaries continued to have popular as well as royal patronage during the medieval times.

Lalita Ramadurai's paper focuses on the animal symbolism in Indian folk and tribal dances, and describes how animals as part of the nature shared by the human beings attracted their attention in various dance forms which continues to enchant the people even in the present times.

Aravinda Kumar, in his paper, highlights the growth of regional histories in contrast to the nationalist histories. The growth of regional historiography in India as elsewhere has its own supporters as well as critics, depending on political, cultural and historical reasons. As long as regional histories help in the reconstruction of national histories, they can have their role to play. When they become a study unto themselves, they tend to incite regional parochial feelings, leading to tensions and confrontations between different human groups.

S. Babu's paper discusses the salient features of the textile trade of the British East India Company on the Coromandel Coast. He describes the types of textile products produced at various centres in Andhra and Tamil Nadu regions that were exported to England on a massive scale.

Bithin Thakur's paper graphically describes the heinous atrocities of the Japanese forces during their brief occupation of the Andaman Islands in the final stages of the World War II. His paper also informs us that the British were much more civilized than the Japanese in terms of treatment of the natives. This paper is a touching narration of the untold suffering sustained by the native population of the Andamans under the oppressive Japanese occupation during World War II.

Divya Sandesh, in her paper, brought to light the active role played by the female members of the royal family of Cochin, Kerala. Breaking the shackles of prejudices, these royal ladies came out in the early 20th century and made their own contribution in the fields of education, music and dance and brought about revolutionary changes in the native education system. They even got married into Brahmin and Kshatriya families, thereby creating a new social order.

The region of the present day Pondicherry city has been one of the important geographical areas of the ancient land of Tamils. Arikamedu and Bahur were important early historical places: the former known for its ancient port, the latter known as a centre of learning under the Pallavas. During the medieval times, this region witnessed brisk political activity as revealed by the existence of huge temple-complexes at Bahur, Villanur, Markanam, Tirubuvanai, etc. These temple-towns and trade centres continued to retain their significant place up to the end of the Vijayanagara period and even later.

The modern Pondicherry began to rise in prominence with the arrival of the European trading companies beginning with the Dutch. It was under the French that Pondicherry became the political capital of 'French India'. During this period, the fortunes of Pondicherry town witnessed many tumultuous phases of development. It preserved its cosmopolitan legacy even after its de jure merger in the Indian union in 1962. The present day Union Territory/State of Pondicherry is constituted out of the four heterogeneous *enclaves* of the erstwhile French domain in India. Pondicherry and Karikal regions are surrounded by Tamil Nadu state while Mahe and Yanam regions are surrounded by the states of Kerala and Andhra Pradesh respectively. The papers of R. Ezhil Raman, B. Ramachandra Reddy and R. Natarajan, A. Arul Jyoti and B. Krishnamurthy are on different aspects of medieval and modern Pondicherry.

R. Ezhil Raman's paper on 'education in pre-colonial Pondicherry' describes the early historical institutions and system of education in Pondicherry between AD 750 and 1600.

The paper by B. Ramachandra Reddy and R. Natarajan is on the interesting folk cult of Ayyanar which is very popular in Tamil Nadu and contiguous regions in South India. After giving a brief description of the origin and evolution of the cult, they have discussed the cult centres of Ayyanar in Pondicherry and the social background of the priests of and modes of worship. They conclude that Ayyanar was a folk hero of Jaina affiliation who in course of time was brought into the puranic pantheon and was given an exalted ritual status. However, his original and folk origins cannot be altogether obliterated.

A. Arul Jothi's paper concentrates on the growth of new social groups in Pondicherry during the French occupation of Pondicherry region. As a result of the marital relations between the native Indians and the French, the natives got to acquire French citizenship and connected privileges.

B. Krishnamurthy in his paper has analysed the native resistance to the French rule in Pondicherry. His study makes use of one on the contemporary sources in the form of the *Diary of Veera Naicker II*, a native police chief under the French. This *Diary* is considered to be one of the primary sources to cover the tumultuous period in the history of French in India during 1778-1792.

In the task of editing a volume, I received encouragement, support and help from a large number of people but for which this volume would not have become a reality.

My foremost respectful thanks should go to our esteemed vice chancellor Prof. J.A.K. Tareen, who gave the administrative sanction for the conduct of the seminar; insisted me to bring out the proceedings of the seminar in the form of a publication; sanctioned a publication subsidy as well and blessed this venture by contributing a thought-provoking foreword. Words fail me in expressing my profound sense of gratitude to this visionary and enlightened soul for his love and affection towards me and in seeing this volume in the present form.

I express my sincere thanks to Shri S. Loganathan, Registrar, Pondicherry University; Dr. M. Rajendran, Deputy Registrar (Planning & Development); Prof. P. Subramanyam Naidu, Former Dean and Prof. D. Sambandhan, present Dean of the School of Social Sciences & International Studies and Prof. D. Srinivas, Head, Dept. of Philosophy for evincing a keen interest in seeing this publication coming out.

The contribution of my colleagues in the Department of History was immense in the organization of the National Seminar as also in bringing out this publication. My foremost thanks should go to Prof. K. Rajan, the then head of the department, who gave me immense moral support in the organization of the National Seminar. I am also thankful to Prof. Venkata Raghotham, head of the department, Prof. G. Chandhrika and Dr. K. Venugopal Reddy, for all their encouragement and help. Doctoral research scholars of this department, Mr. Bithin Thakur, Mrs. Divya Sandesh, Mr. R. Ezhil Raman, Mr. Yateesh Kumar, Mrs. S. Geetha, Mr. Selvakumar, Mr. S. Manikandan, Ms. D. Supriya and others were immensely helpful in more than one way. I place on record my sincere thanks to them.

I received help and loving assistance on many occasions from Dr. V. Nallam, President, The Historical Society of Pondicherry, a distinguished doctor known for his charity medicine and a great lover of the disciplines of History and Archaeology. I am extremely thankful to him for his consistent support and encouragement in all my academic ventures.

My special words of appreciation and sincere thanks should go to Dr. D. Vishwanatha Sastry, Department of History, P.S. Telugu University, Srisailam, Andhra Pradesh, who was extremely helpful at every stage of the organization of the seminar and afterwards.

A host of distinguished scholars have contributed their research papers to this volume, some of which were revised versions of the seminar presentations and some contributed afresh. To all of them, I record my respectful thanks for their love and affection towards me. I am particularly thankful to my teachers and guides: Prof. S. Nagaraju, my research supervisor in M.Phil programme in University of Hyderabad (now Director, M.H. Krishna Institute of Indology, Bangalore) and Prof. D.R. Raju (P.S. Telugu University, Hyderabad), my Ph.D research supervisor, who are responsible for my academic standing at this stage.

I am deeply indebted to Shri Vikas Arya of Aryan Books International who not only came forward to bring out this publication as a joint venture with Pondicherry University, but also stood beside me with unflinching love and patience to see this volume coming out in this beautiful form.

I owe a lot to my wife, Mrs. N. Rajanipriya, and my children, Chi. N.S.S. Gayatri and Chi. N. Srilalita Krishna Prasanna, who, besides making my life pleasant and cheerful, lent their helping hand in all my academic activities and for relieving me of the domestic chores to concentrate on my academic work. To the Omnipresent Almighty, I owe everything of my physical and mental planes.

(N. CHANDRAMOULI)

Contents

Contributors

1. **Dr. A. Arul Jothi**
   Department of Historical Studies, K.M. Centre for P.G. Studies (Autonomous)
   Laws Pet, Pondicherry-605 008.
   Email: satchithananthi@yahoo.com

2. **Prof. A. Gurumurti**
   Registrar, Rashtriya Sanskit Vidyapeetha, Tirupati-517 507.
   Email: agmurti@yahoo.com

3. **Dr. A. Sundara**
   Former Professor & Head, Department of Archaeology, Karnatak University
   Pavat Nagar, Dharwad-580 003.
   Email: sundara_adiga@yahoo.com

4. **Dr. Aravind Kumar**
   Associate Professor, Department of History, Archaeology & Culture
   Dravidian University, Kuppam-517 425.
   Email: aravind19kumar@yahoo.co.in

5. **Dr. B. Krishnamurthy**
   Associate Professor, Department of Politics & International Studies
   Pondicherry University, Pondicherry-605 014.
   Email: bkris53@gmail.com

6. **Dr. B. Ramachandra Reddy**
   Department of Historical Studies, K.M. Centre for P.G. Studies (Autonomous)
   Laws Pet, Pondicherry-605 008.
   Email: b_ramachandrareddy@yahoo.com

7. **Dr. Bansi Lal Malla**
   Indira Gandhi National Centre for the Arts, Janpath, New Delhi-110 011.
   Email: drblmalla@gmail.com

8. **Mr. Bithin Thakur**
   Research Scholar, Department of History, Pondicherry University, Pondicherry-605 014.
   Email: thakurbithin@gmail.com

9. **Dr. C. Somasundara Rao**
   Former Professor, Department of History, Andhra University, Visakhapatnam-530 003.
   Email: srchellapilla@yahoo.co.in

10. **Dr. D. Dayalan**
    Superintending Archaeologist, Archaeological Survey of India, Fort. St. George, Chennai.
    Email: sooraidayalan@gmail.com

11. **Mrs. Divya Sandesh**
    Research Scholar, Department of History, Pondicherry University, Pondicherry-605 014.
    Email: divyasandesh2007@yahoo.co.in

12. **Dr. E. Sobhan Babu**
    Department of History, P.S. Telugu University, Srisailam-518 101.
    Email: sobhanbabu.ellanti@gmail.com

13. **Prof. G. Chandhrika**
    Department of History, Pondicherry University, Pondicherry-605 014.
    Email: g.chandhrika@gmail.com

14. **Dr. G.L. Badam**
    Former Professor, Department of Archaeology, Deccan College
    26/1-4, Hermes Paras-3, Kalyani Nagar, Pune-411 006.
    Email: glbadam@yahoo.com

15. **Prof. K.A. Manikumar**
    Department of History, Manonmaniam Sundaranar University
    Abhishekapatti, Tirunelveli-627 012.
    Email: kamkumar2002@yahoo.com

16. **Prof. Kirankranth Choudary**
    Department of Ancient History & Archaeology, Sri Venkateswara University
    Tirupati-517 502.
    Email: gandhakuti@yahoo.com

17. **Mr. Kumar Akhilesh**
    Sharma Centre for Heritage Education
    28, I Main Road, C.I.T. Colony, Mylapore, Chennai-600 004.

18. **Dr. Lalita Ramadurai**
    Programme Officer, C.P.R. Environmental Education Centre
    1, Eldams Road, Alwarpet, Chennai-600 018.
    Email: lrdurai@yahoo.com

19. **Dr. M. Amritalingam**
    C.P.R. Environmental Education Centre, 1, Eldams Road, Alwarpet, Chennai-600 018.
    Email: m.amirthalingam@gmail.com

20. **Prof. M.L.K. Murti**
Former Professor & Head, Centre for Regional Studies, University of Hyderabad
Hyderabad.
Email: murty_mlk@yahoo.com

21. **Dr. P. Sumabala**
Assistant Professor, CPR Institute of Indological Research
1, Eldams Road, Chennai-600 018.
Email: sumabala2k@yahoo.com

22. **Dr. P. Vijaya Prakash**
Professor, Department of Archaeology, Andhra University, Visakhapatnam-530 003.
Email: profpvprakash@yahoo.com

23. **Dr. P.C. Venkata Subbaiah**
Associate Professor, Department of History, Archaeology & Culture
Dravidian University, Kuppam-517 425.
Email: pcvenkatasubbaiah@gmail.com

24. **Dr. P.S. Kanaka Durga**
Professor, Centre for Folk Culture Studies, University of Hyderabad
Gachibowli, Hyderabad-500 046.
Email: srikanakadurga@gmail.com

25. **Mr. R. Ezhil Raman**
Research Scholar, Department of History, Pondicherry University, Pondicherry-605 014.
Email: ezhilraman1980@gmail.com

26. **Dr. R. Nagaswamy**
Former Director, Department of Archaeology & Museums, Chennai.
Email: nagaswamy@msn.com

27. **Dr. R. Natarajan**
Head, Department of Historical Studies, K.M. Centre for P.G. Studies (Autonomous)
Laws Pet, Pondicherry-605 008.
Email: rnvp1@rediffmail.com

28. **Dr. S. Babu**
Department of Historical Studies, K.M. Centre for P.G. Studies (Autonomous)
Laws Pet, Pondicherry-605 008.
Email: drbabu1961@yahoo.com

29. **Mr. S. Manikandan**
Research Scholar, Department of History, Pondicherry University, Pondicherry-605 014.
Email: manikavi81@gmail.com

30. **Dr. S. Murali Mohan**
Department of History & Archaeology, Acharya Nagarjuna University
Nagarjuna Nagar, Guntur-522 510.
Email: murali_srirama@yahoo.co.in

31. **Prof. S. Nagaraju**
Director, M.H. Krishna Institute of Indology, Mythic Society, Bangalore.
Email: nagarajus03@yahoo.co.in

32. **Dr. S. Vasanthi**
Archaeological Officer, Department of Archaeology & Museums, Chennai.
Email: vasanthi42@rediffmail.com

33. **Dr. S.M. Nagabhushana**
S.J.M. Mahanta 1st Grade College, Ramnagar, Dharwad-580 001.
Email: smnagabhushana@rediffmail.com

34. **Dr. Shanti Pappu**
Sharma Centre for Heritage Education
28, I Main Road, C.I.T. Colony, Mylapore, Chennai-600 004.
Flat No. 2, Moti Mahal Building, Alandi Road, Pune-411 006.
Email: pappu.shanti@gmail.com

35. **Dr. V. Selvakumar**
Associate Professor, Department of Archaeology, Tamil University, Tanjavur-613 005.
Email: selvakumarodi@gmail.com

36. **Prof. Y.A. Sudhakara Reddy**
Head, Centre for Folk Culture Studies
University of Hyderabad, Gachibowli, Hyderabad-500 046.
Email: ysreddy99@yahoo.com

1

Prehistoric Research in South India: Concepts and Methods

M.L.K. MURTY

ABSTRACT

Robert Bruce Foote, who pioneered prehistoric research in South India, laid the foundation for a geological and geomorphological approach with the objective of studying the Stone Age industries in relation to stratigraphy, chronology and past climates. While the conceptual approaches of Foote provided the framework for subsequent researches, there has been an emphasis in the use of sophisticated tools for data recovery, absolute dating, regional scale analyses in the interpretation of occupation sites, and explanation of cultures. In the context of these developments, this paper focuses on three different issues related to (a) the Acheulian and human dispersals; (b) processual changes from hunting-gathering to plant domestication in woodland environments; and (c) the hunter-gatherer (Mesolithic)-agro-pastoral (Neolithic-Chalcolithic) interface.

INTRODUCTION

The beginnings of research in the study of the prehistory of South India implicitly reflect the nineteenth century debate in Europe on the antiquity of man and his culture, the quest for human origins, the explorations and excavations conducted by antiquarians, geologists and naturalists, and the fascinating discoveries and interpretations made by them (see Daniel 1964; Wendt 1974). This mission, pursued by those with a flair for scientific discoveries, was against the backdrop of doctrines such as 'special creation' and the theory of a Universal Deluge in *Genesis.* The most distinguished and ardent advocate of the Universal Deluge was the Zurich city doctor and canon Johann Jakob Scheuchzer (Wendt 1974: 23-29). He discovered, in 1726, some giant fossil bones near the village of Oeningen on Lake Constance, and believed all fossils to be the result of a catastrophic universal deluge, which was identified with the Biblical flood. There were enthusiastic collectors of fossils who speculated about giant monsters, and scholars even debated whether Adam and Eve had not perhaps been giants. Henrion, a French scholar of the seventeenth century, calculated on the basis of existing giant bones that Adam had been 123 feet 9 inches tall and Eve 118 feet and 9 inches. This theory made Scheuchzer wonder how things had been before the great catastrophe took place, and he took to search for the remains of 'antediluvian man'. Scheuchzer concluded that these giant bones belonged to the 'diluvian man' to which he gave the name *Homo diluvi testis* and worked out that this man died precisely in 2306 BC (Wendt 1974: 29). Further studies by others soon have revealed that these giant bones actually were the fossils of a giant extinct salamander of the Tertiary era. Scheuchzer and his pupils, who called themselves Diluvians, stimulated the systematic study of fossils as petrified remains of creatures which had existed on earth, and fostered the study of prehistoric times. As a matter of fact, numerous discoveries of curious objects and fossils that were being made by amateurs, antiquarians, and naturalists from the fifteenth century onwards gave rise to various speculative and intriguing interpretations, but what is important with the Diluvians is their reservations about the Biblical chronology, and scholars like Comte de Buffon even felt that the earth was not created in 4004 BC, as reckoned by Archbishop Ussher of Armagh and other medieval scholars, but was at least 75000 years old (Wendt 1974: 38). During these times of intense debate, Jacques Boucher de Crevecoeur de Perthes, customs officer in Abbeville and an amateur archaeologist, who was in search of 'Adam's Ancestors', has been collecting artificially shaped lumps of stones since 1832 from the 'antediluvian' gravel deposits of the Somme River in northwestern France. He delivered a lecture in Paris in 1839 declaring that the 'flints' he discovered were thousands of years older than all previous archaeological discoveries. In the year 1859, the discoveries of Boucher de Perthes in France and others in Britain (John Frere, Father J. MacEnery and William Pengelly to mention a few) were acknowledged in the scientific gatherings as the 'stone tools' of early man (popularly called as flints), the antiquity of man was established, and prehistory began to emerge as a discipline of stratigraphical geology. By the late 1860s, the Three Age System in the succession of cultural epochs (Stone Age, Bronze Age and Iron Age), proposed by Christian Jurgunsen Thomsen during 1816-19, was progressively elaborated into Palaeolithic, Neolithic, Bronze and Early Iron Ages. This Three Age System provided a chronological yardstick for the cultural periodisation of discoveries being made in different parts of the world.

The term prehistory was first used by Daniel Wilson in 1851, in the title of his book *The Archaeology and Prehistoric Annals of Scotland* and by 1865, the idea of prehistory of man was so far advanced that the popular book *Prehistoric Times,* published by Sir John Lubbock, became the best seller. Sir Charles Lyell used the terms Palaeolithic and Neolithic three years later, in the tenth edition of his *Principles of Geology*. Lubbock modified the Three Age System into Four Ages of Palaeolithic, Neolithic, Bronze and Iron Ages. Eventually, the Stone Age itself was broken into three periods: the Old Stone Age (Palaeolithic), the Middle Stone Age (Mesolithic) and the New Stone Age (Neolithic), and the Palaeolithic has been further subdivided into Lower, Middle and Upper Palaeolithic.

The beginnings of prehistoric studies in South India, as elsewhere in the Indian subcontinent, betray parallels to the nineteenth century researches in Europe, Africa and Southeast Asia in pursuit of human fossils, animal fossils, and stone tools in the context of the search for the antediluvian man. The conceptual approach, by and large, during this period was to work out the stratigraphical succession of the cultures of early man in relation to the environmental episodes – the glacial and interglacial epochs in the temperate regions and pluvial and interpluvial epochs in the tropical zones. Prehistoric cultures were interpreted in terms of typo-technological attributes of stone tools and the associated animal and human skeletal remains in a stratigraphical order.

With regard to the beginnings of prehistoric research in South India, it has been observed by some scholars that Colonel Meadows Taylor discovered the first stone tool, a Neolithic ground or polished stone axe, in 1842, at Lingsugur in the Raichur District, Karnataka (Sankalia 1974: 12). But it was pointed out that it was one Dr. Primrose who, in 1842, discovered a few stone artefacts while clearing his garden at Lingsugur; these artefacts consisted of knives and arrowheads made on jasper, agate and chalcedony; and they are not Neoliths (Patil 2002-2003). The first ever discovery of a Palaeolithic tool (a handaxe) in India was made by Robert Bruce Foote on 30th May 1863 in a pit dug in the lateritic gravel at Pallavaram near Madras, and a few months later, on 28th September 1863, he along with William King located another Palaeolithic site in the lateritic gravels of a stream at Attirampakkam in the Kortallayar Basin and discovered another tool (a cleaver) *in situ* (Foote 1866, 1869). Foote classified them as 'Madras Type'. A.B. Wynne reported, in 1865, an agate knife (flake) at Mungi-Paithen in the clays and gravels of the Godavari; Valentine Ball unearthed stone tools at four sites in Orissa in 1875; H.B. Medlicott discovered stone tools (especially a quartzite handaxe) in 1873, in association with fossil mammalia in the Narmada cliff at Bhutra; and Cockburn reported stone tools from the Singrauli basin, south Mirzapur, in 1883 (Sankalia 1974: 12). The artefacts discovered by Cockburn and Wynne were also associated with the remains of extinct animals. Robert Bruce Foote also discovered the first Neolithic artefact in Andhra Pradesh, in 1865, from a place about 17 km south of Nellore, and published a paper on his discoveries in the *Journal of the Asiatic Society of Bengal* (Foote 1887). De Terra and Paterson, nearly seventy years after the first discoveries made by Foote in 1863, conducted investigations in Punjab and some areas of peninsular India through their Yale-Cambridge Expedition. Their objective was to study the stone tool industries in relation to stratigraphy, chronology and past climates. They discovered in the Sohan valley of the Siwalik (Shivalik) ranges of the Himalayas, a sequence of pebble tool traditions consisting of chopper and chopping tools and flakes, and postulated a correlation of these tool bearing deposits to the Pleistocene glacial sequence in Kashmir. They gave the name 'Soan' to these pebble tool industries. The investigations of the Yale-Cambridge Expedition were also extended to the Narmada valley in Central India and the Kortallayar river basin near Madras. Patterson (1939) described the handaxe industries of the Kortallayar basin as the 'Madras Palaeolithic Industries'.

It was Robert Bruce Foote who systematically carried on the search for the early human cultures in South India (Foote 1868, 1914, 1916). For nearly 40 years, he systematically explored the rivers of Tamil Nadu, Andhra, Karnataka and Gujarat, while attending to his main work as a geologist. He made a vast collection of artefacts and classified and catalogued it. He was the true pioneer of Indian prehistory (Sankalia 1974: 12). At the behest of Robert Bruce Foote, his son Henry Bruce Foote excavated the Billa Surgam caves near Betamcherla, Kurnool district, Andhra Pradesh, which yielded bone tools and fossilized bones of animals. In his interpretation, Robert Bruce Foote observed that these excavations "confirmed the existence of man in these caves at a low stage of civilization and threw light upon the former geographical distribution of some important genera and species of animals, no longer existing wild in south India" (Foote 1884a, 1884b, 1885). Interestingly enough, Foote pointed out that the bone tools recovered from the Billa Surgum caves are comparable to those of the Magdalenian culture of France. Further, the catalogue of sites, lithic artefacts, pottery, etc. made by Foote (Foote 1914, 1916) provided clues for researchers like Cammiade to explore for a stratigraphical sequence of the Stone Age industries, which was the focus of research in Europe and other parts of the Old World. The explorations of Cammiade in the first quarter of the twentieth century in the rivers of Kurnool area can be regarded as the foundation for the stratigraphical-typo-technological sequencing of

Stone Age industries in South India. Cammiade along with Burkitt studied these Stone Age industries and proposed a four-fold stratigraphical sequence of Stone Age industries, which they labelled as Series I, Series II, Series III and Series IV (Cammiade and Burkitt 1930). Subsequent research has established that this Series I-IV corresponds with the Lower Palaeolithic, Middle Palaeolithic, Upper Palaeolithic, and Mesolithic cultural phases respectively (Isaac 1960).

Changing Paradigms

Extensive explorations since the 1960s in different parts of South India with an orientation to regional scale analysis, systematic excavations of a few sites, detailed studies of typo-technological traditions, and cross-cultural comparisons with other regions within India and other parts of the Old World led to the identification of the Lower, Middle and Upper Palaeolithic and Mesolithic cultures with clarity. While stratigraphical sequences and typo-technological traits of artefact assemblages continue to play a major role in the appraisal of Stone Age cultures, attention has been paid in interpreting the prehistoric cultures as responses to climatic and environmental changes of the Pleistocene and Holocene periods (Sankalia 1974). Though geo-stratigraphical and relative chronologies also continued to provide time-frames for prehistoric cultures, the advent of radio-carbon dating and other methods like thermoluminiscence, potassium/argon, thorium/uranium, palaeomagnetism, electron spin resonance and oxygen isotopic dating contributed to the streamlining of absolute chronologies for the Stone Age cultures (Agarwal and Ghosh 1973; Mishra 1995b; Pappu 2001; Possehl and Rismann 1992). Further, in such contexts in which the Stone Age occupations are contiguous with the habitations of the indigenous communities, ethnographic studies have been undertaken to generate general comparative analogies, as in the case of other parts of India, to offer predictive models (see Allchin 1994; Dhavalikar 1983; Mohanty 2002; Murty 2006-2007).

The Lower Palaeolithic Culture

The Lower Palaeolithic culture-complex in South India is characterized by the Acheulian culture, in which an early phase and a late or advanced phase have been recognized (Mishra 2006-2007; Misra 1989, 2001; Paddayya 2006-2007; Pappu 2001). In Kerala, it is characterized by chopper-scraper-flake tradition with occasional handaxes (Gurukkal and Varier 1999: 60-67). The tool types of the Acheulian are handaxes, cleavers, picks, polyhedrons, discoids, chopping tools and a variety of scrapers, and utilized flakes. These artefacts are made on pebbles, cobbles, nodules and flakes, and quartzite is the predominant raw material. In the Hunsgi valley of Karnataka, limestone is the chief raw material and, occasionally, basalt and granite have also been used. That the manufacture of tools took place at majority of the occupation sites is attested by the occurrence of core dressing flakes, waste flakes, chips, unfinished tools and cores. The techniques employed for the manufacture of tools are block-on-block, stone hammer and cylinder hammer, the latter especially for finishing the tools by secondary retouch. The tools are finished by unifacial flaking and bifacial flaking, and the latter becomes more regular in secondary retouch in the late Acheulian. Though our knowledge of functional attributes of these tool types is imperfect, it has been pointed out that the functions they served include hunting, butchering the game, breaking bones for bone marrow, digging of roots and tubers and processing of plant foods, and making wooden implements. Faunal remains preserved in Acheulian gravel bearing deposits in peninsular rivers like the Narmada, Godavari and their tributaries comprise elephant

(*Elephas hysudricus* and *Stegodon insignis-ganesa*), horse (*Equus namadicus*), cattle (*Bos namadicus*), hippopotamus (*Hexaprotodon namadicus*) and wild boar (*Sus namadicus*) (Badam 1979). These faunal assemblages indicate palaeoenvironments with moist deciduous woodlands, woodland savannas and grasslands. Dependence on these fauna for subsistence by hunting or scavenging for the Acheulian groups might have been possible.

In the Acheulian covering a long span of more than one million years, two broad stages, i.e., Early Acheulian and Late Acheulian, have been distinguished (Paddayya 1984: 399-51; Gaillard *et al.* 1990). The characteristic tool types in both the phases are handaxes and cleavers. The early Acheulian tools are crude with zigzag cutting edges; often retain cortex; have large and deep flake-scars; secondary retouch is minimal; tend to be heavy; and the shapes are not standardized. The Late Acheulian tools are fully flaked with no cortex or minimal cortex, have small and shallow flakes scars; straight cutting edges; thin and less heavy; and the shapes are quite standardized. In addition to handaxes and cleavers, scrapers are various types made on cores and flakes (e.g., discoids and ovates) are more varied in the Late Acheulian. Analysis of techno-complexes from excavated sites in the Hunsgi (Isampur and Kolihal) and Baichbal (Mudnur X, Yediyapur IV, Teggihalli II) valleys in Karnataka further indicate the likelihood of a middle Acheulian phase (Paddayya 2006-2007).

Conceptual Approaches in the Study of Acheulian

It would be apt to recall that since the 1960s, in the interpretation of Acheulian culture in South India, the methodological and theoretical approaches of Foote were continued with further refinements and use of sophisticated techniques for data recovery. Foote, in his prehistoric studies of the Kortallayar valley, gave importance to geological investigations of the tool bearing lateritic gravels and the coarse boulder conglomerate on one hand, and emphasized geomorphological approach in the interpretation of occupation sites, on the other. He pointed out, on the basis of these studies, that great changes took place in the physical geography of the Indian peninsula since the time the implement makers first inhabited the country (Foote 1868). The foundation for such a geomorphological approach laid by Foote is being pursued by using scientific techniques for data recovery and analysis, often with the use of terms such as 'site formation processes', 'site taphonomy', etc. (Korisettar 1980; Korisettar and Rajaguru 1998; Mishra 1995a; Paddayya 2001; Pappu 1985, 1999, 2001; Wadia *et al.* 1995). Foote, in addition, also studied lithic artefacts taking into account artefact abrasion, patination, weathering, raw material procurement and artefact technology, and used concepts related to curation and function, bone taphonomy, and ethnography (Pappu 2004: 48). What can be noticed in the researches from the mid-1960s is that a 'site' is not perceived merely as a 'locus' where 'artefacts' occur but as a component of a 'habitat' in which prehistoric human groups lived and performed their activities. To cite an instance, the dispersal of Palaeolithic sites in the Rallakalava, Gunjana and Swarnamukhi valleys of the southern Eastern Ghats were studied as various localities representing different episodes of occupation within a Stone Age habitat in time and space (Jayaraj 1985; Murty 1966; Raju 1981). The archaeological record is studied as an occupational history in the context of landscape ecologies, and the occupations are discerned as upland and lowland adaptations, long-term occupation sites, short-term occupation sites, fleeting transitory loci, temporary encampments, etc. by different scholars (e.g., Murty 1981).

Further, the conceptual approach in the investigations of the Acheulian culture in the Hunsgi-Baichbal valleys is a good illustration in the systemic study of Acheulian with a settlement system perspective (Paddayya 1981, 1982). Paddayya noted that in this landscape, there is a clustering of Acheulian sites in the central part of the valley and scattered sites away from this zone. Paddayya interpreted the clustering of Acheulian sites as the coming together of the Acheulian groups to the area around Hunsgi in the dry season and their dispersal over the entire region during the following wet season and that this observation is not only in accordance with the inferred knowledge of the palaeo-ecology of the valley but would also admirably explain the marked difference between the valley floor sites and those of the Hunsgi cluster. The valley floor sites are comparatively smaller and comprise only a few artefacts, thereby implying smaller groups and brief periods of occupation, whereas those of the Hunsgi cluster are not only larger in size but also richer in terms of artefactual yield.

Taking examples from the seasonal pattern of movement within a habitat, in accordance with resource availability, of hunter-gatherers such as !kung Bushmen of the Kalahari Desert and the Chenchus of the Krishna valley, Paddayya interpreted these two categories of occupations as 'dry season aggregation' (Hunsgi cluster) and 'wet season dispersal' (valley floor sites). For an appraisal of possible modes of subsistence during the Acheulian times, he took into account the wild plant and animal foods being exploited by the contemporary social groups in this region and predicted that the presently exploited wild plant and animal foods provided the subsistence base during the Acheulian times. Accepting the fact that no historical continuity can be established from the Acheulian to the present subsistence base, he advocates the relevance of cross-cultural approach in situations of this kind. Taking into account the environment and ecology of this region during the present times, which is heavily degraded (due to agricultural expansion, large-scale irrigation and deforestation), Paddayya predicted that the pristine ecologies during the Acheulian times must have been more congenial. He interpreted the numerous contiguous Acheulian occupations as representing band level social organization.

Similar problems were addressed with special reference to the Acheulian culture in the Kortallayar Basin, Tamil Nadu (Pappu 1996). Following the trail of Foote, Pappu has been conducting reinvestigations of the archaeological record in the Kortallayar valley, covering Acheulian to Middle Palaeolithic sites, involving a regional scale of analysis and off-site distributional approach (Pappu 2004, 2007). In this exercise, Pappu plotted the entire Kortallayar basin, an area of 150 sq km, documenting artefact location, associated sedimentary contexts, geographical features, vegetation, and current land use practices. These aspects are being investigated by studying river mechanics and depositional history, laboratory analyses of sediments (ferricritized and ferrugenous gravel beds, quartzites, calcretes, etc.), satellite images, and stone tool technologies.

In explaining behavioural variability during the Middle and Late Pleistocene in the Kortallayar valley, she conducted ethnographic studies of Irulas, the hunter-gatherers inhabiting the Kortallayar region and who have a vide range of mobility, and considered their traditions to evaluate the Stone Age pattern. For this study, she also took into account the habits of other hunter-gatherers in Tamil Nadu, Andhra Pradesh and Kerala such as Malapandarams, Eravallans, Vaddas, Kadars, Yanadis and Chenchus (Pappu 2001). Drawing general analogies from the land use behaviour of these hunter-gatherers in their habitation-cum-exploitative range (e.g., period of residence at a given occupation, single-family/multi-family residence types, seasonal mobility strategies, and distance traversed for food procurement) in different ecological zones in South India, she suggested a model for the prehistoric period: Permanent to sedentary multi-family residential bases which are all-season multi-purpose home bases, semi-permanent to short-term base camps and activity loci.

Coming to the chronological aspects, Thorium/Uranium dates of travertine deposits (from Kaldevanhalli), *Elephas* molar (from Sadab), *Elephas* and *Bos* molars (from Teggihalli) and Electron spin Resonance date of *Bos* teeth (Isampur) from sites in the Hunsgi-Baichbal valleys gave an average date of 1.2 myr for the Early Acheulian (Paddayya 2006-2007: 97). Other absolute dates for the Early Acheulian in peninsular India are Ar^{39}/Ar^{40} dating of volcanic ash associated with Acheulian tools at Bori (Bori tephra) in Maharashtra, which gave a date of 670 kyr, and reversed palaeomagnetism dates for the sites of Nevasa, Bori and Morgaon (Mishra 1995b). Thermoluminiscence and Th^{230}/U^{234} dates for the Acheulian at Umrethi in Saurashtra (Marathe 1981) and 16R locality at Didwana in Rajasthan (Misra and Rajaguru 1986; Raghavan *et al.* 1989) indicate a time range of 390,000 to 150,000 years (Misra 2001: 495). Thus, while the sites in Hunsgi-Baichbal valleys, dating 1.2 myr, are the earliest for the Acheulian in peninsular India, the absolute dates for the Acheulian range from 700 kyr to 190/66 kyr (Paddayya 2006-2007: 95). Thus, on the basis of the spectrum of radiometric date, the time-span of Acheulian in India can be safely assigned to 1.2 myr to 150,000 ka. These new insights on chronology and categorization of stages based on well-defined technological traditions and typological characteristics of the Acheulian in India have an important bearing in the perception of human dispersals.

Human Dispersals: The Indian Context

It has been observed that the age of Early Acheulian in peninsular India is close to the earliest sites in Africa; the Early Acheulian tools of India display near typological and technological similarities to the African tools, thus indicating their actual relationship; and the African and Indian Acheulian techno-complexes not only differ significantly with the European Acheulian but are also older (Mishra 2006-2007). The Acheulian culture, having widespread occurrence in different parts of the Old World, is associated with *Homo erectus*. The fossil remains of *Homo erectus* are known from Africa, Europe and Asia (China and Indonesia). The fossil forms of *Homo erectus* in Africa and Europe are now called *Homo ergaster* and the term *Homo erectus* is reserved only for those fossils found in the Asian region, with certain skeletal and dental features, which differ slightly from *Homo ergaster* (Larsen 1998; Leakey 1993; Tattersall and Schwartz 2001).

Recently Arun Sonakia of the Geological Survey of India discovered parts of a fossilized human cranium (right calvaria) on the northern bank of the Narmada River, near the village Hathnora, Hoshangabad district, Madhya Pradesh (Sonakia 1984, 1985). This was followed by the discoveries, around 1997, of a right clavicle, and subsequently a left clavicle and left ninth rib at Hathnora (Sankhyan 2005). Sonakia reported that this hominin fossil (right calvaria) was found *in situ* in the Unit I, which is a 1.5-m thick deposit forming the basal part of the boulder conglomerate (of 18 m thickness) datable to Middle and Upper Pleistocene. According to de Lumley and Sonakia (1985), the fossil displays numerous similarities to the Asian *Homo erectus*. According to Kennedy (1992), this calvaria represents archaic *Homo sapiens*. As an alternative, Sankhyan (2005) suggests that this species may be assigned a new nomen, *Homo narmadaensis*. The estimated time range of Hathnora hominin fossil is an upper limit of 500,000 years ago to a lower limit of 236,000 years ago (the latter based on gamma spectrometric U-series of a bovid scapula recovered from the hominin site). What is important is that the deposit that has yielded the Hathnora calvaria is associated with typical middle to late Acheulian industries. Furthermore, the Narmada valley and numerous basins of the peninsular rivers have extensive occupation sites of early to late Acheulian cultures (Misra 1989, 2001). The Narmada cranium has attracted the attention of scholars in the background of the ongoing debate on the origin and dispersal of modern humans (*Homo sapiens*).

In the context of the above discussion it would be useful to briefly refer to the debate on the origins of modern humans that has been going on for more than two decades. This debate is dominated by two conflicting models: (1) Out-of-Africa Replacement (OAR) Model and (2) Multiregional Continuity Model (Anton and Swisher 2004; Dennel and Rowbroeks 2005; Dunsworth 2007; Longbroek 2004; Wolpoff *et al.* 2001). Both the models and theories tend to accept that the evolutionary origin of the genus *Homo* is in Africa and that these early hominins, i.e., *Homo erectus* subsequently migrated into Europe and Asia 200,000 years ago. However, these models differ in the explanation of the evolution of *Homo sapiens*. Both the theories cite DNA evidences, that is, analysis of genetic blueprint passed down from generation to generation.

According to the Out of Africa Replacement model, a single biological population of anatomically modern *Homo sapiens* developed first in Africa and then spread to the other parts of the world between 100,000 to 200,000 years ago, superseding or replacing all other hominin species, and that the pre-existing hominin populations became extinct. The implication of this argument is that all modern people are ultimately of African descent.

Coming to the context of ancient (extinct) populations, there were the Neanderthals of western Eurasia, who were the descendants of *Homo erectus*. It is held that the Neanderthals made no genetic contribution to the modern humans. It is also the view that though Neanderthals and modern humans coexisted in some parts of the world (Middle East) for thousands of years, they probably did not interbreed. Neanderthals, by 130,000 years ago, following a prolonged period of independent evolution in Europe, became so anatomically distinct that they are classified as a separate species, *Homo neanderthalensis*. Shortly after fully modern humans entered Europe, roughly 40,000 years ago, the Neanderthals began a rapid decline, culminating in their disappearance, roughly 30,000 years ago. Scientists have recently succeeded in extracting DNA from several Neanderthal skeletons. Analysis, particularly of mtDNA (mitochondrial DNA), has shown that the Neanderthal DNA is very distinct from the *Homo sapiens*; and on the basis of these genetic studies, it has been proposed that the Neanderthals did not interbreed with *Homo sapiens*.

The uniqueness of Africa in human evolution has also been emphasized on the basis of molecular studies. These evidences suggest that Africans exhibit a higher level of genetic diversity than non-Africans for many mitochondrial and nuclear loci. This implies that the African line has been around for longer than other populations, enabling greater genetic variation to accumulate, and this observation is used to support the OAR model.

The Multiregional Continuity Model proposes that modern humans evolved simultaneously in different regions of the Old World from populations of *Homo erectus*. It contends that after *Homo erectus* left Africa and dispersed into the other parts of the Old World, regional populations evolved into modern humans. The emergence of *Homo sapiens* was not restricted to any one area, but was a phenomenon that occurred throughout the entire geographic range where humans lived.

This means that people in China descended from the *Homo erectus* populations there, while Australians may have descended from the *Homo erectus* populations in South East Asia. According to multiregional theory, some level of gene flow between geographically separated populations prevented speciation after the dispersal of *Homo erectus*.

It has been postulated that natural selection in regional populations, ever since the original dispersal of *Homo erectus*, is responsible for the regional variants (sometimes called races) and anatomical diversity we see today in modern geographical populations. According to multiregional hypothesis, this diversity resulted from the evolution of distinctive traits, through adaptation and genetic drift, in different geographical regions that became established in early populations of *Homo erectus*. This persistence is called regional continuity.

Both the above models have protagonist; the validity of either of these is yet to be authenticated, and the debate as such is inconclusive. An alternative explanation probably lies in a theory which is a combination of the Out of Africa and Multiregional Models which is reflected in the alternate 'Hybridization' and 'Assimilation' models. This theory tones down the role of replacement in human evolution by incorporating gene flow and hybridization but still allows that Africa has a prime position in human genetic history.

In Africa, the Acheulian appears prior to 1.4 myr and overlaps with the previously existing stone tool industries for half a million years. There is also an overlap between *Homo habilis* and *Homo erectus* in Africa, which is indicative of an association of different hominins with different stone tool technologies. In a review of the Early Acheulian techno-complexes in Africa and India, Mishra has pointed out that the evidence in Africa is suggestive of its introduction from outside the continent and suggests the possibility of Acheulian development in India (Mishra 2006-2007: 72).

It has also been pointed out that early dates (2.0-2.5 myr) for sites like Riwat near Rawalpindi in Pakistan and existence of similar sites in Punjab, Himachal Pradesh and Jammu suggest the possibility of local origins from the pre-existing Stone Age cultures of the Indian subcontinent (Paddayya 2006-2007: 96) and that the Riwat artefacts are securely associated with a context that may be as old as the oldest in Africa (Mishra 2006-2007: 50-53). These propositions assume importance in the perspective of the on-going debate on Out-of-Africa model. They support another new alternative hypothesis which advocates that Asia, rather than Africa, may have been a centre for earlier dispersals (Dennell and Roebrocks 2005) and 'socialization' of technological improvements is a key issue in the explanation of hominin dispersals (Carbonell *et al.* 2008).

The Middle Palaeolithic Culture

Coming to the Middle Palaeolithic phase, the evidences point out that it has evolved from the preceding Acheulian (Misra 2001). Since its identification at Nevasa by Sankalia (Mishra 1995a; Sankalia 1956) as a distinctive flake-tool industry, discoveries in different parts of South India brought to light several occupation sites (Misra 1989, 2001; Sankalia 1974). The Middle Palaeolithic techno-complex shows a continuity of Late Acheulian lithic traditions with refinement in bifacial flaking and secondary marginal retouch; inclusion of small-sized handaxes and cleavers; scrapers of various types such as side (convex, concave, serrated, notched), discoid and ovate; slender flakes and flake-blades produced by flake-core, discoid core and specialized core-reduction schemes like the Levallois; and use of heavy duty, light duty and amorphous flakes with minimal or no retouch.

The tool types of the Middle Palaeolithic in South India are scrapers of various types – single side, double side, side-cum-end, straight, oblique, concave, convex, concavo-convex, notched, and core scrapers; drills; awls; borers; simple unilateral or bilateral points; tanged or shouldered points; miniature hand axes and cleavers; and utilized flakes. Anvils and hammer stones are also found at some of the manufacturing sites. The debitage comprises various kinds of flakes – simple, end-struck, side-struck and indeterminate flakes; Levallois flakes; flake blades;

core rejuvenation flakes; chips; and flake cores. The flake cores are discoidal, globular, pyramidal and amorphous. The techniques used for tool manufacture are stone hammer, cylinder hammer, and Levallois. The tools are finished by secondary retouch; they are characterized by shallow and small flake scars, step flaking, marginal secondary retouch and sharp edges. The raw materials used for the manufacture of tools are medium to fine grained quartzite, chert, jasper and chalcedony. Some of the Middle Palaeolithic bifacial flake points, scraper types and retouched flake tools of this region show typo-technological parallels to the Mousterian core and flake tools, recalling the Mousterian of Acheulian Tradition of Southwest Asia where the Mousterian culture is associated with *Homo neanderthalensis.*

Most of the Middle Palaeolithic sites in this region are either surface occupation scatters or river gravel sites. Wherever the Middle Palaeolithic industries are found in a stratified context, they succeed the Lower Palaeolithic (Gravel I) and occur in Gravel II. The Gravel II deposits in the river systems of the Deccan have been ascribed to late Middle Pleistocene to early part of Upper Pleistocene on the basis of geomorphological parameters. There is a single radio-carbon date on molluscan shells from a post-Middle Palaeolithic context from Nandipalli in the Sagileru valley, a tributary of the Penneru in Andhra pradesh. This date is 23,670±640 years BP. This is suggestive that the Middle Palaeolithic in this region is older than ca. 23,000 yrs BP. A Thermoluminiscence date from Didwana (Rajasthan) dates the Middle Palaeolithic to around 100,000 BP (Possehl and Rissman 1992: 467); and Clark and Williams (1986: 30) suggest that the Middle Palaeolithic in the Son Valley (north Central India) may be 40,000 or 50,000 years BP. By a review of TL, radiocarbon and Uranium/Thorium dates in a pan-Indian context, a time-bracket of ca. 125,000 years to 40,000 years before present has been suggested for the Indian Middle Palaeolithic (Mishra 1995b). This time-scale is applicable to the Middle Palaeolithic cultural phase in this region.

The Upper Palaeolithic Culture

The Upper Palaeolithic culture, which succeeds the Middle Palaeolithic, has a wide distribution in the river valley ecotones of the southern Eastern Ghats (Murty 1966, 1968, 1979); the Billa Surgam cave (Thimma Reddy 1976), Muchchatla Chintamanu Gavi Cave I (MCG I) (Murty 1974), Muchchatla Chintamanu Gavi Cave II (MCG II) (Murty 1985, 2005) and the Kurnool cave areas (Murty and Thimma Reddy 1976); and the Karnataka plateau. The occupation layers in the MCG I (a small cave) belong only to the Upper Palaeolithic, whereas in MCG II (a larger cave) Upper Palaeolithic layers occur at the bottom succeeded by Mesolithic and Late Mesolithic. A fire-place in the Upper Palaeolithic occupation at MCG II containing burnt bones and chunks of clay yielded a Thermoluminiscence date of 17,000 BP (Nambi and Murty 1983). Electron Spin Resonance dating of faunal dental remains from the MCG II cave corroborate this date (Gogte and Murty 1986). The distinguishing feature of the Upper Palaeolithic stone tool industries in this region, as in other parts of peninsular India, is the technique of production of blades from prismatic or fluted cores. These are backed points, pen knives, thick (orange piece like) macro-lunates and macro-triangles. Blades are also finished by pressure retouch and nibbling into shouldered or tanged points, scrapers (end scrapers being most characteristic), burins and awls. The Upper Palaeolithic industries also consist of a variety of flake and core tools like side scrapers, ovate scrapers, notched scrapers, discoid scrapers, horse hoof core scrapers and unifacial and bifacial flake points. Some of these flakes are produced by the Levallois technique and the discoid core technique, indicating the persistence of the preceding Middle Palaeolithic traditions. The raw materials used for the Upper Palaeolithic stone tools are fine-grained quartzite, chert, jasper, chalcedony and limestone. In the MCG II cave occupation large chunks of chocolate brown chert, quarried from the outcrops in the limestone beds, were brought to the cave in considerable quantities. These large nodules are fire-treated, by exposing to flame, for artefact production.

Some of the sites in the lower Godavari valley, which consist of lithic assemblages with flake-blade and flake element, and occasional blades, can be ascribed to a facies of the Upper Palaeolithic. The artefact types are large-sized blades; flake-blades; backed blade and retouched blade tools; different types of scrapers (side, concave, convex, serrated, end) on flakes, flake-blades, and nuclei; flake points; utilized blades, flake-blades, flakes and nuclei; and irregularly worked flake-blades, flakes, and nuclei (Singh 1979, 1984). The last two categories of artefact types, i.e., utilized artefacts without retouch or working and irregularly modified artefacts are predominant. Thus, the Upper Palaeolithic of this region represents an amorphous lithic facies since the artefacts by and large are non-descript and cannot be classified as per the standard categories. The raw materials are chiefly chert and jasper; chalcedony, agate and quartzite are also used. Lithic occupational scatters of this type of techno-complex have a wide distribution in the woodland forested ecotones of this region which are inhabited by communities whose specialized adaptation is shifting cultivation.

Evidences of bone tool industry, the other important trait of the Upper Palaeolithic culture, are recovered from the Kurnool caves. As mentioned earlier, the Billa Surgam caves, near Betamcherla, became famous during the last quarter of the nineteenth century when Robert Bruce Foote and his son Henry Bruce Foote excavated these caves and discovered bone tools in association with the Late Pleistocene fauna (Foote 1884a, 1884b, 1885). Excavations conducted subsequently in the Billa Surgam (Thimma Reddy 1980) and MCG I caves yielded both stone tools and bone tools along with the remains of Late Pleistocene fauna confirming the discoveries made by Footes (Murty 1974).

The bone tools recovered in the excavations of the Billa Surgam caves, which are described by Foote, constituted 1700 specimens of worked and cut bones of which 200 were implements. The bone tools described by Foote comprised awls, barbed and unbarbed arrowheads, daggers, scraper-knives, scrapers, chisels, gouge, wedges, axe heads and sockets. Robert Bruce Foote observed that some of these bone tools are comparable to the Magdalenian culture of France. The bone tools obtained in the excavations of MCG I cave consist of scrapers, perforators, chisels, scoops, shouldered points, awls, barbs, spatulas, worked bones, and splinters. In a total collection of 1652 worked bones obtained from MCG I cave, 878 (47.40%) are bone blanks and 151 (8.15%) are crudely finished tools, the rest representing broken bones and splinters. The MCG I cave bone tools display a crude technology. This is because the cave is a short-term occupation and the possibility for complete representation of well-finished artefacts is less likely in short-term occupations than in permanent occupations.

Radiocarbon dates for the Upper Palaeolithic obtained from different parts of India (e.g., Bhedaghat, Dharampuri, Chandrasal, Mehtakheri, Nagda, Belan valley, Inamgaon, Nandipalle and Patne) and the TL and ESR dates from the Kurnool caves indicate a time-span of 40,000 BP to 8,000 BC (Mishra 1995b; Possehl and Rissman 1992). The faunal remains from the Kurnool caves found in association with the Upper Palaeolithic, are of the Late Pleistocene age (Lydekker 1886; Murty 1975).

The Upper Palaeolithic in the Rallakalava and Gunjana valleys of the southern Eastern Ghats is marked by stabilized and extensive occupations; and a small percentage of the artefacts form a microlithic component. The latter aspect links the succeeding Mesolithic with this phase (Murty 1981; Raju 1986-87).

The Mesolithic Culture

The Mesolithic culture is widespread in peninsular India (Misra 2001: 498-500). There is a significant increase in Mesolithic settlements in South India in varied physiographical zones ranging from the east coast and west coast, riverine ecotones, lowland and upland plateaus, and the deciduous woodlands of northern Eastern Ghats. The well known coastal adaptations of the Mesolithic are the *teri* sites south of Chennai (Allchin & Allchin 1982: 86-88), environs of Visakhapatnam coast (Prakash 1981, 1986-87, 2007 and this volume) and the coastal ecotones of the Western Ghats in Kerala (Rajendran 1989; Thampi 1983).

The Mesolithic culture, in its typo-technological traditions, indicates its development from the preceding Upper Palaeolithic with technological refinement in core reduction techniques and in finishing blade and bladelet artefacts by pressure retouch. The diagnostic tools of the Mesolithic are microliths, which are made on blades and bladelets. The most common artefact categories are backed points, obliquely blunted blades, lunates, triangles and trapezes; flake scrapers; worked flakes and nodules; and amorphous flakes. Waste materials resultant of tool manufacture (debitage), such as core dressing flakes and chips, occur at the tool production spots. In the rock shelter and riverine occupations in the forested zones of Kerala, the Mesolithic is characterized by the dominance of flake tradition; though tools on blades and bladelets, typical of the microlithic tradition are a component (Gurukkal and Varier 1999: 67-74; Rajendran 1989; Thampi 1983). Quartz is the raw material for the Mesolithic techno-complexes in Kerala; and in other parts of South India chert, jasper, chalcedony, agate, quartz and crystal are the raw materials. In the late Mesolithic occupation of MCG II cave, large chunks of chocolate brown chert, quarried from outcrops in the surroundings of the cave, were brought to the cave and fire-treated by exposing to the flame for blade and bladelet production. This occupation has also yielded a well-finished shouldered arrowhead on limestone; a perforator with needle sharp end on limestone, finished by grinding; sling balls; quartzite hammer-stones and grinding slabs. Another important artefact category found in the Mesolithic occupations on the river terraces in the Rallakalava valley near Renigunta are spherical bored stones. These are not too heavy to be regarded as weights for digging sticks. They suggest their probable use as net sinkers for fishing in deep waters of streams or lakes. Mesolithic rock paintings in the Central Indian caves and rock shelters point out that bow and arrow became common during this period (Wakankar and Brooks 1976; Neumayer 1983, 1993; Mathpal 1984).

The microlithic tools from different sites in South India display close typological and technological affinities to those of Bagor (Rajasthan); Baghor, Bhimbetka and Adamgarh (Madhya Pradesh); and Sarai Nahar Rai (Uttar Pradesh), which have radio-carbon dates covering a time range of ca. 8500 BC to 2000 BC. A Neolithic-Chalcolithic potsherd from the Late Mesolithic occupation in the MCG II cave gave a Thermoluminiscence date of ca. 1800 BC. On this basis, the Mesolithic culture in South India can be ascribed to the same time period. This evidence indicates that Mesolithic cultures continued in time after the appearance of the Neolithic cultures and that there were cultural contacts between the former and the latter.

The Mesolithic in the dry deciduous woodlands of the northern Eastern Ghats from the lower Godavari valley to Mahanadi Basin is characterized by the association of faceted tools and shouldered celts typical of the Eastern Indian Neolithic complex with microliths. One instance of this kind has been brought to light from ten find-spots in the lower Godavari valley, all situated in red soil zones enclosed by hills, with or without perennial streams flowing nearby, and with not even a faint indication of regular settlement (Subrahmanyam and David Raju 1983). These celts at these sites occur in association with microliths, perforated stones and potsherds of gritty fabric with red slipped surfaces. Shouldered celts of this kind (some miniature in size) are found along with microliths at Uppalapadu in the Eleru valley, a stream of the Godavari, and this site is right in the habitation of Konda Kummaris who practice shifting cultivation (Kasturi Bai 1992). The dispersal of shouldered celts of the Eastern Indian Neolithic complex in Mesolithic contexts (i.e., with a microlithic techno-complex), in the lower reaches of the Godavari in the habitation zones of shifting cultivators, is suggestive of a pattern of landscape ecology, in the prehistoric past, that could be more or less similar to the present day shifting cultivators of the deciduous woodlands of this region.

Another noteworthy feature in the Mesolithic of this region is the occurrence of bifacial heavy-duty tools on quartzite and dolerite. Such an association of heavy-duty tools and microliths, at times also with polished celts, is documented in Orissa. Such evidences have been brought to light from the Indravati basin (Nanda 1983), immediately north of the Godavari valley, and from the Phulbani district in central Orissa (Ota 1986), which constitute the easternmost outliers of the Eastern Ghats, in the Mahanadi Basin. Several of the thirty open-air primary Mesolithic sites discovered by Ota have yielded heavy-duty implements like horse-hoof cores, choppers and pointed tools of charnockite and quartzite in association with non-geometric and geometric microliths of quartz, chert and chalcedony. In the Keonjhar district of north Orissa, an extension of the Chotanagpur region, Mohanty (1988, 1989) discovered fifty-seven primary occupation scatters, some of which have also yielded heavy-duty implements in considerable numbers along with microliths. These heavy-duty implements consist of choppers, horse-hoof scrapers, picks, knives, limaces and flakes, all made of dolerite, and some of these sites have also yielded celts finished by grinding. Further north, in the Santal Parganas of Bihar, Chakrabarti (1986, 1994) reported a wide dispersal of Upper Palaeolithic and Mesolithic occurrences in deciduous woodlands, which are again characterized by a predominant amorphous element of medium to heavy modified flakes and worked nuclei. The raw materials used in making the microliths are chiefly chert and jasper, chalcedony, agate and quartzite are also used.

Subsistence Economy during Palaeolithic and Mesolithic

Palaeolithic and Mesolithic occupations have a wide dispersal in the riverine ecotones, coastal landforms, lowlands and uplands, forested zones, and caves indicating adaptations to varied habitats.

The Upper Palaeolithic blade and backed blade tools and the microlithic tools of the Mesolithic, in functional terms, suggest their use by hafting in wood, bone and antler as composite tools. Such hafted tools survived in numerous Upper Palaeolithic and Mesolithic sites in different parts of Europe. They might have been hafted to make barbed points, harpoons, projectiles, arrows, hunting spears, etc. The variety of scrapers, burins, borers and awls indicate their use in wood and bone working. The Upper Palaeolithic and Mesolithic tools thus indicate the manufacture of specialized hunting tools for hunting big and small game, and fishing. The faunal assemblages from the Billa Surgam, MCG I and MCG II caves associated with the Upper Palaeolithic and Mesolithic include intentionally broken bones of wild game, representing food refuse. Some of these bones were charred, indicating that animal meat was roasted and consumed.

These faunal remains belong to jungle cat (*Felis chaus*), porcupine (*Hystrix crassidens*), black naped hare (*Lepus* cf. *nigricollis*), wild ox (*Bos* sp.), wild buffalo (*Bubalus* sp.), nilgai (*Boselaphus tragocamelus*), chinkara (*Gazella gazella bennetti*), blackbuck or Indian antelope (*Antilope cervicapra*), four-horned antelope (*Tetracerus quadricornis*), sambar (*Cervus unicolor*), spotted deer (*Axis axis*), barking deer (*Muntiacus muntjak*), mouse deer (*Tragulus meminna*), Indian wild boar (*Sus scrofa cristatus*), pangolin (*Smutsia gigantea*), monitor lizard (*Varanus dracaena*), and a few bones of birds and dermal scutes (horny plate) of turtles.

Since most of the ecosystems in which Stone Age occupations are dispersed and inhabited by native (indigenous or non-modernized) social groups, suitable analogies from their living traditions are taken into account for a general comparative approach. While this approach is being used because of its applicability (lack of sufficient information or any other data to use), the predictions thus made are not meant to be deterministic: Societies and cultures similar in some aspects are uniformly similar, and the use of analogy does not suggest any continuity from the ethnographic present to the Stone Age past.

Some of the communities in South India, considered for general comparative analogy, are the Malapandaram, Eravallan, Vadda, Kadar, Chenchu, Yanadi, Boya and Yerukula (Jayaraj 1985; Murty 1981, 1985; Pappu 1996; Raju 1988). They hunt big and small game (which include the species recorded in the Kurnool cave occupations), birds, and fish in the rivers, lakes and ponds. They use specialized hunting contrivances such as a variety of traps, nets, snares, bows and arrows for hunting and fishing. The hunting practices of these communities point out the possibility of the use of prototypes of some of these specialized aids in the prehistoric past, without which the game would not have fallen a prey.

The likely meat food procurement strategies that can be predicted during the Palaeolithc and Mesolithic phases are: Hunting game by chasing and stalking or felling the prey after a chase, with bow and arrow; ambushing the game at waterholes and during fruiting season; net hunting of small game; use of net traps and noose traps for big and small game, and a variety of birds; and opportunistic scavenging.

In so far as the exploitation of plant foods in the prehistoric past is concerned, no evidences are as yet available. But again, drawing analogies from the communities mentioned above, which are adapted to forested environments, it can be suggested that a variety of wild plant foods such as yams and tubers, fruits, nuts, flowers, leafy vegetables, shoots, and mushrooms; insects; and honey might have been gathered for subsistence. From the Upper Palaeolithic rock paintings of Central India, and those of the Kurnool cave areas in which some of these subsistence activities (hunting, fishing, collection of plant foods and honey) are depicted, it is possible to predict that such activities were in vogue during the Upper Palaeolithic and Mesolithic times (Chandramouli 2002; Mathpal 1984; Neumayer 1983, 1993; Wakankar and Brooks 1976). Grinding slabs, found in association with the Upper Palaeolithic occupations in the Rallakalava and Gunjana valleys in considerable numbers (Raju 1988; Murty 1981) and MCG I cave occupation (Murty 1985), suggest their use in processing plant foods and also for milling wild grains.

UPPER PALAEOLITHIC AND MESOLITHIC IN WOODLAND ENVIRONMENTS: ETHNO-ECOLOGICAL CONSIDERATIONS

The present environs in which the Upper Palaeolithic and Mesolithic occupational scatters occur from the Godavari valley up to the Santal Parganas, are closed and they open forests of deciduous woodlands, gallery forests and gallery bush ecotones; such dispersal makes it obvious that, in all probability, the processes of opening up of closed forests for human habitation were in operation from at least the terminal Pleistocene times. The heavy-duty component of the Mesolithic assemblages suggests the possible functional role of such artefact categories in felling trees. Drawing analogies in land use pattern from the practices of the shifting cultivators of this belt, it can be predicted that fire must have been an important tool in forest clearance in the prehistoric past as it is during the present times.

The region stretching from the northern Eastern Ghats to the northeast is the zone of slash-and-burn cultivation or shifting cultivation called *podu, jhum,* etc. These shifting cultivators clear patches of forests both for making settlements and for shifting cultivation called *podu*. For forest clearance, trees are felled by chopping a hole into the trunk about 30 cm to 40 cm above the ground, and then a fire is lit in the hole. The fire burns into the trunk and the tree falls under its own weight or via a push. Trees with a girth of 15 cm fall in a day or two, while those of half a metre or more take about a week or even more. Iron shaft-hole axes procured from the weekly market have now become common, but triangular iron axes hafted in wood (which recall the lithic prototypes of the Neolithic) are also widely used by some of these shifting cultivator groups. The undergrowth is cleared with a bush knife, the stumps of the felled trees are covered with the slashed undergrowth, and the whole plot is burned. Thus, fire is the most important tool for shifting cultivators in forest clearance, although hunting with the aid of fire, by setting fire to the bush and driving the game towards the hunting party, which was practised some decades ago, is now undertaken only for ritual hunting. Presumably, the terminal Pleistocene and early Holocene occupations in these woodland environments could not have come into existence without some forest clearance, and if the ethnographic practices are any guide one might expect that fire was as effective a tool in the past as it is today.

Proceeding on the premise that fire was used as a tool for clearing patches in forests during terminal Pleistocene and early Holocene times, the possible postulate that can be projected is that it facilitated the invasion of pyrophilous plant species, thus giving rise to new exploitable plant food sources for the human inhabitants. Lewis, by a review of the archaeological evidences and ecological factors concerning the role of fire in the domestication of plants and animals in Southwest Asia, made several propositions (Lewis 1972). These are: (a) the establishment of fire-climax ecosystems would result in overall changes of environment without specific climatological changes; (b) the changes would be characterized not by desiccation and resource depletion but by increased plant and animal productivity; (c) disequilibrium accompanies such increased productivity; and (d) that such disequilibrium could be of sufficient magnitude to provide stimulus which has been sought by archaeologists to explain the beginnings of seed agriculture. Lewis hypothesized that the appearance of domesticated wheat, barley and oats in the oak-pistachio woodland belt of Southwest Asia was due to heat generated by fire and that this was the causal factor in the mutations which ultimately led to the appearance of these domesticated forms. Though the environment of this forested belt under discussion is not comparable to that of Southwest Asia, the two casual factors emphasized by Lewis – (a) the use of fire and (b) the opening up of woodlands – may be as crucial in this region as in Southwest Asia for the origins and dispersal of seed agriculture.

The general pattern of cultivating crops in the shifting cultivation is one of both monocrop and polycrop agriculture in two cycles annually. In the lower Godavari valley, these are called (a) *punasa panta* (June to August) and (b) *pedda panta* (January to June). The major crop for *punasa panta* is rice (a variety called *budama dhanyamu*, the seeds of which are usually stored, but are also obtained from the Odiya who migrated into the Godavari valley from Orissa). Incidentally, *budama dhanyamu* also grows without cultivation along hill slopes and stream banks, where it is also harvested. Two other crops, namely, *Panicum miliare* and *Eleusine coracana*, are also grown for *punasa panta* but the yields are small.

The second crop, *pedda panta*, is also called *konda panta* (hill crop) and mixed cropping in the *podu* fields is the prevalent pattern: A variety of crops in different combinations are raised by broadcasting and covering with the ashes of burnt trees, shrubs and undergrowth. These crops are millets such as *Setaria italica*, *Echinochola frumentacea* and two varieties (red and white) of *Sorghum bicolor*; *Zea mays*; grams like *Cajanas cajan*, *Vigna catjang*, *Phaseolus mungo*, *Vigna radiatus*, *Macrotyloma uniflorum* and *Cicer arietinum*; oil seeds like *Sesamum indicum*, *Linum usitatissimum*, *Brassica juncea* and *Ricinus communis*; several kinds of beans, the common being *Vicia fabra* and *Dolichos lablab*; squashes like *Cucurbita maxima* and *Lagenaria vulgaris*; leafy vegetables, the most common being a few varieties of *Amaranthus* sp. and a hill variety of chili; yams or tuber crops; and several kinds of rice.

The *konda panta* is raised in the upland *podu* fields, and the mixing of crops varies annually and from settlement to settlement. Usually one or two varieties of millets and grams are broadcast in alternating rows, and beans, squashes and yams are planted along the hedges. While some varieties of rice are cultivated in the upland *podu* fields, others are exclusively cultivated in the lowlands by plough agriculture.

There is one pyrophyte, a weedy millet known as *cippa gaddi* (*gaddi*: grass), which is of special interest. This grows on its own (i.e., colonizes) in the *podu* fields in which *Setaria italica*, *Panicum miliare* and *Echinochola frumentacea* are cultivated. This becomes abundant in the second year and more abundant in the third year with a corresponding increase in the yield of grain. This grain, called *cippa biyyamu* (rice is also called *biyyamu*), is smaller than that of *Panicum miliare* and has a tough husk. It is harvested for consumption, and Konda Reddis and other shifting cultivators in some of the hill settlements used to store this grain in considerable quantities. What is important the spread of this weedy millet is associated with fire, i.e. the burning in the preparation of *podu* fields.

Cultivation of Rice

According to a news item (*Sunday Express*, May 30, 2004, P.19), it is claimed that around 400,000 varieties of rice existed in India during the *Vedic* period; and the rice varieties identified by the Central Rice Research Institute in Chhattisgarh alone have gone up to 20,000. The latter are landraces or cultivars. According to one report (*Rice Today Magazine*, vol. 3, no. 1, 2004), scientists have identified 20 wild species of rice each of which contain hundreds of different genetic lines. It is reported that there is a great deal of genetic variability in wild species and getting some of these diverse genes into the rice genome by crossing wild and cultivated rice helps to create rice resistant to weeds, drought, diseases, and tolerant to environmental stresses.

Rice belongs to the genus *Oryza*, which includes 27 species. Of these, 25 are wild and two are cultivated. Out of the 25 wild species, seven are found in India. In the Eastern Ghats, of which the lower Godavari valley is a part, there are three wild rice species. These are *Oryza nivara*, *Oryza rufipogon* and *Oryza sativa* f. *spontanea*. These grow in swampy areas, along the streams, in ditches, edges of ponds and tanks, and in or around rice fields. There are different local names for these wild rice varieties. The local name for *Oryza nivara* over a long tract is *passer (or phasser/passei/phassei)*. The wild rice in the Gond area (Adilabad district, Andhra Pradesh), for instance at Jodeghat, a hill settlement near Asifabad, is called *akasatadi* (rice that grows when it rains). Other names used for rice by the Gonds and Kolams of Adilabad are *vanji* and *dhan*. *Balludan* (black rice) and batadan, *sapoordan*, *ninnudan*, *bogadu sapoor* and *oldu sapoor* (scented variety) are the names used for wild rice (possibly landraces) in the Araku valley. Some of the other names for rice in the Godavari valley are suggestive of the wild variety, for example, *uridhan* refers to the rice that grows near settlements; *janglidhan* means rice that grows wild; and *deobhat* indicates the rice given by god. All these rice varieties are gathered by the shifting cultivators.

Chang (1976) identifies the area of origin of domesticated rice falls between 20^0 N and 23^0 N, stretching from the central Ganga valley to the South China Sea; this implies that northeastern India would be one likely place for early cultivation. Zide and Zide (1973) cite the observation of a rice entomologist that in terms of the number and diversity of rice pests and time judged necessary by entomologists for their development, the Jeypore tract of Orissa would qualify as a possible area of origin and proliferation of rice. It is more plausible, following the observations of Whyte (1972), that wild annual rice suitable for domestication would have been present in many parts of China, Southeast Asia and India, and it is quite reasonable (Glover 1985; Whyte 1972) to expect early and independent domestication of rice occurring in many regions.

In so far as the exploitation of wild and domestic varieties of rice in the prehistory of this region, and for that matter elsewhere in the country, is concerned, some assumptions can be made on the basis of archaeological evidence from the Belan valley of the Vindhyas (Sharma *et al*. 1980). At Chopani-Mando, carbonized grains of wild rice are present in lumps of burnt clay in association with mullers and querns in the advanced Mesolithic phase. At Koldihwa, a Neolithic site three kilometres east of Chopani-Mando, potsherds have been found which contained rice husk from both domestic and wild species. This Neolithic occupation has three radiocarbon dates: 6570±210, 5440±240 and 5430±185 BC. These early dates for the domestication of rice in the Vindhyas though need to be considered with caution, the archaeological context of the Vindhyan evidence cannot be underestimated, in view of the thousands of landraces of rice spread over a large tract stretching from the northeastern India to the Godavari valley and further down beyond the southern Eastern Ghats. In view of above aspects, it can be postulated that the exploitation of wild rice may be expected to be of at least early Holocene age.

Cultivation of Tuber Crops

The shifting cultivators of this region cultivate in the hedges of swidden fields several tuber crops of which some are domesticated and some forest varieties. The commonly grown domesticated varieties comprise *Manihot esculenta*, *Dioscorea rotundata*, *Dioscrea alata* and *Colacasia esculenta*. The species gathered from the forest consist of *Dioscorea glabra*, *Dioscorea pentuphylla*, *Dioscorea hipsida*, *Typhonium trilobatum* and *Ipomea digitata*. There are several other varieties of wild species known by their vernacular names which are harvested and stored up to six months, and the sprouts that appear from the stored ones are cut and planted in the kitchen gardens, thus growing them by vegetative propagation. These shifting cultivators, as a general practice, replant the vine after the yams are harvested, and this practice is also prevalent with the hunter-gatherers of the Eastern Ghats. Quite a few of the wild varieties of yams are toxic and acrid, and these are processed to remove toxicity and made edible.

These shifting cultivator communities do not merely depend upon the above-mentioned crops and vegetable foods. They subsist on a large variety of wild plant foods such as leaves, flowers, fruits, seeds, nuts, berries, mushrooms; insects; honey; and are experts in hunting big and small game and birds, and in fishing. In the light of the ethno-ecological traditions of these shifting cultivators, it can be postulated that the causative factors for the appearance of rice/millet and tuber crop cultivation (fire fallow cultivation) are less likely to be environmental or any kind of other ecological stresses linked to food scarcity, and could rather be associated with prolonged periods of adaptive patterns in woodlands and gallery forests, and extensive use of fire in landscape manipulation.

Mesolithic-Neolithic-Chalcolithic Interface

Evidences from South India reveal that from at least ca. 3000 BC, early farming cultures began to emerge in the plateaus of Karnataka, Rayalaseema and Telangana, and the alluvial basins of the Krishna, Penneru, Tungabhadra and Cauvery valleys (Allchin and Allchin 1982; Dhavalikar 1988; Krishna Sastry 1983; Murty 1989; Nagaraja Rao 1984; Sankalia 1974; Sarma 2003). These are characterized by village settlements and agro pastoral economy, chiefly based on millet farming and stock raising of predominantly cattle and sheep/goat to some extent (Kajale 1974, 1991; Thomas 1989; Vishnu-Mittre 1989); pottery; and copper/bronze tools in the later stages (from ca. 1800 BC). Faunal remains recovered from some of the excavated sites include deer, antelope, fowl, tortoise, and freshwater mussels indicating dependence also on wild game to some extent in meeting the meat food requirements. Carbonized grains are recorded in some sites, and the querns and rubbing stones, which are common at most of these settlements; from the earliest levels of occupation, indicate their use in processing of grain foods. Evidences further point out that the Mesolithic social groups were inhabiting these regions when inroads were made by the Neolithic-Chalcolithic systems into these landscapes, and that there was interactive exchange between the former and the latter. One such example is the Late Mesolithic occupation at the MCG II cave. During the time of this occupation, Neolithic-Chalcolithic village farming cultures moved into the Kunderu valley, of which the Kurnool cave region forms a part. In the Late Mesolithic occupational levels of MCG II, along with microlithic artefacts and remains of wild fauna, were found Neolithic-Chalcolithic objects (Murty 1985). These items are potsherds; copper objects such as spiral ear-ring, rod, and bangles; and a steatite disc bead. Neolithic-Chalcolithic pottery has also been recovered from the upper levels of Billa Surgam and two other caves. These evidences indicate that when Mesolithic communities inhabited these zones (as in the case of Langhanaj and Lothal in Gujarat, and Bagor in Rajasthan) the Neolithic-Chalcolithic groups moved into these regions with agro-pastoral economy. Consequently, there has been cultural interaction between the Mesolithic hunter-gatherers and the Neolithic-Chalcolithic groups and the former obtained these objects from the latter. These objects, in all likelihood, are prestige goods or status markers for the Mesolithic. Further, bio-anthropological studies of human skeletons from the Mesolithic habitations of Langhanaj in Gujarat and Bagor in Rajasthan, and the neighbouring Harappan township of Lothal in Gujarat, have clearly shown that there was not only cultural interaction but also biological interaction (gene flow) between the Mesolithic hunter-gatherers and their agricultural neighbours (Kennedy 2000; Lukacs 1992).

These developments that began with the inroads made by the Neolithic-Chalcolithic cultures into the habitats of the Mesolithic resulted in new processes of land use, interactive exchange and the consequent emergence of complex societies. This period is the beginning of reorientation of cultural boundaries and production systems in which farming, cattle and sheep/goat pastoralism played an important role on the one hand, and the hunting-gathering traditions continued on the other.

These processes became intensified from the early historic times, with agrarian expansion, reclamation of forests for settlements and colonization, with the 'state' being the principal intermediary in articulating different social groups and their habitats with the frontiers of the state. The early and medieval historical sources indicate that intermixture of different communities was taking place, and new occupational groups were emerging in an institutionalized and structured social order with hierarchies of power.

REFERENCES

Allchin, B. 1994. *Living Traditions: Studies in the Ethnoarchaeology of South Asia*, New Delhi: Oxford and IBH Publishing House.

Allchin, B. and F.R. Allchin. 1982. *The Rise of Civilization in India and Pakistan*, Cambridge: Cambridge University Press.

Agarwal, D.P. and A. Ghosh. 1973. *Radiocarbon and Indian Archaeology*, Bombay: TIFR.

Anton, S.C. and C.C. Swisher. 2004. 'Early Dispersal of Homo from Africa', *Annual Review of Anthropology* 33: 271-296.

Badam, G.L. 1979. *Pleistocene Fauna of India with Special Reference to the Siwaliks*, Poona: Deccan College.

Cammiade, L.A. and M.C. Burkitt. 1930. 'Fresh Light on the Stone Age in South-East India', *Antiquity*, 4: 327-339.

Carbonell, E., M. Mosquera, X.P. Rodriguez, J.M. Bermódez de Castro, F. Burjachs, J. Rossel, R. Sala and J. Vallverdó. 2008. 'Eurasian Gates: The Earliest Human Dispersals', *Journal of Anthropological Research* 64: 195-228.

Chakrabarti, D.K. 1986. 'The Lithic Industries of Santal Parganas with Notes on the Daman Industry', *Man and Environment* 10: 143-149.

——. 1994. 'Some Ethnographic Dimensions of the Archaeology of the Chhotanagpur Plateau and the Adjoining Areas in West Bengal in Eastern India', in Bridget Allchin (ed.), *Living Traditions: Studies in the Ethnoarchaeology of South Asia*, New Delhi: Oxford & IBH Publishing Co. Pvt. Ltd., pp. 219-233.

Chandramouli, N. 2002. *Rock Art of South India (With Special Reference to Andhra Pradesh)*, New Delhi: Bharatiya Kala Prakashan.

Chang, T.T. 1976. 'The Origin, Evolution, Cultivation, Dissemination and Diversification of Asian and African Rices', *Euphytica* 25: 425-441.

Clark, J.D. and M.A.J. Williams. 1986. 'Palaeoenvironments and Prehistory in North Central India: A Preliminary Report', in J. Jacaobson (ed.), *Studies in Archaeology of India and Pakistan*, Delhi: Oxford and IBH Publishing House, pp. 19-41.

De Lumley, H. and A. Sonakia. 1985. 'Premiere de Coaverte d'un Home erectus sur le Continent Indien a Hathnora dans la Moyenne Valle de la Narmada', *L'Anthropologie* 89: 13-61.

Daniel, G. 1964. *The Idea of Prehistory*, Harmondsworth, Middlesex, England: Penguin Books.

Dennell, R.W. and W. Roebrocks. 2005. 'An Asian Perspective on Early Human Dispersals from Africa', *Nature* 438: 1099-1104.

Dhavalikar, M.K. 1988. *The First Farmers of the Deccan*, Pune: Ravish Publishers.

——. 1983. 'Ethnoarchaeology in India', *Bulletin of the Deccan College Research Institute* 42: 49-68.

Dunsworth, H.M. 2007. *Human Origins 101*, Westport, Connecticut: London.

Foote, R.B. 1866. 'On the Occurrence of Stone Implements in Lateritic Formations in Various Parts of Madras and North Arcot Districts', *Madras Journal of Literature and Science*. 3rd Series, Part II: 1-35, with an appendix by William King, pp. 36-42.

——. 1868. 'On the Distribution of Stone Implements in South India', *Quarterly Journal of the Geological Survey* 24: 484-495.

——. 1869. 'On Quartzite Implements of Palaeolithic Types from the Laterite Formations of the East Coast of Southern India', *International Congress of Prehistoric Archaeology: Transactions of the Third Session, Norwich, 1868*, London: Longmans Green and Co., pp. 224-239.

——. 1884a. 'Rough Notes on Billa Surgam and Other Caves', *Records of the Geological Survey of India* 17 (1): 27-34.

——. 1884b. 'Mr. H.B. Foote's Work at the Billa Surgam Caves', *Records of the Geological Survey of India* 17 (4): 200-208.

——. 1885. 'Notes on the Results of Mr. H.B. Foote's Further Excavations in the Billa Surgam Caves', *Records of the Geological Survey of India* 18 (4): 227-235.

——. 1887. 'Notes on Some Recent Neolithic and Palaeolithic Finds in South India', *Journal of the Asiatic Society of Bengal* LVI (2): 259-282.

——. 1914. *The Foote Collection of Indian Prehistoric and Protohistoric Antiquities: Catalogue Raisonne*, Madras: Government Museum.

——. 1916. *The Foote Collection of Prehistoric and Protohistoric Antiquities: Notes on Their Ages and Distribution*, Madras: Government Museum.

Gaillard, C., V.N. Misra and M.L.K. Murty. 1990. 'Comparative Study of Three Series of Handaxes: One from Rajasthan and Two from Andhra Pradesh', *Bulletin of the Deccan College Research Institute* 49: 137-144.

Gogte, V.D. and M.L.K. Murty. 1986. 'ESR Dating of Kurnool Caves, South India', *Man and Environment* 10: 135-140.

Glover, I.C. 1985. 'Some Problems Relating to the Domestication of Rice in Asia', in V.N. Misra and Peter Bellwood (eds.), *Recent Advances in Indo-Pacific Prehistory*, New Delhi: Oxford & IBH Publishing Co. Pvt. Ltd., pp. 265-274.

Gurukkal, R. and M.R. Raghava Varier (eds.). 1999. *Cultural History of Kerala*, Vol:1, Thiruvananthapuram: Department of Cultural Publications, Government of Kerala.

Isaac, N. 1960. *The Stone Age Cultures of Kurnool*. Ph.D. Dissertation, Poona University.

Jayaraj, Jacob S. 1985. *Early Hunter-Gatherer Adaptations in the Tirupati Valley, South India*. Ph.D. Dissertation, Pune University.

Kajale, M.D. 1974. 'Ancient Grains from India', *Bulletin of the Deccan College Research Institute* 34 (1-2): 55-74.

——. 1991. 'Current Status of Indian Palaeoethnobotany: Introduced and Indigenous Food Plants with a Discussion of the Historical and Evolutionary Development of Indian Agriculture and Agricultural Systems in General', in J.M. Renfrew (ed.), *New Light on Early Farming – Recent Developments in Palaeoethnobotany*, Edinburgh: Edinburgh University Press, pp. 155-189.

Kasturi Bai, M. 1992. 'Prehistoric and Protohistoric Investigations in the Eleru Valley, North Coastal Andhra Pradesh', *Man and Environment* 27(1): 97-95.

Kennedy, K.A.R. 1992. 'The Fossil Hominin from the Narmada Valley: *Homo erectus or Homo sapiens*', in C. Jarrige (ed.), *South Asian Archaeology 1989*, Madison: Prehistory Press, pp. 145-152.

——. 2000. *God-Apes and Fossil Men: Palaeoanthropology of South Asia*, Ann Arbor: University of Michigan Press.

Korisettar, R. 1980. *Prehistory and Geomorphology of the Middle Krishna Valley, Karnataka*. Ph.D. Dissertation, Poona University.

Korisettar, R. and S.N. Rajaguru. 1998. 'Quaternary Stratigraphy, Palaeoclimate and Lower Palaeolithic in India', in M.D. Petraglia and R. Korisettar (eds.), *Early Human Behaviour in a Global Context (the Rise and Diversity of the Lower PalaeolithicRecord)*, London and New York: Routledge, pp. 304-342.

Krishna Sastry, V.V. 1983. *The Proto and Early Historic Cultures of Andhra Pradesh (Archaeological Series 58)*, Hyderabad: Archaeology and Museums, Government of Andhra Pradesh.

Longbroek, M. 2004. *'Out-of-Africa' – An Investigation into the Earliest Occupation of the Old World, BAR International Series 1244,* Oxford: Archaeopress.

Larsen, C.S. 1998. *Human Origins: The Fossil Record* (Paperback), Illinois: Waveland Press Inc.

Leakey, R. 1993. *Origins Reconsidered: In Search of What Makes Us Human* (Paperback), New York: Anchor Books.

Lewis, H.T. 1972. 'The Role of Fire in the Domestication of Plants and Animals in Southwest Asia: A Hypothesis', *Man* 7: 195-222.

Lukacs, J.R. 1992. 'Dental Palaeopathology and Agricultural Intensification in South Asia: New Evidence from Bronze Age Harappa', *American Journal of Physical Anthropology* 87: 133-150.

Lydekker, R. 1886. *The Fauna of Kurnool Caves, Palaeontologia Indica,* Series C, Vol. 4, part 2, pp. 23-58.

Marathe, A.R. 1981. *Geoarchaeology of the Hiran Valley, Saurashtra, India,* Pune: Deccan College.

Mathpal, Y. 1984. *Prehistoric Rock Paintings of Bhimbetka, Central India,* New Delhi: Abhinav.

Mishra, S. 1992. 'The Age of Acheulian in India: New Evidence', *Current Anthropology* 33(3): 325-328.

——. 1995a. 'Prehistoric and Quaternary Studies at Nevasa: the Last 40 Years', in S. Wadia, R. Korisetter and V.S. Kale (eds.), *Quaternary Environments and Geoarchaeology of India,* Bangalore: Geological Survey India, pp. 324-332.

——. 1995b. 'Chronology of the Indian Stone Age: The Impact of Recent Absolute and Relative Dating Attempts', *Man and Environment* 20(2): 11-16.

——. 2006-2007. 'The Indian Lower Palaeolithic', *Bulletin of The Deccan College Post-Graduate and Research Institute* 66-67: 47-94.

Misra, V.N. 1989. 'Stone Age India: An Ecological Perspective', *Man and Environment* 14: 17-64.

——. 2001. 'Prehistoric Colonization of India', *Journal of Biosciences* 26(4): 491-531.

Misra, V.N. and S.N. Rajaguru. 1986. 'Environment et Culture de l'Homm Prehistorique dans le Desert de Thar, Rajasthan, Inde', *L'Anthropologie* 90: 407-437.

Mohanty, P. 1988. 'Five Seasons of Exploration in Keonjhar District, Orissa', *Indo-Pacific Prehistory Association Bulletin* 8: 47-53.

——. 1989. *Mesolithic Settlements of Keonjhar District, Orissa*. Ph.D. Dissertation, University of Poona.

——. 2002. 'Fifty Years of Ethnoarchaeological Research in India: A Review', in S. Settar and Ravi Korisettar (eds.), *Indian Archaeology in Retrospect: Archaeology and Interactive Disciplines*, New Delhi: ICHR and Manohar, pp. 169-207.

Murty, M.L.K. 1966. *Stone Age Cultures of Chittoor District, Andhra Pradesh.* Ph.D. Dissertation, Pune University.

——. 1968. 'Blade and Burin Industries near Renigunta on the Southeast Coast of India', *Proceedings of the Prehistoric Society* 34: 83-101.

——. 1974. 'A Late Pleistocene Cave Site in South India', *Proceedings of the American Philosophical Society* 118(2): 196-230.

——. 1975. 'Late Pleistocene Fauna of Kurnool Caves, South India', in A.T. Clason (ed.), *Archaeozoological Studies,* Amsterdam: North Holland Publishing Co.

——. 1979. 'Recent Research on the Upper Palaeolithic Phase in India', *Journal of Field Archaeology* 6(3): 301-320.

——. 1981. 'Hunter Gatherer Ecosystems and Archaeological Patterns of Subsistence behaviour on the Southeast Coast of India: An Ethnographic Model', *World Archaeology* 13 (1): 47-58.

——. 1985. 'Ethnoarchaeology of the Kurnool Cave Areas', *World Archaeology* 17(2): 192-205.

——. 1989. 'Pre-Iron Age Agricultural Settlements in South India: An Ecological Perspective', *Man and Environment* 14(1): 66-81.

——. 2004. 'In the Trail of Robert Bruce Foote in Kurnool Caves', in A. Sundara (ed.), *Proceedings of R.B. Foote Memorial National Seminar (1995) on Indian Prehistory and Protohistory (Recent Advances),* Hospet: Directorate of Archaeology and Museums, Government of Karnataka, pp. 68-78.

——. 2006-2007. 'Contributions of the Deccan College to the Ethnoarchaeological Research in India', *Bulletin of the Deccan College Post-Graduate and Research Institute* 66-67: 29-45.

Murty, M.L.K. and K. Thimma Reddy. 1976. 'The Significance of Lithic Finds in the Cave Areas of Kurnool', *Asian Perspectives* 38(2): 214-216.

Nagaraja Rao, M.S. 1984. *Protohistoric Cultures of the Tungabhadra Valley,* Delhi: Swati Publications.

Nambi, K.S.V. and M.L.K. Murty. 1983. 'An Upper Palaeolithic Fireplace in Kurnool Caves, South India', *Bulletin of the Deccan College Research Institute* 42: 110-116.

Nanda, S.C. 1983. *Stone Age Cultures of Indravati Basin, Koraput District, Orissa*. Ph.D. Dissertation, University of Poona.

Neumayer, E. 1983. *Prehistoric Indian Rock Paintings*, New Delhi: Oxford University Press.

——. 1993. *Lines on Stone*, New Delhi: Manohar.

Ota, S.B. 1986. 'Mesolithic Culture of Phulbani District (Orissa) With Special Reference to the Heavy-Duty Component', *Bulletin of the Deccan College Research Institute* 45: 79-88.

Paddayya, K. 1981. 'Water Supply as a Key in the Acheulian Occupation of the Hunsgi Valley, Peninsular India', *Bulletin of the Deccan College Research Institute* 40: 39-51.

——. 1982. *The Acheulian Culture of the Hunsgi Valley, Peninsular India: A Settlement System Perspective*, Pune: Deccan College.

——. 1984. 'Stone Age India', in H. Mueller-Karpe (ed.), *Neue Forschungen zur Altsteinzel*, Munich: C.H. beck Verlang, pp. 345-403.

——. 1985. 'Acheulian Occupation Sites and Associated Fossil Fauna from Hunsgi-Baichbal Valleys, Peninsular India', *Anthropos* 80: 653-658.

——. 2001. 'The Acheulian Culture Project of the Hunsgi and Baichbal Valleys, Peninsular India', in L. Braham and K. Robson-Brown (eds.), *Human Roots: Africa and Asia in the Middle Pleistocene*, Bristol: Western Academic and Specialist Press, pp. 235-258.

——. 2006-2007. 'Evolution within the Acheulian in India: A Case Study from the Hunsgi-Baichbal Valleys, Karnataka', *Bulletin of the Deccan College Post-Graduate and Research Institute* 66-67: 95-111.

Pappu, R.S. 1985. 'Geomorphic Setting of Acheulian Sites in Peninsular India', in V.N. Misra and Peter Bellwood (eds.), *Recent Advances in Indo-pacific Prehistory*, New Delhi: Oxford University Press and IBH Publishing House, pp. 9-12.

——. 2001. *Acheulian Culture in Peninsular India: An Ecological Perspective*, New Delhi: D.K. Printworld.

Pappu, S. 1996. *Pleistocene Environments and Stone Age Adaptations in the Kortallayar Basin, Tamil Nadu*. Ph.D. Dissertation, Pune University.

——. 1999. 'A Study of Natural Site Formation Processes in the Kortallayar Basin, Tamil Nadu, South India', *Geoarchaeology* 14: 127-150.

——. 2001. 'The Environment in Prehistoric Research: A Case Study of the Kortallayar Basin, Tamil Nadu', in K.K. Misra and M.L.K. Murty (eds.), *Peoples and Environment in India*, New Delhi: Discovery Publishing House, pp. 24-38.

——. 2004. 'Robert Bruce Foote and the Kortallayar Basin in Indian Prehistory: Old Problems and New Approaches', in A. Sundara (ed.), *Proceedings of R.B. Foote Memorial National Seminar (1995) on Indian Prehistory and Protohistory (Recent Advances)*, Hospet: Directorate of Archaeology and Museums, Government of Karnataka, pp. 45-67.

——. 2007. 'Changing Trends in the Study of a Palaeolithic Site in India: A Century of Research at Attirampakkam', in M.D. Petraglia and Bridget Allchin (eds.), *The Evolution and History of Human Populations in South Asia, Inter-disciplinary Studies in Archaeology, Biological Anthropology, Linguistics and Genetics Series*, Dordrecht, The Netherlands: Springer, pp. 121-137.

Patil, C.B. 2002-2003. 'The First Neolith in India – A Review with Special Reference to Karnataka', *Puratattva* 33: 63-66.

Patterson, T.T. 1939. 'Stratigraphic and Typologic Sequence of the Madras Palaeolithic Industries', in H. de Terra and T.T. Paterson (eds.), *Studies in the Ice Age in India and Associated Human Cultures*, Washington: Carnegie Institute of Washington Publication No. 493, pp. 327-330.

Possehl, G.L. and P.C. Rissman. 1992. 'The Chronology of Prehistoric India: From Earliest Times to the Iron Age', in R.W. Ehrich (ed.), *Chronologies in Old World Archaeology (Third Edition)*, Vol. I & 2, pp. 465-474.

Prakash, P.V. 1981. *Lithic Cultures and Palaeoenvironment of Gambhiram River Valley, Visakhapatnam Coast*. Ph.D. Dissertation, Andhra University.

——. 1986-87. 'The Mesolithic Industries of Gambhiram River Valley on the East Coast of India', *Bulletin of the Indo-Pacific Prehistory Association* 7: 23-26.

——. 2007. 'Aspects of Formation Processes of Stone Age Sites of Northeastern Andhra Pradesh', in K. Paddayya (ed.), assisted by Richa Jhaldiyal and Sushama G. Deo, *Formation Processes and Indian Archaeology*, Pune: Deccan College Post-Graduate and Research Institute.

Raghavan, H.S., N. Rajaguru and V.N. Misra. 1989. 'Radiometric Dating of a Quaternary Dune Section, Didwana, Rajasthan', *Man and Environment* 13: 19-22.

Rajendran, P. 1989. *Archaeology of Kerala,* New Delhi: Classical Publishing Co.

Raju, D.R. 1981. *Early Settlement Pattern in Cuddapah District, Andhra Pradesh: A Palaeoanthropological Study.* Ph.D. Dissertation, Pune University.

——. 1986-87. 'Fresh Light on the Upper Palaeolithic in the Eastern Ghats', *Bulletin of the Indo-Pacific Prehistory Association* 7: 17-22.

——. 1988. *Stone Age Hunter-Gatherers: An Ethnoarchaeology of the Cuddapah Region, South-East India,* Pune: Ravish Publishers.

Sankalia, H.D. 1956. 'Animal Fossils and Palaeolithic Industries from the Pravara Basin at Nevasa, District Ahmednagar', *Ancient India* 12: 35-52.

Sankalia, H.D. 1974. *Prehistory and Protohistory of India and Pakistan,* Poona: Deccan College Postgraduate and Research Institute.

Sankhyan, A.R. 2005. 'Human Fossil Evidence from Narmada Valley', *Humankind* (*The Journal of Indira Gandhi Rashtriya Manav Sangrahalaya, Bhopal*) 1: 103-115.

Sarma, I.K. 2003. 'Neolithic-Chalcolithic in Andhra Pradesh', in M.L.K. Murty (ed.), *Pre-and-Protohistoric Andhra Pradesh Up To 500 BC* (Published by the Andhra Pradesh History Congress in association with the Dravidian University, Andhra Pradesh), Chennai: Oriental Longman Private Limited, pp. 88-106.

Sharma, G.R., V.D. Misra, D. Mandal, B.B. Misra and J.N. Pal. 1980. *Beginnings of Agriculture* (*Epi-Palaeolithic to Neolithic: Excavations at Chopani-Mando, Mahadaha and Mahagara*), Allahabad: Abinash Prakasan.

Singh, Thakur Raja Ram. 1979. 'Prehistoric and Early Historic Sites in Karimnagar Region, Andhra Pradesh', *Journal of Archaeology in Andhra Pradesh* 1(1): 1-12.

——. 1984. 'Living Conditions of Palaeolithic Man in Godavari Valley: From Basar to Bhadrachalam', *Journal of Archaeology in Andhra Pradesh* 2: 7-26.

Sonakia, A. 1984. 'The Skull-Cap of Early Man and Associated Mammalian Fauna from Narmada Valley Alluvium, Hoshangabad Area, Madhya Pradesh (India)', *Geological Survey of India Records* 113(6): 159-172.

——. 1985. 'Skull Cap of an Early Man from the Naramada Valley Alluvium (Pleistocene) of Central India', *American Anthropologist* 87(3): 612-616.

Subrahmanyam, B.R. and David Raju. 1983. 'The Neolithic Phase in Coastal Andhra: Distribution Pattern', *Journal of Andhra Historical Research Society, Dr. N. Venkataramanayya Commerative Volume* 38 (I): 37-45.

Tattersall, I. and J.H. Schwartz. 2001. *Extinct Humans* (Paperback), Oxford: Oxford University Press.

Thampi, S.P. 1983. *Prehistoric Archaeology of South Central Kerala with Special Reference to the Valley of Anjunad,* Ph.D. Dissertation, Poona University.

Thomas, P.K. 1989. 'Utilization of Domestic Animals in Pre-and-Protohistoric India', in J. Clutton-Brock (ed.), *The Walking Larder: Patterns of Domestication, Pastoralism and Predation,* London: Unwin Hyaman, pp. 108-112.

Thimma Reddy, K. 1980. 'Billa Surgam: An Upper Palaeolithic Cave Site in Southern India', *Asian Perspectives* 20(2): 206-207.

Vishnu-Mittre. 1989. 'Forty Years of Archaeobotanical Research in South Asia', *Man and Environment* 14 (1): 1-16.

Wadia, S., R. Korisettar and V.S. Kale (eds.). 1995. *Quaternary Environments and Geoarchaeology of India,* Bangalore: Geological Survey of India, pp. 324-332.

Wakankar, V.S. and R.R.R. Brooks. 1976. *Stone Age Paintings in India,* New Delhi: B.R. Taraporewala and Sons.

Wendt, H. 1974. *From Ape to Adam: The Search for the Ancestry of Man* (Omega Edition), London: Futura Publications Ltd.

Wolpoff, M.H., J. Hawks, D.W. Frayer and K. Hunley. 2001. 'Modern Human Ancestry at the Peripheries: A Test of the Replacement Theory', *Science* 291: 293-297.

Whyte, R.O. 1972. 'The Graminae, Wild and Cultivated, of Monsoonal and Equatorial Asia. I, Southeast Asia', *Asian Perspectives* 15: 127-151.

Zide, A.K. and N.H. Zide. 1973. 'Semantic Reconstructions in proto-Munda Cultural Vocabulary I', *Indian Linguistics* 34: 1-24.

2

Recent Scientific Approaches to Archaeological Research in India

G.L. BADAM

ABSTRACT

During the last few decades, significant developments have taken place in the adoption and application of a large number of scientific methods in various areas of archaeological research. Previous researches were mostly objective and of the Classical type of the Traditional Archaeology. Subsequently, geographical, geological and lithological dimensions of the archaeological cultures began to be studied for a comprehensive understanding of the multi-faceted dimensions of the occurrence of archaeological cultures. In the recent past, new dating techniques, taphonomy, dental histology, bio-molecular studies, palaeo-diet, palaeo-pathology, etc., have found their way in the archaeological studies. These multi-disciplinary approaches have revolutionised our understanding of the spatio-temporal dimensions of the Archaeological cultures and opened up exciting avenues of research in the analysis of the socio-cultural aspects of the archaeological cultures. It is to be admitted that today there is hardly any branch of science that does not have a direct or indirect bearing in the development of archaeological research. In this paper, scientific approaches that have been applied in recent years in the study of archaeology are briefly discussed and analysed.

INTRODUCTION

In this paper, effort has been made to review the trends that have emerged during the last few decades in the application of the scientific methodology to various areas of archaeological research. Techniques of archaeological excavations gradually became refined with the passage of time. The studies were mostly objective with emphasis on diagnostic features present in stratigraphy, in artefacts, be it Stone Age tools, pottery, epigraphy, numismatics, art, architecture, iconography and other antiquities both from pre-historic and historical periods. However, all these studies were of the classical type but this was when the only method available to study them, of course with gradual refinement of skills. Subsequently, the emphasis shifted to detailed stratigraphic studies, geographical ranges and lithological associations. With the passage of time, areas of ecology, bio-geography and evolution in technology received more attention. During the last few decades, the researches have progressed qualitatively with the application of several new techniques like dating methods, taphonomy, dental histology and enamel ultra-structures, bio-molecular studies, isotope studies, palaeo-diet, palaeo-pathology, population dynamics studies, etc. In addition to this, several new pre-historic and protohistoric sites have been discovered and studied in detail. Multi-disciplinary approaches have been used which have shed new light on the spatial and temporal dimensions of the antiquities and their associations. Today, there is no branch of science which does not have a direct or indirect application to archaeology. We have areas like archaeo-metallurgy, archaeo-chemistry, archaeo-zoology and palaeontology, anthropology, archaeo-botany, bio-metrics and computer applications, experimental archaeology, marine archaeology, ethno-archaeology, forensic archaeology and DNA studies, studies on debitage, wear analysis and various other areas.

In the pages that follow, scientific approaches that have been applied in recent years in the study of archaeology are briefly outlined.

DATING TECHNIQUES

A major advance in dating methodology is seen in the application of absolute dating techniques like C-14, TL, ESR, K-Ar, U-series, Palaeo-magnetism, etc. Many of the problems of chronology, especially of the prehistoric archaeology, have been resolved to some extent by using these methods. The beginning of the Quaternary in India has been established by magneto-stratigraphic studies in the Indian subcontinent, initially applied to Pabbi Hills of Pakistan and later to the Indian Siwaliks bordering Punjab and the Jammu region. The INQUA Commission of 1991 now accepts the base of Matuyama as the beginning of Quaternary, which is an important datum line, for pre-historic research in India more or less starts with this datum line. New evidences are coming up in dating refinements by magnetic polarity and magneto-stratigraphic studies. There are specialized laboratories in Geological Survey of India (GSI), Bhaba Atomic Research Centre (BARC), Physical Research Laboratory (PRL), Birbal Sahni Institute of Palaeobotany (BSIP), Roorkee University and the Institute of Physics, Bhubaneswar which are equipped to undertake this type of work.

ESR DATING

The ESR (Electron Spin Resonance) dating method was for the first time attempted in India by Gogte and Murty (1986) on bone samples from the Upper Palaeolithic site of Kurnool Caves in Andhra Pradesh. The samples selected for ESR dating belonged to five layers at MCG II (Mucchatla Chinta manu Gavi) in the Kurnool cave-complex. The ESR dates were obtained from two trenches, Trench F and Trench B. The dates for the two levels at Trench F: (1) 893 BP for F 20 cm-40 cm and (2) 5247 BP. For F 40 cm-60 cm provide a time sequence for the upper levels of cave sediments. The date for trench B4 (120 cm-135 cm) being 9498 BP supports the association of this level with the Mesolithic. The dates for the preceding levels 16,686 BP for B4 (150 cm-165 cm) and 19,224 BP for B4 (165-180 cm) confirm the Upper Palaeolithic age of these levels. The ESR dating for B4 (165 cm-180 cm) is almost in agreement with TL date of 17,390 BP (Murty and Nambi, 1983) from burnt clay within the sediment from the same level.

In addition to the above, the fission track and TL dating methods have amply demonstrated their usefulness to archaeology in one way or the other.

CHEMICAL DATING

Fluorine dating of archaeological materials (bones and fossils) was attempted for the first time in India by Joshi and Kshirsagar (1986) and subsequently on samples collected from various geographic regions (Kshirsagar and Paddayya 1988-89; Kshirsagar and Badam 1990 and Kshirsagar 1993). These studies have established the positive role that Fluorine analysis can play in relative dating of faunal material from different geological and archaeological periods. For example, the Acheulian sites of Hunsgi (Karnataka) and Chirki (Maharashtra) have F/P ratios in the range of 6.73-8.39 and 8.11-8.29, respectively. Both these ranges indicate a Middle Pleistocene age for the fossil-yielding levels. Another example can be cited from the site of Hathnora in M.P. where the cranium of Homo erectus narmadiensis gives a F/P ratio of 7.53 which places the cranium in late Middle Pleistocene time-bracket. The range of most of the fossils dated by this method can be favourably compared on the basis of archaeological, geological and palaeontological data. The usefulness of fluorine analysis for establishing a chronological framework for the Indian Quaternary deposits has been realised for the last three decades and this study will continue to occupy an important place in archaeological research in the years to come.

Amongst the other relative dating methods in archaeological organic elements, nitrogen analysis was attempted on some of the Narmada Valley fossils. This method has some limitations because nitrogen disappears rapidly from bones in a tropical climate and hence may not give accurate results. The figures 0.97% nitrogen for a fossil from the surface and 1.20% for a buried fossil, both from the Devakachar area in the Central Narmada Valley, were considered by K.P. Oakley to be similar to Upper Pleistocene in Africa and Europe.

U-Series

Recently, Szabo *et al.* (1990) obtained half a dozen radiometric dates using the U-Series technique on assemblage of the Acheulian culture of the Hunsgi-Biachbal Valley in North Karnataka. These dates confirm the Middle Pleistocene-late Pleistocene time-bracket for these cultures. F/P ratios obtained on bone samples from these sites (8.39-5.06 for Acheulian and 5.28-0.22 for Middle Palaeolithic to Neolithic) confirm the dating (Kshirsagar and Paddayya 1988-89). Two of these dates were calibrated on travertine samples from the site of Kaldevanhalli in the Hunsgi Valley. The remaining four dates were obtained on enamel samples of teeth from Sadab, Teggihalli and Kudalgi in the Baichbal Valley. A fragment of molar of Elephas from Sadab has given a date of 290,405 BP. The Bos sample from Teggihalli gave a date of 287,731 BP whereas the Elephas sample from the same area gave a minimum age of 350 kyr.

At Bori in the Kukdi Valley (Maharashtra), typical Acheulian artefacts and fossils of Bos, Elephas and Equus have been recovered from a well section, from cemented sandy pebbly gravel which is underlain by a compact brown silt, fissured clay and pebble. A 2-m thick tephra layer, dated to 670,000 yr BP, is embedded in the clay sediments. Fossil samples from different locations at Bori gave a F/P ratio which is close to the saturation point of 8.92, indicating an older antiquity, possibly Middle Pleistocene for the fossils. The other ratios are in the range of 4 and 5 being comparable with the ratios obtained for the late Pleistocene period (Kshirsagar and Badam 1990). The Th/Ur dates at Bori also indicate a higher antiquity (400 kyr BP). At Nevasa Th/Ur dates, more than 350 kyr BP, on calcrete cemented gravels containing Acheulian artefacts along with fossils of Bos, Elephas and fossil wood, indicate an antiquity (Lower to Middle Pleistocene) much higher than assumed earlier.

The above new dating techniques have revolutionised our thinking on the chronology of Stone Age cultures in Peninsular India, for example, the antiquity of Acheulian in India. Also, some of the fossils have now been placed in a near accurate chronological framework. Of course, further refinements in biochronology are expected from time to time.

DENTAL HISTOLOGY AND ENAMEL ULTRA-STRUCTURES

In the case of palaeobiological materials, one of the major advances has been the application of scanning electron microscopic studies to document the diversity of ultra-structure in teeth and bones and to understand the relationship between enamel ultra-structure and functional dental morphology. The results of these studies have given new dimensions to the interpretation of phylogeny, taxonomy, dietary habits and the diseases from which the animals suffered in the past. Furthermore, the bio-mineralised structure of vertebrate egg shells (for example Ostrich) and dental tissues is ideally suited for such studies. There are various patterns in the dental prism structures which cover all the animal groups. It has also been shown that the prismatic arrangement of the animals, including humans, is controlled by stresses which occur during mastication, fights, heavy load of work, disease, etc., many of which are reflected in taphonomic studies of animal bones and human skeletal material from archaeological sites. Apart from getting an idea about the ancestor-descendant relationship in animal and human groups, the study also suggests a gradual transition in dietary habits of certain species from graminivorous, omnivorous to herbivorous. The SEM studies also help in a precise identification of various closely related taxa where the simple tooth and osteological morphology may not help. Indirect derivation of palaeo-environmental conditions is also possible from such studies. In higher mammals, to dissipate chewing stresses, better structural mechanisms have developed which are reflected in the enamel structure of the teeth. The scanning electron microscopic studies can help in documenting changes on account of domestication process and are fast becoming a standard tool for examination of bones for signs of butchery, disease and muscular stress.

Biomolecular Studies

During the last two decades or so, biomolecular studies have contributed immensely to various aspects of Quaternary studies, including palaeobiology and archaeology. However, in India, such studies are still in an experimental stage. Such studies can contribute to our understanding of the past in a number of ways, e.g., hominid origins and macroevolution, the palaeo-biology and biogeography of human species, environmental reconstructions, past human diets, etc. DNA has been recovered from fossil leaves (e.g., Magnolia), from termites fossilised in amber (both dating to Miocene period), from the skin of Egyptian mummies and from brain tissues (both dating from 5000 to 7000 years) and various other organic materials. Some of the sequences are compatible with those from modern populations. All said and done, there is a need for more systematic work on the survival of ancient bio-molecules in the whole range of organic material that can be recovered from archaeological and geological contexts. More emphasis needs to be laid on the effects of age, type of site, context, soil conditions, macro and micro climate.

Collaborative research on the extraction of DNA from ancient bones and fossils with Centre for Cellular and Molecular Biology (CCMB), Hyderabad is gradually bringing out interesting results but not enough for interpretation at present (Siva Kumar *et al.* 1999). It takes a long time to analyse a normal bone; the older the bone the longer is the time taken for extraction of DNA. For better understanding, we may give here examples from the work of Paabo (1985), a pioneer in research on bio-molecular studies. During the past decade, scientists have learnt that ancient

DNA survives the ravages of time. Scholars have used DNA from bone and soft tissues to establish reliable sequence of seven extinct mammals, the oldest being the woolly mammoth found in the permafrost of Siberia. One can learn much more about the genetic relations among extinct species that DNA can survive for long periods after the death of an individual. Allan Wilson (University of California at Berkeley) studied the quagga, a member of the horse family, that lived in Southern Africa until becoming extinct at the end of the past century. Samples from a 140-year-old quagga skin in a German museum yielded bacterial clones containing sequences from the mitochondrial DNA, which exists in many clones outside the cell nucleus. By comparing these clones with sequences of modern zebra, it was shown that quagga was closely related to the zebra and more distantly related to other equids. These were the first sequences determined from an extinct species.

In 1985, K.B. Mullis introduced a method, the polymerase chain reaction (PCR), which allows the multiplication in the test tube of a particular piece of DNA. This technique is extremely sensitive and can generate billions of copies from a single DNA molecule. It was also shown later that PCR can reconstruct intact DNA from several partially degraded ancient molecules.

Future studies on ancient DNA will "help us learn more about the dynamics of genetic change in populations over time". We may be able to understand better the history of ourselves and other species and also "to frame more rational strategies to limit the ongoing erosion of biodiversity".

STABLE ISOTOPES IN ARCHAEOLOGY

Over the last decade, stable isotope ratio analysis has become a primary method for monitoring of ancient human diets. While stable isotope ratios of animal bones have generally been used as standards against which to measure human dependence on animal and plant resources, increasing attention is now being given to the use of these techniques in the evaluation of the effect of man/animal interaction on animal diet. Changes in animal diet and nutritional levels during early stages of domestication is one topic which might be addressed with this technique; another is the degree of dependence of wild animals on the crops grown by early agriculturists. Studies of this kind have been initiated on archaeological bones in India. In addition, there is an ongoing collaborative research programme in this field with the University of Arizona, Tuscon (USA), in which the present author is involved. Interesting results are expected to emerge from this study.

Chronological Aspects of Mammalian Fossils and the Taphonomic Implications

Index fossil assemblages (or even a single index fossil) play a vital role in chronological assessment of the stratigraphical horizons. Added to it are the several absolute and relative dating methods which have become available in recent times, thus helping to place the fossiliferous and stratigraphic horizons on a sound chronological footing.

In recent decades, these dating methods have demonstrated their usefulness to biostratigraphy in one way or the other. The biostratigraphic chronology of the Indian Pleistocene (which was hitherto mainly based on mammalian fossils and their cultural associations) has now undergone a change. The palaeontologic and stratigraphic dating, index fossil assemblages, the First Appearance Datum (FAD) of an allochthonous faunal element and the Last Appearance datum (LAD) of an index fossil are crucial in building up of a biostratigraphic chronology. However, these should be supplemented by physical (absolute) and chemical (relative) dating methods, some of which are outlined above.

In recent two decades or so, the science of taphonomy has contributed immensely to the assessment of various modes of deposition of sediments and their fossils, activity areas of animals in biocene situation, primary/secondary context of fossils, nature of enclosing sediments and other aspects leading to the stratigraphic details of the fossiliferous sediments. In fact, this subject is now considered as a prerequisite to palaeoecological studies. However, in the Indian situation, some discrepancies have crept in while relating fossils to stratigraphic levels. For example, in the Siwaliks of NW India, some of the earlier collections came from mixed contexts without a clear-cut stratigraphic control (Badam and Rajaguru 1991). In several cases, the matrix enclosing the fossils is different from lithology of the stratigraphic levels from which the fossils are extracted (Saxena 1968). Hence, the chronological framework was somewhat erroneous till the methods of dating became available. In certain areas of the Narmada Valley, two modes of deposition can be distinguished, the majority of fossils found in the lag deposits of boulder and cobbly horizon are fragmented and obviously have undergone some transportation. Fresh and unabraided fossils are derived from the overlying silty sandy horizon (channel fill and overbank alluvial fill deposits) and in most of the cases, the animals represented by these fossils were autochthonous in nature. In other words, they were derived from stratigraphically controlled situations. It may be mentioned that the partial cranium of Homo erectus narmadiensis, found in a channel bar environment at Hathnora in M.P. (Sonakia 1984), which provides a landmark discovery in palaeoanthropology, is heavily mineralised and has been found associated with Late Acheulian artefacts. However, its position in the bar deposits combined with taphonomic features indicated that the cranium was re-deposited in the gravel sheet after having been transported over some distance (Badam 1989). This aspect, if overlooked, would give erroneous results regarding the stratigraphic control of the fossil and, therefore, the sedimentary context of the fossil and the cultural material warrant a detailed taphonomic study.

Hominid Fossils

Hathnora stands unique in South Asia for having yielded the unequivocal Middle Pleistocene hominids crucial for understanding Homo erectus/Homo sapien transition. The first discovery of the hominid partial skullcap (Sonakia 1984) has filled up to a large extent the gap in our knowledge of the hominid evolution in this part of the world and in South Asia as a whole. However, there has been a difference of opinion about its nomenclature. On the basis of archaeological associations, this species fits in the description of 'archaic' Homo sapiens (Badam *et al.* 1986), which was also agreed to by Kennedy *et al.* (1991) on the basis of craniometric and non-mensural characters. This was followed by important postcranial discoveries of hominin fossils from the same locality, e.g., two clavicles and one left 9th rib by Sankhyan (1997, 2005).

The hominid discoveries have given Narmada Valley recognition worldwide. Work on the Narmada Valley is going on in right earnest from the multidisciplinary point of view through a project launched by the Anthropological Survey of India in June 2005. It is hoped that with patience and luck, many more discoveries of the hominin fossils and cultural artefacts from the Narmada Valley and also from other parts of the country would come to light in future.

Rock Art

During the last three decades or so, research on rock-art in several parts of the world has assumed great proportions. The study has progressed from the stage of discovery of rock shelters, identification of animals depicted in rock-art and their chronological sequences to more applied aspects like scientific methods of dating of the rock-art, the rate of weathering of the shelters, animal distribution pattern during the periods of depiction and their extensions in the past geological horizons if any, and the art site management, techniques of conservation and preservation of rock-art. Efforts have been made successfully to include the study of rock-art in the school/college curriculum so as to help develop awareness amongst the students and general public about the need to preserve this cultural heritage for the posterity and also to highlight its importance in the tourism industry.

Signatures of rock-art (in the form of paintings, engravings, etc. drawn on rocks and rock shelter panels) are one of the most authentic and direct evidence of artistic mind of Early Man and his lifeways. Though these evidences are found almost everywhere in the world, today the bulk of evidence comes from South Africa, Australia and India. India stands distinct in concentration and diversity of rock art. Scientific studies regarding chronology, ecology, conservation and collection of samples have been initiated and encouraging results are beginning to emerge.

In India, where rock-art has now come to be recognized as an independent subject in art, archaeology and ethnography, the painting activity generally starts from Upper Palaeolithic (the evidence of cupules pushes back the beginning of the work of art to Middle and Lower Palaeolithic period) and continues till the Early Historic period. This activity had the maximum development during the Mesolithic which was a phase of faunal turnover, with direct evidence of domestication, disappearance of archaic fauna and its replacement by more advanced forms, some of which continue even till today. There was a clear-cut morphological and ecological change during this phase when the rock-art is supposed to have proliferated.

In recent years, attempts have been made to obtain absolute dates for the paintings under EIP (Early Indian Petroglyphs) Project, trace the continuity of rock-art to tribal and folk art and apply multidisciplinary approaches to the rock-art research laying much stress on conservation and management. The Early Indian Petroglyphs (EIP) Project was initiated by the Rock Art Society of India (RASI) and the Australian Rock Art Research Association (AURA) under the auspices of the International Federation of Rock Art Organizations (IFRAO). Under this project, a number of samples from different geological situations have been collected from various rock shelters of Madhya Pradesh for dating and other studies, the results of which are expected. Madhya Pradesh has a vast number of rock-art sites. It is a natural paradise endowed with various hilly ranges like Satpura, Vindhya, forest resources, rich fertile soils, perennial river valleys like Narmada, Tapti, Chambal, Shipra, Son, Mahanadi, Betwa, Indrawati, etc. So these places are a meeting ground for different cultures since the earliest times. Sources of water, availability of raw material for making tools, edible roots and fruits provided ideal habitat for the early man in these settings.

Rock-art is a mixture of art, aesthetics and philosophy. Thus, in unravelling mankind's evolution from Homo erectus to Homo sapiens these early images offer vital clues. We first enter into the present contexts of traditional arts, move backwards in time to rock-art and then reach a stage in which the visual texts and the traditional contexts are compared. All these help us to realise the cosmic dimension of rock-art.

Ostrich in the Indian Archaeological/Geological Context

An interesting discovery in recent years has been the finding of ostrich egg shells, plain or engraved, from the late Pleistocene levels in India, archaeologically equivalent to the Upper

Palaeolithic culture. With several discoveries of such shells, various aspects of taxonomy, palaeoecology, distribution of the bird in the past and its importance in archaeological and palaeontological context became clearer.

The first discovery of ostrich egg shells in India was made in 1860s by Archibald Carlyle from the Ken River in Banda Dist. of Uttar Pradesh (Kumar 1988; Neumayer 1990). It was suggested that the Ken River egg shells resemble those of Struthio molybdophanes (the Somali Ostrich). Sali's discovery (1980) of ostrich egg shells from an Upper Palaeolithic site in Patne in the Jalgaon Dist of Maharashtra evoked a lot of interest followed by the discovery of about sixty sites in Rajasthan, Madhya Pradesh and Maharashtra, some of which were dated (e.g., Patne, Maharashtra: 25,000 BP; Chandresal, Rajasthan: 38900 BP and 36,500 BP; Ramnagar, M.P.: 31,000 BP). Kumar *et al.* (1988) and Badam and Sathe (1990 have given a detailed list of shell discoveries in India; the latter authors have also added details about the taxonomy, palaeogeographic distribution and probable ancestry of the ostrich. Sahni *et al.* (1990) conducted microstructural studies on an extensive collection of the ostrich eggs shells.

Lydekkar (1884) was the first to describe the fossil bones of ostrich in a geological context (*Struthio asiaticus*) from Dhok Pathan Stage of the Middle Siwaliks. This is perhaps the earliest record of the fossil ostrich in India (Badam 2005). To explain the absence of ostrich in India during the gap of 6 myr or more is rather problematic. Whether the evolutionary history of ostrich during the gap is unrecorded, whether the ostrich disappeared from India after the Miocene or whether it was an immigrant to India during the late Pleistocene and disappeared again during the Holocene are questions that await answers. Overkill hypothesis (Francis 1983), climatic changes at the end of the Pleistocene (Kumar *et al.* 1988), or spread of an epidemic (Badam and Sathe 1990) are some of the possible reasons (singly or combined) forwarded for the disappearance of the ostrich in the time gap between the Miocene and late Pleistocene and during the Holocene. In any case, these discoveries have helped us appreciate better the significance of ostrich in archaeological and geological contexts.

CONCLUSION

The role of archaeological science and its benefits for the society and overall mankind hardly needs any emphasis. Starting from the days when it meant only the study of monuments and coins to the time when it is closely collaborating with sciences like botany, ecology, forestry, geology, zoology, anthropology and humanities, archaeology has come a long way. In the few decades, this subject has become truly interdisciplinary, and as I said earlier, today there is hardly any branch of science which is not relevant to archaeology.

Concerted efforts by archaeologists and scientists are recommended for unravelling the mysteries of the past with which man is directly concerned. The traditional and modern systems in any endeavour should not be treated as exclusive systems but as mutually complementary and essential parts of a scientific and historical continuum. Modern science has a great role to play in revitalising the traditional systems without negating the fundamental principles of long-term sustainability.

ACKNOWLEDGEMENTS

I wish to thank Mrs. Bindiya Chopra and Shri Ashish Shinde, IGNCA, New Delhi for their help in the preparation of this paper.

REFERENCES

Badam, G.L. 1989. 'Observations on the Fossil Hominid site at Hathnora, Madhya Pradesh, India', in Ashok Sahni and Rajan Gaur (eds.), *Perspective in Human Evolution,* Renaissance Publishing House, Delhi, pp. 153-171.

——. 2005. 'A note on the Ostrich in India since the Miocene', *Man and Environment* 30(2): pp. 97-104.

Badam, G.L., R.K. Ganjoo, Salahuddin and S.N. Rajaguru. 1986. 'Evaluation of fossil hominid – the maker of Late Acheulian tools at Hathnora, Madhya Pradesh, India', *Curr. Sci.* 55 (3): 143-145.

Badam, G.L. and S.N. Rajaguru. 1991. *Problems of Neogene Litho and Biostratigraphy of the Siwaliks in NW India, Birbal Sahni Birth Centenary Symposium on Siwalik Basin*, Wadia Institute of Himalayan Geology, Dehra Dun, pp. 7-9.

Badam, G.L. and V. Sathe. 1990. 'Geological and Biological Implications of Ostrich in India with reference to its importance in Archaeological Context', in N.C. Ghosh and S. Chakraborty (eds.), *Adaptation and Other Essays,* Visva Bharati Research Publications, Santiniketan, pp. 75-87.

Francis, P. 1983. 'The Ostrich, Ostrich Eggs, and Ostrich Egg-Shell Beads', *Man and Environment* 7: 142-146.

Gogte, V.D. and M.L.K. Murty. 1986. 'ESR Dating of Kurnool Caves, South India', *Man and Environment* 10: 135-140.

Joshi, R.V. and A. Kshirsagar. 1986. *Chemical Studies of Archaeological bones from India: Fluorine and Fossilisation Process,* Deccan College, Pune.

Kennedy, K.A.R. and J. Chiment. 1991. 'The fossil hominid from the Narmada Valley India: Homo erectus or Homo sapiens?', in P. Bellwood (ed.), 1, *Indo-Pacific Prehistory 1990*, Canberra: Indo-Pacific Prehistory Association, pp. 42-50.

Kshirsagar, A. 1993. 'The Role of Fluorine in the Chronometric Dating of Indian Stone Age Cultures', *Man and Environment* 18 (2): 23-32.

Kshirsagar, A. and G.L. Badam. 1990. 'Biochronology and Fluorine analysis of some Pleistocene Fossils from Central and Western India', *Bulletin of the Deccan College Post-Graduate and Research Institute* 49: 199-211.

Kshirsagar, A. and K. Paddayya. 1988-89. 'Relative Chronology of Stone Age Cultures of Hunsgi-Baichbal Valley, North Karnataka, by Fluorine Analysis', *Bulletin of the Deccan College Post-Graduate and Research Institute* 47-48: 143-146.

Kumar, G. 1988. 'Ostrich in India and its Relation to Prehistoric Man', in K.L. Bhowmik (ed.), *Culture of the Past,* New Delhi: Inter-India Publication, pp. 101-131.

Lydekkar, R. 1884. 'Siwalik Birds', *Memoirs of the Geological Survey of India* 10 (3): 136-202.

Murty, M.L.K. and K.S.V. Nambi. 1983. 'An Upper Palaeolithic Fireplace in Kurnool Caves, South India', *Bulletin of the Deccan College Post Graduate and Research Institute* 42: 110-116.

Neumayer E. 1990. 'A Note on Ostriches in India', *Man and Environment* 15 (1): 25-28.

Paabo, S. 1885. 'Preservation of DNA in Ancient Egyptian Mummies', *Journal of Archaeological Science* 12: 411-417.

Sahni, A, G. Kumar, Sunil Bajpai and S. Srinivasan. 1990. 'A Review of Late Pleistocene Ostriches (*Struthio* sp.) in India', *Man and Environment* 15 (1): 41-47.

Sali, S.A. 1980. *Stone Age Cultures at Patne, Dist. Jalgaon, Maharashtra.* Ph.D. Dissertation. University of Poona, Pune.

Sankhyan, A.R. 1997. 'A new human fossil find from the Central Narmada basin and its chronology', *Curr ent Science* 73 (12): 1110-1111.

——. 2005. 'New fossils of Early Stone Age man from Central Narmada Valley', *Curr. Sci.* 88 (5): 704-707.

Siva Kumar, S., V. Subramanian, S.R. Walimbe and Lalji Singh. 1999. 'Current Trends in Ancient DNA Studies – A Review', *Current Science*, Vol. 76 (7): 879-885.

Sonakia, A. 1984. 'The Skull Cup of Early Man and Associated Mammalian Fauna from Narmada Valley Alluvium, Hoshangabad Area, M. P. (India)', *Records of the Geological Survey of India* 113: 159-172.

Saxena, M.N. 1968. 'A Note on the Validity of the Upper Siwalik Vertebrate Fossils for Stratigraphic Correlation', *The Eastern Anthropologist* 21(3): 319-321.

Szabo, B.J., Curtis Mckinney, Timothy S. Dalbey and K. Paddayya. 1990. 'On the Age of the Acheulian Culture of the Hunsgi-Baichbal Valleys, Peninsular India', *Bulletin of the Deccan College Research Institute* 50: 317-321.

3

Action Archaeology and Sustainable Development

S. NAGARAJU

ABSTRACT

Action archaeology is practically applied archaeology. The underlying theme is to utilize past wisdom for future development. It is an approach which can expand the horizons of archaeology and open up new opportunities to the archaeologists. The theoretical premise for action archaeology is derived from the anthropological perspective of cultural evolution. The progressive stages of cultural evolution as revealed by archaeology demonstrates how varieties of strategies, both material and ideological, were chosen to suit different environmental situations. The efficacy of this pluralistic approach is proved by the very success that man has achieved on this planet so far.

The logic behind action archaeology is, as neither the basic needs and aspirations of the humankind nor the general environmental situation on this planet has changed significantly (at least within the Holocene), successful experiments done in the past for efficient use of specific environmental resources for fulfilling human needs could guide future planning too. In the present paper, how a modern problem like shrinking agricultural lands in the process of urbanization can be resolved on the basis of past practices in land use has been discussed; extensive use of rock-cut architecture for developing basic industrial infrastructure has been advocated.

Action archaeology is an extension of archaeology geared to utilize the wisdom of the past for future development, thus transforming what has been to this day a pure academic discipline into a utilitarian technology. It makes archaeology much more relevant to the present and to the future, and opens up new opportunities for the archaeologists to participate in meaningful development programmes.

The theoretical premise for action archaeology is derived from the anthropological perception of culture, wherein culture itself, in all its manifestations as acquired ability of man, is deemed as an adaptation strategy developed by the human species for ensuring its survival and success. Its character is determined by the way man negotiates with the specific environment in which he has to live. As neither the basic needs and aspirations of the humankind nor the general environmental situation on this planet has changed significantly, at least within the Holocene, past experiments in evolving strategies in man-environment relationship could still be instructive. The progressive stages of cultural evolution, as revealed by archaeology, demonstrate how varieties of strategies, both material and ideological, were chosen to suit different environmental situations. The efficacy of this pluralistic approach is proved by the very success that man has achieved on this planet so far. The logic behind action archaeology is that successful experiments done in the past for efficient use of specific environmental resources for fulfilling human needs could guide future planning too. It is here that the field knowledge and insights gained by the archaeologist can become important inputs for planning sustainable development programmes. This is of great relevance, especially for geographical regions where past civilizational traditions have been lost or forgotten due to a variety of reasons (invasions, colonization, globalization, etc.). This line of thinking is not just an academic exercise, but a serious attempt to resolve problems that have cropped up in man-environment relationships in recent years.

As far as India is concerned, there are several examples that could be derived from archaeological studies which illustrate the efficacy and suitability of past practices evolved out of experiments of several generations compared to many modern practices, which are mostly those imposed, or imported, as fashionable in medieval and colonial periods.[1] The present paper attempts to add another example – of exploiting live rock for creating architectural space, a practice widely in vogue once in India, which has the potential of solving the current problem of pressure on agricultural land created by the fast pace of urban and industrial development in recent years.

PROBLEMS IN CURRENT LAND USE POLICIES

The quantum of changes wrought by mankind on this planet in the last 200 years is perhaps hundred times more than what the previous generations of the species did in the last 200 millennia. The modern scientific and technological advancements have tended to exploit the environment ruthlessly without recognizing the consequences of over-exploitation. One of these is the prevalence of unscientific land use policies.

The onset of industrialization has brought in a qualitative change in man-environment relationships. The continued process of establishing industries using modern operating procedures for infrastructural development is causing problems for sustainable development. Land use patterns are changing. The ever-growing demand for land for industrial use is practically invading into productive agricultural lands. The construction methods used, involving large scale utilization of cement and steel, are creating environmental pollution as well as global warming. Occupying agricultural lands for industrial purposes is also creating social problems by dislocating population and uprooting the rural folk from their traditional ways of livelihood.[2] In addition, growth of industrial clusters with high density of population is resulting in the creation of an imbalance between the demand and supply of essential resources like water and energy. Transportation of men and material, a necessary adjunct to industrial processing, is furthering the pressure on the already strained delicate environmental balance.[3]

ACTION ARCHAEOLOGY ALTERNATIVE

In this context, the traditional ways of land use patterns, as revealed from the past settlement pattern studies by archaeologists and as delineated in the *Shilpasastra* works, show a distinctive policy having been evolved. Two basic principles were in practice then, viz.

1. All human settlements (villages and towns) are to be raised close to cultivable lands and perennial water sources.

2. All other activities, not connected with the day to day living of the populace, are to be located away from the above (e.g., military establishments, large kilns, mines, mortuary buildings, cemeteries, etc.).

How the second principle was in operation can be understood best in the hill forts seen almost all over India. Whereas these were mostly for military use, a large number of rock-cut architectural works were created in live rock for the purpose of establishing monasteries, etc. Both of these practically did not interfere in any way with the agriculturally productive lands. Perhaps, similar works may now be undertaken for locating military and industrial establishments.

A few examples of past experiments may provide us a clear idea of such land use patterns. The Ajinkyatara fort[4] (Fig. 1) near Satara (Maharashtra) can be cited as one of the best examples. Supposed to have been built originally by Bhoja Raja (AD 1178-1193), it was further strengthened and expanded by the Bahamani Sultans and the Marathas. Perched on the top of a bare rocky hill about 994 m from sea level, it was surrounded by a fortification measuring about 1000 x 500 metres. Besides its strategic importance, the ruins of wells, tanks, buildings and store-houses seen here indicate that it had been well provided with all amenities to serve as a strong military base accommodating about fifteen to twenty thousand soldiers. It was thus a bone of contention among the rulers of the region, each one trying to gain control over it. The Bahamanis and Adilshahis had occupied it. It was taken over by Shivaji and later occupied by Aurangazeb to be recaptured again by the Marathas. Even afterwards, it continued to be the seat of the Rajas of Satara till 1848, when it was annexed by the British and abandoned shortly afterwards.

The Mehrangarh fort (Fig. 2) near Jodhpur (Rajasthan) is another good example of defense architecture. It is interesting to note that both these are located on the top of rocky hills, without endangering any vegetation growth or interfering with the day to day activities of the agricultural population around these hills. A detailed study of these forts revealed that the materials required for the construction of fort walls and interior buildings were extracted from the very same hills, thus avoiding the need for any large scale transportation. Further, large water tanks and cisterns were dug in suitable locations, which are perhaps the most efficient examples of water harvesting. These forts, which maintained a large resident population, are not known to have met with any water shortage though located on the summit of the hills.

In India, creating architectural space in live rock has been a continuous activity from about the 3rd century BC to about the 13th century AD. A large number of experiments have been done, perhaps much more than what has been done in the other parts of the world, in choosing ideal types of rock formations and creating varieties of architectural works.[5]

Fig. 1. The Ajinkyatara Fort.

Fig. 2. The Mehrangarh Fort.

The potential of rock-cut architecture can be seen from several experiments and achievements of the past. For example, the Lomas Rishi cave[6] (Fig. 3) in the Barabar hills near Gaya, Bihar is known for its immaculate workmanship. The cave has been cut into a scarp of a low sandstone hill. The entry into this is through an arched doorway about 2.5 metres wide and 2.5 metres high. But inside, a large hall with a semi-circular hut-like chamber on one side has been carved. All parts of the cave, whether they are rectangular corners or barrel-shaped roof, are neatly cut with almost geometric accuracy. The whole of the cave has been neatly polished, thus doing away with any other surface treatment like plaster or lime wash. The cave has survived to this day intact for the last 2300 years, without requiring any repair or maintenance.

The 2nd century BC Buddhist monastery at Bhaja[7] (Fig. 4), in Pune district, Maharashtra, is a good example of neat layout, locating the main work-place (chaitya hall) in the centre and arranging the other adjuncts, including the residential units for monks, on either side of this. Some of them are located one above the other with staircases leading up to them. In front of most of the residential units, underground water cisterns have been dug which can store enough water collected during monsoon rains to last throughout the year. Even to this day, they are intact and serve as the only source of water for visitors coming here round the year. Cut into the scarp of a trap rock hill on the Western Ghats, this Buddhist *Vihara* had been located close to an ancient highway connecting Konkan and the Deccan plains up the ghats.

The trap rock formations in the Deccan are ideally suited for rock-cut architecture and nearly eighty per cent of all the rock-cut architectural works of the country are located in this belt. Trap rock can be easily hewn with hardly any limitations on dimensions. The 1st century

Fig. 3. The Lomas Rishi Cave.

BC Karle Chaitya hall[8] (Fig. 5), acclaimed as the best aesthetic creation of the age in this country, is also one of the largest architectural works. This apsidal chaitya hall 150 feet deep from front to back, and about 50 feet wide and 50 feet high, covers a floor area of about 7000 square feet. The interior space available is about 2.6 lakh cubic feet.[9]

Looking from the floor area possibility, the Tinthal[10] (three storeyed) *Vihara* (Fig. 6) at Ellora is the biggest known. The total floor area available in this cave is about 28,000 square feet. Cut in a slightly sloping side of a hillock, a large front courtyard has been created. Thus obtaining nearly a 70 feet high vertical scarp behind, a three-storeyed *Vihara* is hewn into, each floor ascended by rock-cut flight of steps. Each storey has a large hall about 100 x 45 feet with rooms or shrines in the sides and at the back. The main shrines located at the far end of the central bays are nearly a hundred feet inside the front scarp.

The 8th century AD rock-cut temple of Kailasa at Ellora (Fig. 7) is an architectural wonder known for its aesthetic imagination and gigantic size. Here, a full scale temple about 150 feet long, 90 feet wide and 90 feet high, has been cut out of a mass of rock retained in the centre of a huge trench, 270 feet long 150 feet wide and 110 feet deep dug in the trappean hill of the place. The temple looks like a three-storeyed structure, provided with all the regular components like the sanctum sanctorum, the *maha mandapa*, the *nandi mandapa*, the *gopura* superstructure

Fig. 4. The Buddhist Monastery at Bhaja.

Fig. 5. The Karle Chaitya hall.

Fig. 6. The Tinthal Vihara.

Fig. 7. Rock Cut Temple of Kailasa, Ellora.

Fig. 8. Rock-cut Rathas at Mamallapuram.

and also an entrance pavilion, all hewn out from a single live rock. Besides, running corridors and sub-shrines have also been cut in the back and side walls of the trench. The temple itself is aesthetically designed and adorned with beautiful sculptures. In the creation of this magnificent monument, about 1.8 million cubic feet of rock have been hewn out, all by using manual labor and the old chisel and hammer technique.

A similar experiment of cutting out architectural forms is seen in Mahabalipuram, Tamil Nadu (7-8th century AD). Out of a huge bubble of granite outcrop, a number of architectural works (Fig. 8) have been cut out, simulating contemporary structural forms. One wonders whether, with the availability of highly efficient gadgets for rock-cutting, a whole city can be created in similar rock formations.

Looking at the above examples, we can also see that in this method of creation of architectural space, there are quite a number of advantages compared to the deleterious effects of modern day practices. We may list up the advantages here:

1. No loss of agricultural land
2. Raw material is local rock only, without involving long distance transportation
3. No wastage, all by-products can be reused
4. Structures permanent, long lasting and almost maintenance-free
5. Self air-conditioned, maintaining uniform temperature and humidity
6. Aesthetically pleasing (Fig. 9)
7. Basic needs like water and light can be harnessed locally[11]

Such architectural creations can be used for varieties of modern day requirements like:

1. Special Economic Zones (SEZ)
2. Manufacturing and service industries
3. Schools, colleges and research institutions
4. Hospitals and trauma recovery centres
5. Assembly halls, prayer and meditation centres
6. Civilian storage facilities and military warehouse
7. Special purpose spaces, viz., nuclear and fallout shelters, aircraft hangers, etc. and umpteen other uses one may imagine

Rock-cut architecture is feasible in almost all parts of India. Rock formations like granite, sandstone, trap and khondalite which are suited for rock-cut architecture are seen widespread throughout Peninsular India, the Vindhyan regions, Chhattisgarh and Jarkhand, parts of Gujarat,

Fig. 9. Ajanta chaitya.

Rajasthan, Bihar, Orissa and North-eastern states.[12]

Most important in this context is the fact that by opting for this AA alternative, vast areas of productive agricultural land can be saved. Learning from the past experiments in the selection of suitable rock formations and the methods adopted for achieving durability and usability of the rock-cut architectural works, and utilizing modern technology, tremendous possibilities open up for bringing in revolutionary changes in architectural practices. This old-new technology would be the most economical and environmental friendly alternative. It ensures in full measure the triple components of good architecture – stability, utility and beauty.

NOTES

1. In my *Presidential Address* in the XXXVI Annual Conference of Indian Society for Prehistoric and Quaternary Studies, Bhubaneshwar, December 2008 (to be published in the next issue of *Man and Environment*), I have given some examples: 1. Suitability of Harappan town planning and traditional village layouts in windy desert regions, 2. Utility of circular huts, as seen in Neolithic-Chalcolithic periods and in folk architecture in some parts of India, as most scientifically suited for gale- and cyclone-prone regions, 3. Ancient water management strategies in monsoonal regions, etc. Perhaps one of the best instances of relevance of AA is seen in the context of the Hyderabad Karnataka experience. This region, which was once highly productive and prosperous, because of the excellent water management systems adopted then, has turned to be one of the most backward regions in the country. Continuous neglect of those systems for nearly six centuries has resulted in widespread environmental degeneration and serious biospheric imbalance, turning the region from a state of prosperity to that of poverty. How archaeology has been helpful in diagnosing the problem and how the applied aspects of that discipline can be useful for finding solutions for the problem have been delineated in the above paper.
2. The deleterious consequences of thoughtless land use have already begun to be felt as we know from people's struggles going on in Nandigram (West Bengal), Kaiga, Mangalore (Karnataka), etc. and protests to Special Economic Zones programme in Tamil Nadu.
3. Some figures look alarming. A newspaper article (*Vijaya Karnataka*, 12-7-2007) mentions that out of the 73.5 crore acres of agricultural land available in India, 1.97 crore acres have been converted for industrial use and about 1 crore families have been dislocated in the last 10 years. If the same trend continues, almost 30% of the available agricultural land would be lost within this century itself, but at the same time the population is going to double with proportional increase in the demand for food. This is perhaps a very important problem to be taken into consideration for planning further developmental programmes.
4. M.S. Naravane, *Forts of Maharashtra*, New Delhi.

5. The initial experiments in creating rock-hewn architectural space are seen in Egypt dating back to early 3rd millennium BC (M.A. Murray, *The splendor that was Egypt*, London, 1959, pp. 40, 186). Gradually, it evolved there as a regular architectural form and was in use till the Roman occupation of the land. From about the 15th century BC, this rock-cut architectural form spread to Cyprus and on to Anatolia and to west Asia including Palestine, Jordon, Syria and Iran. But all these were for mortuary use. Ever since its introduction in India in the 3rd century BC, rock-cut architecture has been used here for a variety of other purposes like building temples and monasteries, rest houses for travelers, etc.
6. J. Fergusson and J. Burgess, *Cave temples of India*, Delhi, 1969, p. 37.
7. S. Nagaraju, *Buddhist Architecture of Western India*, Delhi, 1981, p. 113.
8. *Ibid.*, p. 221.
9. If converted to a granary, it can hold 20000 tons of grains.
10. Fergusson and burgess, *op. cit.*, p. 381.
11. Rain water harvesting, as mentioned in the case of the Bhaja monastery above, is an age-old practice in all the rock-cut architectural sites. As for lighting, a common feeling is that they are caves and hence dark. But in my visit to nearly eight hundred rock-cut architectural works, I have noticed that several methods like large doorways, front and clerestory windows have been adopted to allow enough day-light. Sometimes special arrangements of cutting side trenches and opening the front and sides as in Ellora and Elephanta (Mumbai) are also seen. Polishing the wall to a mirror-like finish also reflects light very efficiently. All the above methods allow for adequate illumination inside the living space without the need for artificial lighting.
12. The recent sedimentary alluvial plains of the Indo-Gangetic region have no rocks at all and the Tertiary sedimentary formations spread over the Sub-Himalayas are poor material for rock-cut architecture. The lateritic formations spread in many parts of India are of varied structure. Among them, too, some are suitable for rock-cut architecture.

4
New Approaches to Rock Art Research

B.L. MALLA

ABSTRACT

The study of rock art has a great relevance in the context of re-definitions for the study of all arts. So far, we have mechanistic, analytical approaches which assume that the underlying significance of this kind of creativity cannot be inferred by statistical counts of frequency of figures, etc. Nothing could undermine the complexity and richness of this tradition more. At the moment, there is not much available in India by way of interpretive treatment of prehistoric art. Recently, the IGNCA has initiated a multidisciplinary approach for the study of rock art. The new multidisciplinary approach aims at a global view of culture and of the very essence of the spirit of our species (Homo sapiens sapiens). Usually the psycho-analytical and ethnographical approaches are being followed for the study of rock art. In the cultures like Indian where there is a continuity of the artistic traditions the interpretations of the rock art are explored through ethnographical study of the communities living adjacent to the rock art areas. In the cultures where there is no continuity of traditions mainly due to industrialization, etc., the interpretations are mainly sought through the psycho-analytical approaches.

THE BACKDROP

The present concern of all rock art researchers is to explore the 'future of the past' and to look beyond the duty of discovering, protecting, and educating about archaeological treasures. Everybody is curious to know in which direction the discipline of archaeology is going, because the philosophy of research and technology/science is fast changing.

The concern for exploring new ways and means for rock art research and for deciphering rock art opened a new chapter in the history of research in prehistoric and tribal art, with new scope for the collaboration of archaeology with anthropology, art history, philosophy, semiotics, psychology, psychiatry, history of religion and cultural history. The new multidisciplinary approach aims at a global view of culture and of the very essence of the spirit of our species (*Homo sapiens sapiens*).

In the past, the rock art research has coupled archaeology and anthropology with aesthetics and art history. By this approach, a common research ground has been established between prehistoric art and the history of religion. In this direction, investigations have been made on the signs of myths and shamanism, logical and cognitive functions as revealed by art, and paradigms of semiotic and graphic art, etc. But the present challenge is to widen the scope of multidisciplinary involvement, and to look beyond the context and read the messages. Because prehistoric art narrates a piece of life, a thought or an emotion which has been a part of our tradition, it reveals changes in people's way of thinking, feeling, and sentiments.

PSYCHO-ANALYTICAL APPROACH

Under this method of research, psychiatrists are exploring the minds of the prehistoric artists. While starting from the concept of sublimation in relation to creativeness and artistic production, the scholars follow a psychiatrist's, micro-psychoanalyst's point of view and take into consideration some common elements between art and psychosis, psychosis and infantile thought, infantile thought and art.

Some scholars believe that inside the human mind (preconscious, conscious, and unconscious) we could find, metaphorically speaking, traces similar to those of the prehistoric incisions engraved on rocks. It is not the formal similarity among such traces but the fact; they try to represent the inner affect which animates them. It has been observed that the affect linked to at least four variables – nourishment, sex, territory and death – does not change. It is the pattern of representations, which changes into stages of psycho-sexual development with the passage time (Anati 2004).

Besides, the images, which appear in myths as well as in the rock art motifs, may contain the echo of the process that generated them and it may give us a sign about their construction. The representation of the cosmos seems to be constructed through several condensations and displacements, which form similar but not identical images: the course of the sun, the journey of dead spirits and the dream sojourns.

Some considerations have also been made from the analogies between tribal rituals and ceremonies. They assume that during ontogenesis, a human being passes through philogenetic development stages and in particular that the child in evolutive age uses the design and gestures to express his/her psychic life, since he/she is still unable to use a linguistic code. This phenomenon is similar to what happened to our ancestors of the prehistoric era in rituals and in their graphic representations.

In conditions of obsessional neurosis, rituals and ceremonies have an important function, in relation to the need to lessening of the tensions. Through the gesture that the neurotic compulsive repeats during his ceremonials, he tries to find a system, which can express at the same time the wish and the need for self-punishment. Such need allows to reduce the sense of guilt, by using an expressive means which can be compared to the one used by primitive man in ritual and by the child in concrete logic stage.

It seems that there is an immediate need to study further psychology of iconicity, and to make distinction between 'mental and artistic representations'. It is believed that the 'abstract art' comes from the mind but 'representational art' comes from the natural forms.

It is clear from the above discourse that the need of the hour is to study palaeo art in a holistic perspective while applying the multi-disciplinary approach. It is to be investigated as one of the greatest bio-cultural experiments of humanity. We have to develop a formal grammar and unified theory for palaeo art studies.

Ethnographical Approach

Another important avenue for the interpretation of rock art is the ethnographical approach. It is suggested to find out the temporal spectrum of both rock art and tribal art. By this exercise, the upper and lower limits of both the sets of art may be identified. Both the specific points on the respective sets of art are to be compared in detail. The processes are to be carried out (carefully/ logically/scientifically) for understanding the genesis of rock art and the development of tribal art, and to determine the spectrum of continuum.

In the ethnographical study of rock art, two main facets emerge. One is direct relationship between native tribal groups and the rock art in their habitat and another is the inference, which can be extracted from the cognition of the natives about this art. It does not matter if they did not do it or if it belongs to another age which is not connected to them. The first addresses/ undertakes ethnic and ethnological studies of the techniques of conservation (facing tourism and the cultural changes). This is an urgent task. But the approximation to the problem must be synchronic and phenomenological (Malla 2000, 2004, 2005 & 2006).

At the same time, archaeology claiming to be cognitive, aiming at how a culture is understood needs tautegoric ethnography to plan its interfaces. The true understanding cannot come by imposing the pre-conceived, uni-dimensional models of the cognitive development of the human language or through artificial order or data. We have to understand the circular movement of our past and present, regional and global, part and the whole, self and the other, surface and the context in the rock art traditions of the world. It could help in making clear the meaning of rock art depictions; why only some and not all are ruled by the fixed laws, why is it not possible to generalise when dealing with different people. The native of today, as that of yesterday, is a free being, who select the motives that his cosmology dictated or by imperative shamanism. The other factors, which could be investigated by ethno-archaeology, includes abrogation, meaning or reason behind superimposed drawings, destruction, and changing of sites.

IGNCA PROJECT ON ROCK ART: CONCEPT AND STRUCTURE

One of the major academic programmes of the Indira Gandhi National Centre for the Arts (IGNCA) relates to exploring the artistic manifestations emanating from man's primary sensory perceptions. The classification of arts in Indian tradition is based on different aesthetic senses. Amongst the senses that lead to aesthetic experience are vision (*Drshya*) and hearing (*Shrvya*). Architecture, sculpture and painting originate from vision, and music and poetry originate from hearing, and theatre emerges from both of them together. Hence, Indian aesthetics is a well-experimented psychoanalytical process of judgment. Most probably, man's first awareness of the world around came through his primeval sense of sight and ability to hear.

Under this programme, the centre is thinking for the establishment of the twin galleries of *Adi Drshya* and *Adi Shrvya*. The rock art forms a crucial component of the *Adi Drshya* programme. Rock art research will contribute greatly to the establishment of the *Adi Drshya* gallery, while exposition of primary sense of sound (ear), music and musical instruments will form the *Adi Shrvya* gallery (Malla 2004).

The prehistoric rock art has been interpreted with different theoretical orientations – generally based on vague and misguided notions of "primitive mentality". Primitive man is denied of having "deeper aesthetic feelings" and "highest moral and intellectual speculations". Following the evolutionary approach – addressing the propositions about human cognitive development and the process of evolution and emergence of language – 'scientific' claims are made for the 'origins of art'. But we should not ignore the fact that in the Old World, the cosmo centric view dominated the lifestyle. Even the authors of rock art and sages of the *Upanishadic* philosophy reveal the same experience of the cosmos and man's place in it: Both look at the universe and its sacred artefacts. Interestingly, the text of the classical Indian theory of art is consistent with the context of what is known today as aboriginal art. The fundamental intuition, motifs and styles of rock art persist in their art.

Many traditional societies have no formal term for art, no separate word for artist. Majority of them can paint and carve. It is an integral part of their lifestyle. The priest may have the privilege of producing paintings and songs in ceremonies. Or, some members of a clan may hold such a status. The Saora icon is the drawing on the walls and is locally called *ITTALAN* (ID = to write; *KITALAN* = a wall). The term varies from one area to the other. The Saoras living around Chandragiri refer to it as *ANITAL* (*KINTAL* = wall, the drawings on the walls are called *ANITAL*). Similarly, the Pithora painters of western India call painting, 'writing' *LIKHANA* and painter, 'writer' *LAKHERA*. In Indian classical (textual) tradition also, the aesthetics or the science of art appreciation uses the word 'art' in a wide and all-inclusive sense. The essential hallmark of art is to make, create or fashion a form or *rupa*, sensible or intelligible (Malla 2004 & 2005).

Rock art is one of the richest cultural resources in the world, which depicts the earliest expressions of humankind. This prehistoric art perhaps comes to signify the underlying philosophies and the world-view of the ancient people, and tells us about the soul of a community, its thoughts, beliefs and emotions. It is associated with the cultural values, particularly in countries like India and Australia, where this art is a part of the living cultural heritage of its native population. The rock art images could be treated as a source for cultural communication with the past, present and the future. The past to celebrate remembrance, memory and legacy; the present to confirm and legitimise the culture; and the future as an expression for the cultural and human fear of death. India has one of the world's six major prehistoric rock art concentrations of Stone Age era, and is the first country in the world to discover the same (in AD 1867 at Mirzapur, Uttar Pradesh). The other places of the globe are South-Western Europe, Russia, North Africa, South Africa and Australia. The term 'Rock Art' is generally used for all types of artistic activities found on rocks and is classified into two main forms; 'pictographs' and 'petroglyphs'. The pictographs refer to painted figures and are also termed as rock paintings, while and petroglyphs include engravings, carvings, brushing, dotting and cup marking. The pictographs are found on rock shelters, while petroglyphs are usually confined to open rocks and boulders.

It is necessary to mention here that the fundamental approach of the IGNCA in its academic endeavours is multi-disciplinary, multi-dimensional, multi-directional, multi-layering, and multi-meaning within the systemic cultural whole. Its conceptual plan aims to open the doors to the realisation that rock art is pure and absolute and, hence, capable of dispensing great experience beyond its original culture and time. The IGNCA's concern with prehistoric rock art is not restricted to the archaeologists' concern with establishing a linear chronological order, nor is it restricted to the identification of style and school as a criterion for establishing chronology. Instead, it is a concern for man's creativity across time and space and civilizations and cultures through the perception of the sight.

The Sanskrit term *Adi Drshya* is an indicator of multiple levels of interpretations of the world *Adi* (Primeval). The IGNCA has envisaged one *Adi Drshya* gallery which will create for the viewer, a degree of experiential contact with prehistoric art restricted to rock art caves. It would provide the basis for entering into the changing aspects of the living arts of man. It is believed that man's awareness of the world around came through his primeval sense of sight and sound. These two scenes have stimulated artists' expressions, visual and aural, in the prehistoric past as also in the contemporary cultures. Exploring through the faculty of sight, we can construct the kinds of world-view that have nearly ceased to exist, and try to infer from that the articulation of lifestyle that continue to the present only in radically altered ways. Besides, the emphasis will be given to create in the viewer both a perception of time as well as the unchanging material and non-material needs in the physical and environmental setting common to all of humankind without linking the past and the present in an evolutionary framework. While considering the diversity of form and manifold concept of time, there is no good reason to restrict the understanding of rock art in terms of linear time, making it out fixed points of time in history. On the conceptual side, the gallery will attempt to bring out the universals amongst world cultures that existed in the pre-historic times. It is intended that by placing side by side cross-cultural products, it can be demonstrated that there are universals in this system of visualisation, holding great relevance today. In fact, it will be endeavour to create among Indians a greater appreciation of the global past. With a view to prepare for the eventual display in the rock art gallery, a great deal of research and gradual built up of permanent collections is essential.

On the same line, the IGNCA has taken up an ambitious project of the rock art survey and documentation, and also the ethno-archaeological study of the rock art. The purpose of the project is: (*i*) to make textual, contextual video and photo documentation, (*ii*) to communicate with people in the hinterland for archaeological research, and to build up a bio cultural map, a mental and ecological atlas of the rock art landscape, on the basis of documentation of related folklore and natural and man-made features, (*iii*) to make suggestions for structural, ecological, and, in rare cases, direct conservation, preferably using local materials and techniques (*iv*) to develop a video, photo and digital archive, (*v*) to make documentaries on the basis of the video documentations in the field, (*vi*) to organize displays (permanent, mobile, temporary), and (*vii*) to bring out publications, both in print and electronic media. A multidisciplinary approach is being adopted for this project. The field documentation is being done in collaboration with the local experts and institutions of the areas/zones concerned.

Briefly, the goal to be set is not merely the development of a multimedia gallery but also to establish *Adi Drshya* into a school of thought and research on alternate means of understanding prehistoric art. So far, we have mechanistic, analytical approaches which assume that the underlying significance of this kind of creativity cannot be inferred by statistical counts of frequency of figures, etc. Nothing could undermine the complexity and richness of this tradition more. At the moment, there is not much available in India by way of interpretive treatment of prehistoric art. The interpretive research and gallery display must go hand in hand.

REFERENCES

Anati, E. (ed.). 2004. 'Pre-proceedings of the XXI International Valcamonica Symposium', Darfo Boario Terme (BS): CCSP & CAR (Italy).

Malla, B.L. 2000. 'Ethnographical approach for studying Indian Rock-Art', in R.N. Agrawal (ed.), *Indian Rock Art Vis-a-Vis Ethnography*, Sagar: Sagar University, pp. 99-118.

——. 2004. 'Rock Art and Ethnography – An Ethnographical Approach for Studying Rock Art in Indian Context', *Pre-proceedings of the XXI International Valcamonica Symposium*, Darfo Boario Terme (BS): CCSP & CAR (Italy), pp. 295-312.

——. 2005. 'Nature of Art and Art of Nature', paper presented in the International Congress on Nature in Eastern Art, Tehran: the Academy of Arts (Iran).

——. 2006. 'New Developments in Rock Art Documentation and Research', paper presented in the 10th Congress of Rock Art Society of India, Delhi: Institute of Archaeology.

5

A Preliminary Note on Impact Assessment Studies at Prehistoric Sites in Tamil Nadu

SHANTI PAPPU & KUMAR AKHILESH

ABSTRACT

The scale and extent of destruction of prehistoric archaeological sites in India have reached levels unforeseen in the past. This is a result of a combination of factors including rapid development activities, inadequate and outdated legislations, lack of popular awareness of what constitutes a prehistoric site, apathy in implementing conservation measures, and a decline in research in Indian prehistory. This paper presents an overview of the nature of impacts created by various land use patterns at prehistoric sites in Northern Tamil Nadu. This forms part of a broader research and heritage management project implemented by the authors.

INTRODUCTION

The diversity and richness of prehistoric sites in India, spanning the Pleistocene and early Holocene, have been well documented ever since the late 19th century (Foote 1866). Indian prehistoric research has contributed enormously towards understanding the nature and antiquity of early cultures; and in establishing the vital position which India occupies in a wider global perspective (see Bednarik 1993; Foote 1866, 1869, 1870, 1916a, b; Ghosh 1989; Mishra 1994, 1995, 2006-2007; Misra 1989; Paddayya 1984; Petraglia 1998; Sankalia 1974; Settar and Korisettar 2002; Neumayer 1993). Despite this, prehistoric archaeology remains a neglected subject in India. This is not only seen in the decreasing number and nature of research projects which are initiated by Indian scholars, but also in the field of managing and conserving such sites. Prehistoric sites are generally small, forming an 'invisible' part of the natural landscape, as compared to more 'glamorous' structural and monumental remains of later periods. This has led to what was termed the 'Taj Syndrome' (Pappu 2006); a focus on monuments, sculptures or remains which are thought to represent the highest achievements in human creativity, at the cost of those considered to lack artistic, visual or popular appeal. This attitude is combined with ignorance on the part of the general public and government officials as to what constitutes a prehistoric site. When combined with the rapid rate of development projects in the country, these attitudes have accelerated the destruction of prehistoric sites all over India.

In addition to problems in perceptions of prehistory, Indian legislations are in many ways not in sync with recent developments in archaeology (Biswas 1999; The Ancient Monuments and Archaeological Sites and Remains Act 1958; The Ancient Monuments and Archaeological Sites and Remains Rules 1959; The Antiquities and Art Treasures Act 1972; The Antiquities and Art Treasures Rules 1973). In particular, these Acts and Rules lack any provisions for compulsory archaeological impact assessment prior to any small or large scale development project. In the context of prehistory, while surveys of sites and salvage archaeology have been implemented by the Archaeological Survey of India in the case of major dam projects (e.g., Nagarjunakonda, Narmada valley projects) (Ota 2000), this is not so in the case of other constructions of a smaller but equally damaging nature. It is left to vigilant archaeological officers of the Archaeological Survey of India or State Departments of Archaeology to take action in such cases. In most instances, however, these have met with little success owing to the lack of appropriate legislations or delay in implementation of existing Acts, in addition to other internal tensions (Ota 2000).

Unlike sites of later periods, prehistoric sites are highly fragile, and form a non-renewable resource; (ICOMOS Charter of 1990), where artefacts, macro and microfossils and their sedimentary context constitute an intrinsic whole. They are especially vulnerable to changes resulting from rapid development and climate change, and are highly susceptible to unplanned but well-intentioned efforts at promoting tourism. Recognition of their unique nature is noted in various international conventions (The World Heritage Convention, UNESCO; UNESCO Recommendation Concerning the Protection, at National Level, of the Cultural and Natural Heritage 1972). However, we note that prehistoric sites (Palaeolithic/Mesolithic) constitute a small fraction of the 679 cultural World Heritage Sites declared by UNESCO in their list of sites marked out for special protection (World Heritage List, UNESCO). These include those sites renowned for either finds of hominin fossils with/without artefacts, or those marked by spectacular rock-art. The ICOMOS lists a description of World Heritage Hominid Sites with a detailed bibliography (ICOMOS World Heritage Hominid Sites), with only eight sites as being of special importance, primarily owing to their rare fossil hominin remains found with/without prehistoric lithic assemblages. In India, of the 22 World Heritage Sites, only one is prehistoric. The Bhimbetka complex of rock shelters was declared a World Heritage Site (No. 925), in 2003, as per criteria (iii)(v). Incidentally, this is the only prehistoric complex in India where systematic heritage management strategies have been implemented (Bhimbetka, India, No. 925; UNESCO, World Heritage, Rock Shelters of Bhimbetka; http://whc.unesco.org/archive/advisory_body_evaluation/925.pdf; (http://www.w3c.org/TR/1999/REC-html401-19991224/loose.dtd).In the list of monuments/sites declared protected by the Archaeological Survey of India, we note that in the case of Tamil Nadu (http://asi.nic.in/asi_monu_alphalist_tamilnadu.asp), out of a list of 403 protected sites, 186 sites are of the Iron Age (Megalithic cairn circles, dolmens, and other burial types). While these may be classified to some extent as prehistoric, there is not a single Palaeolithic, Mesolithic or rock-art site listed here. In contrast to this, in the case of Madhya Pradesh, at least nine site-complexes are listed with rock-art (http://asi.nic.in/asi_monu_alphalist_mp.asp). Strikingly, the only site in India, Hathnora, where the fossil cranium of possible archaic *Homo sapiens* was found, is absent in this list.

To ensure that this heritage is conserved for future generations, we must adopt a practical policy by which research, conservation and development proceed in mutual harmony. This should be for the benefit of the advancement of scientific knowledge and conservation, yet without conflicting drastically with development of infrastructure and welfare projects. It is thus essential that in a country like India, any management strategy should work to achieve a balance between conservation and development needs and should take into consideration the needs of local stakeholders, developers and archaeologists.

MANAGING INDIA'S PREHISTORIC SITES: A CASE STUDY FROM NORTHERN TAMIL NADU

Managing prehistoric sites requires a fundamentally different approach to that of sites of later periods, owing to the extreme fragile nature of the deposits with artefacts. However, in the initial stages, the requirements are the same, viz., the compilation of a comprehensive database of prehistoric sites in the study area, combined with detailed studies of impacts which are destroying such sites. This paper focuses on impact assessment studies which form part of a broader research and Heritage Management Project implemented by the Sharma Centre for Heritage Education in collaboration with RRSSC-Bengaluru, under the ISRO-GBP programme. This project utilized a combination of satellite remote sensing, GIS and archaeological field surveys/excavations and laboratory studies in order to investigate prehistoric land use patterns over a period ranging from the Middle to Late Pleistocene and Early Holocene. An area of 8000 km^2, in Northern Tamil Nadu (Fig. 1) (districts Thiruvallur, Chennai and Kanchipuram), was considered. A special focus was laid on understanding the area around the excavated site of Attirampakkam (Pappu 2007; Pappu and Kumar 2006, 2008; Pappu *et al.* 2003, 2004). The project is the first of its kind in India, in the case of prehistoric (Palaeolithic) research. The region under study is one where industrialization has changed the face of the landscape over the past decade. This rapid development of infrastructure, construction of industrial areas, factories, houses and other urban expansion programmes, mechanized cultivation, irrigation projects and dams, has resulted in a destruction of archaeological sites on scales unforeseen in the past (Pappu *et al.* 2009).

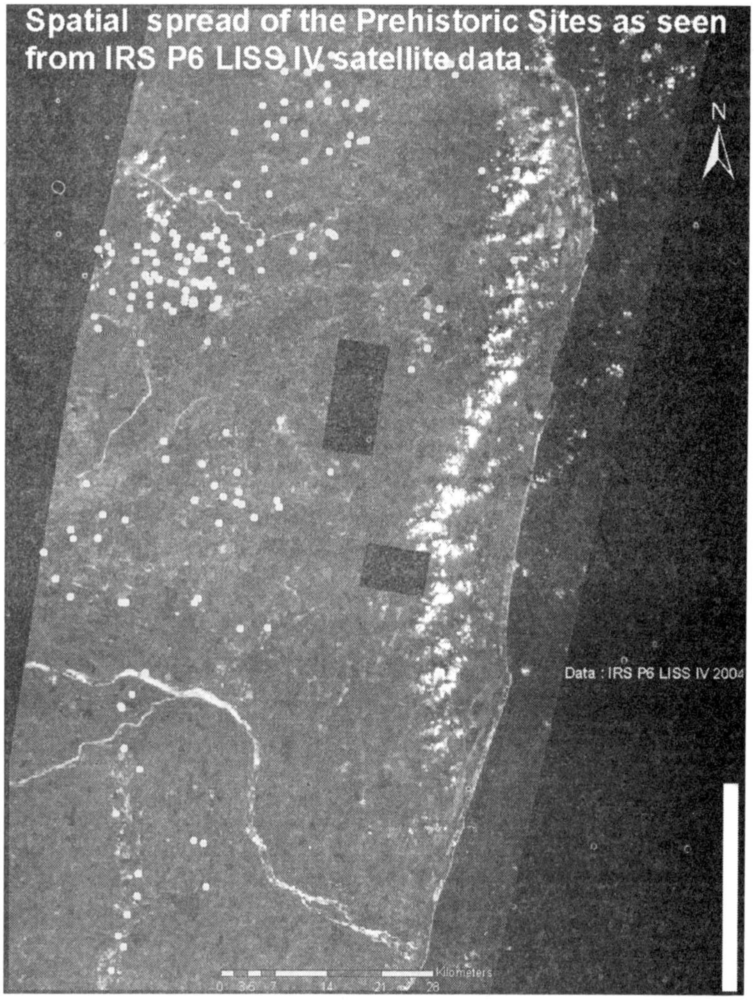

Fig. 1. Spatial distribution of Lower, Middle and Late Palaeolithic sites in the study region (basins of the rivers Arani, Kortallaiyar, Adyar, Cooum and Palar), Tamil Nadu (satellite data from IRS PS-LISS IV).

Satellite remote sensing studies adopted a three-tiered approach for creating a satellite database of the study region. The regional context of each site was studied through medium resolution satellite data of IRS 1D LISS 3 (Nov 2004) of 23 m. To understand the local context of sites, IRS 1D PAN + LISS 3 (Nov 2004) merged satellite data of 5.8 m resolution was used. A very high resolution IKONOS 1 m satellite data (April 2005) was used to get an in-depth understanding of the site of Attirampakkam and its surroundings. Following geo-referencing of the images and use of image fusion techniques, enhanced images could be generated. This was accompanied by digitisation of relevant information from the reference maps related to topography, hydrology, etc. The satellite images were interpreted and updated thematic maps were prepared on various themes like land use/land cover, geomorphology, geology, elevation, drainage, transport network, modern settlement patterns, surface water bodies, canal networks, etc. All archaeological sites and important sections studied for palaeoenvironmental purposes were examined in relation to these parameters. A codification scheme was evolved for various thematic maps. A database was created for all environmental, land use, and archaeological parameters. Village cadastral maps for key sites were also geo-referenced and tiled together. GIS-based spatial analysis techniques like overlay, proximity and query were used for generating various combination thematic maps. This relational database was then organised with systematic structuring of the tables and records with one to many relation. The multiple tables were linked through unique identification numbers and concatenation (as required). The entire RDBMS was linked to the geospatial database for prognostic analysis. This was used to address specific archaeological research issues and for heritage management studies.

Field studies over the entire study region included surveys, test-pits, studies of Quaternary geomorphology; studies of artefact typology and technology, laboratory studies of sediments, and collection of samples for dating and for palaeobotanical studies. Data from ongoing large scale excavations at the site of Attirampakkam was also included to provide stratigraphic and chrono-cultural controls over the database.

Each site, though technically defined as a dense concentration of artefacts, also included areas which had only a few scatters of artefacts. Alternately, we also noted extensive low density scatters of artefacts over several kilometers. These scatters across the landscape were also mapped. Within the study region in particular, the visibility of Palaeolithic sites was dependent largely on the exposure of sediments and, thus, notions of what constitutes a site required rethinking (see Pappu 2001). On defining the limits of the site to be studied, GPS readings were taken with the help of Garmin Etrex handheld GPS (error around 10 m). The DGPS Survey and IKONOS data helped record accurate locations at sites considered to be of great importance.

Although in general salvage archaeology should be the last choice for any heritage management project, it was inevitable in this case, and such operations had to be implemented at sites which were in the process of being completely destroyed. Sampling strategies varied greatly. In most cases, the site had already been disturbed to a greater or lesser degree. When destruction was widespread, random sampling was preferred. However, in the case of quarries where some degree of spatial patterning could be observed from preliminary observations, grids were laid out and a sample of artefacts was collected from across the site. Synchronized walking across transects; timing the collection of artefacts/unit area, etc. were other strategies used. At most sites, samples comprised either squares of 1 x 1 or 2 x 2 m at a measured distance across the site, or in the form of circles of 1-2 m^2 radius. In addition to this, detailed photographs and videos were taken of the sections studied, context of artefacts, landscape, vegetation and surroundings, nature of impacts, and other features. In addition to prehistoric sites, data from areas which were considered important from the perspective of understanding palaeoenvironments was also collected. This included river/gully sections, wells, palaeochannel deposits and the like. At sites which were thought to be of critical importance in understanding scientific research problems, test-pits were sunk. Data was entered into a database, and key parameters were codified for use in GIS analysis.

THE ARCHAEOLOGICAL RECORD OF THE STUDY REGION

The study area chosen covered an area of 8000 km^2, in the districts of Thiruvallur, Kanchipuram and Chennai. This covered the basins of the rivers Arani, Kortallaiyar, Cooum, Adyar, Palar and Cheyyar (12^0 15′ 00″ to 13^0 30′ 00″ N; 79^0 30′ 00″ to 80^0 22′ 00″ E). The region is marked by a range of geological formations (Geological Survey of India 2006; Kumaraguru and Trivikrama Rao 1994; Muralidharan *et al.* 1993; Pappu *et al.* 2003; Subramanian and Selvan 2001). The geology of the region towards the north comprises Archaean formations comprising the Satyamangalam, Charnokite and Bhavani groups; and Upper Proterozoic formations including the Epidote-hornblende gneiss, important insofar as they structure the landscape and were occasionally used as raw material for artefacts. These are disconformably capped by the Satyavedu and Sriperumbudur formations (Lower Cretaceous), of which the latter also includes the marine component of the Avadi formation (Geological Survey of India 2006). The GSI also recognizes a Quaternary fluvial formation (Swarnamukhi formation). In the immediate vicinity of the excavated site of Attirampakkam, the region is characterized by Lower Cretaceous Satyavedu and Sriperumbudur formations, Cenozoic laterites, Pleistocene lateritic gravels; and gravels, silts, sands and clays of the Swarnamukhi/Kortallaiyar Formation (Pleistocene-Holocene) (Geological Survey of India, 2006). To the west of Attirampakkam lie the NNE-SSW-trending Allikulli hills (200-380 m AMSL), which are cobble-to-boulder size fanglomerates or palaeodeltas of early Cretaceous age (Kumaraguru and Trivikrama Rao1994; Muralidharan *et al.* 1993). The low-lying areas of the eastern Cuddapah piedmont in the vicinity of the Allikulli Hills are underlain by a shaly marine formation (Avadi formation), which is coeval and intertonguing with the conglomerate beds. Further south, near Kanchipuram, crystalline Archaeans, sedimentary rocks of the Gondwana supergroup (Satyavedu, Sriperumbudur and Avadi formations), and the Cuddalore formation are exposed. The Quaternary Kanchipuram gravels are also noted sporadically in this region. Laterites, lateritic gravels also termed ferricretes and ferricritised gravels are distributed differentially across the study region. The region falls in an area of seasonally dry tropical conditions, receiving 105 to 125 cm of annual rainfall with a major peak occurring from September to November (see Pappu 2001).

As a result of this project, a total of 160 areas were studied for both archaeological purposes and for generating palaeoenvironmental data. Of these, 148 are prehistoric localities, each of which may have one or more clusters of 'sites'. Sites comprised Acheulian, Middle Palaeolithic and Late Palaeolithic assemblages. Acheulian assemblages were noted at 112 sites within 95 localities. While such sites are largely concentrated in the basins of the rivers Arani and Kortallaiyar, occasional scatters of artefacts are found further south as well, and a single cleaver was found as far south as the site of Ulandai, immediately north of the river Palar. While the distribution of such sites is linked to exposures of Pleistocene deposits and Cretaceous formations on which artefacts are scattered, they are also related to their proximity to raw material sources. Such sites occur within a range of geomorphological and stratigraphic contexts ranging from reworked contexts within recent channel gravels, within ferricritised or ferruginous coarse cobbly-pebbly gravels, roughly corresponding to what is termed Quartz Gravels (Geological Survey of India 2006), within ferricretes (termed also as laterites/lateritic gravels); within ferricritised sediments, on the surface of the Cretaceous formations comprising sandstones and shales of the Satyavedu and Sriperumbudur formations. The unique context of Acheulian artefacts within clayey silts derived from weathering and reworking of the Avadi formation was noted in the excavations at Attirampakkam.

Middle Palaeolithic sites number 130 within 127 major localities, often overlapping with the Acheulian and representing various phases or variants. They have a wider distribution, right up to the R. Palar and further south. For the first time, sites appear associated with a wider range of sedimentary contexts. They occur in channel gravels and ferricretes and ferricritised gravels, on the surface of ferricritised and ferruginous coarse cobbly-pebbly gravels representing Cretaceous formations or within what the GSI terms Quartz gravels. They occur for the first time in non-ferruginous or ferricritised fluvial gravels, silts and sands. For the first time, such sites are noted further south, on the surface of charnokites. Raw material usage includes a continuation of the quartzites noted during the Acheulian, with the addition of more artefacts on gneiss and chalcedony. Sites occur at considerable distances from raw material sources.

Important components of the archaeological record are what may be termed Late Palaeolithic assemblages. These comprise assemblages with a small component of blades and typical blade cores, a 'non-geometric' microlithic element, a significant percentage of small flake tools and occasional Levallois flakes. There are several variants or phases within these assemblages based on the technology represented and microlithic component. These industries may be termed a variant of the typical Upper Palaeolithic noted further north in Andhra Pradesh (Murty 1970), and may be assigned to the Terminal Pleistocene (although dates are awaited). Such assemblages are noted at 44 sites, in 40 localities. Although fewer in number, they have a greater range of distribution as compared to the Middle Palaeolithic and extend south of the R. Palar. The maximum number of such sites is located on the surface of, or within ferricritised gravels; they also occur on the surface of weathered gneiss, and in a range of fluvial deposits, or in deposits derived from local reworking of older Cretaceous formations. There is an increase in the diversity of raw material used, which in addition to quartzites also includes quartz, chalcedony and some examples of fossil wood, with a few artefacts on chert. There are very few truly microlithic assemblages. Such sites have a high percentage of standardized microlithic blades and a flake component. There is a gradation with assemblages of the previous phases, and such sites may only be regarded as distinct only when the microlithic component is predominant. They occur on the surface of indurated ferricrete duricrust surfaces, or on the surface of fine ferricritised gravels.

In addition to these sites, excavations at the site of Attirampakkam (Pappu 2007; Pappu and Kumar 2006, 2008; Pappu *et al.* 2003, 2004) resulted in the establishment of a distinct stratigraphic context for assemblages, which could thus be correlated with discoveries over the entire region. The site of Attirampakkam XE "Attirampakkam" (locally known as Manamedu; 13°13′50″N and 79°53′20″E) yielded a stratified cultural sequence (maximum depth of 9 m) comprising a continuous profile of assemblages ranging from the Lower, Middle and Late Palaeolithic assemblages. In the first phase of excavations, six main sedimentary units were recognized, comprising argillaceous sediments (layer 6), disconformably overlain by a thick sequence of ferricritised gravels (layer 5), capped by clayey-silts (Layers 3, 4), which were in turn overlain by fine ferruginous gravels (Layer 2) and clayey silts (Layer 1). Subsequent excavations revealed Layer 7, a unit comprising cobbly-pebbly gravel in a silty matrix. This capped a clayey-silt similar to Layer 6, and tentatively termed Layer 8. Acheulian industries were noted in Layers 6, 7 and 8, with a Late Acheulian to an Early Middle Palaeolithic in Layer 5, and with industries transitional to the Middle Palaeolithic in Layers 3 and 4. Middle Palaeolithic assemblages were noted in Layer 2. Late Palaeolithic artefacts were noted on the surface and elsewhere in the surroundings. The stratified sequence of assemblages, which are being dated, helps us in placing assemblages across the study region within a cultural and chronological sequence.

Impact Assessment Studies of Prehistoric Sites in the Study Region

An essential factor in any heritage management plan is to assess factors creating direct, indirect or potential impacts on archaeological sites. Impacts considered in the study region included a range of parameters related to agriculture, construction (built-up) areas, forest lands, wastelands, quarries, roads, water bodies, as well as other factors, which are listed in Table 1. In addition to these tangible impacts, factors also considered were vandalism in the form of random collection of artefacts by students, scholars, visitors, etc. leading to the destruction of sites. Tourism in its negative form is also a severe impact arising from development, with greater impacts expected in the case of non-monumental sites. At every site visited (whether of importance only for prehistory and/or for environmental studies), a study was made of the nature, magnitude and severity of impacts noted. Satellite image studies of the region took into consideration impacts around each site within a buffer range of 50 m and a potential impact zone with a buffer radius of 500 m and 1 km. The area of each impact within this radius was then calculated, and impact indices could be generated following assignment of weights to different impacts (Pappu *et al.* 2009). The field studies took into consideration the direct impact on the actual spread of artefacts seen at the site. A comparative study with data obtained from topographic sheets of 1917 (1 inch is to 1 mile or 1: 63,360), and observations in the writings of Foote (1866, 1869, 1870, 1916a, b), also helped provide a long-term perspective on impacts.

Table 1: Land Use Patterns at Prehistoric Sites in the Study Region
(Parameters considered based on Satellite Data)

Note: Each major parameters or discriminant (Discr_L1) could often be subdivided into a number of levels (Discr_L2, L3, L4, etc.).

DISCR_L1	DISCR_L2	DISCR_L3
Agriculture	Aquaculture	Aquaculture
	Crop land	Kharif
		Kharif + Rabi (double cropped)
		Rabi
	Fallow	Current Fallow
		Permanent Fallow
	Plantations	Plantations

Built-up	Towns/cities (Urban)	Mixed Built-up land
		Open Spaces/Vacant Land
		Residential
	Villages (Rural)	Villages (Rural)
Roads (considered only within a 500 m buffer radius)	National Highway	
	State Highway	
	Major District Road	
	Other District Roads	
Forest	Deciduous (Moist/Dry)	Forest general
		Open
		Scrub Forest
	Forest Plantations	Forest Plantations
Wastelands	Barren Rocky/Stony Waste	Barren Rocky/Stony Waste
	Land with gullies	Land with gullies
	Land with scrub	Land with scrub
	Land without scrub	Land without scrub
	Salt Affected Land	Salt-affected Land
Water bodies	River	Sandy area
	Tanks	Tank bed vegetation
		Water spread area

Additional Parameters Considered as a Result of Field Studies

DISCR_L1	DISCR_L2
Built-up	▪ Village burial grounds.
	▪ Channels cut by forest departments within reserved forests.
	▪ College/University/School buildings and associated structures, walls, etc.
	▪ Construction: small scale; e.g., shacks, small shrines, etc.
	▪ Industrial complexes and industrial testing grounds, rough cart/lorry-tracks, etc.
	▪ Plots demarcated for construction, using cobbles/boulders; cement markers, fenced areas, etc.
	▪ Plots demarcated for agricultural field boundaries.
Quarry	▪ Quarries and associated rough tracks for trucks/earth moving machinery, small shacks, etc.
Water Bodies	▪ Irrigation channels and major canals.
	▪ Irrigation channel leading to/from tanks.
	▪ Palaeochannel deposits which are being quarried.
	▪ Reservoirs: Sathyamurthy Sagar (Pundi reservoir), Red Hills, Cholaveram, Madurantakam and Chembarambakkam reservoirs.
	▪ Tanks.
	▪ Wells and associated small structures (pump houses).

Taking into consideration data from topographic maps (1917), satellite remote sensing (IRS 1D LISS 3 (Nov 2004) of 23 m IRS 1D PAN + LISS 3 (Nov 2004) merged satellite data of 5.8 m) and field studies (2004-2008), we note a range of impacts which can be discussed as follows (see Tables 2, 3, 4). A brief summary of the preliminary results is presented here.

Table 2: Area impacted at prehistoric sites based on land use patterns (IRS 1D LISS 3 (Nov 2004) of 23 m IRS 1D PAN + LISS 3 (Nov 2004) merged satellite data of 5.8 m, buffer radius 50 m around each site).

DISCR_L1	DISCR_L2	DISCR_L3	DISCR_L4	Area impacted (sq.km)
Agriculture	Aquaculture	Aquaculture	Aquaculture	1.88
	Crop land	Kharif	Kharif	54.80
		Kharif + Rabi (double-cropped)	Kharif + Rabi (double-cropped)	100.52
		Rabi	Rabi	127.94
	Fallow	Current fallow	Current fallow	187.83
		Permanent fallow	Permanent fallow	7.35
	Plantations	Plantations	Plantations	133.05
Agriculture Total Area				**613.37**
Built-up	Towns/cities (Urban)	Mixed built-up land	Mixed built-up land	6.33
		Open spaces/ vacant land	Open spaces/ vacant land	4.38
		Residential	Residential	34.53
	Villages (Rural)	Villages (Rural)	Villages (Rural)	54.81
Built-up Total Area				**100.05**
Forest	Deciduous (Moist/Dry)	Forest blanks	Forest blanks	7.81
		Open	Open	7.08
		Scrub forest	Scrub forest	32.41
	Forest plantations	Forest plantations	Forest plantations	3.59
Forest Total Area				**50.90**
Wastelands	Barren rocky/ Stony waste	Barren rocky/ Stony waste	Barren rocky/ Stony waste	7.81
	Land with gullies	Land with gullies	Land with gullies	22.25
	Land with scrub	Land with scrub	Land with scrub	226.11
	Land without scrub	Land without scrub	Land without scrub	119.31
	Salt-affected land	Salt-affected land	Salt-affected land	81.99
Wastelands Total Area				**457.47**
Water bodies	River	Sandy area	Sandy area	8.36
	Tanks	Tank bed vegetation	Tank bed vegetation	11.06
		Water spread area	Water spread area	0.22
Water bodies Total Area				**19.64**

Table 3: Land Use Patterns at Prehistoric Sites based on Field studies (2004-2008)
(Note: data based on selected sites only)

DISCR_L1: Land Use	DISCR_L2: Land Use	Total no. of sites
Agriculture	Crop land	3
	Plantations	7
Agriculture		**10**
Built-up	Burial ground	2
	Channels cut by forest department	2
	Colleges/Schools, etc.	1
	Construction: small scale	4
	Industry	12
	Plots demarcated for future housing colonies	1
	Plots demarcated to serve as field boundaries	1
	Roads, cart-tracks, etc.	63
	Towns	2
	Villages	22
Built-up		**110**
Forest	Deciduous (moist/dry)	20
	Forest Plantations	9
Forest		**29**
Quarry		**54**
Wastelands	Land with gullies	16
	Land with/without scrub	42
	Salt-affected lands	1
Wastelands		**59**
Water Bodies	Irrigation channels	8
	Irrigation channels with tanks	1
	Palalaeochannels (quarried)	5
	Sathyamurthy Sagar (Pundi reservoir)	1
	Tanks	6
	Wells	2
	Wells and associated structures	3
Water Bodies		**26**

Agriculture: Agricultural impacts varied through time. From the 1917 topographic survey maps alone, cultivated areas are not always clearly marked. However, in general, we know that at least 34 sites are within areas represented as being cultivable. Information from satellite remote sensing indicates that a very high number of sites (n=119 areas within 99 sites) were affected by agricultural activities of some sort (kharif and/or rabi, aquaculture, fallow land or plantations), which impacts 613.37 km^2 within prehistoric sites, of which the maximum impact arises from crop lands. In striking contrast, field investigations revealed agricultural activities at only 10 sites. To account for this discrepancy, two factors, i.e., time and scale need to be considered. Field studies focused on the land use within the immediate area where artefact scatters were noted. Thus, cultivation was often noted along what we termed the boundaries of the site over which Pleistocene deposits and artefacts were exposed. Generally, this comprised ferricretes, ferricritised gravels or surfaces of Cretaceous formations, etc. with artefacts, which are bordered by alluvial deposits within which cultivation was taking place. Secondly, land which has been left fallow (permanent or current) would have been classified as wasteland in the context of fieldwork. The presence of agriculture at five sites, which are not noted in the satellite image, clearly indicate recent developments.

Construction/Built-up: Built-up areas create irreversible and extensive destruction of sites. These include a range of activities including roads, villages, towns, cities, and within them various categories of built-up land, open spaces/vacant land, and residential areas. Field studies indicate a higher number of sites destroyed by construction (built-up) as contrasted to satellite data. This is clearly explained not only by the time gap represented by the satellite and field studies, but also by the higher level of observation in fieldwork which specifically pin-pointed constructions and potential areas marked out for construction (e.g., plots for housing colonies, etc.) on the ground. Roads (considered within a 500 m buffer radius, and including national and state highways, and major and other district roads) were also a major impact at all sites. In all cases, associated activities, e.g., quarrying of stones and sediments for constructions, rough tracks created by lorries used in quarrying, or for heavy earth moving machinery, etc., led to extensive damage of delicate prehistoric sites and sediments within which artefacts occur.

Intensive damage is created by recent industrial activities, which predominate in Thiruvallur, Kanchipuram and Chennai districts. Miscellaneous activities, such as small constructions, modern temples, burial/cremation grounds, etc., occupy a small part of the total area, but create extensive damage when present.

Quarries: Quarries (for quarrying gravel, ferricretes, ferricritised gravels, charnokites, sands/silts) have resulted in severe and obviously irreversible damage to sites (Fig. 2). For example, the extensive quarried area extending around Mailapur, Devadandavakkam and Kerukambakkam is clearly visible in the IKONOS image (Fig. 3). Similarly, the 11 other quarries picked up by the satellite image are on a very large scale and thus clearly visible. From satellite data alone, we

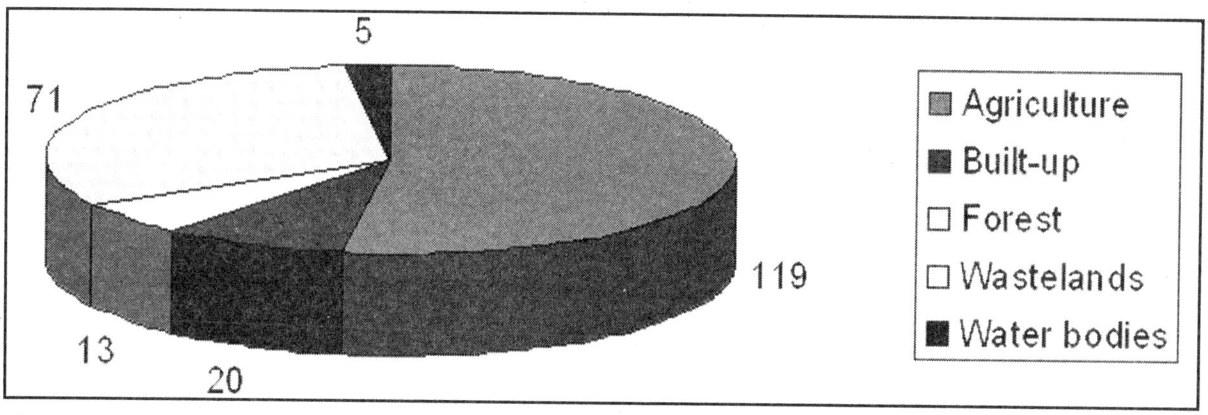

Fig. 2. Land Use Patterns at Prehistoric Sites in the Study Region (based on satellite data: IRS 1D LISS 3 (Nov 2004) of 23 m IRS 1D PAN + LISS 3 (Nov 2004) merged satellite data of 5.8 m, 50 m buffer radius around sites). The counts indicate the number of areas within sites affected by different land use patterns. Each site may have one or more types of land use within the same broad category.

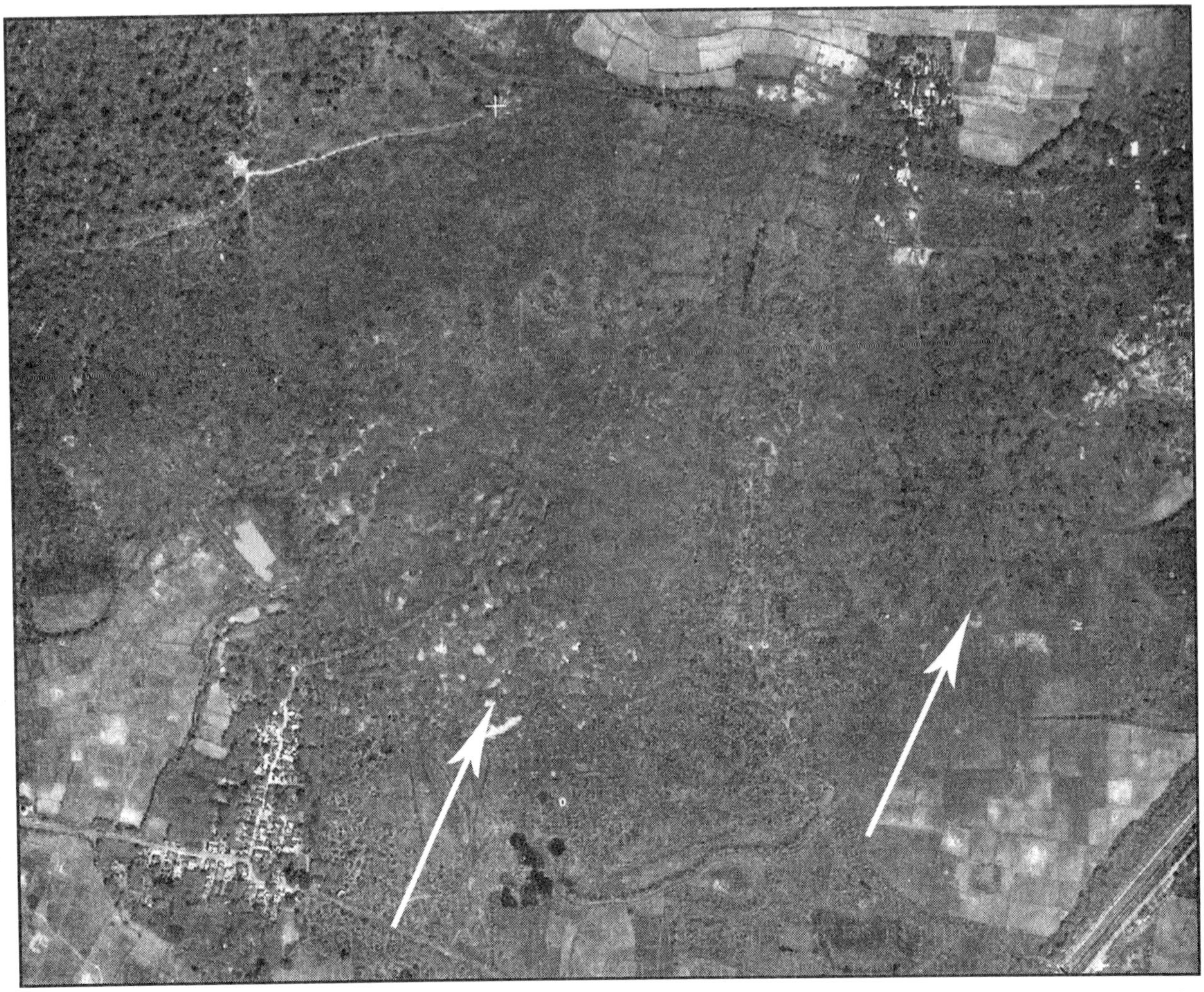

Fig. 3. IKONOS image (1 m) showing destruction of the site of Mailapur and surrounding by quarrying of ferricretes and ferricritised gravels. The arrows indicate quarried areas.

note that quarries have destroyed an area of 60.11 km^2 within prehistoric sites; but more recent field studies point to a total of 54 sites being quarried. In most cases, such quarrying is illegal and often very rapid. A recent feature has been the filling of quarries with sediments from neighbouring areas, levelling them, and then using this newly created area for cultivation (Figs. 4, 5).

Quarries also result in selective screening of the quarried material which is often done only at the construction site in the form of large scale screening to obtain fine-grained sediments. This results in the accumulation of artefacts along with gravel derived from sediments along the periphery of areas where sediments are being used for construction. These gravels and artefacts are often crushed later and used for road construction. A major source of destruction was the construction of an embankment within the Sathyamurthy Sagar (Pundi reservoir), which resulted in dumping of ferricretes with artefacts and gravel within the dam (most sediments for which came from the site of Parikulam). The lining of the Telugu Ganga project (Krishna water canal) also used these sediments after screening. Quarries for charnokites have resulted in less damage owing to the paucity of Palaeolithic sites in such regions (although this has destroyed numerous

Fig. 4. Quarrying and levelling activities destroying a prehistoric site.

Megalithic burials). Quarrying of sands and silts from palaeochannel deposits (again illegal) has destroyed rare sites of later periods, such as that seen at Govindavadiagaram and others. The Red Hills, Erumaivettipalayam and Cholaveram areas near Chennai have been totally destroyed by quarrying of both alluvial deposits and ferricretes.

Wastelands: Both field and satellite data indicate a relatively high percentage of sites in wastelands with/without scrub. Till recently, these lands were used primarily for grazing and for firewood, as they were largely on ferricretes or gneissic terrain and thus were unsuitable for agriculture. Thus, while 95 sites were marked in the toposheets as being on such wastelands, the number is reduced to 68 sites from satellite data, and 59 in the case of field studies. This indicates that since 1917, a number of areas marked as wastelands have since been cultivated, quarried, or constructed on. Further, village burial grounds are also located on such lands. The high number of sites noted in such wastelands is obviously a factor of their good preservation through time and high visibility. It is also predominantly because wastelands are often located in the context of ferricretes or ferricritised gravels, or on the surface of the Satyavedu formation and Quartz gravels, which are also ideal localities where raw material was available for prehistoric populations, and where sites are found. Wastelands, which are dissected by gullies, are also areas where there is a high potential for finding sites, owing to the erosion of Pleistocene sediments, which in turn reveals a high percentage of artefacts.

Fig. 5. Implementing salvage operations at a Prehistoric site in the study region insets transect based surveys, an Acheulian giant core.

Forested areas: Forested areas impact only 50.80 km^2 within 13 areas in 12 sites as per satellite data and within 29 sites as per field data. One of the major factors for this small number is issues related to low visibility owing to vegetation cover, as also difficult access into interior forested areas. Thus, exploration within the Allikulli and Satyavedu hill ranges will certainly yield a higher number of sites. Further, many forested areas overlap with wastelands owing to illegal deforestation. Of the 14 major reserved forest zones in this region marked in 1917 toposheets, most have been encroached on.

Water Bodies: The impact of wells, irrigation channels, tanks, etc. in addition to the major reservoirs Sathyamurthy Sagar, Red Hills, Cholaveram, Chembarambakkam and Madurantakam have resulted in complete submergence of sites. Although our data indicates only a small number of sites being currently affected, it must be remembered that impacts caused by major reservoirs have already destroyed a large number of sites. For example, in the immediate vicinity of the famous sites of Pundi and Attirampakkam, the Sathyamurthy Sagar was built in 1944 with a capacity of 2573 Mcft, submerging vast areas. Ancillary effects of these dams and anicuts, such as downstream effects of water release, sedimentation, ground water fluctuations, impacts on tributaries and overflow, all affect sites in the vicinity.

Potential Impacts: One may provide a rough estimate of potential impacts to prehistoric sites in the coming years, by considering land use patterns in a buffer radius of 1 km around sites (Table 4). Here, we note that destruction will be phenomenal if no immediate measures are taken. In addition to a great increase in agricultural activities and construction, it is also noted that new developments such as airports and other commercial, mining, and mining and industrial areas will engulf sites.

Table 4: Potential Impacts (based on satellite data IRS 1D LISS 3 (Nov 2004) of 23 m IRS 1D PAN + LISS 3 (Nov 2004) merged satellite data of 5.8 m, buffer radius 1 km around each site)

DISCR_L1	DISCR_L2	DISCR_L3	DISCR_L4	Area impacted (sq.km)
Agriculture	Aquaculture	Aquaculture	Aquaculture	12.15
	Crop land	Kharif	Kharif	103.54
		Kharif + Rabi (double-cropped)	Kharif + Rabi (double-cropped)	154.25
		Rabi	Rabi	113.87
	Fallow	Current fallow	Current fallow	105.87
		Permanent fallow	Permanent fallow	216.28
	Plantations	Coconut	Coconut	96.48
		Plantations	Plantations	147.91
Agriculture Total				**950.35**
Built-up	Towns/cities (Urban)	Commercial	Airport	21.97
		Industrial	Industrial	33.58
		Mixed built-up land	Mixed built-up land	392.25
		Open spaces/ Vacant land	Open spaces/ Vacant land	275.92
		Residential	Residential	378.3
	Villages (Rural)	Villages (Rural)	Villages (Rural)	91.02
Built-up Total				**1193.04**
Forest	Deciduous (Moist/Dry)	Dense/closed	Dense/closed	65.61
		Forest general	Forest general	1282.58
		Open	Open	92.77
		Scrub forest	Scrub forest	244.51
	Forest plantations	Forest plantations	Forest plantations	244.78
Forest Total				**1930.25**

Wastelands	Barren rocky/ Stony waste	Barren rocky/ Stony waste	Barren rocky/ Stony waste	419.59
	Land with gullies	Land with gullies	Land with gullies	38.41
	Land with scrub	Land with scrub	Land with scrub	247.22
	Land without scrub	Land without scrub	Land without scrub	199.55
	Mining process	Mining process	Mining process	85.32
	Mining/industrial waste	Mining/industrial waste	Mining/industrial waste	121.79
	Salt-affected land	Salt-affected land	Salt-affected land	248.59
Wastelands Total				**1360.47**
Water bodies	Reservoirs	Reservoir with vegetation	Reservoir with vegetation	55.24
		Water spread area	Water spread area	80.52
	River	River-bed cultivation	River-bed cultivation	38.4
		River-bed vegetation	River-bed vegetation	34.86
		Sandy area	Sandy area	38.96
		Water channel area	Water channel area	57.25
	Tanks	Sandy area	Sandy area	77.96
		Tank bed cultivation	Tank bed cultivation	33.98
		Tank bed vegetation	Tank bed vegetation	42.93
		Water spread area	Water spread area	47.12
Water bodies Total				**507.22**

Natural Factors: In addition to man-made effects, natural processes owing to climate change have left their impacts on prehistoric sites, but to a considerably lesser effect (Case Studies on Climate Change and World Heritage, http://whc.unesco.org). Thus, geomorphological fluvial and colluvial processes, soil formation and weathering since the Early and Middle Pleistocene have affected sites to varied degrees (see Pappu 1999, 2001). The effect of deforestation and quarrying, unplanned construction and expansion of agricultural activities has resulted in greater erosion of Pleistocene deposits, which is leading to the destruction of many important sites.

The Future of India's Prehistory

The study of impacts affecting these prehistoric sites is only the first stage of the Integrated Heritage Management Plan proposed in this project (Pappu *et al.* 2009). For the first time, we present a multidisciplinary approach towards providing quantitative data on impacts affecting prehistoric sites and examining variations through time. These studies have been supplemented by detailed studies of IKONOS 1 m images of key sites overlapping revenue maps of village land comprising areas affected. Further, studies of the lithic assemblages at the sites studied, aided in providing a detailed understanding of the scientific significance of each site. An assessment was also made to demarcate key sites suitable for palaeoenvironmental studies and chronology. These field and laboratory studies are being used to generate appropriate strategies which may be adopted at each site, for purposes of research, public education, conservation and heritage management. A detailed proposal on the methodology for involving the local community in this is also proposed

(Pappu 2000; Kumar and Pappu 2008). Recommendations for legislative amendments and for new legislations have also been proposed. The complete Integrated Management Plan will then be presented to the necessary authorities for further action (Pappu *et al.* 2009).

This paper highlighted the ground reality on the context and state of preservation of prehistoric sites in Northern Tamil Nadu. Personal communication with archaeologists indicates that this situation prevails not only at other sites in the state, but all over India. If we extend the perspective to include all 'non-monumental' archaeological sites, we would find the rate of destruction to be even greater, and compounded by illicit trafficking in antiquities such as coins, stray sculptures, etc. It is perhaps not an exaggeration to state that within a few decades, knowledge of India's prehistoric heritage will be relegated to museum collections or academic journals, with few sites left in the field. The mere declaration of a site as being protected is not necessarily effective at conserving it at the ground level. Construction of fences around the site is not feasible in the case of most prehistoric sites; further, this does not ensure protection against the complexity of natural factors and their interaction with human-induced changes in the landscape. While new discoveries and research initiatives in prehistory are certainly to be encouraged, they must be combined with creative steps in conserving and managing sites. An Integrated Management Strategy ensuring interaction of government authorities, scientists (archaeologists and environmental scientists), NGOs, universities, local stakeholders and developers, is the need for the day. In the absence of careful planning and thinking along these lines, the future of our prehistoric past remains grim.

ACKNOWLEDGEMENTS

We are extremely grateful to the continuous advise and guidance of Shri P.G. Diwakar, Head RRSSC-Bengaluru. This project could not have been successfully completed without the support and constant guidance of Dr. C.B.S. Dutt, Project Director IGBP-ISRO. We are grateful for the support of Professor R. Ramesh in the ISRO-GBP Programme. We thank the Archaeological Survey of India and the Department of Archaeology, State Government of Tamil Nadu, for granting us the required permits for field investigations. We thank Mr. Saleem Sheikh for his help in fieldwork and in the laboratory analysis. We also extend thanks to S. Pappu and Kumar Akhilesh for institutional aid provided by the Sharma Centre for Heritage Education. We extend special thanks to our field staff, and to the villagers of Krishnaveram, Manamedu and Pundi.

REFERENCES

Archaeological Survey of India. (http://asi.nic.in/asi_monu_alphalist_tamilnadu.asp); (http://asi.nic.in/asi_monu_alphalist_mp.asp).

Bednarik, R.G. 1993. 'Palaeolithic Art in India', *Man and Environment* XVIII(2): 33-40.

Bhimbetka, India, No. 925. UNESCO http://whc.unesco.org/archive/advisory_body_evaluation/925.pdf.

Biswas, S.S. 1999. *Protecting the Cultural Heritage (National Legislations and International Conventions).* New Delhi: Aryan Books International.

Case Studies on Climate Change and World Heritage. UNESCO. World Heritage Convention. http://whc.unesco.org.

Foote, R.B. 1866. 'On the Occurrence of Stone Implements in Lateritic Formations in Various Parts of the Madras and North Arcot Districts', *Madras Journal of Literature and Science,* 3rd.series II, 1-35 with an appendix by William King: 36-42.

——. 1869. 'On Quartzite Implements of Palaeolithic Types from the Laterite Formations of the East Coast of Southern India', International Congress of Prehistoric Archaeology: *Transactions of the Third Session,* Norwich, 1868, pp. 224-239.

——. 1870. 'Notes on the Geology of Neighbourhood of Madras', *Records of the Geological Survey of India* III (1), 11-17.

——. 1916a. *The Foote Collection of Indian Prehistoric and Protohistoric Antiquities: Catalouge Raisonne*, Chennai: The Commissioner of Museums. Government Museum, Chennai.

——. 1916b. *The Foote Collection of Prehistoric and Protohistoric Antiquities: Notes on Their Ages and Distribution*, Government Museum, Madras.

Geological Survey of India. 2006. *Geology and Mineral Resources of Tamil Nadu and Pondicherry*, Government of India Press.

Ghosh, A. (ed.). 1989. *An Encyclopaedia of Indian Archaeology*, Vols. 1 and 2. Delhi: Munshiram Manoharlal Publishers Pvt. Ltd.

ICOMOS Charter for the Protection and Management of the Archaeological Heritage (1990) http://www.international.icomos.org/e_archae.htm.

ICOMOS World Heritage Hominid Sites. Description of World Heritage Hominid Sites with a Bibliography of Supporting Documents at the ICOMOS Documentation Centre http://www.international.icomos.org/centre_documentation.

Kumar, Akhilesh and Shanti Pappu. 2008. 'Perspectives on Archaeology from an Indian Village: Examples from Attirampakkam', paper presented at the session *Perspectives on the Past: Archaeology Beyond Academics' Communicating Archaeology* (S. Pappu and M.Bezerra de Almeida organisers). World Archaeology Congress, WAC-6, Dublin, Ireland: 29th June-4th July 2008.

Kumaraguru, P., Trivikrama Rao A. 1994. 'A Reappraisal of the Geology and Tectonics of the Palar basin Sediments, Tamilnadu', in Ninth International Gondwana Syposium, Hyderabad, Jan. 1994, Rotterdam: Geological Survey of India and Balkema, pp. 821-831.

List of World Heritage Sites in India (UNESCO) http://whc.unesco.org/en/list/.

Mishra, S. 1994. 'The South Asian Lower Palaeolithic', *Man and Environment* XIX (1-2): 57-71.

——. 1995. 'Chronology of the Indian Stone Age: the Impact of Recent Absolute and Relative Dating Attempts', *Man and Environment* 20(2): 11-16.

Mishra, S. 2006-2007. 'The Indian Lower Palaeolithic', *Bulletin of the Deccan College Post-Graduate and Research Institute* 66-67: 47-94.

Misra, V.N. 1989. 'Stone Age India: An Ecological Perspective', *Man and Environment* XIV (1): 17-64.

Muralidharan, P.K., A. Prabhakar, P. Kumarguru. 1993. 'Geomorphology and Evolution of the Palar Basin', in *Workshop on Evolution of East Coast of India*, April 18-20, Abstract of Papers. Tanjore: Tamil University.

Murty, M.L.K. 1970. 'Blade and Burin and Late Stone Age Industries around Renigunta, Chittoor District', in S.B. Deo and M.K. Dhavalikar (eds.), *Indian Antiquary 4:* Professor H.D. Sankalia Felicitation Volume, Bombay: Popular Prakashan, pp. 106-128.

Neumayer, E. 1993. *Lines on Stone. The Prehistoric Rock Art of India*, New Delhi: Manohar.

Ota, S.B. 2000. 'Cultural Heritage Management Vis-a-Vis Dams: The Narmada Issue, India', in World Commission on Dams and Cultural Heritage Management Final Report August 2000 Working, paper submitted to the WCD, (A. Brandt and F. Hassan, eds.), pp. 59-61. (pdf). http://www.dams.org.

Paddayya, K. 1984. 'India: Old Stone Age', in *Neue forschungen zur Altsteinzeit*. Sonderdruck (O. Bar-Yosef Ed.), Munich: Verlag C.H., pp. 345-403.

Pappu, Shanti 1999. 'A Study of Natural Site Formation Processes in the Kortallayar Basin, Tamil Nadu, South India', *Geoarchaeology, an International Journal* 14(2): 127-150.

——. 2000. 'Archaeology in Schools: An Indian Example', *Antiquity* 74: 485-6.

——. 2001. *A Re-examination of the Palaeolithic Archaeological Record of Northern Tamil Nadu, South India*, Oxford: BAR-International Series 1003.

——. 2006. 'Prehistory in Tamil Nadu: The Need for Links and Communication', in M. Kannan and Carlos Mena (eds.), *Negotiations with the Past: Classical Tamil in Contemporary Tamil, Institut franÁais de Pondichery and Tamil Chair, Department of South and Southeast Asian Studies. Berkeley: University of California*, pp. 1-24.

——. 2007. 'Changing Trends in the Study of a Palaeolithic Site in India: A Century of Research at Attirampakkam', in M.D. Petraglia and B. Allchin (eds.), *The Evolution and History of Human Populations in South Asia, Inter-disciplinary Studies in Archaeology, Biological Anthropology, Linguistics and Genetics Series*, Elsevier, pp. 121-137.

Pappu, Shanti and Akhilesh Kumar. 2006. 'Preliminary Observations on the Acheulian Assemblages from Attirampakkam, Tamil Nadu', in Naama Goren-Inbar and Gonen Sharon (eds.), *Axe Age: Acheulian Toolmaking from Quarry to Discard*, London: Equinox Publishing Ltd., pp. 155-180.

——. 2005. 'Prehistoric Archaeology and Community Education: earning from Excavations at Attirampakkam, Tamil Nadu', *Humankind* 1: 131-145.

——. 2008. 'The Acheulian of the South-East Coast of India: Attirampakkam and Beyond', in H. De Lumley (ed.), *'Les Cultures A Bifaces Du Pleistocene Inferieur Et Moyen Dans Le Monde. Emergence Du Sens De L'Harmonie*, in press.

Pappu, Shanti, Yanni Gunnell, Maurice Taieb, Jean-Philippe Brugal, Yannick Touchard. 2003. 'Ongoing Excavations at the Palaeolithic Site of Attirampakkam, South India: Preliminary Findings', *Current Anthropology*, 44(4): 591-597.

Pappu, Shanti, Yanni Gunnell, Maurice Taieb and Akhilesh Kumar. 2004. 'Preliminary Report on Excavations at the Palaeolithic Site of Attirampakkam, Tamil Nadu (1999-2004)', *Man and Environment* XXIX (2): 1-17.

Petraglia, M.D. 1998. 'The Lower Palaeolithic of India and its Bearing on the Asian record', in M.D. Petraglia and R. Korisettar (eds.), *Early Human Behaviour in Global Context: The Rise and Diversity of the Lower Palaeolithic Record*, London: Routledge, pp. 343-390.

Sankalia, H.D. 1974. *Prehistory and Protohistory of India and Pakistan*, Pune: Deccan College.

Settar, S. and R. Korisettar (eds.). 2002. 'Indian Archaeology in Retrospect', in *Prehistory. Archaeology of South Asia*, Vol. I, Indian Council for Historical Research. Delhi: Manohar.

Sharma Centre for Heritage Education and Regional Remote Sensing Service Centre, Indian Space Research Organisation. 2009. *Satellite Remote Sensing and Prehistoric Archaeology: Research and Heritage Management;* (manuscript in preparation).

Subramanian, K.S. and T.A. Selvan. 2001. 'Geology of Tamil Nadu and Pondicherry', *Geological Society of India*, Bangalore.

The Ancient Monuments and Archaeological Sites and Remains Act 1958 (ACT No. 24 of 1958) http://asi.nic.in/pdf_data/6.pdf.

The Ancient Monuments and Archaeological Sites and Remains Act 1958 (24 of 1958) along with The Ancient Monuments and Archaeological Sites and Remains Rules 1959. The Ancient Monuments Preservation Act 1904 and the The Madras Ancient and Historical Monuments and Archaeological Sites and Remains Act 1866. Bare Act with short notes 2005. Delhi:Universal Law Publishing Co. Pvt.Ltd.

The Ancient Monuments and Archaeological Sites and Remains Rules 1959. http://asi.nic.in/pdf_data/7.pdf

The Antiquities and Art Treasures Act, 1972 (52 of 1972) along with The Antiquities and Art Treasures Rules 1973. Bare Act with short notes 2005. Delhi:Universal Law Publishing Co. Pvt.Ltd.

The Antiquities and Art Treasures Act, 1972 (Act No. 52 of 1972). http://asi.nic.in/pdf_data/8.pdf

The Antiquities and Art Treasures Rules 1973. http://asi.nic.in/pdf_data/12.pdf

The ICOMOS (International Council on Monuments and Sites) Charter for the Protection and Management of the Archaeological Heritage (1990). http://www.international.icomos.org/e_archae.html

The World Heritage Convention (UNESCO) http://whc.unesco.org/en/conventiontext/

UNESCO Recommendation Concerning the Protection, at National Level, of the Cultural and Natural Heritage. The General Conference of the United Nations Educational, Scientific and Cultural Organization, meeting in Paris, at its seventeenth session, 1972. http://www.icomos.org/icahm/.

UNESCO, World Heritage. Rock Shelters of Bhimbetka (http://www.w3c.org/TR/1999/REC-html401-19991224/loose.dtd).

World Heritage List, UNESCO. http://whc.unesco.org/en/list/.

6

Mesolithic Cultural Adaptations in North-Eastern Andhra Pradesh: A Geoecological Study

P. VIJAYA PRAKASH

ABSTRACT

The north-eastern part of Andhra Pradesh covering the administrative districts of Srikakulam, Vizianagaram, Visakhapatnam and East Godavari forms into a geographical area with diversified ecological zones. The coast of Bay of Bengal and its maritime environment on the eastern side, the hill tracts of Eastern Ghats with forested environment on the western side and in between these two resource systems, the inland plains with thick soil cover are the three distinct geo-ecological zones. At present, fishing communities on the coast, agro-based peasant communities in the inland plains and pre-agricultural tribal communities in the hill tracts are the main inhabitants of the region. Against this geo-ecological and socio-cultural background of the north-eastern part of Andhra Pradesh, the present paper attempts to understand the history of human intervention in these systems. Since Mesolithic period is believed to be vital that brought several diversified ecological zones under human occupation, the Mesolithic cultural manifestation in the three geo-ecological zones is presented.

A total of 161 sites have so far been identified in the study area. Parameters like environment, chronology, typology, technology, raw materials and other associated culture characteristics are dealt in detail to delineate the patterns of Mesolithic adaptations in the region.

INTRODUCTION

The north-eastern part of Andhra Pradesh, covering the administrative districts of Srikakulam, Vijayanagaram, Visakhapatnam and East Godavari, forms into a geographical area with diversified ecological zones. The coast of Bay of Bengal and its maritime environment on the eastern side, the hill tracts of Eastern Ghats with forested environment on the western side, in between the inland plains with thick soil cover are the three distinct geo-ecological zones in the north-eastern part of Andhra Pradesh. Ephemeral rivers like Vamsadhara, Nagavali, Champavathi, Gosthani, Gambheeram, Sarada, Thandava and Varaha originate in the hilly forested tracts of Eastern Ghats drain in southeast-east direction to join the Bay of Bengal. The tributaries like Machkand, Patala, Tajangi and Sabari with a network of hill streams in the interiors of the Ghats join the Godavari River towards the south of the study area. The inland plains are periodically enriched by the local drainage, which brings litter-based sediment from the adjoining forested hill tracts. Along the coast, several bays formed as offshoots of Eastern Ghats protrude right into the sea. They are seen mostly in the northern part, while in the southern part the coastal strip is open type. At present, fishing communities on the coast, agro-based peasant communities in the inland plains and pre-agricultural tribal communities in the hill tracts mainly inhabit in these three geo-ecological systems.

Against this geo-ecological and socio-cultural background of the north-eastern part of Andhra Pradesh, the present paper attempts to understand the history of human intervention in these systems. Since the Mesolithic period is believed to be vital that brought several diversified ecological zones under human occupation, the Mesolithic cultural manifestation of the three geo-ecological zones is presented.

THE MESOLITHIC CULTURAL EVIDENCE

The Mesolithic culture of the region, like any other region or area, is characterized by several kinds of microliths and they are associated with materials like pottery, mace heads, saddle querns, mullers and stone tablets. Cammiade (1924), Cammiade and Burkitt (1942) are the first to report the evidence of microliths in the agency tracts (hill tracts occupied by tribal communities) of Rampachodavaram, East Godavari District. Subsequently, S.N. Rao (1972) collected microliths in the vicinity of tribal habitats of the same area. The Eleru (an ephemeral river in East Godavari District) has also yielded evidence of Mesolithic culture (Kasturi bai 1982 and 1992). In the upper reaches of the Godavari River, a few Mesolithic sites with traces of preceding and succeeding cultural phases are recorded (Reddy and Murty 1988). A solitary site on the hilltop of laterite capping near Rajahmundry also belongs to the Mesolithic period (Reddy and Prakash 1989-90). In Visakhapatnam district, the Mesolithic evidence is reported in coastal plains (Murty 1976), coastal and inland plains (Prakash 1981and 1986; Reddy and Prakash 1985), and the coast (Rath 1996; Reddy *et al.* 1999). Similar evidence is also reported in the hill tracts of Eastern Ghats of the district (Murty 1986; Mouli 1998; Prakash 1998a, 2002). In Vizianagaram and Srikakulam districts, the evidence is scanty and is reported mostly at the periphery of Eastern Ghats (Murty 1976; Rao 1986). From these evidences, it is clear that the region under discussion has been a habitat of Mesolithic populations. The data from these studies and the author's recent investigations in Visakhapatnam district are analyzed to understand variation in habitation, environment and chronology on one hand, and techno-typologies, associated cultural objects and raw materials on the other to understand the adaptations of Mesolithic culture to different geo-ecological zones and micro-environments of north-eastern Andhra Pradesh.

(A) MESOLITHIC HABITATS

Against this geo-ecological and socio-cultural background of the north-eastern part of Andhra Pradesh, the present paper attempts to understand the history of human intervention in these systems. Since the Mesolithic period is believed to be vital that brought several diversified ecological zones under human occupation, the Mesolithic cultural manifestation of the three geo-ecological zones is presented in the following table:

Table 1: Zone-wise distribution of Mesolithic habitats of the study area

S. No.	Zones (elevation in relation to Average Mean Sea Level, in metres)	Mesolithic Habitats						Total %
		Stream/ River bank	Foothill	Hilltop	Rock shelter	Cave	Bad lands	
1	Coastal plains (0-50)	2	0	0	0	0	4	6 3.73
2	Inland Plains (51-200)	52	23	3	0	0	0	78 48.44
3	Hill tracts (800-1300)	4	26	38	7	2	0	77 47.83
	TOTAL %	**58** **36.03**	**49** **30.43**	**41** **25.47**	**7** **4.35**	**2** **1.24**	**4** **2.48**	**161** **100.00**

At macro level, 161 Mesolithic sites are distributed in three distinct geo-ecological zones such as coast or coastal plains 6, inland plains 78 and hill tracts 77, thus reflecting more or less similar distribution in inland plains (48.44%) at an elevation between 51 and 200 Mts. AMSL and hill tracts (47.83%) at an elevation between 800 and 1300 Mts. AMSL with a least distribution in coastal plains (3.73%) at less than 50 Mts. AMSL. The same sites at micro level show preference of 36.03% on stream/river banks followed by 30.43% at the foot of hills, 25.47% on top of hills, 4.35% at rock outcrops or rock shelters of hills, 2.48% in red sediment deposits or bad lands on the coast, and 1.24% in the cave formations of the Eastern Ghats.

It is clear from Table 1 that in all the three zones, the streams/rivers which presented the floodplains with thick soil deposit are the preferred micro-environments of the Mesolithic populations. Gently sloping hills adjoining the stream or river course in inland and hill tract zones, isolated hills with flat hill-tops devoid of vegetative growth due to hard rock surface with little or no weathering in both inland plains and hill tract zones are also made as habitats. In hill tracts, wherever the khondalite or quartzite rocks outcrop and formed hood-like structures are used as shelters. The Mesolithic people have also occupied two cave structures at abandoned stream courses in the hill tracts of Eastern Ghats. Huge deposits of red sediments running into 100 to 150 feet high right on the coast has yielded the microlithic evidence denoting their occupation and utilization by the Mesolithic man. The above analysis of location aspects of Mesolithic sites, known mostly through the microlithic industries, indicate their distribution across three distinct geo-ecological zones by occupying five distinct micro-environments.

Analysis pertaining to the location of Mesolithic sites in different catchment areas and their culture characteristics has been made, the details of which are presented in Table 2. The analysis indicates 47.20% of Mesolithic sites of the study area are distributed in the catchment areas of Machkund River (41.61%) and Tajangi hill stream (5.59%) of the Eastern Ghats. Among other catchment areas, the sites are distributed at 13.04% in Eleru River followed by Gambheeram (5.59%), Nagavali (7.45%) and 4.97% each in Vamsadhara, Gosthani and local hill streams.

Sarada and Champavathi rivers have presented 3.12% and 1.86%, respectively. On the seacoast, 3.73% sites are distributed. It is clear from the analysis that the Machkund, Tajangi and local hill streams, and small rivers like Gambheeram and Gosthani have presented more number of sites than the major rivers like Godavari (0.62%) and Vamsadhara (4.97%).

Though 161 sites under discussion (Table 5) belong to the Mesolithic cultural phase, exclusive Mesolithic culture bearing sites are 68.32% and the remaining 31.68% belong to other prehistoric cultural phases besides Mesolithic evidence. The analysis of culture characteristics of sites clearly indicate that during the Mesolithic period, more number of virgin sites was brought into habitation as revealed by 110 exclusive Mesolithic sites out of a total of 161 sites. The initial occupation of hill tracts of Eastern Ghats by the Mesolithic population is inferred from the analysis of Machkund and Tajangi catchment areas, which are represented by 47.20% exclusive Mesolithic sites, neither with preceding nor succeeding prehistoric cultural phases. It can further be inferred that the hill tracts were under occupation of Mesolithic population till the entry of modern man as evidenced by the absence of successive archaeological record (Prakash 1998b). The other inference is that the local hill streams, including the seacoast and small rivers like Eleru, Sarada and Gambheeram, have the sites with the preceding (Lower, Middle and Upper Palaeolithic) and succeeding (Neolithic and Megalithic) cultures of Mesolithic phase. While, major rivers like Godavari, Vamsadhara and Nagavali on one hand, middle range rivers like Champavathi and Gosthani sites on the other are with Mesolithic and subsequent cultural evidence (Neolithic and Megalithic).

(B) Environment and Chronology

The Mesolithic sites of the study area are known from the primary and secondary contexts and the culture-bearing deposits are red soils in the coastal and inland plains, while brown soils (dull red) in the hill tracts. These deposits are red in colour and sandy loam in the coastal plains, bright red in colour and silty clay in the inland plains, brown (dull red) in colour and silty coarse sand in the hill tracts. These deposits are the cultural horizon not only for the Mesolithic cultural phase but also for the Neolithic and Megalithic cultural phases on the coastal and inland plains while only for the Mesolithic culture in the hill tracts. The cultural material from all 161 Mesolithic sites of the study area is recovered through surface collection (81.99 per cent), wherever culture-bearing deposits are eroded exposing the cultural material in the nearby gullies and nalas; excavation (13.04 per cent) in rock shelters, caves and at a few sites where red/brown soil deposits are intact, and trial trenching (4.97 per cent) at a few partly disturbed sites (Table 4).

The stratigraphic horizon for coastal and inland Mesolithic cultural material is the red soil deposit and they occur at 1 mt 20 cm below the top surface. In the hill tracts, the brown soil deposit is the topmost layer and is about 20 to 30 cm thick. This deposit is mostly dissected by the localized hill streams and is the horizon for Mesolithic culture. The cultural materials are usually found on the top surface but at times occur at all levels of brown soil. The primary context of Mesolithic evidence in hill tracts has come from the caves and rock-shelters.

The red soil deposits on Visakhapatnam-Bhimunipatnam coast gained much importance as they are considered the index for understanding palaeoclimate and environment and they are variously known as 'bad lands' (King 1886), 'high lands' (Mahadevan and Satpathi 1949; Vishnuvardhana Rao 1968) and red sediments (Rao 1978). The mineralogical properties, composition and statistical parameters of zircon studies indicate original derivation from local khondalite rocks. King (1886) has described these deposits to represent the denudational remnants of a great sandbank of the post Pleistocene times or isolated banks formed around the sunken hills. Mahadevan and Sathpathy (1949) conclude that these high lands might have formed by the cumulative work of wind and water. Vishnuvardhana Rao and Durgaprasada Rao (1968) characterize these sediments as wind-borne. According to Raman and Rao (1980), they were deposited in different stages both by wind and water, but mainly wind for which the source area was the then continental shelf. Srihari (1980) attributes a post-Pleistocene aeolian origin on the basis of clay mineral composition of the coastal and inland red soils. A recent study by A.T. Rao *et al.* (1993) has demarcated a pebbly layer within the red soil and attributed fluvial origin to the pebbly layer and aeolian origin to the brown/red sands above the gravel layer. Similar type of red sediments divisible into lower and upper units signify two different regressive periods with a break controlled by a minor fluvial cycle represented by pebbly layer noticed at Bhavanapadu, extreme north-east corner of Andhra Pradesh (Vaz *et al.* 1998). A geo-archaeological study carried at Bhimunipatnam red sediments on the coast have indicated that the Mesolithic populations have existed when the climate was humid during the early part of Holocene period (Reddy *et al.* 1999; Nageswara Rao *et al.* 2006). The calcretes of red sediments, usually formed by capillary rise of carbonate rich ground water under arid/desert conditions (Seminiuk and Meagher 1981), could be attributed to the prevalence of arid climatic conditions during a cycle after the formation of red sediments.

The calcretes present in Visakhapatnam red sediments are Radiocarbon dated to a minimum age of 5840±170 and 5810±120 years BP (Durgaprasada Rao *et al.* 1982). The microliths at 'Teris' of Tamil Nadu coast are collected from the surface of the dunes which are relatively dated between c. 5000 years and c. 16,000 years BP (Gardner 1986). In a similar geomorphological context as that of Tamil Nadu and Visakhapatnam coasts, microliths are recovered from the Sri Lankan coast. The red beds on Sri Lanka coast (Singhvi *et al.* 1986), Teris on Tamil Nadu coast (Gardner 1986) are bracketed between 5000 and 28,000 BP. The red sediments of the study area, on cross-comparison with that of Sri Lanka and Tamil Nadu besides its Radiocarbon date, are considered tentatively between 5000 and 10000 BP (subjected to correction).

(c) Techno-typologies including raw materials

The plotting of sites on the map of the study area presents five distinct clusters and they can be visualized as coastal (A-coastal deposits of Bay of Bengal), coastal and inland plains (B-Gambheeram – an ephemeral river and several local hill streams draining the inland and coastal areas), inland plains (C-flood plains of Eleru – an ephemeral river), periphery of hill tracts (D-upper reaches of Vamsadhara and Nagavali rivers) and hill tracts of Eastern Ghats (E).

The microlithic tools recovered through surface collection, excavation and trial trenching are grouped together at site level and they are pooled against their area of recovery, such as coastal, coastal and inland plains, inland plains, hill tracts and periphery of hill tracts. The microliths are broadly classified on the basis of their technique of manufacture, nature of primary and secondary flake/blade scars, retouch and blunting and designated as blades, backed blades, points, scrapers, borers and burins. A further sub-classification in each of these categories is arrived on the shape, retouch, and blunting and probable function. The number and their respective per cent of groups of tool types and their sub-types against their area of recovery are presented in Table 3. For this analysis only exemplary catchment areas are selected, which stand as representative sample for the five geographical environments.

The microlithic industry of the study area consists of 11,756 tools (byproducts, such as cores, irregular flakes and chips are not included which may go up to several thousands) and they are recovered from coast (4.09%), coastal and inland plains (21.25%), inland plains (6.16%), hill tracts (57.07%) and the periphery of hill tracts (11.43%). Since the hill tracts form the larger geographical area, their drainage pattern is considered to subdivide the area into Machkund, Tajangi and Patala valleys, and they are represented by 14.83%, 26.85% and 15.39% of tools respectively.

The microlithic industry is dominated by blade element as seen from the table that blades (39.46%) and backed blades (17.65%) put together form 57.11%. Even in other categories (42.89%) of tool types, such as points (14.46%), scrapers (18.63%), borers (5.38%) and burins (4.92%), the blade element is dominating, as the flake element is hardly 4.44% (points on flakes and retouched flakes).

The backed points and knives under backed blades category are considered as high efficiency tool types. These types show a higher per cent of 10.51% out of a total tool kit of 11,756 of the sample. In the hill tracts they are 4.62 5, followed by 2.52% in the coastal and inland plains, 1.82% in inland plains, and 1.56% at the periphery of hill tracts. The coast is not represented by such technologically efficient tool types. In the remaining categories of tools also, the similar trend of tool manufacturing from coast to hill tracts can be inferred from the data presented in Table 3. Chisel-edged tools under burins category are a typical type of Visakhapatnam region.

Since the geometric element is considered as technological advancement of microlithic industry of Mesolithic culture, the microliths of the study area are classified into two techno-clusters, such as geometric (lunates, triangles and trapezoids) and non-geometric (all remaining tool types presented in Table 3). These techno-clusters are placed according to their exemplary catchment areas of coastal, coastal and inland plains, inland plains, hill tracts and periphery of hill tracts in order to understand their advancement with respect to the geographical environment. The details are presented in Table 4.

Table 4: Distribution of a number of tools and their percent of techno-clusters against five geo-environments

S. No.	Techno clusters	Coast	Coastal and inland	Inland plains	Hill tracts	Periphery of hill tracts	Total per cent
1	Geometric No.	34	216	70	351	123	794
	%	0.29	1.84	0.60	2.98	1.05	6.75
2	Non-geometric No.	447	2282	654	6358	1221	10962
	%	3.8	19.41	5.56	54.08	10.39	93.25
	Total/	**481**	**2498**	**724**	**6709**	**1344**	**11756**
	%	4.09	21.25	6.16	57.06	11.43	100.00

The analysis clearly indicates that only 0.29% of geometric forms are found on the coast with an ascending trend towards inland plains 0.60%, periphery of hill tracts 1.05%, coastal and inland plains 1.84%, and hill tracts 2.98%. It can be inferred from the analysis that the sites at coast followed by inland and periphery of hill tracts show a degree of advancement from coast to periphery of hill tracts, while hill tracts show a higher degree of advancement. The techno-clusters of coastal and inland sites share the affinities of both coast and hill tracts, thereby acting as a buffer zone between the two techno-clusters. Therefore, it can be presumed that the Mesolithic culture initiated at coastal plains migrated on cross profile to the hill tracts via the inland plains and the periphery of hill tract zone.

A wide range of raw materials, such as chert of different shades (blue, brown, black, green, yellow), quartz of milky and glassy types, agate and jasper, are preferred for the production of microliths. However, quartz and chert are profusely used for the microlithic tool production. Agate and jasper are occasionally used. Preference of raw material for a particular tool type has no correlation but the hill tract microlithic industry is dominated by the chert component.

(D) Other associated materials

The associated materials of the microlithic industry of Mesolithic culture are pottery, mace-heads, saddle querns, mullers, stone tablets and hood stones. Though there is scanty evidence of pottery in the inland plains, the shapes of the pots could not be drawn as the evidence is in the form of shreds and they are fragile. The pottery appears to be coarse-grained red ware, often handmade. The pottery associated with microliths in the hill tracts is coarse red ware and brown ware. Two types, such as bowls (straight and curved forms) and pots (thick and thin rimmed), are unearthed along with the microliths in five excavated sites of the hill tracts and they are handmade, coarse, gritty and sun-baked with a red slip all over the body (Mouli 1998). The coastal sites have not yielded any evidence of pottery. It can be surmised that the evidence of pottery has some implication on temporal scale of Mesolithic culture of the study area. The coastal sites pre-date the inland sites and these in turn pre-date the hill tract sites. Therefore, the Mesolithic culture of the study area qualifies to be the localized development as seen by the association of pottery with microliths in different geo-ecological zones.

The mace-heads, saddle querns and mullers are striking items of the Mesolithic culture and they are seen in all the three zones under study. The mace-heads are made on khondalite rocks. The perforation of the mace-head is made from both the sides leaving a lenticular projection towards center of the mace-head. Khondalite flat stone blocks (about 30 cm in length and breadth), often square type with a thickness of about 15 to 180 cm, are used as saddle querns. Handfuls of round to sub-round quartzite waterworn pebbles are used as mullers. The stone tablets, often circular with about 50 to 70 mm diameter and a thickness of 10 to 20 mm made on khondalites, are seen only in the coastal sites. Hood stones are typical of the Vangasari cave site in the hill tract and they are considered as non-economic but objects of religious significance (Prakash 1998 a&b). They are also part of the Mesolithic culture.

(E) Osteological remains

As discussed in the preceding pages, the red/brown soil sediments of the study area are the Mesolithic culture bearing horizons. These sediments are enriched with iron oxides, thereby showing acidic nature. The Mesolithic sites of the study area could not preserve any organic matter or osteological remains with an exception to a cave site in the hill tracts of the Eastern Ghats. A solitary cave at Vangasari has preserved several bone pieces, including teeth and nails, belonging to small fauna such as rodents, cats, birds and tortoise. Some of the bone pieces are ground and polished (Prakash 1998b).

CONCLUSION

The Mesolithic culture in the north-eastern part of Andhra Pradesh is characterized by microlithic industry with geometric forms and is spread in three distinct geo-ecological zones, such as coastal, inland and hill tracts of the Eastern Ghats. The spatial distribution of Mesolithic culture is significant on temporal scale as the coastal sites precede the inland sites and the hill tract sites show maturity of Mesolithic culture as seen by the percentile distribution of geometric forms to non-geometric, the evidence of pottery and other associated cultural objects. In the absence of absolute dates, parameters like site distribution, techno-typological variation, pottery and other household objects are considered to understand the inter-temporal progress or development.

The palaeo-climate and palaeo-environmental studies on the Mesolithic culture bearing red/brown sediments at Visakhapatnam coast have revealed the humid conditions during the formation of red/brown sediments that are contemporary to the early stages of Mesolithic culture. The compactness of the lower part of the deposit coupled with the presence of a pebbly layer amply suggests the humid condition. Subsequent to this episode of climatic event, the conditions had deteriorated to semi-arid as revealed by the dunes over the pebbly bed and the presence of calcretes in the compact portion of the red/brown sediment.

The Mesolithic cultural variation seen in three distinct geo-ecological zones and their technological advancement from coast to inland plains and in turn to hill tracts could be corroborated to the changing climatic conditions during the Mesolithic cultural phase. The emerging arid climatic conditions on the coast might have instigated the Mesolithic populations, who are adapted to humid environments, to migrate into the hitherto uninhabited environments of hill tracts, which are, in fact, humid due to their elevation in relation to mean sea level (MSL). The changing climatic conditions from humid to arid and diversified geo-ecological zones, such as the coastal, inland plains and hill tracts of north-eastern Andhra Pradesh, seem to have been the causative factors for the progressive development of Mesolithic culture of the region.

REFERENCES

Cammiade, L.A. 1924. 'Pygmy implements of the Lower Godavari', *Man in India* 4: 83-105.

Cammiade, L.A. 1924 and M.C. Burkitt. 1930. 'Fresh light on the Stone Age in Southeast India', *Antiquity* IV: 327-340.

Durgaprasada Rao, N.V.N., Y. Srihari and A.K.A. Behara. 1982. 'Columnar Convertions in the Visakhapatnam Red Sediments on the East Coast of India', *Sedimentary Geology* 31: 303-316.

Gardner, R.A.M. 1986. 'Quaternary coastal sediments and stratigraphy, southeast India', *Man and Environment* X: 51-72.

Kasturibai, M. 1982. *The Stone Age cultures of the Eleru River Valley in East Godavari District, Andhra Pradesh.* Unpublished Ph.D. Thesis, Nagarjunanagar: Nagarjuna University.

——. 1992. 'Prehistoric and Protohistoric Investigations in the Eleru valley, North Coastal Andhra Pradesh', *Man and Environment* XVII (1): 91-95.

King, W. 1886. 'The geological sketch of Vizagapatam District', *Geological Survey of India* 19: 143.

Mahadevan, C. and N. Sathpathi. 1949. 'The origin of the Waltair highlands', *The Indian Geographical Journal* 24: 1.

Mouli, K.C. 1998. *Mesolithic adaptations in the Eastern Ghats of Visakhapatnam region: An Ethnoarchaeological study.* Unpublished Ph.D. Thesis, Visakhapatnam: Andhra University Library.

Murty, D.B. 1975-76. 'Late Stone Age culture in the Visakhapatnam District, A.P.', *Journal of Andhra Historical Research Society* XXXV: 323-326.

Murty, K.S. 1986. *Stone Age archaeology of Araku Valley, Visakhapatnam District, Andhra Pradesh*. Unpublished Ph.D. Thesis, Visakhapatnam: Andhra University Library.

Nageswara Rao, K., Ch.U.B. Rao, P.V. Prakash and K.T. Reddy. 2006. 'Morphostratigraphy and Evolution of the Quaternary 'Red Sands' near Bhimunipatnam, East Coast of India', *Journal of Geological Society of India* 68: 857-873.

Prakash, P.V. 1981. *Lithic cultures and palaeoenvironment of Gambheeram river valley, Visakhapatnam Coast*. Unpublished Ph.D. Thesis, Visakhapatnam: Andhra University Library.

——. 1986. 'The Mesolithic industries of the Gambheeram River valley, Eastern coastal India', *Bulletin of the Indo-Pacific Prehistory Association* 7: 23-26.

——. 1998a. 'Vangasari: A Mesolithic Cave in Eastern Ghats, Andhra Pradesh', *Man and Environment* XXIII (2): 1-16.

——. 1998b. 'Habitation history of north zone Eastern Ghats', in *The Eastern Ghats* – Proceedings of The National Seminar on Conservation of Eastern Ghats, Hyderabad: EPTRI-ENVIS Center, pp. 260-266.

——. 2000. 'Culture-Historical Process in Northern Ghats of Andhra Pradesh: A Predictive Model', *Man in India* 80 (1&2): 57-73.

——. 2002. 'Microliths in the tribal habitat of north zone Eastern Ghats', Proceedings of the 26th Session of A.P. History Congress, pp. 23-30.

——. 2007. 'Aspects of Formation Processes of Stone Age Sites of Northeastern Andhra Pradesh', in K. Paddayya (ed.), *Site Formation Processes and Indian Archaeology*, Pune: Deccan College Post-Graduate and Research Institute, pp. 111-128.

Raman, C.V and A.T. Rao. 1980. 'Textural analysis of red sediments from Visakhapatnam District, Andhra Pradesh', *Journal of the Geological Society of India* 21 (1): 48-53.

Rao, A.T. 1978. 'Red sediments from Visakhapatnam, Andhra Pradesh', *Journal of the Geological Society of India* 19 (2): 79-82.

Rao, A.T., P.N. Rao, D. Deva Varma and K. Purnachandra Rao. 1993. 'Coastal sediments along Visakhapatnam-Bhimunipatnam region, Andhra Pradesh, India', *Journal of Indian Association of Sedimentology* 12: 1-9.

Rao, S.K. 1986. *Prehistory of Srikakulam Region: An ethnoarchaeological study*. Unpublished Ph.D. Thesis. Visakhapatnam: Andhra University Library.

Rao, S.N. 1972. 'Late Stone Age hunter-gatherers of the Lower Godavari valley: A functional approach', *Bulletin of the Department of Anthropology*, Dibrugarh: Dibrugarh University.

Rath, Alok. 1996. *Quaternary environment and Prehistoric cultural development: A micro-level study on the East coast of India*. Unpublished Ph.D. Thesis, Visakhapatnam: Andhra University Library.

Reddy, K.T. 1994. 'Coastal ecology and archaeology: Evidences from the east coast of India', *Man and Environment* 19 (1 & 2): 44-55.

Reddy, K.T. 1994 and P.V. Prakash. 1985. 'The Upper Palaeolithic and Mesolithic in the Gambheeram valley, Northeastern Andhra Pradesh', in V.N. Misra and Peter Bellwood (eds.), *Recent Advances in Indo-Pacific Prehistory*, Oxford & IBH, pp. 157-158.

Reddy, K.T. 1994 and M.L.K. Murty. 1988. *Archaeological investigations in Polavaram submergence area – A Note*, Proceedings of the Andhra Pradesh History Congress, Anakapalle, pp. 10-11.

Reddy, K.T. 1994 and P.V. Prakash. 1989-90. 'Explorations in Rajahmundry lateritic zone', *Indian Archaeology – A Review*: 1-2.

Reddy, K.T. 1994, P.V. Prakash and K.N. Rao. 1999. 'Palaeoenvironment and culture development: A Geoarchaeological study in northeast coastal Andhra Pradesh', *D.S.T. Project Report, Government of India*, Visakhapatnam: Department of Anthropology, Andhra University.

Seminiuk, V. and T.D. Meagher. 1981. 'Calcrete in Quaternary coastal dunes in South Western Australia: A capillary rise phenomenon associated with plants', *Journal of Sedimentary Petrology* 51: 47-68.

Singhvi, A.K., S.U. Deraniyagala and D. Sen Gupta. 1986. 'Thermoluminiscence Dating of Quaternary red sand beds: a case study of coastal dunes in Sri Lanka', *Earth and Quaternary Science Letters* 80: 139-144.

Srihari, Y. 1980. *Origin of Visakhapatnam red sediments, East coast of India.* Unpublished Ph.D. Thesis, Visakhapatnam: Andhra University Library.

Vaz, G.G., G.P. Mohapatra and M. Hariprasad. 1998. 'Origin and palaeoenvironmental aspects of red sediments from Bhavanapadu-Ichchapuram, Andhra Pradesh', *Journal of Geological Society of India* 52: 463-471.

Vishnuvardhana Rao, M. and N.V.N. Durgaprasada Rao. 1968. 'A Note on the origin of Waltair highlands', *Current Science* 34: 438-439.

7

Recent Discovery of Prehistoric Sites in the Lower Kaveri Valley, Tamil Nadu

V. SELVAKUMAR

ABSTRACT

Archaeological investigations carried out by the author in the Lower Kaveri Valley from 2005 to 2008 in order to understand the prehistoric and early historic settlement systems have resulted in the discovery of several archaeological sites datable from the prehistoric to the modern periods. It was assumed that prehistoric remains were not present or insignificant in the Kaveri delta and also in the area to the south of the river Kaveri, due to the unfavourable environmental factors including the lack of suitable raw materials. The surveys have resulted in the discovery of Palaeoliths at several localities in the villages of Pillayarpatti, Thirukkanurpatti and Manojipatti and microliths at Inattukkanpatti, Pillayarpatti, Valavanpatti and Punalkulam in the Vallam tableland southwest of the Kaveri delta and microliths at Vazhamangalam and Thirumalairayanpattinam in the Kaveri delta's coastal regions. This paper presents a preliminary report of these Stone Age discoveries, and calls for detailed investigations in the southern and western part of Tamil Nadu for Paleolithic remains.

INTRODUCTION

The prehistory and early history of the Lower Kaveri Valley have not been sufficiently researched, though scholars have extensively studied its medieval history (Nilakanta Sastri 1955; Subbarayalu 1973, 2001; Champakalakshmi 1996) and excavated a few early historic sites: Kaveripoompattinam (Soundararajan 1994); Terazhundur (*Indian Archaeology – A Review* 1982-83; 1983-84) and Vallam (Subbarayalu 1984). In an effort to understand the settlement systems of the prehistoric and early historic Lower Kaveri valley, the author initiated archaeological surveys in 2005, which resulted in the discovery of several archaeological sites datable from the prehistoric to the modern periods (Selvakumar 2007a, 2007b, 2008a, 2008b). This paper presents a report on the prehistoric sites discovered in the Kaveri valley and its adjacent regions from 2005 to early 2008.

THE STUDY AREA

The Lower Kaveri Valley falls in the districts of Thiruchirappalli, Thanjavur, Thiruvarur and Nagapattinam in Tamil Nadu, and Karaikkal region in Puducherry (Pondicherry State).

Geographically, this region consists of raised plateaus on the flanks of the Kaveri delta and the delta plains.

The geological formations in the Lower Kaveri valley consist of Cretaceous, Tertiary and Recent formations. Cretaceous formations are found to the west and southwest of Vallam and they include impure limestones and sandstones of silt, clay of calcareous and argillaceous variety, topped by a very thick lateritic cap. On the coast, cretaceous formations are overlain by Cuddalore sandstones of Tertiary age, which are exposed to the west of the Grand Anicut canal and near Orathanad. These sandstones are covered by a thin layer of wind-blown sandy clays, unconsolidated sands, clay-bound sand and mottled clays with lignite seams. This tertiary formation is overlain by laterite. In the east, alluvial deposits of the river Cauvery and its tributaries rest over the tertiary sandstones. They consist of medium to firm sands, gravely sands, clays and sandy clays. The thickness of these formations range from 30 m to 400 m. Good-quality laterites are reported from Vallam and Gandarvakottai areas. Pebbles of transparent quartz, such as amethystine citrine and smoky varieties, are reported in the conglomeratic sandstones near Vallam (Blanford, H.F. 1865; Compiled from various geological reports).

Previous Research

Robert Bruce Foote, the pioneer of prehistoric research in India, reported the first palaeoliths in this region in the nineteenth century (Foote 1916) at a place called Vengarayankudikkadu (Vanganam Kudikkad). Subsequently, no prehistoric surveys were undertaken till Sridharan from the Tamil Nadu State Archaeology Department reported a few microlithic artefacts near Thanjavur (Sridharan 1978). Recently, a few palaeolithic artefacts including implements resembling the late Acheulian hand-axes were reported by Ramji (2006; Rajan in press) north of the Kaveri, in Perambalur and Ariyalur regions.

ARCHAEOLOGICAL SITES EXPLORED FROM 2005 TO 2008

The author's surveys yielded 15 palaeolithic and 3 microlithic (Mesolithic) sites to the west and northwest of Thanjavur, within an area of 10 km by 10 km; 2 microlithic (Mesolithic) sites on the coastal region of the Kaveri delta near Karaikkal; and 2 microlithic sites in Pudukkottai district. The surveys, which were carried out with a GPS set and with the assistance of the Google Earth Satellite maps, focussed on off-sites or small sites, apart from the major sites.

A. Palaeolithic Sites

Three geological layers were found at the palaeolithic/microlithic sites discussed below. The top-most layer, which measured about ca. 10-100 cm in thickness, had red loam (close to 5YR 5/8 Red) deposit, below which was a ferruginous gravel layer or weathered laterite surface (10-50 cm) that had the late? palaeolithic artefacts, such as cleavers, choppers and large flakes of cherty quartzite, and quartz cores, chips which resemble microliths, in different concentration. Below this gravel layer is the laterite formation. There are also microlithic quartz artefacts in the top-most red loam (close to 5YR 5/8 Red) deposit, but in less concentration, and these artefacts could represent the microlithic (Mesolithic) culture. The exact nature of the Palaeolithic assemblage, i.e., if it belonged to the Lower Palaeolithic or Middle Palaeolithic cultures, is not clear. They seem to belong to the late phase of the Palaeolithic culture. Further research is needed to identify the nature, characteristics and contexts of this assemblage.

1. Thirukkanurpatti-Varattukulam Locality I

Thirukkanurpatti is situated about 12 km southwest of Thanjavur on the Pudukkottai state highway. Just before the village, immediately to the southeast of the highway is a dry tank called Varattukulam. This tank had been dug up to a depth of more than 2 m using earthmovers by the Government of Tamil Nadu. The bottom of the tank had a hard laterite formation. From the tank bed, bunds and the adjacent areas, palaeolithic artefacts, quartz flakes and chips were found. Scrapers and a pointed end of a broken hand-axe (?) made of brecciated quartzite were the important artefacts noticed at this site.

2. Thirukkanurpatti Locality II

Another locality with palaeolithic artefacts was noticed within the Muniyandavar temple tank, which lies about 1.5 km southwest of Locality I and about 50 m southeast of Thanjavur-Pudukkottai highway. This tank had been dug out with the help of earthmovers. Large quartzite and quartz artefacts were found on top of the laterite rock within the tank. The laterite formation was covered by red loam deposit. At this site, interestingly, some of the quartz artefacts (?) were found embedded in the laterite.

3. Vengarayan Kudikkadu

Vengarayan Kudikkadu, reported as 'Vanganumkudikkadu', was the site that was originally reported by Robert Bruce Foote in the nineteenth century. Earlier, it was thought that 'Vanganumkudikkadu' could be the corrupted form of the village 'Nalla Vanniyan Kudikkad', located to the east of Thanjavur; but a closer look at Foote's description of location suggests that Vengarayan Kudikkadu was visited by R.B. Foote. This site lies northwest of Thanjavur about 10 km close to Nanjikkottai, and south of Thanjavur Air Force Station. Robert Bruce Foote reported palaeoliths in a washed laterite context here.

4. Pillayarpatti (Tamil University Campus) Locality III (Fig. 1)

Several Palaeolithic artefacts were found in a ferruginous gravel deposit within the South Campus (Staff Quarters) of Tamil University, about 7 km from Thanjavur on the Thiruchirappalli road. Here, in the southwestern corner of the south campus from eroded area, palaeolithic artefacts such as cleavers, scrapers, choppers and flakes of large size were found. In addition, quartz flakes and chips were found in this locality.

5. Pillayarpatti Locality IV

This locality lies to the southwest of the Ladies Hostel building in Tamil University's South Campus in the area which has been disturbed due to ploughing by the Forest Department for planting trees. A large ring-stone and a large pebble tool were found on the surface context in the disturbed red loam (close to 5YR 5/8 Red) deposit.

6. Pillayarpatti Locality V

This locality lies to the west of Locality III, just outside the western boundary of the Tamil university campus. At this site, extensive quarrying had been done to supply ballast to lay the

Fig. 1. A palaeolithic artefact in situ at Pillyarpathi LOC IIII.

Fig. 2. Pillyarpatti LOC VIII.

railway track from Thanjavur to Thiruchirappalli in the 19th century. Here, heavy-duty artefacts and microliths were found from the disturbed area.

7. Pillayarpatti Locality VI

Pillayarpatti (Erosion New Nagar) Locality VI lies to the northwest of the Forest Department Shelter. This site yielded a few palaeolithic artefacts.

8. Pillayarpatti Locality VII

This locality lies south of Pillayarpatti village and north of the Thanjavur-Thiruchirappalli road. In the eroded stream-bed, heavy-duty artefacts, quartz flakes and chips were found.

9. Pillayarpatti Locality VIII (Fig. 2)

This locality is within the Tamil University campus, about 50 m southeast of Karikalan Arangam. It has been extensively quarried for laterite for the Thiruchirappalli-Thanjavur railway line. Here, artefacts were found in the weathered top surface of laterite/ferruginous gravel deposit.

10. Pillayarpatti Locality IX

This locality is the *odai* or stream lying immediately to the west of the Tamil University campus. This *odai* has eroded the deposit exposing the artefact clusters. A few Palaeolithic and mostly quartz artefacts were found.

11. Pillayarpatti Locality X

This locality is within the Tamil University north campus, about 100 m west of the Library complex. A few palaeolithic artefacts were found in the gravel deposit exposed in the area adjacent to a small tank.

12. Pillayarpatti, Pocola Locality XI

This locality lies to the west of a small hamlet called Pocola to the west of the Tamil University (north campus). This site had a few palaeolithic artefacts embedded in the red loam (close to 5YR 5/8 Red) deposit.

13. Manojipatti Localities I & II

Manojipatti is located on the northwestern boundary of Thanjavur town. In the western part of the village, from a dugout area, a large number of artefacts and massive formations of brecciated quartzite were found. This locality appears to be a factory site.

14. West of Manojipatti

This locality is about one km northwest of Manojipatti. At this site, a few artefacts were found. This area is closer to the floodplains of the old course of the river Kaveri.

15. Mappillainayakkanpatti

Mappillainayakkanpatti lies about 7 km southwest of Thanjavur on Pudukkottai road. Near a tank, a few artefacts were found and this area was highly disturbed.

B. Mesolithic/Pre Ceramic Microlithic Sites

During the surveys undertaken by the author, prehistoric microlithic/mesolithic sites were found in the coastal areas as well as on the boundary of the Kaveri delta. The discovery of the sites were rather unexpected, because the general impression was that the prehistoric population would not have occupied the Kaveri delta due to the absence of raw materials, and even if they had occupied the evidence would have been destroyed by the intensive disturbances caused by the flood activities of the river Kaveri. To the author's surprise, prehistoric artefacts of microlithic tradition were found at Thirumalairayanpattinam, about 2 km from the coast and Vazhmangalam, about 4 km from the coast.

1. Thirumalairayanpattinam, Karaikkal, Union Territory of Pondicherry (Figs. 3 & 4)

Thirumalairayanpattinam is about 5 km south of Karaikkal on the Karaikkal-Nagapattinam highway. At this village is an area called Polagam, which has been recently acquired for the establishment of the Pondicherry Industrial Development Corporation's complex. Within this complex, soil had been dug for filling up the area to the east, for road construction purposes. This dug-out area filled with rainwater is very clearly visible from Google Earth maps. At this site, mostly quartz artefacts were found.

2. Vazhmangalam, near Tittachery, Nagapattinam Dt.

Microlithic flakes and a ring well of late historical period were found at Vazhmangalam near Tittachery in Nagapattinam district. According to the legends, this place is associated with the palace of Nayaka kings, who ruled from Thirmalairayanpatttinam in the 18-19th centuries AD.

Fig. 3. A view of the section at Polagam.

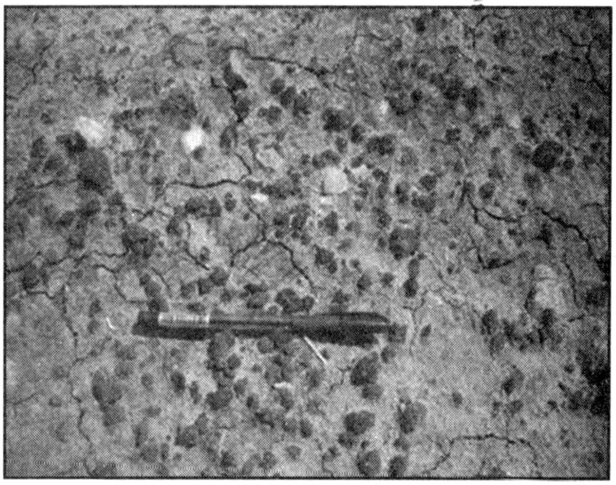

Fig. 4. Quartz artefacts in situ at Polagam along with ferrecrete.

3. Pillayarpatti Locality I

This locality lies to the south and immediately adjacent to the Thiruchirappalli-Thanjavur state highway, about 100 m to the west of the Tamil University campus. This area has been extensively quarried for laterite to be used as ballast for the railway tract between Thanjavur and Thiruchirappalli by the British administration. A few quartz artefacts were found in this area but their exact chronological context is not certain. Perhaps, they belong to the Mesolithic period.

4. Pillayarpatti Locality II

This locality lies to the west of the Tamil University campus at Pillayarpatti, and about 200 m southeast of Locality I discussed above. This area was also extensively quarried like Locality I. Here, a few quartz artefacts were found and their context was not clear. No large-sized tools could be collected. This locality perhaps belongs to the Mesolithic period.

5. Valayanpatti or Valavanpatti

Valayanpatti lies about 5 km southwest of Gandarvakottai on the Thanjavur-Pudukkottai road. At this spot microliths were found in a gravel deposit. Mostly quartz artefacts were found at this site.

6. Punalkulam

Punalkulam (Ponakulam) lies about 25 km southwest of Thanjavur on the Pudukkottai road. Here, on the banks of an *odai* adjacent to the Kings Engineering College, artefacts were collected. This locality and the villages around, such as Korapatti, Arayanipatti, Ponakulam and Pudukkudi, are between the altitudes of 300 and 350 feet AMSL. In this locality no tanks were found, unlike the low-lying areas, and it has a very thick deposit of red loam (close to 5YR 5/8 Red) of about 2 m and gravel deposit of 0.5 m. Quartz artefacts are found in the ferruginous (ferrecrete?) gravel deposit along the river-bed.

7. Inattukhanpatti

Inattukhanpatti lies about 7 km southwest of Thanjavur to the southeast of Thanjavur-Puddukkottai highway, and to the east of the Thanjavur Air Force Station. Within a tank located to the south of the village and adjacent to the boundary of the Air Force Station, quartz microliths were found on top of the laterite formation.

DISCUSSION

The prehistoric sites described above suggest that the Lower Kaveri valley, especially the Vallam table-land and Pudukkottai region, were occupied by the Palaeolithic population. However, the true context of the Palaeolithic occupation, i.e., if they belonged to the Lower Palaeolithic or Middle Palaeolithic or Upper Palaeolithic, has to be researched further. It has to be noted that similar palaeolithic artefacts were reported from the area located to the north of the river Kaveri in Ariyalur district (Ramji 2006; Rajan in press). The heavy-duty tools reported from Sivarakkottai and T. Pudupatti (Raman 1970) and Tottanampatti (Selvakumar 1996a, 1996b, 2001a, 2001b), and also at Teri sites in Thirunelveli district, point to the possibility of later palaeolithic occupation all along the east coast and, therefore, it is necessary that this region is investigated in detail for a better understanding of palaeolithic adaptations. The microlithic finds establish that mesolithic (microlithic) communities were occupying the coastal Kaveri delta, and perhaps they might have seasonally migrated from the delta's coastal region to the interior of Tamil Nadu. Their adaptation patterns, too, need systematic investigations.

ACKNOWLEDGEMENTS

I would like to acknowledge the support and encouragement from Prof. Rajan Gurukkal, Dr. P.J. Cherian and Prof. Y. Subbarayalu, Head, Department of Indology, French institute, Puducherry, and my colleagues in the Tamil University, Tanjavur and the Centre for Heritage Studies, Tiruvananthapuram, Kerala. I am grateful to the Nehru Trust for the Indian Collections at the Victoria Albert Museum, New Delhi and the Archaeological Survey of India, New Delhi for offering financial assistance to undertake the research.

REFERENCES

Blanford, H.F. 1865. 'On the Cretaceous and other rocks of South Arcot and Trichinopoly Districts, Madras', *Memoirs of the Geological Survey of India* 4: 1-217.

Champakalakshmi, R. 1996. *Trade Ideology and Urbanization: South India 300 BC to AD*, New Delhi: Oxford Press.

Foote, R.B. 1916. *Indian Prehistoric and Protohistoric Antiquities: A Note on Their Age and Distribution*, Madras.

Nilakanta Sastri, K.A. 1955. *The Cholas*, Chennai: University of Madras.

Rajan (in press). Rock Art in Tamil Nadu – A Status Report, *Man in India*.

Raman, K.V. 1970. 'Distribution Pattern of Cultural Traits in the Pre and Protohistoric Times of Madurai Region', *Aaraichi* 1: 499-509.

Ramji, M.S. 2006. *Perambalur Vattaratthollyal*. M.Phil. Dissertation, Submitted to the Department of Epigraphy and Archaeology, Tamil University.

Selvakumar, V. 1996a. 'Archaeological Investigations in the Upper Gundar Basin, Madurai District, Tamil Nadu', *Man and Environment* 21(2): 27-42.

——. 1996b. *Investigations into the Prehistoric and Protohistoric Cultures of the Upper Gundar Basin*, Unpublished Ph.D. Thesis, Poona, University of Poona.

——. 2001a. *Mesolithic Adaptation Patterns of the Mesolithic Hunter-Gatherers of the Upper Gundar Basin, Tamil Nadu*. Report of the Post Doctoral Research submitted to ICHR.

——. 2001b. 'Culture and Chronology of Lithic Industries from Southern Tamil Nadu', in S. Rajagopal (ed.), *Kaviri – Studies in Epigraphy, Archaeology and History*, Chennai: Panpattu Veliyittakam, pp. 256-266.

——. 2007a. 'Kavirippadugaiyil Tholliyal Kandupidippukal', *Avanam* 18: 139-140.

——. 2007b. *Archaeology of Kaviri Valley*. Report of Study undertaken with a small Study Grant from the Nehru Trust for the Indian Collections at the V & A Museum, New Delhi.

——. 2008a. 'Kaverippadugaiyil Puthiya Tholliyal Aayvugal 2007-08', *Avanam* 19: 156-158.

——. 2008b. 'Archaeological Research', in *Thanjavur and Pudukkottai Regions: A Report of the Explorations in 2008*, Tamil Civilization.

Sridharan. 1978. 'Tanjore Microliths', in R. Nagasamy (ed.), *South Indian Studies*, Vol. I, Madras: Saher, pp. 126-127.

Soundararajan, K.V. 1994. *Kaveripattinam Excavations 1963-73 (A Port City on the Tamil Nadu Coast)*, Delhi: ASI Memoirs.

Subbarayalu, Y. 1973. *Political Geography of the Cola Country*, Madras: Tamil Nadu State Archaeology Department.

——. 1984. 'Vallam Excavations', *Tamil Civilization* 2(4): 9-98.

——. 2001. *Studies in Cola History*, Chennai: Surabhi Pathippakam.

8

Man-Land Relationship in the Upper and Central Pennar Basin of Andhra Pradesh: With Special Reference to Neolithic Culture

P.C. VENKATA SUBBAIAH

ABSTRACT

Man-land relationships form an important topic of discussion among the social scientists since the second half of the 20th century. Especially in the field of archaeology, it is important for studying the life ways of the extinct societies in which the application of the methodological frames of research related to the concept of cultural ecology is more appreciated as it ultimately makes the archaeologist arrive at certain basic assumptions. Hence, the study of archaeological record in view of the interrelationship of systemic context and archaeological context through adaptive strategies that reflected in the material culture of human societies offer a better understanding of the cultural processes in spatio-temporal systematics. The present paper is one such attempt to visualize the impact of ecological factors that reflected in the socio-cultural and economic system of Neolithic populations inhabiting the Upper and Central Pennar Basins of the present Ananatapur and Kadapa districts of Andhra Pradesh.

INTRODUCTION

Studies concerning the man-land relationship formed an important topic of discussion among social sciences since the second-half of the 20th century, especially in the fields of Geography, Anthropology, History, and more so in Archaeology, it being one of the interdisciplinary subjects in which more emphasis is placed on the reconstruction of past human cultures that measure and explicate different activities performed in a spatio-temporal context. Man-nature analysis could be identified into several conceptual phenomena, such as geographical and cultural determinism, environmental possibilism, etc. In view of the above-said conceptual representation, man has been basically viewed as a creature of environment whose behavior could be judged in the realm of environment and whose growth and development could be traced to the conceptual framework, which also identifies the capability of man to modify the environment around him. Hence, it is felt that environmental features alone were not the causative factors for cultural change and man's cultural behaviour is the deciding factor occupying an important part in the developmental processes either at biological level or cultural level. However, the environmental factors have been broadly treated as setting limits for the development of cultural phenomena. But explanation for the occurrence or non-occurrence of certain cultural items/features, in a particular time period and in a particular environment, may not provide adequate information as they formed part and parcel of a given cultural system. As such, the social scientists began to put more stress on investigating the combination of natural and cultural features in order to reconstruct the total history of humans as an integrated study of geographical and historical phenomena (Clark 1985).

The concept of Cultural Ecology emerged as a major trend in archaeological enquiry through the adoption of methodological frames of research from other related fields, especially anthropology (Steward 1955; Butzer 1964, 1975, 1982; Evans 1978; Roberts 1987; Anderson 1973), sociology, geography, etc., that ultimately made the archaeologists to study the archaeological record of biological and other related sciences useful in the reconstruction of a complete picture of the life history of extinct human societies (Binford 1972; Bintliff and Gaffeny 1986 and Bintliff and others 1988; Dimbleby 1978; Ucko and Dimbleby 1969; Ucko and others 1972). In India, several scholars have significantly contributed their part in studying the archaeological record, through scientific enquiry, from different parts of the country belonging to different periods of cultural components (Subbarao 1958; Zuener 1950, 1963; Joshi 1955, 1970; Joshi *et al.* 1974; Richards 1933; Thomas 1989; Rajaguru and Ravi korisettar 1987, Dhavalikar 1984, 1989, 1993; Pappu 1974, 1985; Paddayya 1982a, 1982b; Sharma *et al.* 1983; Misra 1987a, 1989; Murty 1981, 1989; Makkhan Lal 1984; Rajendran 1989; Arun Kumar 1985; Badam 1979; Kajale 1979; Korisettar 1980; Deo 1991; Varaprasada Rao 1992; Raju 1981, 1988 and Venkatasubbaiah 1992a&b, 2007), etc. More recently, by treating the archaeological record as the outcome of macro-level and micro-level regional analysis, archaeologists are trying to visualize the man-land relationship (for a general concept of man-land relationship see Paddayya 1994: 1-28; Ravi Korisettar and Rajaguru 2002: 243-296). The present paper is one such attempt to study the Neolithic culture of the Upper and Central Pennar Basins of Andhra Pradesh for which the available material culture has been utilized to glean the relationship of the environment and culture during 2nd-1st millennium BC and also to highlight the environmental potential of various micro-ecosystems in the area in order to establish man's dependence on them in his quest for suitable habitats and adaptive strategies peculiar to a variety of physiographic zones through time.

THE AREA

The physiographic and orthographic features of the Upper Pennar Basin, in the present-day Anantapur district, is largely similar to that of the neighbouring Bellary and Raichur districts of Karnataka and western half of Kurnool district. It is an open country of plains from which rise a number of granite hills and hillocks, mostly castellated. The open stretch of land between the hills is devoid of trees and is to a large extent covered with black cotton soils and its elevation gradually falls into Pennar valley in the north and north-eastern region but steadily rises afterwards. The south region has an average elevation of 600 mts. to mean sea level, which is the coolest part of the region. Whereas, the central part is about 330 mts., and the easternmost part is 270 mts. The whole area can be divisible into four geographical units, the northern comprising Uravakonda and Gooty taluks and a portion of Tadpatri taluk extensively covered with black cotton soils. Except Muchchukota range of hills, covering the western part, is the main hill range which is the flat-topped Erramalais binding the north and eastern portions of Tadpatri taluk, there are only a few isolated hills (120 mts. in height) and the plains of Tadpatri taluk is lower in elevation than any other part of the region. The central unit consists of Anantapur, Dharmavaram, Kalyanadurgam and Rayadurgam taluks is almost an arid, treeless zone covered largely by poor, stony red soils with isolated patches of black soils. The general appearance is a level plain but broken into some extent by hills. There are many isolated granite hills and hillocks. The southern unit including Hindupur, Madakasira, Penukonda and Kadiri taluks cover a better variety of red soils and high proportion of reserved forest which also forms part of Mysore plateau sharing higher elevation, cooler climate and hence support thick vegetation due to high rainfall. The physiographic character of the Upper Pennar region is an arid, treeless with general poverty of the soil zone which is also covered with isolated peaks and rocky clusters, the main characteristic feature of the region.

Geologically, the whole area is traversed by Archaeans and Dharwars except Tadpatri, Gooty and Anantapur which are equipped with Kadapa and Kurnool system of rocks. The Archaean group of rocks consists of granites, granitic-gneiss containing hornblende epidotemica pegmatite veins suppose to contain diamonds. They also contain hornblende schists composed of gold, schistose and quartz, mica, ferruginous quartzite, haematite, metadiorite, trap dyke of dolerite, diorite and basalt (exploited by the Neolithic populations for their edge tools). Whereas, the Kadapa and Kurnool system consists of Lower Kadapa group of rocks comprising quartzite grits, shales, grits with pebble beds and sandy shales which uncomfortably overlain the Archaeans. The dolerite, quartzite and limestone formations consists of chert, quartzite grits, conglomerates, shales containing trap sills, sandstones, limestones, and calcareous tufa and shales. The minerals that occur in the Upper Pennar Basin consists of gold, diamond, barites, asbestos, steatite, limestones, abrasives, clay, iron ore and soap stone.

Six distinct varieties of soils occur in the Upper Pennar Basin viz,. black clay, black loam, black sand, red clay, red loam and red clay, among which red sand soils are more inferior. Black soil is mostly confined to the northern most and northern packets of the region. However, the red and black mixed soils are fertile. The central part of the north-eastern unit is completely covered with black cotton soil leaving a little part of red soils, particularly, near the hills and along the margins of rivers. Whereas, the south, south-central portion is covered by fertile red soils and the red soil of inferior variety occur rest of the region. The principle river system is Pennar and other tributaries important tributaries being the Chitravati, Hagari and china Hagari join it. Jayamangali and Kusavati directly fall into Pennar. The other subsidiary rivers are Swarnamukhi, Tadakaleru, Pandameru, Maddaleru and Papaghni which flow in the southern part of the region. Due to it's geographical location in the central part of the peninsula, this region is extremely dry due to heated plains and hence experiences scanty rainfall neither benefited by the south-eastern monsoon nor south-west monsoon because of impediment of the high western ghats that make the region agriculturally precarious and hence often passes through draughts. The average annual rainfall is 586 mm. Except the southern portion, the region is mostly treeless covered commonly with trees of tamarind, mango, banyan, margosa and the common indigenous trees are babul, ber, wild date and the other shrub vegetation along the hills and foot-hill regions consists of tangedu, kanuga, kusum, maddi, neredu, tortollis, pear, aloes, etc. The fauna that occur in the region consists of species belonging to four classes are mammals, birds, fishes, and reptiles.

Whereas, the Central Pennar Basin, the present Kadapa district can be divided into three geographical units, the north-western plains covering Jammalamadugu, Proddatur, Kamalapuram, Pulivendla and Kadapa taluks which is contiguous to the black cotton plains of Kurnool and Anantapur districts with an elevation of between 500-600 mts. MSL., bounded by the chain of Erramala hills in the north and southern extremity; the eastern valley portion formed between the Velikonda hills and Seshachalam, Nallamala and Lankamala hills comprising Badvel, Rajampet and Siddhout taluks with an elevation lying between 650-750 mts. MSL., traversed with red clay, red loam and black loam soils and the southern plateau covering the entire Rayachoti taluk, having the elevation between 900-1000 mts. MSL. has red sandy and black loam soils. This region is geologically equipped with Archaean system of rocks comprising crystallines (granite-gneisses, traps, etc.) and Dharwars (schists, quartzites) and the Kadapa-Kurnool system of rocks comprising shales, limestones, quartzites, dolomites, conglomerates, calcareous flags with basic igneous intrusive of traps and silicious materials like chert, chalcedony, agate, feldspar, etc. and the mineral deposits such as quartz, calcite, copper pyrites, white clay, haematite, purple red oxide, red ochre, steatite, lead, zinc, etc. Drained by the Pennar, through the central part of the region, it has the flow of several main tributaries such as Kunderu, Papaghni, cheyyeru, Sagileru and other many streams, rivulets, nalas, etc. The vegetation is dry-deciduous and tropical thorn types (Fig. 1C) and the climate is basically semi-arid with an annual rainfall of 680 mm. maximum through south-west monsoon.

Neolithic Settlement System and Material Culture

The Upper Pennar Basin had been widely occupied by the Neolithic pastoral groups from the adjacent nuclear zone of Southern Neolithic Culture Raichur (Watgal 4350±100; Piklihal 2000 BC: Allchin 1960: 129; Utnur 2170±150: Allchin 1961) and Bellary districts of Karnataka, a cultural dispersal in search of pastures and their economic pursuits, areas congenial for occupation in all way of life of people and their domestic livestock.

As a result, there are 75 sites (Ash mound-cum-habitation) distributed into two clusters, highly concentrated in the north-west of Uravakonda and Kalyandrug taluks but also sparsely represented in the Gooty, Rayadrug, Dharmavaram, Tadpatri, Guntakal and Anantapur taluks, in and around granite terrain at Akkammakonda, Andepalle, Antarganga, Budedu, Budagavi, Bandmidapalli, Budidagaddapalli, Budili, Bukkacherla, Buthamahalhill, Chakrayapeta, Chetnepalli, Chinnadukonda, Dayyalakuntapalle, Donekal NE, Gadegunte, Gadekottur, Ganji-kunta, Garudapuram, Gotkuru, Gotluru, Gulapalayam, Guntakal RS, Hampapuram, Havalgi, Hulikallu, Idukallu, Jambuladinne, Kadamalakunta, Kadarabanchi, Kalyandurg, Kamalapadu, Kambaduru, Karakumukkala, Katamadevudu hill, Konakonda, Koratlapalle, Krishnareddipalle, Kudipalli, Kunduripi, Lattavaram, Malapuram, Mallappakonda, Mallipalli, Masanakota, Muchukota, Mudigal, Muntimadugu, Narasanayakunikunta, Nimbagal, Palacherla, Palavoy, Paraveli, Peddamatlagondi, Peddanadlagondi, Pillalapalli, Rachepalle, Rachanapalle, Rayadurg, Tadipatri, Tanakal, Tarimala, Thimmapuram, Tsadum, Hulikallu, Uravakonda, Vajrakaruru, Veligondla, Velpumadugu, Vidapanakallu, Vitlampalli, Vantareddipalli, Kolimipalyam, Yatakal and Yetakallu (Ravikorisettar *et al.* 2002: 151-237: Appendix III: 436-478).

The material culture from all these sites include Pecked and Ground stone tools and objects include Axes, adzes, Chopper-chopping tools, core scrapers, Chisels, flake tools, picks, rubbing stones, saddle querns, axe-hammers, sling stones, mace-heads, (Fig. 1A: edge tools); Blade tools

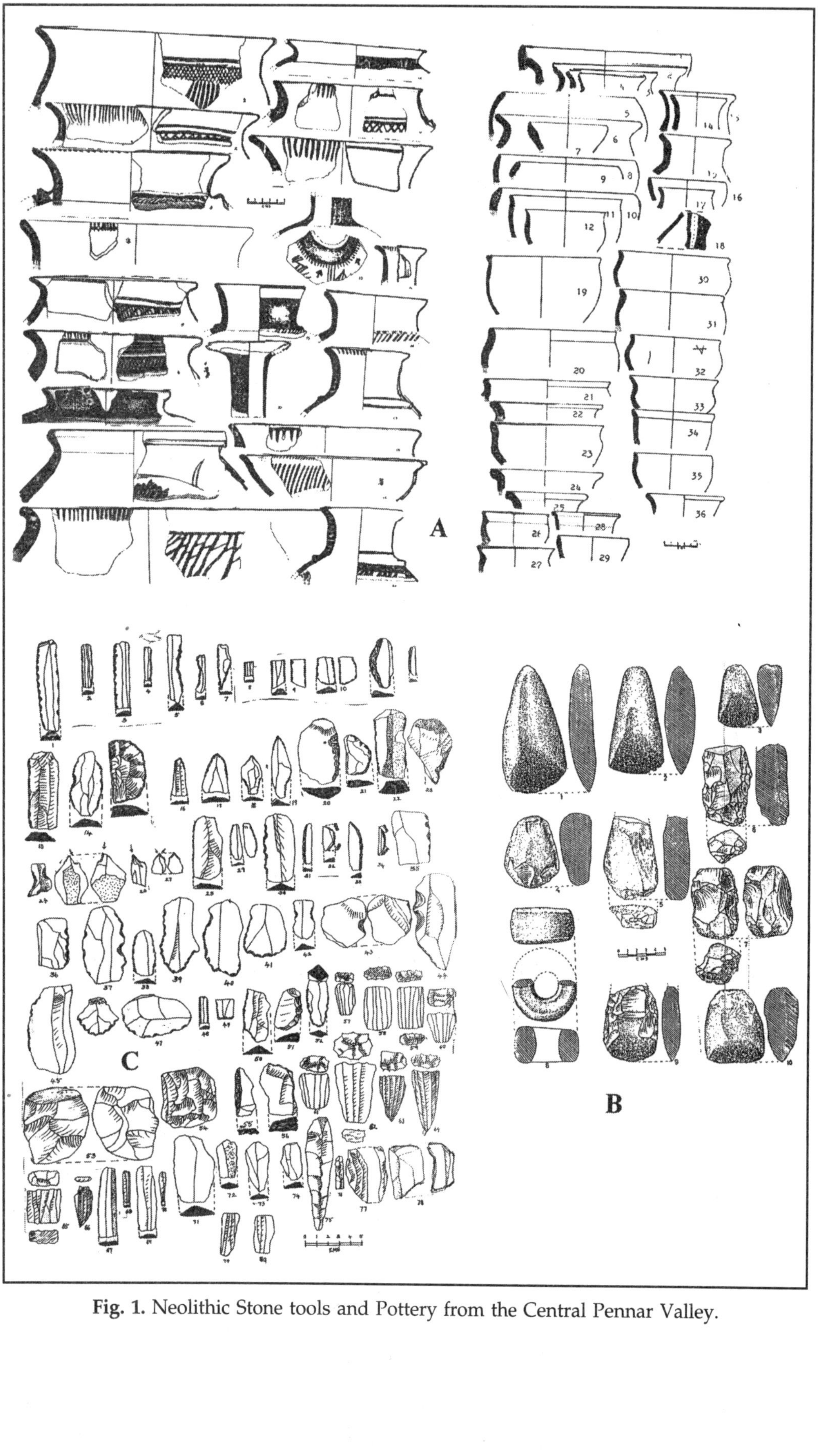

Fig. 1. Neolithic Stone tools and Pottery from the Central Pennar Valley.

include worked flake tools and blade tools, backed blades, truncated blades, lunates, trapezes, points, borers, scrapers, notched flakes, choppers (Fig. 1B); Pottery (Fig. 1C) include blotchy grey ware, unburnished grey ware with impressed, perforated, incised designs on the body of vessels, burnished grey ware with red ochre designs on the body of the vessel forms, unburnished dull red ware with impressed, perforated, painted designs on the body of the vessel forms burnished red ware with similar designs on the body of the vessel forms. The other material include Animal remains of cattle include both species but Buffalo species is less in number, sheep/goats, canis, hog and wild species include deer family; Bone tools of three types such as axe-heads, blades, chisel, punch and points; Beads of carnelian, chert and steatite; Terracotta and clay objects. The plant remains procured from the excavations include Zizyphus species and large quantities of disintegrated wood of Acacia or Dalbergia species.

The absolutely chronology from the excavation of an ash mound and habitational debris at Palavoy, the principle site of the region where four ash mounds are found give rise to 1965±105 (Rami Reddy 1976: 122). The locational analysis of Neolithic settlements in the Upper Pennar Basin provide an idea that these folk besides living in an open on the flat terraces made by leveling the tops of granite hillocks and also slopes and foot of the granite hillock and big hills and also sometimes natural rock-shelters. As the settlements spread to other areas in the region could be noticed close to water courses of small local streams. That the area can be described as arid and semi arid dry climate which is characterized by the thorn and scrub forest interspersed by large grasslands wherever water had been accumulated in the form of pools and ponds due to spring activities and water in more or less quantity could be obtained throughout the year. Hence, such climatic conditions might have, more or similar to those of today, prevailed during Neolithic period in the region. The analysis carried out on the fossil soils obtained from excavations at Kupgal, a Neolithic ash mound site in the Bellary district of Karnataka (Majumdar and Rajaguru 1966: 54-55) revealed similar environmental conditions of present day. Similarly, on the basis of the evidence of carbonized wood samples from other Neolithic sites, e.g. Kodekal (*Zizyphus* sp.: Paddayya 1973: 77), Maski (*Acacia* sp.: Thapar 1957: 140-141) show the prevalence of similar conditions of environment during 2nd Millennium BC Post-holes, which are roughly circular with a diameter of 8 to 20 cm and depth of 8 to 48 cm, obtained in the excavations at Palavoy (Floor 8, Fig. 5: Rami Reddy 1976: 115) indicate circular or rectangular plan of houses with mud walls or wattle-and-daub (as similar walls of split bamboo matting plastered with mud and cowdung found at Tekkalakota: Nagaraja Rao and Malhotra 1965; Piklihal, Brahmagiri: Wheeler 1948), bamboo net smeared with cow dung or mud, being kept as wall, served the purpose of protection from wind, cold and heat procured round their settlements and also obtained through gathering activity, thatched roof supported by the posts of *Acacia* or *Dalbergia* sp. (disintegrated wood found in the depressions of post-holes from excavations). The floors were made of soil mixed with sand, plastered with cowdung and the uneven surfaces of floors were filled with material (reddish murum, silt, rubble, etc.) obtained from surroundings indicate that the Neolithic populations had a good knowledge of geography of the area in which they inhabit and move with their domestic animals. Cultivated grains are not obtained from Palavoy excavations but the presence of large quantity of domestic equipment, helped in the process of vegetable materials, such as querns, rubbers used for grinding and pounding grain indicate the practice of agriculture. The seeds of *Zizyphus horida* and by its ripe fruits are eaten directly or used in the sauce preparation, which is seasonally obtained even now indicate their gathering activities. Stock-raising, an important part of their economy can be assessed through the animal remains as mentioned above. As cattle being one of the major representative along with other species buffalo, sheep and goat formed their diet as there is evidence of charring, cutting, splitting, and chopping on the bones indicate that the cattle were domesticated both for their milk and meat. Splitting of long bones for the extraction of marrow as well as for the manufacture of bone tools for several purposes like scraping (scrapers to detach flesh from the bones), drilling (chisels for making holes in the hides, etc.), points for stitching hides or other vegetable matter into a kind of textile, etc. Similar butchering activity has been inferred from the important Neolithic ash mound-cum-habitation site of Budihal (Paddayya *et al.* 1995: 23-31) indicate the predominance of cattle herding. Another important aspect in connection with herding practices of cattle being the occurrence of different sizes of animals (small, big and normal sizes) on the basis of analysis indicating not only the pastoral nature of the culture but their use in heavy agricultural operations? However, this point does not support due to lack of plant remains but the abnormal characters such as anchylosis and extososis (Rami Reddy 1976: 117), identified on bones of matured animals support the view that these animals were used for prolonged draft work or heavy traction, probably for transportation, ploughing heavy soils, etc.

Another specific character of the Neolithic culture flourished in the Upper Pennar Basin being the prevalence of massive structure of ash mounds and their occurrence indicate the intensive and periodic cow dung burning places. However, it has been viewed differently by several authors (for details see Paddayya 1991: 573-626, 2000-2001: 189-225; Rami Reddy 1977: 193-209 and 1990: 85-99; Sundara 1971: 308-314). But Paddayya's recent investigations by re-visiting several ash mound sites in the Gulbarga, Raichur and Bellary districts of Karnataka and Mahabubnagar and the present area under discussion, proved to be successful in exposing his views, supporting the views of Allchin (1963) and R.B. Foote (1916) and Zeuner (1960) but also putting forward, following the landscape approach and brought to light several novel features which are of crucial and important for understanding the whole problem of ash mounds.

The Central Pennar Basin has given the evidence of 45 Neolithic settlements located, mainly on the small streams and local nalas, are confined geographically described as the north-west plains stretched with black cotton soils at Akkempeta, Balijapalle, Boditippenbapadu, Bodupalle, Bokkudupalle, Chagaleru, Chapadu, Chilamakuru, Chinnamudiyam, Danvulapadu, Dannawada, Gadeguduru, Gollalaguduru, Gudemcheruvu, Hanumantaraopet, Idamadaka, Inagaluru, Jangalapalle, Kamballadinne, Kanyathirtham (Peddandulru), Koduru, Kokatam, Koraguntapalle, Kottagundavaripalle, Kottapalle, Madhavapuram, Nidivelagala, Nagarajupalle, Paluru-J, Paluru-P, Peddamudiyam, Ramireddipalle, Sambaturu, Timmapurampeta, Tondaladinne, Torrivemula, Ulimella, Upparapalle, Vaddirala, Vedururu, Vellala, Veparala and Mylavaram. They are divided into hamlets, small villages, big villages, secondary regional centers and primary regional centre, a nexus of settlements, in a ribbon band fashion close to water courses, inter-connected for the flow of material and people in a tradition connected to the socio-economic activities described as pastoral-cum-agricultural communities in a general sense but most probably both economic activities were the susbsistance pattern followed by the Neolithic populations who were inhabiting comparatively bigger settlements when compared to the settlements of Upper Pennar Basin, as they belong to the later part of the Southern Neolithic complex based on the radio-carbon dates (Venkatasubbaiah 2007: 266; Peddamudiyam 3490±90=1540 BC and 3060±120=1110 BC).

The material culture consists of pottery coarse red ware, burnished red ware, black-on-red ware, Unburnished red ware, grey ware, brown ware, buff ware, all black ware and black-and-red ware, being one of the Megalithic ware probably reaching the terminal stage or overlapping phase of Neolithic-Megalithic period, as the case may be due to its presence mostly in the cist-burials from the present region and perhaps reached these settlements due to cultural contacts or borrowed method of manufacture. The pecked and ground tools comprising both edge tools and non-edge tools made on sandstone, quartzite, dolerite and granite useful for domestic and agricultural purposes and blade tool industry belong to short blade industry made on chert, agate, limestone, quartzite and chalcedony due to the available raw material. The animal remains (Venkatasubbaiah *et al.* 1992: 55-59) consists of *Bos indicus, Bubalus bubalis, Capra/Ovis, Gallus*, indicating the process of domestication of cattle, a dominant economic activity along with small numbers buffalo, sheep and goats in which fowls also formed a part. The plant remains of cereals (barley and wheat) pulses (horsegram, greengram, blackgram, hyacinth bean and pigeon pea) millets (browntop millet, foxtail millet, setaria millet and sawa millet) and other tubers, fruit/nut, (for details see Venkatasubbaiah 2007: 160) formed the subsidiary diet along with the animal diet, of both domestic and wild fauna, especially deer species. The other plant remains indicate the collection of naturally available fruits and nuts along with seasonally engaged fishing of aquatic animal food. As the presence of both plant and animal remains propose for the combination of pastoral and agricultural activity of these first settlers of Central Pennar Basin. A variety of plants indicate mixed farming depending on monsoon rainfall in which cattle not only played a main role in agricultural activity but also in transporting people and things in a nexus of settlements connected in different social and economic activities, especially during the congregations which are even now prevalent in the present rural areas for exchanging material and other cultural transactions. This view is supported by the absence of ash mounds when compared to the adjacent granite terrain area of Upper Pennar Basin. As such cow dung might have been put into use in manuring their fields along with using for several domestic purposes and hence the tradition of burning the cow dung on the intensively made platforms as noticed at Palavoy (author's personal observation in the general survey along with Paddayya in 1994) practically ceased.

Man-Land Relationship in the Upper and Central Pennar Basin: An Interpretation

The study of man-land relationships require a good understanding of several aspects, i.e., the interaction of the people of a particular culture in a given time-scale possessing a particular technology that help the production of tools that are useful for their economic pursuits. Selection of particular environment and the adjustment strategies enhance the determinism of the human behaviour in which an interaction of people with naturally available elements in an area leads to the material production. It is the material culture that helps in drawing inferences about past human behaviour from their archaeological remains (Binford 1968: 21-22; Schiffer 1975, 1976). This method of interpreting archaeological record coincides with what Butzer (1982: 401-402) indicates three goals of environmental analysis in archaeology, either dealing with hunter-gatherer or food-producing economy. The second goal, i.e., understanding the economic area or regional food base stands more appropriate method at the present interpretation.

Around 2000 BC, the Upper Pennar Basin witnessed the arrival of Neolithic populations and they have occupied the granite terrain which is uneven and undulating but perhaps offered a suitable topography for their economic base: Pastoralism. They also occupied the shoulder portions of granite hillocks and also the foot-hill regions in course of time due to the necessity of space as and when population grew. The high elevation of granite terraces offered a better look at the topography of the surrounding areas to watch their animals while grazing and give an excellent picture of raw material availability, water source in the form of small pools and ponds, movement of the people in the process of pastoral activity. The raw material necessary for the manufacture of pecked and ground stone industry and blade tools are available at a particular out crops of dolerite formations and the Neolithic populations exploited the same for making tools thereof and brought to settlements. However, if the raw material availability is beyond their exploitation territory, it might have been brought to the settlements, either by obtaining rough shapes and finishing is done through grinding and polishing methods. As such large amounts of dolerite flakes are noticed in the sites of Central Pennar Basin. It is clear from this assumption that the Neolithic groups not merely explored and exploited the life-sustaining resources of the region where they have been inhabiting but also subsequently absorbed the main feature of the landscape into their sense of economic activities, especially pastoralism, herding of animals and agriculture activities. The other main character of their cultural feature, pottery manufacturing required suitable clay probably collected from the soil formations or obtained the silt formed at the bottom of the water ponds and the admixture easily available in the form of sand and straw from the grasses available in the neighboring grasslands. The shapes and size of pottery indicate not only their social affinity but also their dietary needs. The Neolithic populations inhabiting the Central Pennar Basin were able to achieve a significant fabric, black-on-red ware, decorating black paintings on their pottery which offered a territorial identity within Southern Neolithic complex.

The Upper Pennar Basin offered a better habitat for pastoralism which is a mode of subsistence achieved by tending and herding domesticated animals, especially, cattle, buffalo and sheep/goat. They depended on animals for food (milk and meat) and for their material culture (leather and skin for clothing, tents, bags, as well as bones and horns for other implements). Rich bone tools (accounting 25 per cent of the tool industry) are reported form Palavoy in the form of axe-heads, blades, scrapers, points, a punch and a chisel, most of them made on bovine bones particularly the splinters of long bones and shoulder blades (Rami Reddy 1976: 119) and similar tools are also found from the sites of Central Pennar Basin. However, there was a overlap between sheep/goat pastoralism and agro-pastoralism (Murty 2002: 297-307). The agro-pastoralism is distinguished by the characteristic feature of settled village life, dry farming and cattle husbandry and in the present context; the Central Pennar Basin offered a best example. All the Neolithic settlements in this region are found situated on the fertile black cotton soils suitable for agriculture, especially dry farming. In this context, it is worth noting that the Neolithic farmers never extended beyond the black cotton soil area. This shows the attachment of these early farming groups to the black cotton soil areas, possibly this soil was better suited for their agro-pastoral economy.

The evidence of cattle bones from both ash mounds and habitations around them and also from the other Neolithic settlements in the plains has been considered to explain the process of domestication of cattle. It is also visualized that for growing population, limited quantities of sowing crops with digging sticks was not enough and hence large tracts of black cotton soils or red soils which are fertile, might have brought under cultivation through slash and burn technique and wooden implements in sowing operations, perhaps heavy ploughs drawn by good breed of cattle as noticed at present day. As suggested by Andrew Sherrat (1981: 98) that the earliest cereal cultivation were closely tied to restricted areas of seasonally moist soil, requires minimal soil preparation and hence Neolithic sites first proliferated in the scattered environments where such cultivation could take place. It is likely that greater soil preparation was necessary for cereal growing since cattle were at that time becoming wide spread and hence useful for traction as well. However, sheep/goat were kept primarily for meat and later for wool useful in manufacturing cloth and also as a sacrificial animal as seen at Ramapuram (IAR 1981-82, Plate IIIB).

The socio-cultural and economic groups of agro-pastoral and pastoral-cum-agriculturists inhabiting the Upper and Central Pennar Basins can be visualized through a ecosystem concept of offering two different traditions such as ash mound tradition and non-ash mound tradition even though these differ in spatio-temporal features. As such they were engaged on different economic activities such as pottery, stone tool and bone tool manufacturing useful for their daily life include cooking, gathering, hunting, storing, carrying out other domestic activities along with pastoral and agricultural. This suggests a strong social structure inter-linked with division of labour within a single settlement or between settlements. Their transhumance activity range would have been made possible in knowing their territories better for economic exploitation in connection with cattle, sheep/goat pastrolism as well as incipient agriculture. But necessary advancement in dry farming activities in which seasonality played a dominant role in this semi-arid part of Southern Deccan. Cattle, only as a prime economic source, also offered a taste of aesthetic sense of depicting them on the rocks in the form of incisions and paintings/Gruisings and also in the form of burials in association with human populations of Neolithic times as noticed in the recent excavations at Budihal.

REFERENCES

Allchin, F.R. 1960. *Piklihal Excavations*, Andhra Pradesh Government Publications Archaeological Series No.1: Hyderabad.

——. 1961. *Utnur Excavations*, Andhra Pradesh Government Publications Archeological Series No. 5: Hyderabad.

——. 1963. *Neolithic Cattle-Keepers of South India: A Study of the Deccan Ash mounds*, Cambridge: Cambridge University Press.

Anderson, J.N. 1973. 'Ecological Anthropology and Anthropological Ecology', in J.J. Honigmann (ed.), *Handbook of Social and Cultural Anthropology*, Chicago: Rand McNally, pp. 143-178.

Andrew Sherrat. 1981. 'Plough and Pastoralism: aspects of the Secondary Products Revolution', in Ian Hodder (ed.), *Patterns of the Past: Studies in honour of David Clark*, pp. 261-305. Cambridge: Cambridge University Press, pp. 77-95.

Arun Kumar. 1985. *Quaternary Studies of the Upper Godavari Valley (a Study in Environmental Archeology)*. Ph.D. Dissertation, Pune: University of Poona.

Badam, G.L. 1979. *Pleistocene Fauna of India*, Poona: Deccan College.

Binford, L.R. 1968. 'Archaeological Perspectives', in R. Sally and L.R. Binford (eds.), *New Perspectives in Archaeology*, Chicago: Aldine, pp. 5-32.

——. 1972. *An Archaeological Perspective*, New York: Seminar Press.

Bintliff, J.L. and C.F. Gaffeny (eds.). 1986. *Archaeology at the Interface: Studies in Archaeology's Relationships with History, Geography, Biology and Physical Sciences*, Oxford: B.A.R. International Series.

Bintliff, J.L., Donald A. Davidson and Eric G. Grant (eds.). 1988. *Conceptual Issues in Environmental Archaeology*, Edinburg: Edinburg University Press.

Boserup, Elster. 1965. *The Conditions of Agricultural Growth: the Economics of Agrarian Change Under Population Pressure*, London: Allen and Unwin.

Brooks, B.K. 1987. 'Landscape Archaeology', in J.M. Wagstaff (ed.), *Landscape and Culture: Geographical and Archaeological Perspectives*, Oxford: Basil Blackwell, pp. 77-95.

Butzer, K.W. 1964. *Environment and Archaeology: an Introduction to Pleistocene Geography*, Chicago: Aldine.
——. 1975. 'The Ecological Approach to Prehistory: Are We Really Trying?', *American Antiquity* 40: 106-111.
——. 1982. *Archaeology as Human Ecology*, Cambridge: Cambridge University Press.
Clark, J.G.D. 1952. *Prehistoric Europe: the Economic Basis*, London: Methuen.
——. 1953. 'The Economic Approach to Prehistory', *Proceedings of the British Academy* 39: 215-238.
——. 1989. *Economic Prehistory: Papers on Archaeology*, Cambridge: Cambridge University Press.
Clark, Stuart. 1985. 'The Annales Historians in The Return of Grand Theory', in Q. Skinner (ed.), *The Human Sciences*, Cambrdige: Cambridge University Press, pp. 177-198.
Deo, S.G. 1991. *Geomorphic Study of Palaeolithic Settlements in the Ghataprabha Basin, Karnataka*. Ph.D. Dissertation, Pune: University of Poona.
Dhavalikar, M.K. 1984. 'Towards an Ecological Model for Chalcolithic Cultures of Central and Western India', *Journal of Anthropological Archaeology* 3: 133-158.
——. 1989. 'Farming to Pastoralism: Effects of Climatic Change in the Deccan', in J. Clutton-Brock (ed.), *The Walking Larder: Patterns of Dometication, Pastoralism and Predation*, London: Unwin Hyman, pp. 156-168.
Dimbleby, G.W. 1978. *Plants and Archaeology*, London: John Baker.
Evans, J.G. 1978. *An Introduction to Environmental Archaeology*, Ithaca: Cornell University Press.
Foote, R.B. 1916. *The Foote Collection of Indian Prehistoric and Protohistoric Antiquities: Notes on Their Ages and Distribution*, Chennai: Government Museum.
Higgs, E.S. (ed.). 1972. *Papers in Economic Prehistory*, Cambridge: Cambridge University Press.
Joshi, R.V. 1955. *Pleistocene Studies in the Malaprabha Basin*, Poona: Deccan College and Karnatak University.
——. 1970. 'The Characteristics of Pleistocene Climatic Events in Indian Sub-Continent: a Land of Monsoon Climate', *Indian Antiquary* (Third Series) 4(1-4): 53-63.
Joshi, R.V., S.N. Rajaguru, R.S. Pappu and B.P. Bopardikar. 1974. 'Quarternary Glaciation and Palaeolithic Sites in the Liddar Valley (Jammu-Kashmir)', *World Archaeology* 5(3): 369-379.
Kajale, M.D. 1979. *Bioarchaeology of the Ghod Valley, Maharashtra*. Ph.D. Dissertation, Pune: University of Poona.
Korisettar, R. 1980. *Prehistory and Geomorphology of the Middle Krishna, Karnataka*. Ph.D. Dissertation, Pune: University of Poona.
Makkhan Lal. 1984. *Settlement History and Rise of Civilization in the Ganga-Yamuna Doab*, New Delhi: B.R. Publishing Corporation.
Misra, V.N. 1987. Evolution of the Landscape and Human Adaptations in the Thar Desert, *Presidential Address: Anthropology and Archaeology Section, 74th Session of the Indian Science Congress*, Bangalore.
——. 1989. 'Stone Age India: an Ecological Perspective', *Man and Environment* 14 (1-2): 57-72.
Murty, M.L.K. 1981. 'Hunter-Gatherer Ecosystems and Archaeological Patterns of Subsistence Behavior on the Southeast Coast of India: An Ethnographic Model', *World Archaeology* 13(1): 47-58.
——. 1989. 'Pre-Iron Age Settlements in South India', *Man and Environment* 14(1): 65-81.
——. 2002. 'Sheep/Goat Pastoral Cultures in the Southern Deccan: The Narrative as a Metaphor', in S. Settar and Ravi korisettar (eds.), *Archaeology in Retrospect*, New Delhi: Manohar & ICHR, pp. 297-307.
Nagaraja Rao, M.S. and K.C. Malhotra. 1965. *The Stone Age Hill-Dwellers of Tekkalakota*, Poona: Deccan College.
Narasimhaiah, B. 1983. 'Excavations at Ramapuram, Kurnool District', *Indian Archaeology A Review*. 1981-82: 3-7.
Paddayya, K. 1973. *Investigations into the Neolithic Culture of the Shorapur Doab, South India*, Leiden: E.J. Brill.
——. 1982a. *The Acheulian Culture of the Hunsgi Valley (Peninsular India): A Settlement System Perspective*, Poona: Deccan College.
——. 1982b. 'Ecological Archaeology and the Ecology of Archaeology', *Bulletin of the Deccan College Research Institute* 41: 130-150.
——. 1991-92. 'The ash mounds of South India: Fresh Evidence and Possible Implications', *Bulletin of Deccan College Post-Graduate and Research Institute* 51-52: 573-626.
——. 1994. 'Investigation of Man-Environment Relationships in Indian Archaeology: Some Theoretical Considerations', *Man and Environment* 19(1-2): 1-28.
——. 2000-2001. *The Problem of Ash mounds of Southern Deccan in the Light of Budihal Excavations, Karnataka*, Vols. 60-61, Deccan College Post-Graduate and Research Institute, pp. 181-225.

Paddayya, K., P.K. Thomas and P.P. Joglekar. 1995. 'A Neolithic Animal Butchering Floor from Budihal, Gulbarga District, Karnataka', *Man and Environment* 20(2): 23-31.

Pappu, R.S. 1974. *Pleistocene Studies in the Upper Krishna Basin*, Poona: Deccan College.

——. 1985. 'The Geomorphic Setting of Acheulian Sites', in V.N. Misra and Peter Bellwood (eds.), *Recent Advances in Indo-Pacific Prehistory*, New Delhi: Oxford and IBH Publishing Co., pp. 9-12.

Rajaguru, S.N. and R. Korisettar. 1987. 'Quarternary Geomorphic Environment and Cultural Succession in western India', *Indian Journal of Earth sciences* 14 (3-4): 349-361.

Ravi Korisettar and S.N. Rajaguru. 2002. 'Understanding Man-Land Relationship in Pennisular Deccan: With Special Reference to Karnataka', in S. Settar and Ravi Korisettar (eds.), *Indian Archaeology in Retrospect*, New Delhi: Manohar & ICHR, pp. 243-96.

Ravi Korisettar, P.C. Venkatasubbaiah and Dorian Q. Fuller. 2002. 'Brahmagiri and Beyond: The Archaeology of the Southern Neolithic', in S. Settar and Ravi Korisettar (eds.), *Indian Archaeology in Retrospect 'Prehistory' Archaeology of South Asia*, New Delhi: Manohar & ICHR, pp. 151-238.

Rajendran, P. 1989. *Prehistoric Culture and Environment: a Case Study of Kerala*, New Delhi: Classical Publishing House.

Raju, D.R. 1981. *Early Settlement Pattern in Cuddapah District, Andhra Pradesh*. Unpublished Ph.D. Dissertation, Poona: University of Poona.

——. 1988. *Stone Age Hunter-Gatherers: An Ethno-Archaeology of Cuddapah District Region, South-East India*, Pune: Ravish Publishers.

Rami Reddy, V. 1968. *Pre and Protohistory of the South-western Andhra Pradesh*. Unpublished Ph.D. Dissertation, Poona: University of Poona.

——. 1976. *The Prehistoric and Protohistoric Cultures of Palavoy South India*, Hyderabad: The Government of Andhra Pradesh.

——. 1977. 'The Problem of Ash mounds in South India: a Fresh Look', *The Eastern Anthropologist* 30(2): 193-209.

——. 1990. 'Ash mounds in South India', in A. Sundara (ed.), *Archaeology in Karnataka*, Mysore: Directorate of Archaeology and Museums, pp. 85-99.

Richards, F.J. 1933. 'Geomorphic Factors in Indian Archaeology', *Indian Antiquary* 62: 235-243.

Roberts, B.K. 1987. 'Landscape Archaeology', in J.M. Wagstaff (ed.), *Landscape and Culture: Geographical and Archaeological Perspectives*, Oxford: Basil Blackwell, pp. 77-95.

Schiffer, Michael B. 1975. 'Behavioral Chain analysis: activities, organization and the use of space', *Field Archaeology* 65: 103-119.

——. 1976. *Behavioral Archaeology*, New York: Academic Press.

Sharma, G.R. and J. Desmond Clark (ed.). 1983. *Palaeoenvironment and Prehistory in the Middle Son Valley (Madhya Pradesh, North Central India)*, Allahabad: Abinash Prakashan.

Steward, Julian H. 1955. *Theory of Culture Change: the Methodology of Multilinear Evolution*, Urbana: University of Illinois Press.

Subbarao, B. 1958. *The Personality of India* (2nd Revised Edition), Baroda: M.S. University.

Sundara, A. 1971. 'New Discoveries of Ash mounds in North Karnataka: Their Implications', in S. Ganesan, S. Rajan, N.S. Ramaswami and M.D. Sampath (eds.), *Professor K.A. Nilaknta Sastri Felicitation Volume*, Madras: K.A.N. Sastri Felicitation Committee, pp. 308-314.

Thapar, B.K. 1957. 'Maski-1954: A Chalcolithic Site of the Southern Deccan', *Ancient India* 13: 140-141.

Thomas, P.K. 1989. 'Utilization of Dometic Animals in Pre-and Protohistoric India', in J. Clutton-Brock and C. Grigson (eds.), *Walking Larder: Pattern of Domestication, Pastoralism and Predation*, Oxford: B.A.R. International Series, pp. 355-361.

Ucko, P. and G.W. Dimbleby (eds.). 1969. *The Domestication and Exploitation of Plants and Animals*, London: Duckworth.

Ucko, P., R. Trigham and G.W. Dimbleby (eds.). 1972. *Man, Settlement and Urbanism*, London: Duckworth.

Varaprasada Rao, J. 1992. *Prehistoric Environment and Archaeology of the Krishna-Tungabhadra Doab, Andhra Pradesh*. Ph.D. Dissertation, Pune: University of Poona.

Venkatasubbaiah, P.C., S.J. Pawankar and P.P. Joglekar. 1992. 'Neolithic Faunal Remains from the Central Pennar Basin, Cuddapah District, Andhra Pradesh', *Man and Environment* 17(1): 55-59.

Venkatasubbaiah, P.C. 1992. *Protohistoric Investigations in the Central Pennar Basin, Cuddapah District, Andhra Pradesh*. Ph.D. Dissertation, Poona: University of Poona.

——. 2007. *Southern Neolithic Culture of Pennar Basin, Andhra Pradesh,* New Delhi: Bharathiya Kala Prakashan.

Wheeler, R.E.M. 1948. Brahmagiri and Chandravalli 1947: Megalithic and other Cultures in the Chitaldurg District, Mysore State.*Ancient India,* IV: 180-310.

Zeuner, F.E. 1950. *StoneAge and Pleistocene Chronology of Gujarat*, Poona: Deccan College.

——. 1963. *Environment of Early Man with Special Reference to the Tropical Regions*, Baroda: M.S. University.

9

The Protohistoric Krishna Valley: Problems and Prospects

A. SUNDARA

ABSTRACT

Extensive explorations over the past 157 years, since the discovery of the Iron Age Megalithic burials at Jewargi by Meadows Taylor and numerous stratigraphic excavations since the time of M.H. Krishna at Chandravalli in 1928 and Brahmagiri in 1942 preceded by his scrupulous explorations in 1930s in Brahmagiri in search of the Minor edict of Ashoka, provided an outline of every stage of the Prehistoric and Protohistoric cultures of the Krishna valley. New scientific methods and techniques are increasingly harnessed for identification, precise dating and objective interpretations. Yet, the picture thus far obtained remains fragmentary posing more problems.

The present paper discusses the importance of the Protohistoric sites; the Chalcolithic; the Neolithic cultural elements and material remains in the Chalcolithic; the ash mounds of the upper Krishna; and the Iron Age megalithic in particular such as the Savalda, possibly the Late Harappan; the peculiar Megalithic type in Kaladgi; the Passage chambers and the White painted pottery of the Upper Tungabhadra; the Neolithic of Maski-Watgal area, etc. in the Krishna valley (Karnataka).

PRELIMINARY REMARKS

It is well known that Meadows Taylor (1941) was the first to locate in 1851-59 Iron Age Megalithic burials at Jewargi, Andola as well as Rajankolur, Chikanhalli and Hagaratgi etc. of the Krishna valley with her tributaries – the Bhima on the north and the Ghataprabha, the Malaprabha and the Tungabhadra on the south. He was followed a little later by Robert Bruce Foote (1916) who discovered Stone Age sites at Khyad, a prolific Lower Palaeolithic site in the Malaprabha; Yadeyur (Hunasgi taluk. Kalburgi dt. Karnataka, a Neolithic site in Sanganakal-Kapgal (Koppala dt.), Patapadu (Kurnool dt., Andhra Pradesh) and a few other sites in the Krishna valley.

In the early decades of the 20th century, the State departments of Archaeology and of Geology of the erstwhile Hyderabad state (1934: 121-135) had carried out explorations discovering a large number of rock-art, Neolithic (in the chalcolithic stage) and early Iron Age megalithic sites at Hire Benkal, Kallur, Atnoor, Billamarayana gudda, Maski, etc. The Kannada Research Institute (of the former Bombay Government), Karnatak University, Dharwad (1939-

40, 1941-46, 1947-52 and 1953-57) stumbled upon a chalcolithic site at Sapta Sagara, a rock engraving at Kullolli (both in Belgaum dt.) and some Iron Age megalithic sites at Bhairavanpada near Hallur (Haveri dt.), etc. The former Hyderabad State Department of Archaeology did some probing in Maski and Kallur. The chance discovery of antennae copper swords at the latter is not only startling but also significant. The excavations by M.H. Krishna (1931 and 1942: 100-109) at Chandravalli in 1928 and Brahmagiri in 1942 preceded by his scrupulous explorations in the 1930s in Brahmagiri (Chitradurga dt.) in search of *'Isila'* of the Minor edict of Ashoka located therein, have provided for the first time an excellent stratigraphical outline of the Prehistoric, Protohistoric and Early Historical cultures of the Krishna valley.

The 1944-47 were a turning point in the history of the archaeological investigations due to the trend-setting researches by two scholar archaeologists: B. Subba Rao (1948) and Mortimer Wheeler (1948). The former systematically explored the Sanganakallu in consideration of the important discoveries made earlier by Robert Bruce Foote there and carried out vertical, stratigraphic excavations and established clear sequence of the prehistoric and protohistoric cultures with insights, especially into the everyday life of the protohistoric peoples. Steadily new scientific methods and techniques, nay even scientists from other disciplines, particularly with the adaptation of New and Processual Archaeology are increasingly harnessed and involved making the study multi-disciplinary for precise dating, identification, and objective interpretations. Studies and researches in these areas are increasingly continued more comprehensively. It is heartening to note that younger scholars of universities and research organisations are showing interest in archaeology and taking up researches in the different fields of archaeology: prehistoric and historical. Yet, the picture so obtained still remains fragmentary.

There are two major welcome trends in the field. But, it is rather distressing to note that there is no periodical co-ordination of the regional studies and researches at the regional and national levels. Consequently, certain important diagnostic problems arising in such studies remain neither pursued nor catalogued for future research. In some instances, such problems will have to be attended at the earliest in view of the colossal and total destruction of archaeological sites and monuments, e.g., Sanganakallu, Koppala, Upper Krishna valley sites, etc. owing to large-scale stone quarrying and sugar-cane cultivation that cannot be stopped for several reasons. The present paper discusses the importance of such problems by taking the protohistoric archaeology of the Krishna valley as a case study that needs to be attended to immediately. They are identified in the findings of my archaeological field explorations in the Bhima-Krishna-Tungabhadra valleys during 1957-2005 as follows:

The Chalcolithic Cultures

1. The Chalcolithic Savalda and possibly the Late Harappan, the ash mounds of the upper Krishna;
2. The Neolithic of Maski-Watgal area, etc. in the Krishna valley (Karnataka).

The Iron Age Megalithic

3. The peculiar Megalithic type in Kaladgi;
4. The white painted black and red ware pottery of the Upper Tungabhadra.

The Savalda Culture

This distinctive chalcolithic culture, as is well known, is first identified at Savalda on the bank of the Tapi Valley in Dhule dt. Maharashtra in 1959 by S.A. Sali (1964: 207-10). In this and the other sites in the valley, the Late Harappan pottery, the black and red ware pottery, etc. are found. The unique feature of this culture is the bright red ware pottery with paintings in purplish black of unusual types meticulously and beautifully drawn. They are: arrow, fish, stylised plant and other geometrical designs. Trial excavations at Savalda and Bahurupa did not yield any materials of significance. Interestingly enough, large-scale excavations for the second time in Daimabad located on the bank of the river Pravara, during 1960s by the Archaeological Survey of India Aurangabad Circle, revealed a sequence of five chalcolithic cultures: from the earliest, the Savalda, the Late Harappan, the Daimabad, the Malwa and the Jorwe. Interestingly enough, Savalda precedes the Late Harappan dated here to 2200-2000 BC. It goes without saying that the Savalda culture is contemporaneous with the latter part of the mature Harappan. Among the finds, the most noteworthy are: rectangular structures including the one with some hearths probably for religious purpose; a small crystal object from one of the hearths looking like a *Shivalinga* with chamfered top recalling the *Shivalinga* of the Parashurameshvara temple in Gudimallam near Renigunta (Andhra Pradesh).

Prior to the Daimabad excavations of 1960s, in my field explorations (1971) during 1965-66 in the upper Krishna valley, as many as 20 chalcolithic sites were discovered. Subsequently, in mid-1990s, H.S. Kambley in connection with his Ph.D. research under my guidance explored further the upper Krishna valley and found a few more chalcolithic sites of similar nature and had a trial pit in a site at Mangsuli. In most of these sites, along with the ashy grey and pinkish red micaceous pottery of the Neolithic in the chalcolithic stage, are found the Savalda pottery in two fabrics: the black on red painted and plain bright red and the grey. Curiously enough, the latter too is painted variously in either ivory black or brown or white. The painted designs are quite simple, mostly parallel lines. Thus, there are two distinguishing features in the Savalda cultural complex of the upper Krishna valley, viz., the occurrence of the grey ware and the paintings on them in three different colours. From the sites of the Godavari and the Tapi valleys, with Savalda pottery, so far these two features have not been reported. Even in the excavations at Daimabad, Savalda grey ware pottery has not been found since there is no mention of this pottery (excepting one sherd apparently of grey ware fabric) in the published report (1985). If it is so, did Savalda pottery of both the fabrics originate in the upper Krishna and spread northwards as far up as the Tapi Valley and not beyond? Does this mean that the grey ware pottery preceded the bright red ware? Was the grey ware pottery tradition given up early that explain for its absence in the Godavari and the Tapi valleys? But the C^{14} date for the beginning of the Savalda pottery in the upper Krishna as known from the small-scale trial excavations in Terdal is c. 1800 BC. Owing to their contact with the people of the Neolithic culture of the middle and the upper Krishna valley, did the Savalda people begin producing pottery in grey ware fabric also? Did the Savalda people bring with them the copper technology? Did the Neolithic people of the Krishna valley owing to their contact with the Savalda people get the knowledge of the copper metal technology and/or copper objects and thus reach the chalcolithic stage on a small scale as well as the tradition of painting the pottery as known from the excavations at Maski, Brahmagiri, Tekkalakota, etc.? To answer all such questions and to reconstruct the everyday life of the people to the maximum extent, extensive survey, particularly in the upper Krishna valley, and excavation of select sites on a large scale are absolutely necessary.

THE LATE HARAPPAN EVIDENCES

In many of the chalcolithic sites of the Tapi and the Godavari valleys, are found the late Harappan pottery evidences as well. Similarly, in the Upper Krishna there may be distinctive late Harappan cultural remains, particularly pottery. During my explorations, I might have missed to notice and identify them since my practical knowledge of the pottery is very poor. It may be recalled here that certain geometrical designs typical of the Harappan culture of the type found on the copper tablets from Mohenjodaro, i.e., endless four-knot designs have been found at different places (1996) on stone slabs in the Iron Age Megalithic context, e.g., at Naviltirth (Belgaum dt.), Holaluru (near Shivamogga), surviving as late as the Keladi Nayaks' period (1510-1763 CE) as at Gudnapura near Banavasi, Hale Nagara, the last capital of the Keladi Nayaks (Sundara 1998). Obviously, it is quite probable that this tradition might have come along with the Late Harappan. Keeping these problems in view, the upper Krishna needs to be explored both intensively and extensively.

The Ash Mound Problem

It is well known that Newbold and Robert Bruce Foote (1916), who discovered some ash mounds of immense size and scoriaceous in nature in the vicinity of the protohistoric sites, the Krishna-Tungabhadra doab had analysed them to be due to the burning of cow dung slowly at a very high temperature. The latter observed that the burning was perhaps ritualistic periodically by the Neolithic people. Since then, numerous ash mounds have been brought to light. Allchin (1973) studied all the other sites known till then in detail, besides his report on his excavations of an ash mound and the adjacent Neolithic site at Utnoor (Mahboobnagar dt., Andhra Pradesh, 1961). He infers that the ash mounds are due to the periodical burning of the cow dung accumulated in the cattle pens of the Neolithic peoples and it was ritualistic. Further, he thinks that this tradition has symbolically survived in a modified form till this day in the Deepavali and Holi festivals. Rajguru and Mujumdar (1967) and Rami Reddy (1968; 1972; 1976; 1990) excavated each an ash mound at Kapgal and Palvoy (Anantpur dt., Andhra Pradesh). The former inferred that the cow dung was not burnt in situ, i.e., in the cattle pen but transferred to the nearby spot where it was burnt. The latter, in the light of his findings from the excavations, inferred that they are due to iron smelting activity. Paddayya, the excavator of the ash mounds at Kodekal (1973) and Budihal (Surpur tk., Kalburgi dt.) (1993a&b) observes that they are due to the burning of the cow dung accumulated in the cattle pens of the Neolithic people on the occasion of their rituals. He is in agreement with the theories put forward both by Robert Bruce Foote and Allchin. Thus, different theories are put forward for the origin and purpose of the ash mounds and their cultural contexts that are too well known to be recounted in detail here.

In my explorations in the middle and upper Krishna valley, it was noticed in some of the chalcolithic sites remnants of ash mounds (1987). Kudachi (Raibhag tk., Belgaum dt.) is a typical example where seven chalcolithic sites were founds two of which had ash mounds. In my explorations in the upper Bhima, the Malaprabha and to some extent the middle and upper Tungabhadra valleys, no remains of ash mounds were noticed. Further, Sali had discovered four Chalcolithic sites with ash mounds of scoriaceous ash in the Tapi Valley. Considering these two factors, I am inclined to think that the unusual tradition, of which the resultant is an ash mound, is probably a distinct cultural feature belonging to the people of the Savalda culture that spread along the river course towards the Krishna Tungabhadra doab. The small-scale excavation of a small remnant of an ash mound (that was very extensive when I noticed in 1966) in 2005 seems to indicate that the ash mounds belong to the overlapping phase of the chalcolithic and the Iron Age Megalithic and they seem to be the throw-outs perhaps in the copper smelting operation (Padigar and Sundara 2005). Incidentally speaking, there are similar mounds of iron slags extant in several localities mostly of the medieval and recent periods, as at Kittur (of Rani Chennamma), Adgal near Badami, etc. In many lumps of scoriaceous ash are found oval-shaped depressions of different sizes about 15 x 5 x 3 cm on average having a thin crackled layer of copper residual darkish brown in colour known from preliminary scientific test on the site. Similar ash lumps but with layer of dark dull brown in colour were noticed by me in Sanganakal. What is, therefore, needed is excavation of entire ash mounds in selected areas from the upper Krishna to the Krishna-Tungabhadra doab, keeping the problems in view. Unfortunately, most of the ash mounds are razed to the ground. However, intensive survey of the region may reveal some ash mounds here and there not very much disturbed, e.g., the ash mounds in Kapgal, Wandalli (Raichur dt.), etc.

THE NEOLITHIC CONTEXT

Robert Bruce Foote had identified a Neolithic site in Sanganakal area and grooves on the rock caused owing to the frequent grinding and polishing of stone-axes. The Department of Archaeology and Museums of the former Hyderabad state had collected Neolithic stone-axes in large numbers from Maski site. In the stratigraphic excavations of the protohistoric site in Watgal (Devaraju *et al.* 1995), not far away from Maşki, a shallow pit in the natural soil of one of the trenches overlain by the Neolithic cultural layer was found to contain waste flakes of stone and fragments of dolerite dyke obviously from the process of the preparation of neoliths in the site. No other cultural remains are found associated with these remains. It looks as though these belong to a pre-pottery or aceramic Neolithic stage. In Maski proper, in spite of the occurrence of numerous neoliths on the surface, not a single neolith had been found in the 1954 regular stratified excavations by the Archaeological Survey of India. The situation is not the only one of its kind. In T. Narsipura (Mysore dt.) of the Kaveri Valley, Robert Bruce Foote identified a Neolithic habitation site sprinkled with the neoliths. Excavations in 1960s by the Directorate of Archaeology and Museums, Government of Karnataka (Seshadri 1971) have produced just one neolith in the late phase of the culture although many neoliths from the surface had been collected. In Sanganakal also, in view of the occurrence of a large number of neoliths even from the excavations, there may also be a pre-pottery Neolithic cultural phase. Nagarjunakonda (Sarkar 1975) is another site promising in this regard. It may be recalled here that on the extensive terrace of the Shevroy hills, Tamil Nadu (Narasimhaiah 1980), are found neoliths scattered all over the area without any other cultural remains such as pottery, etc. All these evidences seem to indicate that in South India, too, there is every possibility of finding a pre-pottery or aceramic Neolithic cultural stage like the one in Gufkral, Burzhom in Kashmir Valley. Sanganakal, Maski-Watgal area, therefore, need to be investigated as thoroughly as possible and excavated to define very clearly the horizon of the pre-pottery or aceramic Neolithic cultural stage.

MEGALITHS OF THE KALADGI TYPE

On a hill called 'Cromlech Hill' by an English geologist are found some 43 megaliths that form a class by themselves in terms of types and their ground plans (Sundara 1970). What is particularly noteworthy is that they are almost uniformly medium-sized. The diameter of the circles is on average more or less the same, i.e., 3.5 m. Further in the circle are almost invariably found 13-15 boulders juxtaposed. 13 is an important number in the death ritual performed by Hindu communities in India even today. In Chik-Rampur (Sundara 1987), near Hampi, are six painted rock shelters. In one of them numbered as 1, is surprisingly the painting of stone circle Megalith within a circle having on the exterior petal-like projections partly and frill-like design in the remaining part of the circle. There are obviously 13 stone boulders in the circle connected by intertwining lines. The interior is divided into two parts by a slim ladder-like design that out-stretches the circle at both ends. In one part is the picture of a human body laid extended with pottery vessels to the right. In the other part are zigzag parallel lines probably indicating flowing water. It looks as though that the entire picture displays summarily traditional belief of the journey of the soul after death to the world of the God of death, that is, *Yama loka*. In Indian tradition, till the recent past, usually after the occurrence of a death of a person in a family, *Garuda Purana* was narrated with commentary during the first 12 days. It gives a graphic picture of the itinerary of the soul to the world of the God of death. On the way is a river known as *Vaitarani*, unspeakably the most filthy and foul. If the person of the soul has done some good deeds while alive, he/she will be assisted by either a dog or a cow to cross the river without difficulty. If not, the soul will have to wade through the filthy water, the most pungent and bitter experience indescribable. Now, in the light of the Puranic story, does the painting in Chick-Rampur signify the prototype of the story that was later on elaborated and incorporated in the Purana? Piecing together all these evidences, the number 13 suggested by the number of stones of the Megalithic circle in Kaladgi is quite significant. It is, therefore, necessary to study the site by a team of different experts: anthropologists, traditionalists and archaeologists to document every minute field data that each of the experts would require for a collective study. Further, the Megalithic site of the Kaladgi type is only one of its kind found so far. There cannot be just one but many. Therefore, intensive explorations in the area are absolutely necessary followed by excavation of a select site to understand the religious and ritualistic significance of the megaliths of the Kaladgi type, which will be far-reaching.

The Megalithic white-painted black and red ware pottery

The white-painted and unpainted black and red ware pottery is well known as an important utilitarian component of everyday use in the Harappan of southern Gujarat, including the lower Tapi Valley as at Lothal, etc. and of the Banas culture in Rajasthan in North India as burial furniture of the chalcolithic cultures of the Western Deccan as at Tekwada (Dhule dt.), Chandoli of the Upper Bhima (Maharashtra), Theur near Pune (Maharashtra), Tekkalakota (Ballary dt.) of the lower Tungabhadra and as domestic and burial furniture of the Iron Age Megalithic culture as at Hallur and nearby sites of the Upper Tungabhadra. In my personal study of the white-painted black and red ware from T Kallupatti, Adichannalur, I have found that there is hardly any difference between this pottery and that from the upper Tungabhadra. In a trial pit in a protohistoric site at Benakanhalli (Honnali tk., Davanagere dt.), by Poonacha (1996), this pottery is found in the pre-Megalithic context. But it is not very clear. Recently, in a Megalithic site of the Malabar region in Kerala and in Heggadehalli (Kodagu) (Devaraju *et al.* 1997) are found white-painted black and red ware. Thus, this pottery has a wide distribution through the ages from the Harappa up to the end of the Iron Age Megalithic culture.

In my study (1972: 119-125) of the pottery from Hallur in comparison with that of the Harappa and the Banas Valley, I have found that the former is more intimately akin to that from Harappa. But its occurrence in abundance in the Megalithic burial and domestic context in Hallur region is enigmatic. Excepting one or two potsherds with white paintings occasionally here and there in the middle and lower Bhima, it has not been found so far in the doab region, in the Krishna, in the Malaprabha and the Ghataprabha. In consideration of the geographical distribution of the pottery, the route of the diffusion of pottery is not the Bhima, not the Krishna or the Malaprabha or the Ghataprabha. Then what was the route of the diffusion of this pottery from the north? Is it by the coastal route? Further, did they bring developed iron-smelting technology with them? These two are very important questions in the later protohistoric cultures of the Western Deccan and South India. With these problems, what is needed is a thorough and intensive field exploration in the western coast from Pune region to the Malabar of Kerala on the one hand and in the eastern part adjacent to the Western ghat from Shivamogga to Kodagu region keeping in view the sites in Benakanahalli and Heggadehalli, on the other. After identifying sites with white-painted black and red ware, excavation of the selected sites is necessary.

CONCLUSION

To sum up, in the above review I have just touched upon the vast period of protohistory of the western part of north Karnataka. And there are other areas of archaeology: palaeolithic cultures, historical archaeology covering inscriptional and architectural, ancient habitation sites of towns and villages of historical importance, etc. If a similar critical review of the findings from both explorations and excavations from each of the regions in our country is made, similar problems can be identified. Research institutes and university departments with mutual understanding and coordination with the help of young research scholars can make such critical review of the archaeological investigations carried out in their respective regions from time to time. M.Phil. and Ph.D. scholars can be assigned to work on such problems. While new areas and new problems are taken up for research, identification of the areas for further investigations from the researches done so far should also be carried out. Thus, there are two parts in the research domain complementary to each other. Attention has to be given to all such problems as early as possible before all the surface evidences disappear on account of ignorant vandalism and the deliberate destruction in the wake of the developmental programmes unavoidable for the prosperity of the nation. In the first place, a thorough documentation in all possible ways by using the advanced scientific techniques of all such surface evidences traced in the course of planned explorations is very essential.

REFERENCES

Allchin, F.R. 1961. *Utnoor Excavations*. Department of Archaeology and Museums, Government of Andhra Pradesh, Hyderabad.

——. 1973. *The Neolithic Cattle Keepers of South India*, Cambridge University, Cambridge.

Annual Reports of the Department of Archaeology and Museums, Government of Andhra Pradesh, Hyderabad, for the years 1915-16; 1916-17; 1927-28; 1930-31; 1933-34; 1936-37; 1938-39; 1944-45.

Annual Reports of the Kannada Research Institute, Karnatak University, Dharawad, for the years 1941-47, 1947-52.

Annual Reports of the Directorate of Archaeology and Museums, Government of Karnataka, Mysore for the Year 1942: 100-109.

Devaraju *et al.* 1997. 'The Watgal Excavations: An Interim Report', *Man and Environment*, No. 30. Indian Society Prehistoric and Quaternary Studies, Pune.

——. 1998. *Report on the Megalithic Excavations at Heggadehalli*, Directorate of Archaeology and Museums, Government of Karnataka, Mysore

Foote, R.B. 1916. *The Indian Prehistoric to Prehistoric Antiquities: Their ages and distribution*, Government Museum, Chennai.

Krishna, M.H. 1931. *Report on the Excavations at Chandravalli*, part 1. Mysore: Directorate of Archaeology and Museums, Government of Karnataka.

Nagaraja Rao, M.S. *et al.* 1965. *The Stone Age Hill Dwellers of Tekkalakota*, Deccan College Post-Graduate & Research Institute, Pune.

Nagaraja Rao, M.S. 1971. *Protohistoric Cultures of The Tungabhadra Valley* (Report on the Excavations at Hallur). Dharwad.

——. 1990. 'Graves of the Early Iron Using People's at Komaranahalli', in A. Sundara (ed.), *Archaeology of Karnataka*, Directorate of Archaeology and Museums, Mysore.

Narasimhaiah, B. 1980. *Neolithic and Megalithic Cultures in Tamilnadu*, Delhi: Sundeep Prakashan.

Paddayya, K. 1973. *Investigation into the Protohistoric Cultures of the Shorapur Doab*, Leiden: E.J. Brill.

——. 1993a. 'The Ash Mound Excavations at Budihal, Gulbarga District, Karnataka', *Man and Environment*, No. 18. Indian Society for the Prehistoric and Quaternary Studies, Pune.

——. 1993b. 'Further Field Excavations at Budihal, Gulbarga district, Karnataka', *Bulletin of the Deccan College Post-Graduate and Research Institute*, No. 53. Pune.

Padigar, V. and A. Sundara. 2005-06. 'Excavations at Kudachi', *Puratattva*, Bulletin of the Indian Archaeological Society, New Delhi.

Poonacha, K.P. 1996. 'New Light on the Protohistoric Cultural Aspects of the Upper Tungabhadra', in Dr. Shivananda Kulkarni *et al.* (eds.), *Gauravam* (Prof. B.K. Guru Raja Rao Felicitation Volume), New Delhi: Harman Publishing House.

Rajguru, S.N. and N.N. Mujumdar. 1970. *Ash Mound Excavations at Kapgal*, Deccan College Post-Graduate and Research Institute, Pune.

Rami Reddy, V. 1968. *Pre- and Protohistory of the South-Western Andhra Pradesh*. Unpublished Ph.D. Thesis, Poona: Deccan College.

——. 1972. 'Pre-and Protohistoric Culture of the South-Western Andhra Pradesh', *Journal of the Karnatak University (Social Sciences)*, Vol. VIII, Dharwad.

——. 1976. *The Prehistoric and Protohistoric Cultures of Palavoy, South India*, Hyderabad: Government of Andhra Pradesh.

——. 1990. 'Ash-mounds in South India', in A. Sundara (ed.), *Archaeology in Karnataka*, Mysore: Directorate of Archaeology & Museums, pp. 85-99.

Sali, S.A. 1964. 'A New Ceramic of the Chalcolithic from Dhulia', *Journal of the Asiatic Society*, Vol. 98, Mumbai.

——. 1986. *Daimabad, 1976-77*, New Delhi: Archaeological Survey of India.

Sarkar, H. 1975. *Nagarjunakonda* (Prehistory), New Delhi: Archaeological Survey of India.

Seshadri, M. 1971. *Report on the Excavations at T. Narsipura*, Directorate of Archaeology and Museums, Government of Karnataka, Mysore.

Subba Rao, B. 1947. *Stone Age Cultures of Bellary*, Deccan College Postgraduate and Research Institute, Pune.

Sundara, A. 1971. 'Chalcolithic Phase the Upper Krishna Valley', in S.H. Ritti and B.R. Gopal, *Studies in Indian History and Culture* (P.B. Desai Felicitation Volume), Dharwad.

——. 1972. 'Is There a Non-Megalithic Black and Red Ware Cultural Phase in North Karnataka?', *Archaeological Congresses and Seminar Papers*. Department of Ancient Indian History, Culture and Archaeology (Dr. S.B. Deo *et al.* eds.), Nagpur: Nagpur University.

——. 1970. 'A New Type of Passage Chamber Tomb in Kaladgi, Bijapur district, Mysore state', *Indian Antiquary (New Series)*, No. 4 (Prof H. D. Sankalia Felicitation Volume), Mumbai.

——. 1987. 'Studies in Ash Mounds', in B.M. Pande and Chattopadhyaya (eds.), *Archaeology and History* (Essays in Memory of Shri A. Ghosh), New Delhi: Agam Kala Prakashan.

——. 1996. 'The Harappan Endless Four Knot: Its Survival in the Historical Times in Karnataka and Interpretation', in Dr. Shivananda Kulkarni *et al.* (eds.), *Gauram* (Prof. B.K. Guru Raja Rao Felicitation Volume), New Delhi: Harman Publishing House.

Taylor, Meadows. 1941. *Megalithic Tombs and Other Ancient Remains in the Deccan* (Reprint). Department of Archaeology and Museums, Government of Andhra Pradesh, Hyderabad (This is a collection of his three valuable papers on megaliths noticed by him in Kalburgi district, published during 1851-1862).

Wheeler, R.E.M. 1948. 'Megalithic and Other Cultures in the Chitaldurg District, Mysore State', *Ancient India,* No. 4, New Delhi: Archaeological Survey of India.

10

Interpretation of Terracotta Figurines of Early Andhra

S. MURALI MOHAN

ABSTRACT

Majority of the excavated Early Historical sites in Andhra Pradesh have yielded small terracotta figurines in large numbers. The earliest datable terracotta specimens in this region are reported from Veerapuram: a specimen of small hand-made archaic bull figurine dated to Chalcolithic period (1300-1000 BC*). The majority of the excavated terracottas belong to the Satavahana and Ikshvaku periods. The terracotta figurines of this period are human figures and animal figures, both hand-made and double-mould made. Previous researches on these terracotta figurines were generally confined to classification and iconographic description. In this paper, an attempt is made not only to scientifically classify the terracottas, but also to interpret them basing on iconography, use patterns, symbolism and other social aspects.*

Small clay figurines are common finds in the protohistoric and early historic sites across the world. These figurines consist of representations of humans, animals, birds, etc. Female and male figurines are more common, sometimes with minute differences in the representation of body parts. Archaeologists have recovered terracottas from burial places as accompaniments to the dead; from the domestic floors; in and around religious places; in debris and from the exposed layers of the historical mounds. Some scholars (Lesure 2002) believe that terracottas are common objects found in many early agricultural villages and they disappear slowly as political organizations become more centralized and villages develop into cities. On the contrary, in the case of India, particularly in the context of Early Andhra, the terracotta figurines, in volume and variety, multiply from early agricultural (Neolithic) to early historic period.

The antiquity of the terracotta objects of 'art' in India can be traced back to the Neolithic times (Perod II, Mehergarh, c. 5000 BC to 4000 BC). Important Early Historic sites which have yielded terracottas are Ahichchatra, Bhita, Harinarayanpura, Jhusi, Kausambi, Mathura, Pataliputra, Rajghat, Sravasti, Taxila, Tamralipti, Vaisali, etc.

The sites which have yielded various types of terracottas are classified as major terracotta findspots (Muralimohan, n.d.), such as Amaravati (Sarkar 1992), Chebrolu (Murali Mohan 2002), Dhulikatta (Krishna Sastry 1979, 1983), Kondapur, (Yazdani 1941, Ahmad 1941), Nagarjuna Konda (IAR 1954-55, 1955-56, 1956-57, 1959-60), Peddabankur (Krishna Sastry

1979, 1983), Vaddamanu (Sastry, T.V.G. *et al.* 1992), Yeleswaram (Waheed Khan 1963) and minor sites which have yielded one or two terracottas or broken pieces are Annangi (IAR, 1977-78), Guttikonda (IAR 1981-82), Kothanandayanapalli, Nelakondapalli (Krishna Sastry 1983), Pondugal (IAR 1973-74), Ramapuram (IAR, 1981-82), Salihumam (Subramanyam 1964), Satanikota (IAR 1977-78), Vanitamandalam (Hanumantha Rao 1979), Veerapuram (Sastry T.V.G. *et al.* 1984), Mallapadu (Bhaskara Murti pers. comm.), Elchur (Chandramouli pers. comm.) and others. Many early historical sites have not yielded teracottas in large numbers. Even such sites as Veerapuram and Salihundam, which were excavated in large scale, did not yield full forms and only broken pieces were recovered.

For the present study, Lesure's (2002) four cells of matrix or the 'corners' of an analytical field has been chosen. According to Lesure, by studying the iconography, uses, social analysis and symbolism of the terracottas one can better understand the symbolism of figurine imagery and other aspects of the society. Further taking Lesure's (2002) point into consideration, attention is paid towards the patterns of difference rather than similarities to better understand the symbolism and uses.

The terracotta figurines are manufactured either in clay or in kaeolin. Two types of techniques are used to make the terracottas. The first type of figurines was hand-made by pinching the clay by hand and applying decoration on the figurine. In the second type, two moulds were used: one for the front and the other for the back of the figure. A thin layer of clay was pressed in these moulds and the casts produced were joined together with the same material. Most of these double-mould terracotta figurines have holes in the body, which was useful in letting out the inflated air during the firing. Two pieces of pre-fired slipped variety are found; one is a small piece from Chebrolu and the other is a broken human bust from Amaravati. The second variety of post-slipped variety is reported from Elchur (Chandramouli, N. pers. comm.). The remaining terracottas recovered belong to the third variety without any slip. Painted terracotta figurines are reported from Ramapuram (IAR 1980-81), Kondapur (Ahmad 1941). At Ramapuram, the body of the bull was decorated with vertical bands of red colour. At Kondapur (IAR 1980-81), some of the broken pieces were painted with clear traces of green, red and yellowish paints. An interesting feature to note here is that the painted pottery is found in Early Andhra region right from the Neolithic times (Sharma, I.K. 1968; David Raju 1985) and continues into the early historical times.

The themes found in the terracotta art of early Andhra were remarkable for their variety. Various types of terracotta figurines recovered from different sites of early Andhra are classified basing on the technique of manufacture and physical features: archiac or hand-made and double-mould made. The double-mould made figurines were further classified as 1. Bodhisattva, 2. Kubera, 3. Uma, 4. Mother goddess (*Lajjagauri*), 5. Mother goddess with raised empty hands, 6. Mother goddess with a parrot and fruits, 7. Mother goddess holding breasts, 8. Standing woman, 9. Mother and child, 10. Male head with hat, 11. Yaksha, 12. *Mithuna*, 13. Animals and birds.

Archaic terracottas are found in sites such as Peddabankur, Yeleswaram, Nagarjuna Konda, Kondapur, Nelakondapalli, Ramapuram, and others in large numbers. They consist of human and animal figures. Human figures are called mother goddess figurines if they have female features (Margabandhu 1996). These figurines are hand-modelled and possess pinched faces, short upper arms, breasts and legs. Besides human figures, animal figures such as bull, elephant, boar, ram, dog and other animals are also found. Yeleswaram (Waheed Khan 1963) has yielded a few figurines having holes at the neck perhaps to mortise it to torsoes. The heads of many figures of human and animals were broken. At Ramapuram, the body of the bull was decorated with vertical bands of red colour (IAR 1980-81). Bulls decorated with vertical bands in the rock paintings of Andhra Pradesh are common. Do these vertical bands signify any symbolism? A bull figurine of the Kulli culture was painted in black vertical lines all over the body (Dhavalikar 1977).

Terracotta *Bodhisattva* images are reported from Kondapur (Yazdani 1941). These *Bodhisattva* images are with the conventional hair rings. The face in these figurines resembles typical a inhabitant of South India with flat nose, thick lips and oval face. These features are also found in the stone images of Buddha found at Amaravati, Nagarjunakonda, and other places. A terracotta image found at Kondapur looks like a *Kubera* (Yazdani 1941) or *Yaksha*. This image is having a *yajnopavita*, necklace, turban and bangles. In this broken image bag is missing. A figurine of double mould representing Uma holding Skanda in her lap is found at Yelleswaram (Waheed Khan 1963). She was seated on a pedestal and behind her is a standing nandi with stretched legs. Uma was profusely decorated. Nandi was also decorated with a belly neck strap.

The most popular folk belief is apparent from the Mother Goddess cult. Various types of mother goddess figurines are reported from Early Andhra Region like *Lajjagauri*, mother goddess with upraised empty hands, Goddess *Kumari*, mother goddess holding her breasts with her hands. Two types of the typical *Lajjagauri* figurines are found. These *Lajjagauri* figurines can be compared with Bolon's (1997) *Uttanapad* pot, and form IV Anthropomorphic types.

Uttanapad pot type is characterized by human legs in *Uttanapad* pose with a shape above the legs that resembles both a pot and a female's lower torso with pudeudum, abdomen and lower rib cage topped with lotus buds or flowers. *Uttanapad* pot type of terracottas are reported from Nagarjunakonda and Kondapur in Andhradesa. The Nagarjunakonda figure is topped with lotus buds and four buds in the four corners. The Kondapur figure is broken and on the right side corner a *purnakumbha* is also depicted. This type of specimens are reported from the other sites in India like Ter, Sannati, Osmanabad, Kausambi, etc. The second type can be compared with the fourth type of Bolon (1997) classification of anthropomorphic form. In this anthropomorphic type, the *Lajjagauri* figures are totally anthropomorphic, with a human head and a full natural female torso. This type of *Lajjagauri* figurines are reported from Chebrolu (Fig. 1) (Murali Mohan 2002), Nagarjunakonda (IAR 1956-57), Yeleswaram (Waheed Khan 1963) Vaddamanu (Sastri, T.V.G. *et al.* 1992) and Kondapur (Yazdani 1941, Ahmad 1941) made on clay. The figurine, which was found at Chebrolu, is having a *makara* type of headdress secured with a band and wearing four rows of small beaded ornaments on the forehead. The flowing hair is made into a back knot. She is wearing two strings of small beaded necklace. The girdle is composed of one thread and another big beaded ornament. Her arms

Fig. 1. Chebrolu Lajjagauri.

are holding the large protruded belly which looks like pregnant belly with prominent navel point and the legs are outstretched; the genitals are prominent. An interesting feature in this figure is that below the beaded necklace and above the naval point is a design which looks like two ovary sacks connected (Fallopian tube?) the same design also looks like two snake hoods with connected tails. This type of mother goddess figurines can be placed under the *Lajjagauri* type of Janssen's (1993) classification, where the anthropomorphization is complete. The resting of both hands on the protruded abdomen, prominent genitals and likely snake-hoods all go to affirm that these are associated with the fertility cult.

This type of mother goddess with minor differences are found at the above-said sites in early Andhradesa, and the same type of specimens are reported from the neighbouring contemporary Satavahana sites, such as Paithan (Dhavalikar 1976), Ter (Deshpande 1999), etc.

Mother goddess with upraised empty hands: (*Srivatsa*/Sri Lakshmi) type of women figurines made of clay were reported from Chebrolu (Fig. 2) (Murali Mohan 2002), Nagarjunakonda (IAR 1955-56), Peddabankur (Krishna Sastry 1979, 1983) and Nelakondapalli (Krishna Sastry 1983). Some were headless and few are busts with broken torsos and raised hands. Some are having fillets over the forehead and beautifully combed hair towards the top as a *sikha* and with prominent nose ornament. Most of the figurines were having beaded necklaces. As said earlier, all these figures are having raised empty hands above the shoulder and the nudity is not depicted. In the figurines from Nagarjunakonda and Chebrolu, even though the head is broken, the raised hands above the shoulder are intact.

Mother goddess with a parrot and fruits type, reported from Peddabankur, is made of Kaeolin (Fig. 3) (Krishna Sastry 1983). The head, the right leg and the back portion of the figure are missing. Her left hand rests on the thigh. A parrot perching on the left arm is nudging the breast of the goddess with its bill. The goddess holds a bunch of fruits in her right hand. She is decorated with a necklace ending in a locket above the prominent navel. Bangles, a beaded waist-band of double rows and *keyuras* are present above the feet. Nudity is also indicated. On stratigraphical grounds, this figure is dated to middle Satavahana levels. This type of female figure with a bunch of three mangos in her right hand and a parrot on her left hand, which is

Fig. 2. Chebrolu empty hands.

Fig. 3. Woman with fruits, parrots, Peddabankur.

pecking at her left breast, made of Kaeolin, is found in Paithan of Aurangabad district. Another male figure with mangoes and parrot is also reported from Paithan (Dhavalikar 1976, 1977).

Mother goddess holding the breasts type is found at Dhulikatta (Fig. 4) (Krishna Sastry 1983). It is made of fine clay. The back portion and the body below the breasts is missing. The goddess holds her prominent breasts with her hands below. She wears a beaded *yajnopavita* passing over her left shoulder through the middle of the breasts, a torque around the neck, a beaded fillet over the forehead with a crest jewel and beautifully combed hair towards the right. The goddess is depicted with a smiling expression, with parted lips, narrow eyes and bulbous cheeks. This type of goddess holding breasts are also found in Peshawar and Mathura.

Standing women type is a unique standing terracotta figurine of a woman, the only example in Andhradesa where both mould and relief technique were used. Reported from Vanitamandalam of Srikakulam district (Hanumantha Rao 1979), the front half from face and skirt region is struck in mould, while the legs, hands and pedestal, etc. seem to have been hand-made. The figure is hallow inside from head to pelvic region and solid below. It is the best example of feminine beauty having an oval-shaped smiling face and well-built body. Unfortunately, the hands are broken but the broken portion clearly indicates that they are of solid nature, made separately and joined later when it was wet. Even though Hanumantha Rao (1979) has dated the figure to 2nd-3rd century AD, in the absence of solid evidence for comparison from the adjoining sites, the dating is doubtful.

Fig. 4. Mother Goddess Dhulikatta.

Mother and child type of figurines are found in Kondapur (Yazdani 1941), Vaddamanu (Sastri, T.V.G. *et al.* 1992) and in Yeleswaram (Noorjahan 1979). In Kondapur, a headless female figure with a child sitting on her left knee was found. In the right hand, she holds a fan or an incense burner. She was identified by Yazdani (1941) as Hariti with child. In Vaddamanu, mutlilated mother and child figurine in the standing posture was found, datable to (Period II) circa 100 BC to AD 200. The child is clinching to the left shoulder of the mother while the right hand is placed on her right leg. In Yeleswaram, a headless figure of mother and child was reported by Noorjahan (1979). The figure is almost in round shape but for the back portion which is flat. The mother is standing and her right hand decked with a series of bangles is resting over the right thigh. She holds the babe in her left arm with her hand clasping the baby over its legs. She is adorned with torque and long necklace passing in between the breasts. Similar mother and child type figurines are found in many sites, such as Ahichchhatra, Kausambi, Taxila, Bhita, etc. Agarwal (1948) feels that these mother and child figurines are either mother or child or in some cases they may be nurses. He quotes *Divyavadana* and other works of Buddhist literature, to show that several classes of nurses were employed to attend on royal princes. Mother with a baby in her arms may be representing fertility cult. These figurines might have been used as votive offering by child-less couples.

Hand-made, red-slipped male head (?) is reported from Dhulikatta (Krishna Sastry 1979), which is wearing a hat-like headgear with a prominent brim and a jewel attached to the hat on the left (Fig. 5). The eyes and ears with discular *kundalas* are made in applique and lips parted in a smiling expression. There is a hole on top of the hat, probably representing a Roman trader (IAR 1975-76). One dome-shaped hallow terracotta figurine is reported from Peddabankur (Krishna Sastry 1983). The top of the dome or cap was made as a head of *Yaksha*, with a broad fillet over the forehead, hair shown in ringlets, bulbous eyes and parted thick lips. The elongated earlobes carry *Chakrakundalas*. The head of the *Yaksha* is enclosed in tongues of flames shown as a circle of loops. The body below the loop circles is incised with lotus design. *Yaksha* figure in side lotus medallion is present on one of the *ayaka* slabs of the Buddhist *stupa* at Dhulikatta, which is dated to the early second century BC. This terracotta figurine with rayed circles enclosed in a lotus medallion may be a representation of the Sun god. This figurine is datable to circa 2nd century BC on stratigraphical basis.

Mithuna or *dampati* showing male and female figurines are a popular type in North Indian sites. In early Andhra, this type was reported from Nagarjunakonda (IAR 1956-57) and Yeleswaram (Waheed Khan 1963). The male figure is in standing posture and the female is sitting on the left knee of the man. Right hand of the man is resting on his leg and his left hand holds the woman in place.

Animal and bird figurines were also recovered from sites such as Kondapur Peddabankur, Yeleswaram, Chebrolu, Nagarjunakonda, Vaddamanu, Salihundam, Veerapuram, Sarupalli and others. Besides archiac animal types, double-mould animal figures were also reported from the above sites. The common and popular animal types were bulls, horses, elephants, lions, monkeys, rams, dogs, hens, cocks, parrots and others. Broken pieces and full portion of the animals were recovered.

Standing bull type was the most popular animal figure. Most of the bulls are having neck belts, sometimes with more ornaments. Some terracotta bulls resemble the standing Satavahana stone bull figure from Amaravati. Horses are having saddles but without stirrups. This feature is reminiscent of the horses that were found in Ajanta paintings and in Nagarjunakonda sculptures, which are also depicted without stirrups

Fig. 5. Male head with hat.

(Khan 1941). Lions were also found in large numbers, standing rams with hair in the neck portions and with horns. An interesting mother monkey feeding child monkey was recovered from Nagarjunakonda (IAR 1956-57).

Archiac terracottas consist of human and animal figures. Human figures are called mother goddess' figurines, if they have female features and male (Margabandhu 1976). Animal figures such as bull, elephant, boar, ram, dog, tortoise and others were found. Presence of hand-made terracotta figures along with double-mould type may be indicating that these hand-made figurines might have been made by users (women) themselves for their personal use. Chandan (1981) believes that women made the images and argues from field contents that domestic tasks fell to women. Chandan (1981), after studying Vinca figurines (South Eastern Europe), and Cyphen (1993), after studying the standing figures of Chalcatzingo (Mexico), believe that women were associated with the domestic area and that they actually made the figurines, along with the further suggestion that these figurines represent ancestors; this argument was supported on the basis of ethnographic studies and observations of Marcus (1996, 1998).

Two types of typical *Lajjagauri* figurines are found. These *Lajjagauri* figurines can be compared with Bolon's (1977) classification of Form I Uttanapad pot, and Form IV anthropomorphic form. *Uttanapad* pot type of terracotta figurines are found at Kondapur and Nagarjunakonda. The anthropomorphic type is reported from Chebrolu (Murali Mohan 2002).

According to Bolon (1977), the most elemental and symbolically potent *Lajjagauri* representation is the *Uttanapad* pot goddess (form I). This is the personified *purnakumbha* or brimming vase of fortune, depicted in an unusual manner, like a visual pinovoptical illusion. The *Uttanapad* legs are joined to a truncated torso that may be perceived either as the pudendum, belly, and lower rib cage of a female figure or as a traditional *purnakumbha*. Each pot-like lower torso is topped by a lotus flower. The vase brimming with lotus flower is a traditional symbol of fortune, life and procreative power in Indian art. Biswas (1981) has identified (*Uttanapad* pot type) a squat torso (Headless or broken) of a nude female adorned with Channavira as the counter part of the Kubera and it resembles in all major details the Kubera images from Bengal made in terracotta. This anthropomarphic type is particularly found at Chebrolu, her arms are holding the large protruded belly which looks like a pregnant belly with prominent navel point and the legs are outstretched and genitals are prominent. An interesting feature in this figure is that below the beaded necklace and above the navel point is a design which looks like two ovary sacks connected (Fallopian?) by a tube; the same design also looks like two snake hoods with connected tails. "The practice of adoration of the serpent is very primitive in India," observes J.N. Banarjee (1956). The *Maitrayani Samhita* suggests the snake's association with trees and water.

The epics *Mahabharata* and *Ramayana* have much to say on the origin of *naga* and their physical features, magical powers and sanctity. The Buddhist tradition also throws welcome light on the *Naga* cult (Biswas 1981). Terracotta pieces found at Chandrakethugarh (Biswas 1981). Son valley, Hastipur, Kausambi, Patna and other places (Kala 1950), a long neck and tapering hood showing circular eyes the hood is followed by four circular bands round the neck. The middle part of the body is broad and stamped with circlets. The figure rests on two stumpy legs. It has been identified as the stylized form of *Naga.* According to Ananda Coomaraswamy, such figures indicating splayed hips represent the *Nagini* in the form of mother goddess. The resting of both hands on the protruded abdomen, prominent genitals and likely snake-hood all go to affirm that the anthropomorphic type of *Lajjagauri* is associated with fertility cult.

The other type of mother goddess with upraised empty hands was reported from Chebrolu, Nagarjunakonda, Peddabankur, Yeleswaram and Nelakondapalli. Krishna Sastry (1983) by drawing parallels from a pheonecian mother goddess, Baal or Astrarte, dated to 1300 BC carved on an ivory plaque found at Beide in Syria, with raised hands with fodder has interpreted the Peddabankur goddess with upraised hands but without any fodder bait, as the goddess of plenty. *Srivatsa*, literally the babe (*vatsa*) of Sri or the goddess of beauty, is connected with the cult of 'Sri' goddess (or the mother goddess in general) which signifies beauty, fortune and abundance. The feature was profusely used in the relief carvings of *stupas* at Sanchi, Bharhut, Amaravati, and Nagarjunakonda while the motif is present on a number of terracotta pieces and on the chest of Vishnu and Tirthankara images.

The earliest use of the *Srivatsa* symbol is seen during the Sunga period followed by Kushana and other periods. This *Srivatsa* symbol consists of two scroll like patterns curled round at the ends, above inwardly and below outwardly and held together by a ring in the lower portion (Agarwal 1974). The earliest use of *Srivatsa* symbol in early Andhradesa was seen on a mettalic piece that was obtained in the relics of Bhattiprolu reliquaries (c. 200 BC), and at Amaravati *Srivatsa* symbol occurs prominently along with other symbols on the foot-prints of Buddha. This tradition of carving *Srivatsa* symbols on the Buddha *padas* in Amaravati and Nagarjunakonda continued during the later periods also. The tradition of earlier 'solid' motif type during the Sunga and Kushana periods can be well explained by the name of the motif itself, i.e., *Srivatsa* or "The Babe of goddess Sri". Thus, the original shape being that of a lad or crudely figured child, schematised into a pattern with suggestive details of its head, bust, upraised arms and straddled legs (Agarwal 1974). The occurrence of *Srivatsa* on the breast of Cha(n)da Yakshi at Bharhut, according to P.K. Agarwal (1974), is an evidence indicating the association of *Srivatsa* with a divinity of the class of fertility goddess. This is further strengthened by the presence of *Srivatsa* motif as the principle decorative element on their coiffures of the four Mathura terracottas datable from second and first centuries BC. On a *Mithuna* plaque (200-100 BC) from Ahichchhatra, a female figure is wearing a long necklace consisting of three symbols, two on either side, namely, a dagger, a 'Vajra' and a puppet-like motif in the centre. V.S. Agarwal (1948) has identified this puppet-like pendant as *Srivatsa* and, according to him, it is of interest as it virtually reproduces the form of the archiac mother goddess. According to P.K. Agarwal (1974), "in the light of its presence on the bust of a female figure and the literal meaning of *Srivatsa* as 'the babe of Sri', it seems reasonable to infer that this had its origin in the stylised rendered design of babe, that had been associated in early iconography with the mother goddess as indicative of mother character." 'Puppet' pendant is also worn in the necklace of a seated figure from Kausambi (1st century AD).

The survival of the *Srivatsa* shape in perfect form is noticed in three sculptures datable to the Pallava period (Agarwal 1974). One is a bronze plaque showing *Srivatsa* Lakshmi or *Srivatsa* Vasini Lakshmi from Enedi, Tanjavur, Tamil Nadu, the second one on stone from Kaveripakkam, north Arcot district (Sivarama Murti 1941); and the third one from a relief found at Peddamudiyam Cuddapah district in Andhra Pradesh. According to Agarwal (1974), "here we have an interesting iconographic type that has been termed as 'Srivatsa Lakshmi', i.e., the goddess of Sri Lakshmi shown in the form of *Srivatsa* that reveals a perfect assimilation of the seated figure with the 'shield' type *Srivatsa* shape, the arms and legs of the goddess being conceived as the curled-up ends of the symbol with her head taking the place of its upward central projection." After the above discussion, it can be inferred that these upraised empty hand figurines from early Andhradesa are the earlier form of *Srivatsa* type than the *Srivatsa* Lakshmi of the seated figure.

Mother goddess with parrot and fruits are reported from Peddabankur. A parrot perching on the left arm is nudging the breast of the goddess with its bill. The goddess holds a bunch of fruits in their right hand. Krishna Sastry (1983) believes that a parrot being one of the attributes of the goddess *Kumari*, the above-mentioned goddess with a parrot may be the goddess *Kumari*, who bestows children. Parrots are also sacred to Kamadeva, the god of lust.

Few animal figurines were also recovered from sites such as Kondapur, Peddabankur, Yeleswaram, Chebrolu, Nagarjunakonda, Vaddamanu, Salihundam, Veerapuram and others. Besides archiac animal types, double-mould animal figures are reported from the above sites. The common and popular animal types were horses, elephants, bulls, lions, rams and dogs, hens and cocks; the most popular type of bird is parrot. Broken pieces and full portions of the animals are normally recovered. Sometimes, animals such as horses, bulls, and elephants are decorated with ornaments. An interesting mother monkey feeding a child was recovered from Nagarjunakonda (IAR 1956-57).

Archaeologists did not pay much attention to record the location or find-spots of these terracottas during the excavation, which is useful for the interpretation up to some extent. In Egypt and Mesopotamia, terracotta figurines have been found either in the gravel or beneath the floors of the residential houses. In Babylonia, figurines were kept inside brick boxes and buried under floors to keep away troubles from the houses (Kala 1950). A cave above Delphi sacred to pan and the nymphs in Greek has yielded over 90,000 figurines while from a votive pit at a sanctuary of Hera in southern Italy, fragments representing more than 20,000 figurines were recovered (Uhlen Brock 1992). In Jordan, a neolithic site at Ain Gahazal two stabbed terracotta figurines are recovered *in situ* lying side by side in a tiny pit covered by a lime stone slab, beneath a floor in the corner of a room (Schmandt 1997). In the same site, a clay bull was recovered in another house in a storage bin (Schmandt 1997).

The female figurines of various types discussed in this paper seem to be related in one way or the other with fertility cult. The fourth type of figurine was a nude sitting figure holding protruded abdomen while the fifth type with upraised empty hands represent most probably a developed form of *Srivatsa* or the babe, of Goddess Sri which is represented as an auspicious symbol in the beginning and slowly developed into a human form. The occurrence of *Srivatsa* on the breast of Chunde (Agrawal, P.K. 1974) and the occurrence puppet-like motif in the centre of the necklace on the female terracotta figure (200-100 BC) in Ahichchhatra attests that it is an archiac mother goddess, a divinity of the class of fertility godesses (V.S. Agarwal 1948). Else, this may be a secularised *Lajjagauri* type in the process of evolution, because we find naked *Lajjagauri* type figures with upraised empty hands in other parts of India (Tiwari 1985, Kala 1980).

The sixth type of female figures holding fruits in one hand and a parrot sitting in the opposite side near the breasts may be the goddess *Kumari*, who bestows children. Another type of mother and child or *Ankadhari*, which are found in many sites, may also represent the fertility cult. Various types of mother goddesses related to the fertility cult ascertain the realm encompassed the growth and reproductive forces of the nature in all its aspects.

It may be presumed that the terracotta figurines might have been used for worship, or as votive offerings to gods or goddesses or simply for decoration. The number of broken head pieces recovered in the major terracotta sites outnumber the headless and complete specimens.

In sites like Chebrolu and Nagarjunakonda, which have yielded intact upraised empty-handed female figurines without heads, attesting that these heads were broken intentionally and not accidentally, the same was observed by Uhlen Brock (1992) in southern Italy where a deep well fallen into disuse contained tens of thousands of female heads broken from figurines. It may be presumed that snapping of the heads was part of a purposeful mutilation that took place when the figure was offered so that it could not be reused by anyone else, may be a replacement for human sacrifices.

Even today, worship of terracotta figurines of the *Mansha* (the snake goddess), *Ghata* and horse are prevalent in the Bauri community (Bhattacharya 1991) of Bengal. Terracotta votive offerings are also common in the same community. Near Ahmedabad (Gujarat), in a village shrine, child-less couples perform rituals and offer doll-sized round-faced clay idols, which are lined near the wall of the compound (Mitra 1984) and worship of horses and votive offerings is also common in Ayyanar cult in Tamil Nadu.

With the presence of so many animal figurines, both archaic type and double-mould type, sometimes with heads or without heads or broken limbs, it can be explained that this might have been used for votive sacrifices or else for decoration. Excavations in Jordan at the Neolithic site of Ain Ghazal (c. 8300-6000 BC) yielded a large number of clay animal figurines, the most interesting being two animals each stabbed with three flint bladelets in the throat, the abdomen, the chest or the eyes (Schmandt 1997). This indicates that the practice of animal sacrifices also played a ritual role.

REFERENCES

Agrawala, P.K. 1974. *Srivatsa the Babe of Goddess,* Varanasi: Sri Prithivi Prakashan.

Agrawala, V.S. 1948. 'Terracotta Figurines of Archichchhatra, District Bareilly, U.P.', *Ancient India:* 4.

Ahmad, K.H. 1941. *The Antiquities and Architectural Remains of Kondapur*, Proceedings of the Hyderabad Archaeological and Historical Society.

Battacharya, D.K. 1991. 'Terracotta worship in Fringe Bengal', in I. Hodder (ed.), *The Meaning of Things: Material Culture and Symbolic Expression*, London: Harper Collins Academic, pp. 12-21.

Banarjee, J.N. 1956. *Development of Hindu Iconography*, New Delhi: Motilal Banarsidass.

Biswas, S.S. 1981. *Terracotta art of Bengal*, Delhi: Agam Kala Prakashan, pp. 81-82.

Bolon, C. Radcliffe. 1999. *Forms of the Goddess Lajjagauri in India,* New Delhi: Motilal Banarsidass.

Chandan, John. 1981. *The Vinca Culture of South-East Europe: Studies in Chronology, Economy and Society*, British Archaeological Reports International Series 117, p. 75.

Cyphens Guillen, Ann. 1993. 'Women, rituals and social dynamics at ancient Chalacatzingo', *American Antiquity* 4: 220.

David Raju, B. 1985. *Neolithic Cultures of Central Coastal Andhra*. Unpublished Ph.D. Thesis, Nagarjuna University, pp. 299-301.

Deshpande. 1999. 'Satavahana Terracotta Art with Special Reference to Ter', in Ajay Mitra Sastri (ed.), *The Age of the Satavahanas*, New Delhi.

Dhavalikar, M.K. 1976. 'Paithan Terracottas', *Journal of the Indian Society of Oriental Art,* VII, Calcutta.

——. 1977. *Masterpieces of Indian Terracottas*, Bombay: B.R. Tara Porevela, pp. 48-56.

Gopalakrishnan, M.S. 1974. 'Mother Goddess and Snake worship', *Journal of the Madras University* XLVI X(1), Madras.

Gupta, P.L. 1972. *Gangetic Valley Terracotta Art*, Varanasi, p. 7.

Hanumantha Rao, B.S.L. 1987. 'Inscribed sealing from Chebrolu', *Proceedings of A.P. History Congress. XII Session*, Nagaram.

Hanumantha Rao, D. 1979. 'A Terracotta Figurine from Vanitamandalam, District Srikakulam', *A.P. Journal of Archaeology* I: 89-91.

Indian Achaeology Review: 1954-55, 1955-56, 1956-57, 1959-60, 1973-74, 1975-76, 1977-78.

Janssen, FHP.M. 1993. 'On the origin and development of the So-called *Lajjagauri*', *Proceedings of the 11th International conference of the association of south Asian Archaeologists in western Europe.*

Kala, S.C. 1950. 'Terracotta Figurines from Kausambi', The Municipal Museum, Allahabad.

——. 1980. *Terracottas in the Allhabad Museum*, New Delhi: Abhinav Publications.

Krishna Sastry, V.V. 1979. 'Terracottas from Peddabankur and Dhulikatta', *The A.P. Journal of Archaeology* I (I): 78, 84-86.

——. 1983. *The Proto- and Early historical cultures of Andhra Pradesh*, Hyderabad: Govt. of A.P., pp. 179, 181, 182-185.

Lesure, G. Richard. 2002. 'The Goddess diffracted, thinking about the figurines of Early Villages', *Current Anthropology* 43(4): 587-610.

Marcus jyoce. 1996. 'The importance of context in Interpreting Figurines', *Cambridge Archaeological Journal* 6: 285-91.

——. 1998. *Women's ritual in Formative Oaxaca: Figurine making, divination, death and the ancestors*, Arbor: University of Michigan Museum.

Margabandhu. 1996. 'Early Historic Terracottas from Gujarat Study', *Madhu: Recent Researches in Indian Archaeology and Art History.*

Mitra, N. 1984. 'Bahuchare Mata and Her Rooster', *The India Magazine* 4(5).

Murali, Mohan S. 2002. 'Terracottas Figurines of Chebrolu, Guntur District, Andhra Padesh', *Puratatva*. No. 32, pp. 173-174.

——. (n.d). *Early Historical Terracottas of Andhra Pradesh*, New Delhi: Bharatiya Kala Prakashan (in press).

Noorjahan. 1979. 'Ankhadhari From Yeleswaram Excavation', *A.P. Journal of Archaeology I.*

Sarkar, H. *et al.* 1992. *Amaravati*, Delhi: Archaeological Survey of India, p. 30.

Sastri, T.V.G., Kasturibai and J.V.P. Rao. 1984. *Veerapuram: A type site for cultural study in the Krishna valley*, Hyderabad: Birla Archaeological & Cultural Research Institute, p. 136.

Sastri, T.V.G., M. Kasturibai and M. Veerender. 1992. *Vaddamanu Excavations*, Hyderabad: Birla Archaeological and Cultural Research Institute, pp. 281-283.

Schmandt, Denise B. 1997. 'Animal symbols at 'A' in Ghazali', *Expedition* 39(1).

Sivarama Murthi, J. 1941. 'Goddess Lakshmi and Her Symbols', *Journal of the U.P. Historical Society* XIV.

Sharma, I.K. 1968. 'Patapadu Revisited: A New Painted Pottery Culture of South East India', *Puratattva*, No. 1.

Subramanyam, R. 1964. *Salihundam, A Buddhist Site in Andhra Pradesh*, A.P. Govt. Archaeological Series No. 17, p. 4.

Tiwari, J.N. 1985. *Goddess Cults in Ancient India*, Delhi: Sundeep Prakashan.

Uhlenbrock, J.P. 1992. 'History, Trade, and the Terracottas', *Expedition* 34(1-2).

Waheed Khan, M.D.A. 1963. *A Monograph on Yeleswaram Excavation*, Hyderabad: The Govt. of A.P., pp. 45-47.

Yazdani, G. 1941. 'Excavation at Kondapur, an Andhra Town', *Annals of the Bhandarkar Oriental Research Institute* XXII (III-IV), pp. 177-180.

11

Prevalence of Mother and Child Terracotta Images and Their Significance in Tamil Nadu

S. VASANTHI

ABSTRACT

The exploration and excavation undertaken in Tamil Nadu for the past three decades by various agencies yielded a number of terracotta figurines. Among them, the noteworthy finds were the occurrence of terracotta mother and child images. This paper enlists the places from where they were collected. It also describes and discusses their historical significance.

Tamil Nadu is known for her heritage and culture. There are numerous artefacts of religious and secular representation of images in stone, bronze and terracotta. The terracotta figurines are of divine, human, animal and other objects like beads, earlobes, toys, etc. The findings of the terracotta images during the exploration and excavation in Tamil Nadu indicated the skilled workmanship of both royal artist as well as the local artisans. The making of the terracotta figurines was a highly specialized technique employed consisting of the use of a double mould: one for the front and the other for the rear side in order to have the wholesome image. Mostly, terracotta figurines cast in moulds were obtained.

The terracotta mother and child images were found in the exploration and excavations of the following sites, namely, Thirukampuliyur (Tiruchy District), Alagankulam (Ramnathapuram District), Kambatti (Nilagiri District), Chayavanam (Nagappattinam District), Manmangalam (Karur District), Aravakkuruchi (Karur District) and Uttamanayakkanpalayam (Madurai District).

THIRUKAMPULIYUR

This is a seated woman holding a baby in her left side. It was found in the trench TKP-5, Layer (2); the height of the image is 4 cms. The baby is shown clinging to the mother's breast and its face is shown turning away from the breast. It is a broken figure with the head and the portion below the waist missing. Her left arm is not broken. She wears a necklace around her neck and bangles in her hand which are marked by thin and clear incisions. Her right hand is shown pressing her left breast. The breasts and belly portions are not covered. It was originally treated

Fig. 1. Alangankulam.

with a red slip, the traces of which are seen on the left half of the figure. According to the excavators, it is an interesting figure portraying a natural scene of the bosom relation of a mother and her child. Similar figures are not seen in South India and it may be considered to be very unique and a rare specimen.[1] The terracotta figure is assigned to the 10th-11th century CE.

ALAGANKULAM

This is a solid broken portion of a terracotta representation of a female figure that was recovered from the trench AGM 8 in the depth of 2.28 mt in Layer 3 of period III datable according to the excavators between 100 CE to 500 CE (Fig. 1). The left side of the figure from the waist to the knee portion is found and they are covered by the *sari* frills worn by the lady. The draping of the frills of the *sari* is shown in an elegant manner. A single foot with three anklets is noticed near the hip portion[2] of the mother, which may indicate the baby's foot.

KAMBATTI

During the excavations at Kambatti in the Toda country, J.W. Breeks noticed a lid of a pot carrying a similar figure of a female carrying a baby. This finding of the terracotta in the barrow suggests that this is a megalithic cult.[3]

CHAYAVANAM

Another site, Chayavanam, near the famous Kaveripumpattinam, in Nagappatinam district yielded a terracotta figurine in the excavation. A seated female holding a child is depicted as if the baby is feeding by way of clutching her breasts. The excavators have noted medieval pottery in contemporary layers.[4]

Fig. 2. Manmangalam.

MANMANGALAM

It is a small village about 8 km from Karur to Pugalur. Three terracotta figurines were collected in the exploration (Fig. 2). All the three terracotta figures represent females seated on circular seats, two of them showing their respective their hips.

The first female seated figure is shown with her hands placed on her knees. She is shown with a hair-do with finger nail ornamentation, a prominent nose, impressive forehead, round eyes and earlobes with *Patrakundalas*. The child is seen seated on her hip clutching the breast of the mother. The mother is shown with a lower garment extending up to the knee. The figure is just 12 cm in height.

The other figure about 10 cm in height and somewhat damaged resembles almost the first figure in every respect, though less refined than the first posing to hold the baby though the figure of the child is lost. The third terracotta figurine without holding the child is about 12 cm in height.[5]

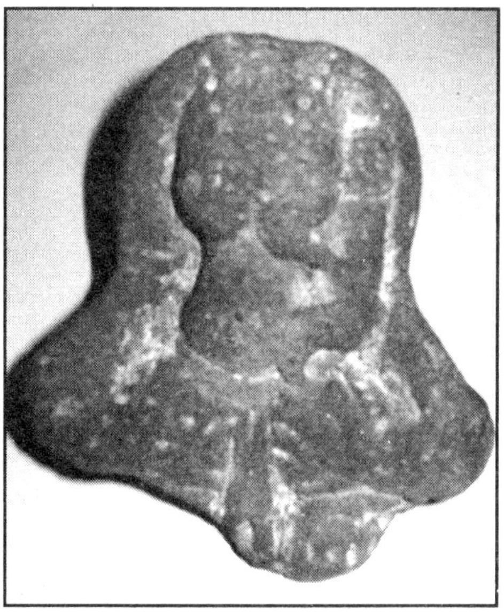

Fig. 3. Arvakkuruchi.

ARAVAKKURUCHI

Another mother and child terracotta from Arava-kkuruchi in Karur district, red in colour, a round complete figurine, was found (Fig. 3). It is depicted in sitting posture and holding a baby on her left side. The blouse worn by the mother is shown up to her sleeve. The headless figurine without any ornamentation has the local artistic style and is stylistically datable to 10th-11th century CE.[6]

UTTAMANAYAKKANPALAYAM

A terracotta image of mother and child was found at Uttamanayakkanpalayam in Dindukal district (Fig. 4). The figurine resembles that of the less skilful. The solid image is holding the child on her hip. Her thick lips and slightly protruding chin, which can be closely associated with the local tribal characteristics, and long elongated ears, mango-designed necklace around her neck are some of the interesting features noticed. She wears three bangles on her arms. The headdress of the figure is also typical of the Vijayanagara dynasty style. Thereby, it belongs to 13th-14th century CE.

Fig. 4. Uttamanayakkanpalayam.

OBSERVATIONS

- Mr. Abdul Majeed, in his article on Manmangalam terracotta, observes that the people belonging to the Karnika sub-caste are living in Manmangalam village. These people claim that they were the descendants of Chitragupta, the chief accountant of Yama (god of death). He also states that this community lives in various parts of Tamil Nadu in places like Madras, Kanchipuram, Erode, Kangayam and Coimbatore. They are found in large numbers in Kodunturai, which is to the north of Musiri in Tiruchi district. It is said that even in the present day, the Karunikas of Kodunturai worship in their houses similar terracotta figures of female deities carrying children. People call this deity *Koppatti Amman, Pappara deivam* and *Brahmana deivam*, and he also suggests that it is difficult to ascertain why they called the terracotta images with child as the Brahmin goddess.

- Jainism and Buddhism were practised by the people from 3rd century CE to 6th century CE in Tamil Nadu. The representation of *Yakshi* was very popular in that period. In Jainism, Ambika *Yakshi* of 22nd Tirthankara Neminatha is depicted with her sons. In Buddhism also, the *Yakshi* Harithi is shown with her children. The influence of these two *Yakshis* might have developed into the practice of worshiping the mother and child images in terracotta. This is due to the prevalence of this religious worship of this kind of images as in Manmagalam may be seen even today.
- The representation of mother and child images has some significance. The projection of the mother and child in a family as a lovable and caring person. Growth of religious dogmas and ideas had their influence in every aspect of the life of the people.
- This mother and child images might have been created as offering or votive images for fulfilling of oaths of their personal/religious beliefs.
- Though the terracotta images were made by the local people, they had some foreign influence as in the case of the terracotta image from Alagankulam excavation. The drapery of the image resembles that of the Roman style of drapery. The local traditional religious concepts were noticed yet with foreign influence of attire.
- To some extent, it can be suggested that most of the images of mother and child belong to 10th-14th century CE, except Alagankulam, which is datable to 500 CE.

CONCLUSION

The representation and worship of mother and child in terracotta is still in vogue in Tamil Nadu due to the continuation of the tradition followed in the early period. The bondage of a caring mother and a child is highly prevalent in present Tamil Society despite the lifestyle being highly influenced by western fashion and technical commitments in day to day life.

NOTES

1. T.V. Mahalingam (ed.). 1970. *Report on the excavations in the Lower Kaveri Valley (Tirukkampuliyur and Alagari)*, Chennai: Madras University, p. 58.
2. T.S. Sridhar (ed.). 2005. *Alagankulam (An ancient Roman port city of Tamil Nadu)*, Chennai: Tamil Nadu State, Department of Archaeology, pp. 65-66.
3. Abdul Majeed. 1978. 'Manmangalam Terracottas', in R. Nagaswamy (ed.), *South Indian Studies*, Madras: SAHER, p. 102.
4. *Ibid.*
5. *Ibid.*
6. S. Vasanthi, 1999. *Tamilaga Azhavil Sathanigal* (Tamil), Chennai: Poovalagi Pathipakkam, p. 16.

12

Taj Mahal: Conservation and Management

D. DAYALAN

ABSTRACT

Taj Mahal (1631-1648), one of the most spectacular monuments in India, has a long recorded history of conservation. The earliest record of its repair, just after four years of its completion, is available in a letter dated AD *1652 from Prince Aurangzeb to his father Shah Jahan. Since then, several conservation measures were undertaken to the various buildings of the Taj Mahal complex from time to time as per the necessity and requirement.*

Since Independence, the Government of India has initiated many studies on the nature of foundation, structural stability, the verticality of minarets, the nature and strength of the building materials, environmental effects, etc. by applying GIS and GPR techniques. In this exercise of monumental proportions, various national and international scientific organizations were involved. The author, entrusted with the responsibility of maintenance and conservation of Taj Mahal and other historical buildings in the Agra region for many years, had the opportunity to examine the monument thoroughly. This paper deals in detail with the various conservation and environmental issues of Taj Mahal and also the measures taken by the Archaeological Survey of India from time to time.

India has a rich and kaleidoscopic variety of cultural heritage right from the pre-historic period spread all over the nation. The diversity of cultures and heritages in the country is not only a matter of great pride but also an irreplaceable source of spiritual and intellectual richness for all human kind. The protection and enhancement of cultural and heritage diversity in India should be actively promoted as an essential aspect of human development. Few thousands of monuments and archaeological sites in India are protected by the Central and State Governments and other agencies. However, there are considerable number of unprotected cultural properties that need public care.

The paper deals in detail with the conservation and management issues of Taj Mahal, the most important tourist destination in India, as a case study for better understanding the conservation and management aspects of cultural properties. In Agra, there are three World Heritage Monuments, i.e., Taj Mahal, Agra Fort and Fatehpur Sikri in addition to quite a good number of other monuments. Out of these three, the first two are located on the right bank of river Yamuna in the city of Agra within a distance of about 800 m in between, whereas the last one is situated 40 km from Agra.

The Taj Mahal (1631-1648) was inscribed on the World Heritage List in 1983. Its inscription as a cultural property of universal significance was justified in the following words, "The Taj Mahal is the greatest architectural achievement of the whole range of Indo-Islamic architecture. Apart from its tremendous romantic appeal, it is a masterpiece of architectural style, in conception, treatment and execution, all alike."

Taj Mahal is surrounded by shops, green belt, emporium, offices, hotels, etc. on the east and west; the thickly populated Taj Ganj area and shopping complexes on the south; and Yamuna River, Mehtab Bagh and green belt area on the north. Taj Mahal has to be visualized along with the riverbank, river Yamuna and adjoining monuments and landscape as they are an integral part of this monument complex (Fig. 1). It is essential that the buffer zone between Agra Fort, Taj Mahal and Mehtab Bagh should be formulated to safeguard the landscape and the environment from any unregulated and inappropriate development. Hence, the modern construction, mining, vehicle movement and pollution in the buffer zone are regulated by various government rules, gazette notifications and Supreme Court directions from time to time.

The main mausoleum is placed on the bank of river Yamuna (Fig. 2). All along the river, there are a series of well foundations with filling of rubble masonry in between (Fig. 3). The

Fig. 1. Satellite image of the Taj Mahal.

main mausoleum is raised over the marble platform, which in turn rests on a low height red sand stone platform known as *chameli* platform because of the floor design on it. The wall of the structure of the main mausoleum is constructed of *lakhauri* brick with lime mortar. The mausoleum has double domes. There are four minarets on the four corners of the marble platform. The inner walls, the lower dome and the outer surface of the mausoleum and the minarets are totally clad with white marble. The intrados of the upper dome was plastered up to the height of 18.59 mt. and above that the intrados was veneered with sandstone slabs. The sandstone was used for veneering the inner face of the minarets and also for the steps. Covering the entire surface of the lower part of the drum, there is a regular and continuous series of eight relieving arches which add to the strength of the structure.

Taj Mahal has a long recorded history of conservation. The earliest record of its repair is available in a letter dated AD 1652 from Prince Aurangzeb to his father Shah Jahan wherein he pointed out some defect in the dome and vaults of the mausoleum. Since then, the conservation work of both minor and major nature were undertaken to the various buildings of the Taj Mahal complex from time to time as per the necessity and requirement. Today, it is in good state of preservation. However, due to its age, minor defects such as cracking of stones due to corrosion of iron dowels and clamp, weathering effect on the stones, decay of the mortar of the roof, missing of inlay due to human vandalism and decay of the adhesive and other minor defects

Fig. 2. General view of the Taj Complex.

Fig. 3. Brick well foundations.

are bound to occur. The environmental effect on the building, wear and tear and some degradation due to the movement of a large number of visitors are some of the major issues.

Conservation is defined as an action taken to prevent any further decay. It includes all acts that prolong the life of our cultural and natural heritage. The minimum affective action is always the best. If possible, the action should be reversible and not prejudice possible future intervention. Before taking up conservation to any ancient monument, it is necessary to study and understand various aspects such as: its location, environment, material used, method/style of construction, cause of deterioration and status of deterioration. Some of the ethics of conservation followed are:

a. All the methods and material used during treatment must be fully documented.
b. The historical evidences must not be destroyed, falsified, or removed.
c. Any intervention must be the minimum necessary and reversible. The existing material has to be retained maximum possible.
d. Any intervention should be in conformity with the aesthetic, historical and physical integrity of the cultural property.
e. No conservation work should be undertaken by the conserver/restorer who is insufficiently trained or inexperienced, unless they obtain competent advice.

Keeping these principles in view, a thorough study of the Taj Mahal was carried out and an inventory was prepared on its conservation-related aspects. The study of properties of the building materials are as follows:

The Lakhauri Brick

The *lakhauri* bricks are perfectly baked and fed into hot fat mixed with some materials which were absorbed into the porous body of the bricks. This thin, almost imperceptible, overcoat made the brick adequately waterproof. The bricks are examined and the test report is below:

(a) Colour	-	orange to red
(b) Average water absorption	-	10.13%
(c) Average compressive strength	-	159.00 kg/m3
(d) Crushing load	-	33.00 MT
(e) Density	-	2077 Kg/m3
(f) Size	-	(a) 18 x 11 x 2 cm
		(b) 19 x 11 x 3 cm

Mortar

Fig. 4. Traditional mortar preparation.

The mortar was prepared in a traditional manner (Fig. 4) by mixing 1:1:2 (1 lime: 1 coarse sand: 2 *surkhi*). The lime used was hydraulic (slaked lime free from lumps and other possible impurities). Some ingredients like *gur* (jaggery/sugarcane juice), *urd* (kind of pulse), *tentile, batasha* (sugar bubbles), *besan* (pulse), *rumi-mastagi, belgri*-water, jute, gum and *kankar* were also added. The cementing material, which had thus been prepared, was very strong and enduring with bounding material of best quality. The size of the brick used in the structures was reduced so that mortar could occupy a greater cubic volume of masonry. The thickness of mortar joints is observed to be 1 to 2 times the thickness of the bricks used in the construction.

Inlay Stones

The main decoration in the Taj Mahal complex consists of intricate inlay, relief carving and incised painting. The inlay of floral arabesques fashioned from precious/semi-precious stones in white marble and the inlaid black marble inscriptions that frame the central vaulted portal or *iwan*, commanding both in form and in content are some of the prime attractions in Taj Mahal. The treatment of the marble surface, like soft muslin embroidered richly with *pietra-dura* work, and multitude surface details are the testimony to the fine quality of the monument. The precious/semi precious stones used for inlay works are: Alabaster *(Sang-i-Rukham)*; Agate *(Sang-i-gawa, sang-i-gheri, sang-i-panghan)*; Amethyst; Black marble *(Sang-i-Musa, sang-i-moosa)*; Bloodstone *(Sang-i-Gad; Sang-i-Dogasra)*; Carnelian of Arabia Felix *(Yamani)*; Chalcedony; Chrysolite/Cat's eye stone (*Lahsunnia*); Conch-shell *(Sankh)*; Coral *(Moonga)*; Carnelian *(Sang-i-Aqiq)*; Crystal *(Billoor)*; Diamond *(Hira)*; Emerald *(Zamurrad)*; Garnet *(Tamra, Sang-i-Tandra)*; *Ghar; Ghori; Godar;* Golden stone *(Tilai)*; Green Marble (Pazhar); *Gulabi;* Jade *(pitunia)*; Jasper *(Sang-i-Badal; Sang-i-Ratak; Sang-i-Galahra; Sang-i-Udha)*; *Khara;* Lapis Lazuli *(Sang-i-Lajward)*; Load stone *(Maqnatis)*; Magnet Stone (Nakhod, Maknatis); Melachite *(Dana-i-Farang)*; Mother-of-pearl *(Sip)*; *Nakhud;* Onyx *(Sulaimani, Sang-i-Lahsania)*; Onyx Marble (Cloud stone, *Badal, Sang-i-abri*); *Pai-Zahar; Pankhni;* Pearls *(Moti)*; Pink Marble; *Pitunia;* Redstone *(Surkh)*; *Reg;* Ruby *(Yakut)*; *Sang-i-Ajuba/Ujuba,* a kind of Turquoise (It is mottled with green and yellow concretions in a brown ground-mass); Sapphire *(Nilam)*; Slate (Calcareous shale); *Sumaq;* Topaz *(Pukhraj)*; Turquoise *(Firoza)*; Turquoise *(Sang-i-Abri)*; Turquoise *(Sang-i-Chitla)*; Yellow Marble *(Khattu, Sang-i-Zard)*, etc.

Marble

The marble used in the Taj Mahal is of several kinds although quarried from the same area, Makrana, with differences in colour, shade and grains. At least three to four differences in quality have been observed. The analysis of few pieces of marble indicated that they are not a pure variety of marble but a dolomite one containing carbonates of calcium and magnesium as well as silica, iron, arsenic, tellurium, etc. The veneering stone of the main mausoleum, particularly the area of marble that was used for inlaying, are of superior quality than the others. The spot or streaks of different natural colours are found on the slabs of marble mainly because of the presence of mineral impurities. The iron dowels or clamps were used for fixing the marble slabs in position. The different types of effects observed on the marble surface of the monument are:

1. Discolouration of the surface – either uniformly or in spots.
2. Breaking of marble slab edges.
3. Formation of cracks on the marble surface.
4. Bulging of marble slabs.
5. Pitting or erosion of marble surface in some areas.
6. Loss of translucent shining.

Different types of studies were made to asserting the root causes of the above problem. They are:

1. Petrologic study to identify the elements present in the marble.
2. Study of crack formation pattern, porosity, soluble salts present in the marble, absorbing capacity and analysis of dust accumulation at various places on the surface of Taj Mahal, mineralogical study, study of SPM, etc.

Cracks of various types and magnitude are seen on the marble surface and the possible reasons for the cracks are as follows:

1. Inherent defects in the stone developed due to the residual stress at the time of quarrying, trimming, etc.
2. These vertical cracks in the marble could be due to the download pressure exerted by the slabs placed above.
3. The mineral impurities in the marble have got preferentially leached by rain water and other factors leading to the formation of cracks.
4. Settlement of the foundation.
5. Chemical weathering.
6. Insulation weathering.
7. Due to rusting of iron dowels, loss of translucent shining surface, formation of cavities and pits on the surface, creaking and flaking of the surface, etc. are happening due to various factors, including environmental pollution.

Sandstone

Sandstone in general consist of quartz, feldspar with mica. Sandstone (sedimentary rock) is being used in Taj Mahal of different tint and colour though reddish with or without spots are used for construction whereas buff colour are also used alternatively with red one for the floorings. The sandstone came from Tantpura, Paharpur, Karuli-Hindaun, Sar-Mathura and also perhaps Fatehpur Sikri. Due to the atmospheric pollution, the possible effect on sandstone are the weight loss, water absorption and loss of compressive strength. Sandstone became little dark due to the formation of Gypsum skin due to the effect of Sulphuric acid (H_2SO_4). It plays a major role in the reduction of compressive strength and flaking. Attack of algae on sandstone surface creates black patches.

The structural stability, the nature of foundation and other constructional aspects of Taj Mahal have been studied in detail by various reputed organizations/agencies in addition to the Archaeological Survey of India. Each and every part of the mausoleum has been measured meticulously and systematic drawings have also been prepared (Fig. 5).

It is necessary to know the type, dimensions and the depth of the foundations as well as to establish the boundaries of the subsoil strata beneath the structure for the analysis of the

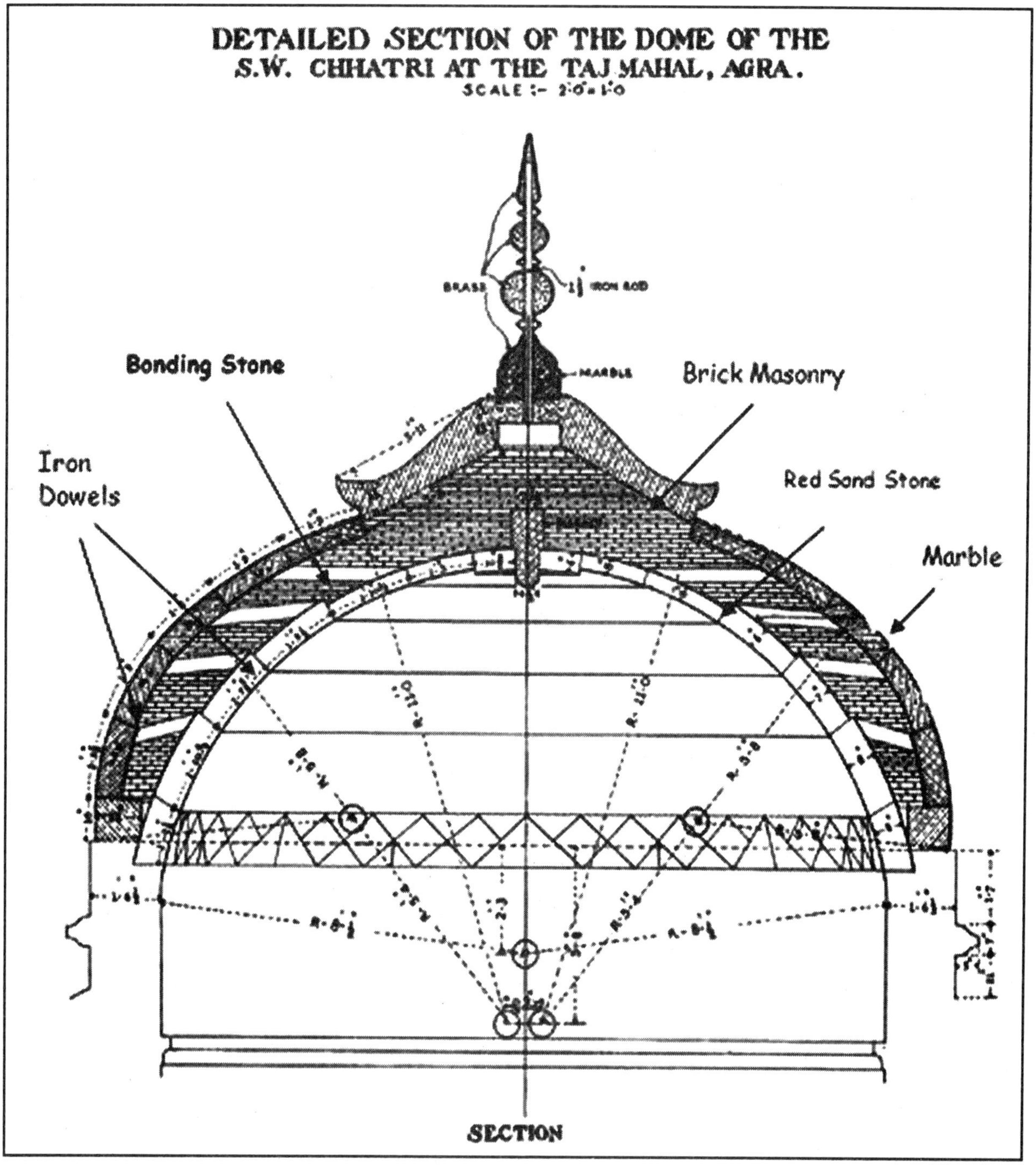

Fig. 5. Section of the drum of the Taj.

performance of the foundation of Taj Mahal. The geo-technical investigation was conducted with the intention of obtaining the details like subsoil strata beneath the structure, including the shear strength, compressibility and elastic properties of the soil strata; impounding of water on the behaviour of subsoil; probable type, dimension and the depth of the foundation; performance of the foundation, etc. The study of foundation and stability of structure revealed that the Taj Mahal is raised on a soiled foundation made of stone rubble and mortar. The approximate thickness of the foundation is 12 to 13 m. Series of ring-wells foundation are provided all along the river side to prevent erosion by the river water. The gaps in between the wells were filled with rubble-masonry. The soil mass below the masonry raft of 34.60 mts. thickness consists of a sandy layer of 9.44 mts. thickness and a clayey stratum of 65.60 mts. thickness resting on rock. The soil below the monument is in the submerged state due to the high water table level. The settlement analysis based on consolidation test data indicates that perhaps 99.4% of the anticipated ultimate settlement may have taken place already and the future settlement, if at all, is likely to be insignificant. The stress analysis indicated that the entire foundation system is in a state of vertical compression. There are, however, zones of small tensile stresses in regions around the contact areas.

The four free-standing minarets at the corners of the platform which has mausoleum in its centre look like ladies-in-waiting to the beautiful princess. It is not only a innovative design hitherto unknown to Mughal architects but also open a new avenue in the architectural vocabulary. In order to monitor the verticality of the minarets and other edifices, a number of benchmarks are fixed on the surface of the different structure of Taj Mahal. Benchmarks 1 to 88 are situated on the ground floor of Taj Mahal and 89 to 104 are located on the first floor. The Geodetic and Research branch of Survey of India has carried out periodical surveys, especially triangulation, traverse and precision leveling to check the verticality of its four minarets and other structures since 1940-41. From the above triangulation, traverse and levelling data of the years 1940-41, 1952-53, 1957-58, 1959-60, 1964-65, 1971-72, 1976-77, 1986-87, 1994-95 and 2004-05, it can be concluded that all the four minarets, the dome and the other structures of Taj Mahal remained quite stable in plan as well as in elevation from 1940-41 to 2004-05. The changes found are within the standard errors of geodetic observations.

Taj Mahal and the other monuments at Agra are not only the prime destination of tourism but also the source of economy of the nation in general and Agra in particular. These monuments are directly or indirectly responsible for the creation of many tourism-based jobs/establishments like hotel and restaurants, shopping complexes, handicraft industries, tourist operators, transport operators, guides, photographers, hawkers, etc. Taj Mahal is visited by 6000 to 8000 people everyday. Tourist inflow is very high in winter months, i.e., 10,000 to 15,000 visitors per day. Due to heavy tourist rush, long queues can be seen at the ticket booking windows and at the security checking points. The Archeological Survey of India has proposed to establish a Visitors' Facilitation Centre at the Fatehabad Courtyard (popularly known as Goshala) located near the Eastern Gate of the monument in consultation with the international and Indian experts after conserving the historic buildings of the Goshala complex without any alteration. Basic tourist amenities like drinking water, lockers, toilets, departmental publication sales counter, touch screen information kiosks and first aid centre, etc. will be provided in the proposed Visitors' Facilitation Centre.

13

Integration of the Boyas into the Andhra Society – A Study

C. SOMASUNDARA RAO

ABSTRACT

Scholars involved in the study of the social developments in Andhra history, hold the opinion that the Boyas were integrated into the Hindu society as Brahmanas during the early period of the Eastern Chalukyan rule and probably merged into the Andhra society, leaving no trace of their tribal antecedents after the 7th century AD. *They appear in the inscriptions as masters of the Guntur-Nellore region during 8th-9th century* AD. *Some time later, it is said that they lost their social position and became cattle-rearers in the Andhra temples. They regained their position as officials and small chieftains in 12th-13th centuries. It is now argued that the term 'boya' of 7th century inscriptions does not indicate the name of the tribe to which the person belonged, but an official who was connected with a village, identical with bhojaka or bhogika. From 11th century onwards, it is possible that the boyas could have become a caste of shepherds and later served the kings as officers and established their chieftaincies. The paper attempts at a study of the views relating to the acculturation of the Boyas into the Andhra society.*

The terms *boya* (singular) and *boi* (plural) occur in the inscriptions of Andhra Pradesh from 7th century AD to 15th century AD in different contexts. In the copper-plate grants of the Eastern Chalukyas of Vengi (AD 624-1076), particularly of the 7th century AD, a number of *Boyas* figure as recipients of *agrahara* villages from the ruling family. Again, in the 8th-9th century AD, Boya chieftains are known from the Pallava as well as Eastern Chalukyan inscriptions. Like the Renati Cholas and Banas, the ruling families of the *Boyas* had to change sides and submit to the authority of the Pallavas and Eastern Chalukyas, as times demanded. Their authority was suppressed during the reign of Gunaga Vijayaditya and the area of rule in Guntur-Prakasam-Nellore districts was annexed to his kingdom. Again, after 11th century AD, *Boyas* are known to have served as cattle-keepers in the temples of medieval Andhra. There are also references to some generals and rulers who had the suffix *boya* to their names.

This data has been utilized by some scholars to represent that the term *boya*, wherever it occurs, should refer to the *boya* tribe, which had ups and downs in course of centuries, i.e., they were admitted as Brahmanas in 7th century AD; they became chieftains in 8th-9th century AD; and later they fell from power, accepted service in the temples and again became generals or subordinate chiefs. This view-point is expressed by scholars like R.N. Nandi,[1] B.S.L. Hanumantha Rao[2] and B. Rajendra Prasad.[3] Though there are minor variations in their arguments, they were unanimous in considering this data as indicative of the different positions held by the *boyas* in the society of medieval Andhra. This has been questioned by P.V. Parabrahma Sastry[4] and C. Somasundara Rao.[5]

Now, we will deal with the evidence under various heads, viz., I) *Boya* integration into the society as Brahmanas; II) *Boya* rule in Guntur-Prakasam-Nellore area; III) *Boyas* in temple service; IV) *Boyas'* official position and rulership.

INTEGRATION INTO THE SOCIETY AS BRAHMANAS

The view that the *boyas* were admitted as Brahmanas rests upon the 7th-century copper-plate records of the Chalukyas of Vengi like the Kondanaguru grant of Indrabhattaraka,[6] the Koneki[7] and and Reyuru grants[8] of Vishnuvardhana II and the Chendaluru grant of Sarvalokasraya.[9]

In the Kondanaguru grant, four persons are mentioned at the end, with the suffix *bol,* who were probably the witnesses of the deed, according to Hultzsch.[10] They were not the recipients of the village, but only officers who must have attested the grant in question. Their names are Alapaka-*bol*, ...ppi-*bol*, Somayajula Vellekki-*bol* and Marata-*bol*. The donee was Chendisarman, son of Vishnusarman and grandson of Durgasarman, the last having been described as Irralur-*boya*. It is not clear why the grandfather of the donee was described as *boya* in singular and the witnesses as *bol* in plural. The names preceding the term *bol* or *boya* is no doubt the village-name, Alapaka or Vallekki or Marata or Irralur.

Hultzsch points out that the term *boya* might mean village clerk or Karanam, because a person was called *boya* of a village. Again, he says that this is doubtful, because two individuals were styled as Marata-*boya* in the Reyuru grant, which leads to the conclusion that *boya* might be the same as *vastavya* or resident.[11]

In the Koneki plates of Vishnuvardhana II,[12] there is a mention of 15 Brahmanas, apart from the principal donee Vidusarman who received the village. Vidusarman is described as Kanderu-*boya*-brahmana and Atukuru-*vastavya* (resident of Atukuru). Among the 15 Brahmanas who received shares in the gift-village, all the names excepting two end with *sarman*, the rest mentioning *boya*. Some of them are described as the *boyas* of Mudokuru, Kumunuru, Atukuru, Nadukuru, Veluchali, Kanparu and Irukuturu. It may be noted that most of the village-names end with *uru*, the usual suffix for a village. Here, there is a clear distinction between *vastavya* and *boya* as the donee was a resident of Atukuru and a *boya* of Kanderu. This shows that the view of Hultzsch that the two terms are synonyms was wrong. Again, it may be observed from this inscription that while the donee Vidusarman was a *vastavya* of Atukuru, the *boya* of Atukuru was Vishnusarman, mentioned as one of the allottees of the land-grant (6th donee). Hence, the editor of the grant, H.K. Narasimhaswami, opined that the term *boya* was a corruption of the term *bhogika*.

The Reyuru grant of Vishnuvarhana II[13] speaks of a large number of Brahmana scholars whose names end with *sarman*. Some of them, like the Koneki grant, were mentioned as *Boyas* of different places. It may be noted that the *gotra* of only the principal donee was given in the Koneki grant, while the allottees in the village were not given the name of the *gotra*. Here, in the Reyuru grant, a large number of them are described with their *gotra* name, though some are ignored.

The Chendalur plates of Sarvalokasraya,[14] belonging to c. AD 673, mention the gift of a village to six Brahmnas, five belonging to Kaundinya-*gotra* and one to the Kalabava-*gotra*. The peculiarity of the inscription is that the names of the recipients of the village are not mentioned; but five of them are described as *Boyas* of villages like Vangara, Kollipura, Pidena, Kuriyeda, Kodinki (Koneki); only one of them is described as *vastavya* of Katura. This is strange because earlier we got the names of persons, either as *vastavyas* or as *boyas,* marking a distinction between the two. Here, the *boya* of a village is meaningful if it refers to an office held by the person. When a resident is mentioned, the name of the person should be specified.

From these inscriptions, scholars held different opinions on what is meant by the term *boya*. They hold that these were *boyas*, who were an uncivilized tribe, but admitted into the brahmanical fold. They regard that the Eastern Chalukyas faced difficulties in consolidating their power in Palli-*rashtra* and Karma-*rashtra* located in the Guntur-Prakasam areas, because they had bitter conflict with the Pallavas. Then they pitched upon the idea of taking these *boyas* who were hunters into the Hindu society and associated them with the Vedic ritualism.

This proposition poses a number of problems. There is no clear evidence to show that the Chalukya-Pallava conflict ended by the integration of the *boyas* as Vedic priests. No doubt, the Guntur-Prakasam-Nellore area was the arena of conflict between the Chalukyas of Vengi and Pallavas, starting with the invasion of Pulakesin II. It continued till the time of Nandivarman Pallavamalla and beyond, up to the reign of Gunaga Vijayaditya in the middle of 9th century AD. The proposition that the priests would strengthen the empire by their advocacy of internal peace is doubtful. When the *boyas* were good hunters and archers, the Chalukyas should have taken them better into military service than into priesthood. If by such a stratagem, the Chalukyas could raise the status of the *boyas* as priests, why was it not devised by the Pallavas or Vishnukundis at an earlier date to resolve their conflicts? The circumstances leading to their acculturation are not clear.

Again, if by 7th century AD, their status was on par with the Brahmanas, why is it that later, when they became military generals and rulers, they did not describe themselves as of a particular *gotra*? When chiefs and kings, hailing from lower social groups, rose to high positions, they sought legitimization by assuming the *gotras* and/or connected themselves with the solar or lunar race. Such an instance is not at all available in our records in the case of the *boyas*.

There is a doubt whether, after being proclaimed as a Brahmana and after assuming the *gotra*-name, a *boya* would still prefer to suffix the term *boya*, which is of a lower status in society. If for the moment we accept that the *boyas* were elevated to the Brahmana status by 7th century AD, would the society have recognized their status? Would the *sudra* families, which were living with the other upper castes, have reconciled themselves, when the uncivilized *boyas* were elevated to the highest position in society?

Scholars hold that along with the term *boya*, their professional group is also mentioned in some of the inscriptions. In this case, the Koneki and Reyuru records are put to use. Pullalur-*boya* meant the grassmen section; Manda-*boya* represents herdsman; Eddondi-*boya* refers to bullocks (from *eddu*); Dudi-*boya* relates to cotton-production; Koyila-*boya* relates to the temple. One may point out that this type of particular profession of the *boyas* was never intended by the composers of the inscription, because it has nothing to do with the Vedic ritualism. On the other hand, most of these were village-names. For instance, Dudi may be identified with the village Dundigam in the Kavali taluk of Nellore district/village Dudyala in the Nandikotkur taluk of Kurnool district. Mandu may be identified with Mandadi in Palnad taluk of the Guntur district; Koyila could be Kovelampadu in the Kanigiri taluk of Nellore district/Koilkuntla in the Kurnool district. Ala-(*boya*) may be the same as Alavapadu (Ongole taluk), Alavala (Narasaraopeta

Taluk)/Alapadu (Tenali taluk). Pandiri (*boya*) may be identified with Pandillapalle/Pandrapadu (both in the Bapatla taluk of Guntur district/Pandipadu in the Kurnool district). Therefore, there is no substance in identifying the particular professions of the *boyas* in the names, which were those of villages.

It may be noted that the term *boya* does not refer to the tribal name, but to an officer or a big landholder. It could be derived from *bhojaka* or *bhogika* mentioned in the Pallava and Salankayana grants. The Hirehadagalli plates of Pallava Skandavaram refer to *bhojakas* of different villages (*gama-gama-bhojaka*).[15] Reference is made to one Mulakura-bhoja in one of the grants of the Salankayanas.[16] *Bhogikas* are mentioned in the Eastern Ganga grants. The Narasimhapalli plates of Hastivarman state that the king gifted a village at the instance of one *bhogika* called Buddhamanchi.[17] The Purle plates of Indravarman, dated in Ganga year 137,[18] refer to the engraver of the plate, Khandichandra, as the son of Aditya-*bhogi*. These instances show that *Bhojaka, Bhogika* and *bhogi* are employed to indicate the designations of officers. The absence of reference to personal names of the *boyas* suggests that they were officials, besides being landholders. The *boya* of a particular place was so well known that records do not refer to his individual name. D.C. Sircar[19] and H.K. Narasimhaswami[20] opine that they were big landholders or *jagirdars*.

BOYA RULE IN GUNTUR – PRAKASAM – NELLORE AREA (ANDHRA PRADESH)

The *boyas* in 8th-9th centuries AD seem to have occupied parts of Guntur-Prakasam-Nellore region and probably served the Pallavas and the Eastern Chalukyas at different times. The Udayendiram plates of Nandivarman Pallavamalla (AD 731-796)[21] refer to the conquest of the *boya* area, which was held by Prithvivyaghra, by the Pallava general Udayachandra and later the conquest of Vishnuraja's territory, which is presumed to be the Eastern Chalukyan Kingdom. Vishnuraja is identified with Vishnuvardhana III. This reference to both the *boya* Chief and Chalukyan ruler indicates that probably the *boya* ruler was a feudatory of the Vengi Chalukyas and, hence, the defeat of both the feudatory and the king.

The next reference to the *boyas* is found in the Addanki inscription of Pandaranga, the Military General of Gunaga Vijayaditya (AD 848-891).[22] He is said to have captured 12 *boya*-Kottams, among which Kandukur and Kattem seem to be prominent. The *boya* Chief's name is sometimes taken to be Vaso *boya*; but such a name is not mentioned in the inscriptions. The General, in another inscription, is said to have burnt the city of Nellore, probably connected with the *boya* territory. It is also said that he drove the *boyas* to forests which shows that they were tribals or forest-dwellers. Except in the Pallava and Chalukya inscriptions, there is no inscription of any *boya* Chief. This area was occupied by Gunaga Vijayaditya and it was bestowed on the great general Pandaranga. Here, it is a clear reference to the role of the tribal *boyas*.

BOYAS IN TEMPLE SERVICE

Inscriptions of medieval Andhra (AD 1000-1600) mention *boyas* in large numbers in connection with the gifts of cattle to the temple for lighting a lamp. The Pancharamas, Bezwada, Tripurantakam, Bapatla, etc. (any Shaivite or Vaishnavite temple) employed these *boyas* who received cattle from the donors, reared them and supplied a stipulated measure of ghee to the concerned temple. Sometimes, the *boyas* themselves gifted cattle to the temple. In some cases, the *boya* was called *golla*, which is the word used in Telugu even now for shepherd or cowherd.

Scholars hold that the *boyas* who were admitted into Brahmanahood later lost their social position and became shepherds. Even if this is accepted, it is difficult to explain how and why the *boyas* of the earlier period had to come over to coastal Andhra or different parts of the present day Andhra Pradesh, instead of confining themselves to the Guntur-Nellore region. Therefore, it is doubtful whether all the *boyas* of temple-inscriptions were of the *boya* tribe itself.

BOYAS' OFFICIAL POSITION AND RULERSHIP

There are a number of officials who had the suffix *boya* to their names. Nagana-*boya*[23] served Bhimavallabha of the Kona Haihaya family; Bodde-*boya*[24] was serving the Chagis of Gudimetta. One Kuna-*boya*[25] fought a battle and was killed in the battle. Jilla-*boya*[26] fought a battle at Kochcheruvula kota against the Karnataka armies and brought victory to the Velanadu ruler. B.S.L. Hanumantha Rao regards that the Kompula chiefs were of the *boya* extraction and served the Kakatiyas. Many of them made donations to temples as officers or individual chieftains.

From the above, we have to note that the *boyas* of the 7th century inscriptions were not related to the *boya* tribe, but Brahmana officers and landholders; *boyas* of the 8th-9th century who figure as chieftains, either under the subordination of the Chalukyas of Vengi or Pallavas of Kanchi were definitely of the *boya* tribe; *boyas* after 11th century AD, who figure as cattle-keepers and temple servants, could be either of the tribe or separate communities among the Sudras. After 11th century, there are references to the officers and ruling families who had the suffix *boya*, which shows that they could be of the tribal affiliation or of the Sudra caste. Anyway, the *boyas* assumed offices and became rulers only after the 11th century AD.[27]

This gets some confirmation from other sources when many families of the Vaisya and Sudra orders gained social mobility. The Vaisyas of Penugonda, the Balanjas, the Telikis and other artisan communities have eulogized themselves like the Brahmanas and Rajanyas of the earlier period. In this context may be quoted two inscriptions, viz., the Ayyangaripalem inscription of Kalagarabharana[28] and the Bezwada inscription of Trikoti-*boya*,[29] both palaeographical belonging to 10th century AD. The first inscription is found in the Jalpesvara temple and eulogizes the work of the architect Kalagarabharana. The Bezwada inscription says that Trikoti-*boya* descended from a person who guided Arjuna to the Indrakila hill, where the latter did penance to get the Pasupata-*astra*. Trikoti-*boya* is compared in the inscription to Karna in strength and generosity and to Hanuman in loyalty to his master, probably the Vengi Chalukya ruler of the times.

NOTES

1. *Proceedings of Indian History Congress*, Bhagalpur Sesion, 1968, pp. 94-103.
2. *Proceedings of South Indian History Congress*, Hyderabad Session, 1986, pp. 58-64.
3. *Social Mobility in Medieval Andhra*, Hyderabad, 1995, pp. 76 ff.
4. *Journal of Indian History*, Vol. LVI, 1975, pp. 21-25.
5. *Proceedings of Andhra Pradesh History Congress, Tenth Session*, Guntur, 1986, pp. 70-75.
6. *Journal of Ancient Indian History*, Vol. XVIII, 1988-89, Calcutta: Calcutta University, pp. 1-8.
7. *Ep. Ind*, Vol. XVIII, pp. 1 ff.
8. *Ep. Ind.*, Vol. XXXI., pp. 74 ff.
9. *Ind. Ant.*, Vol. VII, pp. 185 ff.
10. *Ep. Ind*, Vol. VIII, pp. 236 ff.
11. *Ep. Ind.*, Vol. XVIII, p. 4.
12. *Ep. Ind.*, Vol. XVIII, p. 2.

13. *Ep. Ind.*, Vol. XXXI, pp. 74 ff.
14. *Ind. Ant.*, Vol. VII. pp. 85 ff.
15. *Ep. Ind.*, Vol. VIII. pp. 236 ff.
16. *Ep. Ind.*, Vol. I, pp. 1 ff.
17. *Ep. Ind.*, Vol. IX, pp. 56 ff.
18. *Ep. Ind.*, Vol. XXIII, pp. 62 ff.
19. *Ep. Ind.*, Vol. XIV, pp. 360 ff.
20. Sircar, D.C. 1965. *Indian Epigraphy,* Vol. I, Delhi: Motilal Banarsidass, p. 344.
21. *Ep. Ind.*, Vol. XXXI, p. 77.
22. *SII*, Vol. II, p. 372.
23. *Ep. Ind.*, Vol. XIX, pp. 271-77.
24. *SII*, Vol. V, No. 156.
25. *SII*, Vol. VI, No. 94.
26. *Ibid.*
27. *SII*, Vol. X, No. 162.
28. B.S.L. Hanumantha Rao. 1995. *Social Mobility in Medieval Andhra,* Hyderabad: Telugu University, p. 91, *Epi. Andh.*, Vol. V, pp. 33ff.
29. *SII*, Vol. X, No. 33; *ASR*, 1915-16, p. 98; *ASPP.*, Vol. VII, pp. 227-231.

ABBREVIATIONS

ASR: Archaeological Survey Reports. Archaeological Survey of India, Delhi.
ASPP: Andhra Sahitya Parishad Patrika (Journal of Telugu Academy) Hyderabad.
Ep. Ind: Epigraphia Indica.
SII: South Indian Inscriptions.
Epi. Andh: Epigraphia Andhrika.
Ind. Ant: Indian Antiquary.

14

A Unique Inscription of Kulottunga Chola II at Srirangam

R. NAGASWAMY

ABSTRACT

There is a general misconception among the historians as well as laymen about the religious conditions of the Chola rule during the medieval times in Tamil Nadu. Folk stories also developed as to how the Chola emperor Kulottunga II became a Saiva bigot and prosecuted Ramanuja, the Vaishnava teacher par excellence. This paper on solid epigraphical evidences argues, on the contrary, that the Chola emperor Kulottunga II was in fact a devotee of Lord Sri Ranganatha of Srirangam and he along with his queen made lavish donations to this Vaishnava temple.

It is generally held that Kulottunga Chola II (AD 1133-1150) was responsible for persecuting the Vaishnava Acharya, Ramanuja because of his violent antagonism towards Vaishnavism. Even a movie recently released introduces an episode at the beginning that Kulottunga II and the Saivites were responsible for the Anti-vaishnava feeling which caused a devotee of Ramanuja to be thrown into the sea. This is shown as a historical introduction to the factious story to follow. An inscription of Kulottunga Chola would be read with interest in this connection, which will show a different picture of the King Kulottunga Chola II, in contrast to the recent movie referred above.

The inscription is found on the south wall of the fourth *prakara* of the Sriranganatha temple and was copied in the year 1936 by the Government Epigraphist, a summary of which was published in English as ARE. No. 56. The full text is published in the *South Indian Inscriptions*, Vol. XXIV, No. 123. The following English summary precedes the text in the above volume.

"Kulottunga II, commences with the introduction 'Pumamannu padumam'. Purports to be an order issued by the deity leasing out some temple lands to the 'Kovanavar' who were to plant areca palms thereon and pay a specified yield to the temple year after year. The inscription is dated in the seventh year of the king's reign (Kulottunga II) and the dating works out to AD 1140, Feb. 10, Sunday."

The inscription begins with the well known *prasasti* of Kulottunga II and mentions "*Rajakesarivarmarana Tribhuvana cakravarti Kulottunga Choladevar,* who was seated with his queen Bhuvana-muludiayal, like Siva seated with Uma on the Himalayas." As this *prasasti* is found in hundreds of Second Kulottunga's records, it is certain the king was Kulottunga II. The presence of this inscription at Srirangam would show Kulottunga II was no bigot as is projected. Moreover, at the very beginning of the *prasasti* he says, *"This king was the very lord Vishnu born in the line of Surya (solar race) as a result of the penance under taken by the three worlds."*

This is a very important statement which shows that he was the Vishnu on earth born as a result of penance undertaken by the entire world. So the attribution of anti-Vaishnavism to this monarch is totally ahistorical. There are two more inscriptions of this king at Srirangam which would give a lie to the proposition that he persecuted Ramanuja because he was against Vaishnavism. It is also seen that the order issued through this record in the name of the god was approved by the very same king.

According to the record, the Sri Vaishnavas of the temple requested Lord Sriranganatha that coconut and areca palms should be planted by the *Kovanavas* of the temple who should pay annually specified number of areca nuts to the temple as lease. It was customary to make all requests in the presence of the lord as if all the transactions were done with the approval of the deity. Similarly, the orders issued by the king were also said to be issued by the deity. So the order in this case was recorded as if issued by Lord Sri Ranganatha, the tutelary deity of Srirangam. But it also goes to record the order was agreed to by the king who as per procedure consented and ordered the same may be executed. This would also show the king was no fanatic.

At this stage, it is necessary to say that the Chola emperors called Sriranganatha as their family deity (*Kuladhanam*), a phrase which we find in an inscription from the same temple issued in the reign of Kulottunga III. It is not surprising that they called the deity as their *kuladhanam* because they came in the solar race and the deity was worshipped by *Ikshvaku* Sri Rama and other ancestors. It is also known that Parantaka Chola I in the beginning of 10th century AD performed *tulabhara* rite in the temple with gold. The Chola Viraranjendra, the third son of Rajendra Chola, mentions in his Kanyakumari inscription that he presented a special golden jewel set with precious gems to Lord Ranganatha. So the claim that Srirangam temple was the family deity of the Chola emperors is attested both in literature and epigraphs.

It is seen that most of the inscriptions of the Chola period found in the Srirangam temple tell us that all the administrative officers called *Sri Karyam* in the records, were high-ranking officers like *Senapati* (commanders), and others who bear royal titles like *Brahmadhirajar* and so on. They are specifically called *Adhikarikal* and were the highest officers to issue orders locally to the temple authorities. They were also mostly appointed annually, and were responsible heads of the administrative setup of the temple. That shows the Srirangam temple was considered the royal temple and administered by the Chola kings directly through their officers. All these prove beyond doubt that the so-called persecution of Ramanuja is a simple and pure myth.

The inscription is also interesting from another angle. The Lord Ranganatha is said to have accepted the request of the Srivaishnavas and the king accepted the same and he issued the orders in the proper course. At the end of the record also, there is a statement, that it is an order obviously of the king though there is certain amount of damage in the record. The inscription ends saying, *"Triubhuvana muludiayal Anai,"* i.e., order of Tribhuvana muludaiyal. *Tribhuvana muludaiyal* was the name of Kulottunga II's chief queen. We have seen that she was seated with the king on the royal throne like Uma seated with Siva on *Kailasa*. As this was an order issued by her also, the same is found mentioned at the end.

The Chola inscriptions, particularly of this period, say that when the king was coronated, the chief queen was also coronated at the same time. The record states that she got simultaneously the crown, the royal throne and the power to issue orders. It is virtually a joint rule in which the queen acquires equal powers and her order has the same validity as that of the king (*okka mudi kavittal udan Anaiyum, udan irukkaiyum kadan akave perraruli*). The ancient Hindu Law books like *Dharmasastras* empower such a position for the queen. That is the reason in most sculptural representations, the king when shown, is seated on the throne with his queen. This is a religious requirement and legal empowerment. So the order of the queen in this case would point out that it had her approval as well.

It should not be construed that such a privilege was available only for the royal queens and not to ordinary women. The *Dharmasastras* gave the same power to housewives as well. In all the Hindu families, this is the law that the wife has equal right like her husband in all religious and social acts. It is practised to this day in every household in a symbolic way though its significance is not understood. In any act of gift or other important rites, the wife will have to pour a spoon of water in the hand of the husband which stands for this right. The pouring of water over the hand is symbolic of authorizing her husband to perform the act on her behalf. This would be performed in the presence of the assembled elders who are the members of the assembly standing witness to the act. So the Hindu society has recognized this inherent right of women from times immemorial. That is what is signified by the term "*Tribhuvana muludiayal anai*" at the end of this record. There are some more inscriptions in different parts of Tamil Nadu, especially in the Chola period, attesting to the recognition of this right.

The inscription of Kulottunga at Srirangam has given us valuable information on two important aspects of Indian history.

15

Kingship and State Formation in Medieval Andhradesa

P.S. KANAKA DURGA

ABSTRACT

Kingship is the conventional and obligatory empowerment (coercive and conciliatory) of the king to rule over his kingdom. It articulates the king with different power structures of the temporal and sacred realms of his kingdom. The nature of kingship and its symbols of sustenance depend upon the demands of the socio-political needs of the people. During the medieval times, the ideology of kingship lay in the separation and integration of 'temporal' and 'sacred' realms of the groups or individuals involved. However, the ideology and interpretation of dharma underlying kingship shifted its paradigms throughout the historical formations.

So far, the historians defined the medieval South Indian state in different models. All these models emphasized Andhradesa as a peripheral precinct of other South Indian dynastic powers. The Indian notion of culture represents two strands, the marga (Sanskritic) and the desi (non-Sanskritic), representing the elite and folk ways of life identified with the Literacy (written) and Oracy (mnemonic/oral) modes of communication. The marga notion represents the 'ideal selves' or the 'mental constructs' of the elite, operating nationally over almost all societies as 'pan cultural ideology'. The desi traditions are the practical ways of life that emphasize more on practice of the ideologies based on the norms of marga life, but represent typical regional/vernacular adaptations of the respective ecological zones.

This paper focuses on the emergence of an independent sovereign and 'popular state' in medieval Andhra articulated by 'popular kingship', which is designed on the philosophy of integration and legitimation of emergent ideologies and groups of people who created and perpetuated them.

INTRODUCTION

Kingship is the conventional and obligatory empowerment pre-bended upon the king to rule over his kingdom. It is a coercive and conciliatory mechanism that enables the king to legitimately integrate different spheres of power within the state. The nature of kingship and its symbols of sustenance depend much upon the demands of the politico-cultural and socio-economic needs of the people. During the medieval times, the ideology of kingship lay in the separation and integration of 'temporal' and 'sacred' realms of the groups or individuals involved in it by protecting *dharma* through *danda*. Hence, the purpose of kingship is two-fold: (i) to validate the king himself as the ruler and (ii) to legitimize the new social roles of emerging social groups. However, the ideology of *dharma* underlying kingship was dynamic and frequently shifted its paradigms throughout the historical formations to meet the changing needs of the populace and save the state from socio-political anarchy.

The Indian notion of cultural formations, the *marga* (Sanskritic) and the *desi* (non-Sanskritic) symbolizing the elite and folk ways of life, were identified with the Literacy (written) and Oracy (mnemonic/oral) modes of expression. They were represented as parallel streams of cultures patronized by royalty to appease both the walks of society. However, the *marga* notion represents the 'ideal selves' or the 'mental constructs' of the elite, operating notionally over almost all societies as 'pan cultural ideology'. It is the 'elitists' view-point which represents homogeneity through language and *Sastric* traditions based on written law, dress code and rules of social stratification. They are projected as authoritative norms to be followed by one and all if one chooses to be called as elite or civilized. The *desi* traditions are the practical ways of life that emphasize more on practice of the ideologies based on the norms of *marga* life, but local represents typical vernacular adaptations of the respective ecological zones. It contributed for different versions and variations in cultural practices. *Desi* displays periphery and heterogeneity echoing voices of different cultural communities through their colloquial genres of cultures, norms and values that mark their respective identities. The State strategically shifted its sponsorship to these two streams of cultures throughout the historical formations to integrate different strata of people in their realms.

While the Calukyas evoked *desi* (native/local) consciousness, the Kakatiyas synchronized both the *marga* and *desi* patterns, thereby resulting popular ideologies through a vernacular state wherein administration is run on sharing and participation. Such an incorporative integrative syncretic ideology formed the premise of the Kakatiyan kingship. This can be designated as popular kingship as it could co-ordinate different politico-social segments of the society.

In the light of the above discussion, this paper focuses on the process of construction of kingship and state formation in Andhradesa from the time of the Calukyas of Vengi to the Kakatiyas of Warangal. The former was established in the riverine base of Coastal Andhra and the latter in the uplands that sustained on tank irrigation. The geographical and dynastic shifts are correlated with changes in the ideology and icons of kingship in Andhradesa. The paper further traces emergence of kingship from a monarchical state to vernacular state articulated through heroic, *dharmic*/moral, ritual and popular kingship.

The onset of medievality in Southern India is attributed to the rise of Calukyas at Badami and the establishment of their collateral line in Andhradesa as Calukya dynasty at Vengi (Coastal Andhra) by AD 624. The socio-political crises of the pre-medieval period were partly due to distribution of power-conceded shifts in administrative strategies (altering the icons of kingship and governance) and centres (ecozone-wet to dry). The history of Andhradesa, from the Satavahanas (2nd century BC to 2nd century AD) to the end of Vijayanagara dynasty (in late sixteenth century AD), witnessed several politico-historical upheavals. They prompted the upsurge of significant cultural ideologies and practices that determined the philosophy of 'kingship' and 'state formation' of the medieval polity. The studies conducted by J. Gonda (1996), A.M. Hocart (1979, 1977) and L.D. Dumont (1957) on various aspects of political authority stressed the inseparability of ritual and politics irrespective of the type of kingship.[1]

IDEOLOGY OF INDIAN KINGSHIP

R.S. Sharma (1991: 49-61), basing on the information provided by Puranas, epics like *Mahabharata* besides Jain and Buddhist traditions, holds that the emergence of family and private property necessitated formation of state and emergence of king and kingship. The king was required to maintain social order dictated by ideal norms and values and at the same time they were loosened as 'transcendental norms' to accommodate and fix new entrants in social hierarchy. To provide a sense of security among his people by punishing wrongdoers and extending protection from thieves, robbers and external aggressors were counted as chief obligations of a king. To let go an offender unpunished amounted to sin. Hence, 'protection' can be regarded as the central conceptual component of the idea of kingship in India. It was, therefore, a special duty of the king to protect and look after those who needed them most. Manu explicitly states that it is the duty of the king to protect the property of everybody. It is the weaker ones who deserve king's protection most; the office of the king was created to escape the *matsya nyaya* where the stronger would roast the weaker like fish on a spit. The Hindu theory of state conjures two concepts, the *mamatva* (*mineness*) or *svatva* (*svam)* that is the property and *dharma* as law, justice, duty and also as ritual. *Dharma* was the foundation for individual and collective security and identity without which the state witnesses socio-political anarchy. In return of the protection that the king extended to his subjects, he was empowered with authority to impose and collect taxes from them in the form cash or kind.

Adiparva of *Mahabharata* (135-138) prescribes three modes of acquiring kingship: those who were (i) *sakulina* (born in same caste as that of the Pandavas/Kauravas, the *ksatriyas), sura* (valorous) and *sena parikrshita* (capacity to be the commander of the army). Manu further clarifies that (XII-10) one who knows the Vedas is qualified to be a king.

During the medieval times, the ideology of kingship lay in the separation and integration of 'temporal' and 'sacred' realms of the groups or individuals involved in it. The former represents 'actual' status and the latter represents the 'ritual' status. If the temporal power needed legitimation through spiritual authority, the people representing the latter sought 'protection' from the former and hence such 'reciprocity of the mutual sustenance' fostered 'identity formations' through display of symbolic behaviours in the loci that are frequently visited. Temporal powers authorize the extent of royal power in terms of the designations *mandalika* (feudatory), *mahamandalesvara* (bigger feudatory*), raja* (king), *maharaja* (independent king), and *cakravarti* (monarch). It cannot be determined by the actual spatial boundaries, because no dynasty or ruler could keep up his spatial domains continuously for longer periods for mutual distrust and frequent shifting of alliances of the *mandalikas* among themselves and also with their overlords. This made spatial/political boundaries much fluid. Protection is related to the ideal of social order as defined by the sacred domain. The position of *dharma* was safeguarded by *danda* (Thapar 1978: 31) and the latter was regulated and operated according to the prescriptions of the former. *Danda* has secular and sacred connotations, intended by the 'sacred' realm not as a political expedient but for the preservation of social orders (P.V. Kane 1974, Ch. 33). The divine origin theory of the king later led to the notion of 'homologisation of king and god' in the conceptualization of medieval kingship.

Heroic kingship: Satavahana times

The kingship that uses *danda* for the regulation of social order and righteousness can be designated as 'heroic kingship'. During the ancient period, the Satavahanas (c. 205 BC-c. AD 220), who rose to power from Paithan in the West, got extended their sway over Deccan including Andhradesa. The regime began and expanded in the fertile lands of Deccan, in the alluvial belts of Krishna,

Godavari (Maharashra and Andhradesa), Narmada and Tapti (Central India), and Kaveri (South). The vast area of the empire covering different geographical landscapes – deltaic, arid, dry, forest, hilly terrains – inhabited by multicultural population needed 'heroic kingship' to integrate the 'centralized-bureaucratic power structure' (R.C. Majumdar 1951: 303-34; K.A.N. Sastry 198: 50-66; A.S. Altekar 1972: 174-6; Krishna Murali 1977: 191-8). The following are some of the features of heroic kingship:

(i) The actual base of 'heroic kingship' was coercive power and extended authority through officialdom. The inscriptions of Gautamiputra Satakarni substantiate that the accession to power and annexation of new territories mark the symbols and ideological precepts of heroic kingship.[2]

(ii) The ritual base was the Brahminical religion situated in *yajna*, the royal sacrifice sanctioned by 'Vedic ritualism' and they represented the king as the sacrificer who exchanges gifts with the allies and subordinates. The 'Brahmin-ksatriya alliance' is evidenced in 'Heroic kingship' wherein the process of legitimation of royalty was through sacrificial rituals. The complexities that arose in exercising the coercive powers were cushioned through rituals sanctioned by the *dharmic* ideologies pumped in polity.

(iii) Public display of royal power largely depended upon the valour and intimidation expressed through conquest and war[3] and also as the upholders of *varna dharma* as revealed by the *prasastis* (eulogies) of the inscriptions that depict the entitlements (*birudavali*) and filiations (*vamsavali*) of the kings. The Satavahana society was heterogeneous and included several pockets of foreign populace (Yavanas, Sakas and Palhavas), perhaps leading to caste proliferation and contamination.

(iv) Traditionally, *varnasamkara* is considered as the premise of social anarchy. The *rajadharma* empowered the kings to uphold the fourfold *varna dharma* to establish social order. The sacrifices were widely accepted by contemporary *dharmic* ideologies as purificatory rituals. The kings were designated to perform Vedic sacrifices as expiatory rituals on hand and as legitimizing their claims over the colossal empire through kingship. The Naneghat inscription of Naganika gives a string of Vedic sacrifices conducted by her husband Satakarni I.[4] The heroic kinship represents 'brahman-ksatriya alliance' in state formation. It was held that performance of sacrifices like *Aswamedha* establishes the ruler as an undisputed independent monarch king, Rajasuya, associated by 'ritual dice', ascertains the 'sovereignty' and *Vajapeya* associated by public performance of chariot race in front of invitees from different corners of his empire fixes the king as absolute and paramount sovereign over his newly designated empowerment.

Moral (Dharmic) kingship: Chalukyan times

Politico-historical backdrop

The emergence of independent Vengi Calukyan state took almost three centuries after its inception in c. AD 624 as a peripheral precinct of the Badami Calukyas of the Westen Deccan. Almost three centuries after the fall of the Satavahana Empire, the Calukyas of Badami attained imperial status at the time of Pulakesin II in Western Deccan (AD 624). He conquered Kalinga and Kosala in the north and extended his regime up to Kanchi in the South by disrupting the powers of Pallavas and Colas. He swayed over the land between sea coasts in the east and west. He consecrated his brother Kubjavishuvardhana as ruler of *Vengi* in AD 624. His line of kings flourished in Andhradesa for three centuries as Vengi Calukyas or Eastern Calukyas in different statuses, as feudatories, independent and finally as imperial powers. The Calukyan power underwent a series of political upheavals in its career, because the establishment of the kingdom itself was rooted in a fertile riverine basin, which was always contested by the rulers of the border kingdoms of the north and south, the *Kalingas* and Pallavas and Colas respectively and also from local potentates like Vishnukundins who were still powerful in that region. For more than two centuries, Vengi Calukyas struggled to free themselves from these political threats and attain supremacy as rulers. Later, the constant menace from the newly emerged kingdoms, the Rashtrakutas of Malkhed and the Calukyas of Kalyani for possessing the *Vengi mandala,* created political unrest in Western Andhra. Finally, they owed matrimonial alliance with the Colas of Tanjore in the South. They flourished as Calukya-Colas for a century till the Kakatiyas, who were the feudatories of the Western Calukyas, established an independent kingdom in Telangana region by AD 1158. The constant struggle for consolidation of the state and internecine warfares necessitated the Calukyan state to frequently shift the nature and icons of kingship throughout its regime-formative period, independent dynastic rule and Imperial rule in the banner of Calukya-Chola emperors.

These situations demanded the Calukyas to find new ideologies and icons of kingship to integrate different segments of power, within and outside their temporal domains. Different phases of their political ascendancy, formative, independent and imperial statuses were corroborated respectively with heroic, *dharmic* and ritual kingship.

Origin Myths as Legitimisers of Calukyan line

The struggle of Calukyas for political ascendancy and legitimation of power is reflected in their origin myths that gave them genealogical links and purity of birth. The origin myth and the eulogies of the Calukyan line reflect their struggle to establish their 'identity' on the paradigm of 'kingship' by ascertaining ksatriya-hood to attain sovereign status.

Vikramankadevacaritra of Bilhana gives an interesting account of the origination of the Calukyas. The myth of the Calukyas traces their origin to Brahma. When Lord Brahma was giving his morning libations, Indra came and asked him to put an end to godlessness on the earth since no one was performing Vedic sacrifices and oblations to gods. He requested him to create a hero who could save the earth from lawlessness. Then Brahma looked into his chuluka, the hollow of his palm which he held to pour water for libation. A powerful warrior fit to protect the world sprang up from the hollow of his palm. From him who was born from Chuluka, the Calukyas descended. Among them was Harita who was the first progeny of the line. Manavya, whose humbleness put an end to the pride of the wicked kings on the earth, was the founder of their gotra, Manavyasa. The Ranastipundi inscription of Calukya Vimaladitya goes further in tracing their origin to Brahma claiming the lineage of Somavamsa. When Vijayaditya of the line was migrating to south, he came into conflict with Trilochana Pallava of Pallava line. He under took deforestation and land reclamation situated to the south of Krishna river and established agraharas extended who was asserting power by land reclamation and deforestation and caused the settlement of brahmin families from Ahicchatra and different parts of south India. In this, Vijayaditya died and his pregnant wife was rescued by a Brahmin scholar Vishnubhattaraka Somayaji of Mudivema Agrahara. She delivered a son and named him as Vishnuvardhana after her savior (B.V. Krishna Rao: 1973: 56).[5]

The origin of the Calukyas from the palm of the divine hand of Brahma, their acquisition of royal power by the strength of the coercive power of their shoulders claiming ksatriyahood and representation of Brahman as a saviour of their progenitors were clear landmarks in the process of transformation of Calukyan kingship from 'heroic' to 'ritual' through *'dharmic'* ideologies. Such transformation conceded with the base of kingship from *yajna* to *vamsa* through genealogies. It further explains the gradual transition of the Brahman alliances from 'Ksatriyas to Sudras'. The origination of the Calukyan line from the palm (*culuka*) of Brahma (but not the shoulder) suggests their origin from the service community; the *sudras* and the depiction of Brahmin as a redeemer of their fortunes substantiates this shift of alliances. The *Anusasana parva* (Section CXLIII) of *Mahabharata* sanctions the upward social mobility of humble castes into higher social ranks through behavioural purity attained by observing austerities and rituals.

In the formative times of the kingdom, as shown in their records, *heroic kingship* empowered the kings to consolidate their power. The kings like Pulakesin I and II, Vishnuvardhana, Ammaraja, etc. were eulogized as the performers of Vedic sacrifices. They held high-sounding imperialistic entitlements and mythical filiations that supported their coercion. It was imperative for them to exert coercive power to suppress all oppositions in the state. The inscriptions from Tammiyaleru (c. AD 660), Amudalapadu (AD 660), Venapalli (AD 675) and Pallipadu (AD 682), from Mahaboobnagar district, praise Pulakesin II as one who was sanctified by the ritual bath taken after the successful completion of *Asvamedha* sacrifice (*Asvamedhavabhrita pavitrikrita gatra*). Kirtivarma I, the donor of the above records, mentions that they belonged to *Manayasa gotra*, which is honoured by the entire populace of the world (*salala jagadabhivandyamana Mananyasa gotranam)* and obtained their boar crest *(varaha lanchana)* by the grace of the feet of Lord Narayana. They were said to be sons of Goddess Hariti and they were protected by lord Karttikeya ever since the times of their great grand father. He achieved victory over the confederacy of their enemies relying on the strength of their shoulders and his feet were adorned by the thrones of his enemies who were defeated in the war (*svabhujabala vijita ripusamiti ravanataneka narapati makuta labhu gatita charanah*). These records further refer to the illustrious victory of Pulakesin II over Sriharsha of Kanauj.[6] The Vengi Calukyan king Jayasimhavallabha, who could suppress all the rebellious forces during the formative period of their dynasty, held titles like *Sri Prithvi vallabha* (lord of earth) and *Sakala lokasraya* (asylum of all mankind). He is eulogized as "one who acquired the title *Vishama siddhi*, that is, who acquired success even in most difficult circumstances on account of his having captured several fortresses of his enemy kings (*aneka ripu durga pramarthanavapta Vishamasiddhi*). He is said to have entitled as *Sarva siddhi* (accomplisher of all his duties as a king) by the prowess of his own arms. He held the banner which always brought him victory in hundred battles (*Samara satasankatothkantha vira vijayadhvaja*). He claimed to be victorious in many battles (*aneka samara samghatta vijayinah)*. He is said to be the *Vajapeya yajvan*, performer of the Vajapeya sacrifice, a symbol of paramount sovereignty of the ruler.[7] The reign of Calukya Vishnuvardhana II (AD 673-682) marked the attainment of paramountacy of the Calukyan rule and this was symbolically expressed by holding the title *samadhigata pancamahasabda,* that is, one who is heralded in public by the great five sounds produced out of *Sringa* (horn), *Mridanga* (tabret), *sankha* (conch shell), *Bheri* (kettle drum), and *Ghana* (group/gang). Sound symbolizes public display of power which is iconically represented in the form of musical instruments as cited above and the important kingly offices as cited below. *Panca mahasabda* further depicts five major offices of an independent king (*karya sthana*). They are *mahapratihari* (the superintendent of the kings' chamber), *maha sandhivigrahi* (the minister of war and peace of the foreign affairs), *mahasvasaladhikritudu* (superintendent of stables), *mahabhandagaradhipati* (treasurer) *and mahasadhanikudu* (commander of the forces). His other titles like *Pralayaditya* (sunrise at the time of deluge) and *anekasamara samaghattopalabdha yasah* (obtained fame by being victorious in several battles) substantiate the emergence of Calukyas as the supreme authority in Andhradesa during his times by his own prowess. The attribution of rise and fall of any political power to the valour of the king is a typical notion of 'heroic kingship' that underlied the political ideology of the state during its formative periods.

After the Calukyas established an independent empire, the 'heroic kingship' that revolved round the Brahminical religion and bloody sacrifices developed unrest among different sections of the society (Kanaka Durga 2005: 502-540). In order to integrate these discrepancies, the state shifted its sacrificial-centred 'heroic kingship' to '*Dharmic*/Moral kingship' that prescribed ethical conduct and just behaviour for being a king and to act as an upholder of peace and prosperity. Subjugating the hearts of people became the core concern of the 'moral kinship' than conquering the mere physical territories of the other kingdoms by violence. The canonical texts of Jainism like *Nitivakyamrita, Sravakacara, Sagaradharmamrita, Kumarapala Pratibodhana,* and *Sambodhasattari* advocated that the kingship and polity should be a means for enforcing morality and restraint on the behaviour through religious ideology. These texts emphasised the need for reciprocal relations between the state and society, thereby revealing their expectations towards the polity. Somadeva considers kingship as a necessity and legitimate feature of everyday life when executed justly. He is a *digambara* Jain teacher who flourished in the court of the Western Calukyan king Arikesari II. Somadeva discussed in detail about the qualities of a king and essentials of polity in his *Nitivakyamrita,*[8] a treatise on polity and statecraft. He emphasized the need of a king to the people who should remain grateful to his subjects who support him in execution of royal messages. He warns that an ungrateful king is of no use to the people in troubles and his frugal court becomes a hole full of snakes. He expects that the king should not be lazy and never encourage bribery in his domains. He considers a king as a maker of the times.[9] He held that it is better to be a kingdom without a king rather than having an unvirtuous and unworthy ruler who would destroy people. Though Somadeva gave a wide range of statuses for the king provided that he possessed proper moral qualities.[10] He should be pure in lineage, righteous in conduct, considerate in behaviour and remain self-controlled in miseries and pleasures. The *Jaina dharma* holds that the people's affirmative predication should always be dependent upon *svadravya* (own money), *svakshetra* (own domain), *svakala* (own time), and *svabhava* (self/original nature). If it is *paradravya* (other's money), *para kshetra* (other's domain), *parakala* (other's time) and *parabhava* (false self), it can be negatively predicated. The benevolent rulers are supposed to have such affirmative prediction that inculcates in them the sense of self-sameness with the others. Jainism always questioned absolutism and by upholding uncertainty/indecisiveness and predicaments in human life. It is because, one viewpoint results in anger, bigotry and strife. By getting training in many-sidedness, one can realize that all ordinary propositions are relative to the aspects from which they are made. It also enables to know the objects of one's attention by considering them from all points of view. Such thinking paved the way for the formation of the doctrine of *Anekantavada*, the 'many-sidedness' or 'non-absolutism' that believes in the plurality of souls.[11] The *Syavada,* the method of dialectical predication, reflects the incorporative nature of their kingship. *Nayavada,* the method of standpoint/viewpoints, *anekantavada,* the theory of manyfoldedness/indetermination of reality and knowledge, is the postulation of many-ness (*aneka*) and end of manyfoldedness (*anekanta*) an inherent complexity within each of the 'real' in the universe speak about the need for politico-social integrity and incorporatedness for kinship. The doctrine of *anekantavada* was best suited for the mercantile and business communities whose professional lives are highly dynamic responding to multiple mind/souls from different perspectives. The concepts like *anyonyatmakatva* (mutuality) and *anyonyavyaptibhava* (mutual pervasiveness), when applied in the context of a 'concrete real', supports the Jaina view of the universe as a fully interrelated or relativistic (*sapeksa*) system of reals, which in turn are causally efficient (*arthakriyakari*). The variety of titles that the royal personages and the imperial powers held stressing on personal character trace the emergence of *dharmic* kingship based on personal virtues and ethical characters and substantiates the shifting base of kingship from *yajna* to *vamsa*. The phrases in the inscriptions like *caru charitra* (good/pure background), *sujanaika mitra* (friend of good people), the hereditary title *satyasraya* (asylum to truthfulness) of the Calukyas depict their emphasis on truth, the citadel of *Jinadharma*.

As the Calukyan kingdom attained imperial status, it incorporated a vast land and people along with their beliefs and practices. The morale of the *dharmic* kingship could not meet the changing needs of polity dominated by *mandalikas* who were always on their toes to shift their loyalties in political warfare. The strict behavioural ethics and ritualistic restraints could not appease all, especially the masses, but for the royalty and business communities who could practise and afford them as symbols of their power. Hence, there was a need for a spiritual ideology that could evoke ardent devotion and sacrifice among the subordinates towards their masters. The devotional ideologies upheld by the sectarian religions, especially the Saivism with its militant dogmas, served as the base of political ideology. Its egalitarianism, zealous loyalty of servant (devotee) to lord (king), self-sacrifice, etc. got imbibed into the political ideology of Western Calukyas and began to evoke religious fervour in Western Andhra. It gradually culminated into the Saiva-Jaina conflicts in the Calukyan domains. These differences were sponsored and championed by none other than the political leaders like Basavesvara, the propounder of Virasaivism and *dandanayaka* of the Kalachuris of Karnataka. It contributed for the gradual uprootment of the influence of Jainism and its institutions in royal courts. The sectarian religions – Saivism and Vaisnavism – evolved as popular religious cults that could appease larger sections of society through their ideologies and practices based on egalitarianism. These conditions demanded the state to shift kingship from *dharmic* to 'ritual' polity to integrate fragmented political powers and segmented societies. The ritual kingship was based on *puranic* theism that upheld the ideology of devotion, *bhakti* manifested in the ritual practices of *dana* (gift giving) and *tirtha darsana* (pilgrimages). It was substantiated by the growth of temple building activity and increased number of *dana sasanas* (inscriptions denoting gifts) on different ritual occasions which are popularly being celebrated by different sections of the people in the society.[12] These components were mentioned as integrative observances for different *jatis* to change their ritual status and mobilize their positioning in higher social order and hence were included into kingship practices. Towards the end of the Calukyan rule, the politico-religious integrative activities were being strengthened under the rubric of ideology of, *saptasantanas*, (seven categories) of gifting – *agraharas* (Brahman settlement), *dharmavivaha* (legitimate marriage), *daivagriha* (temple), *vana* (garden), *nidhinidhana* (hoarding treasure), *putradana* (procreation of son) and *kritidana* (dedication of a literary work)[13] – and expanded the religious base of *Puranic* theism. It gradually constituted the politico-religious ideology of the Kakatiyan state which showed the signs of 'popular kingship'.

Popular Kingship

Politico-economic premise

The Calukyan kingdom could not politically unite the entire Telugu-speaking areas under one umbrella due to historical reasons as discussed earlier. But during the regime of Kakatiyas (AD 1000-1323), who ruled Andhradesa in various ranks as feudatories, kings and emperors, built an independent empire for the entire Telugu-speaking people without disturbing the diversity and multi-culturalism of different geographical zones. The political history of the Kakatiya dynasty was vividly described by P.V. Parabrahma Sastry (1978) in his exhaustive work on the Kakatiyas of Warangal.

The significant features of Kakatiya regime were (i) shift of political dominance from the riverine base to uplands/dry territories and (ii) transformation of Andhradesa as the 'core zone' of an empire for the first time in South India based on language and cultural paradigms. A loosely organized but strongly articulated politico-religious network got deeply penetrated into coastal Andhra region, the peripheral zone of the Kakatiyan kingdom. These conditions influenced the kingship, political economy and thereby new social formations.

After the Kakatiyas emerged as Imperial rulers under Kakati Ganapatideva (AD 1199-1263), there was a constant need for consolidation of resources and power in the rich fertile lands of Coastal Andhra. In the core zone, Telangana, there was a demand for expanding cultivable land through land reclamation and augmentation of water resources by tank construction. These two acts respectively caused (1) caste proliferation due to the increased inflow of the forest dwellers and autochthonous communities into the society and (2) brought forth new professions related to administration, tank construction, maintenance and taxation. These conditions led to the rise to new *jatis* (*Lakshmiranjanam 1980: 150-1*).[14] It was imperative for the State to accommodate these newly emerged *jatis* into socio-political hierarchies and fix them ritually in *varna* (linear) and *jati* (horizontal) paradigms.

The mechanism of political integration by the state during the Kakatiyan times was of two types: (i) The Kakatiyas till the reign of Ganapatideva had pursued a strategy of soliciting alliances with chiefs and princes, many of whom had been defeated in the battlefield. Matrimony was one of the traditional conciliatory measures[15] that he adopted in his state. But such conciliatory mode of integration was not sufficient to manage the crises of power successions that emerged at the time of two last rulers: Rudramadevi (AD 1262-1289) and Prataparudra (AD 1289-1323). (ii) During their regime, the increasingly growing realm of the dynasty into upland and forest zones demanded the polity to permeate deep into the social life of the people though the ritual links. In dry interior plateaus, the settled agriculture was relatively a new phenomenon and many peasants got recently switched from other occupations, particularly pastoralism and hunting (Feldhaus 1989: 151: 82).[16] The greater mobility necessitated by these non-agricultural occupations combined with the frontier conditions of the upland region required such a strong martial tradition that could control the situation and regulate the administration. Hence, the dominance of warrior peasantry, emphasis on fortified sites and extensive militarization[17] and related officialdom are the hallmarks of upland polity. Thus, an intensive vertical network that penetrated deeply into the countryside through the creation of patron-client (lord-subordinate) ties with the peasant warriors and other people of humble origin emerged as the royal paradigm.

Social milieu

In society, the caste-cum-professional organizations that wielded immense influence in the royal courts of the Calukyas 'as establishers of the glories of their masters' and 'important offices of the king' (*prabhumukhyulu*) emerged as powerful nuclear bodies, the guilds, that exerted immense influence in the society. They were consolidated as corporate bodies and developed new social identities through redefining and fixing *kuladharma* (duties of their caste) and mythificaton of their origins through *kulapuranas* (caste myths) and performing of rituals sanctioned by their *samaya dharma*, all of which were guided by contemporary politico-religious ideologies. Caste contamination was strictly prohibited and sometimes culminated into permanent ritual breakdown of kinship relations. Hence, the society witnessed the progressive hierachisation of caste into several sects and sub-sects basing on purity-pollution norms and religiosity. As the horizon of empire expanded, regional differences began to crop up in the society. The Saiva-Jaina conflict that shook the socio-political spheres of the society during the Calukyan times continued during the early phase of the Kakatiyas. The militancy in Saivism was arousing fervour among the populace.

KAKATIYA STATE AS ASSIMILATOR OF LOCAL CULTURES: EMERGENCE OF POPULAR KINGSHIP

In order to assimilate different socio-political power groups, the new economic policies of tank irrigation and deforestation were used by the state to fix social hierarchies of the new entrants into the state fold. It necessitated vernacularising the polity, which emphasized the participation of the kings and subjects in public spaces like rituals, temple festivities and other state-related activites. Vernacularisation (Pallock 1998) of polity is a process in which the antecedent universalistic, hegemonic orders and values (*marga*) were negotiated with the local, participatory and democratic practices (*desi*) through the ideologies and practices construed upon the values and norms of the major populace that could be appropriated by these two societies. Though the state emerged as a legitimate institution to integrate and protect the people from social anarchy by upholding *dharma* and *danda*, the government is created by, and subject to, the will of the people who are source of all political power. The *dharma* of the state in these circumstances is to share power with different politico-social groups and articulate them not by coercion, but by participation. The *danda* in this context can be interpreted as an enlightened politico-spiritual ideology based on the reciprocity of relations which could bind different power groups with one another on one hand and with the king on the other. Ideologically, the Indian state is viewed as one that is based on the social contract between the king and his subjects; the former protects and the latter pay taxes in exchange. Hence, the state runs on the norms of reciprocity between the king and his subjects, but the latter are source of power to function.

Analysis of several epigraphs issued by *nayamkara* holders of the times of Kakati Prataparudra in the core zone, i.e., the Telangana region of Kakatiyan hegemony, attests to the fact of spreading actual sovereignty not only towards periphery, but also in the centre suggesting the increased number of virtual political power centres that sprang due to social hierachisation. The origin myths, eulogies and entitlements of the Kakatiya kings displayed a clear shift from *yajna* (sacrifice) to *kula* (caste) through *vamsa* (lineage). The segmentation of society into different caste-cum-professional organizations with their distinct caste myths (origin myths) known as *kulapuranas* denote a significant shift from *vamsa* to *kula*. Except for a few political powers who claimed *ksatriyahood* after they rose to the status of emperors like the Calukyas, Rashtrakutas and the Kakatiyas, most of the feudatory families (Velanadu, Kondapadumatis of Nadendla, Kotas of Dharanikota, Natavadis of Madapalle, Cagis of Gudimetta, etc.) traced their descent from Durjaya clan, the fourth caste. The kings of *Caturdhavarna* by following the *dharma* prescribed by the *Puranic* theism (*dana* and *tirtha)* attained ritual purity and became *satsudras*. The kings held the titles like *Satsudracudamani* (crest jewel of the sudras), *Caturthakulasekhara*[18] (moon to the fourth caste) and *Sudrakulendrudu*[19] and traced their kingship to their respective valour and ability to command forces.

The Brahmana-Sudra alliances that emerged during the times of Calukyan ascendancy got consolidated during the Kakatiyan hegemony. In the caste myths of Kakatiyas, Madhava Sarma, a Brahmin was the saviour of their progenitor. Madhava Sarma was born in the line of Somavamsa. The myth contains legend of their migration from the north. The worship by *Kushmanda* (pumpkin) fruits by one of the ancestors of Kakatiya family and performance of numerous meritorious activities mentioned in Puranas as purificatory rituals of birth prescribed for social mobility and construction of kingship based on birth purity. Their right to rule as Ksatriyas was constructed through lineages and thus empowered and integrated the rulers to the state through kingship. The *dana sasanas* display lengthy genealogies of their feudatories even in the peripheral zones.[20] These situations demanded the emergence of a kingship imbibed with an egalitarian politico-religious ideology that could be embraced by every segment of power – from the emperor to commoner. Thus, the 'popular kingship' emerged on the paradigm of *Puranic* theism emphasizing devotionalism to integrate different segments of power in the society.

PURANIC THEISM AS BASIC TENET OF POPULAR KINGSHIP

Puranic theism is a belief system construed upon the tenets of *puranas* which replaced Vedic ritualism with devotion and self-surrender of the devotees to their respective personal gods. The *puranas* are known as *srutis*, which means that they were learnt by listening (*sruti*= listen). They were transmitted orally to the populace in the public spaces like temples and religious gatherings; the message of the god was more public than in the Vedic ritualistic religion. The rituals prescribed by the Puranas were also egalitarian and feasible for different sections of society to follow. The practices were not restricted only to the ruling classes, but were popular among different castes and communities that needed socio-political ranking and mobility. The pantheon of the pastoral communities and forest tribes were also genealogically linked with the *puranic* gods and goddesses and construed their *kulapuranas*. Thus, the dogma of *puranic* religion itself became a popular *dharma* embraced by the different sections of society.

It seems that the tenets of *puranic* theism are identical with the paradigms of Indian kingship. Since the very purpose of the latter is to address the politico-religious needs of the people, *puranic* theism is made as the base of popular kingship to regulate their lives in the matrix of *varnashrama dharmas* and *purushardhas*, the *dharma-artha-kama-moksha* through observing *sodasa samskaras* (enculturation) and gifting *sodasa mahadanas* (sixteen great gifts). All of them rested on strict adherence to their respective *dharma*, which was interpreted as religion. Observance of *dharma* constituted the fulcrum of even mundane activities of *karma* (satisfaction of worldly pleasures) and *artha* (accumulation of wealth). The thesis of *karma* (deeds), *janma-punarjanma* (birth-rebirth), *atma* (transmigration of soul), *papa* and *punya* (sin and merit), *saucha* and *asaucha* (purity and pollution) were the issues answered by the *puranic* religion through performances and practices associated with ritual-gifting (*dana*), realisation of vows (*vratas/nomu*) and pilgrimage and sacred bath (*tirtha* and *snana*). Violation of *dharma* was considered a sin that would throw the violators into hell. The merit that had been accumulated by upholding and observing *dharma* of one's own *varna* and *jati* leads them to heaven and finally causes eternal bliss (*moksa*), the aim of any human life. Impregnated with this ideology, *puranic* theism upheld *bhakti*, devotion and *prapatti* (self-surrender) in which the devotee worships one deity with ardent devotion which leads to the growth of sectarian religions, Saivism and Vaisnavism.

Each power centre (from empire to petty feudatory, chief pontifical seat to a lay mendicant, big international guild to a tiny caste guild) expected such constancy of relations from their subjects, irrespective of magnanimity and authority. They had a *dharma* to be followed (*rajadharma, samayadharma, kuladharma*) and an institution to organize and execute the stringent observance of the *dharma*. Each power group observed the same popular practices, such as *prasastis* (honorifics), having elaborate *vamsavali* (genealogies), *birudavali* (entitlement), emblems (*lamchana*), *samaya* (corporate offices) and *samayadharma* (code of conduct). The people adapted those practices that were endorsed by devotionalism like *dana* (gifting), *tirtha darsana* (pilgrimage), *nomus, vratas* (ritual observances), etc. to proclaim their identity and legitimation in socio-political hierarchies.

Dana (gifting), the core determinant of kingship, is of two types, *istadharma* (sacrificial) and *purthadharma* (fulfilment). They include *vrata, nomu, tirthayatra, upavasa,* and *pradakshina* which are allowed to be performed by people of all castes as attested by contemporary legal texts, *Vijnanesvaram* of Ketana and *vratakhanda,* a chapter in *Caturvarga chintamani* written by Hemadri, a poet in the court of Yadavas of Devagiri in thirteenth century.[21] The contemporary inscriptions attest that the intention of gift-giving is dual: (i) to ward off past sins and (ii) to achieve religious merit in future. An inscription from Makhtal dated S. 1220 (AD 1298) registers the gift of a tank *Baddirajuceruvu* for *angarangabhoga* of *Svayambhu Mallikarjunadeva* to ward off sin and to attain unlimited meritorious worlds (*samasta papaksayamay akshaya punyaloka praptambagunatuga*).[22] The increased number of *dana sasanas* between seventh and fourteenth century,[23] including women in the society,[24] bear testimony to a wide range of gifts in cash and kind that were endowed to the temples for warding different evils.

The occasions of gift-giving in the temple are varied – *grahanams, samkramanas, kartika paurnami, vishuvu samkranti, tula dvadasi, sravana paurnima, davana punnami* and festivals like *dipavali, samkranti,* marriages of the deities, coronations, temple rituals, etc. Almost all sacred or secular and auspicious and inauspicious events were treated as the contexts of gift-giving thereby transforming the temple as big as that of the kingdom. Moreover, ritual observances were always followed by *dana* and *dakshina*; the former is customary and the latter is obligatory, but both go together in practice as gifts made either in cash or in kind. The number of the objects of *dana* varied from ten (*dasa danas*) to sixteen (*sodasadanas*). During the period under study, the concept of *sodasadanas* was prevalent as revealed by the entitlement of the kings. The gifts sanctioned by the norms of *Dharmasastras* abound during the medieval times like villages, gardens, livestock, cash, lamps, food grains, utensils, ornaments, ritual paraphernalia like lampsteads for burning camphor, plaques, etc.

Vrata, the other popularly observed ritual, was performed by people to gain or refrain from something that is beneficial to them. These may be of *nitya* (everyday), *naimittika* (in particular time and space) and *kamya* (fulfilment of desires) for piety, progeny, wealth, beauty, fortunes, virtue, fame, long life, and purity; enjoyment of pleasure, heaven and renunciation. Tradition attributes more merit to the gift-giving on the completion of *vratas*. A hierarchy of these observances was prescribed to men, women, unmarried people and widows to achieve different motives. Rudramadevi (the Kakatiyan queen) was said to have performed *Triratri vrata* and emerged victoriously in the war against the *Seunas* of Devagiri. Kuppambika, wife of Malyala chief Gumda,[25] performed the *vratas* prescribed in the *Kalpasutras – jalasayana, lakshminarayana, ekadasi, asunyasayana vratas* – and realized her vows to achieve a long married life, family welfare and longevity of her husband. Women performed many rituals for begetting son who would relieve them from the debts of their forefathers. *Dasiredla nomu* (worship of oxen), *Nandikesuni nomu* (worship of bull),[26]. *Gajanimma nomu* (gifting of lemon fruits), *Vidhivelugu nomu, Garima nomu, Sanjavali nomu, Jagajjoti nomu, Ikavillanu nomu, Panchavillanu nomu, Chikatintinomu, Nandi nomu, Kedaresuni nomu* and several others were performed to beget sons.[27] *Vesyavrata* (penance by the prostitutes) was also suggested by contemporary *dharmic* texts.[28] Some women held titles like *Masopavasi* (who observes *upavasa*, fasting on specific days of each month) and *Suvrata* (observed all fortune-giving observances).[29] The ritual observances were followed by gift-giving to temples, Brahmans, unmarried and unwidowed women. The other *vratas* like *Caturmasya vrata* and *Gauri vrata* found in the epigraphs attest the land gifts to the temples.[30] It is believed that a gift made on auspicious occasions, ritual observances and in a sacred place promises merit to the donor in his/her next birth.

Tirthadarsana (pilgrimage) to the places of religious importance was privileged in *Puranas* which incurs merit.[31] Saivism gave ritual sanction to women to take part in pilgrimage to the temples on festive occasions. It even gave permission to women to leave their husbands if they denied them to follow Saivism. Their participation was dogmatically legitimised by incorporating them as one among five basic practices, *'pancamakara'* of *'Vamacara'* sects of Saivism. Women were permitted to perform the death rituals of their husbands (*sradhha*) on the banks of sacred rivers like Kasi through proxies (Ramesan 1970: 93-102).[32] Sometimes, the proxies were sent to perform circumambulations (*pradakshina*) to temples like Mallikarjuna of Sriparvata. Interestingly, both the royal and common women found pilgrimage as a ground to attain merit as attested by the inscriptions at Pancharamas, Simhachalam, Srikurmam, Srisailam, Mukhalingam, Bezawada, Bapatla, Tripurantakam, etc. and the literary sources confirm the same notion.

TEMPLE FESTIVITIES AND ROYAL PARTICIPATION

The royalty, besides gifting to classical gods and goddesses, not only encouraged the celebration of popular cultural ambiances like *tirunallu,* but also participated in those occasions and events. These ritual and festivities of the deities increased the worship realm of the temple by the participation of different sections of people for different purposes like trading, helping the pilgrimage, etc. Palkuriiki Somanatha's description of celebration of *Sivaratri* at Srisailam in his *Panditaradhya Carita* (Narayana Rao 1974: 211-270) and Srinathas' description of *tirunalla* (fair) at Srikakolanu in his *Kridabhiramam* (1961) are testimonies to the transformation of temple rituals as a public space giving more scope for popularization of egalitarian ideologies and practices among the participants. *Prataprudra caritra* of Ekamranatha (Ramachandra Rao 1984: 34) alludes to a *tirunalla* conducted by Rudramadevi, the Kakatiya queen for goddess of Ekavira at Mogilicherla. She further conducted rituals of goddess Kakati and Mailaradeva at Ainavolu and god Ganesa at Oddapalli. She is said to have performed all these rituals before she launched against the Seunas of Devagiri for achieving victory in battle. The local cults and worship patterns were embraced by the power groups, thereby legitimizing their rule into the nook and corner of the ethnic communities. The above-discussed aspects – gift-giving, ritual visits to public spaces like temples and ritual festivities of the local cults by the kings, display the participatory role of the kings and the people in local celebrations.

SAPTASANTANAS (SEVEN MERITORIOUS DEEDS)

The ideology and practices of *Saptasantanas* that embodied the *puranic* theism formed the bulwark of popular kingship since the inscriptions inscribed in the public spaces like temple revealed as a contemporary spiritual need to be realized by the populace to attain the merit. Its constituents, viz., (i) brahman villages (*agraharas* or *nallillu*), (ii) gifting a son (*putra dana*), (iii) dedication of a literary piece (*kriti*), (iv) hoarding of treasure (*nidhinidhana*), (v) excavation of tank (*tataka nirmana*), (vi) raising a grove (*vanamu*) and (vii) construction of a temple (*Deva griha),*were sanctioned by the *dharmic* texts and approved by people and polity as a common shared ideology and practices for attaining merit.[33] The royalty took pride in claiming that they had established the *saptasantanas*.[34] Mailamba (AD 1221), the sister of Ganapatideva who built the famous Bayyaram tank in Khammam district, was praised as *dharma kirti* (obtained fame for practicing piety).[35]

All the constituents of *Saptasantanas* expanded the parameters of the concept of *dana*, (gifting), which has politico-economic nuances. Founding of new villages was always associated with construction or renovation of new or old tanks and temples, distribution of shares to Brahmins and other village communities. Inscriptions issued by the kings and feudatories attest to such land reclamations and new village settlements that yield revenues to the royal treasury. *Putradana,* a lawful gifting of a son by the parents for adoption to childless couple, regulates legal successions and legitimation of inheritance. The transformation of rights and properties from prebendial to heritable required legitimate successors. To safeguard from illegal and illegitimate successions of royalty and properties, *putradana* was included as one that incurs immense merit to the donors. The *nidhinidhana* was to cater for the needs of the posterity of generations. Interestingly, the caste myths of the peasant communities (the Reddi and the Velama) were centred round the motifs of treasure-troves.

MANIFESTATIONS OF POPULAR KINGSHIP

In the same way as the *puranic* theism with its egalitarian ideology distributes the message of god to all irrespective of their status, the king through 'popular kingship' articulates his presence to people in the nook and corner of his domains. The belief of populace in the divine origination of the kings – *na vishnu prithvipatih* – was channelized in popular kingship. It was accomplished among different segments of socio-political powers through the popularization of (i) deities, (ii) temples, and (iii) Brahminical institutions.

The Popularization of Deities

This was appreciated through 'Homologization of deities' with 'kings'. Homologization is a process wherein two groups (of power) are treated on the same plane and on par with one another. The deities in temples and the kings in the state were homologized through the process of 'deification of kings' and 'royalisation of gods', respectively. On the other hand, the deities were brought much nearer to the people through 'humanization' of their origination, routine and cyclical rituals in the temples on par with the human beings. Such process found expressions in the myths of the goddesses and gods of the village pantheons. The deification process homologized the king with god. As the temple-building activity incurred enormous merit, the kings constructed temples and consecrated gods in them by naming after themselves and their forefathers and thus identified with the god by deification. The titles like *pratyaksa pramadha ganavatara* (direct replica of Siva, the lord of *pramatha ganas*), *trinetra* (Siva who had a third eye), *parama mahesvara,* etc. reflect the anxiety of the kings to legitimize their divine origin. Consecration of *Sivalingas* as commemorative symbols of the deceased was a popular practice among the elite and commoners. The fourteenth chapter of *Mahanirvana tantra* describes the merit one acquires by installation of *Sivalingas,* which is superior to several Vedic sacrifices and open to all irrespective of caste hierarchies.[36]

The royalisation process made the kings to homologize the gods with them by endowing the deities with all the services and goods that were entitled to the king. The paraphernalia of royalty were entitlements (*Birudavali*), filiations (*vamsavalis*), attires, attributes, offices, rituals and services and structures. The deities in the temples held the titles with high-sounding royalty like *cakravarti, mahadevara, puravaresvara. Sriparvata srisvayambhu Sri Linga Cakravarti Sri Mallikarjuna Mahalingadevara, Sri Sriparvata Srisvayambhu bhulimga cakravarti Sri Mallikarjunadevara,*[37] *Srisailesvara Mallikarjunamahadhisaya.*[38] In the same way as the kings claimed in their records that they have acquired sovereignty by relying upon the strength of their own shoulders (*svaabhuja prakramalabdha*), the *Sivalingas* in some royal temples were described as *Svayambhu* (self-emanated).[39] The feudatories claimed in their records that they have obtained the royal insignia, the *panchamahasabda, mahasamanthadhipatya,* etc., from their masters by worshipping their lotus feet.[40] The gods were given eulogies like that of the kings.[41] The gods in the royal temples were ornamented and dressed with an elaborate jewellry from head to feet like that of the kings. Several contemporary inscriptions from Amaravati, Konidena, Nadendla, Bezawada, Bapatla, Simhachalam, Draksarama, Srisailam, Tripurantakam, Puspagiri, Srikurmam, etc. attest a variety of ornaments and precious stones gifted to the deities of the respective temples for routine and festival decorations.

The rituals and services in temples became highly complex and increased due to the process of homologization of god and king. Most of the temple inscriptions refer to the gifts made by the kings for the *anga ranga bhoga* of the deities in the temples. *Angabhoga* are the ritual sacraments that the deities in the temple have to undergo from morning till late in the night. The *rangabhoga* of the god incorporated the performances of dance, music and all services that are entitled to have by the king. The *rangamandapa* and *natamandapas* of the temple were the venues of performing the *rangabhoga* to the god. The increase in the number of services to deity on par with the king extended the realm of the temple office, *deva sthana,* as elaborate as that of the *rajasthana* of the king. Both the offices maintained a hierarchy of officials as many as 'seventy-two', known as *bahattaraniyogalavaru.*[42] The inscriptions of the Calukyan and Kakatiyan kings refer to an office *bahattaraniyogadhipati,* an officer over seventy-two offices.[43] The temple inscriptions from Simhachalam, Srisailam, Nadendla, Bapatla, Tripurantakam, Pushpagiri, Vijayawada, Draksarama, Mukhalingam, Srikurmam, Amaravati, etc. furnish a variety of temple employees ranging from Brahmans and peasant communities like Reddi, Kapu, and Velama to the artisan communities *panchanamvaru, kummari* (potters), *cakali* (washer men) and tribal communities like *boya* and *chenchu* serving administrative and executive duties. They were given shares in the temple gifts and tied their services to the sacred complexes.

In the process of royalisation, the deity was enshrined in palatial temple-complexes which were as big as royal palaces. Thus, the huge temple constructions, worship patterns and sculptural representations stood as the modes of communication of the political ideologies to the public.

Popularization through Sacred Complexes/Temples

Creation of pontifical seats and extensive gifting to them was another popular gesture in the legitimation process of royalty through sacred realm. The ideology of devotionalism created the notion of *guru,* the preceptor that initiates the mendicant into the sectarian religion of his/her choice, a ritual of initiation, *diksa,* which is an elaborate rite of religious passage. During the medieval times, the ritual initiation of the kings was a real display of royalty through extensive gifting and public declarations. These rituals elaborated the power domains of the temple and progressed as sacred complexes with *mathas* (monastry), *vidyamandapa* or *goshtimandira* (a hall meant for academic discourses discussions). *Mathas* were dwelled by mendicants (*sanyasis*) and celibate students (*brahmacharins*). *Matha* associated with respective shrine and worship order having an administrative head-office constitutes the *pitha*. The *mathadhipatis* (pontiff of *matha*) and the *pithadhipatis* (higher pontifficial seat) were as powerful as that of the central cabinet of government and virtually began to wield politco-spiritual control over the regions which were under their sway. The pontifficial seats of different religious faiths such as Jainism, Saivism and Vaisnavism exerted immense influence in making and breaking the dynasties that created them.

The sectarian religions, Saivism and Vaisnavism, through their ritualistic practices took to the cause of integration. Several inscriptions of Western Calukyan and Kakatiyan rulers refer to the popular practice of initiation and lavish gifts made to the religious teachers that initiated them into faith. Of all branches of Saivism, the ideology of Pasupata sect (Kanakadurga 1987: 1-14),[44] a synchrony of devotionalism and Brahmanism, formed royal religious ideology of popular kingship that integrated the Kakatiya kings to the state and society through the creation of a chain of pontifficial seats of Golaki matha throughout Andhradesa. In the process of integration, the institutions, temple, pitha, and *matha* and monasteries of heterodox religions emerged as parallel power structures of the state. After the Kakatiyas attained sovereignty, the want of peace in their extended empire made them to champion the cause of Smartha ideology, a synchrony of Saiva-Vaisnava religions through Harihara cult as an integrative doctrine of kingship. The hegemony and authority of Sanskrit was balanced through the introduction of vernacular Telugu language. The *Janu Telugu* was a significant criterion of their kingship that integrated king to his political realm. It also integrated the people to state. At the same time, the translation of *Sanskrit Mahabharata* into elite Telugu poetic version, which was begun during the reign of the Calukya-Cola emperor Rajaraja, was completed by Tikkana Somayaji, the Court poet of the Telugu Coda king, Manuma Siddhi.

Popularization of Brahminical Institutions

The *agrahara* was the age-old institution that was complied by the power groups in executing the ritual polity and aimed at legitimizing the socio-political hierarchies formed during the times of new state formations. It was accomplished by encouraging the settlement of Brahmins in administrative and religious institutions as ritual custodians for popularizing polity of the kings. Tradition attributes to a Pallava king, Trilochana Pallava, for the founding and granting of new villages by deforestation and land reclamation to the Brahmans as *agraharas*.

Concomitantly, he established several peasant warrior communities, belonging to *caturthakula* and ksatriya families as *mandalikas* in the regions situated to the south of river Krishna. The concurrence of the establishment of both the priestly and political institutions suggests the interdependence of state and priestly classes in polity.[45] The Brahmans provided *vamsavali* (lineages) and *birudavali* (*Prasastis*) to the kings to legitimize their birth and succession by constructing origin myths and *puranic* lineages to strengthen their kingship. They received *agraharas* in token of their services.[46] The origin myths of Calukyas representing Brahmins as saviors of their lineage, their emigration from Ayodhya thus fixing in the lineage lunar race of ksatriyas, shifting the cause of their fortunes and royal power from their own valour to the grace of goddesses, etc. in the inscriptions and literature attests the empowerment of *Prasastis* composed by the Brahmins in the legitimization process.[47] Several inscriptions of the Eastern Calukyas bear testimony to the extensive formation of *agraharas*, settled by Brahmans, and construction of royal temples, like the Pancaramas simultaneous to the expansion of political territories.[48]

The dry zone polity of Kakatiyas that rested on tank irrigation and land reclamation necessitated the institutional support of the *agraharas* and temples for making peace with new entrants of society. Several inscriptions from the Western Andhra issued by Badami and Kalyani Calukyas bear testimony to the grant of villages as *agraharas* to the brahmins as *ekabhoga* and a few *ganabhoga* as a part of their agrarian policy. The Kakatiyan records and Kaifiyat tradition attest to deforestation and land reclamation of these times.[49] The institution of *agraharas* administered by an autonomous body of assembly emerged as a distinct politico-ritual power group that legitimized the status of the kings and other social groups in their respective hierarchies. Inscriptions refer to several boundary disputes, problems of taxation, illegal occupations, etc. that needed extensive peace-making and interference of local *mahajana*, the assembly of *agraharas*. The remission and concessions given to them due to their higher ritual positioning were compensated by strict and stringent restraints imposed upon their behavioural code. Punishments were severe if they went wrong. Ketana in his *Vijnanesvaram* gives details on this aspect.

Brahmins as holders of *agraharas* and other offices like *sumkadhikari, bahattaraniyogadhipati, sandhivigrahi, gajasahini, mahapradhani, dandanayaka, durgadannaikas, karanam,* etc. during the Calukyan and Kaktiya rules, plan an important rule in the socio-political lives of people in disseminating the royal message through popular politico-religious ideologies and performances.

MATRIX OF STATE-TEMPLE-*AGRAHARA*: SHARING THE PROCESS OF LEGITIMATION

The implications of popular kingship in the state's policy resulted in the development of three parallel institutions – state represented by the king, temple by god and *agrahara* by the Brahmin – that shared power through exchange of honours and contributed for the legitimation of the social roles of the groups in different segments of power.

The politico-religious policies of the state evolved the temples and other allied institutions as centrifugal and centripetal forces that regulated the lives of the people. The temple in medieval times flourished as a "landholder, employer and consumer of goods and services, as bank, school and museum, as hospital and theatre, in short, as a nucleus which gathered round itself all that was best in the arts of civilized existence and regulated them with the humanness born of the spirit of dharma, the medieval Indian temple has few parallels in the annals of mankind" (Sastry, K.A.N. 1984: 654). Hence, it became a 'public space' for participation of rulers and the common folk in several activities sanctioned by contemporary *dharma* as attested by thousands of inscriptions inscribed on the walls of the temples during the medieval times. The rituals of legitimation were centred round the temples and sectarian leaders attested by the king or royal representatives.

As discussed in the previous section, by the end of the Calukyan period, there was an extensive territorial expansion of the guilds of oil-mongers (*teliki vevuru*), artisans (*panchahnamvaru*), weavers (*salevaru*), *vaisya* (*nakaras*, a caste-cum-trader's guild) and *pekkandru* (the traders guild whose membership was widely open) in Andhradesa.

They emerged as self-governing institutions with an office (*samaya*), assembly (*sabha*), head (*nakarapurusha/settipattanasvamy/prabhumukhyulu*), code of conduct (*samayadharama*), norms and values (*samaya mariyada*) and traditions/conventions (*acara*), etc. Claiming the clans (*gotra*) of *rishis* (*puranic* sages) was a popular practice to legitimize their higher positioning as distinct bodies. They exchanged honours with the power groups for their legitimation. Like any other power structure, they were associated with a tutelary god and a town/city as the centre of their activities.

To retain identity, each group developed their own caste myths, the *kulapuranas* that legitimized their social positioning basing on the observances of purity and pollution. Though the Temple-State-*Agrahara* institutions were the agencies of legitimation of the social groups, the political powers also enacted as the catalysts in the process of legitimation through exchange of gifts and honours as in the case of artisan communities cited below.

Telikis were one such artisan-cum-trader's community that emerged as guild of *Teliki vevuru* (Telikis of one thousand *gotras*) by the end of Vengi Calukyan times and attained social mobility from *sudravarna* to ksatriyahood. The progression of their mobility was attested and legitimized in the inscriptions by the political powers, who were no other than the emperors/viceroys. Recent researches on social mobility demonstrated how the political institutions like state represented by kings acted as legitimiser of new identities, besides the Brahmins and temples which proved to be the validators of legitimation (Kanaka Durga 2001: 1-35).[50] The other artisan guilds, like the *Panchahanamvaaru*, that deal with woodwork, metal work, gold, etc. and *Pekkadru*, the Andhra counterparts of the South Indian trade guild *Ayyavali 500* were legitimised by political powers, the emperors.

Sharing of land in the name of different socio-religious and service tenures emerged absentee landlordism and evolved several peasant warrior groups among the sudras as local potentates given in charge of administrative offices. The peasant communities which were collectively known as *Kapus* were heterogeneous caste groups – the *Reddi, Velama* and *Kamma*. By the end of the Calukyan period, they got consolidated as distinct power groups in royal courts as ministers, commanders and feudatories and emerged as local potentates, but with mixed identity. The new state formation under the Kakatiyas welcomed several new caste groups into political and agrarian sectors that competed with extant peasant warrior communities. Towards the end of Rudramadevi's reign, the militarism based on *nayamkara* system was shaking the foundations of patrimonial rights since the tenures were not hereditary. These situations necessitated the other peasant warrior communities Reddis, Velamas and the Kammas to safeguard and sustain their heritable and ownable rights and properties that were pretended upon their forefathers by the earlier rulers and establish their inheritance as sons of the soil. In these circumstances, the peasant communities had to construct their 'new identities' through *kulapuranas* and ritual practices that confirm their ethnicity as those who had legitimate right to own and plow the land as distinct 'caste groups'. The mixed identity of the peasant castes got disintegrated into different groups – Reddi, Velama, Kamma and several sects among *kapus* towards the end of the 11th century.

The autochthonous groups and marginalised communities were legitimised by the temples by providing them space in the temple service in different cadres. Despite the stringent efforts of the caste groups to prevent caste contamination, there was no escape in the society from *anuloma* and *pratiloma* marriages and added much to the caste proliferation. The *Vijnanesvaram* of Ketana refers to this situation and gives a list of new caste formations due to these marriages.[51] *Pratapa Caritra* of Ekamaranath (Ramachandra Rao 1960: 150-152)[52] alludes to the prevalence of several castes by the end of the Kakatiyan period. Inscriptions attest to the corporate body of eighteen different castes in the villages known as *astadasapraja,* who made donations to the temples for the welfare of the people and the rulers.[53] Hence, the process of legitimation by the *agraharas* and the temples, the bulwarks of the popular ideology of *dharma,* was not limited only to the higher levels of state and established social groups, but was extended to all sections of society. As the political powers of the medieval state expanded their frontiers, land reclamation and deforestation became a feature and resulted in new settlement formations. With the result, the frontiers of the State got encroached into pastoral and forest zones; thereby, the entry of the autochthonous tribes (*boya, koya, yerukala, chenchu, yanadi, lambadi)* and pastoral communities (the *golla* and *kurubas)* into social hierarchy turned out to be an inevitable phenomenon during the period under study. This cultural milieu warranted the acculturation and legitimation of the new entrants into the caste society. One of the ways the State used to incorporate these autochthonous communities was through popularization of deities by 'humanization of god' and 'deification of human beings'. In the humanization, gods were identified and treated as fellow human beings having all sufferings, bonds of kinship and power relations. Deification of human beings was another popular practice which got reflected in consecration of *virakals* (herostones), *satikals* (sati stones), and conducting rituals respectively in commemoration of their death hero worship (*viraradhana*) and cult of *peramtallu* respectively. They were exalted to the status of gods and deified in the temples. The caste heroes like Mallanna, Birappa of the pastoral communities were deified as the incarnations of Siva. The concept of *avataras,* the incarnation of the *puranic* pantheon, was extended to the process of legitimation.

The social groups got bifurcated into patron and client castes based on the paradigm of purity and pollution. The client caste being the record-keepers and singers (*kulagayakulu*) of the glories of the patron caste (*kulapuranas*) were given shares in the produce. The sectarian religious ideologies influenced these caste groups and performances which got reflected in their cultural practices. Besides the sectarian religions, the cult of village pantheon likes Yellamma, Renuka, Nalla Pochamma, Maisamma, Kakatamma, Ekavira, Idamma were very popular among the people ranging from ruling classes to stray mendicants in the society.

The politico-religious ideologies guided the kingship throughout historical formations, especially in popular kingship, which transformed the institutions like temples, *pithas, mathas,* royal courts into public spheres. Here, the matters connected with people and state were discussed and settled on the norms of respective *samayadharmas.* A member representing royal agency would ratify the issues. The democratic assemblies of the caste-cum-professional organizations that functioned on the norms of *danda* and *dharma* of their respective societies dealt with several issues related to public and communities, including disbursement of the tax payments and so on. The temples emerged as popular institutions that enshrined *marga, desi* and popular traditions, religion, ritual dance, music, amusements, etc. in different spaces of its realm. Further, they were citadels of social life and became a venue for the exchange and dissemination of information through the inscriptions displayed on its walls. The commercial transactions of the guilds were officiated in the *mukha mandapa* of the temples. The temple ritual festivities temporarily merged the hierarchies and relieved the populace from routine tensions of life and encouraged their participation through pilgrimage tradition. The traditional eighteen-village communities (*astadasa praja, samastapraja*) together made donations for the welfare of the people and the king. The royal courts which were homologous to the temples also got transformed as popular institutions representing the voices of different strands of cultures protecting the heterogeneity of society.

CONCLUSION

From the above discussion, it is observed that the medieval state in Andhradesa has undergone two crucial shifts: (i) Emergence of independent sovereign powers, i.e., Vengi Calukyas who held partial sway in Andhra Pradesh and succession of the Kakatiyas who emerged as undisputed masters of the South ruling from Andhra as the core zone. (ii) Shift of political power from riverine base to dry uplands under the Kakatiyas. The dry zone politico-economic policies of land reclamation, deforestation and tank irrigation led to caste proliferation and formation of new *jati*s. It was imperative for the State and religion to accommodate these emergent groups into socio-political hierarchies and mobilize in *varna* (linear) and *jati* (horizontal) matrix. To integrate the new social groups in the state, military fiscalism in the guise of *nayamkara* system was followed by the medieval powers. The state emerged as a multi-centred power structure sharing sovereignty. The political fragility in the name of *samantas* and other officialdom and social hierachisation in the name of multiple castes necessitated integration through popular kingship that could be all through a politico ritual ideology based on enforcing upon the people a spiritual norm to be achieved for a human being. The paradigm of the kingship was manifested through the process of (i) homologisation, (ii) popularization of sacred complexes (temples) through extensive patronage, and (iii) expansion of Brahminical institutions by which exchange of honours, goods and services was achieved among various social groups in the state. At *marga* level, the homologisation of deities was done through deification of kings and royalisation of gods. At the *desi* level, cult centres were popularized by humanization of gods and deification of human beings. Thus, the medieval period of Andhradesa facilitated the emergence of 'popular kingship' to articulate and assimilate different dominant local potentates that sprang in the wake of state formation into its spatial realm.

NOTES

1. The historiography on polity of medieval South India revealed four major state formations: (i) 'unitary state' ruled by 'centralized bureaucratic system' which was controlled by the emperor through 'heroic kingship'; (ii) The 'feudal state' wherein sovereignty was parcellized and power was decentralized, but articulated by the emperor through 'moral (conciliatory) or dharmic kingship'; (iii) The 'commentary state' having a 'multi-centred power structure', which is pyramidal wherein the sovereignty is dual, i.e., actual (temporal) and ritual (sacred) located respectively in the core and periphery of the empire. Different segments of power in this form of state were articulated by 'ritual kingship'; and (iv) 'Integrative and processural' state that is articulated by 'ritual polity', executed through ritual policies adapted by the kings to distribute royal message to the nook and corner of the state. 'Royal temple policy' the conceptual model of integrative state formation emerged from an analysis of the dynamics of this interdependent socio-economic, political, and cultural process is a processual model of the state formation. (A.S. Altekar

1972; R.S. Sharma1985 & 1991; Stein 1984a&b, 1996; Romila Thapar 1975, 1978, 1984; Perlin 1985; Mahalingam 1976; J. Heirtzmann 1997, H. Kulke 1978, 1982 and 1997).

2. It is because the king is considered to be an expander and protector of the land and people. (*E.I.*, Vol. VIII, pp. 61-62). It explains the exploits of Gautamiputra Satakarni and the titles that speak about his personal traits and kingly virtues, valour, expeditions, extent of his empire, successful performer of his duties as king and his charities that would confirm his sovereignty as a monarch in his dominions. *Trisamudra toya pitavahanasa* (his horse drank water from three oceans, Bay of Bengal, Indian Ocean and Arabian sea), *khatiyadapamana madanasa* (who put down the pride and ego of the *ksatriyas*). The word *ksatriya* may refer to powerful and coercive enemies than the traditional warrior community.
3. The king is the commander of the war who led his armies personally to the battle-field. The detailed instructions issued to the *amatyas*, the governors of the provinces, substantiates the heroic nature of kingship (*E.I.*, Vol. VII, Karle 17). The string of titles in the Nasik inscription of Vasisthiputra Pulumavi (*E.I.*, Vol. VII, No. 14) and Gautamiputra Satakarni (Archeological Survey of Western India, V, pp. 60ff) reveal their valorous expeditions as conquerors of earth. The titles of the king were: *ekasurudi* (only valorous), *ekadhanudhanudu* (only king who held bow and arrow) and *akamkusudu* (only one who got *ankusa*-the *danda*, the power to rule). The concept of overall sovereignty and centralized power is depicted through these titles.
4. The Naneghat inscription of Naganika (Archeological Survey of Western India, V, pp. 60ff), who is described as *masopavasi* (who can fast for months), *grihatapasi* (domestic mendicant), *charitabrahmacharya* (who practices celibacy), *dirghavrata yajnadikshita* (took long term vow of initiation to sacrifices). A list of sacrifices and the types of gifts given on those occasions were described in detail. The title *ekabamanasa* held by Gautamiputra Satakarni (*E.I.*, VIII, Nasik 2) depicts the ideal of Vedic ritualism that was depicted as a token of popular religious ideology to achieve political solidarity and integration. In this record, Satakarni is described as one who always contributed for the prosperity of Brahmins and other people (*dvijavarakutumbavividhanasa*). He was further praised as *abhiyodakadana kilinakilinanibhayakarasa*, which means that his hands were washed on the occasions of gift-giving and extending assurance for fearless refugees. Act of *Dana* is an elaborate ritual in which the donor gives gift by oblation with water. The title emphasises the ritual linkage of gift giving with the king's legitimacy. The titles held by the Satavahana rulers speak about the performance of Vedic sacrifices like *Asvamedha, Rajasuya,* and *Vajapeya, etc.* which legitimise their paramount sovereignty, that establish their heroic kingship.
5. *E.I.*, Vol. VI, pp. 347-9.
6. N.S. Ramachandra Murthy (ed.), 2003. *Inscriptions of Andhra Pradesh, Mahaboobnagar District*, Vol. I, Hyderabad. Nos. 1-5, pp. 1-10.
7. *I.A.*, Vol. XIII, p. 137; (ll.7-3; 13-15), *E.I.*, XIX, p. 263, 258.
8. Somadeva, *Nitivakyamrita*, ed. Pandit Pannalal Suri (1922) Bombay, pp. 180-84.
9. Somadevasuri, *Nitivakyamrita*, pp. 344-56, cf. A.L. Basham, 1948. 'Jainism and Buddhism', in Barry, Hay, Weiler and Yarrow (ed.), *Sources of Indian Tradition*, p. 92.
10. Somadeva, *Nitivakyamrita*, *op. cit.*, 17: 180-184.
11. Theodre de Bary, Stephen Hay, royal Weiler and Andrew Yarrow, *Sources of Indian Tradition*, Delhi, Motilal Banarsidass (rpt.) 1988, pp. 73-81.
12. *Ibid.*, P.S. Kanaka Durga, 2005. 'Religious Philosophy of Kingship', *Studies in Jainism*, Vol. II, pp. 502-540.
13. Vedam Venkataraya Sastry (ed.), 1959. *Nannechoduni Kumara Sambhavamu*, Madras, pp. 48-50. The *Saptasantanas* were *Agrahara* or *nallillu* (Brahmin villages), *putradana* (gifting a son), *kriti* (dedication of a literary piece), *nidhanamu* (hoarding a treasure), *tataka nirmanamu* (excavation of a tank), *vanamu* (raising a grove) and *devagrihamu* (building a temple); *South Indian Inscriptions*, Vol. IV, Nos. 1180, 749; *Nellore District Inscriptions*, Vol. I, Kanigiri; P.S. Kanaka Durga. 1988. 'Radical Saivism and its Impact on Medieval Andhra Society', *Proceedings of Andhra Pradesh History Congress, XIII Session*, Anakapalle, pp. 84-89.
14. *Siddhesvara Caritra* of Kase Sarvappa mentions different castes that exist in Telangana region, some of which were not referred in any other part of Andhra Pradesh. Ketana in his *Vijnanesvaram*, a legal treatise of the contemporary times, refers to the punishment imposed for giving nicknames basing on regional variations. It appears to be the backlash of the people in the borders of state that were in the periphery of the empire for the regions mentioned are *Mulakanadu* and *Veginadu*. These two regions were

vanquished during the construction of Imperial power under Ganapatideva. Ketana: *Vijnanesvaram: Prayaschittakanda*: 1997: v.56.

15. The subjugated rulers were allowed to rule in their own territories as hereditary kings of their localities. Their network of matrimonial alliances with the local *samanta* families like Viriyalas of Gudur, Ayyas of Divi, Natavadis of Madanapalle, Calukyas of Nidadavole, Kotas of Dharanikota, etc. stabilized their authority. *S.I.I.*, Vol. IV, Nos. 465, 422, *ibid.*, Vol. X, No. 536, *E.I.*, Vol. XXV, p. 227, *E.A.P.* 121 (P.V. Prabrahma Sastry 1978: 120-145).
16. Gunther-Dietz sontheimer, 1989. *Pastoral Deites in Western India*. Trans. Anne Felhaus, New York, pp. 15-82.
17. Hence, the kings maintained more personal links with the officials than with the nobles. The frequent occurrence of the offices *amgarakshaka* (body guard) *and lemka (*a personal military service who fought alongside the lord) during the regimes suggest the shift of their reliance from nobility to the personal officers who mediates between people and polity. There were many instances wherein the *astadasapraja* and *nayamkara* holders made gifts for the welfare of Kakati Prataparudra. The military officers of the Kakatiyas claimed titles like *Sri Ganapatideva dakshina bhujadanda, Sripratarudradevara dakshina bhujadanda, Sri Rudradeva dakshinabhujadanda* (right hand strength) as shown in their royal inscriptions suggest the strength of the militarization in Kakatiyan polity. *S.I.I.*, Vol. X, Nos. 522, 521, 533, 461, 471.
18. N.S. Ramachandra Murty, 1993. Vol. I, No.LL.16
19. *S.I.I.*X, No. 171.
20. An inscription Konidena, Guntur district dated AD 1235 of Ophili siddhi, a Telugu choda registering a gift to the temple, gives a lengthy eulogy that trace the ancestry of their *vamsa*, from Solar race from Pulasthya till the donor through a series of kings like Harischandra, Rama and Karikalachola. But he mentions the name of the overlord as *Srikakati Ganapatideva* maharaja. Such a process was more predominant towards the end of the Kakatiya period. *S.I.I.*, Vol. VI, No. 628.
21. *H.A.S.*, Vol. 19. Mahaboobnagar. 47. *Sidhhesvara Caritra* alluded that the Kakatiyas were the 'H*emadri kalpoktadana pranitulu*; they were proficient in making gifts prescribed by Hemadri based on *Kalpasutras* (K. Sarvappa 1960: 148). A later Kakatiyan inscription from Umamahesvram (*H.A.S.*, 19, Mn. 35) Mahaboobnagar district dated AD 1375 refers to Madhava nayaka, a Recherla chief, who was praised as the one who was always immersed in performing the *danas* prescribed by Hemadri (*satata Hemadridana nirata).*
22. N.S. Ramachandra Murthy, 2003. *Inscriptions of Mahaboobnagar district*, Vol. I, *op. cit.*, p. 18.
23. Ratnasara Kundakunda (ed.), 1934. *Jnanasagara*, Calcutta, V. 53; See P. Kanaka Durga, *Religious Philosophy*, *op. cit.*, pp. 524-6.
24. *S.I.I.*, Vol. X, Vol. Nos. 1022, 1043, 884, 1015, 1164, 1368, 1241, *Ibid.*, Vol. V, Nos. 1347, 1348, Vol. VI, Nos. 1203, 974, Vol. X, Nos. 188, 260, etc.
25. *H.A.S.*, Vol. 19, Mahaboobnagar, 47.
26. *H.A.S.*, Vol. 13, No. 50, *Basavapuranam* of Palkuriki Somanatha mentions that Medamba, wife of Mandega Madiraja, performed several *vratas* to beget children, but on the advice of brahmins and elders she performed the *Nandikesuni nomu* and begot a son (ed. G.V. Subrahmanyam, 2002: 6-7). *Sidhhesvara Caritra* (K. Lakshmiranjanam, *op. cit.*, p. 131).
27. Srinatha (*Palanativira Caritra*: 1960: 322-323), mentions that Itamba, the wife of Brahmanaidu of Palanadu, performed several ritual observances to beget her son Balachandra. *Sidhhesvara Caritra* (K. Lakshmiranjanam, *op. cit.*, p. 131).
28. *Kumarasanbhavam* and *Dasakumara Charitra* of these times show evidences to the *vesyamatas*, the mothers of prostitutes suggesting their daughters to observe penances for wealth and prosperity. *Vesyavrata* is a ritual worship of Manmatha, the cupid god, for a period of one year. A Brahmin who is well versed in Vedas has to be honoured by gifting gold and jewels, etc. In the 13th month on the constellation of *Hasta* in the cyclical month *Pushya*, the ritual performer should endow the god with rice, a bead stead, gold chain and an image of Kama (P.V. Kane, 1975: 417).
29. *S.I.I.*, Vol. IV, Nos. 1096, 664.
30. During the period of observing *Caturmasyavrata*, the queen Kuppambika, wife of the feudatory Malyala Gumda, gifted land everyday. *H.A.S.*, XIII, No. 59; *S.I.I.*, Vol. IV, No. 1043.

31. Palkuriki Somanatha, *Sri Panditaradhya Caritra,* (ed.) C. Narayana Rao, *Andhra Patrika*, Madras, 1974, p. 234, Vallabharaya; 204-213; *E.A.*, Vol. 1, pp. 33-102.
32. N. Ramesan (ed.), 1970. *E.A.*, Vol. IV, pp. 192-193. *H.A.S.*, XIII, p. 50.
33. The Karimnagar inscription (AD 1170) of Gangadhara, a minister of Kakati Rudra, describes *Saptasantana* as *tana pemchina santanamu danasantanambum kritiyum dana nallillunu vanamunu cheruvunu gudiyunu janavinutamulaina saptasantanamulu* – children brought up by oneself, one's own children, literary work, one's *agrahara*, garden, tank and temple are famous among men as one's children. *H.A.S.*, Vol. 13, No. 56, v.32, S.I.I., Vol. VI, No. 620.
34. An inscription from Daksarama dated AD 1148 registers a gift by a *Sandhivigrahika* Somana preggada, the war and peace minister of a *mandalika*, Bhimana who was described as the devotee of all gods, gurus and Brahmins. The general gifted pereptual lamps at a series of temples at Pancaramas, Cebrol, Bezawada. He claimed that he had constructed several temples at the above-said places and established *saptasantanas* at numerous places (*S.I.I.*, Vol. IV, No. 749).
35. N. Venkataramanayya, 1974. *op. cit.*, No. 59.
36. The installation of a *Shiva-linga* purifies of all great sins, and leads the sinner to the Supreme Abode (5). A man acquires ten million times the merit which is acquired by giving the world and all its gold, by the performance of ten thousand horse-sacrifices, by the digging of a tank in a waterless country, or by making happy the poor and such as are enfeebled by disease (vv.6-7). Thirty-five million known and unknown places of pilgrimage and all the holy places abide near Shiva. The land within a radius of a hundred cubits of the *linga* is declared to be Shiva-kshetra (9-10). This land of Isha is very sacred. It is more excellent than the most excellent of holy places, because there abide all the immortals and there are all the holy places (11). He who in a devout spirit lives there, be it even for but a little while, becomes purged of all sins, and goes to the heaven of Shangkara after death (12).Anything great or small (meritorious or otherwise) which is done in this land of Shiva becomes multiplied (in its effect) by the majesty of Shiva (13). All sins committed elsewhere are removed (by going) near Shiva, but sins committed in Shiva-*kshetra* adhere to a man with the strength of a thunderbolt (14).The merit acquired by the performance there of *purashcharana*, *japa*, acts of charity, *shraddha*, *tarpana*, or any other pious acts is eternal (15). The merit acquired by the performance of a hundred *purashcharana* at times of lunar or solar eclipse is acquired by merely performing one *japa* near Shiva (16). By the offering of *pinda* once only in the land of Shiva, a man obtains the same fruit as he who offers ten million *pindas* at Gaya, the Ganges, and Prayaga (17). Even in the case of those who are guilty of many sins or of great sins attain the supreme abode if *shraddha* be performed in their names in the land of Shiva (18). The fourteen worlds abide there where abides the Lord of the Universe in His *Linga* form with the auspicious Devi Durga (19). The *mahima* of the *Anadi-linga* is beyond the power of words to express (20). O Suvrat! Even in Thy worship at the *Mahapithas* the touch of an untouchable is unclean, but this is not so in the worship of Hara in His Linga image (21).
37. *S.I.I.*, Vol. X, Nos. 503, 504, *I.A.P.*, Mahaboobnagar II, No. 3, LL2631.
38. N. Venkataramayya, 1974: Nos. 61, 63, 64.
39. *Ibid.*, No. 1, LL5-10
40. *Ibid.*, No. 40, pp. 108-9.
41. K. Isvara Dutt, *op. cit.*, p. 19, pp. xcii-xciv; *S.I.I.*, Vol. X, No. 645.
43. *Ibid.*, pp. xlv-xivii, *S.I.I.*, Vol. X, Nos. 333, 343. *N.D.I.*, Vol. I, Kavali: 25.
44. It is based on the *Pasupata* ideology which believes that *pati* (lord-Shiva) relieves *pasa* (animals, people) from *pasa* (fetters and entanglement). It metaphorically conveys the message in the same way as the only god, Shiva protects the devotees from the worldly entanglements, and the king is the only lord that could take care of the people. The Golaki matha based on *Pasupata* ideology was royally patronized whose branches were spread all over Andhradesa during the Kakatiyan times and got migrated to Tamil Nadu in the wake of Muslim invasions. Jainism was politically exterminated.
45. Several *mandalikas* of the region situated to the south of Krishna River, like Kotas of Dharanikota, Pallavas, Kondapadumatis of Nadendla, Durjayas of Velanadu claim that they were installed by Trinayana Pallava. In the same way, the several medieval kings claim that they had reestablished the villages which were formerly granted by Trilochana Pallava (*S.I.I.*, Vol. X, Nos. 248; *Ibid.*, Vol. VI, Nos. 236, 238, etc.).

46. An inscription from Patanceruvu dated AD 1127 refers to privilege of collecting *Kolaradaya*, a tax from the Chintamani of Potmaker to an astrologer, Nannaya Bhattaraka. The gift was given to the astrologer on the coronation day of the king Bhulokamalla Somesvra III for fixing an auspicious day for launching his expedition. N. Mukunda Rao, 2001. *I.A.P: Medak district*, No. 87.
47. *E.I.*, Vol. XIX, p. 253-254; *Ibid.*, Vol. VIII, p. 55; N.S. Ramachandra Murty, *Mahaboobnagar district 2003*, Nos. 1, 2 etc.
48. *S.I.I.*, Vol. X, No. 248; *Ibid.*, Vol. VI, Nos. 236, 238; *E.I.*, Vol. XIX, pp. 253-254; *Ibid.*, Vol. VIII, p. 55; N.S. Ramachandra Murty, *Mahaboobnagar district 2003*, Nos. 1, 2 etc., *E.I.*, Vol. XIX, p. 253-254; *Ibid.*, Vol. VIII, p. 55; *Ibid.*, Vol. V, No. 10.
49. *S.I.I.*, Vol. X, 504; *Nellore Distrct Inscriptions*, Vol. II, Ongole.19; R. Narasimha Rao, 1967: 86-102; P.V. Parabrahma Sastry, *I.A.P. Karimnagar district*, 1974: No. 28; *S.I.I.*, Vol.I.X. 248; *S.I.I.*, XXIII, No. 380.
50. The hypothesis of the social mobility of *asatsudras* (artisan cum trader's communities) identities were formed at corporate level and *satsudras* (peasant communities) was at family level had been proven (P.S. Kanaka Durga 2001: 1-35).
51. Ketana, 1977. *Vijnanesvaram*, (ed.) C.V. Ramachandra Rao, *Prayaschittakanda*, vv. 134-136, Nellore: Publications.
52. Ekamranatha, (1984). *Pratapa Charitra*, (ed.) C.V. Ramachandra Rao, Hyderabad, A.P.: Sahitya Academy, pp. 43.
53. *S.I.I.*, Vol. X, Nos. 495, 98, 508, 489, 507, 533, 488, 122 etc., *H.A.S.* 19, Warangal. 13, 9, Mahaboobnagar, 19, Khammam, 6; Vide, R. Narasimha Rao, 1967, 110-124. The eighteen castes mentioned in the records were: Mahajanas, Nakara, Kampulu, Balijasettikamdru, Dara, Golla, Akkasala, Sale, Srivaisnava, Velamaveguru, Karanam, Telike, Nayilu.

ABBREVIATIONS

EA: Epigraphia Andhrika
EI: Epigraphia Indica
HAS: Hyderabad Archaeological Series
SII: South Indian Inscriptions
IAP: Anscriptions of Andhra Pradesh
NDI: Nellore District Inscriptions

REFERENCES

Altekar, A.S. 1972. *State and Government in Ancient India*, Delhi: Motilal Banarsidass (First Publication 1958).
Appadorai, Arjun. 1978. 'Kings, Sects and Temples in South India 1350-1700', in Burton Stein (ed.), *South Indian Temples: An Analytical Study*, New Delhi: Vikas Publishers, pp. 47-73.
Basham, A.L. 1948. 'Jainism and Buddhism' in Theodre de Bary, Stephen Hay, Royal Weiler and Andrew Yarrow (eds.), *Sources of Indian Tradition*, Washington D.C.: Public Affairs Press.
Dumont, L. 1957. *Hierarchy and Alliance in South Indian Kingship* (Occasional Papers of the Royal Anthropological Institute of Great Britain and Ireland, No. 12), London: Anthropological Institute.
Feldhaus, Anne. 1989. (trans.). *Pastoral Deites in Western India of Gunther-Dietz Sontheimer*, OUP: New York.
Gopalachari, K. 1976. *Early History of the Andhra Country* (2nd edn.), Madras: University of Madras.
Gonda, J. 1966. *Ancient Indian Kinship from Religious Point of View*, Leiden: E.J. Brill.
Gunther-Dietz Sontheimer. 1989. *Pastoral Deities in Western India* (Trans. Anne Felhaus), New York.
Heirtzmann, James. 1997. 'State Formation in South India, 850-1280', in *The State in India 1000-1700*, Delhi: Oxford University Press, pp. 162-194.
Hocart, A.M. 1970. *Kings and Councillors: An Essay on Comparative Anatomy of Human Society*, R. Needham (ed.), Chicago: University of Chicago Press.
Isvara Dutt, K. 1967. *Inscriptional Glossary of Andhra Pradesh*, Hyderabad: Andhra Pradesh Sahitya Academy.

Kane, P.V. 1962. *History of Dharmasastras: Ancient and Medeival Religious and Civil Law in India*, Vol. V, Part II, Poona: Bhandarkar Orientl Research Institute.

——. 1975. *History of Dharmasastras*, Vol. IV, Part II, Poona: Bhandarkar Research Institute.

Kanaka Durga, P.S. 1988. 'Radical Saivism and its Impact on Medieval Andhra Society', *Proceedings of Andhra Pradesh History Congress*, Anakapalle Session, pp. 84-89.

——. 1992. 'Temples, Kings: Legitimation of Autochthonous Communities: A Case Study of South Indian Temple' (co-author, Y.A. Sudhakar Reddy), *Journal of Social, Economic and Historical Orient*, Vol. 35, Part II, Netherlands, pp. 145-166.

——. 1999. *Culture as Identity*, paper submitted to *Workshop on Culture as Identity*, organized by FRRC, St. Xavier's College, Palayamkottai, 1st-8th, January 1999.

——. 2001. 'Identity and Symbols of Sustenance: Explorations in Social Mobility of Medieval South India', *Journal of Social, Economic and Historical Orient*, Vol. 45, Part II, Netherlands, pp. 1-34.

——. 2005. 'Religious Philosophy and Kingship: Studies in Jainism', in V. Kishan Rao and A. Satyanarayana (eds.), *A Thousand Laurels Saadik Naqui (Studies on Medieval India With Special Reference to Deccan)*, Hyderabad: Karshak Art Printers, Vol. II, pp. 502-540.

Kulke, Herman. 1978. 'Royal Temple Policy and the Structure of Medieval Hindu Kingdoms', in A. Eschmann, H. Kulki and G.C. Tripathi (eds.), *The Cult of Jagannatha: The Regional Tradition of Orissa*, Delhi: Manohar.

——. 1982. 'Fragmentation, Segmentation, versus Integration? Reflections on the concepts of Indian Feudalism and the Segmentary State in Indian History', *Studies in History* 4: 237-63.

——. 1997. 'The Early and the Imperial Kingdom: A Processural Model of Integrative State Formation in Early Medieval India', in (ed. Idem), *The State in India 1000-1700*, Delhi: Oxford University Press.

Krishna Rao, B.V. 1973. *History of the Eastern Calukyas of Vengi*, Hyderabad: Andhra Pradesh Sahitya Academy.

Krishna Murali. 1977. *The Calukyas of Kalyani, from circa 973 AD to 1200 AD*, Delhi: Concept.

Lakshmirnjanam, K. (ed.). 1980. *Srisiddhesvara Charitra of Sarvappa, Kase*, Hyderabad: Andhrarachayitala Sanghamu.

Mahalingam, T.V. 1976. *South Indian Polity* (2nd edn.), Madras: Madras University.

Mukunda Rao, N. (ed). 2001. *Inscriptions of Andhra Pradesh, Medak District*, Hyderabad: Department of Archaeology and Museums.

Mazumdar, R.C. 1951. *Ancient India*, Varanasi: Motilal Banarsidass.

Narasimha Rao, R. 1967. *Corporate Life in Medieval Andhradesa*, Delhi: University Grants Commission.

Narayana Rao, C. (ed). 1974. *Sri Panditaradhya Caritra of Palkuriki Somanatha*, Madras: Andhra Patrika.

Pallock Sheldon. 1998. 'India in the Vernacular Millennium: Literary Culture and Polity, 1000-1500', *Daedalus*, Summer.

Pandit Pannalal Suri. (ed). 1922. *Nitivakyamrita of Somadeva Suri*, Bombay: Manikchandra Digambara Jaina Granthamala Samiti.

Perlin, Frank. 1985. 'State Formation Reconsidered', II, *Modern Asian Studies*, 19: 415-60.

Ramachandra Murthy, N.S. 1993. *Inscriptions of Andhra Pradesh, Mahaboobnagar District*, Vol. I, Hyderabad: Department of State Archaeology and Museums, Government of Andhra Pradesh.

Ramachandra Murthy and P. Jogi Naidu. 2003. (ed.). *Inscriptions of Andhra Pradesh, Mahaboobnagar District*, Vols. I & II, State Archaeology and Museums, Government of Andhra Pradesh.

Ramachandra Rao, C.V. (ed). 1984. *Ekamranathuni Pratapacharitramu of Ekamranatha*, Hyderabad: Andhra Pradesh Sahitya Academy.

——. (ed). 1977. *Vijnanesvaram: Prayaschittakanda of ketana*, Nellore.

Ramesan, N. 1970. (ed). *Copper Plate Inscriptions of Hyderabad Museum*, Vol. I, Hyderabad: State Archaeology and Museums, Government of Andhra Pradesh.

Sharma, R.S. 1985. 'How Feudal was Indian Feudalism', *Journal of Peasant Studies* VII, Volume 12, Issue 2 & 3, January, pp. 19-43.

——. 1991. *Aspects of Political Ideas and Institutions in Ancient India*, Delhi: Motilal Banarsidass (Third Revised Edition).

Sastri. KA.N. 1984. *The Colas* (Reprint), Madras: University of Madras.

Sastry, P.V.P. 1974. *Inscriptions of Andhra Pradesh, Karimnagar District*, Hyderabad: State Archaeology and Museums, Government of Andhra Pradesh.

——. 1978. *The Kakatiyas of Warangal*, Hyderabad: Government of Andhra Pradesh.

Somadeva. *Nitivakyamrita*, (ed.) Pandit Pannalal Suri, Bombay: Manikacancandra Digambara Jaina Granthamala Samiti, 1922, 17. 180-84.

Srinatha. 1961. *Palanativiracaritra*, P. Lakshmikantham (ed.), Vijayawada: Visalandhra Publications.

Stein, Burton. 1984. 'Social Mobility in Medieval South Indian Hindu Sects', in (ed. *Idem.*), *All the Kings Mana: Papers on South Indian History*, Madras: New Era Publishers, pp. 282-301.

——. 1984. 'All the Kings Mana: Perspectives of Kingship in Medieval South India', in (ed. *Idem*), *All the Kings Mana: Papers on Medieval South Indian History*, Madras: New Era Publications, pp. 1-67.

——. 1997. 'The Segmentary State: Interim Reflections', in *The State in India 1000-1700*, Delhi: Oxford University Press, pp. 134-161.

Subrahmanyam, G.V. 2002. (ed.). *Basava Puranam of Palkuriki Somanatha*, Hyderabad: Potti Sriramulu Telugu University.

Thapar, Romila. 1975. *The Past and Prejudice*, New Delhi: National Book Trust.

——. 1978. *Ancient Indian Social History: Some Interpretations*, Delhi: Orient Longman, pp. 122-131; 211-240; 240-267; 294-326.

——. 1984. *From Lineage to State*, Delhi: OUP.

Theodre de Bary, Stephen Hay, Royal Weiler and Andrew Yarrow (ed.). 1988. *Sources of Indian Tradition*, Delhi: Motilal Banarsidass.

Venkataraya Sastry, Vedam. (ed). 1959. *Nannechoduni Kumara Sambhavamu*, Madras: Vavilla Ramaswamy and Sons.

Venkataramanayya, N. 1950. *The Eastern Chalukyas of Vengi*, Madras: University of Madras.

——. 1974. (ed). *Inscriptions of Andhra Pradesh: Warangal District*, Hyderabad: State Archaeology and Museums, Government of Andhra Pradesh.

16

Urbanization in Rayalaseema under the Rayas of Vijayanagara (AD 1336-1648)

A. GURUMURTHY & E. SOBHAN BABU

ABSTRACT

The transformation of rural economy into urban economy constitutes one of the significant steps in human history. Gordon Childe was the first theoretician on Urbanisation, who differentiated between the rural and urban economies. He was followed by Weber, Adams, Brainwood, C.F. Khan, Mayor, Reissman, Wheatly, Lewis Wirth, Redfield, Milton Singer, Bruce Trigger and so on, who advanced alternative theories in urban studies.

Urban studies in India are of a fairly recent interest in several academic disciplines, i.e., Geography, History, Economics, Sociology and others. Researches on the dynamic principles of urbanization in India are in majority, conventional and some of them are theoretical and conceptual, the latter being very few. The conventional works were merely compilation of the names of towns and cities under different categories such as religious, administrative, trade and marketing centres. In these works, only incidental explanation is given regarding the causal factors for the emergence of urban centres. Regarding South Indian scenario, Champaka Lakshmi's work is a pioneering one, focusing on Tamil Nadu. Andhra region remained a virgin area for investigation. An attempt is made in this paper to study the factors that led to the growth of urban centres in Rayalaseema during the Vijayanagara period (AD 1336-1648).

I

Gordon Childe was the first theoretician of urbanization who differentiated between the rural and urban economies. He proposed a broad theoretical framework for the identification of urban traits, in a Pre-colonial and Pre-industrial social context of the old world.[1] He was followed by other theoreticians like Weber,[2] Adams,[3] Braindwood,[4] C.F. Khan and Mayor,[5] Reisman,[6] Wheatly,[7] Lewis Wirth,[8] Red Field and Milton Singer,[9] Bruce Trigger[10] and many others,[11] who advanced alternative concepts and theories in Urban Studies. If Mumford and Giedon Sjoberg stressed the role of Socio-Political factors in a rural settlement changing itself into an urban one, Childe, Toynbee, Adams and others emphasized economic factors as vital in the transformation. Red Field and Milton Singer focused on the role of cultural factors in the growth of urban centres. Geographical factors were viewed as mainly responsible for a similar transformation from rural to the urban, by Khan and Mayor. In all these theories, one finds that some particular and individual elements, in isolation of others, in the growth and development of urban centres, have been emphasized instead of taking a comprehensive view of their genesis. Trade, marketing, warfare, irrigation, religion and such other factors, as pointed out by Wheatley,[12] had their important part to play in the growth of cities. Unless the farmers produced surplus food and supplied it to urban centres, the very existence of the state and its maintenance would be thrown into jeopardy without such an organization, as there would be no security for anyone, neither the rural nor the urban settlements. Similarly, the state enables the development of agricultural facilities and for the well-organized storage and distribution system for the surplus production without which there might be anarchy all over. In distributing the produce all over, tradesmen and merchants and their guilds play a key role, to avoid the danger of economic stagnation. These random instances reveal the mutual interdependence of several factors such as social, political and economic in the emergence and growth of towns. These factors play a complementary role to each another, and together facilitate the urban growth.[13] Therefore, it is necessary to take an integrated view of urban growth rather than over-emphasizing one or two of the individual causal factors.

Urban studies in India, which are of fairly recent origin, have engaged the attention of several scholars,[14] many of whom adopted the Western concepts and theories of Urbanization[15] in their analyses of the urbanism of the historical India.[16] Most of these works were concentrated on the study of processes of urbanization in North India.[17] There are some conventional studies of the urban phenomenon, without a meaningful framework. They are more or less compilations of the names of towns and cities under different categories such as religious, administrative, trade and marketing centres, etc. Only incidental explanation is given in these studies regarding the causal factors for the emergence of towns and cities.[18] Regarding South India, Champaka Lakshmi's work is a pioneering and path-breaking one.[19] She raised several theoretical and conceptual questions regarding urbanization in South India. However, her focus is almost entirely on Tamil Nadu, and thus contributes little to the understanding of urbanism in the other equally important regions of South India. As she limits her study to AD 1300, she has no scope to discuss the urbanization processes during the Vijayanagara rule in Tamil Nadu. Two foreign Scholars, Burton Stein[20] and Karashima,[21] whose emphasis is again on Tamil Nadu, make a few general remarks on the urban phenomena during the Vijayanagara rule in the whole of South India. But for a few sporadic studies and research papers by a handful of scholars on urbanization in Andhra, the region remains largely unexplored.[22]

II

During the Vijayanagara period from AD 1336 to AD 1648, the process of urbanization, particularly in Rayalaseema, received great impetus, and is both intensive and extensive. It was largely because the region enjoyed absolute security under the Rayas of all the four dynasties – Sangama, Saluva, Tuluva and Aravidu – who ruled over it. Because of its strategic position geographically, it formed the nucleus of Vijayanagara Kingdom and attained unprecedented political importance.[23] As a result, a large number of forts developed at several strategic places in the region, such as Chandragiri, Adoni, Gandikota, Penukonda, Rayadurgam, Gutti, Kundurpi, etc. These places were not only strong and formidable defense centres but also acted as headquarters of the administrative provinces of the kingdom known as *Rajyas*. Each *Rajya* functioned as a central place for a larger number of smaller administrative divisions, such as *Seema* and *Sthala*, surrounding it.[24] The following were such centres: Alavakonda, Awuku, Siddhavatam, Velugodu, Mosalimadugu, Kandanavolu, Kovilkuntla, Siddhapuram, Adoni,

Panem, Gorantla, Dharmavaram, Bethamcherla, Penakacharla, Pennabadi, Chennuru, Vutukuru, Prodduturu, Chagalamarri, Pottapi, Basanikonda, Kadapa, Pulivendala, Pedekallu, Chirabadi, Nitturu, Tallaproddutur, Rayadurgam, Sirivella, Gurrumkonda, Narayanavanam, Satyaveedu, Gandikota, Chittoor and so on.

Each of these sub-centre or division was surrounded by a large number of village settlements for which it acted as the central place.[25] All the centres, big and small alike, became Capital towns of administration for the Nayankaras. Their emergence led to a number of socio-economic changes in the region such as: (1) Change in the pattern of land use in the surrounding areas; (2) Increase in demand for agriculture and agricultural products; (3) Construction of roads to facilitate transport and communication between the administrative centres and their adjoining areas; and (4) Promotion of daily interaction between the town centres and village settlements. All these centres grew into big urban agglomerations. As all these places had royal palaces, forts, market-places, temples, a large number of houses of various kinds accommodating people of different classes, places for recreation and sports. Morphologically, they are amenable to be identified as urban centres.[26]

During the Vijayanagara times, the administrative centres were consumption points into which all agricultural surplus and revenue in the form of taxes flowed from the hinterland.[27] As a consequence, many towns in their neighbourhood of the administrative headquarters became urbanized. The revenue earnings of the Vijayanagara Central Government depended greatly on trade and commerce, since income in the form of land tax appears to have been moderate. This was due to the fact that the Central Government had very little land under its direct control. There were three kinds of land tenures under the Vijayanagara sovereigns: *Bhandarvada, Manya* and *Amara* lands.[28] Three-fourths of the total land was under the control of the Nayankaras. The Nayankaras enjoyed full freedom to exercise their authority in their respective region. Alavakondasthala,[29] of which Gurappa Naidu was the chief, provides suitable illustrative example. If we examine the revenue of 12 of its villages during the period, trade and industries seem to have yielded greater revenue than agriculture. There were in the town of Alavakonda a number of mercantile shops, and the weaving industry was flourishing. Taxes were levied on different kinds of cloth produced by the weavers. A number of people depended on the industry for their livelihood. The income of this *Sthala* can be gauged by the growth of the number of villages during the 16th century, from 12 to 42. Obviously, the revenue too might have correspondingly increased during the period. Another factor responsible for the growth and development of village settlements during the Vijayanagara period was an increase in population.[30] This population increase necessarily led to agricultural expansion and encouraged economic competition among the people. As a consequence, a number of industries emerged and prospered. Migration of labour from rural to urban areas, gender division of labour, expansion of different economic activities, which took place during the period, were necessitated mainly by the growth of population. As there is no direct documentary evidence for the demographic information during the period under study, the density of population of the area can be approximately assessed on the basic of geographical and topographical factors. The population was naturally concentrated in riparian region, rich in alluvial soil and places where there were potential irrigated land and systematic irrigation facilities than in the dry upland areas. During the Vijayanagara period, the population in Rayalaseema seems to have increased considerably. This is evident from the fact that vast tracts of forest areas were cleared and village settlements were established in these places, as mentioned in a number of local records.[31] Another piece of evidence for the increase of population is that, there was a large scale migration of Brahmanas into the Rayalaseema region because of gifts made to them in the form of *Agraharas* and *Brahmadeyas*.[32] Construction of a number of irrigation works to meet the needs of agriculture also testifies to this fact.[33] The population was dense in wet cultivation areas and it was a third of the same in dry cultivation areas, since agricultural families and labourers settled more in the former than in the latter. The *Kamma, Velama* and *Reddy* communities were directly engaged in agriculture, while the *Brahmanas* and *Vaisyas* who owned rural agricultural lands, however, lived in urban centres leasing out their lands to tenant farmers. Rich land lords too, irrespective of caste, chose to live in towns, leasing out their lands to the tenants.[34] The literary works and inscriptions of the period give us relevant information about the prevalent crop patterning. On their basis, the crops may be divided into two categories: 1. Food crops cultivated in wet and dry lands and 2. Orchards and commercial crops. The pattern of crops indicate the changes that were taking place in the social and economic spheres.[35]

Industries of different kinds flourished in Rayalaseema during the Vijayanagara Period. Their prosperity was made possible by the surplus agricultural production, which supported and sustained the urban population. Further, there was also large scale migration of artisans and other craft specialists, from rural areas to urban areas due to better employment opportunities created by extensive building and construction activities, in the form of construction and renovation of temples, building of royal palaces, mansions of the well-to-do and defense fortresses, construction of roads and the making of sophisticated and luxury goods, jewellery, etc. All these factors contributed to the expansion and development of urban industries, which included iron and steel, armoury, jewellery, carpentry, leather working, minting, metal and building industry.[36] As Rayalaseema was rich in minerals such as iron, copper gold and diamonds, etc., these industries could flourish. Forest wealth enabled the growth of wood industry. There were agro-based industries such as oil and jaggery. Particular mention must be made of the textile industry, which not only flourished but also provided good employment for a large number of families. Many artisanal communities such as goldsmiths, blacksmiths, carpenters, kancharas, stone masonry workers, oil mongers, etc. can be said to be directly responsible for the growth of the urban centres.[37] These artisanal groups formed themselves into guilds and controlled the mercantile activities of the towns and cities, adding for the growth of corporate life. They carefully protected their hereditary crafts and preserved the purity and quality of their products. They exerted great influence on the state and society in both villages and towns through their prosperity. Their economic prosperity is reflected in the large number of endowments they made to the temples.[38] Through such munificent donations they tried to enhance their social status.[39] The rise and growth of urbanization of Rayalaseema owed a great deal to trade and commerce in the region. In the economic sphere, the production of cash crops such as cotton, sugarcane, indigo, etc. led to the commercialization of agriculture and brought monetary economy in the place of barter/exchange economy.[40] Almost all commodities – agricultural and commercial – were available at reasonable rates in all market centres and this enabled the establishment of the market economy. This is attested by the epigraphs and the literary works of the period.[41] The Vijayanagara rulers, their nayankaras, officers and others connected with administration gave particular attention to promote trade and commerce in Rayalaseema.[42] New network of roads were constructed which enabled transport of goods from one place to another on bullock- and horse-drawn carts.[43] The merchant communities like the *Setti* (*Komati*), *Virabalinja, Chalumula Balinja, Nanadesi, Nagarattar* and *Pekkandru*, who had formed themselves into trading guilds, associated closely with the establishment, organization and maintenance of different markets. Weights and measures were regularized and standardized by the state and the merchants, as a result of which commercial transactions became systematic.[44] A variety of coins, native and foreign, made of gold, copper and silver were in circulation, which indicates the flourishing condition of the market economy.[45] All these factors indicate the prosperous condition of trade and commerce in the region during the Vijayanagara rule.

The flourishing urban markets centres in Rayalaseema can be grouped into three kinds: a) local, b) regional and c) intra-regional, on the basis of the number of customers and patrons, the size of market area and the variety of goods transacted.[46] The local markets served a limited area of village settlements, which were close to each other. *Santas* (weekly markets), in which the local products were brought and sold, dominated them[47] and the limited number of people belonging to the nearby villages visited them. During the Vijayanagara period, there were a large number of such local market centres. The regional market centres, which emerged near imperial palaces, fortresses, administrative centres and the temple centres were permanent centres and served a larger number of people than the local markets. They provided a great variety of goods and commodities ranging from daily necessities to luxury goods.[48] In Rayalaseema, Adoni, Udayagiri, Penukonda, Gutti, Chandragiri, Gandikota, Bukkapatnam, Rollamadugu, Dharmavaram, Alava Konda, Rayadurgam and several other places were such regional markets centres.[49]

There were inter-regional market centres, which were also engaged in the import and export trade[50] of the period. They traded in a number of goods. The advent of Portuguese in India gave impetus to these markets. From Rayalaseema such commodities as rice, sugar, cotton, oils, ghee, tobacco, silk fabrics, diamonds, etc. were exported to the other kingdoms in India and foreign markets.[51] Diamonds from Vajrakarur, Ramallakota and Munimadugu were sent to the merchants of Gujarat who exported them to other countries.[52] According to *Attavana vyavahara Tantram*, an administrative manual of Vijayanagara, the chief commodities imported were glass, broad cloth, lead, nutmeg and mace, sugar and silk from China. The principal consumers of these imported commodities were the princes, nayankaras, feudal lords, well-to-do families and temples, etc.[53]

III

During the Vijayanagara period, there was enormous temple-building activity in the empire, particularly in Rayalaseema. This activity contributed greatly to the process of urbanization. It could even be said that among the principal factors which contributed to urbanization during this period, the temples were perhaps the most significant as they played multiple roles, social, economic, cultural and religious, all at the same time as no other institution could.[54] The Vijayanagara rulers patronized both Saivite and Vaishnavite temples. They built new temples, made additions to the already existing temples in the form of *gopuras* and *mandapas* and renovated old ones. The temples, which attracted people of all sections of society, received gifts and endowments from all, notably from the princes, nayankaras, administrative officers, merchants and others.[55] The endowments were in the form of land-grants, villages, cattle and sheep, ornaments, and tax revenue. The temples in their turn promoted extensively agriculture in the lands gifted to them, undertook large-scale irrigation works, such as tanks and canals, and their regular maintenance. Thus, they contributed to the emergence and expansion of agricultural settlements near temple centres. They also attracted and employed on a large scale a variety of skilled artisans, craftsmen, stone masons, sculptors, musicians, dancers and such artists, etc. All of them lived in the temple centre which in turn became important urban centres.[56] The temples instituted a number of festivals, which attracted pilgrims in large numbers to them. As a result, trade and commerce found encouragement in the temple centres.[57] Many temples in Rayalaseema, Tirumala, Tirupati, Tiruchanoor, Srikalahasti, Srisailam, Mahanandi, Ahobilam, Ramesvaram, Pushpagiri, Tadipatri, Lepakshi, Markapuram and several others attained great importance. Of these, Tirumala-Tirupati, Tiruchanoor, Srikalahasti, Srisailam and Mahanandi retain to this day their urban characteristics.

During the Vijayanagara period, there was great social mobility among the people belonging to different sections, rural and urban alike. Many people found patronage in the royal court. There were frequent movements of the army from one place to another. Expanding trade and commerce enabled people from different regions to move from one corner to another of the kingdom and mix freely, forgetting for the time being their social distinctions of caste and creed. Many found employment in the civil service of the state and the armed forces. In the urban social order the king and nayankaras, the nobility and priests occupied the higher positions. Merchants, money lenders, doctors, lawyers, writers and groups of skilled artisans occupied the middle order. All those provided menial service to those of upper classes, such as watchman, barber, washer men, servants, gardeners and others were at the bottom of the social hierarchy. Those who provided entertainment and amusement to those of the upper classes, such as the wrestlers, acrobats, dancers and musicians, actors and the like, prostitutes who had patrons among the well-to-do, all formed a separate recognized social group.[59] One of the consequences of large-scale urbanization in Rayalaseema during the Vijayanagara rule was that the distinction between the elite and non-elite, the well-to-do and the poor seem to have become more pronounced than before. In food habits, housing facilities, and pattern of dwellings and dress and jewellery, access to social amenities, in sophistication and lifestyle, the elite and the well-to-do had several advantages that the rest of the population did not have.[60] An interesting feature of urbanization in Rayalaseema during the Vijayanagara period is that a number of places in the region which became urban administrative centres during the period, retain even to this day their urban activities and administrative importance. Virtually all of them are *taluk* headquarters and *mandal* headquarters today as Chandragiri, Vayalpadu, Narayanavanam, Satyaveedu, Karvetinagaram, Chittoor, Kurnool, Banaganapalle, Panyam, Nandyala, Kovilkuntla, Adoni, Dhone, Chagalamarri, Betamcharla, Siddhavatam, Siddhavatam, Kamalapuram, Pottapi, Dharmavaram, Uravakonda, Penugonda, Rayadurgam, Madakasira, Gutti, Kalyanadurgam, and so on. Another interesting feature noticeable is that many centres of craft and textile industry of the Vijayanagara days in Rayalaseema continue to retain their spinning and weaving activity even to this day. The places like Narayanavanam, Tiruchanoor, Puttur, Jammalamadugu, Prodduturu, Dharmavaram, Rayadurgam, Adoni, Gutti, Emmiganuru are known for handloom industry while Kalahasti, Tirupati are centre for alloy industry. Village *santas* are a continuing phenomenon even now, in spite of the changing pattern of trade and commerce. Yet another observable feature is that many of the temple and local festivals instituted during the Vijayanagara times continue to the present and have remained popular.

NOTES

1. V. Gordon Childe, 1972. *What happened in History*, London: Penguin Books, pp. 77-97.
2. M. Weber, 1958. *The city* (translated and edited by D. Matindale and G. Neuwvirth). New York.

3. R.M. Adams, 1965. *The Evolution of Urban Society: Early Mesopotemia and pre hispanic Mexico*, Rochester.
4. R.J. Braidwood and G.N. Willey (ed.), 1962. *Courses Towards Urban Life Archaeological considerations of some cultural alternates*, Edinburgh.
5. C.F. Khan and Mayor (ed.), 1967. *Readings in Urban Geography*, Allahabad: Central Book Depot.
6. P. Reissaman. 1964. *The Urban Process: Cities in Industrial Society*, New York.
7. Paul Wheately, 1971. *The Pivot of the Four Quarters*, Edinburgh, p. 42.
8. Lewis Wirth and Mumford, 1975. *The City in History*, London: Pelican Books.
9. Redfield and Milton Singer, 1954. 'The Cultural Role of Cities', *Economic Development and Cultural Change*.
10. Bruce Trigger, 1972. 'Determinants of Urban growth in pre-industrial societies', in P.J. Ucko, R. Tringham and G.W. Dimbleby (eds.), *Man Settlement and Urbanism*, London: Institute of Archaeology, pp. 77-94.
11. H. Carter, 1983. *An Introduction to Urban historical geography*, London: Edward Arnold.
12. Paul Wheatly, *op. cit.*, p. 319.
13. Kameswara Prasad, 1984. *Cities, Crafts and Commerce Under the Kushanas, Delhi:* Agam Kala Prakashan.
14. C.P.V. Ayyar, 1911. *Town Planning in Ancient Deccan*, Madras. P.B. Dutt. 1925. *Town Planning in Ancient India*, Kolkata. B.N. Puri, 1972. *Cities in Ancient India*, Meerut. K.C. Jain. 1972. *A History of Towns in Rajasthan in Medieval Period*, Delhi. Sturt Piggott, 1976. *Some Ancient Cities of India*.
15. A. Ghosh, 1973. *The City in Early Historic India*, Simla: Indian Institute of Advanced Studies. V.K. Thakur, 1981. *Urbanization in Ancient India*. Delhi: Abhinav Publishers. Kameswara Prasad, 1984. *Cities and Crafts under the Kushanas*, Delhi: Agam kala. R.S. Sharma, 1987. *Urban Decay AD 300-1000*, Delhi: Munisiram Monoharlal. B. Chattopadhyaya (ed.), 1991. *The Making of Early Medieval Indian History*, Delhi: OUP.
16. C.P.V. Ayyar, *op. cit.*, P.B. Dutt, *op. cit.*, B.N. Puri, *op. cit.*, K.C. Jain, *op. cit.*
17. Kameswara Prasad, *op. cit.*, A. Ghosh, *op. cit.*, R.S. Sharma, *op. cit.*
18. R.S. Sharma, *op. cit.*, B.D. Chattopadhyaya, *op. cit.*
19. R. Champakalakshmi, 1996. *Trade, Ideology and Urbanization in South India 300 BC-AD 1300*, New Delhi: OUP.
20. Burton Stein, 1980. *Peasant State and Society in Medieval South India*, Delhi: OUP, p. 214.
21. Noboru Karashima, 1984. *South Indian History and Society Studies from the Inscriptions AD 850-1800*, New Delhi: OUP, p. 161.
22. E. Sobhanbabu, 2001. *Urbanization in Rayalaseema under the Rayas of Vijayanagara AD 1336-1648*. Unpublished Ph.D. Thesis. P.S. Telugu University, Srisailam.
23. Y. Yasodadevi, 'The Role of Rayalaseema in the Vijayanagara Kingdom', *S.V.O.R.I.* XIV, July 71, Tirupati.
24. N. Venkata Ramaiah, *Studies in the third dynasty of Vijayanagara*, Madras: Universityof Madras, pp. 254-256.
25. V. Ramachandran, 1990. *Urbanization and Urban systems in India*, Delhi: OUP.
26. *Ibid.*, pp. 261-262.
27. Burton Stein, *op. cit.*
28. N. Venkata Ramanaiah, *op. cit.*, pp. 261-264.
29. C. Mackenzie, *Local Record No. 6, Alavakonda Kaifiyat (hereafter L.R).*
30. Based on Epigraphical Information.
31. *Amukta Malayada*, in 256, *Local Records*, 36, p. 26.
32. G. Yazdani, *The Early History of Deccan*, OUP, pp. 681-682.
33. *Frontline*, From the Publishers of Hindu, December, 15.12.1987, p. 76 and also see. R. Sewell, *A Forgotton Empire*, Asian Education Service, New Delhi, p. 245.
34. Burton Stein, *op. cit.*, p. 180.
35. N. Venkata Ramanaiah, *Studies in the Third dynastie of Vijayanagara*, Madras: University of Madras.
36. E. Sobhanbabu, *op. cit.*, pp. 175-178.
37. Vijaya Ramaswamy, 1985. 'Artisans in Vijayanagara Society', *I.E.S.H.R.*, p. 224.
38. *Ibid.*
39. Burton Stein, *op. cit.*, pp. 248-252.
40. N.V. Ramanaiah, *op. cit.*, p. 213.
41. Gurubrahma Sarma, *History of Kondaveedu*, p. 93.
42. *L.R. Rollamadugu*, p. 148. *L.R. Recherla*, 236. *L.R. 18 Gotur*, p. 513. *L.R. 9 Pothuri Palem.*

43. *L.R.* 136, pp. 657-58.
44. N.V. Ramanaiah, *op. cit.*, pp. 353-354.
45. A. Appadorai, *Economic conditions in South India*, Vol. II, Chapter IV, p. 451.
46. K.M. Asharaf, 1954. *Life and Condition of the People of Hindustan,* Delhi, p. 106.
47. *Ibid.*
48. Borbusa. *Forgotten empire*, pp. 255-56.
49. *M.MSS.* 160, 10, 15, 6, 8. *L.R.* 48, p. 341.
50. *L.R. No.* 15.6.8. *Attavana vyavahara Tantram*, p. 327.
51. N.V. Ramanaiah, *op. cit.*, p. 288.
52. *M.MSS. Kaifiyat of Munimadugu*, p. 139-4.
53. Abdul Razack. *op. cit.*, p. 88.
54. K. Sarojini Devi, 1990. *The Religion in the Vijayanagara Empire*, New Delhi, p. 102
55. *T.T.D. Epigraphical Series*, pp. 269-281.
56. K. Sarojini Devi, *op. cit.*
57. *South Indian Inscriptions* XVI, No. 52, *NDI*, Part III, p. 1121. *M.MSS.* 112, pp. 61-63.
58. V. Ramachandran, *op. cit.*, p. 216.
59. V.K. Thakur, *op. cit.*, p. 124.
60. N.V. Ramanaiah, *op. cit.*, p. 356.

17

Trade and Commerce in Ancient Belgaum

S.M. NAGABHUSHANA

ABSTRACT

Belgaum is the headquarters of a district of the same name in North-Western Karnataka. It is one of the famous historical places having a long history and it was under the rule of the major dynasties in South India. It was the capital city of Rattas, a minor dynasty of Karnataka. The inscriptions of the region reveals many facts concerning trade and commerce, markets, etc. The present paper is intended to study the trade and commerce, market fairs, trade articles, trade guilds and merchants of the Belgaum region during the 5th to 12th century AD. *The main sources of the study are the inscriptions, both in stone and copper-plate, of the region belonging to various phases of medieval history.*

INTRODUCTION

Belgaum is one of the major towns in North-West Karnataka and the district headquarter of the same name. The area lies between 15° 41′ to 16° 04′ North Latitude and 70° 20′ to 74° 51′ East Longitude. It is in an elevated portion of the district in particular and north Karnataka. The present paper is intended to study the 'Trade and Commerce' of the region. The study is based largely on lithic inscriptions and copper-plates, temple architecture of the region and its adjacent territories ruled by different dynasties in different periods. The inscriptions and antiquities which are considered in this study range from 1st century BC to 13th century AD. A history of minor dynasties of the region, viz., Kadambas of Banavasi and Goa, Rattas of Soundatti and Belgaum, along with the major dynasties that ruled this region is quite relevant. As a natural corollary, a study of trade and commerce provide us a good picture of the economy of the period under study.

Trade and commercial activities may be taken as an index to the economic prosperity of a country or kingdom. It is the natural corollary of industry, and the medium of the distribution of industrial and agricultural products. A study of the sources clearly testifies to the vigorous trade that the region enjoyed during the period under review. It also reveals the fact that the trade activities, foreign as well as inland, were largely controlled and dominated by various mercantile bodies or guilds that played an important role in the upliftment of the socio-economic life of the people as a whole.[1]

The regional epigraphic sources testify the existence of numerous arts, crafts and occupations, which resulted in lucrative trade, both inland and foreign. Various articles of wood and metal were produced on an industrial scale. Mining and metallurgy were highly advanced. Trade and commerce flourished with the increase in agricultural production. The contemporary epigraphic and literary sources contain numerous references to activities like trade and articles of trade, means of transport, road networks, various guilds and trading centres, fairs, currency system, weights and measures of materials and lands.

TRADE ARTICLES

In the region, contemporary evidence acquaints us with numerous articles, both of necessity and luxury. It would, indeed, mean a very long list to enumerate them all. There were, to mention only a few, dealings in precious stones and gems, such as emeralds, pearls and metals like gold, silver, copper, etc. as also gold and jewelled ornaments, and metallic utensils and images numerous food stuffs-cereals, spices vegetables, fruits, etc. and other miscellaneous articles as earthen ware, textiles and so on[2] as enumerated in the table below.

S.No.	ARTICLES OF TRADE	PLACE/YEAR	REFERENCES
1.	Rice and paddy	Huli plates Telasango-AD 1147 Belgaum-AD 1204 Soundatti-AD 1248 Ambewadi-AD 1185	*K.I.* II, No. 21, p. 79. *E.I.* XIII, p. 26. *S.I.I.* XX, No. 247, p. 299. *I.D.* VII, p. 8.
2.	Jowar (*Jola*)	Mudenur-AD 973	*S.I.* XX, p. 363.
3.	Jiraka	Godachi plates	*E.I.* XXVIII, p. 59.
4.	Jaggari (*Bella*)	Huli plates	*J.K.U.*ss V, p. 175.
5.	Sugar (*Sarkara*)	Belgaum-AD 1204 Soundatti-AD 1228	*E.I.* XIII, p. 26. *S.I.I.* XX, p. 303.
6.	*Betel-leaves* Betel-nuts or Arecanuts	Golihalli-AD 1173 Golihalli-AD 1176 Belgaum-AD 1204 Soundatti-AD 1228	*K.I.* V, No. 64, p. 239. *K.I.* V, No. 33, p. 134. *E.I.* XIII, p. 26. *S.I.I.* XX, No. 248, p. 303.
7.	Coconuts	Belgaum-AD 1204 Nada-AD 1197 Soundatti-AD 1228	*E.I.* XIII, p. 26. *S.I.I.* XX, No. 183, p. 232. *S.I.I.* XX, No. 248, p. 303.
8.	Vegetables and flowers	Munavalli-AD 1222 Telasanga-AD 1147 Golihalli-AD 1173 Belgaum-AD 1204 Examba-AD 1165	*K.I.* I, No. 30, p. 66. *K.I.* II, No. 21, p. 79. *E.I.* V, No. 64, p. 239. *E.I.* XIII, No. 26. *INKK*, p. 105.
9.	Turmeric	Belgaum-AD 1204	*E.I.* XIII, p. 26.
10.	Ginger	Soundatti-AD 1228	*S.I.I.* XX, No. 248, p. 303.
11.	Black pepper	Belgaum-AD 1204	*E.I.* XIII, p. 26.
12.	Asafetida (*Ingu*)	Munavalli-AD 1222	*K.I.* No. 30, p. 66.

13.	Myrobelan(*Hlalekaye*)	Munavalli-AD 1222	*K.I.* No. 30, p. 66.
14.	Oil (edible oil and burning lamps in the homes and temples)	Konnur-AD 1032 Umarani-AD 1174 Golihalli-AD 1173 and AD 1176 Ramathirtha-AD 1115 Kokatanur-AD 1235 Munavalli-AD 1252 Belgaum-AD 1204 Soundatti-AD 1228 Eksamba-AD 1165	*K.I.* V, No. 6, p. 67. *K.I.* II, No. 26, p. 95. *K.I.* V, No. 33 & 64. *K.I.* II, No. 13, p. 48. *K.I.* No. 38, p. 129. *K.I.* I, No. 31, p. 71. *E.I.* XIII, p. 26. *S.I.I.* XX, No. 248, p. 303. *K.B.* 11-2, 1978, p. 22.
15.	Pastone, incense	Belgaum-AD 1204 Ramathirtha-AD 1115 Kokatanur-AD 1306	*E.I.* XIII, p. 26. *K.I.* II, No. 13, p. 48. *K.I.* I, No. 42, p. 144.
16.	Cotton cloth	Soundatti-AD 1228 Kirihalasagi-AD 1199 Telasanga-AD 1147	*S.I.I.* XX, No. 248, p. 303. *R.N.G.*, p. 306. *K.I.* II, No. 21, p. 79.
17.	Food grains	Golihalli-AD 1176 Examba-AD 1165	*K.I.* V, No. 33, p. 134. *K.B.* 11-2, 1978, p. 22.
18.	Tamarind (*Hunise mara*)	Golihalli-AD 1176	*K.I.* V, No. 33, p. 134.
19.	Musical instruments tambules	Kiriholasagi-AD 1199 Belgaum-AD 1199	*R.N.G.*, p. 306. *K.I.* II, No. 13, p. 115.
20.	Bangles and beads	Belgaum-AD 1261 Golihalli-AD 1176	*K.I.* II, No. 40, p. 139. *K.I.* V, No. 33, p. 134.
21.	Gold jewellery	Telsang-AD 1147 Kadaralli-AD 1075 Rayabag	*K.I.* II, No. 21, p. 79. *I.A.* I, p. 141. *I.N.K.K.*, pp. 23 & 105.
22.	Salt	Telsang-AD 1147	*K.I.* II, No. 21, p. 79.
23.	Umbrella (*Chhattra*) easy chair (*Sukasana)*	Kokatnur-AD 1235	*K.I.* II, No. 38, p. 129.
24.	Baskets (*Jelle, Yadige*)	Telasang-AD 1147 Soundatti-AD 1228	*K.I.* II, No. 21, p. 79. *S.I.I.* XX, No. 248, p. 303.
25.	Bindigi (*pot*) (*copper*) koda	Soundatti-AD 1228 Eksamba-AD 1165	*S.I.I.* XX, No. 248, p. 303. *K.B.* 11-2, 1978, p. 22.
26.	Arivana plates, copper or bronze	Belgaum-AD 1204	*E.I.* XIII, p. 26.
27.	Ghee (*Benne*)	Eksamba-AD 1165	*K.B.* 11-2, 1978, p. 22.

MARKETS AND FAIRS

The inscriptions of the region vouchsafe to more information on the markets and weekly fairs, in different cities and towns of the region. There were many big bazars with numerous shops in all major towns and cities where all sorts of articles of both necessity and luxury were sold and bought. There were, for instance, shops of clothiers, jewellers, goldsmiths, perfumery, paddy, cotton, salt, oil, bangles and the like, and on each of them, a certain tax was levied. Reference is often made, for instance, to a tax on shops (*Angadidere*)[3] in the inscriptions.

Bedkihal plates (AD 1000) mention several important market-places (*bananju vattanas*), such as Kurugodu in Bellary district, Piriyakereyuru (modern Hirekerur) and Kaurur (modern Kaulur) near Koppal, in the Dharwad district and Arasikere near Aihole.[4] These records show the trade contacts with the other regions also. It is interesting to note that Sirisingi[5] had attracted merchants from all over the Tamil and Telugu countries besides those in Karnataka. It is also *Mahanadu* (big market place) or the Central Chamber of Commerce. Eksamba (AD 1165)[6] mentions *Balaya vattana* Eksamba, *Koravalli kompana*. Rayabag inscription mentions the *Kuhundi pattana*.[7] Telsang market-place levied different duties on the articles of merchandise.[8] Belgaum inscription (AD 1204) mentions *Venugrama* as an important one as it throws considerable light on the economic orgainzation of a great town of the period and lists out a large number of shops.[9] Soundatti (AD 1228) reveals the *santhe* (weekly fair) and mentioned different articles and on tax in *Sugandavarti Vattanam*.[10] The Chikka Bagiwadi copper-plate grant (AD 1249) of the Yadavas mention *Santheya Bagevadi*, a market town.[11] Many inscriptions mention the trade guild of artisans and *Mahajanas*, trade activities in the villages or places, where there is *Mahajanas* and different trade guilds there is a town or markets places as in the Belgaum region we find such town and market places Halasi,[12] Kadaravalli,[13] Huli,[14] Golihalli,[15] Nada,[16] Munavalli,[17] Eksamba,[18] Konnur,[19] Ramathirtha,[20] Kokatanur,[21] Kirihalasagi,[22] Kanabargi,[23] Rayabag,[24] Hannikeri.[25] For all these towns, which are generally market places, we find commercial records through the contemporary stone epigraphs.

TRADE GUILDS AND MERCHANTS

Artisans and traders were working under the control of their own respective guilds. Indeed, such industrial or artisans, or craftsman and mercantile guilds have played an important part in the economic life of ancient and mediaeval period.[26] The artisans guilds are variously referred to in the inscriptions of Karnataka. In some, the term *seni* has been employed to denote such guilds. Perhaps the most popular term used in the inscription of Karnataka for guilds of artisans is *Kottali*. These guilds are also called *ashittus*. Sometimes, such terms as *Samudaya jati, Samaya, Okkalu* and *nakhara* were also employed to denote the guilds of artisans. The system of referring to such guilds by the name of the profession followed by their members was also not unknown.[27] For example, the guilds of oil-millers/families are frequently referred to as *Telligas*[28] or *Telligarayvattakkalu*. Each professional caste formed a guild of its own. For instance, an inscription from Yewur of the time of Vikramaditya VI enumerates various guilds of artisans naming them by their professions suffixed with the term *Kottale*, denoting the guild. Such organisations in Karnataka start even from the time of Chalukyas of Badami.[29]

In the Belgaum region, during the period under study, there was a network of such guild organisations, both of craftsmen and merchants; the former were devoted to production and the latter to distribution.[30]

Besides these, we have reference to the craft guilds or the artisan guilds in the inscriptions. Belgaum (AD 1204) mention following merchants and guilds and also artisans: *Telligaru* (oil-millers), dinka saligaras (metal workers, gold-workers), and other all traders of *Lala, Maleyala*, etc. Other traders of the aforesaid place of *Venugrama*, mention many traders and merchants in the place.[31] Here, *dinka saligaru* are identified as manufacturers of *Nekararu* – type of cloth.[32] Eksamba-(AD 1165) mentions *Ganadokkalu dene* (oil-millers association or families).[33] Soundatti-(AD 1228) speaks about the *Bada keye* (vegetable sellers), *Samastha Nakararu* (all merchants) in the market.[34] Munavalli-(AD 1222) mentions *uguru munnurvaru* (betel-leave cutter-300 members).[35]

Badli-(AD 1246) mentions the *Kumbararu* (potters association), *Honnu Vyavaharada* (gold jewel makers), *Telliga setti* (oil-millers).[36] Inscriptions refer to few craft guilds in the region.

We have a large number of references to the merchants' guilds also in the inscriptions of the contemporary period. Merchants, who called themselves in the epigraphs as the protectors of the *Vira-Bananju Dharma* (the law of the noble merchants or the heroic creed of the traders), were organised into a number of autonomous guilds, with traditions insignia and *prasasti* of their own. Such guilds are, however, not particularly confined to this region alone but are to be found practically all over the Deccan, Karnataka and Gujrat (*Lalatadesa*), Andhra and Tamil Nadu.[37]

Inscriptions of the period often refer to the trade guilds, such as the *Five Hundred Svamis* of *Ayyavale, Nanadesis, settis, settiguttas, Mummuridandas, Gavares, Gatrigas* and so on.[38] At the present stage of our knowledge, it is not easy to make out the exact significance of each of these terms, and the distinctions among them.[39]

The Bedkihala plates[40] (AD 1000) throw interesting light on some other important aspects of the *Vira Bananjus*. They reveal the fact that these guilds often encouraged their warriors by conferring honorary titles upon them, as also by offering certain specified remissions of taxes, etc. in their favour. This copper-plate inscription is also important for another point of view that seems to show that the *Vira-Balanjus* had their own seal, i.e., the seal of *Mahisasuramardini*, which is soldered to the ring of the plates bears the figure of the deity in bold relief, in the act of killing by spear the demon *Mahisasura* in human form.[41] There can be little doubt that this seal belonged to the *Five Hundred Svamis* of *Ayyavole*, who issued the grant.[42]

Golihalli[43] (AD 1173) inscription reveals the numerous *mummuridandas* of different places of North Karnataka, *Srimad ayyavaleya Ayanurvara Svamigalu* among *pereyayobbarada settiyaru, Kunelegeriya, Sadamboda Staladavaru, Purigeri, lokkeyandi, Hanagol Nadu, Marudigi, Gangapur, Yarambargi, Sampagadiya settiyar, setti Guttiyaru, bidugalu*, and *Beruvanegea Gavaregalur, Gavaregatrigaru* and many other in the *Halasi Nadu*. Telsang inscription (AD 1147)[44] refers to *Telasangada muvattararumbeden settiyarum* (the *settis* of the thirty-six camps), *stala Banjiga settiyarum* of the place and all *Nakaras*. Kokatnur inscription-AD 1235,[45] mention *Sree madaagrahara korggattanur maha prabhu*, headman of the place, and mention the gifts, of articles and lands to the temple. Belgaum inscription[46] (AD 1204) mentions the *Vira-banajudharmmarum*, and *Venugramada sthalada samasta-mummuridamdamgalum* (all *mummuri-dandas* of the place of Venugrama) and the *Mummuri-dandas* of both itinerant traders, and speaks about the other merchants leaders from different places around the Belgaum region.

NOTES

1. S. Gururajachar. 1974. *Some Aspects of Economic and Social Life in Karnataka* (AD 1000-1300), Mysore, p. 102.
2. *Ibid.*
3. *KI* II, No. 21, p. 79.
4. *KI* IV, No. 5, p. 118.
5. *KI* I.
6. *KB*, Vol. 11, 1978, p. 24.
7. K.G. Kundanagar (ed.), 1939. *Inscriptions of Karnataka and Kolhapur District*, Kolhapur, p. 105.
8. *KI* II, No. 21, p. 79.
9. *EI* XIII, No. 3, A, p. 17.
10. *SII* XX, No. 248, p. 308.
11. *IA* VII, p. 304.

12. *JBBRAS* IX, p. 236.
13. *JKU(ss)* IV, p. 178.
14. *JBBRAS* IX, p. 240.
15. *KIV*, No. 64, p. 239.
16. *SII* XX, No. 183, p. 232.
17. *KI* I, No. 30, p. 66.
18. *KB*, Vol. 11(2), 1978, p. 14.
19. *KI* V, No. 6, p. 17.
20. *KI* II, pp. 13, 48.
21. *KI* II, No. 23, p. 87.
22. R.N. Gurav, *Kadambas of Goa and Their Inscriptions* (Unpublished thesis), Dharwad, 1970, p. 344.
23. *EI* XIII, p. 22.
24. K.G. Kundanagar (ed.), *op. cit.*, No. 23, p. 105.
25. *Ibid.*, p. 1022, p. 99.
26. S. Gururajachar, *op. cit.*, p. 116.
27. *JKU* ss. VI, p. 194.
28. *EI* XIII, p. 22.
29. *JKU* ss VI, p. 194.
30. S. Gururajachar, *op. cit.*, p. 116.
31. *EI* XIII, p. 22.
32. B.R. Hiremath, 1986. *Sasanagalalli Karnatakada Vartakaru*, Dharwad, p. 113.
33. *KB*, Vol. 11 (2), 1978, p. 41.
34. *SII* XX, No. 248, p. 308.
35. *KI* I, No. 30, p. 74.
36. *KI* I, No. 33, p. 79.
37. S. Gururajachar, *op. cit.*, p. 117.
38. *KI* I, No. 25, p. 49.
39. S. Gururajachar, *op. cit.*, p. 117.
40. *KI* IV, No. 55, p. 118.
41. *KI* IV, No. 55, p. 18, plates VIII, B.
42. S. Gururajachar, *op. cit.*, p. 123.
43. *KI* V, No. 64, pp. 243-245.
44. *KI* II, No. 21, p. 82.
45. *KI* II, No. 38, pp. 131-133.
46. *EI* XIII, pp. 21-27.

ABBREVIATIONS

IA: Indian Antiquary
EI: Epigraphia Indica
JBBRAS: Journal of Bombay Branch Royal Asiatic Society
KI: Karnataka Inscriptions Volumes
KB: Karnataka Bharati Volumes
JKU: Journal of Karnatak University

18

Education in Pre-Colonial Pondicherry (AD 750-1600)

R. EZHIL RAMAN

ABSTRACT

In medieval times, temples and mathas played an active role in fostering education and literature. Pondicherry is credited with a glorious history of education and has been a great centre of learning as early as eighth century AD. *The copper-plate inscriptions of Bahour speak of it as a 'Vidyasthana', a seat of learning. At Triubuvanai also, there was a matha where Sri vaishnavas were fed and maintained for religious and literary services. From another record, we know that there was a regular college with students and teachers for learning various subjects. Besides, there were many educational institutions such as Sanskrit College, Gathikas, Guhais, Mathas, Agraharas and similar other institutions like Gurukula, thinnai palligal functioning in medieval Pondicherry to impart education to the people. In this paper, an attempt has been made to trace out the history of the functioning of various educational institutions which existed in Pondicherry during the medieval period.*

It is believed that before the coming of the French, there was no formal schooling available in the Pondicherry region and there existed a native method of learning.[1] In the past, there existed various kinds of educational institutions like *Mathas, Guhais, Agraharas, Ghatika, Thinnai palligal,* temple *gurukulas* and temple colleges, in the ancient and medieval times.[2] *Gurukula* was an ancient type of educational institution, where the students stayed with their respective *Guru* to have their education. In the *ghatika* system of institution, all subjects were taught to the students. The educational system of *Guhais* is almost similar to the *Gurukulas*. Almost in all these institutions, knowledge on various subjects was imparted in Sanskrit. In Pondicherry region, which was a part of *Tondaimandalam* in the ancient and medieval times, there is an availability of evidences regarding the functioning of such ancient educational institutions, in Bahour and Tribuvanai. Besides, Pondicherry was the headquarters of a *matha*, popularly known as Ambalthadaiyar *Matha*[3] which had 24 branches in the eighth century AD and where the original manuscript of *Thiruvasagam* was protected in a silver casket and offered worship.[4]

SANSKRIT COLLEGE AT BAHOUR

The region of Pondicherry is credited with a glorious history of education and has been a great centre of learning as early as in the eighth century AD. The copper-plate inscriptions at Bahour speak of *Vidyastana*, which means a seat of learning existed in the Bahour. A well-established Sanskrit College was functioning there even from the beginning of the eighth century. The level of learning and the achievement of college students may be easily judged by reading the *prasasti* composed in elegant Sanskrit verses by a servant of the *Vidyastanam*.[5]

Jouveau Dubreuil states that the learning at Vahour (Bahour) College consists of 14 *gunas* or 14 divisions of knowledge. He also says that it was taught to the residents of the Bahour village because it was the dwelling place of the learned men, where the *Vidyastana* or the seat of learning existed. Further, the king granted three tax-free villages (Vilankattu Kaduvanur, Iraipunaicherry and Settupakkam) under his protection to the learned men of Bahour.[6] The village (Bahur) itself was a *Brahmadeya* grant to the institution. This is exclusively a Brahminical institution where the sacred Sanskrit texts alone were taught.[7] Tax exemption was granted to particular groups for special reasons. The Brahmins were the prime social group enjoying most tax-exemptions. Learned Brahmins were settled in the tax-free villages, which they collectively enjoyed. *Salabhogam* was another tax exemption granted to lands owned by *salas* or schools.[8]

S. Kuppusamy, who lived in Bahour and studied the Bahur inscriptions, listed out the subjects taught in the *Vidyasthana* to the students. They were the fourteen Arts, four Vedas, Six *Angas, Mimamsa, Nyaya, Dharmasastra, Puranas*, medicine, bow and arrow, music and *Porul Nool* (Economics). However, he states, there is no information about the subjects in that inscription. About the teachers who were worked in that college, he mentions the *Nagayas*, one of the *Marayans* (who chants the *mantras*). The college was administered by the Brahmins, so mostly the teachers and students were all from the Brahmin families. For successfully running this college, the king granted three villages, namely, Vilankattu Kaduvanur, Iraipunaicherry and Settupakkam as *Vidyanubogha* (means grant for learning). He opined that the origin of this college belongs to the pre-Nripatunga period.[9]

TRIBUVANAI SANSKRIT COLLEGE

Besides the Bahur College, another Sanskrit college existed at Tribuvanai. Though the exact period of its origin was unknown, its existence was recorded in the 30th regnal year (AD 1048) of the Chola Emperor of Rajadhiraja's inscription, which speaks about the donations made by one of the Rajadhiraja's captain, *Rajendira Chola mavali Vanarayan*.[10] In this college, there studied 260 students, who received their education from their respected *gurus* or *acharyas*. There were 12 subjects taught by 12 teachers to the students of this college.[11] The Tribuvani institution was predominantly a medical college, attached with a hospital. Though *Ayurveda* taught as an important subject, the curriculum also included other subjects[12] like *Rupávatara*, the four Vedas, *Vajasaneyã*, the *Chandayoga*, the *Brahmanas*, the *Upanishad, Baudhayana Grhyakalpa*, and *Gana, Vyakarana, Prabhakara, Mimasa, Vedantha* and *Sandyashta sutras*. In addition, the epics like *Mahabaratha, Ramayana, Manusastra* and *Vaikhanasastra* were taught to the students.[13] Mostly the education in the early days was imparted in the premises of the temple, *mutts* or under the shadow of the trees in public places. Besides students, some of the subjects were also taught to the public of the villages, which may be in the form of *upanyasa*. One of the important aspects of this college was that it already introduced the scheme of providing scholarship to students, like our modern educational institutions.

To all the 12 teachers, daily allowances were given in the form of grains. To them, four *kalams*[14] were given as their salary. Besides teachers, students also received their daily allowances in the form of grains. Nearly 190 students from various disciplines were given 11 *kalams*,

10 *kuruni* and 4 *nali* of paddy per head. S. Kuppusamy also mentions the number of students who received their allowances according to the subject they learnt. He says that 190 students received these allowances. Of these, 60 students studied *Rigveda,* 20 studied *sandega samam,* 60 students studied *Yajurveda,* and rest of the 50 students studied other disciplines.[15]

For the source of regular income and to maintain the college, 72 *veli* land was made as donation to the college. From these lands, the annual produce of grains were 12000 *kalams;* of these, 9525 *kalams* were spent in the form of salaries and other allowances to the teachers and students of the college, the rest of the products used to compensate miscellaneous expenses of the college.[16]

EDUCATION IN *MATHAS*

The *mathas* of South India are similar to the monasteries of medieval Europe. They functioned as great centres of religious learning. The *matha* imparted instruction in Vedic studies. The *matha* was a place of meditation and study of subject relating to religion, higher truths pertaining to the spirit. The *mathas* were presided over by a *sanyasin* who was invariably a cultured person. The management and administration, encouragement of religious and philosophic learning were the principal duties of *sanyasin*. There studied many disciples in the *mathas*, from the brahminical institutions, who learnt the Vedas and other allied Sanskrit literature.[17]

In Pondicherry, there existed many *mathas* in the medieval period such as Ambalathadaiyar *Matha,* Akkasamy *Matha,* Siddhananda Samy *Matha,* Yazhpanam Kathirvel Samy *Matha* and Villianur Kalvi *Matha,*[18] which primarily functioned as educational institutions. In addition to these, there existed Meignana Mamuni Saivama *Matha* in Villianur,[19] Kenikulam *Matha,* Kambali Samy *Matha,* Sithan Kudi *Matha,* Karamanikuppam Iyyarsamy *Matha,* Ellaipillaichavady Sirungeri Sankara Peeda Achariya Samy *Matha,*[20] were performed its religious duties along with education in the regions of Pondicherry. Apart from these, at Tribuvani also there was a *matha* where Srivaishnavas were fed and maintained for religious and literary services. It was called Rajendra Chola *Matha* during the time of Raja Chola I.[21]

ROLE OF *GHATIKAS*

Just like the *mathas*, the *Ghatikas,* the *pathasalas* and the *salas* functioned as Hindu educational institutions.[22] Nothing is known about the *Ghatikas* in Pondicherry, but one Bahour inscription engraved on the north wall of *Ardha Mandapa* of Bahour Sri Moolanatha Swamy temple states about the donation of 2 *ma* of land for the development of the Sanskrit college by the *Mahasabha* of *Vahur Nadu*. It also states that the *Mahasabha* appointed three *Vaishanava* Brahmins named Kesava Battan, Chandra Ulaganatha Battan and Harinarayana Battan of the *Ghatika,* to maintain the land.[23] Mostly, these *Ghatikas* flourished under the patronage of the later Pallavas. It should also have continued to exist and imparted advanced studies in Vedic studies[24] and during the Pallava reign in Pondicherry.

AGRAHARAS

Agraharas were the Brahmin settlements around the temple of the village. The *Brahmanas* were held in high esteem in Vedic studies and culture. Thus, many endowments by the rulers were made in favour of Brahmins, with the provisions for feeding them in the temples. The early

Cholas were very famous for creating several *brahmadeyas* (*agraharas*) in every part of their empire.[25] Since the region around the present-day Pondicherry came under the reign of Cholas, these *brahmadeyas* and temples were increased with great royal patronage.[26] The main motive behind such creations was to disseminate the Vedic studies.[27]

Education to Non-Brahmins

The non-Brahmin communities who belong to the working and artisanal class, such as copper-smiths and stone engravers, were also educated during the medieval period. Though the sources about the admission or provision of education of the above communities in such educational institutions are very scarce, the inscriptions engraved on the walls and copper-plates clearly indicate that these people were well educated and knew the art of reading and writing. The common people also got their education during the early periods. Through the methods of *Upanyasa* and *Kathakalashepa*, the lay men were taught. Through this, they knew about the stories of *Itihasas* and *Puranas*. In addition to Sanskrit, importance was also given to the Tamil language and other general studies. Though there is lack of evidence about the existence of Tamil colleges, the standard Tamil prose and poetry in the inscriptions, and the Tamil literature related to *Saiva* and *Vaishnava* religious sects indicate the flourishing status of Tamil education during the medieval times.

Native System of Education

Though indigenous schools and colleges were abundant in Pondicherry, till the arrival of French in seventeenth century, there is no copious information about the system of education prevailed in this region. However, with the help of the early Tamil literature, we can have some idea about the native system of education.

The native systems of education in Pondicherry were mostly in favor of higher caste rich families and totally denied to other castes. The native system of education was provided in the traditional learning centres called portico schools or *thinnai palligal*. Mostly these schools were run in the *thinnai*[28] of the teacher's house, where the students sat and learnt what the teachers taught them. The teachers were mostly hereditary.[29] The students in these schools learnt to write first on the sand by their fingers and then on the palm leaves. The teachers were called *Pundits* and *vathiyars*, who ran these schools, and were all well-versed in local languages, religion and arithmetic.[30]

The curriculum of these schools differed according to the knowledge of the teacher. Students had to learn whatever he taught them. These *thinnai* schools mostly aimed to train the students for reading and writing; they taught Tamil alphabets and prepared them for facing their day-to-day affairs. Besides, they taught the students simple and basic calculations in mathematics like additions, subtractions, divisions and multiplications. In mathematics, the learning is mostly memorizing the tables and reciting it repeatedly. The period of basic literacy was from two to three years in basic mathematics and Tamil language skills. After completing this, the students were trained for learning their family profession.[31] Thus, these *thinnai* schools made one literate in his traditional learning at the basic level. One more important feature of these schools was that there was no bookish system of learning and no need for referring to any books. Being localized, the students from a particular caste studied in these schools, which existed among the people of a particular caste. For the convenience of the local students, these *thinnai* schools mostly functioned only in the morning, but at their home, students had to undergo drilling and practice by copying what they wrote on their slates.[32] Moreover, the indigenous schools ran successfully in imparting the basic knowledge to the students till the arrival of the Europeans.

CONCLUSION

Thus, the system of education in Pondicherry was well flourishing in the pre-colonial period with advanced level of studies, such as Medicine, Astrology, Metallurgy, *Ayurveda*, and *Upanishads*. There were also well-established educational institutions like Sanskrit Colleges, *Mathas*, *Ghatikas*, and other indigenous educational institutions. Like the modern world, eighth century educational institutions also provided salaries to the teachers and scholarships to the students who studied in the colleges. But, the advent of Europeans and the efforts taken by the foreign missionaries in the field of education resulted in the gradual decrease of those native schools in Pondicherry, and the beginning of modern education in this territory marked a great success from the eighteenth century onwards.

NOTES

1. K.S. Mathew (ed.), 1999. *French in India and Indian Nationalism (1700 AD-1963 AD)*, Vol. II, Delhi: B.R. Publishing Corporation, p. 365.
2. S. Gurumurthy, 1979. *Education in South India: Ancient and Medieval Periods*, Madras, p. 108.
3. At present, it is existing in Amabalathadaiyar *Matham* St., Pondicherry.
4. P.E. Mohan, 1997. 'Education in Pondicherry Region – Tribuvanai: A Study' (Tamil), in A. Ramachandran (ed.), *Pondicherry through Ages*, Pondicherry: Pondicherry History Congress, p. 33.
5. Francis Cyril Antony, 1982. *Gazetteer of India, Union Territory of Pondicherry*, Pondicherry, pp. 12-21.
6. Jouveau Dubrauil, 1917. *The Pallavas*, Pondicherry: St. Joseph's Industrial School, p. 51.
7. R. Rajalaksmi, 1983. *Tamil Polity* (c. AD 600-c. AD 1300), Madurai: Ennes Publications, p. 209.
8. V. Palanichamy, 2005. Society and Land Relation in the Kaveri Delta during the Chola Period – AD 850-1300, *Journal of Indian History and Culture*, Chennai, p. 77.
9. S. Kuppusamy, 1974. *Kalvettukalil Puthuvai Paguthigal* (Tamil), Pondicherry, pp. 17-18.
10. *Ibid.*, p. 73.
11. K.A. Nilakanta Sastri, 1955. *The Colas*, Madras: University of Madras, p. 631.
12. R. Rajalaksmi, *op. cit.*, p. 209.
13. K.A. Nilakanta Sastri, *op. cit.*, p. 631.
14. 1*Kuli* = 81 sq. ft. of land, 100 *kuli* = 1*ma*, 20*ma* = 1*veli*, 12 *kuruni* = 1 *kalam*.
15. S. Kuppusamy, *op. cit.*, p. 73.
16. *Ibid.*
17. T.V. Mahalingam, 1940. *Administration and Social Life under Vijayanagar*, Madras: University of Madras, p. 230.
18. Mu. Tha. Velayuthanar, 1974. *Vaiyam Pugazh Puduvai* (Tamil), Pondicherry: Nattramizh Pathipagam, p. 63.
19. N. Vengadesan, 1979. *Varalatril Villianur* (Tamil), Chennai: Sekar Pathipagam, p. 122.
20. Mu. Tha. Velayuthanar, *op. cit.*, p. 63.
21. K.V. Raman, 1987. 'The Sources of Pondicherry's History', in *Revue Historique De Pondicherry*, Pondicherry: The Historical Society of Pondicherry, Vol. XV, p. 25.
22. R. Rajalakshmi, *op. cit.*, p. 209.
23. Vijaya Venugopal (ed.), *Kalvettukalil Puduvai Paguthigal* (Tamil), Pondicherry: French Institute of Indology, Inscription No. 32.
24. S. Swaminathan, 1998. *The Early Cholas – History, Art and Culture*, Delhi: Saradha Publishing House, p. 130.

25. *Ibid*.
26. K.V. Raman, *op. cit.*, p. 22.
27. S. Swaminathan, *op. cit.*
28. K.S. Mathew, *op. cit.*, p. 366.
29. The place used to sit in the front side of the house.
30. K.S. Mathew, *op. cit.*, p. 366.
31. Francis Cyril Antony, *op. cit.*, p. 12-22.
32. K.S. Mathew, *op. cit.*, p. 366.

19

Medicine in Buddhist Tradition

KIRANKRANTH CHOUDARY

ABSTRACT

It is indisputable that the Buddhist Sangha became the centre for the preservation of Indian medical knowledge. The practice of temporary retreats evolved into permanent monastic establishments by providing the requirements of life, which is very well known from the Vinaya Pitaka, which speaks about medical matters, the rules connected with remedies and treatment. The acquisition and development of teachings connected with medicine can be traced in the Pali canon. According to the Vinaya Pitaka, a new monk of the Sangha was provided with putrid urine of cattle as medicine along with other requirements. The use of animal urine was permitted to treat the snake-bites as given in the medical section in the Vinaya. Its inclusion as one of the essential life resources indicate the knowledge of techniques of healing among the monks. The settled living in the monasteries put an end to the wandering life of the monks. It made medicines essential for their lifestyle. Thus, medicine evolved along with the Sangha and it resulted in rise of the monk-healers. It was codified as part of their scriptures. Thus, it laid foundations to the Buddhist monastic hospices and infirmaries. Finally, medicine became part of the standard curriculum. Thus, the traditional system of Ayurveda medicine owes much to Buddhists and their vihara order for its early systematization, preservation and propagation.

In ancient times, majority of the ascetics had medical knowledge. It was associated with the Buddhist monasteries and became an integral part of their religious doctrines. Some scholars opined that Lord Buddha propounded the Four Noble Truths basing on the medical logic. Suffering, its cause, its suppression, and the way of its elimination correspond in medicine to disease, its cause, health and the remedy.[1] However, the fourfold division which appears in the *Caraka Samhita,* differs from that of the Four Noble Truths. It is indisputable that the Buddhist *Sangha* became the centre for the preservation of Indian medical knowledge. When the *Sangha* began to take shape, its member monks simply followed the teachings of Buddha.[2] The practice of temporary retreats evolved into permanent monastic establishments by providing the requirements of life, which is very well known from the *Vinaya Pitaka.* The *Vinaya Pitaka* mentions about medical matters, the rules connected with remedies and treatment. The *Sangha* life was based and controlled by the teachings of the Buddha. Richard Gombrich avers that "one should treat oneself well enough not to be distracted from spiritual life by hunger, and moderately enough not to be distracted by over-indulgence."[3]

The acquisition and development of teachings connected with medicine can be traced in the Pali canon.[4] According to the *Vinaya Pitaka,* a new monk of the *Sangha* was provided with four resources (*nissaya*): meals of morsels of food (acquired by begging), robes of rags from dustheaps, lodging at the foot of trees, and putrid urine of cattle as medicine (*putimuttabhesajja*). The use of animal urine was permitted to treat the snake-bites as given in the medical section in the *Vinaya*. It was used as one of the ingredients for many treatments according to the early *Ayurvedic* texts.[5] Its inclusion as one of the essential life resources indicates their knowledge of techniques of healing among the monks. The settled living in the monasteries put an end to the wandering life of the monks. It made medicines as requisite in their lifestyle. Further, the evolution of *Sangha* and the development of discipline rules also contributed to the growth of pharmacopoeia and permitted foods for the monks also increased. The *Cullavagga* gives a detailed view of the daily life of monks and nuns, health and hygiene and arrangements in the monasteries. Individual hygiene and cleanliness in surroundings was strictly followed. The systematic arrangements were made to maintain privies and bathrooms in the monasteries. Proper care was taken for drinking water. The monasteries were provided with storerooms for foodstuffs and distribution of foods was assigned to various monks. The monk who was responsible for the distribution of small necessities was in charge of the drugs and medical supply.[6]

The *Vinaya* refers to disease as *gilana* instead of *atura* as in medical texts. Medicines were used and distributed among the sick people to cure their diseases, to get rid of pains and to maintain health, not to give pleasure.[7] *Mahavagga* details under the chapter *Bhesajjakkhandhaka* about the medicines that were permitted to the monks. According to it, the basic five medicines were purified butter (*sappi*), fresh butter (*navanita*), oil (*tela*), honey (*madhu*), and molasses (*phanita*). The practice of begging for food was replaced by the acceptance of offerings brought to the monasteries. The collected offerings were divided into foods and medicines. The latter was used for treating the sick monks.

It seems, in the early stages, the monks used to take care of their fellow *bhiskkhus* only. How this activity of caring became institutionalized in the *Sangha* is known from a story in the *Mahavagga*. According to it, a monk fell in his own urine and feces due to his bowel disturbance (*kucchivikarabadha*). Since he was not useful to the fellow monks in this condition, no one served (*upattheti*). However, the Buddha attended on the monk and nursed him and announced the rule connected to the nursing of sick monks."You, O *bhikkhus,* have neither a mother nor a father who could nurse you. If, O *bhikkhus,* you do not nurse one another, who then, will nurse you? Whoever, O *bhikkhus,* would nurse me, he should nurse the sick."[8]

The *Mahavagga* also identifies the qualities of good and bad patients and also competent and incompetent nurses (*gilanupatthaka*). According to it, a good patient is one who does what is beneficial and he knows moderation. He takes his medicine. He clarifies the cause for the affliction. He wishes him well by saying 'it is progressing' as it progresses, 'it is regressing' as it regresses, and 'it is stable' as it stabilizes. The qualities of a patient difficult to serve are the exact opposites of the above. The qualities of a competent nurse to the sick are competent to provide medicine; he knows what is good and bad for the sick, he nurses the sick with a kind heart and thought, not out of greed, he has to remove feces, urine, mucus or vomit, he has to encourage and delight the sick from time to time with a story about Buddhist doctrine. The exact opposites disqualify one to nurse the sick. Serving of a sick monk was regarded as a great service (*bahupakara*). If the sick monk diseased, his begging bowl and robes were given to the one who nursed him. Thus, materials were given as incentives to those who served the sick. It indicates the importance given to medical care. The *Mahavagga* refers to only the attendant, who acted as a healer, but not the physician. There is no evidence that Buddhist nuns carried out the functions of nursing and taking care of the sick. But it can be presumed that they had attended to the sick nuns.

The *Mahavagga* gives information about the diseases and their treatment. Method of treating headache was that the drug was administered through nose and oil was applied on the head. For jaundice, *Haritaki* impregnated with the urine of cow was prescribed. For snakebites, dung, urine, ashes and clay were prescribed. Eye ointments were given for the eye-disease. The work classified the drugs. The vegetable drugs enumerated and are given in groups. They are roots – turmeric, ginger; barks – *nimba, kutaja;* leaves *patola, tulasi;* fruits *vidanga, pippali; niryasa-hingu, sarjarasa,* etc. Large numbers of medicinal plants are also given in different contexts.[9]

Many lay physicians (*vejja*) provided free medical service to the monks. Akasagotta of Rajagriha, a physician, allegedly lanced a rectal fistula, a procedure monks were forbidden to conduct.[10] The renowned physician was Jivaka Komarabhacca. He is said to have provided free medical care to the Buddha and other monks. He donated his mango grove, *Jivakarama,* at Rajagriha for use of monastic community. It is stated that he performed a large number of miraculous cures. He was born of Salavati, a courtesan of Vaisali. He learned medical science at Taksasila under Atreya. The latter became a physician in the court of Bimbisara. His amazing medical and surgical cures can be found in almost all versions of Buddhist scriptures.[11] Lay women extended medical service to both monks and nuns in three ways. In this context, it may be recalled the services of Suppiya best known for her nursing of monks and nuns.[12]

Dammapada indicates freedom from disease as the highest gain. This work uses the word *atura* for diseased, although the word *gilana* was in vogue in the Buddhist texts. The work advocates to avoid two extremes, viz., *ayoga* and *atiyoga* and to adopt the middle path. There are many texts on *Apadana* or *Avadana* of which *Avadansataka* and *Divyavadana* are more popular. The *Avadansataka* (AD 100) describes several types of diseases, their symptoms and methods of their treatment. It also states that for diagnosis and treatment of the sick, their clothes, food, beddings and appliances were offered to Lord Buddha. The case of pregnancy in terms of drugs, diet and behaviour is detailed in the work. A pregnant lady was advised to avoid all the six tastes and any kind of unpleasant sound. *Divyavadana* suggests different types of houses for various seasons. It suggests *gosirsa candana* in case of fever with burning sensation. *Sammohini* and *Sanjivani osadhi* are also referred to in the work. The *Sardulakarnavadana* classifies and divides the plants into seven different groups, viz., *phalguvriksa, sthalaja vriksa, ksiravriksa, phalabhaisajya vriksa, sthalaja puspavriksa* and *jalaja puspavriksa.* Diseases like *apasmara, kilasa* and *kustha* are described.[13]

Kunalavadana contains an interesting story about a disease of King Asoka and its treatment with onion by his wife. The Pali text *Milindapanha* states that medicine was one of the vital subjects of teaching during the Buddhist period. King Milinda himself was proficient in *cikitsa* along with the other eighteen subjects. It is suggested in the case of poisoning, a mixture of ghee, butter, oil, honey and jaggery are given. It is quite interesting that urine is indicated with reproduction. Nagasena enumerates the eight factors like *vata, pitta, slesma, sannipata,* seasonal imbalance, irregular diet, improper treatment and past deeds as the causes for disease. The *Saddharmapundarika,* a Mahayana sacred text, belonging to the first century AD, mentions the Buddhist monasteries were well-equipped with food, drinks and appliances for diagnosis and treatment of the sick. Another interesting feature of these monasteries was that they were attached with a flower garden or park. Further, it classifies the diseases, plants and parts of the plants. Drugs were taken in various forms such as juice, paste, decoction, infusion or in combination with other drugs by injecting through needle or cauterization or mixing with food. The *Suvarnaprabhasasutra,* belonging to the first-half of the fourth century AD, specifies by avoiding exertion and proper nutrition play a important role in the longevity of life. The *Buddhacarita* and *Saundarananda* of Asvaghosha (second century AD) provide valuable information about Buddhist medicine system. Many authors who contributed in the field of *Ayurveda* represented the Buddhist system of medicine in their works. The *Astangasangraha* and the *Astangahrdaya* of Vagbhata, besides having the *Samhitas* of Caraka and Susurta, also contain a large number of the Buddhist medical formulas. It is generally accepted the work is to be the first compilation of the early treatise of classical Indian medicine.

The *Bower Manuscript* (4th to 6th century AD) is another Sanskrit text containing a large section on medicine. Its section, *Navnitaka,* lists out a series of prescriptions for the diseases to cure. Rivigupta, a Buddhist scholar, composed the *Siddhasara* (AD 650). It is a medical manual based on the theories and principles of *Ayurveda.* Nagarjuna produced a good number of works. His work *Yogasataka* (Tibetan *Sbyor-ba-brgya-pa*) may date from the 7th century. But Filliozat attributed its authorship to the *Mahyamika* Buddhist Nagarjuna, who lived in the 2nd century AD.[14] It is also a manual of practical medicine. Some other works like *Avabhesajakalpa, Arya raja name vatika, Arya mulakosa mahausadhavali* of Nagarjuna are incorporated into the Tibetan Buddhist canon, known as the *Kanjur* and *Tanjur.* The involvement of Buddhism in medicine created medical knowledge in the *Sangha.* It provided some sort of codification and further it gave opportunity to the teaching of medicine in the monasteries. It was an important tool for missionary service to humanity and animals. Medicine became a part of the curricula in the education centres. Taxila was the most renowned education centre in ancient India. This university was famous for medical education. As mentioned earlier, Atreya was part of the university. His teachings were the basis of the *Caraka Samhita.* Jivaka, the famous Buddhist physician, was trained under him and the former studied there for seven years. The monastery at Nagajunakonda, Andhra Pradesh, imparted education where medicine might be an important subject. In the monastery there existed a room, next to the room for those recovering from fever. Some scholars claim that it was a classroom. Considering "its proximity to the infirmary, both practical and theoretical education in medicine could well have taken place there".[15] By the middle of sixth century AD, the Buddhist monasteries became monastic universities. While describing the Nalanda *Mahavihara,* Huen Tsang states that students from all quarters came to study with learned scholars. He mentions that *cikitsavidya* forms part of the five sciences of the curriculum. I-tsing also mentioned the study of the five sciences. He also explained that the science of medicine was composed of eight sections. Medicine was also taught in Vikramasila University. During the periods of Asoka, Kaniska, Harsha and others, the Buddhist tradition flourished along with the Vedic tradition. Many *viharas* were established in various parts of the country.

In the early stages, medicine was part of an ascetically based religious movement. Medicine evolved along with the *Sangha* and it resulted in the rise of the monk-healers. It was codified as part of their scriptures. Thus, it laid foundations to the Buddhist monastic hospices and infirmaries. Finally, medicine became part of the standard curriculum. Thus, the traditional system of *Ayurveda* medicine owes much to Buddhists and their *vihara* order for its early systematization, preservation and propagation.

NOTES

1. The theory was first proposed by Hendrik Kern. He stated that the Four Noble Truths (*aryasatyani*) are "nothing else but the four cardinal articles of Indian medicine, applied to spiritual healing of mankind", citing Vedvyasa's commentary (seventh to ninth centuries AD) on *Yogasutra* 2.15 as proof (*Manual of Indian Buddhism,* Varanasi: Indological Book House, 1986 (Reprint) pp. 46-47).
2. Richard F. Gombrich. 1988. *Theravada Buddhism: A Social History from Ancient Benaras to Modern Colombo,* New York: Routledge & Kegan Paul, pp. 18-19.
3. Heinz Bechert and Richard Gombrich (eds.), 1984. *The World of Buddhism: Buddhist Monks and Nuns in Society and Culture,* London: Thames and Hudson, p. 81.
4. Kenneth G. Zysk, 2000. *Asceticism and Healing in Ancient India,* Delhi: Motilal Banarsidass (Reprint), p. 39.
5. *Ibid.*, pp. 40-41.
6. R.B. Barua, 1978. *The Theravada Sangha,* Dacca: The Asiatic Society of Bangladesh, No. 32, p. 60.
7. *Sabbasava Sutta,* 27; *Majjhimanikaya,* 1.10; *The Collection of Middle Length Sayings* (*Majjhima-nikaya*), 3 vols., Pali Text Society, Translations, nos. 29, 30, 31; 1954, 1957, 1959 (Reprint), London: Luzac, 1967, 1970.
8. Kenneth G. Zysk, *op. cit.*, p. 41.
9. P.V. Sharma (ed.), 1992. *History of Medicine in India,* New Delhi: Munshiram Manoharlal, pp. 117-135.
10. Kenneth G. Zysk, *op. cit.*, pp. 114-116.
11. Debiprasad Chattopadhyaya, 1977. *Science and Society in Ancient India,* Calcutta: Research India Publications, pp. 327-28.
12. I.B. Horner, 1930. *Women under Primitive Buddhism,* Delhi: Motilal Banarsidass (Reprint), p. 334.
13. P.V. Sharma (ed.), *op. cit.*, pp. 117-135.
14. Kenneth G. Zysk, *op. cit.*, p. 64.
15. *Ibid.*, pp. 47-53.

20

Environmental Conservation – A Historical Perspective

P. SUMABALA

ABSTRACT

Environmental history is the study of interaction between human culture and natural world. It seeks to deepen our understanding of how the natural environment has affected humans and vice versa. The role of the religious preachers and the social activists; the laws passed by the rulers for the preservation of wild life; the wars waged by the village folk for safeguarding their cattle; the rules regulated by the administrative assemblies for the upkeep and management of the water resources; the settlements made by the village headmen in the land and water disputes; the worship of rivers, trees and the animals – all speak of the efforts taken by our ancestors for the preservation of the environment.

This paper attempts to study how different elements of nature were venerated, the care taken by them for the protection of water resources, for the conservation of trees and for the safeguard of the animals; on the extreme steps taken by the people in the form of skirmishes or big battles or popular movements for the conservation of the environment and analyzes their impact in the history of India.

TREE WORSHIP

Tree worship is one of the earliest and most prevalent forms of religion in ancient India. It was through the worship of the trees that man attempted to approach and propitiate God.[1] There is no part of world in which trees have not been regarded with special reverence. Importance of the trees during the Rigvedic period can be seen in this hymn "... May plants, the waters and the sky preserve us, and woods and mountains with their trees for tresses."[2] They provided man food, fodder, timber, medicine and shelter. It is the extreme usefulness of the trees like Pipal, Neem, Banyan, etc. that they have been protected by religious injunctions and planting is encouraged by a promise of eternal bliss in the Other World. The fig tree is supposed to be an incarnation of Vishnu, the Indian fig tree of Rudra, and the Palasa of Brahma. In *Bhagavad-Gita*, Krishna says that among the trees he was the Pipal.[3] In the *Varaha Purana*, the planter of a group of trees is promised heavenly bliss. According to *Padma Purana*, "The man planting trees by the way side will enjoy bliss in heaven for as many years as there are fruits, flowers and leaves in what he planted."

Certain symbols of trees and flowers like *Padma, Kalpa vriksha,* etc. were also considered sacred. The Pipal or the *Bodhi* tree has been the chief object of veneration for Buddhists throughout Asia. The symbols or the marks of the Jaina Tirthankaras include lotus, blue water lily, etc. The sculptured forms of trees are found in the temples, which were considered sacred. The neem tree and the *Tulsi* plant were worshipped for their medicinal value. *Tulsi* leaves are used for the worship of Vishnu.

The *sthalavrikshas* located in the temples were also worshipped. They have either economic or social roles and which were the reasons for their sanctity. The *punnai* tree is the *sthalavriksha* of Kapalisvara at Mylapore, Chennai. The wood of the tree is used for building ships. Its economic role was recognized when it became the sacred tree of the sea-faring coastal people of Mylapore. The *tillai* or mangrove of Chidambaram, the mango tree of Kanchi's Ekamresvara and the Kadamba of Madurai, *Jambu* or black plum of Jambukesvaram (*Tiruavanaikka*), are famous examples of *sthalavrikshas*. The images of deities were erected under the trees and worshipped. Later, shrines or temples were built for the deities near the tree for the worship. Each *sthalavriksha* is associated with a particular god or goddess. The *sthalavrikshas* and the *tirthas* associated with the temples were worshiped with equal importance to the main deity of the temple.

In the words of Fergusson (1971: 1), "With all their poetry, and all their usefulness, we can hardly feel astonished that the primitive races of mankind should have considered trees as the choicest gift of the gods to men and should have believed that their spirits still delighted to dwell among their branches, or spoke oracles through the rustling of their leaves."

The symbols like *kalasa* (*Purna kumbha*), cow, lotus and conch are considered sacred by the Hindus. In the performance of *Pujas,* especially while venerating Ganesa, different kinds of leaves are used. The *Durva*, a kind of grass, is an essential article in the worship of all gods. It is said to have originated from the thigh of Vishnu. The leaves such as *Machipatram, Brihatipatram, Bilvapatram, Durvayugmam, Datturapatram, Badaripatram, Apamargapatram, Tulasipatram, Vishnukrantapatram, Damidipatram, Devadarupatram, Maruvakapatram, Sindhuvarapatram, Jajipatram, Gandakipatram, Samipatram, Asvatthapatram, Arjunapatram, Arkapatram, Chutapatram, Kapitthapatram,* etc. and the flowers such as *Malathi, Punnaga, Bilva, Champaka, Kapiththa, Karaveera, Ashwattha, Vakula, Parijaatha, Kaanchana, Shatha-patra, Giri-karnika, Kalhaara, Padma, Nimba, Paatalee, Arka,* etc. were considered sacred and were used for the worship of gods and goddesses.

Buddha, in his previous births, was born as a *deva* of a tree. This shows the importance of tree worship in Buddhism. The trees, which are associated with the birth of the Buddha, are *Sala, Asoka* and *Plaska.* Gautama got enlightenment under the shade of a Pipal tree, which was henceforth called the *Bodhi* tree and he died in a grove of *Sala* tree.

The conservation of sacred grove, a protected forest area in the village, is another important feature of tree worship. Sacred groves are small patches of forest left untouched by the local inhabitants to be protected by the local village folk deities like Amman, Ayyanar, etc. People make votive offerings made of terracotta to these deities. Several such groves are found in different parts of our country. These are the last remnants of the native vegetation of each particular region. The conservation of the sacred grove by the local people involves strict rules and taboos, whereby tree-felling is strictly prohibited and hunting of animals is forbidden. A combination of local taboos and mystical beliefs and legends protects the groves from human interference. Disobedience of any taboo is believed to cause crop failure, sickness in the family or diseases to livestock. The local headman would punish those who violate the rules with fines ranging from money for the village to feasts for the villagers. Thus, these remnants of natural vegetation are being protected by the village folk against the clearing of vegetation for settlement and other reasons.

WORSHIP OF WATER RESOURCES

Worship of rivers and sacred tanks is an important feature, which reveals the regard and concern of Indian people for the natural resources. The sculptural representation of river goddesses like Ganga and Yamuna are found in the ancient temples of India. Human civilizations and cultures grew on the banks of rivers. In a country like India, the close relationship of the rivers with the lives of the people manifest itself in many forms. Most of the pilgrim centres are situated on the banks of rivers and are attributed religious importance.

The lack of perennial rivers in most parts of India led to the system of water harvesting with the aid of tanks. Over the centuries, two types of artificial tanks evolved for harvesting and conserving water, viz., the large man-made earthen reservoirs and the temple-tanks. Kings, individuals and village administration made endowments to maintain tanks and irrigation channels. There are several stone and copper-plate inscriptions to that effect. Temple-tanks like *Svami Pushkarini* in Tirumala, *Tala Kaveri* in Karnataka, *Mahamagam tank* in Kumbakonam and *Rama Tirtham* in Ramesvaram are some of the tanks that are as sacred as the temples.

Traditionally, farmers and local people desilted tanks, and the silt was used as manure in paddy fields. In recent times, temple-tanks have fallen into disrepair. They are used for other purposes.

In contrast to the sacred tanks, the artificial lakes are large earthen pits constructed on the ground to collect and hold rainwater. Unlike the sacred tanks, which were meant for ritual usage, the artificial tanks were constructed for providing irrigation fecilities to agricultural lands. Kudimaramat was the traditional community-based system devised for the maintenance of the irrigation tanks in Tamil country. Till 17th century, local communities collected the resources to maintain them. These tanks were used for cultivation and they played an important part in preventing soil erosion, floods, and water wastage, and in recharging the groundwater.[4]

WORSHIP OF ANIMALS

The worship of animals is another important feature of environmental concern of the Indian people. They were considered sacred for many reasons. They were regarded as the *vahanas* (vehicles) of the gods and goddesses. Some of the animals, like snake, were worshiped out of fear.

The concern for animals, especially for cow, can be seen from the Vedic period. There are innumerable references to the worship of cow. In later Vedic society, it was recognized that a symbiotic relationship exists between man and cow.

Most of the hero-stones found in different parts of South India record the death of a local hero in protecting their cattle. The majority of the inscriptions of 10th century AD found in the Chengam Taluk of the erstwhile North Arcot district of Tamil Nadu refer to the cattle raiders and the people who died while rescuing their cattle.[5] They disclose not only the bravery but also the concern of the village folk for their cattle. They went to the extreme of losing their lives for the protection and possession of their cattle. They were venerated for their sacrifice and courage.

M. Somasekhara Sarma in his *History of the Reddi Kingdoms* states that the tantric cult was in vogue from the times of the later Cholas. Virabhadras, a sect of Saivas, are said to have performed heroic deeds such as cutting of their scrotum, stomach, and head for the protection of the village from natural calamities.[6] This kind of self-sacrifice became a remarkable feature in the medieval period. There are also instances of women sacrificing for closing the breach or leakage in the tanks or lakes.[7]

The association of various wild animals with the gods and goddesses confirms that the preservation and protection of wildlife had religious support. The Harappan pottery and seals contain several animal and tree motifs. Later, the kings had the animal motifs on their royal emblems and on the coins issued by them. The animals became the characters of Indian folklore. The wildlife caught the imagination of the poets, sculptors and the artists. Religion and tradition in India are thus bound with a variety of animal forms, both wild and domestic.

During the reign of the Mauryan dynasty, forests were classified according to uses such as forests for grazing, hunting, religious purposes, etc. Some forests were declared protected and were known as *Abhayaranyas*. Hunting of animals and birds in these forests was prohibited and severe penalties were prescribed for breach of law. During Asoka's rule, special attention was paid to the preservation of wildlife. He banned destruction of forests for the purpose of expanding kingdoms.

ASOKA'S DHAMMA

Asoka played a vital role in advocating non-violence. He gave up the royal habit of hunting. Formerly, numerous animals and birds used to be killed in his kitchen for the preparation of food. But after the Kalinga war, he gave up this aggression and preached Dhamma. His edicts are the store-houses of his great principles.

About protecting species, one of the edicts of Emperor Asoka says: *Twenty-six years after my coronation various animals – parrots, mainas, aruna, ruddy geese, wild ducks, nandimukhas, gelatos, bats, queen ants, terrapins, boneless fish, vedareyaka, gangapuputaka, sankiya fish, tortoises, porcupines, squirrels, deer, bulls, okapinda, wild asses, wild pigeons, domestic pigeons and all four-footed creatures that are neither useful nor edible, were declared to be protected. [The identification of many of these animals is conjectural.] Those nanny goats, ewes and sows, which are with young or giving milk to their young, are protected, and so are young ones less than six months old. Cocks are not to be caponized, husks hiding living beings are not to be burnt and forests are not to be burnt either without reason or to kill creatures. One animal is not to be fed to another....*[8]

Ashoka's first rock inscription at Girnar, Junagarh district, Maharashtra-261 BC says: *Beloved-of-the-Gods, King Piyadasi, has caused this Dhamma edict to be written. Here (in my domain) no living beings are to be slaughtered or offered in sacrifice. Nor should festivals be held, for Beloved-of-the-Gods, King Piyadasi, sees much to object to in such festivals, although there are some festivals that Beloved-of-the-Gods, King Piyadasi, does approve of. Formerly, in the kitchen of Beloved-of-the-Gods, King Piyadasi, hundreds of thousands of animals were killed every day to make curry. But now with the writing of this Dhamma edict only three creatures, two peacocks and a deer are killed, and the deer not always and in time, not even these three creatures will be killed.*[9]

ROLE OF RELIGIONS

Jainism played a vital role in protecting the environment through the principle of *ahimsa* or non-violence. Jainism gives the greatest respect to living beings. Jains were the pioneers in establishing the animal hospitals and retirement homes for the old cattle. Some of the followers of Hinduism influenced by the principles of Jainism became staunch vegetarians. They stopped hunting and non-killing of animals became their highest philosophy.

Buddhist principles advocate non-violence to any sentient being, not just humans, for Buddhism sees humans and other beings as fellow-sufferers in the round of rebirth. While humans are seen to be particularly worthy of respect due to their moral and spiritual potential, these very qualities imply that we should not thoughtlessly exploit other beings, but show our relative superiority through kindness and care.

Such actions are also ascribed to the gods. It is said that Sakka (who gained his divine status by being the helpful Magha, above) was once fleeing with his army from the army of the *asuras*. Seeing that his chariot was about to destroy some birds' nests, he stopped the retreat which then shocked the *asuras* into stopping their pursuit.[10]

In the *Cakkavatti-Sihanoda Sutta*, the ideal ruler is seen as establishing "guard, ward and protection" for both various groups of people in town and country, and animals and birds.

The *Upāsaka-Sila-Sutra* says of the *Bodhisattva*: In places where there are no trees, he erects posts and builds sheds for animals.... Seeing animals that are in fear, he helps and shelters them and persuades hunters [to stop hunting] by providing them with material things and kind words (Sinha 1994: 133-134).

ROLE OF BISHNOIS

Mention should be made in this regard of the Bishnois, who played and are still playing a very effective role in protecting animals and environment by self-sacrifice. For over half a millennium, the Bishnois have evolved their lifestyle into a religion that fiercely protects the environment. It is not a religion that has a heritage of myths, miracles, a book, ornate temples or priests. The Bishnois, estimated to be around 6 million, spread over Rajasthan, Gujarat, Haryana, Uttar Pradesh and Madhya Pradesh, are a practical, wise people who hold lessons for everyone. The Bishnois are practising naturalists and are world's first environmentalists.

The Bishnoi sect was founded by Guru Jambhesvar (b. 1451), also known as Jambhoji or Jambaji, after a drought in the Marwar region of India in AD 1485. He had laid down 29 principles to be followed by the sect. Bis means 20 and noi means 9; thus, *Bishnoi* translates as *Twenty-niners*. Further, the Guru directed the worship of Lord Vishnu (Bishnu). Thus, the sect is called Vishnoi or Bishnoi. Killing animals and the felling of trees were banned. One of his 29 principles states to protect trees and animals. Thus, trees and animals are considered to be sacred by the Bishnois. Out of these 29 principles, 8 were prescribed to preserve biodiversity and encourage good animal husbandry. Jambhoji passed away in 1536, leaving behind guiding principles for his community to save the environment and its animals. He had foreseen the need for environmental protection and made his principles into religious commandments so that people could internalise those principles easily. He preached the ideals of brotherhood, fighting social evils, demanding rights for women, preservation of wildlife and trees and kindness towards all animals. These principles form the religion of the Bishnois who followed them devotedly. They have never allowed anyone to kill any living being or cut any green trees. Due to their efforts of conservation, the desert tract is covered with trees like Khejri, Jal, Rohida, Aak, Ber, Kair, etc., making it the world's greenest desert. Bishnois are strong lovers of wild animals. It is because of their protection that in Bishnoi-dominated areas, deer and antelope (such as blue bulls, black bucks, chinkaras, and chowsinghas) are seen grazing peacefully in their fields despite the fact that the State of Rajasthan where the Bishnois mainly live, faces severe water shortages. Bishnoi women are known to even nurse orphaned blackbucks.

In the 1730s (may be 1737), the ruler of Marwar (Jodhpur), Maharaja Abhay Singh sent his senior official Giridhardas Bhandari to get wood for burning limestone to be used for the construction of his palace. The king's soldiers reached Khejarli village and began to cut Khejri trees. Amrita Devi, the native of the village, requested the soldiers not to cut the trees. When the soldiers did not pay attention to her, she and her three daughters clung to the trees and were killed by the soldiers on the orders of Giridhardas Bhandari. 363 persons (69 women and 294 men) laid down their lives to save the trees. On hearing of this mass sacrifice, the Maharaja himself came to the village and promised the Bishnois that he would never cut trees again. Every September, a Shaheed Mela is held in the village Khejarli to commemorate this great sacrifice. The Chipko movement against the felling of trees started in the Garhwal region was motivated by this incident.

Recently, the commitment of the Bishnoi community once again came to limelight when a famous film personality hunted and killed blackbucks. He was pursued relentlessly by the Bishnois and convicted in spite of his popularity.

With the increasing population and industrialization, the world is witnessing tremendous pressure on its natural resources. Protection and preservation of the environment has, therefore, become a prerequisite and integral part of the development process at the local, national and global level. All over the world, environmental movements (also termed as) are spreading their wings and rewriting the social and economic history.

In India, too, people in different parts of the country are organizing themselves into pressure groups and articulating their demands for just and equitable development without undermining their natural support systems.

Environmental protection is a major threat of the present society because man's desire for more joy and comfort has led him to over-exploit nature's free goods to the extent of reducing its natural capacities for self-stabilization. Man has been indiscriminately manipulating the environment and nature to fulfil his narrow selfish interests. In the process, he has sometimes left the environment so badly mauled and mutilated that it is proving harmful to the humanity itself. As a consequence of this outright disregard of the impact of these activities on the environment, numerous ecological problems have arisen. But the main reason behind this ruthless exploitation of natural resources is man's greed. Gandhiji has very rightly viewed that, "The earth provides enough to satisfy every man's need but not for anybody's greed."

Several environmental or ecological movements are started from the last three decades and the movements like *Chipko* and *Narmada Bachao Andolan* are internationally acclaimed. Other movements in different parts of India were started with support of local or regional environmentalists like Bedti Valley Hydel Project anti dam movement, Champalli Bhopal-capattnam on Godavari, Indravati rivers. Environmentalists are raising voice against the slow death of Dal lake in Kashmir. There is a protest against pollution of rivers like Tungabhadra in Karnataka, Chaliyar river in Kerala, and Chambal River in Madhya Pradesh. *Mannu Rakshanakoota* (Save the Soil campaign) is started in Karnataka to oppose the government's decision to plant eucalyptus trees on farmland and pastures which depletes soil fertility and destroys water resources. Similarly at Hoshangabad area in Madhya Pradesh *Mitti bachao andolan* (Save Soil movement) is started to protest against the feritilizers. Environmentalists are protesting against the location of Mathura oil refinery near Taj, which is causing severe damage to Taj

Mahal. Mining is another area, which witnessed movements. There is a movement against the minings in around Sariska National Park in Alwar district in Rajasthan. Similarly, there are movements of 'Save Western Ghats' and 'Save Eastern Ghats'. People are raising concern over chemical projects and nuclear sites. Balco project, which is an aluminum plant in Orissa, is opposed by the environmental activists. Plans for a hydroelectric project that threatened the park's high diversity of wildlife stimulated an environmentalist social movement in the 1970's called 'Save Silent Valley' at Kerala, which resulted in cancellation of the project and creation of the park in 1985. But the controversy still continues. The spectacular waterfall between the Neelikkal and Pathrakkadavu hills bordering the Silent Valley will disappear if the proposed Pathrakkadavu hydro-electric project is implemented.[11]

Awareness and concern for environment have remained, more or less, restricted to a few individuals in most of the developing countries like India. As a result, despite the rise in the number of conflicts and movements over environmental issues, concern for the environment has remained peripheral for most of the contemporary movements.

NOTES

1. M.S. Randhawa, 1964. *The cult of trees and tree worship in Buddhist-Hindu sculpture*, p. 1.
2. *Rigveda*, V.41.11.
3. *Bhagavad Gita*, 10th chapter, 26th *sloka*.
4. Nanditha Krishna, 2003. 'Souvenir and Proceedings of the International Seminar on water resources and development and management in India through the ages', *Conserving water in South India: The sacred and the secular*, pp. 119-120.
5. T.V. Mahalingam, *A Topographical List of Inscriptions in the Tamil Nadu and Kerala States*, pp. 46-58. R. Nagaswamy, 1985. *Chengam Nadukarkal*, 1971/66.
6. Somasekhara Sarma, *History of Reddi kingdoms*, Waltair, p. 340.
7. Sivasankara Narayana, *Anantapur District Gazetteer*, p. 822, Arthor F. Cox, *North Arcot District Gazetteer*, p. 384.
8. The Seven Pillar Edicts: 5, D.C. Sircar, 1967. *Inscriptions of Asoka*, Delhi.
9. D.C. Sircar, 1967. *Inscriptions of Asoka*, p. 46.
10. Peter Harvey, *Avoiding Unintended Harm to the Environment and the Buddhist Ethic of Intention*, School of Arts, Design, Media and Culture, University of Sunderland.
11. *Only An Axe Away*, is a well-researched film documentary on the struggle to preserve the Silent Valley. The film shares the anxiety of the people of Kerala about the future of the Silent Valley. Producer: Third Eye Communications, Director: P. Baburaj and C. Saratchandran, Malayalam/40min/2004/DV.

REFERENCES

Amirthalingam, M. 1998. *Sacred Trees of Tamil Nadu*, Chennai: C.P.R. Environmental Education Centre.

——. 2005. *Sacred Groves of Tamil Nadu*, Chennai: C.P.R. Environmental Education Centre.

Amirthalingam, M. 1998 and N. Muthukrishnan, 2004. *Temples Tanks of Chennai*, Chennai: C.P.R. Environmental Education Centre.

Birdwood, G.C.M. 1992. *The Arts of India*, Calcutta: Rupa & Co.

Bisht, R.S. 1995. *National Parks of India*, Delhi: Publications Division.

Donald Hughes, J. 2006. *What is Environmental History*, Polity Press, U.K., U.S.A.

Fergusson, James. 1971. *Tree and Serpent worship*, Delhi: Indological Book House.

Gadgil, Madhav and Ramachandra Guha. 1996. *This Fissured Land*. Delhi: Oxford University Press.

Gupta, Shakti. 1996. *Plants in Indian Temple Art*, Delhi: B.R. Publishing Corporation.

Mahalingam, T.V. 1985. *A Topographical List of Inscriptions in the Tamil Nadu and Kerala States*, New Delhi, S. Chand & Company Ltd.

Nagaswamy, R. 1971. *Chengam Nadukarkal*, Madras: State Department of Archaeology.

Nanditha Krishna and Jayanthi Prabhakaran, 1997. *The Ecological Traditions of Tamilnadu,* Chennai: C.P.R. Environmental Education Centre.

Nanditha Krishna. 2003. 'Souvenir and Proceedings of the International Seminar on water resources and development and management in India through the ages', *Conserving water in South India: The sacred and the secular*. Dept. of Indian History, Chennai: University of Madras, pp. 119-120.

——. 2008. *Sacred Animals of India*, Chennai: C.P.R. Environmental Education Centre.

Randhawa, M.S. 1964. *The cult of trees and tree worship in Buddhist-Hindu sculpture*, New Delhi: All India Fine Arts and Crafts Society, p. 1.

Richard, H. Grove, Vinita Damodaran and Satpal Sangwan. 1998. *Nature and the Orient*, New Delhi: Oxford University Press.

Roy, P.C., S. Sorensen (trans.). 1978. *An Index to the Names in the Mahabharata*, Delhi: Motilal Banarsidass.

Sinha, B.C. 1979. *Tree Worship In Ancient India,* New Delhi: Books Today.

Sinha, P.C. 1994. *Green Movements*, International Encyclopedia of Sustainable Development Series, Anmol Publications Pvt. Ltd., New Delhi.

Sircar, D.C. 1967. *Inscriptions of Asoka*, Publications Division, Ministry of Information and Broadcasting, Delhi.

Somasekhara Sarma, M. 1948. *History of Reddi kingdoms*, Waltair: Andhra University Press.

Soren Sen, S. 1978. *An Index to the Names in the Mahabharata*, New Delhi: Motilal Banarsidass.

21

Nature Conservation in the Tamil Tradition – A Historical Perspective

M. AMRITHALINGAM

ABSTRACT

Sangam literature (300 BC-AD 300) mentions the term 'thinai', which encompasses five different types of landscapes, each with its own ecology, social, cultural and ethical behaviour of people. These landscapes are known by their characteristic geographical features – Kurinji (mountainous region), Mullai (forest track), Marutham (agricultural land), Neithal (coastal region) and Paalai (arid land). Each thinai is associated with its own native flowers, trees, animals, birds and climate. In ancient days, a strong and healthy tree was indicative of the king and his rule. Such trees were known as kaaval marangal (vigilance trees). Tree worship was widely prevalent during the Sangam period. Trees were worshipped in temples and they were invariably associated with the presiding village deity. As the banyan tree was associated with Shiva and Vishnu, trees like vembu, vilvam and kontrai were sacred to a particular deity whose idol was installed beneath these trees. The ancient Tamils attached great importance to the preservation of natural resources and biodiversity. This paper summarizes the history of nature conservation by the Tamils drawing references from classical Tamil literature.

INTRODUCTION

Tamil Nadu, endowed with a noteworthy environmental heritage, is ecologically unique among the States (Sanjeeva Raj 2004). Various Tamil literary works, such as *Tolkappiyam*, *Paththupattu*, *Silappadikaram*, *Manimekhalai*, grouped together under Sangam literature, contain elaborate details regarding the nature of polity, economy and society and their gradual advancement. There are descriptions about the varying bio-geographic zones and their differing natural resources.

ANCIENT ETHICS OF CONSERVATION

Tamils had shown their reverence and close attachment to the land, ecology and religious tradition. Each of the *thinai* was named after a flower unique to the region. The ancient landscapes described in the *Tolkappiam* are separate eco-zones scientifically classified. *Tolkappiam* also briefly narrates the lifestyle of the people of each eco-zone and their distinguishing characteristics. Each of the five *thinai*-s or eco-zones is associated with its own characteristic flower, tree, animal, bird, deity, climate – apart from their other individualistic geographical features. The *Tolkappiyam* also speaks of each eco-zone boasting of one particular aspect of emotion, one poetic expression, and also one deity – the hills (*kurinji*) with bondage and Cheyon (Murugan); the arid/desert (*paalai*) with parting and Korravai (Durga); the forests (*mullai*) with waiting and Mayon (Vishnu-Krishna); the seashore (*neythal*) with wailing and Varuna; and the cultivated lands (*marudam*) with quarrel and Ventan (Indra). Similarly, each *thinai* also reflected its unique social behaviour and culture and it is also seen that the environmental factors influenced their culture and behaviour.

On special occasions, the kings of ancient Tamil kingdoms adorned themselves with particular flowers – the Cheras with flowers of Indian Palm (*Borassus flabellifer*) which is known in Tamil as *pondhail* or *panam poo*; the Cholas with *aathi* and the Pandyas with *vembu* (*Azadirachta indica*). The objectives of battle were indicated by wearing specific flowers such as *vetchi, vanji, ulinai, kaanchi, thumbai* and *vaagai*. The seasons of sprouting of leaves, flowering, shedding of flowers and maturing of fruits were deemed as indicators of environmental changes. Before departing for a major war, soldiers used to pray in front of the *unna maram* (Grewia *tilifolia*) to achieve victory. The king, in times of war, appealed to this tree to bloom in emerald verdure to presage victory (*purapporul vennpamalai* 243). If the king was to emerge triumphant in battle, then the *unna maram* (*Grewia tilifolia*) would display fresh foliage and stand erect and if he were to encounter defeat, then it would appear emaciated and dry (*padittruppathu*, 40). This tree was also revered by devotees for its divine fore knowledge and unfailing prophecies.

In each kingdom, a particular tree became part of the regal paraphernalia. The king worshipped that tree and a healthy and sturdy tree reflected the prosperity of his rule. Such a tree was known as *kaaval maram*. In battles, kings sealed their triumph by symbolically slashing the *kaaval marangal* of their opponents. *Madurai Kanchi* (153) refers to the victory of Pandyan Nedunchelian (*padittruppathu* 11-12). Similar reference is made to celebrate the triumph of Imayavaramban Neduncheralathan over the *kadambargal* by cutting the *kadamba tree* which was their *kaaval maram*. Much of the available literature contains several references to *kaaval marangal* (Subramania Pillai 1948; Fergusson 1971 and Aravanan 1980, 1981).

SACRED TREES

The worship of trees was equally prevalent among the Tamils as it was among the people of other civilizations. There are numerous references in Sangam literature to the belief that trees were the abodes of deities (*Natrinai* 83-2 and 303:3; *Agananuru:* 270:12; *Sirupanatruppadai* 17; *Kalithogai* 83:14; *Manimekalai* 3:144; *Purananuru* 191:1 and 198:1; *Natrinai* 343-4; *Tirumurugatruppadai* 256 and *Kurunthogai* 87:1).

For example, the banyan (*Ficus bengalensis*) tree, which was associated with both Siva and Tirumal, subsequently developed into the *sthalavriksha* of the temple with which it was associated. Trees worshipped in the temple and associated either with the temple or the deities came to be known as *sthalavrikshas* or sacred plants. Further, trees like *vembu, vilvam* and *kontrai* were sacred to a particular deity whose idol was installed beneath the tree (*purananuru* 199-1; *agananuru* 287-7; *paripadal* 4-67). Later, when temples were erected for the deities who had originally occupied places under the trees, devotees took special care not to remove or disturb those trees. In fact, these trees formed the centre of the temple near the *garbagriha,* and they were provided enough space for future growth (Subramaniya Pillai 1961). The tamarind tree of the Vishnu temple at Alvar Tirunagari (between Tirunelvelli and Tiruchendur) is illustrative of this practice.

In Tamil Nadu, there are a number of tree shrines and the prominent ones include the mango (*ekamra*) tree at Kanchi, a black plum (*jambu*) at Jumbukeswaram near Tiruchirappalli, the Indian palm (*panai*) at Tirupanaiyur and the 'blinding' tree (*tillai*) at Chidambaram. Besides gods who are widely-revered, such as Shakti, Shiva, Vishnu and Murugan, the sacred trees are also associated with local village guardian deities. One of these is arkamma, named after the plant 'ark', i.e., *errukku* in Tamil (*calotropis gigantea*) and *panaieriyamman* who is the goddess named after the palmyra palm or *panai* and also called *Taalavaasini*, a name that extends to the association to all palms.

The presence of a particularly bountiful tree may have given rise to the concept that a deity is present who offers her blessings in the form of fruits, as in the case of the tamarind tree where *Puliyidaivalaiyamman* is worshipped and a *kadamba* tree that is linked to a goddess called *Kadambariyamman*. The sacred trees are symbolic of a single genetic resource and play a pivotal role in the conservation of local floral wealth and biodiversity.

Every famous temple in Tamil Nadu has a holy tree of its own and is associated with either a local or a *puranic* legend. Sometimes, places are even named after the tree, such as the town of Kanchipuram which has acquired its name after the *kanchi* tree. Thiruverkadu, Tillai, etc. are other examples to further substantiate this point. Every tree has a legend of its own. For example, the mango tree at the Ekambareswarar temple in Kanchi is said to yield mangoes of different variety, taste and size and is believed to be possess an element of divinity and hence worshipped (Jayasendhilnadhan 1988).

Many places are named after the *vriksha*. For example, Thillai (Chidambaram) is derived from the *tillai* tree *(excoecaria agallocha,* the mangrove). Although the name Tillai is still in vogue, the *tillai* tree itself is now extinct in Chidambaram except for a small patch of *tillai* trees in Pichavaram situated at a distance of about five kilometres from Thillai. To restore and respect the traditional heritage, a small *tillai* tree is now grown on the right side of the eastern gateway of the Nataraja temple at Chidambaram. Similarly, the *kadamba (anthocephalus cadamba)* of Madurai, *jambu (syzigium cumini)* of Tiruvannaikka, *venu (bambusa bambos)* of Tiruvetkalam and Tirunelveli, *mullai (jasminum auriculatum)* of Mullaivayil, and *nelli (emblica officinalis)* of Thirunellikka are the *vrikshas* after which the *sthalams* have been named.

Tamil tradition and culture have successfully preserved biodiversity through the ages. An interesting feature of the temples of Tamil Nadu is their association with plants. The Tamils considered the tree sacred and worthy of worship. Even if the sacred tree happened to fade away or perish, it did not cease to be sacred and worship was still continued. The withered tree after some days would wear away, except for the lower part of the trunk. The surviving part of the tree, in the form of a stump called *kandhu*, was worshipped by the people. The people believed that to nurture the spirit dwelling in the stump of the decayed tree, the usual offerings and worship should be carried on uninterruptedly as evidenced by the *Pattinappalai* 246-249; *Aganaanuru* 287:4; 307:22; *Tirumurugatruppadai* 226; *Pattinappalai* 249; *Tiruvilaiyadarpuranam* 18.

A *kadamba* tree (*Anthocephalus cadamba*) once flourished in the Meenakshi Sundareswarear temple at Madurai. Today, only the stump remains and is covered by a silver plate. In Tirupadhiripuliyur, the remains of the *padhiri* tree (*Sterospermum suvedens*), under which goddess Sivagami performed penance to get rid of her sins, are covered by copper-plate. In Tiruvothur, the base of the ancient *panai* (*Borassus flabellifer*) is covered by copper plate, which is circumambulated and worshipped by the devotees (Sundara Sobhidharaj 1991). In Kutralam, the remnant base of the perished *kurumpala* tree (*Artocarpus integrifolia*) has been protected in a separate room. Later, the Tamils sculpted the image of the former sacred tree and worshipped it. A pertinent example for this is in the Ekambareswarar temple, where there is a sculpture depicting with a woman hugging the mango (*Mangifera indica*) tree and in Tiruvanaikka, the goddess is worshipping the *lingam* under a *naval* (*Syzigium cumini*) tree.

There are several examples of trees found in sculptures: In Kutralam, people worship the *lingam* under the *kurumpala;* in Kurukkai, the tree is worshipped by the goddess and *rishis;* in Tirukuvalai, the *lingam* under a tree is worshipped by the king and others; in Anbilalandhurai, the *lingam* under the tree is worshipped by a king; in Tirukottai, a *rishi* sits under the *kottai chedi* (*Ricinus communis*) and in the five metal sculptures of the Tirumangalam temple, one of the *nayanars* is seen under the *kontrai* tree.

The sacred plants are symbolic of a single genetic resource and play an important role in the conservation of biodiversity. The social, economical, medicinal and environmental importance of these trees was recognised and the sacred tree concept evolved as a means of conserving the land's rich plant genetic diversity. The sacred trees represent various geo-climatic habitats. Sacred plants provide food, shelter and nesting substratum for several species of birds and squirrels. For instance, banyan (*Ficus bengalensis*), pipal (*Ficus religiosa*) and Indian fig (*Ficus glomerata*) are afforded total protection in India. *Ficus* is now considered a key resource playing a significant role in the conservation of many insects, birds and mammals.

SACRED GROVES

Sacred groves probably represent the single-most ecological tradition of ancient Tamil culture. Each grove is dedicated to the local folk deities and spirits (*vanadevathai*) and has folklore associated with either the deity or the grove. Commonly found deities are the Aiyanar, Sastha, Muniyappa, Karuppuswami, Veeran (*Kaaval Teivam*/Protective Deity), Andavar (a powerful wish-fulfilling deity) and the goddesses are Selliyamman, Kali, Ellaikali, Ellaipidari, Sapta Kannis, Pechiyamman, Rakkachiyamman and Nagadevadhai (fertility and good health). Among these, Aiyanar is the most ubiquitously found deity. The annual festival is celebrated in all the groves of all districts marked by community offerings of *pongal* and animal sacrifice. Sacrifice of fowl, goat and sheep are made to all the deities except *Aiyanar.* In certain sacred groves, people fulfil their vows by tonsuring (shaving the head to make a ceremonial offering of hair to the god). Terracotta horses of various sizes are lined up in front of the deity within the sacred groves praying for a good harvest.

The taboos, rituals and beliefs associated with the groves, supported by mystic folklore, have been the awe-inspiring factors for preserving them in pristine condition. People believed that any damage to the sacred grove, harm to the fauna residing within it or felling of any tree or taking dead wood may invite the wrath of the local deity, causing diseases and failure of agricultural crops. The rich plant life helps to retain subsoil water during the hot summer months as the pond in the grove is often the only source of drinking water. The groves are a unique form of biodiversity conservation, and are conspicuous examples of the Indian tradition of conserving the ecology as a natural heritage.

Sacred groves were first described by Brandis in 1857. According to Fergusson (1971), sacred groves are believed to be pre-Vedic in origin. More recently, Gadgil and Vartak (1981) reviewed the sacred groves of India's states and reported some 13,270 intact sacred groves, with the highest number found in Himachal Pradesh (nearly 5000 sacred groves). Other estimates put the total number of such groves in India at over a lakh. Sacred groves are called by different names in different parts of India: *Deorali* in Darjeeling, *Law Lyngdoh* in Khasi Hills, *Sarna* in Central India, *Mawphlong* and *Gomphas* in North-East, Gamkhal, Nagvan in Manipur, *Pengada* in Gond, *Jaher* in Santal, Oran and Jogmaya in Rajasthan, Aravalli Hills, Van, Deovani, Deorai in Maharashtra, Sharanas, Dev, Samas in Madhya Pradesh, Kan, Dev Vana, Devara kade in Karnataka, Kaavu and Sarpa kaavu in Kerala and Koil kaadu and Sami solai in Tamil Nadu (Ramakrishnan, *et al.* 1998).

In India, sacred groves were found to be intact (Andhra Pradesh 750, Arunachal Pradesh 58, Assam 40, Chhattisgarh 600, Gujarat 29, Haryana 248, Himachal Pradesh 5000, Jharkhand 21, Karnataka 1424, Kerala 2000, Maharashtra 1600, Manipur 365, Meghalaya 79, Orissa 322, Rajasthan 9, Sikkim 56, Tamil Nadu 448, Uttaranchal 1, West Bengal 670). Of these, 79 range in size from 0.01 to 900ha. and collectively embrace 10,511ha. of vegetation cover. Of this area, only 138ha. comprise totally undisturbed vegetation and 3,188ha. have an open canopy. Most of these groves (66 out of 79), covering an area of 10,251ha. are located in the catchments areas of major rivers and rivulets; 58 (9,621 ha.) are at the origin of perennial streams and 38 (6,454ha.) are on hillsides (Malhotra *et al.* 2001). Amirthalingam (1998) after extensive study documented 500 sacred groves of Tamil Nadu. Another estimate suggests that the number of groves in the country may be as high as 100,000 to 150,000 (Malhotra 1998).

In Tamil Nadu, the sacred groves are sporadically distributed in almost all the villages, where about 500 sacred groves dedicated to various male and female deities were identified. Of these, 343 are dedicated to 93 male deities and 157 are dedicated to 77 female deities. The approximate area occupied by these is 21,694 hectares. Among the 77 female deities, Mariamman is common and worshipped in 14 sacred groves while Aiyanar is the common male deity, worshipped in 86 sacred groves. Most sacred groves are seen in Dharmapuri, Perambalur, Pudukkottai, Tirunelveli and Tiruvannamalai districts, the most in Perambalur district.

SACRED GARDENS

The custom of offering flowers to deities as a sign of devotion is an age-old practice. The inscriptions of Srirangam provide numerous instances of grants for gardens and orchards to the temple. Special staff were employed for maintaining the gardens. They were called *tirunandavana-kaingkarya* and lands granted to the gardens were known as *tirunandavana-puram.* A record dated AD 1316 at Varadaraja Perumal temple, Kanchipuram, mentions a royal grant for the maintenance of a flower garden (*pushpavanam*) and the upkeep of four lotus tanks for the supply of water, flowers and vegetables to the temple. The record gives a list of trees and plants like *javanthi, alari, jaathi, champaka, maadulai,* mango, coconut, orange and lemon. Andal's *Tiruppaavai* mentions the flower garden in the backyard of the house (*pulakkadai tottathu vaaiyil, sengalunirvaai nelndaambal vaai koombina kan*). The term *manaipadappa* used in the inscriptions refers to the house garden. In fact, Andal's father Perialwar nursed a flower garden and supplied garlands to the temple at Srivilliputtur (Raman 1997).

SNAKE WORSHIP

Worship of snakes is fascinating and finds reference in all Indian traditions in general and Tamil Nadu in particular. Snake stones are found all over India, mostly under peepal and neem trees. Snake worship is very popular during the Sangam Age. *Kurunthogai* (282) states that the people who tend to the snake god (*Nagam*) lived under the *marudham* tree (*Terminalia arjuna*). In

Tamil Nadu, peepal and neem trees are planted so close to each other that they entwine as they grow. A *naga* or snake idol is installed under them and worshipped. Women desiring children erect snake stones under these sacred tress and these stones have stylized cobras carved on them representing the Goddess Nagammal (snake goddess). They were offered prayers and appropriate rituals were performed. Women take an early morning bath and reverentially circumambulate these trees" (Ayyar 1982). There is a belief that an infertile woman can conceive if she offers prayer to the goddess Nagathamman. Snake veneration is also an integral part of Indian religion. An important festival, called *Nagapanchami,* is celebrated on the fifth day of the bright half of *Shrawan* (August) (Sivapriyananda 1992). As demi-gods they are depicted in human, half-human and full serpent form.

Tamils also worship the *puthu* (ant hills), the residing place of snakes, and offer oblation on all auspicious days. There is also an association between snakes and trees, both being symbols of fertility and the roots of trees, like the termite mound, are seen as a gateway to the other world.

TEMPLE TANKS IN TAMIL NADU

Hundreds of years ago, when the spectacular array of temples, deemed as expression of our religions creativity, were being built in the vast, dry plains of Tamil Nadu, the creators of those magnificent temple-complexes had also excavated sizeable water-tanks around the temples. Not only had these people understood the significance of water but, more importantly, they had lent it great aura of sanctity. Water was treated as the foremost of the five elements (*panch tatva*) and perhaps the primary reason for constructing these tanks must have been their essentiality.

Much of the plains of Tamil Nadu are characterized by an average rainfall of under 1000 mm and a near absence of perennial rivers. Not surprisingly, this region was described as *vaanam paartha bhoomi* (land desolately looking at the skies). In this context, creation of several kinds of water tanks made practical sense. The best known water-holding structures were the specially excavated water tanks around the many temple sites. In fact, the two entities, temple and the water-tank, complemented each other, both serving an essential part of rural and urban life, of rituals and domestic use. "Actually, the temple and the tank are linked in the term *kovil kulam*, meaning temple tank". Sacred place, deity and sacred water, the temple and the tank fulfilled all the requirements of pilgrimage.

Several temples had two tanks, one of which was for cleansing by the pilgrim while the other was for the deity's ritual bath or *abhishekham* and to serve as the site of the float festival. At some of the temples, they helped to nurture the gardens which provided flowers for the many rituals. "But these *kovil kulams* served more than just the ritual needs; these played an important role in the prosperity of the area; these helped recharge and maintain the groundwater level and proved to be a boon for local ecology as well." There are more than a hundred water-tanks in the Chennai region alone, although most of these have fallen into a state of utter neglect in recent times.

Made of brick or plain earth, most temple tanks are rectilinear in shape. The original structure was an imaginatively planned design, with appropriately situated inlets to gather rainwater from surrounding areas and outlets for release of excess water. Even the surrounding architecture was made in sync with the objective of enhancing the rain-harvesting potential of these tanks. For instance, many of the older homes had sloping roofs that facilitated flow of rain-water into the tanks, some of which were even connected with one another through channels to enable optimum harvesting of water. While religious and traditional practices may have been instrumental in the evolution of this concept, the sacred tanks became a social necessity, offering a meeting place for village people to spend long leisure hours on hot evenings in the open air.

Interestingly, the original names of many of the tanks too were sacred, a few of them named after sacred trees. Thiruvallikeni, the original name of the Parthasarathy temple tank at Triplicane, means 'tank of the sacred white lily'. Alas, unplanned development and growth of the urban areas around the temple-complexes has ruined many of the sacred tanks. While steps have been taken for the restoration of these tanks, it is unfortunate that detergents, plastics and other refuse continues to flow turning these sacred tanks into sewage tanks and intensifying our water woes.

CONCLUSION

The ancient Tamils attached great importance to the preservation of natural resources and biodiversity. These resources were considered not only a source of material well being but also a reflection of the character of the state and its citizens. In this article, the author has made an attempt to explore the importance of the sacred elements such as sacred plants, sacred groves, sacred gardens and temple tanks and their role in ecological traditions. Ecological traditions are very important to humankind and ecological sites have played key roles in regulating various functions such as hydrological cycles, rainfall, temperatures, local climatic conditions and supported bio-diversity. Of course, they also provide significant economic support to the society and to the local people in various ways. Unfortunately, ecological traditions have been subjected to severe biotic pressures, with indiscriminate exploitation, excessive demands for commercial purposes and various other such causes. It is time we revived ecological traditions and realise the role they play in conservation.

ACKNOWLEDGEMENTS

I wish to express my gratitude to Dr. Nanditha Krishna, Honorary Director of C.P.R. Environmental Education Centre, for her constant encouragement and to deepen my interest about the history of nature conservation in the Tamil literature. I am also thankful to Dr. V. Arivudai Nambi for his comments on my earlier draft.

REFERENCES

Amirthalingam, M. 1998. *Sacred Groves of Tamilnadu – A Survey*, Chennai: C.P.R. Environmental Education Centre.

Aravanan, K.P. 1980. *Anthropological Studies on the Dravido-Africans*, Madras: Paari Nilayam.

——. 1981. *Tree Worship in India and Africa – A Comparison (Tamil)*, Chennai: World Tamil Research Centre.

Brandis, D. 1857. 'Indigenous Indian Forestry: Sacred Groves', in *Indian Forestry Working*, Poona: Oriental Institute, pp. 12-13.

Fergusson, J.A. 1971. *Tree and Serpent Worship*, Varanasi: India Book House.

Gadgil, M., and V.D. Vartak. 1981. 'Sacred Groves of Maharashtra: An Inventory', in S.K. Jain (ed.), *Glimpses of Ethnobotany*, Bombay: Oxford University Press, pp. 279-294.

Jagadisa Ayyar, P.V. 1982. *South Indian Customs*, Delhi: Asain Educational Service, pp. 89-90.

Jayasenthilnadhan, J.A. 1988. *Thirumurai Thalangal* (Tamil), Kanci: Indhu Samaja Mandiram.

Malhotra, K.C. 1998. 'Anthropological dimensions of sacred groves in India: An overview', in P.S. Ramakrishnan, K.G. Saxena and U.M. Chandrashekara (eds.), *Conserving the sacred for Biodiversity Management*, New Delhi: Oxford and IBH Publishing Co., pp. 423-38.

Malhotra, K.C., Y. Gokhale and S. Chatterjee. 2001. *Cultural and Ecological Dimensions of Sacred Groves in India*, Bhopal: Indira Gandhi Rashtriya Manav Sangrahalaya.

Raman, K.V. 1997. 'The Ecological Tradition in Tamil Literature and Epigraphy', in Nanditha Krishna and J. Prabakaran (eds.), Chennai: C.P.R. Environmental Education Centre, pp. 16-24.

Ramakrishnan, P.S., K.G. Saxena and U.M. Chandrashekara (eds.). 1998. *Conserving the Sacred for Biodiversity Management*, New Delhi: Oxford and IBH.

Sanjeeva Raj. 'Unique eco-heritage', *The Hindu*, October 3, 2004.

Sivapriyananda. 1992. 'Serpents in Indian Imagination', *The Indian Magazine*, pp. 18-27.

Subramaniya Pillai. 1948. *Tree Worship and its Ophiolatry*, Chidambaram: Annamalai University, pp. 95-102.

Sundra Sobhidharaj. 1991. *Tamilil Seithigal*, Vol. II, Research Papers, Nagercoil: Sobhitham Publishers.

22

Glory Bitten but Not Battered: A Historical Investigation of the Cult of Ayyanar

B. RAMACHANDRA REDDY & R. NATARAJAN

ABSTRACT

Human sojourn directed by twin forces of fear and gratitude takes refuge in religion. In this context the present paper deals with an analysis of the cult of Ayyanar in the Tamil-speaking area in general and Pondicherry region in particular. Ayyanar's origin is analysed based on puranic tradition and popular belief. His abode and attendants and His pivotal role as a protector and benefactor of the village community are elaborated for a detailed analysis. The caste matrix of the priests of his temples and the influence of Vedic tradition are highlighted. Louis Dumont's interpretation that Ayyanar is a Brahmin Aiyer is contested on various grounds. Ayyanar is essentially projected as a deified king of the Jain tradition whose singular importance was overshadowed by the process of Brahminisation. His royal insignia and monarchical valour is strengthening the argument. His role fitting into the heroic tradition right from the Sangam Age is substantiated by reverential cult of hero-stones is also highlighted. Gustav Oppert's analysis of Ayyanar is dismissed. His symbiotic position between Saivism and Vaishnavism is vindicated. The assimilation process of Popular tradition into the Elite tradition is emphasized.

Human existence right through various chronological segments of History is singularly characterized by twin intrinsic forces of fear and a sense of gratitude. The pangs of helplessness drove mankind to take refuge in the hands of supernatural protection. Worship of animals and nature in the early stages of human history was drawn out of the aforesaid compulsive psyche. Subsequent religious faith in the cycle of birth and rebirth glued their minds to ancestral worship as a holy continuum in the societal evolution. Benevolent and sacrificial tendencies of selfless persons came to be held in high esteem and they were deified and venerated. This form of worship continued to persist with the age-long worship of Mother Goddess often identified with adoring principles of love, compassion, fertility and motherhood. Male deities found their inclusion in the process of extension of Hindu pantheon at a later date with the influx of a number of gods and goddesses with assigned functions and motives. The concept of worship of folk gods is primitive in the Indian religious history and the genesis of *Agamic* form of worship was a later addition. The cult of Ayyanar as an integral component of this tradition is still extant in the society in Tamil Nadu. The origin of Ayyanar is steeped in mystery and he is known by different names. The mode of worship is also not uniform. Pondicherry region is taken for analysis to adjudge the prevalence of the cult and the types of worship of this popular deity.

GEOGRAPHICAL SETTING OF PONDICHERRY

The Union Territory of Pondicherry is constituted out of the four erstwhile enclaves of the French domain in India. The four enclaves are not a homogenous whole. Pondicherry and Karaikal regions are flanked by the nearby Tamil Nadu state, whereas Mahe and Yanam regions are surrounded by Kerala and Andhra Pradesh states respectively. The present study is limited to Pondicherry region alone. Pondicherry lies between 11° 46′ and 12° 03′ Northern Latitude and between 79° 36′ and 79° 53′ Eastern Longitude (Antony 1982: 2). The total area of Pondicherry region is about 290 sq. kms. with a total population of 7,35,332 as per the 2001 census. It has a substantial dalit population of 1,20,980 (Census 2003: 1). Though statistical particulars of the castes are not available, agro-pastoral communities like the Vanniyars or Pallis (Thurston 2001: 1-28) who also act as temple priests of folk deities, are considered numerous in this region. The archaeological and epigraphic sources speak about the historical past of the region (Begley 1987; Raman 1987).

HISTORICAL APPRAISAL OF AYYANAR CULT

Ayyanar, a folk deity, continues to be worshipped even today and is accommodated in the list of gods and goddesses of the highly evolved and complex pantheon of the Hindu tradition of the later period. If the worship of the male god is understood as an adjunct proposition to the prevalent Sakthi Cult, Ayyanar stands out prominently as a part of this holy tradition. His worship can be traced even in the early centuries of the Christian era and is well documented in religious history. He is popularly known by different names like *Sattan, Purattan, Kanakari, Brahma Sasta* and *Dharma Sasta*. Analysis of the name Ayyanar becomes imperative to know its significance in terms of his function as a great benefactor of humanity. The word *Ayya* stands for 'father', 'respectable', 'a man of esteemed position', 'master', 'lord' and 'teacher'[1] (Burrow and Emeneau, 1961: Entry No. 46 and 163). Suffixing 'n' in Tamil language to proper pronouns is a grammatical exercise and *Ayya* naturally becomes Ayyan. Suffixing 'ar' is to extend respectability to such pronouns which otherwise become singular expressions. Therefore, *Ayya* is transformed into a term of respectability as Ayyanar. It is noteworthy that the god's name will not be pronounced in singular terms, except while referring to his Sanskritized names which reveal the emotional attachment of the villagers towards him, like those of Sivan, Murugan, etc. Dumont says that Ayyanar may mean a Father, just as referring to a village Goddess as Amman. If Ayyanar is juxtaposed to Amman, He should be the Lord or Master to the Lady and not as father to the mother (Dumont 1959: 77). Gopinatha Rao (1968: 485-486) deviates from the Dravidian interpretation and attributes Sanskrit tradition in describing the name Ayyanar as a modification of the Sanskrit word *Arya* (Respectable). Since the origin of Ayyanar is not within the purview of any singular exact origin, there is a need to decipher corroborative sources which give some clues to the birth of Ayyanar or Hariharaputra.

After churning the ocean of milk (*ksheera sagara*), both gods (*devas*) and demons (*asuras*) were in war with each other to have total possession of ambrosia that makes the drinker eternal and divine. To overcome this piquant situation, Lord Vishnu appeared in the form of Mohini to seduce the *asuras* and carried out his plan of distributing ambrosia to the *devas*. Lord Siva, who was witnessing all these events, was enamoured by the beauty of Mohini and Hariharaputra (Son of Vishnu and Siva) was born of their union. He is as black as sea in colour with a flowing hair and a *sendu* or horse whip in his hand[2] (Arunachalam 1977: 19; Krishna Sastri 1916: 230).

Another *puranic* story of *Bhasmasura* is equally important in this context. He was blessed by Lord Siva that anyone touched by *Bhasmasura* on head would be reduced to ashes. The *asura* wanted to test it with the boon-giver himself and Lord Siva was on his heels to save his life and appealed to Lord Vishnu for protection. Lord Vishnu came in the guise of Mohini. *Bhasmasura* was so much enticed by her bewitching beauty and wanted to enjoy her immediately. He was asked to come clean before courting. The *asura* touched his own head unconsciously while cleaning and was reduced to ashes. Another version says that the *asura* while dancing with Mohini, put his hand on his own head imitating Her dance posture and was reduced to ashes[19] (Oppert, 1972: 508-509). Yet another story says that Siva and Vishnu went to Daruka forest as Bhikshatana Murthi and Mohini to entice sages and their consorts. Lord Siva himself was engulfed by the glitter of Mohini and Hariharaputra was born as a testimony of their union (Arunachalam 1977: 21).

According to the oral tradition of *Terukuttu* singers, it was Rudra Maharshi who spotted the deserted child in Aivalam forest and reared him as his foster son. He was taught the basics of warfare, *sastras* and magic. He was endorsed the job of conquering fifty-six kingdoms of the Earth (*Avani aimbattaru desam*).[3] He won over fifty-five countries and the Malayalattars were conquered in magic. The defeated people became his slaves and attendants. While crossing the river Madhulai on his return, he was drifted to Velvimalai in the cross-currents, the dwelling place of Velvinathar.

At this juncture the story associated with the saint should be discussed. In the past the saint, Rudra Maharshi was performing a *yagna* under a tree. The eggs of Velvi bird fell into the holy fire pit accidentally from the tree top and two female babies came out of them. They were named as Purani and Putkalai and were brought up by the saint. Just before Ayynar reached the forest spot, these damsels had a dream of marrying him. Now they had a chance to see him in person and fell in love with him. They expressed their desire to their step-father and their marriage was fixed. The white elephant given as dowry became his vehicle later. Viran and Malayalattar became his associates.

Another story connects Aiyanar with *Sapta Kanyakas* (seven virgins).[4] Ayyanar during his stroll with Viran happened to see the 'seven sisters' in a pond. They were lured by his beauty and pleaded him to marry. As he was already married with two wives, he negated their proposal. There are panels of *Sapta kanyakas* in eight temples of Ayyanar in the studied area.

There is another *puranic* version according to which sage Narada informed Lord Siva that his son Ayyanar was due for marriage. Viran, son of Rudra Maharshi and Ayyanar's friend, jointly planted a flower garden and Ayyanar left it later under Viran's care. Both were in the process of conquering territories. Two thousand warriors were ruling over the Malayalam territory assisted by the magical powers, namely, Kali, Dhuli, Ladan and Madan. Both Ayyanar and Viran disguised as *Jogis* (hermits) overcame all the witchcraft and defeated them. They became his attendants. Kali recognized Ayyanar and permitted him to stay in her premises. Marriage with Purani and Putkalai was subsequently arranged with Ayyanar by their brother Viran (Arunachalam 1977: 41-42). There is no uniformity in the stories of origin of Ayyanar and different anecdotes often criss-cross and overlap.

Fig. 1. Aranganur Ayyanar Temple.

PLACES OF WORSHIP OF AYYANAR

A majority of the villages in the Pondicherry region have at least one Ayyanar temple each, with the exception of the historically important village Bahur. His image, with those of his two wives, is usually chiselled on a granite slab. However, Yamashita argues, on the basis of his field study of Central Tamil Nadu, that the worship of Ayyanar can even be without an image. He writes: "God resides in all the bricks of an Ayyanar temple" (Yamashita 1996: 59). He adds that there is a preconceived notion of anthromorphism in the case of gods in the orthodox Hindu pantheon and it is not in the case of Ayyanar and his entourage on account of the different idea of the divine. Hence, the presence or absence of an image and the extent to which the image is anthromorphically carved are largely matters of arbitrary choice and are strictly not of importance (Yamashita 1996: 65). His abode is either roofless or flat-roofed. In the urban localities, a small *Vimana* (superstructure) is added. It is so in the case of Brahminised temples of Ayyanar in rural areas also. They are usually located on the south-west boundary of the villages. Gopinatha Rao (1968: 485) also says, "It is an invariable rule in the Malayalam country that in every temple, be it of Siva or Vishnu, there must be in its south-west corner a shrine for Sasta" (Ayyanar). Rarely the temple is located to the north-east of the village (Yamashita 1996: 60). Occasionally, they are positioned on the banks of ravines or irrigational tanks. *Athankarai* (river bank) Ayyanar near *Abhishegapakkam* and *Erimudy* (tank edge) Ayyanar at Aranganur (Fig. 1) are the standing examples of that type. The image of Aiyanar obviously faces towards the east. A sacred grove is normally found around an Ayyanar temple. It is a heinous sacrilege to remove even a twig of these groves (Francis 1906: 100). His attendant Viran is seen in a standing position with a drawn sword on the northern side. His vehicle elephant in stone is placed in front. Offerings in the form of small terracotta horses are found in rows (Fig. 2). Now-a-days, big horses made of

Fig. 2. Aranganur terracota horses.

cement have started replacing terracotta ones. Bigger structures of Madurai Viran in stucco figure are also found. Madurai Viran is a historical figure said to have been a contemporary of Tirumala Nayaka, who ruled Madurai in seventeenth century (Kannan 1996: 213-214). Beside him is a dog in sitting position and a seated lion is a rare addition. It seems that Madurai Viran was a later addition to the Ayyanar cult around seventeenth century. In the recent times, Madurai Viran statue has two guards in colourful police or *sepoy* uniform with two guns. Thus, the abode of Ayyanar is a sacred complex accommodating many gods, who were connected with Ayyanar in some way or the other in the oral tradition, except Madurai Viran.

AYYANAR – THE GOD OF THE VILLAGE COMMUNITY AS PROTECTOR AND BENEFACTOR

Normally, Ayyanar has the attributes as protector of *dharma* and preserver of order. He is believed as a warrior on foot or riding on a white elephant or a horse, with a *sendu* or a whip in his hand. He is the prime guardian deity (*kaval daivam*) of the entire village. As a nocturnal god, he goes round the village on his vehicle accompanied by his attendants and punishes the evil-doers and thieves. He is said to be the king of demons. Pate says that Ayyanar is their master although he is not one of them (Pate 1917: 142; Francis 1906: 99-100). Oppert calls him the protector of human beings from all kinds of calamities and more so from the mischievous machinations of the evil spirits (Oppert 1972: 454). Terracotta horses made as offerings by the devotees facilitate the movement of Ayyanar and his retinue during nights. His escort battalion consists of guards or vassals or demons. He goes for patrolling during nights at an awful pace with his people waving their swords in hands surrounded by torch-bearers. It is believed that anyone who meets this hunting party will face a certain death. So the sight of Ayyanar is much feared. He is a scourge to the thieves and way-laiders, and is held in special esteem as a protector of live-stock. In the event of an epidemic to the cattle in the locality, the villagers pray to him to protect their cattle from pestilence (Arunachalam 1977: 46).

Apart from his sacred role of being a guardian spirit, he is a generous boon-giver as well. People invoke his blessings for getting wealth or destroying enemies or securing the chosen women or to ward off of evil effects or omens caused by lizards. Francis calls Aiyanar a god in settling disputes. "A settlement is usually made without any loss of time before the god and is ratified by offering at his shrine" (Francis 1906: 101). The blessed beneficiaries express their gratitude by offerings terracotta images of horses and bulls. He is believed to bless the devotees with children. They in turn offer swings (*oonchal*). Two such swings are found in the Ayyanar temple of Thirubuvanai village. Yet another peculiarity in the Pondicherry region is that the devotees write their prayers in paper and tie it to the legs of the bigger cement-mortar horse, in front of the temple. The entire village community goes for collective prayers to relieve them of the distress of severe drought. He is also the custodian god of water bodies in some rural pockets of Pondicherry, the best example being the Athangarai Ayyanar near Abhishekapakam, who is the protector of ravine waters and Erimudy Ayyanar in Aranganur is the protector of the water of the huge tank of Bahur belonging to the Chola period. Thus, Ayyanar is worshipped as a god with diverse functions and limitless boons.

The Caste Matrix of Priests in the Temples of Ayyanar

According to Louis Dumont, the priests in the Ayyanar temples belong to potter community based on his observations in Madurai, Tirunelveli and Ramnad districts of Tamil Nadu. They are non-vegetarians and make terracotta images of horses. The field survey in Pondicherry region gives a different picture altogether. Out of fifty Ayyanar temples surveyed, forty-two have Vanniya (Palli) priests (84%), five have Brahmin priests (10%), two have *Dalit* priests (4%) and one is a Pattinavar or fisherman priest (2%). Ninety per cent of them are non-vegetarians. The number of Vannia priests out-numbering the priests of other communities must be due to the high percentage of the agricultural population. As the population of *Dalit* is more in Abhishekapakam and Pichaiveerampet the priests of these villages are from *Dalit* community. In Veerampattinam village ninety-eight per cent of the population belongs to fisherman community or Pattinavar and naturally the priest is from this caste. Villages like Olanthaikeerapalayam, Thattanchavady and Mettupalayam bordering the urban limits of Pondicherry have Brahmin priests as it is commonly found in all the temples within urban areas. Brahmin priests have substituted former Vanniya priests in the temples of Eripakkam and Thengathittu. In two temples at Aranganur and Kirumapakkam, the two priests belong to Vanniya and the Brahmin communities respectively.

Form of Worship

Form of worship varies, depending on the wealth and location of the temples. Daily worship, annual ceremonies, individual and communal worship are noticed in the Pondicherry region. In some temples, *pujas* are performed twice a day with rituals like libation (*abhishekam*), offering of food (*naivedyam*) and burning of incense (*harathi*). It is followed by rendering of prayers and chanting of sacred verses (*mantras*) imitating the Brahminical tradition. Improvised version of *mantras* is also included (Oppert 1972: 506-508). In some temples, the *puja* is limited to select days like Mondays and Fridays.

The individual families offer worship and give swings and clay figures of children to Ayyanar when their prayers are answered. The clay replicas of human parts are offered when the respective ailments are cured. Francis gives an example of presenting huge sandals for the nocturnal wanderings of Ayyanar but there is no such practice observed in the studied area. The much satisfied parties often present a pair or more of terracotta horses with or without riders to Ayyanar. The opening of the eyes of terracotta horses, called *Kudirai Viduthal,* is deemed to be a sacred event that will be performed by the potter. The individual or family worship often includes animal sacrifices. They offer cooked rice (*pongal)* as offering (*naivedya)* to Ayyanar and it is distributed to the devotees at the end of the *puja.* A cloth curtain is suspended in front of the vegetarian god, Ayyanar. Then a fowl or a goat is sacrificed to Viran. It is believed to be a good augury if the sacrificial victim is cut with a single stroke of the sword. After that, arrack (Indian made foreign liquor now-a-days), a bottle full of toddy, opium, *ganja* (hemp), a cigar and dried fish are offered to Viran. These offerings and the head of the sacrificed animal are taken away as the share of the non-Brahmin priest. In recent years, some trading or business companies are also resorting to this practice once in three or five years with the money accrued by keeping aside a fraction of their profit.

The impressive annual festival is perhaps *Atru tiruvizha* (river festival) celebrated in the Tamil month of *Thai* for *Erumudi* Ayyanar of Aranganur with all pomp and splendour of Brahminical tradition. His idol is taken in procession through the neighbouring villages for a holy dip in the river South Pennar in the presence of a large number of devotees.

ANALYSIS

The villages of Pondicherry region have Ayyanar temples located mostly on the north-west borders amidst sacred grooves. The terracotta images of horse given as offerings are believed to facilitate his patrolling during nights to ward off evil spirits and thieves. He is both the guardian and benevolent boon-giver of the village community. He is considered an independent deity in his exclusive abode of worship with his friend and attendant Viran.

We propose to project Ayyanar as a deified king of the Jaina tradition. His origin and deeds of excellence were overshadowed by increasing Brahminisation. According to the ancient Tamil text Tolkappiyam of the Sangam Age, the essential regalia of the king included a war weapon, the flag, the umbrella, the drum, the horse, the elephant, the chariot and the crown (Subramanyam 1980: 74). The concept of royalty was yet to bloom in full during this period. Ayyanar is having at least five royal insignia as stated in Tolkappiyam. They are sceptre (weapon), the flag of fowl, the white elephant, the white horse and a crown.

Ayyanar is seen with a crown symbolizing royal supremacy. The sceptre in his hand stands for the royal justice and authority. Use of elephant was the prerogative of an independent sovereign at least up to 6th century AD in almost all parts of India. Ayyanar's white elephant similar to Iravata of Lord Indra, must be deemed as an exclusive privilege of the king of kings. It is further strengthened by the folk tradition, according to which he conquered fifty-six (*Aimbattaru*) territories/countries of ancient India. Use of a spotless white horse is yet another privilege of the emperors and it was reserved for use in *Asvamedha* sacrifice. His flag contains a fowl emblem or insignia. As a guardian deity of the village, he protects water bodies to help in living and irrigation. These are the prime duties of a king. These duties and attributes of Ayyanar fit him into the stature of an earthly king. Other components like the sacred grove, the fowl banner and sceptre lead us to surmise that he belonged to the agro-pastoral community dwelling in pasture lands. It is believed that the concept of kingship originated in the shepherd dominated *Mullai Tinai* (Physiographical division). It is further attested by the Tamil equivalent of the word king as *Ko* again derived from *Kon* that means a cowherd (Subramanyam 1980: 39).

Louis Dumont gives an interesting interpretation that Ayyanar is a Brahmin *Aiyer* based on the phonetic resemblance of his nomenclature and vegetarianism distinctly in contrast to his attendant Viran (Dumont 1959: 85-86). His conclusion needs re-examination in the context of three vital premises connected to the cult of Ayyanar. They are his seating position, vegetarianism and the very name itself. He is seen with a folded right leg tied with a meditation band and his left leg is drooping. Jainism gives specific importance to meditation. It is equally significant to assume that vegetarianism of Ayyanar is mainly drawn on the principle of strict *Ahimsa* (non-killing) of Jainism and not so much from Hinduism and Buddhism by contrast. Hence, Ayyanar's Jaina heritage becomes an acceptable probability. At this juncture it becomes imperative to analyse the word Ayyanar further in depth to assess his Jaina lineage. The term Ayyanar may be a derivative of *Accan,* which means in Tamil and Malayalam either an honourable man or head of the family. The Kannada variant of it is *Ajja,* which means grandfather (Burrow and Emeneau 1961: Entry no. 46). *Ajja* is another form of Prakrit Ayya (Sanskrit *Arya*). In the region immediately to the south of Krishna River, the Sanskrit version of *Arya* for the Dravidian *Ayya* is still current. *Arya* (venerable) as an honorific prefix to the names of Buddhist or Jaina teachers and saints occurs in the inscriptions all over India (Gopalachari 1976: 202). For example, the author of Purapporul Venbamalai of Sangam period was one Aiyan Adigal, a Jaina teacher. The easiest mechanism to attain and sustain royalty for an aboriginal is to espouse heretical sects especially Jainism, the dominant heterodox sect of the region (Stein 1983: 53). The same argument holds good for Ayyanar who was basically an aboriginal, and who chose Jainism as an easy means to get ritual sanction to his royalty. Dumont says that the structural disposition of his attendant gods represent a bipolar framework visibly identified in the social relations in the village society based on the principles of purity and impurity. He goes further to explain the relationship between Ayyanar and Viran as one of interdependence of pure and impure.

Yet another argument in place to describe Ayyanar's affection towards Jainism is evidenced by a temple dedicated to Parsvanatha, the 23rd Jaina Tirthankara, at a place called Melchittambur, roughly 15 km away from Jinji. The architectural pattern belongs to the Pallava period. Within the temple premises, there are four small temples with diminutive roofs separated by a small wall. Three of them are dedicated to female deities (*yakshis*). The signboard of the first shrine says it is Brahmadevar, whose leg portion is covered with *dhoti* (loin cloth). A careful examination revealed that the deity was seated on an elephant and not on Brahma's vehicle swan and the folded leg posture and the presence of meditation band confirm that the statue was that of Ayyanar. Just above his head, a small Jaina *Digambara* statue was found. Arunachalam also says that in Jainism, Ayyanar has the status of a tutelary god of watch and ward and is found in all Jaina temples (Arunachalam 1977: 28).

Ayyanar fits into the heroic tradition traced from the Sangam Age onwards as a protector and a benefactor of the people. Erecting memorial stones, locally called *veerekkal,* was a common practice in Tamilaham in honorific memory of those who protected people and place from wild animals and intruders (Soundara Rajan 1982: 59-76; Settar 1982: 183-197). Nagaswamy (1984) also believes that the erection of hero-stones and the adoration of the dead hero as the saviour spirit of the community may be considered as an extension of the pre-historic cult of erecting megalithic tombs and the worship of these hero-stones led to some of the cults of village gods. Soon the hero came to be celebrated in ballads and his fame spread to nearby regions and these people, wherever they migrated, took the worship of that hero with them spreading the cult. Detailed references to the rationale of the hero-stone cult are furnished in Tolkappiam, the oldest grammar text and they were further expanded and detailed by Ayyan Adigal in his Purapporul Venbamalai (Soundara rajan 1982: 66). Tirukkural also refers to hero-stone worship (Bharati 1995: Couplet 71). Interestingly, the authors of all the three works professed Jainism and the hero-stone cult can be inferred as part of Jainism in ancient Tamil land. Tolkappiyam refers to two methods of erecting hero-stones, namely, *vettiyal* and *poduiyal*. According to the first practice, the name of the dead hero is engraved on the stones after offering prayers to god. In the second tradition, the hero-stone gets divinized once it is installed (Soundara Rajan 1982: 67). The hero of the stone can be seen as fighting with a wild animal or with a weapon in his outstretched hand in combating position. The idol of Viran in front of Aiyanar is having similar attributes. The very name Viran means a hero. Soundara Rajan also vaguely suspects that the heroes merged with Aiyanar cult as demi-gods[5] (Soundara Rajan 1982: 69). If Viran and Madurai Viran were human beings deified, there is every possibility to believe that their master Ayyanar must also be a human being who was deified for his benevolent deeds.

Gustav Oppert opined that the Brahmin priesthood invented a disgusting account of the incestuous origin of Ayyanar to heap disgrace and destroy his influence (Oppert 1972: 505). A clear understanding of the South Indian *Bhakti* movement give a different dimension opposite to Oppert's view. The story was invented for some other reason. In the evolution of *Bhakthi* cult in South India, gods of five *tinais* (physiographical divisions) and Jaina *yakshis* were given an esteemed position in the complex Hindu pantheon. The deities of little tradition were accommodated in the pantheon of the great tradition (Champaka Lakshmi 1996; Narayanan and Veluthat 2000). After a period of bitter rivalry between Saivism and Vaishnavism, an acceptable compromise was reached. It vindicated the unity of the cults of Siva and Vishnu (*Sivaya Vishnu rupaya* and *Vishnu rupaya Siva*). During this period of transition, Ayyanar, the mighty God of the Little tradition, might have been loosely integrated in both these cults. It is ostensibly visible in the religious marks of his two consorts. Purani wears a Vaishnava *kasturi* mark on her forehead and Putkalai has the holy streaks of sacred ash (*Vibhuthi* or *Tiruniru*) in Saivite style. The popularity of 'Hari haraputra' definitely shrouded the real origin and sacred memories associated with Ayyanar.

CONCLUSION

The sociological interpretations need to be analyzed for their exact relevance and significance. The dichotomy of pure and impure concepts attributed to Ayyanar and his attending gods is found to be deviant in the field study. Since times immemorial, 'impure' concept is associated with a mystical power which carries with it a profound religious significance in ancient society. During this period, the idea of 'divine' was so sacred and above these pure and impure impulses before the emergence of Brahminical religion which was essentially drawn out of these two opposite perceptions. As Ayyanar was enjoying an enlightened status as the powerful god, these delimitations of Hinduism become less effective criteria. For that matter it is difficult to apply them even to his attendant gods since their relationship with Ayyanar is often one of co-existence. The scheme to keep and present them as two opposite functional gods is very difficult. The symbiotic relationship between the two does not provide space for such a conjecture.

Based on the field study, the following conclusions can be drawn assertively. Ayyanar was a great heroic, benevolent earthly king with Jaina affiliation. He was a great conqueror, protector and benefactor of the village people. He is the god of the village community and fulfils their needs and aspirations. He was commanding an exalted position as the chief god in the early period. With the emergence of complex orthodox Hindu religion, the worship of Ayyanar was relegated to a position of lesser importance. His vegetarianism and the *Puranic* contentions of his origin as Hariharaputra were invented to position him within the framework of Hinduism. Yet, his popularity in the rural society and mythology is still distinctly visible.

ACKNOWLEDGEMENTS

We thank Mr. Y. Gopala Reddy, Nellore, Prof. Kothandaraman, Former Director of Pondicherry Institute of Linguistics and Culture, Pondicherry and Mr. K. Srinivasulu, Lecturer in History, C.S.R. Sarma College, Ongole (A.P.) for their suggestions and comments.

NOTES

1. It may also be a derivative of *Acca* that means 'honourable person' or 'head of the family'. If the second letter in a Tamil word is transformed into a vowel, *Accan* becomes *Aaan* as per the rule of Prakrit language and would be pronounced as *Ayyan*. We thank Prof. Kothandaraman for the information.
2. This is a summarized version of the story of Ayyanar as told by the priests of various Aiyanar temples in and around Pondicherry. Some used to say that the seed of Siva was received in the hand and Hariharaputra, who arose out of it, was called *Kaiyanar* (*Kai* in Tamil means hand), and its corrupt version Ayyanar is a far-fetched etymological exercise.
3. Traditionally, the entire Indian sub-continent was divided into fifty-six countries or *chappanaru desams*. They were 1. Anga 2. Vanga or Pundra 3. Kalinga 4. Karnata 5. Kerala 6. Kamarupa 7. Gowda or Gada or Verendri 8. Vanavasa or Banavasi 9. Kuntala 10. Konkana 11. Magadha or Kikata 12. Surastra 13. Malwa 14. Lata 15. Bhota 16. Virata 17. Sabara 18. Kukura 19. Kuruvu or Kurukshetra or Vivasana or Gamisnuvu 20. Avantya or Avanti or Ujjayini or Visala 21. Pandya 22. Madra 23. Simhala 24. Ghursara 25. Paralika 26. Mithila 27. Panchala 28. Surasena 29. Gandhara 30. Bahlika 31. Haihaya 32. Talava 33. Salva 34. Pundraka 35. Pragjotisa 36. Matya 37. Chedi 38. Barbara 39. Nepala 40. Gaula 41. Kasmira or Kira 42. Kanyakubja or Kusasthala 43. Vidarba 44. Khurasana 45. Maharastra 46. Kosala 47. Kekaya 48. Ahicchatra 49. Trilinga 50. Karhata 51. Prayaga 52. Kambhoja 53. Bhoja 54. Chola 55. Huna 56. Kasi or Avamukta. It is improbable to think that Ayyanar might have conquered all the areas from Central Asian part to Deep South. It may be reasonable to think that such a sub-division of South India might have existed whose details are not forthcoming. We thank Mr. Y. Gopala Reddy, Nellore, Andhra Pradesh for providing this information.
4. The *Sapta Matrkas* or seven virgins are 1. Brahmi, 2. Maheswari, 3. Kaumari, 4. Vaishnavi, 5. Varahi, 6. Indrani and 7. Chamundi. At Sanyasikuppam village, 35 km from Pondicherry, there is an exclusive temple for *Sapta Matrkas* that faces towards north. The sanctum sanctorum consists of life-size separate images of seven virgins, a seated Vinayaka and a seated Ayyanar in the front with meditation band across the two folded legs without his consorts.
5. K.V. Soundara Rajan (1982) also says that near Dharmapuri offerings were also associated with a Hanuman temple. Hanuman, it may be recalled, is also called Mahavira.

REFERENCES

Antony, Francis Cyril. (ed.). 1982. *Gazetteer of India, Union Territory of Pondicherry*, Vol. I, Pondicherry.

Arunachalam, M. 1977. 'The Sasta (Aiyanar) Cult in Tamil Nadu', *Bulletin of the Institute of Traditional Cultures*, Madras, pp. 2-51.

Begley, Vimala. 1987. 'Sources of Pondicherry History, Prehistoric to Early Historic Period', *Revue Historique De Pondicherry*, Vol. 15, pp. 1-20.

Bharati, Yogi Suddhananda. 1995. *Tirukkural with English Couplets*, Madras (First published 1897).

Burrow, T. and M.B. Emeneau. 1961. *A Dravidian Etymological Dictionary* (D.E.D), Oxford: OUP.

Census of India 2001, *Series 35: Pondicherry Final Population Totals*, Pondicherry, 2003.

Champaka Lakshmi, R. 1996. 'From Devotion and Dissent to Dominance: The Bhakti of Tamil Alvars and Nayanars', in R. Champaka Lakshmi and S. Gopal (ed.), *Tradition Dissent and Ideology: Essays in Honour of Romila Thapar*, Delhi: Oxford University Press, pp. 135-163.

Dumont, Louis. 1959. 'A Structural Definition of a Folk Deity of Tamil-Nad: Aiyanar, the Lord', *Contributions to Indian Sociology*, Vol. III, pp. 75-87.

Francis, W. 1906. *Madras District Gazetteers – South Arcot*, Madras.

Gopalachari, K. 1976. *Early History of the Andhra Country*, Madras.

Gopinatha Rao, T.A. 1968. *Elements of Hindu Iconography*, Vol. 2, Part II, Delhi: Motilal Banarsidass.

Kannan, M. 1996. 'Through a Text: The Silence of Maturai Viryan and Its Other Echoes', *PILC Journal of Dravidian Studies*, No. 6, 21 July, pp. 213-226.

Krishna Sastri, H. 1916. *South Indian Images of Gods and Goddesses*, Madras.

Nagaswamy, R. 'Village Gods and Heroes – Worship of Hero Stones of Tamil Nadu, India', *UNESCO Courier*, March, 1984. http://findarticles.com/p/articles/mi_m1310/is_1984_March/ai_3156298/pg_1?tag=artBody; col1.

Narayanan, M.G.S. and Veluthat, Kesavan. 2000. 'Bhakti Movement in South India', in D.N. Jha (ed.), *The Feudal Order: State, Society and Ideology of Early Medieval India*, New Delhi: Oxford University Press, pp. 385-410.

Oppert, Gustav. 1972. *On the Original Inhabitants of Bharatavarsha or India*, Delhi (First published 1883).

Pate, H.R. 1917. *Madras District Gazetteers – Tirunelveli*, Madras.

Raman, K.V. 1987. 'Sources of Pondicherry History, Early Period', *Revue Historique De Pondicherry*, Vol. 15, pp. 21-31.

Settar, S. 1982. 'Memorial Stones in South India', in S. Settar and Gunther D. Sontheimer (ed.), *Memorial Stones: A Study of Their Origin, Significance and Variety*, Dharwad, pp. 183-197.

Soundara Rajan, K.V. 1982. 'Origin and spread of memorial stones in Tamil – Nad', in S. Settar and Gunther D. Sontheimer (ed.), *Memorial Stones: A Study of Their Origin, Significance and Variety*, Dharwad, pp. 59-76.

Subramanyam, N. 1980. *Sangam Polity*, Madurai.

Stein, Burton. 1983. *Peasant State and Society in South India*, Delhi: Oxford University Press.

Terukuttu singing by P. Gnanaraj (a traditional story-teller and ballad singer) and his interview in September, 2005.

Thurston, Edgar. 2001. *Castes and Tribes of South India*, Vol. I-VII, New Delhi: Asian Educational Services (First published 1909).

Yamashita, Hiroshi. 1996. 'The Cult of Aiyanar: A Note on a Rural Godling in Present-day Tamilnadu', T. Mizushima and H. Yanagisawa (eds.), *History and Society in South India*, Tokyo, pp. 58-76.

23

Subaltern History and Postmodernism

K.A. MANIKUMAR

ABSTRACT

Postmodernism, projected as a radical social theory, renders wrong the modernist notions of reason, knowledge, history and morals. With its distrust for "meta-narratives", the postmodernist thinking represents rejection of "totalizing thought in all its forms". It is argued by postmodernists that any broad movements for social change lead to new forms of oppression and hence particular struggles on particular issues are desirable. This new theory has adherents world-wide, resulting in encouragement of "fragmented politics of difference and identity" involving subaltern groups. This paper, while acknowledging the influence of postmodernism as a concept, seeks to defend the relevance of historical materialism as a framework for "mounting a powerful critique of the evils of capitalism". It attempts to trace the genesis of grassroots history and its promotion by Karl Marx, Antonio Gramsci and Michel Foucault and analyse how the writings of the last two influenced feminists and Left intellectuals and paved the way for the emergence of Subaltern Studies Group, whose early writings helped to significantly modify the historiography of anti-imperialism. The notion of postmodernists that "modern or scientific" discourses are power-ridden and hence objectionable is contested. The paper concludes with a critique of the postmodernists' attack on the notions of universality and rationality. In the end, the danger of postmodernism in avoiding the realities of global domination of capitalism is highlighted.

I

The history of common people as a specialized field of study began with the history of mass movement in the eighteenth century. Michelet was the first great practitioner of this grassroots history. French Revolution was the theme of his writing. French tradition of historiography steeped in history, not of the French ruling class but of the French people, established most of the themes and even the methods of grassroots history. George Lefebvre and Marc Bloch represented this illustrious trend.[1] But, as Eric Hobsbawm notes, the field really began to flourish in other countries only after World War II, to be specific in mid-fifties, when Marxism had started influencing the historical research. The Marxist historians focused their attention on subaltern groups, such as peasants and factory workers.[2] Recovering the historical and cultural particularities of the oppressed has been one crucial aspect of 'history from below'.[3]

Antonio Gramsci, by his conceptualization and theoretical rigour, gave a new thrust to the study of people belonging to inferior ranks in the civil society. He coined the term 'subaltern' to denote the marginalized. He also suggested six criteria for writing the history of subaltern classes,[4] such as:

1. The developments and transformations occurring in the sphere of economic production leading to the formation of subaltern social groups.
2. Their active or passive affiliation to the dominant political formations, their attempt to influence the programmes of these formations in order to press their own claims.
3. The birth of new parties of the dominant groups with the intention of containing the ascent of the subaltern groups to retain their control over them.
4. The formations which the subaltern groups themselves make with a view to pressing claims of a limited nature.
5. Those new formations which assert the autonomy of the subaltern groups, but within the old social framework.
6. Those formations which assert the integral autonomy.

Gramsci articulated the view that the ruling class ruled not only by force but also by consensus. The persuasion to reach consensus was indirect and in the process, he said, "the subordinate or subaltern classes learned to see society through their rulers' eyes thanks to their education and also to their place in the system".[5]

Foucault helped to expand the range of historical studies of power relations, beyond the conventionally defined "political and economic into the chores of every day life".[6] Foucault, as a post-structuralist, made a critique of historicism and questioned the notion that there is an overall pattern in history. He argued that excessive insistence on the state playing a dominant role leads to "the risk of overlooking all the mechanisms of power which sustain the state more effectively than its own institution. For Foucault power is not located in the state apparatus. It passes through much finer channels. His position is that 'the state can only function on the basis of other already existing power networks such as the family, kinship, knowledge and so forth".[7]

Foucault, in an essay titled "Nietzsche, Geneology and History", rejected conventional histories for their assumptions of linear development, teleology and pretensions to 'an apocalyptic objectivity'. Such claims, he argued, assume a 'supra-historical perspective'.[8] Feminism felt empowered by his writings. If historians of British India are today producing serious monographs on how women experienced colonial rule and how it affected their lives as well as how women and the 'women question' affected colonial politics, it is because of the influence of Foucault.

In the changing ideological moorings, Habermas' view of public sphere, which held sway over the intellectual domain for sometime, came under fierce attack. According to Habermas, public sphere, that mediates between society and the state, "is a sphere in which public organizes itself as the bearer of public opinion". The criticism made against this view was that Habermas idealized the liberal public sphere and in the process failed to examine other non-liberal, non-bourgeois, competing public spheres.[9] In a critique, Nancy Fraser elaborated other public spheres. She wrote: "Members of subordinate social groups – women, workers, people of colour, and gays and lesbians – have repeatedly found it advantageous to constitute alternative publics. I propose to call these subaltern counter publics in order to signal that they are parallel discursive arenas where members of subordinate social groups invent and circulate counter discourses to formulate oppositional interpretations of their identity, interests and needs."[10]

II

A group of historians led by Ranajit Guha employed Gramsci's ideas and published a series of collective volumes titled *Subaltern Studies*. They critiqued elitist interpretation of movement for Indian independence, terming the historiography of Indian nationalism as the work of a small upper class group. In contrast, the subaltern historians focused their attention on the participation of the people with special emphasis on different forms of popular resistance to British rule.

Ranajit Guha's *Elementary Aspects of Peasant Insurgency in Colonial India* brilliantly portrayed the subjection of the peasant to the triumvirate of colonial state, money-lender and landlord.[11] Tracing the period in which the breach between popular and national history became prominent, David Ludden in his recent review of *Subaltern Studies* series noted that James C. Scot's *Weapons of the Weak: Everyday Forms of Peasant Resistance* "made a departure from earlier studies of revolution into analysis of localized, personal resistance to the power of elites and states". As Foucault's influence was spreading, by the 1990s, an array of scholars inside and outside Subaltern School had made everyday resistance a basic feature of life in South Asia.[12]

The early writings of *Subaltern Studies* group thus helped to significantly modify the historiography of anti-colonial nationalism through a focus on 'pressures from below'. This opened up possibilities for exploration of ways in which elite nationalism might have both inspired and constrained popular initiatives.[13] Ranajit Guha, for instance, exposed how the Cambridge School, epitomized by the writings of scholars like D.A. Washbrook and C.J. Baker, had blended the biography of the coercive colonial state and its Indian elite collaborators as the history of Colonial India.[14] To quote Guha:

> The historiography of Indian nationalism has for a long time been dominated by elitism-colonialist elitism and bourgeois-nationalist elitism... sharing the prejudice that the making of the Indian nation and the development of the consciousness-nationalism which confirmed this process were exclusively or predominantly elite achievements. In the colonialist and neo-colonialist historiographies these achievements are credited to British colonial rulers, administrators, policies, institutions, and culture, in the nationalist and neo-nationalist writings-to Indian elite personalities, institutions, activities and ideas.[15]

The first volume of *Subaltern Studies* appeared in 1982 and the subaltern historians could explicate 'the interplay of coercion and consent' during 200 years of British rule. In their attempts to explain hegemonic processes, subaltern historians explored and articulated the stories of women. It was the subaltern project that prompted Gayatri Spivak to write her challenging article "Can the Subaltern Speak?" In this article she stated the problem of writing the history of colonial women: "As object of colonial historiography and as subject of insurgency, the ideological construction of gender keeps the male dominant. If, in the context of colonial production, the subaltern has no history and cannot speak, the subaltern as female is even more deeply in shadow".[16] Feminism provided what Gayatri Spivak has termed "a persistent critique of history". Spivak, however, warned the uncritical historian to beware of the pitfalls of valorizing "the concrete experience of the oppressed". This way of writing history, as she asserted, often constituted an autonomous subject without due recognition of the dual oppression of colonialism and patriarchy, and the further oppression of Western scholarship.[17] Feminism, according to Spivak, also made a thorough-going critique of the patriarchal assumptions embedded in linguistic and other forms of representation. Historians, in the light of the above paradigm shift, instead of accepting feminine identity as natural and essential, began to treat it as constructed.

Since the archives produced by governments and other overwhelmingly male-dominated institutions tend to say little directly about gender, feminists had to turn their attention to literary and other non-conventional sources for hidden meanings. A 'literary turn' in other words, was indispensable for feminist history.[18] But hardly one could find great works of native literature in colonial India, since, as Spivak argues, the institutional conditions under which they could have flourished did not exist under colonial rule. Betty Joseph, contrary to common perception, based on her experience in archival research, asserts that "women are everywhere in the colonial archive: Albeit in a fragmented and dispersed way, they are in and across various documents and discursive domains".[19] As Ranajit Guha writes, "The official report, while representing its task of law and order, relates accounts of counter-insurgency that contain evidence of rebellious subjects."[20]

III

Subaltern Studies had attracted little international attention in its initial radical populist 'history from below' phase. Its subsequent elevation to the status of South Asian historiographical trend abroad "owes much to its insertion, as a constitutive part of to-day's post-modernist international counter establishment, of anti-Enlightenment polemic with critiques of Eurocentrism and colonial knowledge".[21]

The politics of identity, which has of late become central to subaltern studies, has caused a shift of focus from the politics of class struggle to that of identity. Postmodernism has contributed greatly towards the valorization of this change, helping to constitute a situation where the labour struggles that still take place in many parts of the world, for instance, get very little media or intelligentsia attention. Here one tends to pose the question why identity politics is so often said to exclude themes of class, since the latter, in strict logic, is surely also a kind of identity.[22]

The assertion is that the historians have been bound up with the modern 'nation state project' and hence are incorrigibly statist. Gyanendra Pandey argues that "all histories since the nineteenth century have been National Histories due to the historians" privileging of the view-point of the state.

For the French Philosopher Lyotard, 'modern or scientific' discourses are objectionable and inevitably power-ridden because they are 'foundational', grounded in grand or meta or master narratives.[23] Questioning this assertion Sumit Sarkar states

> Histories dealing with states or nations are not necessarily statist or nationalist. The political implications of a historical account are conditioned primarily by the values, approaches and choices made by the writer not by the subject or kind of source material available. It is possible that one can use non-official, popular, oral material for deeply statist or conservative purposes and vice-versa.

Sarkar further argues,

> National politics had always included both popular insurgency and elite conservatism, struggling against one another, producing conflict ridden political movements and state regimes. Despite the lack of revolution or significant social change, opposition to caste oppression and class struggles by low caste and untouchable dalit workers did occur, and in places like Thanjavur district, Tamilnadu, local struggles led by Communists were potentially revolutionary.[24]

IV

Postmodernists like subalterns criticize the claim of modernism that its rationality is universal. Their criticism is based on the understanding that it is a means for creating an identity for the West that distinguishes it from the 'other'. Instead of suggesting an alternative notion of universality, that is more inclusive, the postmodernists deny the possibility of any notion of universality and, hence, any foundation for rationality. The postmodernists assert that postmodernism has facilitated the entry of the struggles of historically oppressed groups into academy, feminism and post-colonial critiques of orientalism. Notwithstanding its liberating intent, the postmodern reaction to colonization is seen as legitimizing neo-colonialism.

Post-modernism is considered dangerous for it avoids confronting the realities of political economy and the circumstances of global power.[25] The observation made by Roslyn Wallach Bologh and Leonard Mell in this context is worth quoting: "Today's neocolonialism takes the form of recognizing the political and cultural independence of the former colonies of the Empire of the Dollar. Allowing them the political form of independence and the cultural form of a play of difference, this neocolonialism speaks the language of nominalism and formalism, it allows for independence in name or form only."[26]

Both Wallach Bologh and Leonard Mell point out the strategic ploys involved in the works of Samuel Huntington (*The Clash of Civilizations*) and Robert Kaplan (*The Coming Anarchy*), particularly with reference to divide and conquer strategy that stresses differences of identity among the different civilizations.[27] The cultural difference at the heart of the clash of civilizations as described by Huntington refers to that between Western modernism and non-Western fundamentalism. Both Huntington and Kaplan predict that the post-cold war period is going to be characterized by conflict and hostility between the West and a non-West bent on challenging Western hegemony, without providing an analysis of the role of capitalist interests in creating and perpetuating the problems.

Huntington believes that hegemony of the West can be sustained in the short run, with some accommodation in the long run. Kaplan portrays a gloomy picture for the 21st century – the coming anarchy – that describes what Wallach Bologh and Leonard Mell call the New Feudalism.[28] They quote Kaplan's statement to drive home their point. "As crime continues to grow in our cities and the ability of state governments and criminal justice systems to protect the citizens diminishes ... as small-scale violence multiplies at home and abroad, state armies will (be) gradually replaced by a booming private security business and by urban mafias."[29] Such perceptions breed cynicism and help only to protect the West.

Edward Said's influence causing a major shift in anti-colonial discourses from politico-economic to cultural realms, has exacted a high price in terms of abandonment of earlier kinds of analysis of imperialism. The Saidian shift led to power getting increasingly identified with colonial discourses, through which Enlightenment rationalism supposedly established "cultural domination, colonizing indigenous minds, at least English educated middle class ones".[30] As a consequence, questions of poverty or economic exploitation, which might be more central to the everyday lives of immigrants or ethnic religious minorities, get less attention. Involvement or interest in actual movements of the oppressed gets displaced by romanticized depictions of exotic tribal or popular cultures.[31]

NOTES

1. E.J. Hobsbawm, 1988. 'History From Below – Some Reflections', in Frederick Krantz (ed.), *History From Below*, Oxford: OUP, pp. 15-16.
2. *Ibid.*
3. Michael Gismondi, 1988. 'The Idea of Resistance: Dependency as Historical Process', *Critical Sociology*, Vol. 15: 3.
4. Gramsci, 'Notes on Italian History', in Horace and Smith (ed.), *Selections from Prison*, Notebooks.

5. Peter Burke. 2005. *History and Social Theory*, Cambridge: Polity Press, p. 88.
6. Madan Sarup, 1989. *An Introductory Guide to Post-Structuralism and Post-modernism*, Athens: The University of Georgia Press, p. 87.
7. *Ibid.*
8. Rabinow Paul (ed.), 1984. *Foucault Reader*, New York, pp. 76-95.
9. Moishe Postone, 1992. 'Political Theory and Historical Analysis', in Craig Calhoun (ed.), *Habermas and the Public Sphere*, Cambridge: MIT Press.
10. Fraser Nancy, 1992. 'Rethinking the Public Sphere: A Contribution to the Critique of Actually Existing Democracies', in Graig Calhoun (ed.), *Habermas and the Public Sphere*, Cambridge: Cambridge: MIT Press.
11. Sumit Sarkar, 1999. 'Postmodernism and the Writings of History', *Studies in History*, Vol. 15, No. 2, pp. 305-316.
12. David Ludden (ed.), 2000. *Reading Subaltern Studies: Critical History, Contested Meaning and the Globalization of South Asia*, Delhi: Oxford University Press.
13. Sumit Sarkar, *op. cit.*, p. 316.
14. Ranajit Guha, 1992. 'Domination without Hegemony and Its Historiography', in Ranajit Guha (ed.), *Subaltern Studies: Writings on South Asian History and Society*, Vol. VI, Delhi: Oxford University Press.
15. Quoted in Gayatri Chakravorty Spivak, 1988. 'Can the Subaltern Speak?', in Cary Nelson and Lawrence Grossberg (eds.), *Marxism and the Interpretation of Culture*, London: Macmillan.
16. Geraldine Forbes, 1998. *Women in Modern India*, Cambridge: CUP, p. 3.
17. *Ibid.*
18. Sumit Sarkar, *op. cit.*, p. 312.
19. Betty Joseph, 2006. *Reading the East India Company, 1720-1840: Colonial Currencies of Gender*, New Delhi: Orient Longman, p. 3.
20. Ranajit Guha, 1988. 'The Prose of Counter-Insurgency', in Ranajit Guha and Gayatri Chakravorty (eds.), *Selected Subaltern Studies*, New York: Oxford University Press, pp. 45-86.
21. *Ibid.*, p. 314.
22. *Ibid.*, p. 320.
23. *Ibid.*, p. 304.
24. Barrington Moore, 1966. *The Social Origins of Dictatorship and Democracy: Lord and Peasant in the Making of the Modern World*, Boston: Beacon Press, pp. 8-9.
25. David Harvey, 1990. *The Conditions of Post-modernity*, USA: Blackwell, p. 115.
26. Roslyn Wallach Bologh and Leonard Mell, 1994. 'Modernism, Post-modernism, and the New World (Dis) Order: A Dialectical Analysis and Alternative', *Critical Sociology* 20(2): 85.
27. *Ibid.*, pp. 98-99.
28. *Ibid.*, p. 95.
29. *Ibid.*
30. Sumit Sarkar, *op. cit.*, pp. 305-315.
31. *Ibid.*

24

Regional Approaches in the Writing of History

ARAVIND KUMAR

ABSTRACT

To collect the source material and interpret the data based on the information contained in the records are the primary tasks of a historian. For a vast country like India having distinct geographical and cultural features, it is required to study the history in a regional perspective. 'Region' as a concept has been made use of by all social sciences.

An attempt is made in the present paper to understand the regional approaches in writing of history. In a country of sub-continental size like India, focus on distinctive features of its various parts is as much significant as viewing the country as a whole. Before undertaking research in the history of an area taken to be a distinct region, it is essential to satisfy oneself whether it contains all or most of the elements that go into the making of a 'region'.

The primary duty of the historian is to collect the source material and interpret the data based on the information contained in it. Sometimes, historians make use of the concepts that require proper definition and classification. The readers may not be familiar with the full meaning of the various concepts and methods used in constructing the past or the people concerned. The problem becomes more complicated when a given term is used in historical sources of different periods and localities and at the same time having different meanings, which we attribute to them in contemporary times. For a vast country like India having distinct geographical and cultural features, the focus of writing history, for each varying unit is significant. So identifying various zones in terms of 'regions', as a unit of historical research, is a difficult task, but is necessary for the understanding the historical processes on a pan-Indian scale. So, it is required to study the history in a regional perspective. Region as a concept has been made use of by all social sciences. An attempt is made in the present paper to understand the regional approaches in writing of history.

According to Aristotle, man is a political animal. Hence, a sense of belonging to a piece of territory renders him a territorial animal, and the roots of regionalism could be located in human nature itself. The biological basis is also to be found in the case of insects, birds and even mammals, which fight for the territorial possessiveness. Traversing from biology to sociology, it can be said that the defining features of a region are as much natural and evolutionary as man-made. It is the human being that moulds the landscape for his own benefit and modifies it in the process with a stamp of distinct individuality. The distinct individuality demarcating a region from its neighbouring ones consists of cultural forms and social systems, handed over and passed on from generation to generation. In any study to identify the regional specificities, therefore, the roots of regional identity are to be traced. In the process of the development of statehood and kingship, or for that matter any form of administrative mechanism, the uneven dimensions of development is well reflected in the continuously changing configuration of core areas under direct state control and peripheral areas experiencing indirect political hegemony.

Historians are rarely conscious of their primary function of collecting and interpreting facts contained in records of the past. They use concepts and categories that need definition and clarification for correct and complete comprehension of the scenario they describe. Even standard works on history of any period or people take for granted that the reader is well familiar with the full meaning of the various concepts and processes used in (re)constructing the past of a period or the region or the people concerned. This problem is further compounded when a single term used in historical sources of different periods and localities has different meanings or varying shades thereof with practically no resemblance to the meaning we attribute in our own time. However, our concern here is not with the technical terms in historical sources, but with the types in historiography. In a country of sub-continental size like India, focus on distinctive features of its various parts is as much significant as viewing the country as a whole. Thus, identifying their various parts in terms of region as a unit of historical research is not as easy as it might appear to be. Before undertaking research in the history of a given region, it is essential to satisfy oneself whether it contains all or most of the elements that go into the making of a 'region'.

Though as a concept region is common to all social sciences, it is often overlooked that contributions to building theory and methodology in the field have come as much from physical sciences as from social ones. A section of biologists, for example, differ from physiologists on the subject of man-land relationship. If a human being is taken to be a political animal in agreement with Aristotle, adding the corollary that a sense of belonging or attachment to a piece of territory renders him also a territorial animal, then the roots of regionalism could be located in human nature itself. The biological basis could also be pointed citing the cases of insects, rodents, birds, and even mammals (higher apes), which run into rage, offering bitter resistance against their own species in the course of defending the territory they inhabit. It is exclusively the human being that moulds the landscape to suit his own needs and in the process becomes responsible for the creation of several distinctive constructional or other cultural edifices with a stamp of individuality at a 'regional' level.

Regional historiography in India has been motivated by the Nationalist School and its writing in many universities on regional history is taken as an important theme for the syllabi and research on history. Historical research has become interdisciplinary or rather multi-disciplinary. History has to be studied and researched in the time and space context. While studying the historical process, one has to study the influence of geography in the shaping of historical events.

In developing the 'regional' concept of history, the French historians, like Lucien Febvre and Marc Bloch, contributed a lot. They, along with Fernand Braudel, have made great contribution to the development of a new school of historiography known as Annales School, which gave a new agenda in the 20th century historical writing. The Annales historians adopted the multi-disciplinary approach. They wrote history based on the four main areas: sociology, demography geography and economics. Febvre and Bloch drew primarily upon Sociology,

Economics, History, Literature and Psychology. But Braudel drew mainly from geography; he said that "mountains, as much as money, make the man".

Since ages we have seen the existence of many cultural units and their influence on one another. These regional cultural units strive to preserve their unique identity and offer resistance to any outside influences. So the study of regional history helps to understand the progress made by mankind in various parts of the world. For a holistic understanding of the world history, the study of regional history is very important in the contemporary times. The study of regional history is becoming more and more popular as it has the inherent potential to tap different source material for researching the different aspects of history. The vastness of India, with its several regions, called the attention of specialists and academicians working on the different aspects of Indian history.

The scope of regional history is too vast. Indian history has been studied from various perspectives, like nationalist, imperialist, Marxist and subaltern and so on. These schools of history have brought out various dimensions of Indian history. The contributions of the historians of these schools have illuminated the political, economic and socio-cultural aspects of the Indian history and helped indirectly to the development of regional historical perspective. So, to have a proper understanding of the development of the concept of regional history, a broad understanding of the historigraphical trends in India becomes a pre-requisite. In the beginning, the historians were interested mainly in finding new source material. This has resulted in the accumulation of abundant source material added to the body of information already available on the history of many regions of India. It is, however, at the interpretational level that the interest in regional history assumes greater historiographical potential.

The focus on the regional history is more pronounced in South India, where the regional, geographical and ecological identities are strikingly unique. This resulted in the development of distinctive historical edifices at a regional level in the present day linguistic zones of Andhra Pradesh, Karnataka and Tamil Nadu. The researches at the regional level brought out new sources providing information, particularly on the inter-state relations and their mutual influence. The 19th century historiography has pointed out some of these regions as dark ages, which were cleared by the new local source material.

The study of regional history corrects the earlier generalizing tendency about Indian history from the perspective of North India. In the post-independence era, the sub-nationalism of various regions, history is being written with a desire to establish an identity on the part of the social group to which the historian belongs. Dominant groups of a region project history of their community as the history of their region or even of nation. This has been stressed in historical writing by equating the present day state boundaries with the regional boundaries.

According to Romilla Thapar,

> the scope and significance of regional history to three trends, firstly, the acceptance of the conventional Periodization of ancient, medieval and modern. The acceptance of this Periodization imposes assumption on the historical data from regional sources. Secondly the axiomatic theories in vogue must not be accepted for understanding regional history. Thirdly, the inevitable search for a golden age, traced by a dominant group, which is described in the glowing tints of cultural resurgence (1978: 319).

Regional history can play a catalytic role in the creation of a national perspective. Regional history must not be a mere generalization of Indian history. The fixing of boundaries is a complex task in itself, for man-made boundaries change frequently and rapidly with political changes over a period of time. The only stable boundaries are geographical, and even these are liable to be substantially modified by ecological changes. The definition of a 'region' requires the correlation of many faces in the study of historical evolution. Regional history has to be studied with full objectivity. Even a small subjectivity will reduce the regional history into a hypocritical affair.

REFERENCES

Grewal, J.S. 1974. *The Studies in Local and Regional History*, Amritsar: Guru Nanak Dev University.

Sills, David L. (ed.). 1968. *International Encyclopedia of Social Sciences*, Vol. 13, London: Macmillan Co.

Thapar, Romila. 1978. *Ancient Indian Social History: Some Interpretations*, New Delhi: Orient Longman.

25

Tripartite Trade: Types of Textiles of the English Trade on the Coromandel Coast (1611-1652)

S. BABU

ABSTRACT

India has maintained commercial relations with the west from the pre-Christian days. The commodities of India reached Europe both by land and sea routes through Constantinople. This trade was affected in 1453 with the capture of Constantinople by Muhammad II of Turkey. So, there arose a necessity of finding a new sea route and many European nations took interest in this venture. The Portuguese were the first who reached India travelling the Cape of Good Hope, in the later part of sixteenth century, and started direct commercial contact with India. The lucrative trade of the Portuguese with India inspired the Dutch and the English to get a share in the profit of Eastern trade. The availability of all sorts of spices in the Southeast Asian region attracted the European companies to establish their trading settlements on the Coromandel Coast, which is geographically very near to the said region and also to make use of the textiles of coast for the barter of the spices. An attempt is made in this paper to throw light on the composition of the textile trade of the English Company on the coast and its impact on the society basing on contemporary sources.

In general parlance or nomenclature, the term 'Coromandel' refers to the land extending from the Godavari delta to Cape Comorin (Moreland 1931: Introduction; Penny 1908: 1-2; Wheeler 1972: 47). It is derived from the ancient 'Colamandalam', i.e., land of the Colas (Arasarstnam 1986: 7; Burton Stein 1984: 147). The weavers of the Coromandel Coast were gifted with the art of painting calico to the highest pitch of perfection, which were in great demand in Europe and Southeast Asian countries (Wheeler 1972: 47). These products attracted many of the European trading companies.

When the demand for the spices of the East increased highly in the home markets, the English company came to the Asiatic waters for procuring them directly. The English company opened its first factory at Surat on the Western Coast in 1608 to get spices directly from India (Foster 1856: Introduction). But the Portuguese being dominant on the Western Coast and also influential in the Mughal court spoiled all the attempts of the English in the beginning itself (Foster 1856: pp. 20-26).

The successful business of spices of the Dutch East India Company in the Southeast Asian region from the Eastern Coast of India encouraged the English to change its area of operation

(Foster 1856: XXXII). So they escaped from the difficult and troubled commercial atmosphere of the West Coast dominated by the Portuguese and came to the untroubled peaceful commercial enterprise on the Eastern Coast known as the Coromandel Coast (Fig. 1).

The English East India Company established its settlements on the Eastern Coast of India first at Masulipatnam (1611) (Foster 1856: 136; Penny 1908: 2-3). The second factory was established at Pulicat (1621), (Foster 1906: I: XIV and 253; Love 1913: 11-12). Each of these factories were under a chief and for the convenience of administration, they were brought under the control of the President of Bantam (Penny 1900: 3-4). To avoid the hostility of the Dutch at Masulipatnam and the oppression of the Golconda rulers, the English company closed its factory there and opened a new one at Armagon, north of Nellore (1626) (Lyall 1910: 154-56). However, the trade at Masulipatnam was revived in 1630 after diffusing animosity with the local ruler (Lyall 1910: 154-56). Meanwhile, with a grant from the local Nayak, Francis Day founded a settlement in Madras on 22 August 1639 and Fort St. George was constructed for that purpose in 1640 (Foster 1906 VI: 156-159; Penny 1908: 2-3). Later, in 1652, Fort St. George superseded Bantam as the seat of Eastern Presidency (Foster 1906 VI: 175; Dodwell 1929: 89).

The trade in those days was mainly through bartering and the English company could not make profit because there was no demand for English goods in Asia. The trade in Southeast Asia was only through bartering and so the English company bartered Indian goods bought through bullion, for procuring spices from Southeast Asia for consumption in England and Europe (Moreland 1972: 62-63). Through this trade, the English company established a triangular trade. The company also acquired the available gold and silver within Asia and invested in India (Moreland 1972: 63-64). Gradually, the Coromandel Coast became the capital of the English for textile trade in the Southeast Asian region in the early seventeenth century.

The fundamental idea of the Asiatic trade was to double or triple the investments brought from England by entering on trade in Indian textiles. It was done through this trade by regularly carrying Indian textile from one Asiatic port to another. Only the profit of textile trade was to be remitted in Europe in the form of spices or other Eastern products but not the capital (Moreland 1972: 62-63). For operating the Asiatic trade, textiles of the Coromandel Coast played two major roles: (a) they were used to barter for spices of the East for Europe and West Asian markets, and (b) they became a link in the operation of 'triangular spice trade' to get high profit.

The availability of raw material and transport were the primary considerations for the collection of textiles. Masulipatnam, Armagon, Pulicat and Madras were the principal factories from where the consignments for Asiatic and European markets were obtained by the English. To a large extent, the weaving villages were scattered and attached to the company's settlements (Vijaya Ramasamy 1985: 141; Babu 1990b: 145-150). Masulipatnam centre derived its supplies from the villages like Palakollu, Warangal (with twelve villages), Ellur (with eight villages), Mustabad (ten villages), Mangalagiri (fourteen villages), Maleporo (twenty-two villages) and Modapollam (twenty-four). In the same way, Pulicat, and later Madras, derived their supplies from Nellore, Arcot, Vellore, Kanchipuram, Chinglepet, Madurantakam, Dindivanam, Senji, Puducherry, Cuddalore and Salem. Every town had at least five to ten villages to draw its supplies. The textile centres were commercially linked to the factory from where textiles were exported.

A large variety of cotton clothes were manufactured on the Coromandel Coast for local consumption and foreign markets. The textiles for export were manufactured according to the taste and demand of the market concerned (Table. 2).

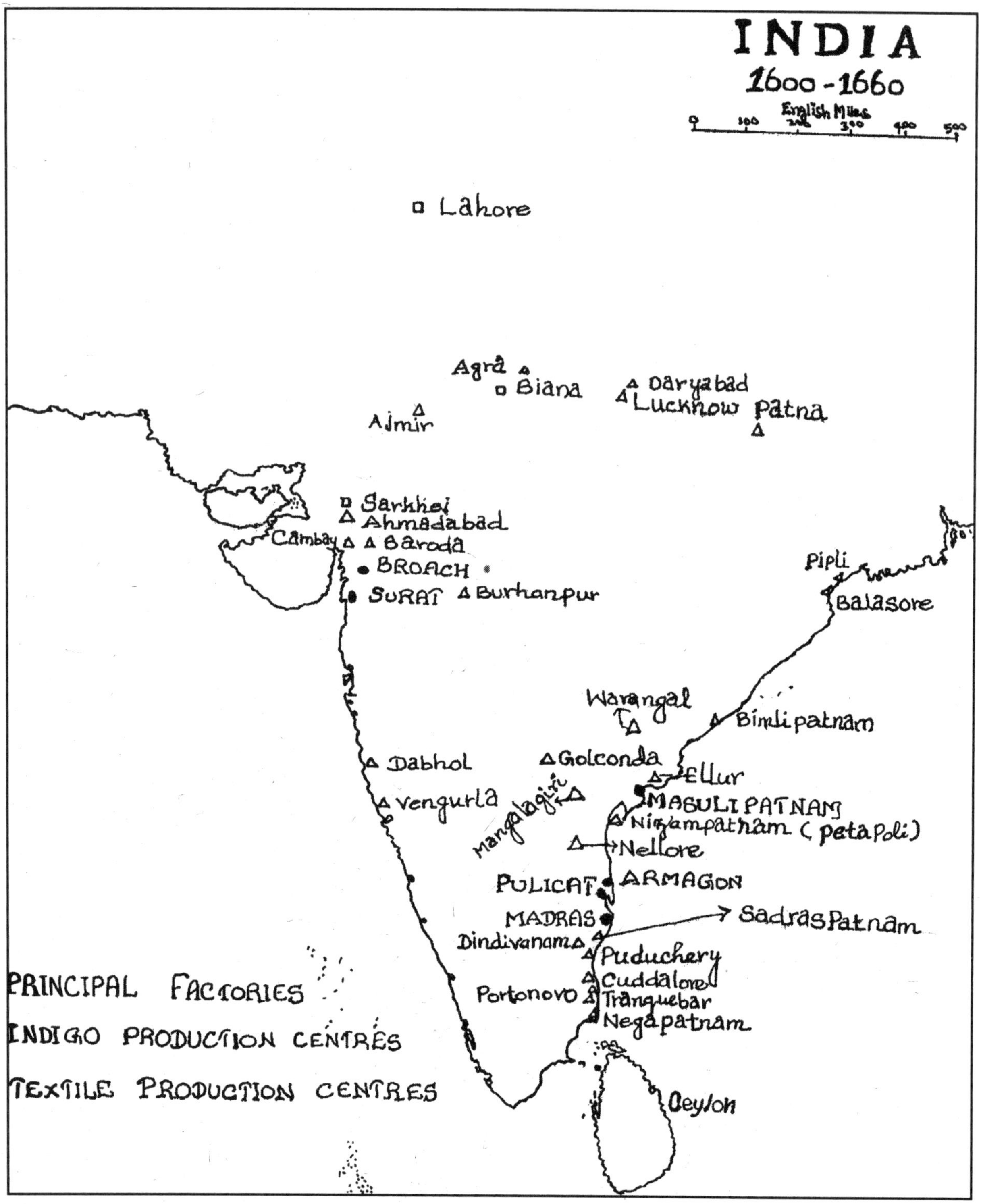

Fig. 1. Map showing the important trade centres on the Coromandel Coast.

The nature of the demand of textiles in Southeast Asian countries varied. By and large, calico[1] (Yule and Burnell 2002: 147) dominated the export item of the company to the Southeast Asian regions (Table 1). Textiles like muslin, dress or fancy goods were on a high demand. They were plain, either bleached or unbleached, in various colors called *baftas* (Foster 1906: I: 250; Yule and Burnell 2002: 47).

Among textile products exported to Southeast Asia, the most important were *salampuris, muris* and *chintz*. The *salampuris* were made out of staple cotton and woven in wide range, from fine to coarse in many colours with length 16 yards and width 1 yard (Foster 1906: IX: 250; Yule and Burnell, 2002: 784-785). *Muri,* also woven out of staple cotton, was a finer and superior quality, usually 9-10 yards long and 1 yard 28 inches wide for making *chintz* on it (Vijaya Ramasamy 1985: 214). It was used for painting and was sold in the Southeast Asian region as painted *chintz* or *Pintado* (Moreland 1972: 32). It was manufactured by the skilled craftsmen in the villages in and around Nellore, Arni, Pulicat and Madurantakam (Arasarstnam 1986: 99; Babu 1990b: 148-150).

Percallas were a high-grade plain cotton cloth of 8 yards long and 1 yard wide, mostly in white and red, and produced mostly in Pulicat and Masulipatnam, of coarser and finer varities (Vijaya Ramasamy 1985: 216). Of the same texture of *percallas,* a type of cloth woven from cotton thread and dyed in bright colours with stripes and checks was called Guinea cloth. It was required in unlimited quantity for tribal population in the Southeast Asian region (Moreland 1972: 55). Besides, *Kaingulong* (rolled cloth), *chelas, medaphons, drogangs, dupatty, gingham, tapichindes, sarassgobars, tapi-sarassas, tapigulong, tapikachil,* handkerchiefs and short dyed pieces of calico goods were also exported from the Coromandel Coast to Southeast Asia (Foster 1906: I: 61; Yule and Burnell 2002: 784-785). *Dungari* was a plain white coarse cloth used by the poor as loincloth, exported to Malay Archipelago (Yule and Burnel 2002: 330-331). *Sucatoon* was a variety of heavy cotton cloth used for packing and as blanket, mostly made in North Coromandel (Arasarstnam 1986: 101). There were many other cloths like *matafon, pattas, allijaes* and *dutties* (Travernier 1977: 50, 76, 118 and 171).

The above mentioned cotton fabrics of both coarse and fine varieties were used for producing *kalamkaris* or *chintz,* painted cotton cloth of several colours. They were in great demand in Moluccan Islands. The centre of production was Pulicat (Vijaya Ramasamy 1985: 65). These were the major export item of trade because of their cheapness, durability and attraction achieved by dyeing, painting and printing.

The Coromandel textiles were mostly sold in the Malay Archipalego. The painted calico of the south Coromandel were very much in demand in the markets of Moluccas, Macassar, Sumatra, Borneo, East and West coasts of Malay Penninsula. Siam, Tennasserin, Pegu, Achin, Java and Arakan (Foster 1856 I: Introduction; Arasarstnam 1986: 102; Babu 1995: 261-272).

Various kinds of textiles like *baftas,* muslins, white and striped *sarassas,* chintz, Indian *lungis,* Narasapur *joories,* white cloth and dragong cloth from Masulipatnam were exported to Central Asia (Foster 1906: II: 208; Sangar 1970: 127-128). Muslins were very much in demand as they were of thinner texture and of lighter weight than calico. They were most suitable for wearing in hot climate (Moreland 1972: 55-56 and 128).

In the early part of seventeenth century, most of the textiles dispatched from the Coromandel Coast were taken for Southeast Asian markets. Only a small quantity of goods was taken to Europe by the English East India Company via Surat. The first attempt to export calico directly to England from the East Coast appears to have been made in the year 1621(Vijaya Ramasamy

1985: 136; Moreland 1972: 128). Afterwards, the ships which were leaving Surat for England carried a part of textiles from the Coromandel Coast.

The textiles sold by the company in the London market consisted of different kinds, differing in size, quality, texture and colours. Naturally the price of each type differed according to its quality and texture. Cotton goods, both plain and designed found a greater demand in England. The plain textiles of India displaced the more expensive linens imported from Holland and Germany for household use. The designed varieties were very much used for hanging and decorative purposes in houses. Thus, the Coromandel textiles became competitors to the linens imported from Holland and Germany in the European markets. The Governor of the English company declared in 1624 that England saved annually a quarter of a million sterling by importing Indian calicoes through eastern trade instead of costly foreign linens (Moreland 1972: 120; Babu 2006: 92-98). Indian calico was used as table cloth, coverlets, napkins and wall-hangings in England (Foster 1856: I: 29; Vijaya Ramasamy 1985: 136).

Different types of textiles were sent by the company to England. They were *percallas, muris, salampuris* and *chintz* (Foster 1856: I: 136; Arasarstnam 1986: 98-102). Long cloth, either plain dyed or figured *chintz,* was highly in demand in the London market in the mid-seventeenth century. The products from Madras were considered the best (Foster 1906: IX: 250). Many other varieties of textiles were also collected by the English company and exported for European markets. They were *beathilles,* Golconda *beathilles, izzarees allijaes, dungarees, sailcloth, ginghams* (striped cloth), *gobar* (curtain cloth) and *sarassas* (multi coloured cloth) (Foster 1906, I: 264; III: 92-95; Arasarstnam 1986: 98-102; Vijaya Ramasamy 1985: 130-140). The sale of textiles was ordinarily made by piece or *corge*[2] (Foster 1906: I: 265; Arasarstnam 1986: 98; Chaudhuri 1965: 197).

The sudden outbreak of famine in 1630 in Gujarat and in North India disrupted the supplies of cotton fabrics from the region. The English company was therefore forced to find out other avenues to get supplies when the west coast (Surat) failed to meet the demands of England and Europe (Foster 1906: V: 57; Chaudhuri 1965: 197). At this juncture, the merchants on the Coromandel Coast reported that they could procure large quantities of textiles as desired by the company (Chaudhuri 1965: 98). So the company started sending indents directly to the Coromandel Coast to get supplies of textiles suiting the taste of European markets. The first direct shipping from the Coast to London was started in 1649, when a consignment of 18,225 pieces of textiles and other goods was dispatched from Fort St. George by the ship Bonito (Foster 1906: III: XXX; Moreland 1972: 98). This was an advantage that accrued to the Coromandel trade, thanks to the English company's trading operations in the Coromandel Coast.

The export of cotton fabrics increased in the first-half of the seventeenth century because they were very much in demand in the continent (Foster 1906: III: 297). From the coast, in 1621, the company exported nearly 12,500 pieces (Foster 1906: I: 209) and in 1639 it increased to 18,225 pieces (Moreland 1972: 129-130). It increased up to 52,000 pieces in 1652 (Chicherov 1971: 122), when the cotton fabrics of the Coromandel Coast increased in the history of English maritime trade and began to emerge as the principal supplier for west European markets (Moreland 1972: 131).

The English company earned huge profits on the sale of the Indian commodities in England especially cotton textile. For example, "in 1630s a piece of cloth bought in India for seven shillings sold in London for pound sterling, i.e., a profit of about 300 per cent. A pound of clove or nutmeg bought in India for eight to nine pence sold in England for six shillings at a profit of about 800 to 900 per cent" (Chicherov 1971: 122). Thus, the company exploited its own country men.

As there was no demand for European goods in the East, precious metals (bullion) occupied first position among the lists of imports from England. So Englishmen criticized the drain of bullion from England by the company to procure the eastern commodities, therefore, the English company was forced to take some amount of European goods to avoid criticism at home. This is a significant thing in the commercial activities of the company with India.

The English company imported lead, tin, copper, quicksilver, ivory coral, gilded mirrors, blades, knives, swords, sword blades, arms and ammunition and a variety of luxury goods (Foster 1906: III: 180). As the demand for the European goods was very less, the English company gave them mostly as *peshkush* or gifts to the local rulers or merchants for cajoling them (Foster 1856: II: 193; Foster 1906: III: 102-103 and 118; Babu 2002: 5-19).

The increased demand for textiles from the coast by the English company gave a fresh fillip to the maritime trade and development of production on the coast. Earlier it was spices which dominated exports of the English company from India but later it was textiles that occupied prime importance in the latter half of the seventeenth century. Agricultural production on the coast was boosted in the tune with the increasing demand for cotton and textiles of different sorts for Southeast Asian and European markets. It is clear from the increase of weaving activities in villages in this region. There is no clear idea regarding the extent of land brought under cultivation of commercial crops due to lack of data, but it is justifiable to say that the cotton cultivation was given a push to furnish the necessary raw material for weaving. In 1630s, the price of candy[3] (Moreland 1972: 336) of cotton was nine pagodas and it had gone up to fifteen pagodas in 1650s. It shows the increase in demand of cotton for weaving industry. So large-scale cultivation of cotton, probably even to the detriment of other crops (e.g., paddy), was done on account of the greater demand in the market.

The increasing demand generated by the English company geared up production in the secondary sector. A large number of villages were engaged in weaving and other activities connected with the textile production. It seems that a considerable change had taken place in the seventeenth century. The small-scale production that was going on for centuries together was not able to cope with the greater demand of the companies. So the individual producers with limited investment were subjected to the money advanced by the merchants and they turned out to be mere daily wagers. The artisans and craftsmen were others brought under the sway of merchant capital. So they became dependent on those who advanced money and lost their freedom to sell the products as they liked. In other words, they were subjected to 'economic bondage' or 'economic dependence'. Thus, the 'merchant monopoly' had turned the artisans merely as 'contract producer' from that of an independent one. Further, the system of advances brought a number of non-producers to supervise the production of textiles, i.e., the emergence of middlemen or brokers. The individual free producer was thus brought under the control of merchant's capital.

There occurred a major transformation among the merchants too. Many native merchants felt that it was more profitable and less risky to act on behalf of the company rather than make voyages of their own. So, the widely scattered weaving villages on the Coromandel Coast gave an opportunity to these indigenous merchants to act as a link between the weavers and the companies. The English signed contracts with these merchants of great substance to avoid any risk by giving advance to small-scale merchants of negligible investments. Thus, the foreign merchant's capital provided an excellent opportunity to a few local merchants to work with companies. They grew up and transformed the small-scale merchants as mere dependents on them. So capital accumulation in a few hands and the decline of small scale merchants were the outcome of this situation. There emerged the position of chief merchant(s) held by one or two of the most influential merchants in the urban centres. He was the sole agent for the supply of goods required by the company (Arasaratnam 1986: 237; Babu 1990a: 7-14).

With the emergence of the European settlements on the coast in the early part of the seventeenth century, the lives of the weavers no longer revolved around the temples but around the European factories. For example, a separate settlement was established in Madras in the year 1640 adjacent to Fort St. George for the workers of the company and was known as 'Black Town'. The expansion of such towns with the growth of population led to the urbanization of settlement in the ports. In the year 1648, three officials were appointed to administer and render justice to the inhabitants. They were *Adhikari* or Governor, *Kanakupillai* or Accountant and *Peddenayak* or officer in charge of law and order. The growth of trade led to the decline of joint family system, especially among the mercantile families.

The change of interest in the commodities of export from India shown by the English gave a new direction to the maritime trade of the Coromandel Coast and production was boosted. The English trade with the Coromandel Coast affected its economy and society.

To conclude, it may be said that the growth of English textile trade on the Coromandel Coast brought about considerable changes in the agrarian and non-agrarian sectors of production. These changes also had their impact on the socio-economic conditions. The interest shown by the European companies, especially the English, in the export of textiles could be considered the chief reason for the emergence of Coromandel Coast as a significant region in the world markets.

Table 1: Varieties of textile exported from the Coromandel Coast by the English company to Southeast Asian countries.

Allejeas	Striped cotton cloth with checks, either red or white, sometimes decorated with gold and silver threads, 16-17 by 1,25 yards.
Bafta	Plain cloth, average length 15 cubits (18 inches), either white or dyed.
Cachchai	A loincloth made of coarse cotton.
Chelas	From Telugu *ceera* or sari. A cloth both striped and chequered.
Chintz	Course painted cloth worn in Malay Archipelago as sarongs, required no stitching. They were also known as *tape-sarassas.*
Drongang	Cheaply dyed cotton cloth. It was described as black and red, either striped or chequered.
Dungarees	Plain white, coarse calico.
Dupatty	A cloth in double width used for wrapping.
Ginghams	Pure cotton cloth woven of dyed yarn, either striped or chequered.
Kaingulongs	A variety patterned in the loom and usually incorporated gold thread.
Muri	Finer variety of this used for making chintz on it, usually, 9-10 yards long and 11 yard and 28 inches wide.
Matafon	A stripped cloth woven chiefly in Golconda and exported to Malay Archipelago.
Patta	A cheap dyed cotton cloth, usually striped.
Percallas	High grade plain closely woven cotton cloth, 8 yards long and 1 yard wide. Mostly in white and red.

Salampuris	Made out of pure cotton ranging from coarse to very fine, either plain white, blue or brown. Length 16 yards and width 1 yard.
Tape-chinds	A cheap painted or printed cloth made for spice islands.
Sarassa and Sarassas gobars	A cheap multi coloured patterned cloth used as waist cloth and curtain cloth.
Tapi Sarassas and Pulang	Multi-coloured skirts, decorated with patterns.

Table 2: Varieties of textiles exported to England

Allejaes	Striped cotton cloth with checks, either red or white, sometimes decorated with gold and silver threads, 16-17 by 1,25 yards.
Beetellaes	Muslin cloth used for veiling. Much in demand in Europe as neck cloths. Dyed in red and some times striped or flowered colours with embroidering. Long 14-15 yards and 1.25 yards wide.
Dungarees	Ordinary staple cotton cloth of the coast, esteemed for its usual length (37 yards long and 1.25 yards wide).
Ginghams	Pure cotton cloth woven of dyed yarn, either striped or chequered.
Muri	Finer variety of cloth used for making chintz on it, usually, 9-10 yards long and 11 yard and 28 inches wide.
Percallas	High-grade plain closely woven cotton cloth, 8 yards long and 1 yard wide. Mostly in white and red.
Salampuris	Made out of pure cotton ranging from coarse to very fine, either plain white, blue or brown. Length 16 yards and width 1 yard.
Sarassagobar	A cheap multi-coloured patterned cloth used as waist cloth and curtain cloth.
Tapi-sarassas	Multi-coloured skirts, decorated with patterns

NOTES

1. Cotton cloth of fine texture.
2. *Corge* perhaps derived from the Telugu *Khorjam,* a term used for a bale of twenty pieces. Five *corges* formed a bale.
3. On the Coromandel, one *candy* or behar usually 20 *maunds.* One *maund* was equal to about a mound.

REFERENCES

Arasarstnam, S. 1986. *Merchants, Companies and Commerce on the Coromandel Coast* (1650-1740), Delhi: Oxford University Press.

Babu, S. 1990a. 'The Indigenous Merchants and the English Company on the Coromandel Coast (1611-1652)', Journal of Tamil Nadu Archives *Avana Amudham,* cup 4, drop 14, January-March, pp. 7-14.

——. 1990b. 'Textile Trade of the Coromandel Coast and the English East India Company (1611-1652)', *Journal of the Institute of Asian Studies,* Vol. VII, No. 2, March, pp. 145-160.

——. 1995. 'Commodity composition of the English trade on the Coromandel Coast (1611-1652)', in K.S. Mathew (ed.), *Mariners, Merchants and Oceans,* New Delhi: Manohar, pp. 261-272.

——. 2002. 'The English Trade on the Coromandel Coast (1611-1652)', *The Visvabharti Quarterly* (New Series), Vol. 10, No. 4, January-March, pp. 5-19.

——. 2006. *Merchants of Politics: East India Company and Dawn of the Raj,* New Delhi: Dominant Publishers.

Burton Stein. 1984. *All the King's Mana: Papers on Medieval South Indian History,* Madras.

Chaudhuri, K.N. 1965. *The English East India Company: The Study of Early Joint Stock Company* (1600-1640), London: Frank Cass & Co.

Chicherov, A.I. 1971. *India: Economic Development in the 16th to 18th Centuries,* Moscow: Naunka Publishing House.

Dodwell, H.H. 1929. *The Cambridge History of India,* Vol. V (1497-1858), London.

Foster, William (ed.). 1856. 'Frederick Charles Danvers', *Letters Received by the Company from its Servants in the East,* Vols. I-VI (1602-1617), London.

——. (ed.). 1906. *English Factories in India,* Vols. I-X (1618-1660), Oxford: OUP.

Love, Henry Davidson. 1913. *Vestiges of Old Madras: 1640-1800,* Vols. I-IV, London.

Lyall, Alfred. 1910. *The Rise and Expansion of the British Dominion in India,* London.

Moreland, W.H. 1972. *From Akbar to Aurangazeb: A Study in Indian Economic History* (Reprint), Delhi: Asian Educational Services.

Moreland, W.H. (ed.). 1931. *In Relations of Golconda in the Early Seventeenth Century,* London.

Penny, F.E. 1908. *On the Coromandel Coast,* London.

Penny, Mrs. Frank. 1900. *Fort St. George,* London.

Sangar, S.P. 1990. 'Export of Indian Cloth to Africa and Middle East in the Seventeenth Century', *Proceedings of the Indian History Congress 32nd session,* Jabalpur, Vol. II, pp. 127-128.

Travernier, Jean Baptiste. 1977. *Travels in India,* Delhi: Asian Educational Services (Reprint).

Vijaya Ramasamy. 1985. *Textiles and Weavers in Medieval South India,* Delhi: Oxford University Press.

Wheeler, Tolboys. 1972. *Early Records of British India: A History of the English Settlements in India,* Delhi: Asian Educational Services (Reprint).

Yule, Henry and A.C. Burnell. 2002. *Hobson-Jobson: A Glossary of Anglo-Indian words or phrases and of Kindred Terms Etymological, Historical, Geographical and Discursive* (Reprint), Delhi: Asian Educational Services.

26

A Study of New Communities in Pondicherry under the French

A. ARUL JOTHI

ABSTRACT

With the establishment of the French rule in Pondicherry, inter-racial marriages took place which gave rise to a new type of population known as Creoles or Metis. They were also called Topas. There was another section called Renoncants. Towards the end of the French rule, some new communities came into existence due to their political and administrative involvement in other parts of the India. People from Kerala, Andhra, Karnataka, Gujarat, Maharashtra and Bengal migrated to Pondicherry for trade and commercial reasons. These were followed by other migratory communities, such as Gujaratis, and Indo-Vietnamese population. This paper is a study of the various dimensions of these new communities in Pondicherry during and after the French rule.

The establishment of the Colonial French rule in Pondicherry resulted in the flow of men and ideas from France and this, in turn, gave rise to a new social and cultural milieu. The French people in Pondicherry entered into marital relations with the local people. These inter-racial marriages gave rise to a new type of social group known as *Creoles* or *Metis*. They were also called '*topas*'. There was also another section of people called *Renoncants*, who were the French citizens of native Indian origin.

Towards the end of French rule, there were some other new communities came into existence due to their political, economic and administrative relations with the other parts of India. People from Andhra, Karnataka, Gujarat, Maharastra and Bengal migrated to Pondicherry for trade and commercial purposes. In Mahe, which was a French settlement, people from adjoining Kerala came to settle down and they also came in large numbers to settle down in Pondicherry. With the establishment of Aurobindo ashram, the *Ashramites* in which the Bengalis form the majority, led to the migration of a large number of Bengalis into Pondicherry.

RENONCANTS

All natives who came forward to abandon their Indian personal laws and accepted to be governed by the French Civil Law are known as *Renoncants*. A good number, mostly from the depressed classes of the Indian society, conscious of their own degradation, willingly opted to become French citizens so as to attain equality of status and position. They thus liberated themselves from the clutches of age-old laws and customs which had till then relegated them as untouchables. The decorate of 21st September 1881 decreed that the *Renoncants* should be regarded as French citizens in the true sense of the term with all its implications and the Court of Appeal had also held that their names should be included in the same list along with the Europeans.[1] Considering the political and social advantages, quite a few among the Hindus also opted to become *Renoncants*.[2] The *Renoncants* were required to adapt a family name, the choice of which was not always so easy. Many chose the names of the former French officials while others preferred the names of historic personages. Some preferred to choose typically Indian or Tamil names. Ponnoutamby Poulle, who was a social reformer, adopted the name 'La Porte' (which means the door) to signify the fact that renunciation had opened the door towards the West.[3] Ponnoutamby Poulle, along with a team of followers, worked for the upliftment of the Valangamougattars. As a social reformer, he was the first to oppose casteism in Pondicherry and did much to improve the lot of Valangamougattars.

Hindus surrendering their personal laws ceased to be French subjects and became French citizens. As such, they were entitled to all rights the French citizens enjoyed in the Colony and in France, particularly the right to be enrolled as a voter in the electoral roles, while Hindus who fell under the category of subjects could exercise their voting rights only in India. This act of 'renunciation' could be made either at the time of marriage or at any other time. If done at the time of marriage, it was to be mentioned in the record drawn up by the Officer of the Registry. Otherwise, it may be received by the Officer of the Registry from the residence of the persons concerned as notification of births and deaths are received and entered in a register said for the purpose in all communes. This may be done either before a Justice of Peace assisted by his Registrar and two witnesses before a notary. In the last two cases, a copy of the deed made before the notary or of the report of the Justice of Peace was forwarded to a competent officer of the Registry who entered it in the register said for that purpose.

By this Act, the *Renoncants*, their wives and their children came to be governed from the date of renunciation; a *Renoncant* was considered a co-owner of a joint estate or a partner in a joint partnership, subject to the provisions of Article 1837 of the Civil Code. His property is to be bequeathed to his heirs as determined by French law without discrimination between citizens and subjects (Articles 745 to 768 of the Civil Code). Under the French Law, only monogamy was admitted among *Renoncants*. As for marital age, Article 144 of the Civil Code was applicable, i.e., the minimum marital age was 18 years for males and 15 years for females.[4]

Metis/Creoles/Topas[5]

The term 'Creole' stands for all those born to French parents in the Colonies. In due course, however, it came to be applied to all born of mixed marriage, i.e., between Europeans and natives. The progenies of such mixed marriages were otherwise known as *Metis*. Such persons were also called '*topas*' or 'Gens de Chapeau' on account of their wearing the hat (*topi*). As early as in 1706, the new town of Pondicherry accounted for about 300 *topas*. They were mostly French officials and soldiers who had married *creoles*. As some of those who contracted marriage with the natives were Portuguese settlers, they invariably adopted family names like Rozario, De Cruz, Pereira, De Costa, De Monte, etc. which were of Portuguese origin, as many of these marriages were between Portuguese settlers in Pondicherry and natives. Most of them were Catholics. They were treated by the pure whites as second-class citizens.

A report sent to the King on 25 July 1827 said that the *Metis* or *Topas* were "made up of a mixture of European and Indian blood. This population combined the vanity of the white man and the indolence of the Indian races and nothing could match its inactivity, if not its immorality". Since 1827, special attention was paid to the upliftment of the community. Members of this community were given training and employment in the newly established *Ateliers de Charite*. Indigent families received cash doles from the *Comite de Bienfaisance*. In due course they earned the goodwill of the administration and secured high positions in the administration, judiciary and other technical cadres. Some joined the army and distinguished themselves in the World Wars I and II.

After merger, a good number of them not only opted for French nationality, but went away and settled in France and other French colonies. The few who still remain here have established links with Anglo-Indians whose social background is very much similar except for the language barrier. The well-to-do among them live in clean and well-maintained western-type houses. Their affinity to the French is reflected in their food, dress, religion and culture. They prefer bread to rice, beef to mutton and foreign liquors. The *Societe de Secours Mutuels des Creoles* takes care of those not so well off in the community.

INDO-FRENCH[6]

The Indo-French community of Pondicherry is a unique group. They are Indian-born, Indian residents of French nationality. The singularity does not end here. They retain their respective socio-religious affiliations like any other Indian citizen in Pondicherry.

The Indo-French community is mostly distributed in Pondicherry city and the rest in Karaikal, Mahe and Yanam. While most of the elders live in India, many of the younger generation are employed in France. The origin of the Indo-French is traced to the French leaving India on August 16, 1962, after *de jure* merger of French India with the Indian Union. The local population, hitherto French citizens, was given the option to become Indian nationals or retain their French nationality. Those who opted for the latter constitute today's Indo-French community. Those preferring to retain French citizenship, as a part of the Indo-French agreement, received liberal concessions from the French government. Indian-born French citizens cannot, however, get jobs with the Indian government.

Most of the Indo-French are fluent in French, as many of them, or their fathers, had worked in the French administration or in the French military service. They usually converse in French or in the regional language with a very liberal mix of French, so much so that the Tamil spoken by them has acquired a French intonation. A few have a working knowledge of English.

The Indo-French people like to dress formally for all occasions. Men wear suits and ties, without exception, and women either wear their best silk saris or the most fashionable frocks. They use jewellery and cosmetics freely and their presence is always noticeable by their expensive and pleasing perfumes. The food habits of the Indo-French community reflect French culture. This is because the community is affluent, due to the liberal pensions they get from the French government. Like the French, they too drink alcohol with their meals. They are non-vegetarians and eat all kinds of meat, fish, etc. They are fond of vegetable salads.

Although they are French nationals, the Indo-French retain their Indian identity, with its varied religions, castes, sub-castes and sub-groupings. In fact, even Hindus converted to

Christianity, through French influence, retain their caste identity. For instance, there are Vellala Christians, Padayachi Christians, etc. The same social hierarchical denominations between castes and sub-castes operate, the Indo-French families being particular about the social distance between the castes and sub-castes. For example, a Vellala Christian does not enter into matrimonial alliance with the off-springs of a Gounder, even though both are Indo-French and Christians by faith. However, observance of pollution and isolation because of caste occupations are things of the past.

The basis of the Indo-French community is its nationality. The social activities and religious functions of the Indo-French are all identical to those in Indian families of the same religion, caste or sub-group. Thus, a French Hindu Iyer marriage in the community is performed with all the rites and mantras as in an Indian Iyer (Brahman) family. The same is the case with the other social and religious groups.

Among the Indo-French Hindus, the undivided family is still favoured, whereas nuclear families are the norm among Christian families. Residence is patrilocal. The relationship between family members is usually very cordial. The rule of inheritance, among the Indo-French, is governed by French law – all members of the family have equal shares. The parents' shares, after their deaths, are divided equally among all offsprings. Division of property among children, while the parents are alive, is not uncommon.

An important feature of the Indo-French community is the contemporary change in the status of women. Even though they follow all the rituals and social restrictions of their respective social groupings, women are given equal importance and status in the family. This may be due to the statutory provisions in the French law, whereby French women are given equal rights and shares in inheritance. The influence of French culture has made these legal rights socially acceptable. Women participate in all social, religious and other activities. They pursue education and employment on equal terms with the men. They have equal say in all the activities of their households and society in general.

There is no direct or indirect evidence to show any strong bondage as a community. The affinities existing in the Indo-French community are largely confined to kinship or caste affiliations, as seen from the gatherings on socio-religious occasions. The cosmopolitan French culture is limited only to aspects like dress, food, etc.; it has not created a cogent identity for the Indo-French as a single community.

The Indo-French observe all the life-cycle rituals prescribed by each individual's religion, caste and sub-caste. However, the birth of every child has to be recorded by name immediately after birth, in the *Livre de famille*, a book of records for each family kept by the French Government. Formal christening is done later.

Marriages are conducted, as far as possible, within the community, subject to the religious/caste restrictions of endogamy and clan exogamy. The parents of the boy or girl look for an alliance with another French citizen as this would benefit the couple in terms of future employment and the careers of children. Those who marry outside the community do so with persons of equal economic status. Marriages have to be registered at the Marie (i.e., the Town Hall or the Municipal Office), irrespective of the celebration of the marriage in a church according to the Christian rules or in a temple according to the Hindu rules or at home. All such details go into the record book, *Livre de famille*. Deaths are also registered at the Marie hall and entered in the *Livre de famille*.

Most of the Indo-French lead comfortable lives as they get substantial amounts as salaries or pensions, and other benefits, compared to their Indian counterparts. Their children's employment is guaranteed by the French Government. Consequently, they are engaged in very little economic activity. The people of the Indo-French community, being French citizens, are bound by French laws. The French Consulate in Pondicherry regulates the application of these laws and looks into the various requirements of the community. There are very few instances of Indo-French citizens violating these laws. They, however, come under Indian law in criminal litigations.

The French are great connoisseurs of art. The French connection has inculcated in the Indo-French of Pondicherry a similar passion for and appreciation of art. In every household of the Indo-French, there are antiques and decorative *objects de art* kept in places of honour. Almost all their houses have murals on the walls. The houses are furnished, arranged and decorated attractively. Members of the Indo-French community enjoy socialising. They mix well with their neighbours and are known for their friendly nature and liberal views. They have a strong club culture and men visit local clubs every evening, to socialise and relax. Their affluence gives them a high status in local society. Beneath their courteous and sociable nature, however, they are slightly aloof, and this singles them out as a separate community. This is largely due to their lifestyle, which is totally different from that of Indians.

As the high standard of living of the Indo-French owes much to their French connection, they do not show much enthusiasm for the development activities around them. The main aim of the younger generation is to secure entry into the French army or civil service. Most of the Indo-French build or own large houses, many of which they rent to the local people. This could be termed their only productive revenue-earning economic activity.

REFERENCES

1. F.C. Antony, 1982. *Gazetteer of India, Union Territory of Pondicherry*, Vol. 1, p. 392.
2. Julien Virson, 1885. *L'Inde Francaise et les Etudes indiennes de l882 1884*, footnote, pp. 19-20.
3. Evariste Deessama, 1950. *Tribulation de L'Inde Francaise*, p. 18.
4. F.C. Antony, *op. cit.*, p. 393.
5. *Ibid.*, p. 394.
6. K.S. Singh (ed.), 1994. *People of India-Pondicherry*, Vol. XXXVI, Anthropological Survey of India, pp. 144-147.

27

Early Resistance to Colonialism in French India – A Study Based on the Diary of Veera Naicker II

B. KRISHNAMURTHY

ABSTRACT

There is a general impression that there was no popular movement against the French colonial rule in India and that the French have transferred their territorial possessions in India to the Union in 1954 on their own will. It was also assumed that the natives were very happy and led a contented life under the French rule and that they had never risen against or resisted the French colonial administration in India. These assumptions are far from the truth. Indeed, there were popular movements against the colonial rule of the French, particularly against its socio-economic and religious policies.

The present paper will study and analyse the popular movements against the discriminative and exploitative policies of the French, particularly in Karaikal and Pondicherry regions. It also aims to highlight the political awareness of the people of French India and their reaction to the French Revolution of 1789. Besides, it introduces the diary of Veera Naicker II, a native police chief under the French administration in Pondicherry, as an important indigenous source material for the study of political and socio-economic history of French India.

Veera Naicker II's Diary covers the tumultuous period in the history of French India from 1778-1792, thus giving a pen-picture of the developments that have taken place at the headquarters of the French power in India, as a result of the French Revolution, which has brought the *ancienne regime* in France to an abrupt and violent end. This is an insider's account on the French colonial rule in Pondicherry. The fact that he belonged to a family of native police chiefs add additional credibility to the facts recorded in the diary. It is based, in the words of the diarist, on "the incidents heard, seen and read".[1]

The diary of Veera Naicker is an eyewitness account of the political, economic and socio-cultural scenario of Pondicherry of those days. It primarily covers:

(a) Popular movements against French colonialism
(b) Impact of French Revolution in France
(c) Impact of French Revolution over French Indian population
(d) Right and Left Hand Caste problems

(e) Hindu-Christian religious ill-feelings
(f) Terrible impact of local political upheavals on the economy of French India and the surroundings
(g) Colonial judicial and administrative systems
(h) Disparities displayed by the rulers over the ruled
(i) Severe punishments inflicted on the army-deserters

FRENCH COLONISATION OF INDIA

As a result of Dupleix's *Forward Policy*, the French had carved out "a colonial empire in India, which was twice as large as France, containing thirty million people in the early 1750s".[2] July 1751 was the apogee of the French power in India and Dupleix's most successful and finest hour. However, the French interests suffered a serious setback when Dupleix was recalled to France unceremoniously in 1754. Moreover, the British imitated his game more successfully and as a result, major parts of India came under their control. During the seven years' war (1757-63), Pondicherry was taken over by the British, who pulled down all the fortifications and levelled all the buildings to the ground. When the war was over, Pondicherry was returned to the French, who had to rebuild the whole town anew. The *Memoires* of Law de Lauriston, who was the Governor of French India stationed in Pondicherry, offers a pen-picture of the sad plight of both the town and its inhabitants – Europeans as well as the natives – during the early 1770s. As such, the French prospects, which we find in the diarist's account, were quite unenviable.

NATIVE POPULATION UNDER THE FRENCH RULE

As a consequence of the French efforts to establish and extend their colonial rule in India, thousands of natives came under its ambit. Due to the political instability and incessant wars among the native states, the merchants, weavers and other people living under their rule migrated to those places which were under the French control thinking that they could gain protection and livelihood. In 1715, the Hindus lived in Pondicherry numbered from 60,000 to 70,000 and Christians 2,500, of which about 500 were French nationals and the Eurasians.[3] By 1725, the population of Pondicherry crossed the one lakh mark.[4] However, by the end of the eighteenth century, the population of Pondicherry got dwindled and by 1791, there were just 600 French, including Eurasians and 7,000 natives.[5] Thus, Indians by birth, upbringing and culture continued to live under the French rule in Pondicherry and other establishments. Native population of the French India was considered as *sujet francaise* (French subjects).

RACIAL OVERTONES OF COLONIAL SOCIAL POLICY

From the initial stages of their existence in Pondicherry, the French were well aware of the racial, cultural, societal, religious and linguistic differences between them and its aboriginal inhabitants as well as recent settlers. In the French Indian settlements, social privileges were determined on the basis of colour and the majority ruled were discriminated on every count by the minority rulers. The French sense of racial and cultural superiority found expression in their concept and creation of *ville blanche* and *ville noir* (white and black township), which maintained the racial segregation of the Europeans as well as their descendents and the native Indians.[6]

The permission given to Ananda Ranga Pillai to enter into the fort area in a palanquin and to wear footwear in the presence of the Governor as a special privilege clearly shows that other natives were denied of their basic right.[7] Equality before law and equal punishment for same offence were not practised. For the same offence, the Europeans and the natives were punished differently – while the Whites were treated leniently, the natives were given severe punishment, thus proving the practice of racial discrimination. The case of a lower caste man who was sentenced to death by hanging for killing his wife, which was finalized in a single day, proves the travesty of justice meted out by the French colonial masters on the natives.[8]

Colonial Religious Policy

The proselytizing policy of the French appealed especially to the socially and economically down-trodden sections among the Hindus, who thronged the Christian missionaries with the hope of achieving upward social movement and of taking benefit of the new opportunities thrown open by the commercial activities of the French Company. One of the prize-catches of the missionaries was Tanappa Mudaliar alias Lazero de Motta, who got a small but beautiful church built for the Capucins. While the native Christian population in Pondicherry numbered around 2,000 in 1715, it almost tripled by January 1726, as a result of the conversions which went on full-swing.[9]

Due to the influence of the Jesuit missionaries, a policy of intolerance was followed towards the native Hindu population living in the French Indian colonies, which resulted in their mass exodus from Pondicherry more than once.[10] In March 1701, Francois Martin, the first Governor of the French Company in Pondicherry, prohibited the ceremonies of both the Hindus and the Muslims during the fortnight of Easter and on Sundays. The last straw on the back of the Hindu population was mounted by the destruction of Vedapureeswaran temple in September 1748.[11]

Prevalence of Slavery

In 1728, while Dumas was functioning as Governor of *Ile de France* (present day Mauritius) and *Ile de Bourbon* (present *la Réunion*), he paid a visit to Pondicherry ostensibly to discuss some constitutional dispute with Lenoir, the French Governor at Pondicherry, but actually to buy slaves. Lenoir bought 100 slaves, boys and girls between the ages of eight and twenty-five, who were boarded on *La Sirene* bound for *Ile de France et Bourbon*, where there was a big need for slaves for working in plantations. Slaves were available at cheap rate in Pondicherry region because of the famine that came in the wake of the Mughal-Maratha wars in the Carnatic. Later, in 1736, the Directors of the French Company in Paris wrote to Dumas, who by then had become the Governor at Pondicherry, cancelling the order, which had been placed earlier for slaves with the *Conseil* at Chandernagore, and agreeing with him that "prisoners of war would be more economical".[12] Pillai cites the case of a young boy, who was arrested in a petty case, being shipped to the Isles to serve there as plantation labour. He also talks about the activities of some tricksters and mischievous fellows who used to intoxicate the gullible by mixing some intoxicant in lime used with the betel leaf – then transport them in a ship to the Isles, while they still remained unconscious. Indians were sentenced in the *Chaultry* court with slavery for a fixed period or in perpetuity in the *Isles de France et Bourbon*.[13] Though in the aftermath of the

French Revolution and the royal decree of February 22, 1792, the slave trade was prohibited, it appears that the trade on human cargoes continued to take place unhindered in French India for some more time.

COLONIAL ADMINISTRATION

The Governor was simultaneously the chief of the French East India Company as well as the representative of the French Crown in India. The Governor and the members of the *Conseil Supérieur* conducted the political and administrative affairs of the colony. *Dubashis* or the interpreters and clerks drawn generally from the native population helped the French administration in their political and economic activities. Besides the European, especially French, army officers and soldiers, *sepoys* or the native soldiers, recruited and trained by the Europeans, were employed to protect the settlements from the native powers as well as from the other European competitors. Again, under the European police officials and sergeants, *Nayanar* or the native police chief and other police personnel were appointed to take care of the law and order situation, especially in the native quarters within the settlements.

Role of Natives in the Colonial Administration

The decree of August 1784 reconstituted the *Conseil Superieur* and permitted some Indian businessmen and important persons nominated by the Governor to be the members of the same. However, the role of the natives in the French Indian administration was quite negligible earlier and only in 1788, the Consultative Chamber, whose members were chosen from the notables among the native population, was created. Still, the native fortunes continued to be dim under the French horizon.

French Revenue System

At first, the French used to collect land revenue directly from the people but it proved to be a hard task for them due to the fraudulent, insincere and evasive tactics practised by the native clerks, who were employed by the Company in assisting it in tax assessment and collection. Moreover, direct tax collection called for show and, at times, use of force towards *poligars*, the local chieftains, demanding huge expenses and other complications. Thus, to ensure a fixed income, the French took to *ijara* or putting-out system of farming of its territories to the chosen one, naturally the highest bidder.[14] Anyhow, in case it could not get a handsome offer, the Company resorted to direct collection appointing its own clerks and others.[15] Moreover, stipulated amount was also collected from the peasant community towards expenses to be incurred on maintaining irrigation canals and roads. Bellecombe, the Governor of French India, laid down certain regulations in 1777 relating to this payment. Besides land revenue, customs duties, sales taxes, especially on the sale of monopoly goods such as tobacco and betel leaf, income tax, and other heads were collected from the native population.[16]

Native Resistance to Colonial Religious Policy

Those native people who came under the jurisdiction of France were not always happy under the French colonial rule and occasionally they have exhibited their displeasure in an organised way. Reference has already been made to the intolerance shown by the French to the native religion, rituals, customs and traditions. During 1701 and the following years, due to continued intervention of the French in the religious life of the native people, some 2000 families left their colonies.[17] The French Governors had to use force as well as persuasion to retain in/bring them back to their settlements. Agriculture suffered in the Karaikal region and much of the land remained uncultivated due to the migration of the population in protest against the religious intolerance shown by the French.[18]

Native Resistance to the French Taxation Policy

The French Indians were quite discontented with the tax system implemented by the French. Whenever new taxes were imposed without taking note of the economic deprivation of the populace, the latter resorted to mass exodus from the French establishments. For instance, in 1785, when taxes on the monopoly goods like tobacco and betel leaf as well as betel nuts were introduced, disregarding the voice of the people against such a step, the natives of Karaikal fled away from the French settlement and took asylum in the villages under the native rule.[19]

In mid-1780s, the French authorities rented out the collection of taxes in Karaikal and its dependencies to one Savarimuthu Pillai. The *rentier* reduced the *varom* or expenditure stipulated for rice cultivation and tried to pocket the amount. In 1787, widespread agrarian unrest broke out in Karaikal and its dependencies on this count and farmers abandoned their land and evacuated entire villages. The French Governor Comte de Conway dispatched de Fresne to Karaikal to bring round the farmers to an amicable settlement and this produced desired effects.

In 1791, once again there was a general uprising of farmers against Arokiam, the *rentier*, who had taken some arbitrary decisions harming the interests of the farming community. In this struggle, the *visiadars* (local constabulary) and toll collectors too joined hands with them. M. de Espinasse with his 53 European soldiers and 260 *sepoys* was hard put against the rebels and the French Governor had to send Touffreville with 100 European soldiers to suppress the popular rising, which, it was perceived correctly, had thrown a challenge to the French authority. Touffreville was later appointed by the French Indian authorities as Commandant of Karaikal, as a reward for his success in quelling the mass resentment.[20]

After some time, the problem once again surfaced with greater rigour. Vilvendra Pillai and Savarimuthu Pillai, the tax-farmers, who had secured the right to collect land revenue quoting higher rates, created fresh problems to the native population. The latter joined together and man-handled them and then went to Touffreville to demand the cancellation of their license to collect the taxes. Instead, they promised to pay the taxes directly, which was earlier practiced and was known as *kudi kuththagai.* On getting a stern reply that the license to collect taxes would be given to the highest bidder and so, direct tax collection was not feasible, the natives withdrew from the town in great numbers. They got support from some neighbouring *poligars* as well. Some 10,000 people with arms blockaded the town and prevented entry of rice, vegetables and fire-wood into Karaikal. When they came to know that the French had arranged for the supply of food-materials from Nagour through sea route, they attacked the boats and confiscated the materials from them. A letter was also written to the people of Nagappattinam against the dispatch of food materials to Karaikal in the name of the people of Karaikal.

The popular movement became so severe that Touffreville had to plead for help from de Fresne, the French Indian governor in Pondicherry. The latter, on the one hand, dispatched military reinforcement to quell the movement and, on the other, had sent Nainathai Mudaliar, a notable resident of Pondicherry, to convince the people and to settle their problem.[21] Still, the problem continued to rage for some more time and only in April 1792 the farmers and the *visiadars* returned to their work.[22]

In Pondicherry also, in 1791, peasants rose against the tax collector Abira Mudali, who arbitrarily collected half of the produce from them. Keeping Leger, the *Intendant* of Pondicherry in good humour and securing the support of local bigwigs, he even went to the extent of harvesting the crops in their fields employing his own goonda elements. The peasants complained to the higher authorities against his activities and demanded to cancel his license to collect the taxes with immediate effect. They promised that they would pay the taxes directly to the French by way of *kudi kuththagai*. Initially, the French higher-ups tried to avoid taking any serious action against the tax collector. However, later, on seeing the determination of the people, the French authorities decided to cancel the arrangement with him.[23] This incident clearly shows that the peasant community of Pondicherry too did not hesitate to agitate against the injustice meted out to them.

Native Reaction to the French Revolution of 1789

The news about the French revolution of 1789 and other developments that had taken place in Paris and other places, reached Pondicherry by the end of February 1790. An all-white *Assemblee generate* (General Assembly) was held on March 2, 1790 in Pondicherry and Moracin was selected as its President with another Councilor as a Secretary. This Assembly wanted to forward the wishes and grievances of the French in India to the *Assemblee Nationale* (National Assembly) in Paris and decided to send Beylier, Kerjean and Delarche le Fils to Paris to represent their case before the National Assembly. These three men actually left Pondicherry on March 17, 1790. Later, a Committee of Representatives was also established. By the end of March, the Governor and other French people adopted the *cocarde nationale* – the tri-colour revolutionary symbol of white, red and blue.[24]

Meanwhile, the natives of Pondicherry, who were unhappy with the step-motherly treatment meted out to them by the French administration, tried to take benefit of these developments. They presented a *memoire* to the Governor requesting him to consider them as the citizens of France and to extend the French protection to them as well. De Fresne promised to treat them so and expected them to contribute their might to the common good as and when required. Later, Moracin too assured them to that effect.[25]

However, the leaders of the Committee of Representatives debarred the Indian citizens from participation both in the General Assembly and in the deputation. Even the requests of the Indian notables in the Consultative Chamber to allow them to join the movement were turned down. In June 1790, suggestion from some of the progressive elements of the Committee advocating admission of the Indians as members of Pondicherry municipality to be created soon too was vetoed as unacceptable. Those who dared to pick up the cause of native representation were expelled from French India as 'dangerous agitators'.[26]

It appears that some French nationals under the leadership of Culan tried to capitalize on the uncertain conditions caused by the developments in France to their personal end. They planned to assassinate de Fresne, Moracin and others and to take power and position in their hands. Assemblee Generale took severe note of their activities, arrested and dispatched them to Paris to be presented before the National Assembly. Culan, who escaped from Pondicherry, was declared as *persona non grata*.[27]

Still, the natives tried to capitalize on the changed environment. On August 20, 1790, the natives presented before the General Assembly a representation accusing certain native officials of the French establishment of malpractices and demanding that those people be arrested and necessary actions taken against them. Next day, those native officials were summoned before the Assembly and were strictly told to be careful and considerate in their actions, so as to avoid any future complaint.[28]

While in France, under the instruction of the Committee of Representatives, Kerjean and Delarche delegated their power to Monneron, who along with Beylier, presented six *memoires* submitted by the French in Pondicherry to the National Assembly of Paris, which accepted both of them as its members representing French India in October 1790.[29] Some of the demands of the French citizens of Pondicherry, like freedom of commerce, were meted out by the National Assembly. A decree for the creation of municipalities and administrative assemblies too was sent to Pondicherry.

Meanwhile, the French nationals in Pondicherry debated on the establishment of municipality and, after a referendum, a positive decision was taken on this count. Accordingly, on November 14, 1790, a Municipality was set up in Pondicherry with five members and a Mayor. A Permanent Committee of 27 members with representatives from other settlements was also established. The decisions of this Representatives Committee after being signed by the Governor and registered in the municipality became the laws of the colonies. However, all these developments were limited only to the French of pure blood and even the Franco-Indian *Creoles* or *Topasses* of mixed blood were kept away from the Representative Committee and the municipality.[30] When the Permanent Committee intended to sent a submission to the National Assembly, the local inhabitants clamoured to be informed of the contents of the submission to be thus forwarded. The Committee declared their demand 'inadmissible'.

In March 1791, some leaders of native Christians tried to form a *comite* and a municipality to take care of the native interest and in their effort to pressurize the French Indian administration they organised *bandh* and closed shops. This effort failed miserably, when the French authorities threatened them with dire consequences. Since the initiative came from minority Christian population without taking the majority Hindu natives into confidence, the latter were indifferent to their efforts.[31]

In April 1791, some 300 *sepoys* refused to do their duty and left the fort, due to ill-treatment meted out to them by Duplessis, their French Commandant and clamoured that the Commandant should be replaced and that they should be treated with respect and dignity. De Fresne had to intervene and to assure the *sepoys* of right conduct on the part of the Commandant.[32]

In June 1791, the Representative Committee was replaced by a Colonial Assembly consisting of twenty-one members – fifteen from Pondicherry, three from Chandernagore and one each from Mahe, Yanam and Karaikal. The French residents above the age of 25 and who were resident in India since two years were to elect the representatives of the Colonial Assembly. Again, it was limited to the French only. However, when the Colonial Assembly met on July 6, representatives from Pondicherry, Karaikal and Yanam only turned up. Chandernagore flatly refused to recognize the authority of the Colonial Assembly of Pondicherry. Still, the latter took the momentous decision of abandoning the old *fleur-de-lys* and adopting the new revolutionary Tri colour flag on August 4, 1791.[33]

The natives were continued to be neglected by the French. Though the constitution of the Colonial Assembly provided for the admission of four local Indian representatives to the Assembly, especially when matters relating to the Indians were to be discussed, it was never implemented and was actually abrogated later. In fact, the new constitution drawn by the Colonial Assembly went to the extent of rationalising and justifying its refusal of franchise and representation to the Indians.[34] Again, its effort to impose the Civil Constitution of the Clergy passed by the National Assembly on the priests of Pondicherry backfired since most of the priests refused to comply by the order and decided to desert Pondicherry for Madras.

In August 1791, a secret letter written by some mischievous elements from Chanderagore and addressed to the French soldiers stationed at Pondicherry, instigating them to revolt against the Governor and to assassinate all the authorities, reached Girardot, a resident of Pondicherry. When this was brought to the notice of De Fresne, he summoned the soldiers and warned them of severe punishment, in case of any disturbance from their side. He also dispatched a ship to Chandernagore in his effort to arrest and bring the culprits to book. The instigators, on getting scent of the plan, ran away and took asylum in Calcutta. On August 31, the French Indian authorities imposed martial law to keep the situation under control.[35]

However, certain mischievous elements continued to create problems in Pondicherry. On the night of February 5, 1792, some miscreants climbed atop the flag mast, tore the tricolour flag and took away a part of it. The authorities even declared a gift of 100 gold coins for those who offered some information on the incident and help to nab the culprits. Special guard was provided for the flag mast and the soldiers were instructed to shoot at sight anyone who approached the area after 10 p.m.[36]

Veera Naicker II concludes his diary with the happy developments in France, where the King had given approval to the new constitution introduced by the National Assembly. He also gives details of the celebration of July 14, 1792. All the French nationals, including the Governor, took the oath of loyalty to the National Assembly, the King and the law of the land. All of them spent a happy time with drinks and food. Naicker notes that some 1500 bottles of liquor were spent on the occasion. A special tax of ten rupees was collected from each French household for this purpose.[37]

In September 1792, Lescalier, one of the Civil Commissioners deputed by the National Assembly to supervise the reorganisation of the colonies, arrived at Pondicherry. He proposed the election of a new Colonial Assembly consisting of only 12 members elected by French citizens of 25 years and above with a minimum of one year's domicile in French India and owning property worth Rs. 500 or with a minimum of two year's domicile and paying a monthly rent of rupees five. The Franco-Indians, who were generally called Topas, were also given the right to vote at the elections to the Colonial Assembly subject to certain conditions like that they should be legitimate children of free parents; own property worth Rs. 500 or pay a monthly rental of Rs. 5 and be able to read and write French. It may be worth noting that the number of active citizens in Pondicherry numbered only 214 plus 14 topas.[38] Still, the natives were left in lurk.

A fresh Colonial Assembly based on these provisions was elected in December 1792 and one of the first tasks that it took on hand was the complete reorganization of the administration of the Indian settlements. Many far-reaching reforms were introduced and the most notable one was the prohibition of slave trade in the French Indian colonies.[39] However, as mentioned earlier, the problem continued to be in practice in French India for some more time to come.

REPERCUSSIONS OF 1857 IN FRENCH INDIA

Some of the Indian Princes and a few thousand disgruntled *sepoys* or native soldiers, supported by the artisan and peasant communities, challenged the British authority in 1857 in different parts of North India. It appears that there was some reaction in French India to the developments in the North. Due to their fear that the natives under their rule too might revolt against them, the European settlers in Pondicherry requested the Governor to offer firearms to them and to allow them to organise into a battalion. It is ironic to note that some 400 pro-French natives pleaded with the Governor to take stringent actions against any one who intended to take part in revolutionary activities in French India.[40]

CONCLUSION

While some scholars attempt to portray the ilk of Arokiam and Savarimuthu Pillai as embodiments of the evils of the *ancienne regime* and to connect the peasants' revolts in French India with the French Revolution, Saroja Sundararajan (1985) maintains that the whole episode is 'mere' agitation since the cultivators felt aggrieved and their disaffection and suspicion manifested themselves in a 'strike' and they calmed down and resumed their work on being convinced that the French Indian Government showed fairness and were sincerely concerned in their 'welfare'.[41] Both these view points take two extreme positions. The popular resistance movement in French India can neither be eulogized as part of French Revolution nor can be dismissed as 'mere' popular resentment, which took the form of 'strike'.

The peasant community of French India did not hesitate to agitate against the injustice meted out to them by the native agents of the French colonial misrule. Their uprising could not be treated as agitation against the arbitrary activities of the tax collector but against the French colonial rule, which had hoisted these elements on them. The fact that these miscreants had also enjoyed the support of the officials of the French colonial administration fanned the popular resentment against the alien colonial masters, who had not hesitated to use military force to suppress the popular resistance movement.

The interest shown by the natives to have sound knowledge about the repercussions of the French Revolution over the French population of Pondicherry proves beyond doubt their political awareness and their intention to participate in the momentous developments that were taking place in their town. However, the divisions among them on the basis of religion, caste and other such factors prevented them from taking benefit of the liberal environment that over took the French colonial masters for the time-being. Soon, the latter regained their superiority complex and started assuming that they were rulers and the natives were the ruled, thus failing the famous revolutionary triad: *liberté, egalité et franternité*.

Repercussions of 1857 over French India clearly demonstrate the existence of an elitist section of native population of French India who remained self-centred and had not hesitated to assume pro-French postures to please their colonial masters. Their avariciousness led to their betrayal of the common cause with their brethren who intended to take benefit of the developments caused by the 1857 revolt.

NOTES

1. Veera Naicker, *Diary of Veera Naicker II (1778-92)*, (edited and published by Orsay M. Gopalakrishnan) Chennai, 1992, p. xxii (hereafter Naicker's *Diary*).

2. H.I. Priestely, 1939. *French Overseas through the old Regime – A Study of European Expansion*, New York, pp. 190-1.
3. Bibliothèque *Nationale Departement des Manuscrits Francais* (henceforth B.N.Mss.Fr.) 6231, f. 55; Castonnet de Fosses, *L' Inde Française avant Dupleix*, Paris, 1887, p. 157.
4. Bibliothèque *Nationale Fond Nouvelles Acquisitions Française* (henceforth Mss. B.N.N.A.) 9090, f. 160; *Memoires et Correspondence du Chevalier et du General de la Farelle*, published by E. Lennel de la Farelle, Paris, 1896, p. 16.
5. Naicker's *Diary*, p. 258.
6. *B.N.N.A.* 9354, f. 76. In the colonial townships developed under the jurisdiction of the European trading organizations, both in Madras and in Pondicherry, we can observe these white and black towns. While in the 'White town' Christianity alone was tolerated, the native customs and ways of life were allowed to be practiced in the other. In Pondicherry, a canal was dug and developed parallel to the sea to clearly demarcate the 'White' from the 'Black' settlement.
7. Ananda Ranga Pillai, *The Private Diary of Ananda Ranga Pillai, 1736-1761*, Trans. and published by J.F. Price and Dodwell, Madras, 1904-08, Vol. 9, pp. 25, 124, 328. Pillai was given permission to ride on horseback or in a palanquin in the fort area and to move around with all paraphernalia like white flag and umbrella, the right to wear slippers in the Governor's presence and to military honours like gun salute on ceremonial occasions, as at wedding or funeral.
8. Naicker's *Diary*, pp. 217-8.
9. *B.N.N.A.* 9090, f.160.
10. *B.N.N.A.* 9225, fls. 292-3; B.N.Mss.Fr. 6231, f. 55.
11. Pillai's *Diary*, Vol. V, p. 311.
12. Paul Olagnier, 1936. *Ungrand colonial inconnu le gouverneur Benoist Dumas, Societe le l'histoire des colonies francaises*, Paris, pp. 43, 74 and 161.
13. Joseph Minattur, '*Tribunal de la Chaudrie* (1728-1827), *Revue Historique de Pondichery* (henceforth *Revenue*), Vol. 12, p. 13.
14. *Proces-verbaux des deliberation du Conseil Supèrieur de Pondichéry*, tome 1, Pondicherry, 1911-1914, tome 1, p. 93.
15. *Ibid.*, pp. 147, 292.
16. B. Krishnamurthy, 1991. 'The Revenue System of the French Administered Territories in India in the First Half of the Eighteenth Century', in *Revue Historique de Pondichery*, Joseph Minattur (ed.), Vol. 16, Pondicherry, pp. 1-18. Veera Naicker (pp. 198-200) gives details about the fixation of tax collection in December 1789 for three years from January 1790 to December 1792 as follows:

For monopoly goods like betel leaf and tobacco	-	Rs. 12,210/-
For customs duties	-	6,160/-
For goods moving through land route	-	10,330/-
For liquor etc.	-	3,200/-

17. *Proces-verbaux*, tome 1, pp. 24-5.
18. S.P. Sen, 1958. *The French in India 1763-1816*, Calcutta: Mukhopadhyaya Publications, p. 107.
19. Naicker's *Diary*, p. 125.
20. *Gazetteer*, Vol. 1, pp. 213-214.
21. Naicker's *Diary*, pp. 246-8.
22. S.P. Sen, *op. cit.*, pp. 482-3.
23. Naicker's *Diary*, pp. 229-30.
24. *Ibid.*, pp. 203-8.
25. *Ibid.*, pp. 204-6.
26. *Gazetteer*, Vol. 1, p. 216. However, it is heartening to note that these people were later acquitted by the National Assembly of Paris in March 1792.
27. Naicker's *Diary*, pp. 211-217.
28. *Ibid.*, pp. 210-12.
29. *Gazetteer*, Vol. 1, p. 217. Veera Naicker gives some additional information about the representation to the National Assembly in his diary (p. 257). These representatives incurred an expenditure of 16,000 rupees

in France. The Mayor of Pondicherry informed the leaders of the natives about this and instructed them to collect half of the amount from the natives and submit to him. He gracefully informed them that the rest would be the share of the French citizens of Pondicherry. This incident clearly shows the double standard of the French. While they were not ready to share the benefits of 'liberty, equality and fraternity' with the natives, they expected them to pay equal share in the expenses.

30. M.V. Labernadie. 1930. *La Révolution et les établissements Française dans l'Inde 1790-1793*, Paris, pp. 62-3, 390-3. However, Veera Naicker (p. 215) maintains that the French authorities instructed the notables among the natives to nominate some members to the Municipal Chamber on behalf of them. It appears that no follow up action was taken by the French on this count.
31. Naicker's *Diary*, pp. 235-7.
32. *Ibid.*, pp. 238-41.
33. *Ibid.*, p. 248.
34. J.B.P. More, 2001. *Freedom Movement in French India: The Mahe Revolt of 1948*, Tellicherry: Institute for Research in Social Sciences and Humanities, pp. 49-50.
35. Naicker's *Diary*, pp. 254-5.
36. *Ibid.*, p. 261.
37. *Ibid.*, pp. 268-70.
38. J.B.P. More, *op. cit.*, p. 218. The French Constitution of September 1791 divided the population into 'active' and 'passive' citizenry according to wealth, social class and sex. While even certain classes of men having their rights restricted, all women fell into the 'passive' category. In response to this anomaly, Olympe de Gouges, the authoress of the 'Declaration of the Rights of Woman' of 1791, clamoured for the protection and promotion of the rights of women.
39. *Gazetteer*, Vol. 1, p. 219.
40. *Ibid.*, p. 229.
41. Saroja Sundararajan, 1985. *Glimpses of the History of Karaikal*, Madras: Lalitha Publications, pp. 29-31.

28

Atrocities in the Andaman Islands under the Regime of Japan (1943-45)

BITHIN THAKUR

ABSTRACT

The islands of Andaman witnessed both the British and the Japanese imperial rule. Andaman was consistently under the rule of British since 1857, but was occupied by the imperial Japan in 1942 in a very dramatic way and from then on for a period of three years, Andaman went through one of its dark periods of its history. The study covers the occupation of the islands by the Japanese, chaos, restoration of order and atrocities by them against the local people in the name of spy case. Netaji's visit to Andaman was a great hope for the local people but the Japanese managed it so well that he found everything normal and fine in the island. However, chaos and atrocities continued till the reoccupation of the island by the British in 1945 after the surrender of Japan in Second World War.

The Andaman group of islands lies between the 10° to 14° North Latitude and between 22° to 24° East Longitudes, 590 miles away from the mouth of the river Hooghly and 219 miles in length. This group of islands is also known as Bay islands because of their geographical spread in the Bay of Bengal.[1] It was first explored by the British in 1849 and we have an account of Andaman and Nicobar Islands in an early Chinese document. As far as Indian history is concerned after the revolt of 1857, the British were in search of some place for the Indian prisoners and they found Andaman as the safest place.

Before dealing with the actual occupation of the islands by the imperial Japanese, some important facts need be mentioned. Some ten years prior to their occupation, they were often coming to these islands ostensibly to collect shells from the shores of the island. At first no attention was paid to them but when their numbers increased, they were asked to take out licenses by the British. So when they came out in their boats, they touched Port Blair first, took out necessary licenses from the administration and went out fishing. Then they returned again, exhibited their ware at Marine Dockyard, paid royalty, took a port clearance from the Harbour Master and departed to their destiny – invariably, Malaya. No one knew of the otherwise innocent vocation until after the war, when it was discovered that these fishermen were expert naval personnel from Japan who surveyed every inch of the Andaman Sea and picked up useful knowledge from the local people so the Japanese landing forces were fully aware of the coastal condition when they came to the islands.[2] A fleet of ships was seen by some villagers, on the east cost of Port Blair in the early part of the night of 22nd March 1942. The troops from the ship started landing on the morning of 23rd March 1942 and marched towards various directions of the island and took over the charges from the British administration. The occupation was completed within twelve hours of landing, without firing a single shot and excepting those on sentry duty, the entire force, some twenty thousand strong, remained in the Japanese fleet outside Port Blair harbour waiting for eventualities. The landing force consisted of both army and navy personnel. The navy struck its headquarters at Aberdeen and the army at Haddo. After the Englishmen and the Anglo-Indians were taken into custody and confined to Ross Island from where there was no fear of their escape, the men of the army and the navy were ordered to rest.

The lawlessness then begun. The general public did not have sufficient time to realize what the change meant. After the evacuation by the British, the work in the different offices had been redistributed. As the heads of departments had left, the seniormost subordinates were promoted as departmental heads. Thus, the work of the Deputy Commissioner and the Settlement Assistant Commissioner was combined with the Chief Commissioner. A Tahsildar was appointed as Deputy Assistant Commissioner – a work-charge subordinate, the Engineer and the Harbour Master, an Exploitation Officer, a Chief Forest Officer; a Sub Inspector of Police, the Superintendent of Police; a Sub-assistant Surgeon, the Senior Medical Officer. This was a purely makeshift arrangement. With the advent of the Japanese, when all the remaining Englishmen were taken into custody and were made prisoners, the civil administration came to a standstill. The match factory, the concern of the Western India Match Company, the only privately owned concern under a Swedish manager, was also at a standstill when the Swedes were taken into custody along with other Europeans of the settlement. This was the picture of the administration on the day of occupation of the islands by the Japanese.[3]

The Japanese soldiers were prohibited from entering any civilian house by the government. So the Japanese officers had to think about the comforts of their soldiers to satisfy their hunger for sex. The Japanese officers, with the help of some local Andaman people, tried to solve this problem but failed as the people of Andaman did not cooperate. Therefore, they brought Korean girls for this purpose. They were kept in the barrack of South Point where the government school was run prior to the Japanese occupation. Some of them were also kept in other villages where Japanese soldiers were stationed. These innocent girls were treated badly and were forced to sexually entertain Japanese soldiers. There is no word to describe the horrible condition of those poor girls. After the war, the Japanese officials denied that the war time government was ever involved in forcing women to serve as comfort girls.[4]

The Andaman even in the best of times did not produce foodstuff or vegetables sufficient for the need of the population. Consequently, rice, *atta*, oil, ghee, potatoes, onions and all condiments were imported from India. Now that the islands contained a surplus population, some twenty thousand over and above the normal, it was clear the foodstuff should come from outside. These were actually brought by the Japanese from the conquered areas so long as the going was good. In addition to foodstuff, clothing materials had also to come from India and other places and the Japanese brought these also in good quantities. Ship-loads were coming in every week, at least at the rate of two per week. Ammunition also came along in large quantities. Military accoutrements were also dumped all over the place. The army left the Islands in about three or four months of occupation, for being deployed elsewhere but the navy continued to remain throughout. The strength was kept up reasonably high. Allied aircraft began to bomb Japanese cargo ships continuously after three or four months of occupation, within which period the Japanese had collected on the Islands sufficient quantities of consumer goods and other war materials. Towards the close of 1942, bombardment of cargo ships was done extensively by air and what remained to be done was done by the Allied submarines. The anti-aircraft guns and the fighter planes were never seen or heard to have brought down an enemy plane.

How the Allied bombers came along at the right moment when the cargo ships went at the port was something that maddened the Japanese. Local people were arrested under suspicion of giving information to the Allies. Tortures infused on the arrested were of many varieties. Some of the major ones are described below:

Beating

Both hands are tied up together and a haul made until just the toes touch the ground. Now blows are delivered on the breech, with a thick wooden cudgel with full bodily force. So long as the man does not slacken in the legs, blows continue. This process continues for days together and stops only when it is found that some of the portion of the flesh of the breech has sloughed off. The victim is now left in his cell with no medical aid. Sleeping or sitting is impossible. Maggots are formed in the open wounds and no one outside knows what is happening to him.

Water treatment

A man is tied up flat on a wooden cot. His head is held tight upright by a man. His hands are pinned to the cot. Water is now poured on his face, without break. His breathing is impossible and if at all he breathes, for breathe he must, water enters his lungs at each breath. The process continues for hours together until the man is done up. He is unable to sit and unable to lie down on account of foreign matter in his lungs. In the course of a few hours, he attains a comatic state and ultimately dies.

Electric treatment

This is done by first pinning down a man with handcuffs to either a wall or the ceiling. Electric current (250 DC) is now passed through his body this way: The tips of the positive and the negative wires are shaved naked and when the positive becomes red hot, both ends are put on the body of the sufferer who had been stripped naked. When the current passes through, he yells and groans, which can be heard throughout the vast jail. The shock is excruciating. This goes on for days, nay, for weeks until a man reaches the verge of lunacy.

Burning

The victim in this case is stripped of all his clothing; he is hauled up by a rope tied to his wrist and legs are tied up apart and stretched out as far as they go. Rubbish paper is now heaped up between his legs and set fire to. The flames reach up to the chest burning the thighs, the scrotum, abdomen and a part of the chest. After setting fire, the torturer leaves the room so that the victim and the fire are left to take care of themselves. The howling and wailing of the sufferer are of no avail. The burn is usually deep and in this case also, no medical aid is given. Gaping wounds attract flies, as the victim cannot keep any clothes over his body. In the course of time, the man becomes the headquarters of maggots. Survivors still have the scars on their bodies.

Piercing the Finger Nails

An iron pin of a large size, preferably an office pin or a gramophone needle, is driven under the nail of a finger in the fleshy part. The finger is then caught with pliers and brought to a burning candle on the flames of which the tip of the finger with the iron pin sticking under the nail is heated up, until the iron pin is red hot. The finger tips burn. One finger is dealt with at a time until the tenth day, by which time the tips of all the ten fingers are burnt out and big ulcers are forced. In some cases, the process re-starts after the first wounds are healed up. Some have malformed nails still to remind them of the cruelty of the Japanese.

Sitting treatment

This consists in making a man kneel down, and then sit on his heels. A stick is now inserted between the ground and the bent knee and the other is inserted between both the curved knees. The arms are stretched skywards, on the palms of which a heavy book or a slab of flagstone is placed. Unlike the burning torture, in which case the tormentor is usually absent, after setting on the fire, in this case he is always present watching the two sticks and the weight of the palms. If the weight falls or the sticks are displaced, the victim is subjected to a number of lashes on his back before the status quo is restored. The process goes on from morning till evening for weeks together and each evening the victim leaves the torture chamber, with a swollen back which in a few days loses a good portion of its skin. He is unable to walk to his cell in the evening when he is asked to go away. At the end of a week, he becomes a well nigh cripple.[5]

These are a few illustrations of tortures perpetrated by Japanese or by Indians on Indians under the order of Japanese. In between these tortures, interrogation by the Japanese continued, even severe forms are adopted. Sprinkling a part of the body with petrol and setting fire to it until the entire skin burns deep, was one form. Another severe form was to incise daily some part of a man's body and to sprinkle the cut with salt or powdered chillies.

When all these tortures failed, wives and children are brought to the jail. Both now enter the torture chamber. The woman is beaten in front of her husband and the husband is beaten in front of the wife. Or the wife is asked to beat her husband and the husband, his wife. Children are beaten in front of their parents. Sometimes the son is asked to beat the mother or the father. The helpless victim does not know what all that fuss is about. People were also taken in boat and in the mid sea near an island called Havelock were forced to jump on the gun point. There are also a few records of mass murder: Some 33 person were shot dead in Dundus Point.[6]

After the World War, when we read of Nazi tyrannies and treatments in the Concentration camps in Europe, we feel consoled by the fact that victors all through the ages and everywhere behaved cruelly to the utmost degree bereft of all human feelings.

With the arbitrary arrests and the incarceration of these people for over three months, during which period news seeped out about the perpetration of tortures on Indians in the cruelest methods imaginable, everyone thought that the Andamans were doomed. The tall talk of the South East Asian Co-Prosperity Sphere was now replaced by terror. Everyone began to say in hushed voices that the Japanese may be Asians but they were no friends of Indians. Toward the close of 1942, the Japanese had started a one-page daily by the name of

The Andaman Shimbun. They used this paper for propaganda purposes and gave out news of their successes in various war fronts, especially in the Pacific, and held out promises of golden days ahead.

The work on the aerodrome was carried on at top speed with all available labour. By the beginning of 1943, the air strip began to function effectively and fighter planes arrived in hundreds. The sea-planes meant to bomb the Indian coastal towns were withdrawn. Before their withdrawal, much damage was sustained by the machine gunning of the enemy, many planes of Japanese being destroyed at Haddo. As the work on the aerodrome was intensive and as the work was extracted without regard to physical abilities of the labouring people, diseases became rife. Those who did not fall by diseases fell by the club blows of the Japanese. Medicines were not supplied to hospitals, and what little they had, had practically been spent out. Anyone getting admitted in the hospital did so merely to die. Short supply of rationing articles was killing or emaciating people. Prisoners in penal days had tasted grumblingly some bitter pills of adversity, but all free persons now tasted the much more bitter pills of adversity.

The Japanese shipping came to a standstill by the middle of 1943 and no cargo of any kind, food, clothing or ammunition, reached the islands. Food was getting scarce all over and the dearth of clothing was keenly felt. The Allied bombers, which had been making raids off and on, increased the frequency of the raids. Big gun emplacements and the aerodrome were their objectives. The Chatham sawmill was practically crippled. Hundreds wounded by each raid, were brought to the ill-equipped hospital. There was no chloroform or anesthetic of any kind even for the amputation of a damaged limb. Butchery was surgery. Sub-marines were often seen hovering around. Cargo ships were going down before the very eyes of the Japanese. There was hardly any naval defense worth the name. Fighter planes, which were taking off at times, were crashing at the time of landing, at the rate of two per trip.[7] *The Statesman*, in its war news, reported:

"In a strike against the Andamans, heavy bombers of the 10th USAAF of the Strategic Air Force, Eastern Air Command, in daylight on April 15, bombed enemy shipping at Port Blair. Near misses on three motor vessels were observed. In the ensuing attempted interception by 3 to 5 enemy fighters, one enemy fighter was probably destroyed and two damaged."

"On July 29 our heavy bomber operated in the area of the Andaman Islands. A 300-ft. steamer docked at Chatham Island was bombed. No direct hits were claimed but bombs were seen to destroy many buildings in the dock area. A tremendous delayed explosion followed, the smoke from which blanketed the entire area. A 150 ft. ship near Ross Island was strafed and damaged. A naval vessel of the same length found 25 miles off Port Blair was also strafed and damaged."

"A communique issued from Rear Echelon HQ, USAFF, China, Burma and India, says: B-24 heavy bombers of the 10th USAFF on August 15 attacked enemy installations on Chatham Island in the Andaman group. Direct hits were observed on warehouses and other buildings, causing great destruction and starting large fires. One a-a battery was destroyed. Smoke from the fires was visible 50 miles away. All our aircraft and crew returned safely."[8]

Towards the close of the year, a Japanese air expert visited these islands and observed that the frequent air accidents at the time of landing took place on account of the existence of an air pocket over the aerodrome. In view of this report, the aerodrome was thereafter abandoned for all serious purposes.

At this period, suspicion about the sending out of news of military importance by the residents of the Islands grew in the minds of the Japanese once more. Their wireless station at the same time intercepted messages sent out by someone other than themselves from somewhere near about the Islands. They were worried. They opened out numberless military outposts all along the sea shore in their vain attempt to catch the person who was spying. All residents were suspected. The Japanese Intelligence Department, the local police and the Jiku students were all engaged as detectives. Unfortunately, for the residents, one of the military outposts at this time spotted a strange looking bearded man with long hair landing on a beach from the open sea by a rubber boat. He was chased but escaped capture. The Intelligence Department became more brisk and everybody was placed under strict observation, particularly those with beards and long hair. The inference was that the stranger had come to contact some local resident.[9]

Some of the prisoners who helped the Intelligence Department in 1942 and succeeded in getting seven men shot, were still in the police department. The rest who became the real terror found themselves in jail for civil offences, such as taking bribes and other gratifications from the terror-stricken victims. They considered themselves immune awhile, being in the police department, but were caught in the act of corruption by the same Japanese, who now employed some of their brethren to spy over them. The system of the Japanese administration was, in the other words, to employ a spy on the public, and then to employ a spy over this spy, and another spy, and so on. Those spies, who became venomous to public and behaved arrogantly on account of constant favours showered on them, were killed on some pretext or other. The cause of their actual death remained a secret.

It is a fact that the allies came to the islands by sub-marines and established themselves in various points in the well known thick jungles. They contacted men who were mostly working in jungles or fishing on sea shores or living in the out-of-the-way villages well known to Mr. Mc-Carthy (a British man). They had Indians with them who made the actual contact. From their hiding place, they gave out wireless messages which brought the allied aircraft or sub-marines at the right moment to attack the Japanese shipping in the Bay of Bengal nearabout the Andamans. But the happenings worried the Japanese who were all the time embarking on a wild-goose chase arresting people at random by hundreds, and torturing them to elicit information. The actual offenders, with their transmitters, were all the time in the forests or below the surface of the sea, in some sub-marines.[10]

The Indian Independence League sponsored by the Japanese was started in the South East Asia under the president ship of Ras Behari Bose with headquarters at Bangkok. Branches were established at Malaya, Burma and the Andamans. In the Andamans, it was functioning drowsily but after the terror created by the first Spy Case, it went into a perfect slumber. Most of the members and volunteers, who were strutting in the streets as some rulers, were taken away for work on the aerodrome; so this branch of the Independence League existed on paper only, with no authority worth mentioning.

The presence of a bearded stranger on the beach, and the constant interception of wireless messages that were sent out from somewhere nearabout the islands, made the Japanese crazy and incensed. They were pulling hard at the leash to apprehend the real culprits. They went all out, employing all sorts of methods, coaxing, cajoling, tempting, and what not. Then they descended to crude methods – suspected men were caught, harassed and finally tortured. The Cellular Jail was their concentration camp and the present Secretariat building, their headquarters *Thokomohan*.

The work of the aerodrome at Lamba Line was somewhat slackened on account of the verdict of the expert about the existence of an air pocket over it, and the consequent daily crashing of fighter planes at the rate of at least two per day, to the amusement of the onlookers and to the annoyance of the Japanese. It was decided by them (in the middle of 1943) to construct a new aerodrome at Mithakhari. The strip selected was between Mithakhari Jetty and Elephant Point. A number of bull-dozers were employed in levelling the ground. The adjoining paddy fields were taken over from the owners. This was done during the season for planting paddy, with absolute disregard to the needs of cultivators or to the scarcity of food grains that would follow in the wake of such an action.

The Japanese collected cultivators from villages in the settled area by motor trucks and dumped them near Mithakhari to work on the new project. Make-shift leaf barracks for their accommodation were erected hurriedly. It was the peak of the rainy season. The barracks, having no adequate roofing, were like sieves, and sitting in them during the day and sleeping by night was impossible during rains. There was no arrangement for cooking food. This had to be done in the open and when a downpour came, men had to run back to the shelter of the barracks, pot and all, only to get further wet there. Going out of barracks either by day or by night was impossible owing to the bog developing all round them in the rains.

Men were brought away from villages by truck loads and were not told where they were to go. No utensils for cooking, no change of clothes or things needed were brought by them. Their women and children were left in the bewilderment. News reached them after a day or two that their men folk were all at Mithakhari for aerodrome work and that they would not be allowed to go home. Utensils and some clothes were brought down by the womenfolk but those who were single, remained helpless. At least the British supplied their prisoners, when they brought them here in 1858 the following years, with food, clothing, bed and a shelter, habitable if not comfortable. The Japanese did not provide any of these to the free citizens. On the other hand, they employed these men from morning till evening. When anyone pleaded that his field was going to ruins, severe *lathi* blows descended on him. Slackening at work was the other occasion when the *lathi* (club) became liberal. Apart from the work on the aerodrome, men were also employed intensively on other defense work, such as gun emplacements, branches and hideouts.[11]

One morning, at the end of August 1943, it was found that two supervisors of Labour, who held charge of the labour force under a Japanese Officer, had been placed under arrest overnight. The arrest of these two men was the beginning of a very cruel episode in the history of the Andamans under the Japanese. Those two persons were beaten daily to give clue of the spies working on the Island in a gang under someone. What information the Japanese extracted from these two is unknown and will remain unknown as one, Ratan Chand, was shot and the other, Faizul Hussain, died under torture. But what is well known is that people from all walks of life and from all over the place were arrested indiscriminately and taken to the jail under the direct supervision of Mitsubishi, the Chief of the Police, who was a civilian in military uniform under Jyochi Renusukai, the Civil Governor.

Scores of arrested men, with arms pinned behind their backs by a rope in utter humiliation, like an animal taken to be butchered, were brought daily, through the bazaar to Cellular Jail. Arrested persons, at the end of the month, overcrowded the jail. Their numbers rose to some hundreds. Strange it may seem and even paradoxical that the men chosen by the Chief of the Police to inflict torture on Indians were not Japanese but Indians, mostly picked up from all over the Islands for their build and sturdiness. They were the men who were wielding clubs, sticks and cudgels with all animal fury. They had no alternative, the master being so cruel. The head of the torture chamber was always Japanese. The torturers were doing their work with great animal satisfaction for fear that if they showed any mercy, they may land themselves into serious trouble.[12]

By the end of November, arrests stopped. But tortures on those already arrested continued. Sikhs and their friends came under severe chastisement on account of the bearded man seen on the beach. All the Sikhs in the Police Department were ordered to cut off their beards and long hair, in order that there may be no confusion about their identity. The occupation forces showed utter disregard for religious sentiments. The exigency of war was apparently the cause of this apathy. Inner human feelings could jeopardize the cause of the option at war. Besides, it must be recorded that the occupation forces here were fighting against an underground intelligence and espionage force. In a vengeful mood, the Japanese military authorities resorted to cruelty and transgressed all canons of human behaviour.[13]

As a large number of Indians came in the hands of Japanese in Malaya, Burma and other South-East Asian countries, the Japanese got Netaji Subhash Chandra Bose from Germany under certain arrangements with the European arm of the axis. The world came to know about this only after his miraculous arrival at Singapore. His arrival gave a fillip to Indians and courage to the Japanese. After a month or two of his arrival, a South East Asian Conference with the representatives of Burma, Malaya, Netherland East Indies (now Indonesia), Philippines and occupied China, was convened at Tokyo. As Netaji represented no Indian territory, he refused to take part in the conference as a representative of India, but on the insistence of the Japanese government, he took part as an observer.

In this conference, it was declared by the Japanese government that the territory of the Andaman and Nicobar Islands, being a part of the Indian sub-continent, will be placed under him. This was done to give Netaji Subhash Chandra Bose the status of the Head of an Indian province so that he could be treated as other Heads of Government in South East Asia. History shall record that a trick more sinister than this was never played by any nation. Events that followed in the Andamans after this declaration by the Japanese government showed, in course of time, that their declaration was a mere mockery. It is asserted that these Islands were never handed over either to Netaji or, on his behalf, to this appointed Chief Commissioner Col. Loganathan, who actually came here later with his staff to take over the charge of the Islands.[14]

Netaji visited the Islands towards the close of 1943. The spy case, mentioned in the previous paragraph, known locally as the second spy case, was in full swing at that time and unheard of tortures were perpetrated within the four walls of the Cellular Jail. Outside it, considerable panic prevailed. As Netaji's visit could not be put off and as the country could not be brought hurriedly to normaley, precautions, by various ingenious methods, were taken to obliterate the abnormality prevailing on the Islands and keep Netaji in the dark about the tortures on Indians. No member of the public was given a chance to speak to him freely. Some Japanese official was always present to report the conversation that took place between him and a few Indians the Japanese allowed him to meet. On Netaji's arrival at the aerodrome, a selected band of officials were made to stand in two rows at the aerodrome. This was the party which had ostensibly gone to welcome Netaji. They were all picked up overnight as the news of Netaji's arrival was kept off from the public on account of the war exigencies. He met them without speaking to any one of them as though he was inspecting a guard of honor. He, with his staff, after landing, was carried to the erstwhile Government House at Ross Island. The road from the aerodrome to Aberdeen Jetty, from which a crossing by boat is made to reach Ross Island, was ordered to be lined up by men, women and children. Of this order Netaji was unaware. If he thought that this entire crowd had come to pay him homage, no one dared dispel the wrong impression. The Japanese were mortally afraid of the leakage of the news of the torture that they were perpetrating here.[15]

It must be recorded here that Netaji, being as a casual visitor who saw the islands for the first time and who was quite unaware of the fact of torture and maltreatment meted out to Indians on ground of espionage, took everything here as normal and never suspected that the Japanese officials would deliberately hoodwink him. Of good nature and of a lofty character himself, he had no suspicion of Japanese behaviour.

A public meeting was arranged on the only *maidan* of Port Blair, in which a large number of people were ordered to attend. Netaji came from Ross and reached the *maidan* in a ceremonious procession made up of Japanese officers in a number of cars. As usual, no Indians from the Andamans were included in this procession. On arrival, he went up the rostrum and unfurled the Indian National flag, the first one to be hoisted on an Indian territory. The Chairman of the Andaman branch of the Indian Independence League, Mr. Rama Krishna, gave a welcome address and presented a purse for the I.N.A., after which Netaji addressed the gathering. Without meeting any of the residents, he was again very ceremoniously driven back to Ross. No one from the Andamans accompanied him.[16]

A visit to the jail was in the itinerary of Netaji. He was to go there on a morning. Now, at the time of the visit of Netaji, there were barely a score of actually imprisoned persons in the jail. But the so-called second spy case being on, there were more than a hundred persons undergoing tortures and interrogations daily. Netaji was shown barely the score of persons who were the actual prisoners and were at various jobs, such as cleaning the garden, planting vegetables, sweeping the compound and cooking for the prisoners and such other routine jail work. He was taken to one or two wings to show him with a big grin, that there were hardly any prisoners to fill such a large jail and that for that reason it was practically empty. No Indian from the administration was allowed to accompany him on this occasion also. He never saw the wing in which tortured people were held. If he had seen persons whose skins were missing from thighs, scrotum, abdomen and chest and could not wear any apparel; a few who had no flesh on their breeches; a few who had no skin on parts of their bodies, the result of burns by petrol; a few who could not walk straight, the result of constant kneeling on sticks; a few who had deep knife cuts all over the fleshy parts of their bodies on which salt had been sprinkled or if he had met even one of them and questioned him about his predicament things could have been different. He was taken to the jail deliberately, so that later, when news reached him by some chance from some source at his headquarters at Singapore, he might be perplexed and even ejaculate that he had seen nothing wrong there when he actually visited it. That was the ulterior motive of the Japanese in showing him the jail.

During the Japanese regime, Andaman underwent the worst time with total chaos and atrocities, which affected Andaman politically and economically. The people of Andaman never experienced such kind of treatment from the British government. Japan is well known for her war crimes during the Second World War and subsequently has acknowledged it also but the atrocities in Andaman are never mentioned in this acknowledgment of war crimes.

NOTES

1. N. Iqbal Singh, 1978. *The Andaman Story*, New Delhi: Vikas Publishing House, p. 9.
2. Unpublished Document, Krishna Rama, *The Andaman Islands under Japanese Occupation – 1942 to 1945*, p. 3.

3. B.B. Lal, 1998. *A Regime of Fears and Tears,* New Delhi: Vikas Publishing House, p. 28.
4. Seoul 17th January 1992 (AP), Published in the *Daily Telegraph.*
5. Unpublished Document, Krishna Rama, *op. cit.,* pp. 42-45.
6. Oral Interview of Mr. Rash Bihari, Port Blair (an eye witness to the Japanese invasion of Andaman).
7. Unpublished Document, Krishna Rama, *op. cit.,* pp. 47-50.
8. *Ibid.,* p. 53.
9. B.B. Lal, *op. cit.,* pp. 73-75.
10. Basil Collier, 1969. *The War in the Far East,* London: Heineman, pp. 33-34.
11. Unpublished Document, Krishna Rama, *op. cit.,* pp. 32-34.
12. *Ibid.,* pp. 36-37.
13. Mohinder Singh Dhillon, 1994. *A Titan in the Andamans. Dr. Diwan Singh Kalepani: A Biography,* Chandigarh: Angad Publication, p. 86.
14. John Jacob and Harindra Srivastava. 1995. *Netaji Subhas, The Tallest of Titans,* New Delhi: Ess Publications, p. 97.
15. Tatsue Hayashida, 1970. *Netaji Subhas Chandra Bose, His Great Struggle and Martyrdom,* Bombay: Allied Publishers, p. 102.
16. Unpublished Document, Krishna Rama, *op. cit.,* p. 62.

29

The Glowing Haveli: A Study of the Multifaceted Contributions of Women in the Cochin Royal Family

DIVYA SANDESH

ABSTRACT

This paper aims at bringing to light the rich cultural heritage and traditions of the Cochin royal family with special reference to the contribution of the princesses in various fields. There are no written evidences regarding the origin of the Cochin royal family. All that we have are recorded from the folk tales and stories. This paper is an attempt to trace the changing status of the Cochin royal women, aspects of matrilineal system followed by the family, their participation in various social and cultural activities, thus becoming the embodiment of the pride and prestige in the Kerala society, even today. Today, the Cochin royal family, whose motto is 'Honour is our Family Treasure', comprises over a thousand members – each one independent and totally dissimilar.

The kingdom of Cochin came into existence in AD 1102 with the breakup of the Kulasekhara Empire. Initially, it was a small kingdom and its ruler was a king whose authority was confined to Cochin and its adjoining areas. There are no written historical evidences regarding the origin of the kingdom. All that we have are recorded from the folk tales and stories mentioned in a Sanskrit work called *Kerala mahatmayam* and the Malayalam work *Keralolpathi*. Cochin is also referred to in the writings of ancient travelers like Ma-Huan and Nicolo Conti (15th century). The family that ruled the kingdom was known as the *Perumbadappu* family, which had four branches or *thaavazhis*, namely, *mootha thaavazhi*, *elaya thaavazhi*, *vettathu thaavazhi* and the *Chazhiyur thaavazhi*. The Cochin royal family which had its roots in the *Chazhiyur thaavazhi* gradually proliferated and branched out to different parts of the state and is surviving as one of the oldest surviving royal clans of the world with an accurate genealogy and a unique tradition.[1]

Like any other family, the Cochin royal family also followed the matrilineal system. In this system, the family properties were owned by the female members while the financial and political affairs were managed by the eldest male member of the family. The male members of the royal families were known as *Thampuran* and the female members as *Thampurattis*.[2] The royal princesses lived under the strict control of the male members of the family. They were not permitted to go out of their houses and mingle with people other than their kith and kin. They could not take their own decisions even in their personal matters. But changes began to take place by the middle of the 19th century. The most important factor which came in favour of royal women was the spread of education. Education among the females was to play a decisive role in the progress and gradual evolution of the clan, leading up to its relatively privileged position in the present society. The royalty was exposed to formal education only after 1900. Till then, the princesses underwent an exclusively private tutorship at their residential palaces.[3] Some affluent families owned their own centres of learning. By 1900, it was decided by the Maharaja of Cochin that the princesses should also be formally educated. By that time the male members had already gone to Madras and had university education as well. The building called Kalikkotta (Fig. 1) was used for the purpose of schooling of royal girls. In every class there would not be more than half a dozen students; the schooling was more or less just for the sake of some kind of engagement during the day time. Learning was secondary. Most of the teachers were females and a familial relationship existed between the teachers and students.

School education till the twentieth century was not even a topic of discussion among the royal princesses. Only private tuition, especially for languages, was imparted in Kalikkotta. The women had very little contact with the outside world. They had simple entertainments except what was available during the celebration of festivals in the temples. They were permitted to learn music but forbidden to perform. They could dress like a simple normal woman of the land except that they could wear a few gold ornaments (Fig. 2). They were not allowed to go out of their

Fig. 1. Kalikkotta Palace.

quarters unless chaperoned by a male and a maid servant. It was from this background that they had to join the social life.[4]

Education opened up new avenues for them. A girl's school was started in the first quarter of the twentieth century. After completing their schooling, they themselves took initiative to pursue higher studies in Madras which showed their courage to take decisions by themselves. The first princess to go to Madras and get a Degree in Sanskrit was Ikkavutty Thampuran, the niece of the Parikshith Maharaja of Cochin. She was, therefore, called *Honours Princess*. The Madras University allowed a special college to function in the palace school at Kalikkotta. It could admit only female members of the family who were taught in non-science subjects by qualified teachers. Under-Graduate level teaching and graduate examinations were also permitted there. Some of the princesses thus graduated got employment as teachers in their own schools and later took their B.Ed degree as well. Often, they were promoted and transferred to other schools and by about 1950 some of them had become head-mistresses in government schools. Some of them occupied important positions like District Education Officers.

Fig. 2. Traditional dresses.

By this time, the existence of the special college came to an end and young women of the family had to go to the main town and join the Maharaja's College.[5] The conveyance was provided by the family with a special bus and in those days Maharaja's College had the rare sight of 20 to 30 young princesses alighting from this special bus. Often, all the princesses used to dress themselves in one colour of their choice and sometimes of certain uniform, which was awaited with expectation by students and teachers of the college. The option of science courses opened the doors of medicine and engineering. By 1970, there were many qualified post-graduate princesses who were ready to take up any job anywhere. Teaching at schools and colleges was given priority. There came up a number of doctors and engineers from the royal family of Cochin, of which Smt. Asha Devi Thampuran became the principal of an engineering college and Smt. Ganga Devi Thampuran became the principal of Maharaja's College and Deputy Director of Education. Smt. Lalitha, who became a doctor, began to practice in an *adivasi* village called Sittilanji in Tamil Nadu.[6]

In the field of cultural activities also, the royal women of Cochin showed their presence. Music has been taught in many families. Some royal princesses took to it so earnestly that they were permitted by the family to make performances, which was not allowed earlier. Smt. Manku Thampuran (Fig. 3), who became the first chairperson of the Kerala Sangeetha Nataka Academy, is a disciple of the great Chembai Vaidyanatha Bhagavathar. Smt Ratnam Thampuran, who also became a member of the Sangeetha Nataka Academy, was a great Karnatic musician. The same path was followed by Smt. Subhadra Thampuran and Rema Ramavarma, the daughter and niece of Ratnam Thampuran respectively. Smt. Mrinalini Thampuran was a noted dancer from the Cochin royal family who studied at Kalakshetra at Madras and could undertake stage performances.

Fig. 3. Smt Manku Thampuran.

By 1970, some princesses began to study Kathakali which was a male dominated temple art of Kerala. In spite of this fact, Cochin royal family produced well known Kathakali artists. When the all-women Kathakali troup visited U.S. and Canada on a performance tour, these women were the main artists in the troupe.

There was also a noted woman painter in the Cochin royal family called Smt. Kunjikkavu Thampuran. Her paintings are preserved in the art galley of Cochin and her famous work *Santhanagopalam* is depicted on the wall of Sri Poornathrayesa temple at Tripunithura (Fig. 4). Her paintings were mostly spiritual and devotional.

Apart from the field of arts, very few women in the royal family of Cochin sought government service as bureaucrats and also as bank employees. Social life was banned for the female members of the family in the olden days. They were not permitted to mingle with anybody other than their kith and kin. Yet, by 1940, princesses like Smt. Thankakutty Thampuran and Smt. Kunjikkavu Thampuran were brave enough to involve themselves in the activities of the All India Women's Conference, encouraged by Lakshmikutti Nethiaramma. Initiated by her, Radhalakshmi Vilasom College for music and fine arts was established in Tripunithura for both men and women in the 1940s.[7]

By this time several marriage reforms also took place. The custom in the family had been the ritual 'veli' before attaining 16 years of the age followed by the 'Sambandham' or the actual marriage.[8] The real partners in life would be young men from the *nambuthiri* caste. There was no option for the girl to think about anyone else. By 1950, Kochammini Thampuran declared that she would marry a prince of her choice, a member of the Kodungallur family. The family members didn't agree to it since there was no precedent. But she insisted that she would marry only that person or remain a spinster throughout life. She was so determined that after six to seven years, permission was given and she married the man of her choice, Kunjirama Varma. This pioneering effort led to a number of marriages from the same family. From the Kodungallur family itself, there are more than 18 young princes married to the Cochin princesses. Thereafter members from other kshatriya families, namely, Punjar, Kilimanjur, Harippad, Mavelikkara, Pantalam, Chirakkal, Bepur, Zamorin and Nilambur have married Cochin princesses. The Nambadi rajas from Chiralayam, Manakkulam and Kumarakom also have wives from this family. Even in the 1940s, one Subhadra Thampuran, a teacher in the Hindi Pracharak Sabha, got married to one Venkateswara Sharma, a Tamil Brahmin, who was also a Hindi Pracharak. It was only in the 1970s that a princess in the Cochin royal family chose a Nair and married him. But this did not bring in so many Nairs as spouses to the family. At the present context, there are not more than three or four Nair men as partners of Cochin princesses. There have been a couple of instances where Cochin princesses had been married to members of scheduled caste through arranged marriages.

Fig. 4. Sri Poornathrayesa temple, Tripunithura.

The young women of the family refrained from entering the political arena. There is only one Shanti Varma who got elected to the municipal council on the Left Front ticket. She lost her interest within a short time and later joined as a bank employee.

From the above context, it is clear that the royal princesses changed and evolved a lot to suit the contemporary situation and almost amalgamated themselves with the mainstream of the social life. Now they are a community, educated, financially sound and enlightened. Though they are not politically motivated, it is desirable that that they should enter the fabric of social life and enrich the society with their humble presence.

A number of laws have been enacted to raise the position of women. The acts, such as the Cochin Nayar Act of 1920, The Madras Marumakkathayam Act of 1932, etc. were passed with a view to ensure equality of status and equal opportunity to women.[9] Other factors like westernization of these laws led to the advancement of the position of women.

Educated women could break traditional values and family restraints, and build up their own future. Work outside the home brought them the opportunities of widening their outlook and developing their personality. The new educational industrial and urban development opened up new vistas and roles for women. The women in the royal family of Cochin are today the embodiment of prestige and proudness in the society of Kerala. The members of the Cochin royal family – whose motto is 'Honour is our family treasure' – are thousands in number, each one independent and dissimilar.

NOTES

1. T. Whitehouse, 1859. *Historical Notices of Cochin,* Kottayam: C.M. Press, p. 33.
2. K.P. Padmanabha Menon, 1912. *Kochi Rajya Charithram,* Trichur: Bharati Vilasam Press, p. 42.
3. Interview with Sri Raviachan, a senior member of the Paliyam family, dated 6th February 2005.
4. Jaffrey Robin, 1976. *The Decline of Nayar Dominance,* London: Sussex University Press, p. 77.
5. Interview with Sri Raviachan, *op. cit.*
6. *Ibid.*
7. Interview with Smt. Subhadra Thampuran, a musician from the Cochin royal family dated 8th February 2005.
8. D. Renjini, 2000. Nayar Women Today, *Disintegration of Matrilineal System and the Status of Nayar Women in Kerala at Present*, New Delhi: Saujanya Books, p. 56.
9. C. Fuller, 1976. *Nayars Today*, New Delhi: Cambridge University Press, p. 89.

30

From Monologic to Dialogic: Current Research Trends in Folk Culture Studies

Y.A. SUDHAKARA REDDY

ABSTRACT

The folklore/folk life/folk culture studies in the initial stages were hosted by the disciplines of Literature or Anthropology and therefore approached the subject from 'lore' and 'folk' perspective respectively. The literary perspective emphasized 'text' as the prima-facie and therefore relied on framing 'genres' to typologise the subject matter of folklore. Those who approached folklore from 'anthropological perspective' brought forth 'folk' to the forefront of the study as the makers of the 'lore' and stressed on the material culture.

Folklore/Folk culture research in recent times became ethnographic sensitive and writing culture is not a monologue and observer (researcher) dominated, but a dialogue between the observers and observed. This phase of folklore studies further led to another interesting hermeneutic discourse in textualisation in terms of sign-signifier relationship. The study of folklore in contemporary postmodern epistemological, hermeneutical discourse would mean to negate the distinctions between folk and lore, subject and object, informant and ethnographer, observer and observed, representation and represented and all such polarities and seek meanings to identify a folk group and to understand how they relate themselves with each other and with others.

Folklore as an emerging independent discipline is still trying its best to have its unifying theory. It appears that the difficulty lies in the very subject matter with which folklore deals. The materials of folklorists are generally recognised to be traditional ideas, actions or consequences. The 'tradition' based ideas, actions and consequences, when considered as folklore matter resulted in two schools of thought studying them. The first school of folklorists does not consider all traditional things but only those held to be expressive, artistic and non-instrumental in nature. This school of thought consists of the traditional (arts) folklorists within which there may be further narrowing to include only the arts that depend heavily on a verbal component (the traditional verbal art). Generally, the traditional art folklorists define 'traditional' in terms of some process or basis of artistic expression in the form of either oral transmission or face to face communication and not in terms of particular culture level. Consequently, they are free to explore this art among all cultural levels and groups. The second school of folklorists consists of folk life scholars who delimit the domain of traditional ideas, behaviours and consequences in terms of culture level and not in terms of whether these traditional ideas, etc., are necessarily expressive in nature. Folk life scholars study folk culture where the term 'traditional' tends to mean some combination of the following traits: rural, pre-industrial, non-mainstream, non-elite, preservationistic (i.e., past-oriented, old time), regional, ethnic, little or *desi* tradition. This broad division in the study material of folklorists resulted in the lack of unity among the different theoretical perspectives in modern folkloristics (the study of folklore), which eventually led to a considerable difficulty in grasping the theoretical state of the discipline. Theories which are currently popular are shared by many disciplines. For example, in the literary, linguistic and communication approach to folklore, all pursue the matters of structure and style, while anthropology, sociology and psychology investigate the issue of function. The water-tight compartmentalisation of culture theories may result in exclusion of theoretical pursuits from certain disciplines and thus narrow the boundaries of investigation. All the expressive theories are based on two perspectives: the diachronic and the synchronic. The diachronic perspectives frequently combined with geographic perspectives resulted in the investigation of folklore over a period of time and space. They basically deal with the origin and development of a given cultural trait. The diachronic studies developed the theories such as evolution, devolution and diffusion. The synchronic perspective is the study of expressive behaviour more or less at one point of time and space. In synchronic studies, the functional, psychological and structural aspects of expressive behaviour of an individual or group form the subject matter.

The Russian philosopher Mikhail Bakhtin in his work of literary theory, *The Dialogic Imagination* (Bakhtin 1981a), used the concepts of *dialogic* and *dialogism*. Bakhtin contrasts the 'dialogic' and the 'monologic' work of literature. The monologic phenomenon is associated with the idea of knowledge as emanating from a single, authoritative, closed source. Monologic also produced a set of disciplinary institutions, practices and discourses to legitimate its modes of domination and control. The dialogic work carries on a continual dialogue with other works of literature and other authors, and clinches the idea of knowledge as collective, relational and dynamic. Dialogic literature is in communication with multiple works. This is not merely a matter of influence, for the dialogue extends in both directions, and the previous work of literature is as altered by the dialogue as the present one is. The term 'dialogic', however, does not just apply to literature. For Bakhtin, all language, indeed, all thought, appeared dialogic. This means that everything anybody ever says always exists in response to things that have been said before and in anticipation of things that will be said in response. As a result, all language (and the ideas which language contains and communicates) is dynamic, relational and engaged in a process of endless redescriptions of the world.

With the pervasion of 'new ethnography' in the field of social sciences and humanities, the barriers between the 'folk' and the folklorists began to shatter and the power relation hitherto hierarchically designed between the informant and the researcher, or the interviewee and the interviewer, were totally altered. James Clifford defended new ethnography as a "dialogical enterprise in which both researcher and natives are active creators or authors of cultural representations" (Clifford & Marcus 1986: 84). This new environment gave a fillip to folklore as not only an academic discipline but also as a tool to represent the cultures properly, which are marginalized by the invasion of modernity. The ethical and moral basis of the entire folklore studies rested on the fundamental maxim of "give back to the people what we have taken from them and what rightfully belong to them". This self-consciousness of folklore opened the gates of modernity to various folk groups which are often stereotyped as illiterate, backward and marginalized. The forces of modernity as represented in the new socio-economic formations, which are regulated by the global capitalist market, de-codified and re-codified the existing language system and semiotics through computer technology and electronic media, and eclipsed the communities, which were based on orality in the west. The changing trends in the education system gave more power to 'written word' than to 'orality'. Even the modern legal system passes its verdicts mostly based on written traditions and contemplates for accepting 'oral traditions' as basis for judgments. The oral evidences are being interpreted in the light of written evidences and, hence, undermine the strength of oral traditions of a given community and its value systems. This changing socio-economic scenario posed new challenges to the folk and their lore on one hand and on the other, the study of folklore itself as an academic discipline.

The challenge is two-fold: Primarily, folklore is private when intimately shared by groups in informal setting, but it is also most public of activities when used by groups to symbolize their identity to themselves and to the others. While modernization advocates for universalization of lifestyles through market economy, folklore reacts to it by increasing the use of oral traditions by groups to represent themselves beyond their immediate communities. The sense of sharing 'group identity', if widespread and strong, may lead to nationalism or if it is to be shared by various groups in a multi-cultural setup, it may generate polyphonic and pluralistic identities, which eventually resort to hierarchal but symbiotic relationships for mutual co-existence. In this situation, folklore exists not only in its context (primary existence) but also outside its context (i.e., secondary existence). Thus, folklore is the representation and application of folk traditions in new contours and contexts within and beyond the communities in which they originated, often through the collaborative efforts of tradition-bearers and folklorists or other cultural specialists.

The folklore/folk life/folk culture studies at the initial phases are hosted by the disciplines of literature or anthropology and, therefore, approached the subject from 'lore' and 'folk' perspective respectively. The *literary perspective* emphasized 'text' as the *prima-facie* and therefore relied on framing 'genres' to typologise the subject-matter of folklore. Those who approached folklore from the *anthropological perspective* brought forth 'folk' to the forefront of the study as the makers of the 'lore' (expressive traditions) and stressed on the material culture. These two perspectives sought the tools, which could lead to comparisons or specificities in a given set of cultures. Likewise, they also looked for collective consciousness and individual creativity in expressive tradition of the folk. In either case, the data presented is to demonstrate how paradigms are constructed to reveal holistically the cultural lifestyles. All along, in these two disciplines folklore is viewed as an 'objective reality' which exists in either 'archaic' 'pure' or 'original' form and untouched by dominant culture which hegemonizes it. This idiosyncratic and ideological standpoint of the scholars made folklore as the surviving cultural trait of barbarians and uncivilized or less civilized. From this premise, the evolutionists and diffusionists operated defining folklore that which 'represent' the rural, non-urban, non-literate and peasant groups. Till the early 20th century, this notion pervaded the folkloristics.

Even before the term 'folklore' was coined by William John Thomas in 1846, there was a serious study of folklore forms at the turn of the 18th century in Germany. Romantic nationalistic impulse directed the Grime brothers to collect the *volklieder* (folk songs), tales, games, sayings, names, and idiomatic phrases still to be found among the German peasantry. They considered the above-mentioned forms as the remnants or survivals of the past. The work of the Grime brothers was highly influential in England. There was a long tradition of analyzing the antiquities like old buildings, old legal documents, old artefacts, old tales, old songs, old customs, etc. These forms were labeled as 'popular antiquities'. In 1846, Thomas replaced 'popular antiquities' by the Anglo-Saxon compound word 'folklore' (Thomas 1846). Since he has modelled his programme for the study of folklore directly upon the work of the Grimes, the term 'folklore' came into being to designate materials believed to survive primarily among the rural peasantry and to reflect life of the distant past.

In the latter part of the nineteenth century, English folklore studies were further influenced by Cultural Anthropology and the evolutionary perspective of E.B. Tylor and his disciples. Tylor thought that the history of mankind reflected a development from simple 'savage' stage through 'barbarism' to 'civilization'. He sought to demonstrate that in cultural evolution, knowledge, custom, art and even religious belief had developed by a natural process having their roots in primitive savagery. The development of all human social groups necessarily followed a similar gradual progressive development and the stages of this development could be 'reconstructed' in the absence of historical evidence by applying the 'comparative method' to human groups coexisting in the present. To quote E.B. Tylor,

> civilisation actually existing among mankind in different grades, we are embedded to estimate and compare it by positive examples. The educated world of Europe and America practically settles a standard by simply placing its own nations at one end of the social series and savage tribes at the other, arranging the rest of mankind between these limits accordingly as they correspond more closely to savage or to culture life. The principal criteria of classification are the absence or presence, high or low development of the industrial arts... the extent of life knowledge, the definiteness of moral principles, the conditions of religious beliefs and ceremony, the degree of social and political organisations and so forth. Thus, on the definite basis of compared facts, ethnographers are able to set up at least a rough scale of civilisation.

With this method, he schematised all cultures by broadly pinpointing different institutions that each culture carried with it and they, in turn, represent the culture traits of that particular culture, name it either savagery, barbarism or civilisation. Progress is seen in terms of a culture's advancement from one stage to the next through a relatively fixed sequence. Only through contact with a much more advanced culture can a less developed culture bypass or slip a stage or condition in the 'natural sequence of development'.

However, expressive and other behaviours of earlier stages can survive into later cultural stages as residuals, having lost their original and primary function and meaning and having taken on secondary function and significance. Cultural residuals are called 'survivals'. The notion that some cultural forms survive in the context of cultural evolution is referred to as the 'doctrine of survivals'. Alexander A. Goldenweiser defines 'survivals' as a "cultural feature which does not fit in with its cultural medium. It persists rather than functions, or its function somehow does not harmonise with the surrounding culture". More advanced cultures reveal their previously less advanced heritage through survivals. Evolutionists tend to equate modern primitive cultures with the savage stage of cultures and look to primitive cultures for the nature of the savage mental and cultural condition. The nineteenth century culture evolutionists equated folk with that of peasants.

Tylor's researches were neither romantic nor nationalistic, but concerned with the development of mankind as a whole, and not just one particular nation or race. Folklore was considered not as a relic of the national spirit but rather as a relic of the systems of primitive thought and belief. In 1965, the famous American folklorist Alan Dundes came out with a definition. By breaking the compound word 'folklore' into 'folk' and 'lore', he tried to define it in the following manner. According to Dundes,

> The term 'folk' can refer to any group of people whatsoever who share at least one common factor. It does not matter what the linking factor is – it could be a common occupation, language, or religion – but what is important is that a group formed for whatever reason still have some traditions which it calls its own. (Dundes 1965).

In order to distinguish folklore from other phenomena of the same kind, they have qualified folklore material in terms of their social context, time depth, and medium of transmission (Sudhakar Reddy: 2004). After discussing these points elaborately, Ben-Amos emphasized the necessity of changing the existing perspective we have of the subject. The majority of definitions of folklore consider it as a collection of things. The folklorists are of the opinion that folklore is a collection of abstracted things. "To define folklore, it is necessary to examine the phenomena as they exist. In its cultural context, folklore is not an aggregate of things, but a process – a communicative process to be exact" (Ben-Amos 1971).

Ben-Amos insisted on defining folklore in its context. In this approach, there is no dichotomy between process and product. He distinguished folklore from other modes of communication. "Folklore is the action that happens at that time. It is an artistic action. It involves creativity and aesthetic response, both of which converge in the art forms themselves. Folklore in that sense is a social interaction via the art media and differs from other modes of speaking and gesturing" (Ben-Amos 1971).

The performance studies opened up new vistas in the study of folklore by combining 'text' and 'context' in their performative situation. This gave altogether a new approach to folklore and made it a live one rather than a static, frozen and dead entity of the past. The past-present continuum both in spatial and temporal deployments gained new meanings and vocabularies in the dynamics of culture. What is interesting in the performance approach is that it combines in itself both the literary and anthropological scholarships. It also harmoniously blends the generic forms and behaviour modes of a culture group on one hand, and art and science disciplines on the other.

Performance theory is more of an 'approach' rather than a 'theory' to study an artistic action and event involving the performer, art form, audience and setting of a given cultural milieu. This approach has given altogether a new scope and definition to folklore studies. The discipline of folklore, prior to this approach, confined itself largely to the traditional remnants of earlier periods still found in those sections of society which do not come under the influence of dominant culture. In other words, what Raymond Williams (1958) considered folklore as the study of experiences meanings and values of residual cultures remained by and large the broad area of study of folklore. This premise almost threatened the very existence of folklore as discipline in the academic circles because, when the traditions of residue cultures or residue cultural traits of an emergent culture either die out or undergo change, the discipline loses its relevance and, hence, invites its own demise. Therefore, to create a social relevance and utilitarian basis, performance studies strived hard and gave almost new life to the discipline itself.

Evidently, there are historical, political and other factors which operated behind this new thinking by the scholars involved in folk culture studies. In the United States of America, in the late seventies, the political parties, both Republicans and Democrats, to enlarge their vote bank brought several ethnic communities into their fold. The new immigrants as well as the ethnic communities already residing in the Unites States right from its formation days wanted their identity to be protected and respected. With the advent of new technology, the US in general threw its markets open to the world which brought forth severe challenges to the people of America especially in the cultural front. Under these circumstances, the political leaders with the advise of the scholars in the field of culture studies encouraged a cultural policy which would preserve the 'identities' of the ethnic groups. Several research programmes were sponsored both by the governmental bodies and the philanthropic institutions run by the industrial or business households. Some of the ethnic communities, such as Blacks and Hispanics, were recognised as marginalized groups and given minority status (Abrahams 1992). Americo Paredes (1958), Bauman & Roger Abrahams (1981) are some of the noted scholars who took immense interest in some of the ethnic communities' cultural traits and engaged in the collection, preservation and dissemination of the data. The methodology they followed was totally different from that of the previous scholars. They adopted performance approach as a tool to study cultural traits in their 'original' and 'changing' contexts. The technological advancement in the collection, preservation and dissemination methods came handy for them and gave a new lease of life to the performance studies. The video and audio equipment, etc. were used to capture the cultural material, both, verbal and non-verbal cultural products. With the result, the ethnic groups which were already striving for 'identity' happily welcomed the new cultural policy and gave a supporting hand to the researcher community. This atmosphere changed even the very definition of culture. A culture, according to the performance theoreticians, is a group of individuals who asserted their own sense of groupness through their cultural manifestations. This process of assertion and self-education is worthy of being recorded and used as a basis of a theory-building analysis. Thus, the sense of groupness which was produced through a conformation with other cultures dramatised the usefulness of analyzing folklore in its political, social and cultural contexts.

Another important reason for the shift to performance approach is philosophical, epistemological and academic outlook, which changed considerably the relative position of a researcher and the material with which he was dealing. Till 1970, American folkloristics were involved in 'mentalistic structuralism' or 'the mentalist's approach' wherein humans were conceived of as language and symbol producing machines and, hence, culture was depicted as a dynamic information-bearing system in which individuals demonstrated their humanity through an ability to understand and produce meaningful utterances (Abrahams 1992: 34). The mentalists-structuralists therefore confined to textual interpretations from an etic point of view. Consequently, this approach in the initial phases of formalism mainly concentrated on the analysis on narratives to cognate plot, character and genre. The mentalists argued for gender-based divisions of the cultural products of the human beings.

From the performance studies point of view, folklore and expressive forms of different cultural strands can be distinguished based on performer-audience continuum. Essentially, one can separate folklore and popular culture on the basis of dissemination method, i.e., performance mode. According to Abrahams (1992), folklore exists in face-to-face encounter that leads to oral transmission. In other words, expressive forms in folklore are grounded on the maxim of performer-audience interrelationships. The manner and level of relationship between the two form the crux of the 'structure of the context'.

As a product of this discourse, scholars brought forth new dimensions in the studies of performance during the early nineties. Hitherto scholars viewed structure of the performance based on 'textual' movement, i.e., the way text is textured and knitted the audience and performer through a story-line with meaningful and communicable modes of expression. Therefore, structures are essentially "textual" and hence contexts are basically referential in function. However, the idea of context and structure as independent units, both effecting the text of performance, is gradually being undermined by the scholars practising new ethnography. The field data collected not as a participant observer but as a researcher, whose presence as a researcher is neither concealed nor disguised but informed to the community, made the performance approach more democratic than ever. In other words, acceptance of the observer as an outsider made him realize his own position and limitations, and allowed him to look for 'polyphonic' and dialogical ways of collecting and representing the data.

This new premise in the methodology of post-modern or new ethnography negated the idea of sequencing events through narrative and paved way for looking for contexts, which has the potential to create structure of a given performance. Therefore, 'structure of context' rather than 'context' and 'structure' became centri-focal to the performance studies. It is 'context' that has its own structure to determine the level of performance. So to say, structure of both text and performance emerge within a structure of 'context' rather than a mere 'context'. Here, I wish to clarify that the early performance theoreticians used the term 'context' as a temporal phenomenon, which situates the 'event', while it is presently viewed as one that reflects the interpersonal relations between performers and the audience. Performance, in this sense, carries the potential to rearrange the structure of social relations within the performance and perhaps beyond it. The structure of social roles, relations and interaction emerged as the casual variants in the performances and their communicative meanings.

In due course, when structuralism came under the influence of naratology, performance-centered approach is impelled to study cultural expressive behaviours in a given phenomenon. Accordingly, structuralist theories squabbled that each narrative has two parts, a story, i.e., the content, and a discourse, i.e., the expression, and the means by which the content is communicated. It posits the co-existence of two independent levels of narrative structure. The first is basement level underlying every narrative, which is considered as a 'deep structure' or the 'basic story'; the second is the narrative discourse itself where the basic story is actualised, articulated, realised, and manifested in some form or in many different forms, styles, and media (Chatman 1978: 19-21). This indispensable perceptive led to the realisation of 'version' and 'variation' as one of the basic features to distinguish a folklore item from those of the others. Bremond maintained that every narrative encompass "a layer of autonomous significance endowed with a structure that can be isolated from the whole of the message and this basic autonomous structure can be transposed from one to the other medium without losing its essential properties" (1964: 4). For this reason, the subject of a story may serve as a theme for a ballad, an epic or a myth. This transpodability of the story is the strongest reason for arguing that narratives are indeed structures independent of any medium. When stories get transformed into discourse (or performance), dualism occurs at two levels. Firstly, it occurs in time orders of narrative structures as 'discourse time' and 'story time', i.e., between the length of the time it takes to perform the narrative and the length of the time engaged by the events referred to in it. Secondly, the set of events that occurred in one order can be narrated in another order or, in what is called, in non-linear sequence. The folklorists who followed performance-centered approach, contrary to the genre-based analytical categories, argued for 'ethnic genre' which cannot be seen in isolation or compartmentalised as this would affect the very meaning and function of the genre itself. They took the lead from socio-linguists and ethnographers of communication and argued for analysing text in the context of a large culture-specific system of communication. Hymes (1973) and Tedlock (1972) were the two important of the many scholars who were the force behind 'ethnography of speaking approach', which apparently became the starting point for performance studies.

The performance theory viewed performance as an art of communication (Bauman 1977). Most performance traditions are verbal expressive and found 'in action'. The performance study basically is the study of events and all that is related to an event – a setting, a social context, the performer and the audience. Hence, any performance study should logically be based on live presentations rather than 'dead' or 'patricide' texts, which speak only when the researcher wants them to speak. All the more, no performance is identical to that of any previous ones as every performance acted in a given context has its own version and variation. In that sense, every performance is unique.

Thus, the performance approach advocates holistic ethnographic accounts to understand any given folk genre. The major shift in folkloristic practices at this point in the post-World War II period was to collecting and theorising by the same persons. Theoretical observations were constantly tempered by the field experience. Theories began to insist on reporting not only on the performer in that community, the power attributed to the performer but also such other situating factors. Until this step, the study of text had been centred on the keyword variation, a term useful primarily for the comparison of the text. As field work and theory came together, two kinds of repertoire analyses were constructed. The one on the individual performer and the other on the aesthetic and moral choices involved on the part of the individual performer. Folklorists then needed to discover the range of possible items from which the choices are made, i.e., the repertory of the community. This drift towards the repertory analysis is encouraged by parallel developments in the ethnography of communication, which calls for the understanding of the expressive resources of the groups and an observation of the native genres.

Thus, the performance-centred folkloristics was not an attempt to do away with previous ways of collecting, organising and analysing but to address questions arising from the introduction of new technological devices into the process of collection and preservation. It became possible to collect more and more contextual material in the course of the field experience and to use these to develop a fuller understanding of the ways in which traditional attempts and practices enter into people's lives.

The ethnographic method is a shift from the traditional researcher dominated by the informant-centred studies of culture wherein the former is an ethnographer and the latter is not merely a feeder of data but a participant of culture, the data bank, who had his own space in the process of research. The issues: rationality/irrationality, text/context, space/time, nature/culture, subject/object, ideal/real, total/fragmentary, etc., which influence on data as well as on the ethnographic writing, were subjected to the philosophies of post-modernism and post-structuralism which produce new hermeneutics in research methodology.

Folklore research in a *Post-modern* and *Post-structural* context became ethnographic-sensitive and the writing culture is no longer a monologue, and observer (researcher) dominated, but a dialogue between the observers and the observed. The line of distinction between the two almost became invisible. The interaction between the two produces 'cultural texts' that are 'self-articulative' and 'self-expressive'. Therefore, the performance theoreticians considered folklore as one that exists due to interaction between the performer and the audience. Post-modern ethnography, unlike the traditional method wherein the text is more privileged, monologic and dominated by ideology of the transidental observer, is a discourse/dialogue and emphasizes the co-operative and collaborative nature of the ethnographic situation. It is a dialogical production of discourse by mutual and reciprocal cooperation of the ethnographer and the participant.

The 'ethnographic context' here is a story-making, which produces 'polyphonic text' and none of its participants would have a final word in the form of framing a story on synthesizing.

The data is polyphonic in the sense that different voices of the participants in the form of a 'discourse' on a tale or song are recorded in data collection. It is just a dialogue and juxtaposition of shared experiences in a specific ethnographic situation. Here, the emphasis is on the emergent character of textualisation which provides negotiated text for the reader for interpretation. The hermeneutic process is extended not only to the reader's relationship to the text but to the participants that initiate the dialogue. Since it is participatory and emergent, post-modern ethnography cannot have a predetermined form.

It is fragmentary as life in the field is fragmentary and cannot be organized on par with the ethnic categorization of kinship, economy, etc. Post-modernism is a return to the aesthetic integration. The holistic movement of textuality is along the text-author-reader and privileges no member. This dialogical method is neither theoretical object nor an object of theoretical knowledge; neither evolved [inspired] by explicit methods nor derivational source of practices. It is not a dialectical synthesis of data but a dialogical process of construction.

According to Bhaktin (1981a&b), dialogical process proliferates in any complexity represented by discursive space. Many voices clamour for expression, thus making the textual production as 'polyvocal representation'. Hitherto, the ethnographer pursued monistic representations and gave the ethnographers the authorial function and to the others the role of sources, i.e., 'informants' to be quoted or paraphrased. Once the dialogism and polyphony are recognized as modes of textual production, monophonic authority is questioned. This scenario too raised critical issues of informants and ethnographers to co-authors and scribe/archivist, respectively thrown open several hermeneutical problems concerned with the process of textualisation and its authenticity. Once the position of the researcher got shifted from the ethnographer to that of a scribe/archivist, the nature of folklore data also got affected. Whatever may be the method of elucidating the data by the ethnographer, it subverted the autonomy of the informant and produced the 'cultural texts' what the ethnographer perceives than what they mean to the participant of the culture. This phase of folklore studies further led to another interesting hermeneutic discourse in textualisation in terms of sign-signifier relationship. Sign need not necessarily be representing a signified but generate multiple signifiers in a signification continuum. Ethnographic discourse is itself neither an object to be represented nor the representation of an object. It moved beyond the representational function of signs.

This posed a new problem in locating meanings based on a single textual production. In fact, such texts are only a version of a larger whole of a cultural text. So we can say it is 'a text', but not 'the text'. This argument further led to probe critically into folklore matters as discursive elements but not as end products because they are not the sole identifiers of folk groups, but a viewpoint of that group. This again gave rise to another set of issues concerning the ideas of representation, power and authority. Who represents what and how, became the nodal points of discourse in culture studies, particularly in folklore studies. The post-modern scholarship advocated for fragmentation and segmentation of power and cultural groups and questioned the universality of traits or norms of behavioural patterns. This inevitably resulted in hegemonising tendency by the dominant culture quite often than not by coercive power. This being the situation, the dominant culture claimed not only authority but also exercised power in representing the subdued cultures. Edward Said's work on orientalism is a classical example which critiqued the modes of representation of the colonial regimes of the 'Occident' (West) over the 'Orient' (East). According to him, 'orientalism' is not a reality in the East but exists in the minds of the West which has perceived Orient from an ethnocentric archetype. This is also true with studies in folklore wherein the elite and the literate exercise power to represent the non-literate. In the process of representation, the group which is represented is quite often undermined and schematically presented in the 'rhetorics' of elite traditions. Ethno-poetics of elite often played 'power politics' and superimposed their styles over the subject material. In such cases, folklore is neither an object to be described nor a unified corpus of symbols and meanings that can be interpreted. It is contested and discursive in temporal frame and diffusive in spatial domains. The study of folklore in contemporary post-modern epistemological, hermeneutical discourse would mean to negate the distinctions between folk and lore, subject and object, informant and ethnographer, observer and observed, representation and represented and all such polarities. It would also mean to seek meanings to identify a folk group and to understand how they relate themselves with each other and with others. Both the esoteric and exoteric viewpoints and exigencies are a must to comprehensively locate the folk in relation to its 'representative power' in order to critically evaluate the dynamics in projections and manifestations of folklore in temporal and spatial scales.

Folklore studies in contemporary context would mean realisation of the field as an object of study, which exists only in its subjective ideological and interpretative manner of the representative power, rather than as an objective reality. In other words, folklore is to be contested as a matter of conflict that arises between the observer and the observed, the former as an embodiment of 'knowledge' and the latter as a representative of an ideology. Knowledge is power, which hierarchically structures the folk groups internally, whereas ideology externally subjugates and controls such powers and relegates authorial position to representing authority on one hand, and on the other create new contexts to expose cultural traits of subjugated folk groups. This trend altogether brought a new branch in folklore, previously known as folklorism or folklorismus and currently debated as public folklore with all the issues related to copyright, patent right and other ethical viewpoints.

To conclude, post-modernist ethnographic approach is dialogical. It is a discourse between the ethnographer and the participant, which produces emergent 'text'. The text is the product of dialogue between the reader-writer in relation to participants and, therefore, the discourse is polyphonic and fragmentary. The polyphony corresponds to plurality of meanings in the process of interpretation. In other words, inter-textuality reflects the meaning of signs in different contexts. The post-modern ethnography is a text of physical, the spoken and the performed, an evocation of quotidian experience, a palpable reality that uses everyday speech to suggest what is re-affable not through abstraction but by means of concrete. It will be a text to read not with the eyes alone, but with the ears in order to hear and, hence, a dialogical process of construction.

REFERENCES

Abrahams, Roger D. 1968. 'Introductory Remarks to a Rhetorical Theory of Folklore', *Journal of American Folklore*, 81: 1-16.

——. 1992. 'The past in the presence: An overview of Folkloristics in the late 20th century', in Reimund Kvideland (ed.), *Folklore Processed*, Helsinki: Suomalaisen Kirjallisuuden Seura.

Bauman, Richard. 1977. *Verbal Art as Performance*, Illinois: Waveland Press.

——. 1986. *Story, Performance and Event: Contextual Studies of Oral Narratives*, Cambridge: Cambridge University Press.

Bauman, Richard and Joel Sherzer. 1974. *Explorations in the Ethnography of Speaking*, New York: Cambridge University Press.

Bauman, Richard and Roger D. Abrahams (eds.). 1981. *And Other Neighborly Names: Social Process and Cultural Image in Texas Folklore*, Austin: Texas University Press.

Bakhtin, M. Mikhail. 1981a. *The Dialogic Imagination: Four Essays by M.M. Bakhtin* (translated by Caryl Emerson & Michael Holquist), Austin: University of Texas Press.

——. 1981b. 'Discourse in the Novel', in Michael Holquist (ed.), *The Dialogical Imagination,* Austin: Texas University Press, pp. 259-442.

Ben-Amos, Dan (ed.). 1971. *Folklore Genres*, Austin: University of Texas Press.

Bremond, Claude. 1964. 'Le Message narratif', *Communications* 4: 32.

Burns, Thomas A. 1989. 'Folkloristics: A Conception Theory', in Elliot Oring (ed.), *Folk Groups and Folklore Genre,* Logan Utah: Utah State Univ. Press, pp. 1-20.

Chatman, Semour. 1978. *Story and Discourse: Narrative Structure in Fiction and Film,* Ithaca: Cornel University Press.

Clifford, James and George E. Marcus. 1986. *Writing Culture: The Poetics and Politics of Ethnography,* Berkeley: University of California Press.

Dundes Alan (ed.). 1965. *The Study of Folklore,* N.J.

——. 1977. 'Who are the Folk', in William R. Bastom (ed.), *Frontiers of Folklore,* Boulder. Colorado: Wester View Press.

Fine, Elizabeth C. 1984. *The Folklore Text: From Performance to Print,* Bloomington: Indiana University Press.

Finnegan, Ruth. 1970. *Oral Literature in Africa,* Oxford: Oxford University Press.

Goldenweiser, A. Alexander. 1937. *Anthropology: An Introduction to Primitive Culture,* New York: F.S. Crofts.

Hymes, Dell. 1966. 'Two Types of Linguistic Relativity (With examples from Amerindian Ethnography)', in William Bright (ed.), *Sociolinguistics,* The Hague: Mouton.

——. 1973. 'An Ethnographic Perspective', *New Literary History* 5: 187-201.

Honko, Lauri. 1976. 'Genre Theory Revisited', in Tuula Jurikka and Juha Pentikainen (eds.), *Folk Narrative Research* 20: 20-25, Helsinki: Studia Fennica.

Mitchell, W.J.T. (ed.). 1981. *On Narrative,* Chicago: University of Chicago Press.

Ong Walter, J. 1982. *Orality and Literacy: The Technologizing of the Word,* London: T.J. Press.

Paredes, Americo. 1958. *With His Pistol in His Hand: A Border Ballad and Its Hero,* Austin: University of Texas Press.

Said, Edward. 1978. *Orientalism* New York: Pantheon Books.

Singer, Milton. 1972. *When a Great Tradition Modernizes,* New York: Praeger.

Sudhakar Reddy, Y.A. 2004. 'Folklore in the Public Sphere: Reflections on Contemporary Civil Society', in M.D. Muthukumara Swamy and Molly Kaushal (eds.), *Folklore, Public Sphere and Civil Society,* Indira Gandhi National Centre for the Arts, New Delhi and National Folklore Support Centre, Chennai, pp. 23-36.

Tedlock, Dennis. 1972. 'On the Translation of Style in Oral Narrative', in Paredes Americo and Richard Bauman (eds.), *Towards New Perspectives in Folklore,* Austin: University of Texas Press.

Thomas, William. 1846. 'Folklore', *The Athenaeum* 982: 862-863.

Tylor, E.B. 1865. *Researches into the Early History of Mankind,* London.

——. 1889. 'On a Method of Investigating the Development of Institutions', *Journal of the Royal Anthropological Institute,* pp. 245-269.

Willams, Raymond. 1958. *Culture and Society 1780-1950,* New York: Columbia University Press.

31

Folklore and Cultural Constructions in Colonial South India

G. CHANDHRIKA

ABSTRACT

The history of India was (re)constructed in the nineteenth century in many discursive fields, like language, literature, religion and region. The publication of Caldwell's A Comparative Grammar of the Dravidian or South Indian Family of Languages *(1856) had a significant impact on the way the history of South India was constructed, especially in the wake of the earlier works of Indologists like William Jones, H.T. Colebrook and others. The latter's treatises on the Sanskrit language, religion, law and (Aryan) culture of the people of North India had already brought into existence a vast discursive space into which was drawn the idea of a differentiated (Dravidian) language, religion and culture of a distinct South Indian region. In this context, this paper seeks to locate and understand the beginnings of the idea of a Dravidian culture in the studies of the folklore of South India.*

I

The nineteenth century occupies an important position in the historiography of modern India for its engagement with the contestations of tradition and modernity. The 'pre-colonial' and 'traditional' dimensions of Indian society and culture were redefined and reinterpreted in multiple ways during the later nineteenth century. Folklore figured in a significant way in constructing a cultural space in colonial South India. Whereas historiography has analysed the role of literature in the construction of cultural identities, the use of printed folklore in the shaping of identities has not been fully explored by scholars. Blackburn and Dalmia (2003) have done pioneering work in this area. Following their lead, this paper seeks to analyse the place of folklore in the construction of a folk identity in colonial South India and its implications in the cultural sphere.

European ideas of folklore, rooted in the nineteenth century intellectual currents of romanticism and nationalism, had come into vogue by the time the British had set up an empire in India. When folkloristics/folklore arrived in India in the 1850s, it had already acquired the status of a modern science. The Indian Antiquary established by James Burgess in 1872 in Bombay and the foundation of the Folklore Society in London in 1878 stimulated the development of Indian folklore research. At the same point of time, Comparative Philology was making great strides in post-Napoleonic Europe leading to linguistic research on the language families of India. The publication of Bishop Robert Caldwell's text on Dravidian grammar (1856) opened a floodgate of discussions and debates about the Dravidians as the pre-Aryan /original inhabitants of India.

These two trends of Indology, viz., the increasing focus on Indian folklore and the discovery of the Dravidian language family, when linked with each other, had a peculiar role to play in the construction of a 'pre-Aryan', 'Dravidian' folk culture in colonial South India. The earliest expression of such a cultural construction is found in the *Old Deccan Days* by Mary Frere (1868). The 'Introduction' to the tales locates their origin to the *lingayat* sect, "a more ancient race, and an earlier wave of immigration, than most of the Hindu nation with which they are now intermingled". The writer, who happened to be Frere's father and a former Governor of Bombay, found them especially valuable as they represent "the popular non-Brahmin superstitions of the lower orders" (Frere 1881: xii-xiii).

THE 'DRAVIDIAN' IDENTIFIED WITH 'FOLK'

The idea of the Dravidian or non-Brahmin as the folk found a favourite position in the literary discourses of the protestant Christian missionaries of the nineteenth century. Charles E. Gover's *The Folk songs of Southern India* (1871) discusses at length what he describes as 'the silent revolution' of sectarian Hinduism through the ages against Brahmanical Hinduism. He observed:

> This silent revolution has been, as far as can now be seen, altogether independent of European influence and agency. In fact, by giving to the people a more refined system of religious thought, it has greatly tended to hinder the spread of Christianity. It had begun long before the rise of the British power. All this points to the fact, with which we started, that the people of India are not accurately described from Brahman sources; and that in thought and habit they are, in a marked sense, different from the sacred caste. This has often been noticed; but there has always been a great lack of material for proving it to those who have not lived in India, or having lived there, took their knowledge from Brahmans. It is necessary that the proof should be really popular and purely indigenous. The dramas published by the Rev. J. Long have done much to reveal local feeling in Bengal, but Madras has not been so fortunate as to possess an enquirer of like character. The following pages contain the result of an attempt to fathom the real feelings of the masses of the people, by gathering and collecting the folksongs of each family of the great Dravidian nation (Gover 1871: 8-9).

THE PURITY OF TAMIL

Yet another favourite theme of the Protestant missionaries was the antiquity and purity of the Tamil language. E.J. Robinson, author of *Tamil Wisdom* (1873) and *Tales and Poems of South India* (1885), wrote:

> The Tamils call Sanscrit *'Vada-morlyi', the northern speech,* supposing it to have originated in the north, and their own language *'Ten-morlyi', the southern speech,* because Pothiyamalay, the mountain in which Agastya lived, is in the south of India. A sufficient reason for the name is, that in fact Tamil is the southern language, being used by ten millions of people, in that part of Hindustan formerly comprising the Chera, Chola, and Pandiya kingdoms, and in the northern half of the island of Ceylon. Cities conversed in it centuries before the Christian era; and, as might be inferred from its beauty and finish, it boasts an ancient and honoured literature (1873: 1-2).

Robinson claimed that pure Tamil, or the language of non-Brahmans, "existed in perfection long before Sanscrit mingled in its stream" (Robinson 1885: 1). Gover declares that in the process of collecting the folk songs, he has deliberately avoided "episodes of the great epics and the erotic chapters.... both of which are purely Brahmanic, entirely foreign to the Dravidian literature and mind" (Gover 1871: xix). He further remarked that "It is common remark of all who study Dravidian literature that the older it is the purer it is" (1871: 13).

The Legend of Valluvar

The legend of Thiruvalluvar figures in a central way in the cultural constructions of colonial South India. Both Gover and Robinson dwell at length upon the subject. Gover describes the story of Valluvar being the offspring of a Brahmin father and a pariah mother as a concoction of the Brahmins (1871: 15). He narrates the legend from the *Thiruvalluvar Charithram* and goes on to show that the main object of the work was to give a Brahmin parentage to Valluvar. He cites this as an example of literary fraud by the Brahmins (Gover 1871: 215). A few pages earlier, he remarks thus:

> The Brahmans frequently explain the tone of Tiruvalluvan, Sivavakyer, Kapila, Auveiyar and other early Dravidian poets by asserting that they were Jains. There is no proof of this, but it can hardly be doubted that both Buddhism and Jainism reflected the same popular tendency that we see in the early poets. The Brahmans extirpated Buddhism in India by fire, sword and relentless persecution.... Thiruvalluvar saved his work from the flood that destroyed every avowed obstacle in its grievous course (Gover 1871: 201).

He concludes by praising the ancient Tamil works as the epitome of the "poetical power of the Dravidian people, their appreciation of the beneficent operations of nature and of their perception of the dignity and beauty of the physical world" (1871: 220). As has been pointed out by Stuart Blackburn, Valluvar became the emblem of the 'Dravidian as folk concept' and was valorized by every major writer on Tamil literature in the nineteenth century as the personification of a 'buried Dravidian culture' (Blackburn 2003: 162).

Protestantism and Heterodoxy

The Protestant missionaries, heir to an intellectual tradition of protest in Christianity, which is traced to the fifteenth century to Erasmus of Rotterdam, saw a parallel in the heterodox sects of Hinduism which had their roots in protest. The Thirukural and the folk songs represented a pre-Sanscritic Dravidian ethical system, "a scheme more moral than religious in which ideology is unknown and the diversity is always spoken of as the great soul of the universe" (Gover 1871: 6-8). This new cultural construction of the 'Dravidian as the folk' enabled the Protestant missionaries to harp about a non-Brahmanical folk religion, untainted by priest ridden ideology, centered on the low-born Valluvar, a probable Jain and his Thirukural. To quote Robinson, "the ethical rules of the Tamils are hung, darkened with foul devices, about the cars and temples of idolatry, and spoken from pagan altars which convey no moral inspiration. The missionaries have to separate them from the rubbish which buries them, and attach them to their home, the atoning and cleansing Cross" (1873: 6).

By the end of the nineteenth century. the idea of a Dravidian culture obscured by the Aryans was repeated by folklorists, who had their fair share in the construction of a pre-Aryan Dravidian folk culture. In identifying the non-Brahmins as sons of the soil, they echoed the

European definition of folk as peasant. Such an identity was a recurrent theme in the next century finding exposition in the works of Protestant missionaries like Henry Whitehead (1921), and was recast in terms of race by European scholars as well as Tamil neo Saivites, literary historians and leaders of the Dravidian movement.

REFERENCES

Blackburn, Stuart. 2000. 'Corruption and Redemption. The Legend of Valluvar and Tamil Literary History', *Modern Asian Studies* 34(2): 449-82.

——. 2003. *Print, Folklore, and Nationalism in Colonial South India*, Delhi: Permanent Black.

Blackburn, Stuart. 2000 and V. Dalmia (eds.). 2003. *India's Literary History: Essays on the Nineteenth Century*, Delhi: Permanent Black.

Caldwell, Robert. 1976. *A Comparative Grammar of the Dravidian or South Indian Family of Languages*, Madras: University of Madras (Reprint).

Frere, Mary. 1989. *Old Deccan Days: Hindoo Fairy Legends, Collected from Oral Traditions*, New Delhi: Asian Educational Services (Reprint).

Gover, Charles E. 1999. *The Folk-songs of Southern India*, New Delhi: Asian Educational Services (Reprint).

Robinson, Edward Jewitt. 2001. *Tamil Wisdom: Traditions Concerning Hindu Sages*, New Delhi: Asian Educational Services (Reprint).

——. 1885. *Tales and Poems of South India, from the Tamil*, London: T. Woolmer.

Whitehead, Henry. 1999 [1921]. *The Village Gods of South India*, New Delhi: Asian Educational Services (Reprint).

32

Historical Material in Veerapandya Kattabommu Kathaipadal: A Study

S. MANIKANDAN

ABSTRACT

In the late eighteenth century, there was a resistance in Panjalankurichi, Tirunelveli region, against the occupation, expansion and domination of the English East India Company. Veerapandya Kattabomman, the palayakkarar of Panjalankurichi, played a significant part in the resistance. Many folk songs and ballads have carried over the history of Kattabomman and his supporters. Through these we can understand characteristic features of the palayakkarars' revolt against the Company's administration. This paper attempts to present a study of the historical material available in folklore. For this purpose 'Kattabomman Kathaipadal', a published version of a ballad on Kattabomman, is used intensively. This paper analyses how far the ballad (Kattabomman Kathaipadal) can be taken as historical material, through a corroboration of events mentioned in the ballad with those found in the archival records.

INTRODUCTION

In the late eighteenth century, there was a resistance in Panjalnkurichi[1] against the occupation, expansion and domination of the English East India Company. Veerapandya Kattabomman, the *palayakkarar*[2] of Panjalankurichi, played a significant role in the resistance. Many folk songs[3] and ballads have preserved the history of Kattabomman and his supporters. This paper attempts to present a study of the historical material available in folklore. For this purpose, *Veerapandya Kattabommu Kathaipadal,* a published version of a ballad on Kattabomman, is used intensively and extensively.[4] A ballad is a form of folksong that tells a story. A ballad tells its story simply and directly, often by means of dialogue, always concentrating on the story's climax. It is always sung in such a way that the words rather than the melody are stressed.[5]

Most of the people, not only in Tamil Nadu but all over India, are living in villages. They are involved in different kinds of productive works such as cultivation, tilling, weaving, pottery making, mat making, wood cutting, metal working, etc. The people, at the time of working, use to sing some songs to entertain themselves as well as to forget the physical hardship of the work they did. These songs are the symbols of their culture.[6] All these songs are classified together as folk songs or ballads. The ballad, generally, has been divided into three categories. They are:

1. Epic ballad, 2. Historic ballad and 3. Social ballad.[7] Stories of Desingu Rajan, Kattabomman, Marudhu Pandyas, Khan Sahib, and Pulithevar are the important ballads that fall under the category of historic ballad. The story of Kattabomman has been taken into full form as a ballad, named *Veerapandya Kattabommu Kathaipadal,* which was edited by N. Vanamamalai and published by New Century Book House in 1961.[8] The next edition, by the same author, was edited and published by Madurai Palkalai Kazhakam[9] in 1971.[10]

Hero of the Ballad

The hero of the ballad is Veerapandya Kattabomman. In the dynasty of Katta Bommu, 46th generation came up in the second half of the eighteenth century. Veerapandya Kattabomman was born on 3rd Janaury 1760 to Jagavira Kattabommu and Arumugathammal, who had two more sons and two daughters. They were Oomaithurai, Duraisingam, Vadivu and Duraikannu.[11] Kattabomman became the *palayakkarar* of Panjalankurichi in 1790, at the age of 30.[12] He was an efficient administrator. He was given 96 villages which were grouped into six divisions (*mandalams*) for administrative purposes. He ruled the *palayam* with the blessings of his favorite god and goddess, Murugan and Jakkammal respectively. He was a devotee of God Murugan of Tiruchendur.[13] He had donated 400 acres to the temple at Tiruchendur. Even today, these lands are maintained in the name of 'Senthilam Pannai'. For Goddess Jakkammal, he had made a temple inside the fort.[14] He and his supporters plundered some of the villages and granaries belonging to the East India Company or the supporting *palayams* of the Company. Kattabomman administrated his *palayam* by helping the people who did not have any means for their living. He was held in high esteem. The people were freed from the paying of *kist*[15] during failure of monsoon and during famine. The poor people were always welcome in the Panjalankurich fort.[16]

Historical Material in *Veerapandya Kattabommu Kathaipadal*

In the eighteenth century,[17] each and every Palayakkarar emerged as a 'petty king' or 'chieftain'. The Company, whose motive was collection of revenue and annexation of the place to extend their territory, began to dominate all the Palayakkarars. Kattabomman resisted their expansion. Most of the Palayakkarars surrendered and paid the tribute. But Kattabomman refused to pay any *kist* and tribute to the Company. The Company found that there was a feeling of unfriendliness between Ettappan and Kattabomman. When the officials enquired Sivasubramania Pillay or Thanapathy, they came to know about the power, pride, bravery and valour of Kattabomman. After some days, Thanapathy plundered Srivaikuntam and Alwar Tirunagari granaries, which belonged to the Company, and killed Sangudevan and Pandyadevan, the Kavalkkarars. Thanapathy's action severely disappointed the Company and sparked off enmity between the Company and Kattabomman once again. Major Bannerman was appointed by the Company to defeat Kattabomman. The first revolt broke out. At the end of the revolt, Kattabomman was hanged at Kayathar after formal enquiry in the presence of all the Palayakkarars.[18]

Later, the people released Oomaithurai and other followers of Kattabomman from the jail by a daring attack on the soldiers. Oomaithurai was accepted as the rightful heir of Kattabomman and thus the Palayakkarar of Panjalankurichi. He took an oath to revenge the Company. So the second Palayakkarari revolt broke out. He fought with the Company's troops for one-and-a-half months. At the end, Oomaithurai with his brother escaped from the fort and joined Marudu

Pandyas, the Palayakarars of Kalayarkoil. Chinna Marudu was a close friend of Oomaithurai. All of them were crushed and hanged by the Company. The Company got the strongest support from Ettappan, who provided the assistance of his own force to defeat Kattabomman and Oomaithurai. Oral narratives explained about some other important personalities who were in Kattabomman's administration. They were: Thanapathy, Vellaiyadevan, Duraisingam Sundaralingam Veeramallu, Kandhanbagadai, Pulikuthi Nayak, Muthubagadai, Pottibagadai and Mullukattu Muthuveeran. These patriots, who dedicated their life to the freedom of the land and their rights, met with a tragic end. This is the information which can be considered as historical material mentioned in both records.[19]

Ballad vs Archival sources

Kattabomman has been described in official records as a rebel and a plunderer. But the folklore treated him as a folk hero and patriotic warrior. (Although he died in the late eighteenth century, he has survived two centuries after his death in the folk tradition of the Tamil country. Legends and folklore have been developed around Kattabomman, Oomaithurai and their supporters.)

To study the history of Tirunelveli, the historians or researchers would consider the following sources: *Military Remainiscenes* by James Welsh (1930), *Tirunelveli District Manual* by Stuart (1829), *Madura Country: A manual* by Nelson (1989), *Tinnevelly Gazetteer* by H.R. Pate (1917), *The Poligar of Panjalankurichi* by Kearns (1873), and *A History of Tinnevelly* by Caldwell (1997). These are the primary and secondary sources which have been used to explain the history of Tinnevelly and the Poligar of Panjalankurichi. All the above-mentioned authors were Englishmen and the author's motive and approach becomes quite obvious by the style and culture of the English. This source cannot give the real character of an opponent.

Oral narratives are the products of the common people. Kattabomman lived in the late eighteenth century. The ballads and folklore were made during that period. These oral narratives have not been written. These were passed from generation to generation orally. When the story of Kattabomman is handed down to the next generation, the affection of the present social background and political situation will be added with the folk songs, stories and Koothu (drama) on him. One can understand that contemporary people have only words that celebrate him. The recorded narratives are stable and standard. But the oral narratives are changeable and flexible. So, year by year or generation by generation, the story of a man can change with the present atmosphere, culture and the condition of society. Where the oral sources are not factual, the researcher has to depend on recorded narratives.

These two sources belong to two different classes. Folklore is the attempt of the common people to keep their memories alive. The differences of perception should be critically analyzed in order to get a true picture of the past.

CONCLUSION

From the ballad itself, we cannot understand the actual historical content. We, at the same time, cannot reject it as useless. We should analyze all the sources which have been for one particular event; each and every character must be placed in the relevant place and respective manner. Even though the ballad has a fixed climax, it cannot be rejected in favour of archival sources which embodied the official version of the revolt.

As has been said earlier, some of the Palayakkarars revolted against English East India Company and died in the revolt. Such kinds of people have an important place in history. A researcher only has to locate them properly in historical time and space. For perceiving the right method of history, historical incidents and historical heroes, we should study the society of a particular time, and understand the culture of the people and their lineage? This will give direction to the writing of history. As such, *Veerapandya Kattabommu Kathaipadal* can be considered as an important historical source. The ballad is not conformed or accepted as the only source, but as one of the essential sources.

NOTES

1. According to the oral narratives, Panjalan was the name of Kattabomman's grandfather with which he added the word Kuichi and made it as Panjalankurichi. There is another version about the same name. The name of Kattabommu's wife was 'panjali'. By her name, the place was named Panjalankurichi. During the period of Vishwanatha Nayak, the system of *palayam* was introduced as 'revenue settlement'. The Pandyan region, with its capital Madurai, was divided into many *palayams*. Each and every *palayam* had a fort, sequestered place and soldiers with weapons. There were 72 *palayams* in Tamil Nadu, in which 18 *palayams* were in Tirunelveli region where Panjalankurichi was one of the important *palayams*.
2. In this paper, the word *Poligar*, which has been written in official records, is replaced as *palayakkarar*, which has been used in all Tamil texts.
3. Folk songs, stories and ballads recalling the heroism of the *palayakkarar* leaders remain alive in Tamil Nadu to this day.
4. The legends and stories about Kattabomman are still prevailing in the Tirunelveli and Ramanadhapuram regions.
5. Anthropologists and ballad scholars have since come to recognize that the ballad is a far more modern, sophisticated art form. An individual with some artistic education composed a particular ballad. Then the people took it over from the composer, who was soon forgotten. Finally, it was shaped and re-created as it travelled by word of mouth from singer to singer. Passed on by word of mouth through many folk generations, they have developed a large number of versions and variants. *The new book of knowledge*, Grolier Incorporated, Connecticut, 1986, p. 21.
6. Those who want to know the culture of common people, they must take into account the folk songs.
7. N. Vanamamalai, *Veerapandya Kattabommu Kathaipadal*, Madurai Palkalaikazhakam, Madurai, 1971, p. 18.
8. The first version about Kattabomman was by Siranjeevi who gave it with *kummi* and lesson form. The second work, with the complete history of Kattabomman and his supporters, was edited by N. Vanamamalai. He took the whole scripts which were written by an unknown author, who was a contemporary of Kattabomman. N. Vanamamalai, *op. cit.*, p. 5.
9. Madurai Kamaraj University.
10. N. Vanamamalai, *op. cit.*, p. 19.
11. In official records, it has been recorded that the names of Oomaithurai and Duraisingam were Kumarasamy Nayak and Sevathaiya repectively.
12. Nicholas B. Dirks says: "Vamcavali literally means the path (vali) of a family (vamcam or parambarai). Every *palayakkarar* family has at least one vamcavali that recounts the 'history' of the family. Each vamcavali consists of a succession of episodes concerning selected ancestral heads of the family. Episodes are linked by successional lists of from one to ten generations, consisting of just the names of the intervening family heads. The vamcavalis are genealogies both in that they list the entire line of the family and in that genealogy acts as the narrative frame of the text." Nicholas B. Dirks: 'The pasts of a palayakkarar: The ethnohistory of a south Indian little king' in George W. Spencer (ed.), 1987. *Temples, Kings and Peasants: Perceptions of South India's Past*, Madras, pp. 97-126.
13. Tiruchendur is in the east coast of South India, and at present, it belongs to the Tuticorin district.

14. N. Vanamamalai, *op. cit.*
15. Arrears of payment.
16. N. Vanamamalai, *op. cit.*
17. As the power of the Nayaks waned, many of the Palayakkarars of Tirunelveli started to rule the *palayam* independently without paying the tribute to the respective Nayaks. The chief among the important *palayams* in Tirunelveli were Ettaiyapuram, Panjalankurichi and Nelkattansevval.
18. All the official records and N. Vanamamalai, *op. cit.*
19. *Ibid.*

REFERENCES

Caldwell, R. 1997. *A History of Tirunelvelly*, New Delhi: Asian Educational Services (Reprint).
George, W. Spencer (ed.). 1987. *Temples, Kings and Peasants: Perceptions of South India's Past*, Madras: New Era Publishers.
Kearns, J.F. 1873. *Introduction to Panjalam Kurichi Poligar and the State of Tirunelvelly*, Palyam Kottai.
Nelson, J.H. 1989. *Madura Country: A Manual*, New Delhi: Asian Educational Services (Reprint).
Pate, H.R. 1917. *Madras District Gazetteers: Tirunelvelly*, Vol. 1, Madras: Government Press.
Stuart, A.J. 1829. *Manual of the Tirunelvelly District in the Presidency of Madras*, Madras: Government Press.
Vanamamalai, N. 1971. *Veerapandya Kattabommu Kathaipadal*, Madurai: Madurai Palkalaikazhakam.
Welsh, J. 1830. *Military Reminiscences*, Vols. I & II.

33

Animal Symbolism in Indian Folk and Tribal Dances

LALITHA RAMADURAI

ABSTRACT

Animals – both real and mythological – have been one of the oft-repeated themes in literature, art and architecture since ancient times. Animal motifs have figured prominently in cave paintings, temple sculptures, etc. In Ramayana *and* Mahabharata, *there are numerous references to zoomorphic characters. Although classical Indian music and dance have largely neglected animals and opted for more sublime themes, many folk and tribal dances in our country continue to revolve around animal themes.*

Dance has been an indispensable feature in the religious, social and cultural activities of the tribal and folk communities. The tribal dance forms often replicate the movement of different animals and are performed by dancers wearing appropriate costumes and masks. The dance forms presumably had their origin in some hunting customs or were relics of animal totemism. Although many of these dance forms continue even to this day, they are performed more for entertainment or commercial gains than as customary rituals.

This paper focuses on some of the well-known animal folk/tribal dances of India. It also attempts to explore the possibility of using such dance forms to create awareness about the imperative need for environmental protection and biodiversity conservation.

ANIMALS IN INDIAN ART, CULTURE AND MYTHOLOGY

Indian culture like many other ancient cultures reveres Mother Nature in all her manifestations. Mountains, forests, oceans, rivers, plants and animals are all sanctified and worshipped. Every living being, be it a plant or animal, is thus ascribed a certain sanctity. Among these, the living things that are closely associated with humans are considered special.

The wild animals were dreaded for their strength and ferocity. Their superior strength was attributed to divine presence. Thus, the snakes – the venomous cobras, in particular – became demi-gods and were associated with wealth, power and fertility. Carnivores such as tiger and lion became the mounts of Goddess Durga and Kali, reflective of their prowess to annihilate the evil forces. Some animals of high utility value, like the cow, were domesticated and in an effort to prolong their use and prevent their wanton destruction, they were lent an aura of divinity.

This is the underlying reason for the close association of animals with Indian culture and their prolific representations in various art-forms – visual and performing.

Animal motifs along with floral designs are central to the Indian monumental sculptures, paintings and literature. The stone seals and pottery belonging to the Harappan Civilisation feature a host of animals like the humped bull and elephant – not to mention the popular mythical unicorn.

In the Hindu epics *Ramayana* and *Mahabharata*, there is a whole cast of animal characters, none more idolized and better revered than the monkey-God Hanuman. Hanuman is renowned for his steadfast celibacy and utter devotion to the divine incarnate Rama. The myth talks of the ploys of this character that helped the downfall of the mighty king Ravana. He also belongs to the galaxy of the seven illustrious immortals (*chiranjeevi*) as per Hindu mythology. Jambavanta, the king of the bears, also played no less important role in Rama's battle to retrieve Sita.

Literary classics like Kalidasa's *Abhijnana Shakuntalam* are a tribute to man's relationship with animals. Shakuntala's love for trees and deers is well stressed by Kalidasa in his *Shakuntalam*. Poets and lyricists have repeatedly taken recourse to drawing parallels between their characters and animals. Most poetic similes about eyes in Indian poetry are drawn from the animal world. A woman's eye is usually likened to a deer's (*mriganayani*) or a fish (*meenakshi*).

Buddhist mythology, iconography and literature also feature a large number of animals. Lord Buddha is often portrayed sitting under the hood of a snake. He is believed to have delivered his first sermon at the deer park (*mrigadava*) near Sarnath, and the deer has since captured the imagination of many Buddhist sculptors. The Buddhist *Jataka* stories too are based on animal characters, which preach values and morals to human living. These stories are part of a huge collection of animal fables that include the *Hitopadesa* and the *Panchatantra*.

Ancient Indian architecture too draws heavily from the faunal world. Animals have been a compulsive feature for architectural ornamentation, pillar design, temple carvings and cornices. The most famous example is the Lion Capital of Ashoka at Sarnath that has been adopted as the national emblem of India. The capital contains four lions standing to back atop an abacus. The abacus itself is adorned with the relief of a lion, bull, horse and elephant separated from one another by the *dharma chakra*, consisting of twenty-four spokes.

Unlike other art forms, classical Indian music and dance have largely forsaken animals in favour of loftier subjects. Notwithstanding this, the religious tales still feature various kinds of spirits, demons, animals and birds. Classical dances such as the *Bharatanatyam* have developed hand gestures (*hastas* and *mudras*) and movements (*karanas*) that depict various animals and birds. The *sarpa shirsha* (snake's head), *mriga shirsha* (deer's head), *hamsa paksha* (goose wings) and *shuka tunda* (parrot's beak) are well-known hand gestures germane to several classical dance forms (Gopinath 1957; Unnikrishnan 1994).

FOLK DANCE

In a country like India, which is blessed with a rich diversity of cultures, languages, and religion, it is but natural to expect a wide variety in the music and dance forms. Folk dance in India is a term that covers various dance forms developed by peasants, shepherds, fishermen and the tribals, who are still maintaining their pristine forms not influenced by the modern ways of living. Unlike the classical forms of dance that require rigorous training, folk dances are generally spontaneous and performed instinctively. They usually involve repetitive steps seemingly monotonous to any spectator. They are primarily meant for the pleasure of the participants or quite often a prelude to some ritual or festivity. Though deemed inferior to the classical forms, these dance forms have to be assiduously preserved as they reflect the mental attitude and inner spirit of the village folk.

Folk groups usually live in close proximity to the physical environment and eke out their livelihood through activities such as farming, fishing, herding, etc. They are greatly influenced by various natural phenomena in a variety of forms. That may be the reason why topography, change of seasons and biodiversity are well depicted in the folk dances. There are dances for rain, spring, harvest and some to hail animals and birds. The choreographic pattern also takes inspiration from natural phenomena like the blossoming of flowers, swaying of trees, waves and tides, flight of birds and the rhythmic movements of animals. The sudden leaps, jumps and crouching positions which form an integral part of many dance forms are attributed to the movements of wild animals.

ANIMAL SYMBOLISM IN FOLK AND TRIBAL DANCES

TIGER

In many parts of India, the tiger is valued and respected as the guardian of the forests. A legend from Nagaland says that the mother of the first spirit, the first tiger and the first man came out of the earth through a pangolin's den. Man and the tiger are seen as brothers. While one stayed at home, the other went to live in the forests. One day they met in the forest and were forced to fight. Man tricked the tiger into crossing a river and then killed it. God *Dingu-Aneni* could perceive that the bones had come from a human womb and brooded over them for ten years. As a result, hundreds of tigers were born; some of them lived in the hills and others on the plains (Thapar 1992). The most sanctified perception about the tiger is probably associated with its role as Goddess Durga's *vahana* (vehicle). The Goddess together with the tiger symbolises unlimited destructive power to triumph over evil.

Tiger dance is a popular folk dance all along India's southern coastline (Fig. 1). It is referred by different names in different states – *Puli Veshalu* in Andhra Pradesh, *Puliattam* in Tamil Nadu, and *Bagh Nritya* in Orissa. It is practiced both by the Hindus and the Muslims and is performed in open air during Dussera and Muharram.

In Kerala, *Pulikali* is performed on the fourth day of the Onam festival. It is identified with Kerala's cultural capital Thrissur, where this practice is said to be in vogue for nearly a century. It is understood that the tiger dance was introduced in Kerala by the Tamil-speaking Muslims as a part of the Moharram festivities. Ali, the son-in-law of Prophet Mohammad, is said to have had close links to the performance. Ali was a great warrior and the Islam portrays him as the guardian angel of the

Fig. 1. Puli Attam.

Almighty, possessing the strength and valour of a tiger. Gradually, the Muslim population lost interest and abandoned this dance form. The Konar and Chettiar communities of Tamil origin adopted this dance as they were used to *Puliattam* (Paul 2005).

In Karnataka, the dance is referred to as *Huli Kunita* or *Huli Vesha* and is performed during Navaratri to glorify Goddess Durga. It is also performed during Janmashtami.

Tiger dance is usually performed by young men, who smear their whole bodies with yellow varnish, black spots and stripes to resemble a tiger. In the past, the paints used were based on plant pigments, but in recent times these have been replaced by tempera powder mixed with varnish. The costume also comprises a tiger mask and a long cloth tail. There are *Patte hulis* (Royal Bengal tiger), *Chitte Hulis* (leopards) and *Thora Patte* (young and old tigers). The dance is actually very simple with few steps, but the facial expressions and the zestful movements of the skilful dancers make it fascinating. The scenes enacted include the tiger hunting down a deer and such similar episodes accompanied by the loud beating of traditional percussion instruments. In Tripura, the Lampak dance, which depicts the hunting of a tiger, is performed by the Koirang tribes.

Snake

Snake dance in India finds special favour as snakes are regarded as powerful deities to symbolise wealth, power and fertility. Snakes (cobras in particular) have been feared and revered in our culture from times immemorial. There are several temples dedicated to snakes and they are referred to as *Nagaraja/Nagadevata*. In South India, many houses have sacred serpent groves (*sarpa kavu*) in their backyards, with a carved snake-stone (*nagakal*). Women offer milk and light a lamp everyday at the *nagakal* to propitiate the snakes. Snakes are an important symbol ubiquitously found in Hindu mythology and iconography. Lord Shiva is often depicted with a cobra coiled around his neck. Lord Vishnu is portrayed as reclining on the coiled body of *Adisesha*, the primeaval multi-headed giant snake. Snake dance, also known *sarpa nritya,* is one of the most preferred folk dances of India (Fig. 2). The dance movements of the performers resemble the crawling serpent. They simulate the writhing, creeping movements of the snake using their hands and head. The performers usually sway to the notes of the *been* – the musical instrument of the snake charmers.

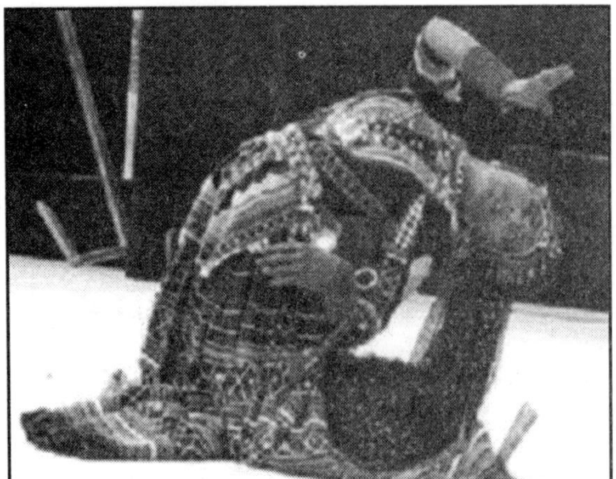

Fig. 2. Snake Dance.

Snake dance is believed to be an offshoot of snake idolatry. For instance, in the north-eastern state of Assam, the dance is ritualistically performed to glorify Goddess Manasa. The *Pulluvar* community of Kerala performs snake dance, locally known as *sarpam thullal* or *pampin thullal* in the honour of *Nagaraja*, the king of the serpents. Other serpent gods – *Nagayakshi* (the queen serpent), *Karinagam* (black serpent), *Paranagam* (flying serpent) and *Anchilamaninagam* (five-hooded and jewel carrying serpent) – are also propitiated in the ritual.

The *sarpam thullal* is usually performed in specially decorated *pandals* or thatched shed close to the *sarpa kavu* or in the courtyard in front of the house. The floor of the *pandal* is first plastered with cow dung and decorated with flowers. The women draw *sarpakalam* (designs with one or two entwining snakes) in the courtyard using different colours. Bronze oil lamps are lit in front of the *sarpakalam* along with offerings of rice and coconut. The snake idol is brought from the *kavu* in a procession called *thalapoli* to the *pandal* accompanied by beats of the percussion instruments. A number of girls with hairdo resembling the hood of a snake – appearing like the *naga kanya* – take part in the procession. While reaching the *pandal*, the *piniyals* (the family on whom the effect of the ritual is sought) dance holding an inflorescence of *arec*. They sway their bodies to the tunes and rhythmic beatings of the *para* (crude drum) and *elathalam* (cymbals), accompanied by the Pulluvan *pattu*. They then enter the *sarpakalam* and rub the figure of the *nagas* with the flower. If they do not get possessed, the devotees come to the conclusion that the ritual was not successful and repeat it over (Narayan 2004; Kumar 2006).

The Kalbelia community of Rajasthan is a community of snake catchers and charmers. The *Nagin* dance, performed by women belonging to this community, is indicative of the profession of the community. The women dancers attired in traditional black *ghagaras* slither like a snake while the men play their *been*. The Malers – a primitive tribe of Bihar – have a very unique way of performing the snake dance. During the harvest festival known as *Ghaghra puja*, the tribes catch live snakes and stitch their mouths. The snakes are then placed in the open ground and the tribes dance around them. The snakes are later taken to neighbouring villages and gifts/ alms are collected.

Horse

The horse is one of the important animals frequently referred to in Hindu scriptures. It is believed that the first horse surfaced during the churning of the divine ocean (*sagara mathana*). It was a white-coloured, flying horse named *Ucchaishrava*, which was taken by Indra to his heavenly abode. Subsequently, Indra severed the wings of the horse and sent it to earth. The wings were severed to ensure that the horse remained on the earth and disabled from flying back to Indra's *svarga* (Krishna 2008; Stutley 1985). It is considered to be the *vahana* of *Kubera* – the Hindu God of wealth and Sukra (Venus) – one of the *navagrahas* (nine planets). The chariot of Lord Surya is also drawn by seven horses (*saptashva*).

Poikaal Kudirai Attam or *Puravi Attam* is the dummy horse dance of Tamil Nadu, where the dancer bears the dummy figure of a horse's body on his/her hips. It is made out of cardboard, jute, paper, glass and bamboo strips with colourful cloth on the sides to cover the legs of the dancer. The dancer fits himself with wooden legs to generate sounds like the hooves of the horse. The dancers sing the valour of kings and heroes to the accompaniment

Fig. 3. Horse Dance.

Fig. 4. Terracotta horses.

of *Naiyandi melam*. The dance is associated with the worship of the folk deity Aiyanar, who is often found mounted on a horse. Terracotta horses are offered to the deity in the villages (Fig. 4).

Some legends associate the origin of the dance to the Shakti cult. It is said that in the *Puranic* times, a terrible war raged between the demons and Goddess Durga. The demons let loose on earth snakes and other poisonous creatures. In order to destroy them, the Goddess is said to have worn wooden legs and danced on the battlefield (*http://www.anothersubcontinent.com/forums/lofiversion/index.php? t1337.html*). In Tamil Nadu, the dance is believed to have been introduced first by the Maratha artists (Muthiah 2003). In many parts of India, dummy horse dances are performed under different names and with different thematic contents. In Uttar Pradesh and Rajasthan, it is called *Kucchi Ghodi* and is perfornmed during the festival of Holi. In Chittoor, Nellore, Prakasam and Guntur districts of Andhra Pradesh, it is known as *Keelugurram* and in coastal areas of Orissa, it is popularly called *Chaiti Ghoda Nach.*

Chaiti Ghoda is performed by the Kaibarta caste during the month of Chaitra. It is performed in the honour of Vasuli Devi – an incarnation of Goddess Durga. Bamboo frames in the shape of a horse are worn by the dancers, who appear as if they are riding a horse. The songs recited during the performance revolve around the various episodes in Hindu mythology.

The *Ghode Modni* dance of Goa portrays the heroic feats of Ranes, the Maratha rulers over the Portugese. It is performed during the Shigmo festival. The dancers, attired in colourful costumes and armed with swords, have effigies of horses fixed to their waists.

Bull

The practice of sanctifying the bull as a deity can be traced back to the Vedic times. The Vedic people were conscious of the importance of the bull and the Vedas exhort the rule "O King! You should never kill animals like the bullock that are useful for agriculture or like cows which give us milk and all other helpful animals and must punish those who kill or do harm to such animals" (*Yajur Veda*, 13.49). The white bull, Nandi is the *vahana* of Lord Shiva.

Pashu nritya is performed in the villages of south Orissa, especially in the district of Ganjam and particularly during the Thankurani yatra, a religious festival when the idols of the folk deity Goddess Thakuran are taken out on the streets. During these times, animal mask dancers go dancing before the procession. The dancers typically wear the costumes of a bull but at times even the costumes of other creatures like the tiger, deer or the peacock. *Kaalaiattam*, a dance similar to the dummy horse dance, is prevalent in Tamil Nadu. The dancers perform it wearing the mask and dummy figure of a bull.

Bison

Fig. 5. Bison dance.

The buffalo or bison is held sacred by many tribes and believed to be a symbol of abundance as it provides milk, meat and leather. The buffalo is sacred to the Todas of the Nilgiris and features in many of their rituals (Walker 2004). In the Mhasoba cult of western and southern India, people worship Mhasoba (a horned buffalo deity, sometimes associated with Lord Shiva/ Mahesh) and His consort Jogubai (Goddess Durga) (Krishna 2006). The bison is a totemic animal for the Marias of Central India. The Singh or Tallaguda Maria (Bison-horn Maria) – inhabitants of Bastar in Madhya Pradesh – celebrate by joyfully performing the bison dance (Fig. 5). The word Gaur means 'ferocious bison'. The image of the bison inspires the dancers to be very zestful and virulent. The men wear colourful head-dresses of bison horns topped by peacock feathers, their faces covered by a string of cowrie shells. The women wear white and red sarees. The men usually move in a circle creating a variety of dancing patterns. They assault each other imitating a number of bison movements – frisking bull, hurling wisps of grass in air, charging and tossing their horns, etc. The *Mithun* dance or bison hunt dance is performed in Nagaland after the killing of a bison.

Deer/Antelope

The deer is associated with innumerable tales in Indian mythology. In *Ramayana*, Ravana makes Maricha assume the form of a golden deer to lure Rama and Lakshmana away from Sita to facilitate the abduction of Sita by Ravana. In *Mahabhrata*, Pandu shoots a stag mounting a doe for copulation. Before dying, the deer curses Pandu that the instant he touches his wives, he would drop dead. The curse comes true after several years when he touches his wife Madri. The deer is sacred to the Buddhists too as they perceive divinity in its grace, gentleness and elegance. The Monpa tribe of Arunachal Pradesh perform the deer dance. The theme of the dance revolves around a sheperd and his two sons, who capture a deer. When the deer is about to be killed by them, the people from the village dissuade them from doing so and plead for mercy. The dance thus captures the compassion and love that the tribes possess for the animal. Deer dance is also performed in Sikkim in the honour of Kalarupa – one of the principal protectors of Dharma. The Khasis of Meghalaya celebrate Shad Beh Sier, a festival meant to rejoice the hunting of a deer and during this festival, a deer hunting dance is performed.

Langur/Monkey

Hindus revere Lord Hanuman, the Hindu monkey-god, as an embodiment of the langur or the monkey. In the epic *Ramayana*, Hanuman played a substantial role in the defeat of Ravana by

Fig. 6. Hanuman dance.

Lord Rama. He commanded a battalion of monkeys, called the *vanara-sena*. Hanuman langurs are often found in and around Hindu temples, where devotees feed them with bananas and nuts. The Hanuman dance is a folk dance of Rajasthan where the dancers sport the costume of a langur, imitate monkey movements and perform some acrobatic feats (Fig. 6). The performance is accompanied by recital of the *Ramayana*. The *Bridabani* dance of Seraikella in Bihar is performed on the second day of *Chaitra Parva* – the week-long festival marking the onset of spring. The dancers dress up in outfits designed with leaves and twigs to represent Lord Hanuman. The performer is controlled by a leash handled by one of the worshippers.

Elephant

Elephants are sacred to the Hindus. Many Hindu temples, especially in South India, own elephants that carry the deities during festival processions and ceremonial circumambulations in the temples. The blessings of temple elephants are sought by Hindu devotees as the animal is associated with Lord Ganesha, who is depicted as having the head of an elephant. The *Gaja nritya* or the elephant dance is prevalent among the Dhangars or the shepherd community of the Sholapur district of Maharashtra. It is performed during temple festivals, religious processions and marriages. The dance symbolically represents the elephant, the swaying of its huge ears represented by the slow movement of colourful scarves held by the dancers. The tempo of the rhythm is very slow and sedate, reflecting the elephant's gait. The dance is performed by the Dhangars to please their God Biruba, a manifestation of Lord Shiva.

Monitor Lizard

The monitor lizard has a special place in Maratha history and folklore. The Marathi word for a monitor lizard is *ghorpad*. Legend has it that Karna Singh, a famous Maratha warrior, breached the supposedly impregnable Kelna fort by tying a rope to the back of a monitor lizard. The lizard scaled the cliff and secured itself in a crevice, facilitating Karna's ascent. Karna's tribe was known as Ghorpad (pronounce ghorpade) and every soildier in the Maratha army was trained in this strategy (Krishna *et al.* 2006). The Kolam tribes in Yavatmal, Nanded and Wardha districts of Maharashtra perform the *Ghorpad Kola* to celebrate hunting of the lizard, which is used both as food and medicine by the tribes. The main dancer crawls like a lizard. He is surrounded by a number of other dancers, armed with sticks, who move around in anti-clockwise direction.

Snow Lion

The snow lion is a dignified royal symbol in many cultures. In Buddhism, the snow lion symbolises the fearlessness of the Buddha (Beer 1999). In Buddhist paintings and sculptures, the body of the snow lion is depicted white while its flowing hair is either in blue or green. The snow lion is the national symbol of Tibet. *Singhi Chham* is the religious masked dance of Sikkim, depicting the snow lion – decreed the guardian deity of the people of Sikkim by Guru Padamsambhava. The dance is performed during the worship of Kangchenjunga, the world's third-highest mountain, which is also believed to resemble the snow lion. The natives dress in furry costumes and perform the masked dance. In Arunachal Pradesh, the Aji Lamu dance is a Buddhist ritualistic dance, popular among the Mompa tribe. The dance symbolises the fact that prosperity comes only when there is complete harmony and co-operation amongst all living beings on earth. It depicts friendship between a saint meditating in the mountains and the snow lion and peacock.

Yak

Man is completely dependent on the yak for survival at high altitudes. It is the sole means of transportation in the hills. It also provides milk and meat for sustenance during winters. The rich mane of the animals provides cloth while the fibre is woven into blankets. The *Yak Chham* or the yak dance is performed to honour the yak. The dance is prevalent in the mountainous regions of Jammu and Kashmir, Arunachal Pradesh and Sikkim. The dance depicts the yak and projects the simple lifestyle of the herdsman in the mountains. The dancers donning yak skin and masks dance gently to the percussion. They sit, jump, tumble and run in circle.

Birds

Peacock

The peacock is considered sacred in Hindu religion. The divine vehicle or *vahana* of Lord Muruga is a peacock named *Paravani*. In Tamil Nadu, peacock dance, referred to as *Mayilaattam*, is performed to extol Lord Muruga. The dancers dress up as peacocks (Fig. 7) resplendent with peacock feather and a glittering head-dress complete with a beak. They exhibit movements similar to those of a live peacock. Peacock dance is also prevalent in the northern parts of India, where it is referred to as the *mayur nritya*. *Mayur nritya* is a key aspect of the traditional Chhau dance of Bihar, Orissa and West Bengal. In Madhya Pradesh, the *morni* dance also imitates the peacock and celebrates the rain and spirit of the monsoon.

Fig. 7. Peacock dance.

Raven

In Mahayana Buddhism, the raven is seen as an auspicious bird and is associated with a form of Mahakala, the guardian deity (Guyot 2007). The raven dance is popular in the state of Sikkim. The bird-faced dancer (wearing a mask) represents the high spirits of the practioners.

Hornbill

The hornbill is a prominent bird that figures in the folklore of most of the Naga people. The *Langdai Lam* is the name given to the harvest hornbill dance performed by the Ka bui tribes, a sub-tribe of the Nagas inhabiting Manipur, Assam and Nagaland. The male and the female dancers wear hornbill feathers in their headgear and dance like the bird, expressing great joy over the harvest. The *Khongpilaam* dance of Tripura also borrows from the movements of the hornbill bird. It is performed by both the male and female dancers, who dance in a circle first slowly and then accelerate.

Rooster

The Buddhists have a representation, called the Wheel of Birth and Death, that symbolises the incessant cycle of existence that all beings are trapped into. The centre of the wheel contains a rooster (or dove in some cases), a snake and a hog. These represent the root causes that keep us trapped in this cycle. The rooster represents greed, the snake represents aversion, and the hog represents delusion or ignorance (Tsomo 2006). In many parts of India, tribal and folk deities are propitiated through cock sacrifice. Cock-fighting is a favourite leisure activity for people living in the rural parts. *Kakong Tokai* or cock-fighting dance is an indigenous dance form of the Khampti tribe, who inhabit parts of the Lohit district in Arunachal Pradesh. It can be performed anywhere and at anytime of the year. The dancers stand opposite each other and stage a mock cock-fight leaping and jumping back and forth with their heads raised and hands in motion like the claws of the cocks. In the cock-fighting, the dancers use masks and costumes of the cocks and perform to the vociferous beating of drums and gongs. The Zemis tribes of Nagaland also perform a mock cock-fight called *Nruima Lim*.

Insects

Labang Bomai is an ingenious harvest dance of Tripura that mixes art and science. Insects such as grasshopper and cricket species abound at the harvest time. The *Labang Bomai* dance is actually meant to catch these insects. The bamboo clappers (locally known as *tokkas*) played by the dancers make a peculiar sound that entices these insects from their hiding place. While the men clap the *tokkas*, the women dance in a circle waving colourful scarves. The dance is accompanied by the *sarinala* (bow string) and the *pung* (drum). The Kai Bui tribe also performs the cricket dance, referred to as *Kit Lam*. It is a recreational dance that imitates the movement of the insect. They also do the *Khoi Lam* or the honey bee dance during the Ganngai harvest festival. The dance depicts how honey bees collect and store the nectar. The dance highlights the fact that just like the honey bees store nectar, the tribals store paddy and other food grains. In Assam, the insect-catching dance is referred to as *Gan-daula-ban-nai*.

FOLK DANCES AS A COMMUNICATION TOOL FOR BIODIVERSITY CONSERVATION

The loss or extinction of species is an inevitable part of the evolutionary process. However, human activities in recent times have seriously interfered with and accelerated the rate of extinction. Today, Indian wildlife is seriously imperiled. Due to a variety of reasons, including habitat loss, poaching and pollution, many wild species are disappearing rapidly. An indefinite number of species is already permanently lost and a large percentage of the rest are on the verge of extinction. Even the continued survival of India's national animal – the Royal Bengal Tiger – appears precarious. Recent reports have revealed that the population of tiger has more than halved in the last 5-6 years from 3,642 in 2001-02 to about 1,411 in 2008 (State of Tigers, Co-predators and Prey in India Report, 2008 and *http://envfor.nic.in/pt/status/intro.html*).

Local communities form critical links in the chain of biodiversity conservation. The native population has profound knowledge and if effectively applied, this could be of great use in making conservation efforts more meaningful. All over the world, governments have begun to recognize the significance of involving the local people in conservation efforts. Even the Convention of Biological Diversity (CBD) emphasizes the importance of traditional knowledge and practices. *Article 8(j)* of the CBD states:

> Each Contracting Party shall, as far as possible and as appropriate: subject to national legislation, respect preserve and maintain knowledge, innovations and practices of indigenous communities and local communities embodying traditional lifestyles relevant for the conservation and sustainable use of biological diversity and promote their wider application with the approval and involvement of the holder of such knowledge, innovation and practices and encourage the equitable sharing of the benefits from the utilisation of such knowledge, innovations and practices. (*http://www.cbd.int/traditional/*).

Awareness creation is the key to motivating local communities to partipate in wildlife conservation. Traditional folk media, such as puppetry, street theater, folk music and dance, have served societies as potent tools of communication for ages. During India's independence movement, folk media was effectively used in many social and political campaigns against the colonial rulers. Even in present times, they are highly relevant in societies like ours, where the majority of the population lives in rural areas without access to mass media and formal education. While mass media can be used successfully in the cities to reach out, they are generally found to be ineffective in the rural areas where the rate of literacy is low.

In traditional and rural societies, dance is an integral part of the day to day lives of the people. These dances provide recreation to the people and help to ease stress and fatigue. They also serve as a powerful propaganda media to draw the attention of the people to a particular issue because they have the advantage of combining education with entertainment. Unlike formal education and workshops, where there is more instruction than interaction leading to disinterestedness on the part of the audience, folk performances establish rapport with the audience almost instantly. They serve as ideal 'icebreakers' while reaching out to the communities the constructive messages. If deployed properly, they have the propensity to dismantle the barriers of illiteracy, religion, caste, language, age and sex.

As discussed in this paper, many folk dances of India revolve around mythological/folklore stories underlining the close affinity between man and animals. Accompanied by songs, drums and other instruments, these dances not only regale the audiences but also highlight the need for harmonious living with nature. Many of folk dances can be used effectively for creating environmental awareness – the crying need of modern times.

The folk dancers and performers could be initially trained and sensitized on different aspects of environment and biodiversity conservation. They could then be encouraged to reorient their performances to impart conservation messages without abandoning the traditional movements and steps, so that the originality of the dance form is not lost. The performances can also be followed by interactive discussions when the need for conservation can be convincingly driven home to the local communities. Such indoctrination may be essential lest the audience forget the messages after the performance is over. Although not all the folk dances discussed above can be used for purposes of environmental communication, dances such as *Puli Kali*, *Mayilattam*, *Singhi Chham*, *Poikaal Kudirai* can effectively incorporate and deliver environmental messages. But unfortunately most of these traditional art forms are near extinction and even those that exist have undergone mutation. There is an imperative need to restore the art forms and revitalize them with new content to allure the younger generation.

ACKNOWLEDGEMENTS

I express my gratitude to Dr. Nanditha Krishna, Honorary Director, C.P.R. Environmental Education Centre for her constant encouragement and guidance. I am also thankful to Mr. M. Amrithalingam and Mr. N.S. Srivatsan for their valuable inputs and editorial assistance.

REFERENCES

Anantharaman, L. 2007. 'Dance Like A Tiger', *Discover India*, December.
Banerji, P. 1944. *The Folk Dance of India*, Kitabistan: Allahabad.
Beer, Robert. 1999. *The Encyclopedia of Tibetan Symbols and Motifs*, London: Serindia Publications.
'Colours Endangering Huli Vesha', *The Times of India*, October 03, 2003.
Ghosh, S. and U.K. Banerjee. 2006. *Indian Puppets*, New Delhi: Abhinav Publications.
Gopinath, N. 1957. *Abhinaya Prakasika*, Chennai: Natana Niketan Publications.
Doubler, M.N. 1957. *Dance: A Creative Experience*, Wisconsin: The University of Wiscosin Press.
Guyot, Isabelle. 2007. 'Bhutan – The Dragon Kingdom', *Isabelle around the World*, March 12.
Krishna, N. 1996. *Folk Arts of Tamilnadu*, Chennai: C.P. Ramaswami Aiyar Foundation.
——. 2006. *Sacred Animals of India*, Chennai: C.P.R. Environmental Education Centre.
Krishna, N. 1996. Amritalingam, M. and A. Godbole. 2006. 'Sacred Animals of Maharashtra', in Nanditha Krishna (ed.), *Ecological Traditions of Maharashtra*, Chennai: C.P.R. Environmental Education Centre, pp. 105-112.
Kumar, B. 2006. 'Snake Worship in Kerala', in Nanditha Krishna (ed.), *Ecological Traditions of Kerala*, Chennai: C.P.R. Environmental Education Centre, pp. 91-105.
McNeely, J.A. and D.C. Pitt (eds.). 1985. *Culture and Conservation: The Human Dimension in Environmental Planning*, London: Croom Helm.
Muthiah, S. 2003. 'The Maharashtrians of Tamilnadu', *The Hindu*, Monday, July 07.
Narayan, S. 2004. *Folk Dance Traditions of India*, Gurgaon: Shubhi Publications.
Paul, G.S. 2005. 'Mimic the Tiger', *The Hindu*, September 11.
State of Tigers, Co-predators and Prey in India. 2008. National Tiger Conservation Authority, Ministry of Environment and Forests and Wildlife Institute of India.
Stutley, M. 1985. *The Illustrated Dictionary of Hindu Iconography*, London: Routledge and Kegan Paul, p. 147.
Thapar, V. 1992. 'The Cult of the Tiger', *The Tiger's Destiny, Kyle Cathie Ltd.*, p. 35.
Tsomo, K.L. 2006. *Into the Jaws of Yama, Lord of Death – Buddhism, Bioethics and Death*, State University of New York Press, p. 4.
Unnikrishnan, C.P. 1994. *A Window to Kathakali*, Kerala: Anaswara Publishing.
Walker, A.R. 2004. 'The Truth about the Todas', *Frontline*, Vol. 21, Issue 05.